# CITY *of* ∞
# LAUGHTER

THE WHORE'S LAST SHIFT.

Publish'd Feb.y 9th 1770. by W. Humphrey.

# CITY of ❧

# LAUGHTER

## SEX AND SATIRE IN
## EIGHTEENTH-CENTURY LONDON

## VIC GATRELL

Atlantic Books
London

Published in Great Britain in 2006 by Atlantic Books,
an imprint of Grove Atlantic Ltd.

9 8 7 6 5 4 3 2 1

A CIP catalogue record for this book is available from the British Library.

Royal Hardback
ISBN 10: 1 84354 321 4
ISBN 13: 978 1 84354 321 3

Royal Trade Paperback
ISBN 10: 1 84354 322 2
ISBN 13: 978 1 84354 322 0

Designed by www.carrstudio.co.uk

Printed and bound in China by Compass Press

Atlantic Books
An imprint of Grove Atlantic Ltd
Ormond House
26–27 Boswell Street
London WC1N 3JZ

Laughter: an affection peculiar to mankind, occasioned by something that tickles the fancy.

*Encyclopaedia Britannica* (1780)

A serious and good philosophical work could be written that would consist entirely of jokes.

Norman Malcolm, *Ludwig Wittgenstein: A memoir* (1958)

What is it, I ask you, which begets gods or men – the head, the face, the breast, hand, or ear, all thought of as respectable parts of the body? No, it's not. The propagator of the human race is that part which is so foolish and absurd that it can't be named without raising a laugh.

Erasmus, *In Praise of Folly* (1509)

**A MORNING FROLIC, or the TRANSMUTATION of SEXES.**

*From the Original Picture by John Collet, in the possession of Carington Bowles.*

416    Printed for & Sold by CARINGTON BOWLES, at his Map & Print Warehouse, N°69 in S.<sup>t</sup> Pauls Church Yard LONDON . Publish'd as the Act directs

# CONTENTS

# LIST OF ILLUSTRATIONS

Note: Approximate measurements (where known) of original prints shown in millimetres.

## 3    COVENT GARDEN AND THE MIDDLING SORTS

## 4    CROSSING THE BOUNDARIES

## 6    BUMS, FARTS AND OTHER TRANSGRESSIONS

## 7    IMAGE MAGIC

## 8    SEEING THE JOKES

## 9   GILLRAY'S DREAMSCAPES

## 16  RADICAL SATIRE AND THE CENSORS

## 17 THE SILENCING

## 18 HAPPINESS, CANT AND THE BEGGARS

## EPILOGUE: FRANCIS PLACE AND 'IMPROVEMENT'

# PICTURE ACKNOWLEDGEMENTS

Figures are reproduced by kind permission of the following (unlisted figures are privately owned):

Andrew Edmunds: 38

Bibliophile Books and Lance Hodgson: 176, 194, 195

British Museum: 1-5, 8, 10, 18, 20, 21, 24, 25, 27, 31, 33, 37, 44, 45, 49, 50, 52-56, 58, 59, 62, 63, 66, 69, 73-78, 83, 86, 89, 95, 97, 98-102, 104, 105, 108, 109, 112, 114, 117, 119-122, 124-127, 131, 133, 135, 136, 139, 140-142, 144, 145, 147, 149, 151, 159, 162, 164, 168-170, 174, 177, 182, 183, 185, 186, 189, 190, 192, 193, 196-201, 206, 208, 212, 214, 215, 217, 218-220, 225-235, 239, 240, 242, 246, 248, 249, 253, 254 259, 261 265, 267, 270, 273, 274, 287

Cambridge University Library: 29, 30, 32, 35, 42, 87, 250, 251, 275-279, 281, 283

Lewis Walpole Library, Yale University: 7, 9, 11-14, 16, 17, 19, 22, 23, 28, 34, 36, 39-41, 43, 46, 48, 51, 60, 64, 65, 68, 70-72, 82, 84, 93, 94, 96,103, 107, 115, 116, 123, 129, 130, 134, 137, 138, 143, 146, 148, 150, 152-158, 163, 165-167, 171-173, 178-181, 184, 187, 188, 191, 202-205, 207, 210, 216, 222-224, 236, 237, 238, 241, 243-245, 260, 282, 285, 286

Library of Congress, Washington DC: 61, 90, 106, 111, 175, 221, 252, 271

Motco Enterprises Limited: 15, 26, 288

Museum of London: 47

National Archives, London: 266, 269, 272

University of Liège, Belgium: 79, 80

# ACKNOWLEDGEMENTS

Why were Londoners in the late Georgian era so fond of ridicule and scurrility, and how did they square that taste with politeness? How did men laugh at women and women laugh at men? And when and why did their bawdy humour fall out of fashion? As these questions imply, those people's high-mindedness was seriously fractured. In what follows, I explore their implications by using a vast body of under-explored evidence. Between 1770 and 1830, London's printshops published some twenty thousand satirical or humorous engravings. Half of them were about politics and international affairs. The rest, less familiar, revelled in the comedies of sex, debauchery, scandal and fashion, or in the pleasurable vexations of living in London itself. Ribald, scurrilous, and much interested in the humour of the fart and the bum, these images were bought by well-born or prospering customers. They open the way to a panoramic survey of metropolitan mentalities and manners that were the reverse of polite – to a history, moreover, in which pictures cue the argument rather than the other way round. They also, however, indicate how their purchasers' views of their world changed, for the prints lost their bite in the 1820s. They capitulated them to the deepening respectability and correctness by which modern manners were tamed.

Writing about a subject as open-ended as this, with no simple chronology or precedent to follow, hasn't always been (entirely) 'a laugh'. George Orwell once said that writing a book 'is a horrible, exhausting struggle, like a long bout of some painful illness' and that 'one would never undertake such a thing if one were not driven on by some demon whom one can neither resist nor understand.' His point is well taken. I have survived Orwell's illness thanks to friends' and colleagues' generous support. My gratitude to the following people and institutions returns them much less than I owe them.

My earliest debt is to the staff at the Lewis Walpole Library at Yale. It was during a fellowship there that the prints' potential as historical sources most fully came home to me. Richard Williams and Joan Hall Sussler gave me free rein to work through the library's magnificent print collection at my own pace and as my curiosity led me, an unsupervised privilege that quite transformed my sense of that era. Next, Sheila O'Connell of the British Museum's Prints and Drawings Department has cheerfully put her vast knowledge of the prints at my disposal. Her help has been utterly indispensable to all that follows. To many readers my thanks are as fulsome. Suzanne Matheson contributed wonderfully erudite references from her great knowledge of the period, while early drafts of this or that chapter benefited from the sharp eyes of John Barrell, Vyvyen and Piers Brendon, Lizzie Collingham, Hilary Court, Martin Daunton, Louise Foxcroft, Emma Griffin, Larry Klein, Sheila O'Connell, the late and much missed Brian Outhwaite, Paul Pickering, Kate Retford and Quentin Skinner. During my three years at Essex University, Jeremy Krikler's support has been exceptional for its kindness and warmth. He, Amanda Flather, Peter Gurney, James Raven and John Walter commented on parts of the book, and Steve Smith forensically cut through many of its contradictions. None is responsible for my misinterpretations and errors, but each left me feeling that writing was worth it.

In Cambridge, Neil McKendrick and Martin Daunton kindly backed my quests for funding and fellowships, while the Cambridge students who took my Special Subject on the print satire taught me far more than they realized. Early picture research was supported by Caius College and the Faculty of History. Serious writing began during a fellowship at the Australian National University, and a fellowship from the Paul Mellon Centre for the Study of British Art supported me during the book's last stages. The Mellon Centre and the Essex Department of History helped pay for the pictures. My publisher Toby Mundy must have worried as the book grew in size and ambition, but his belief in it never visibly wavered. For striking so neat a balance between price and production quality I thank him warmly. My editor Louisa Joyner worked on the book tirelessly. She saved me from my more ponderous expressions and put up with my neurotic interventions more patiently than I deserved. Emma Grove at Atlantic, Rich Carr the designer and Jane Robertson have my gratitude too. During spells of research or writing in London, Italy, South Africa and California, I've enjoyed the hospitality of Lisa and Adrian Binks, Alison and Alex Chrystal, Rosie Morgan and Mark Damazer, Janice Hughes and Stephen Taylor, Claudia and Vivian Bickford Smith, Polly Toynbee, and

Alison Winter. Richard Higgins advised me on the Strathmore case, and Timothy Hyman and David Alexander gave me valuable leads.

By far my deepest debt is to my wife Pam. Without her tolerance of my oddities during its writing, the book would have sunk long ago, and I with it. I dedicate it to her in love, gratitude and admiration. Quite simply she has been, and is, my sine qua non.

# INTRODUCTION

# LADY WORSLEY'S BOTTOM

## London's humours

Should you visit the great mansion of Harewood House in Yorkshire today, you might notice seven fine family portraits hanging together in one of its lavish drawing rooms, each of them painted by Sir Joshua Reynolds. One, from about 1776, depicts the young Dorothy, Lady Worsley. Striking a mannish pose in her scarlet military costume, she adds considerable weight to Harewood's advertisement of its owners' immodest wealth and connections: she was the stepdaughter of Edwin Lascelles, the mansion's true founder. You may also notice, however, that most of your fellow visitors pass her by with scarcely a glance, as if her portrait's formality distances her flesh-and-blood reality from them. To many people pictures like this can suggest an era that today is all but impenetrable: in which ladies were so genteel, men so gallant, manners so refined, and fashions so extravagant, that imaginative engagement with it is impeded. The Harewood guidebook does try to break through Lady Worsley's mask by hinting that her marriage to Sir Richard Worsley was unhappy and that he was to cite another military officer for adultery with her. But no more than that is said, and what is said is too discreet, so most visitors pass on bemusedly to the gilded fancies that lie ahead, and forget Lady Worsley very quickly.

It is lucky, then, that other images of Lady Worsley are available to us, and with them another view of her times. And because sex, bodies and scandal are at their centre, they may be easier for us to engage with today. In 1782, nearly a dozen prints circulated in fashionable London that were not at all designed to trumpet her high standing and connections. Costing a shilling plain or two shillings coloured and exhibited in printshop windows, they were bought by the great if not the good in malice and delight. In one, by the up-and-coming caricaturist, James Gillray, entitled *Sir Richard Worse-than-sly, Exposing his Wifes* [sic] *Bottom – O Fye!*, a man hoists

*Sir Richard Worse-than-Sly,
Exposing his Wifes Bottom.—O fye!*

**Fig. 1** Gillray, *Sir Richard Worse-than-Sly, Exposing his Wifes Bottom – O Fye!*
(W. Humphrey, 1782)

**Fig. 2** Gillray, *A Peep into Lady W!!!!y's Seraglio* (W. Humphrey, 1782)

another man on to his shoulders to allow the latter to peep through a bathhouse window at the naked Lady Worsley as she washes herself demurely. In bluff military fashion, the peeping man remarks to the other below: 'Charming view of the back settlements, S$^r$ Richard.' 'Good lack! my lady,' her attending maid exclaims in alarm, 'the capt$^n$ will see all for nothing' [fig. 1]. Gillray engraved a second print of this friendly scene, and then a quite different one six weeks later. In this last, *A Peep into Lady W!!!!!y's Seraglio*, nine impatient gentlemen queue on a staircase to await their turn with Lady Worsley in bed. As one lover has his way with her, another departs on the right, pulling up his breeches [fig. 2].

These salacious images circulated widely among London's finer people; and, because newspapers and pamphlets reported it gleefully, all knew the scandal that was being referred to. They knew that Sir Richard Worsley had brought a suit against one Captain Bissett for 'criminal conversation' with his wife (a usual preliminary to divorce), and that Worsley's hypocrisy was exposed as he did so. The court heard that while Worsley was quartered in the military camp at Cox's Heath, Lady Worsley had often used the nearby bathhouse at Maidstone. On one occasion her husband had tapped on the bathhouse door, saying 'Bissett is going to get up to look at you'. Hoist Bissett up to the window Worsley duly did, for him to gaze on her nakedness. Worsley's obvious collusion in the adultery meant that the court awarded him a derisory shilling in damages instead of the £20,000 he had hoped for. He became polite society's laughing stock, though not as much as she did. As the gossipy aesthete Horace Walpole wrote in his excited and delighted letters, the case revealed that 'thirty-four young men of the first quality' had enjoyed her favours; and one of them, the Marquis of Graham, had given her his own 'favour' in return. By this Walpole, amused, meant venereal disease. After the scandal, Worsley refused to pay Reynolds for his wife's portrait (understandably), so Reynolds gave it to her stepfather, Lascelles, instead.[1]

This book is about the stories, jokes and satirical exposures that later Georgian English people found funny. It is about the rise and fall of a great tradition of ridicule and of the satirical and humorous prints that sustained it. It focuses, not on the polished wit upon which the politer people prided themselves, but on their malicious, sardonic and satirical humour: a peculiarly English humour, if you like, that was bawdy, knowing and ironic. It explores what it says about their views of the world, and about their own pretensions. It examines how they laughed about sex, scandal, fashion, drink and similar pleasures of life; and it enters the clubs and taverns where that laughter flowed most freely. Just as the glimpse that Gillray affords us of Lady Worsley may reveal more of her times as well as of Lady Worsley than Reynolds's portrait does, so the book suggests the fruitfulness of exploring the era's lowest manners and lowest forms of artistic production, rather than its highest.

'An exceedingly frank acknowledgement, one might almost say a relish, of man's animal functions was as much a part of the age as the elegant furniture or delicate china,' J. H. Plumb once wrote of the eighteenth century. People do appear to have experienced their bodies differently then. Both sexes dressed their bodies differently from us, and they thought about and had sex differently also (less nudity and orality and more standing up than today, it seems). Many believed it natural and good to indulge the body's desires, and men referred to its parts and functions more openly: for Enlightened materialism taught them that it was the senses, not the spirit, that moved behaviour. What follows doesn't quite endorse the fantasy that the eighteenth century was 'a guilt-free sexual playground peopled by comely wenches and swaggering rakes ready to roll in the hay at the drop of a hanky'.[2] Even libertines knew guilt; moralizers were many and vocal; and the boundaries between public appearance and private practice were earnestly if inefficiently patrolled. Still, the fact that those boundaries were repeatedly breached by bawdily mocking exposures is why this book can give the low behaviours, as well as parts, of people like Lady Worsley and Captain Bissett a central rather than an incidental role in its story.

By focusing on casts of mind that were satirical, sardonic or ironic, as well as on some more genial forms of humorous expression, the book offers a history of humour and laughter. Attention to so large and loose a subject must break new and difficult ground, for there isn't much previous research to build on. It is lucky for laughter that most historians prefer to write histories of misery, pain and woe, since nothing so kills laughter as analysing it. Yet humour is as plausibly a historian's subject as any other, and it allows us to say new and important things. As the Aristotelian formula put it, man is the only animal that laughs (and weeps and blushes) because man alone can see the difference between how things are and how they ought to be. In other words, the reflex of laughter is controlled by mental processes; and mental processes have *histories*. The subjects that people think it appropriate to laugh at; what kinds of people laugh; how cruelly, mockingly, or sardonically they laugh (or how sympathetically and generously); and how far they permit others to laugh – all vary with time, sex, class, place, and culture. And since these questions have always been regulated by moralists, laughter has also been central to the processes by which Western manners have been disciplined over centuries. For all these reasons, studying laughter can take us to the heart of a generation's shifting attitudes, sensibilities and anxieties just as surely as the study of misery, politics, faith or art can. Indeed, the art forms which shape this book, whose purpose was to provoke amusement at others' expense, are perfectly contrived to lead us to past mentalities along routes as yet hardly explored.[3]

Two large questions are addressed about the later eighteenth and early nineteenth centuries: how differently the sexes and the classes laughed, and how (in and after the 1820s) their humour softened, thus foreshadowing the deepening taboos of Victorian and subsequent times. But *where* people laughed mattered as well, since that determined their humour's subject-matter and sophistication. The book is about Londoners' satirical humour, and this can't rightly be interpreted without locating it within the frames of London living.

London isn't commonly thought of as a place that was much given to laughter or that was much of a laugh in itself. Disease haunted its tenements and thieves its streets, and the poor were exploited and hungry. Such prosperity as its humbler people enjoyed was precarious, while the educated worried about urban vice or the people's disaffection. The gaps between the income, lifestyles and privileges of rich, middle, and poor were chasmic, and segregated living reinforced social distinction. Nonetheless, London was still a place in which laughter would insist on erupting. It was the great emporium in which satire and the old bawdry found their chief practitioners and markets. Nearly all the graphic satires whose cues we follow were conceived and sold in the metropolis, and the pleasures and vexations of London living were what a large proportion of them were about. Moreover, people in London heard more laughter than weeping, and saw more animation than woe. In streets and alehouses, in gentlemanly clubs and in artisan taverns, laughter flowed around wit, jest and sex, other people's appearances, mishaps and affectations, and the city's own intoxicating vigour. London was experienced as a stage, crowded with incident and human display: amusement, as like as not, was fed by things *seen* – all the better, therefore, for graphic representation. Human comedies, absurdities or misfortunes were enacted in public places and relished with sympathy or malice. In short, that still intelligible and walkable city was experienced with a visual immediacy that we've now lost. People saw it, journeyed in it, and enjoyed it differently; and they bequeath us vignettes like this one, which couldn't be re-enacted now:

> Walking some time since in Lincoln's Inn Fields, I followed a party of chimney-sweepers, who at the turning under a gateway, suddenly met three Chinese, apparently just arrived in London. It was clear they had never before seen chimney-sweepers, and it seemed that the chimney-sweepers had never, till that moment, seen such figures as the Chinese. Each party and every spectator was in a convulsion of laughter.[4]

One in ten of all English people lived in London by the mid-eighteenth century, and one in six are thought to have spent some time in it. No other European city grew so fast – from about 675,000 people in 1700 to just short of a million in 1801. (Paris was half the size.) By the very end of the eighteenth century, about 3,000 to 4,500 aristocratic and gentry families lived there during the parliamentary season. The mercantile and financial elites – some thousand families – had also grown in affluence and confidence, joining the patricians as the chief motor forces behind the building of fine houses, the social rituals within them, and the capital's seasonal consumption patterns. By 1800, these patrician and major mercantile families made up some 2 or 3 per cent of the London population, if their retinues are included. This 'elite' wielded political power and was the subject of most commentary. If we add to them the loosely defined 'middle classes' (these categories are fragile) – that is, the higher professional and the most successful literary and artistic figures, and then again some of the more successful merchants and manufacturers – we swell the proportion of London adults who could afford significant cultural consumption to some 10 per cent by the century's end.

The so-called 'middling' sorts – tradesmen, shopkeepers, and craftsmen – were also increasingly significant as the decades passed. About 30,000 such families have been estimated for 1801, making one in seven of the total.[5] Poverty and low levels of literacy prevented most from being primary cultural actors. Yet life was improving for some of them, and with it the confidence to express their views and tastes; and at more educated levels these were opinionated as well as aspiring people. Their spokesmen had deplored parliamentary corruption and the limitations on their political rights ever since the 1760s, and their electoral influence was unmatched elsewhere in Britain because London's parliamentary constituencies were uniquely democratic. By the 1810s, the hope or experience of improvement induced many to dissociate themselves from the manners of their ruder forebears, and 'respectability' began to claim them. As evangelical Christians struggled to plant moral earnestness in London's soil, they were to find multiplying allies among these aspirant folk. London's plebeians, alas, must be left outside our range. Their humour was just as sardonic and mocking as that of people above them, and more rumbustious and bawdy. But they were too poor to buy the prints on which this book is based and must be left to other kinds of study.[6]

Despite its many social distinctions, London was a place of exhilarating social fluidity, a booming, consuming, commercial capital in which innumerable forms of social intermingling were possible, even if they were mostly deplored. Its pleasure gardens and masquerades were 'great scenes of rendezvous', Henry Fielding wrote at mid-century, 'where the nobleman and his taylor, the lady of quality and her tirewoman [maid], meet together and form one common assembly'. 'The different departments of life are jumbled together,' Matt Bramble complained in Smollett's *Humphrey Clinker* (1771): 'there is no distinction or subordination left'. London was 'one universal masquerade', Hannah Cowley lamented ten years later: everyone was 'disguised in the same habits and manners'; it was 'a mere chaos, in which all distinction of rank is lost in a ridiculous affectation of ease'. Towards the end of the century, after long residence in London, the German pastor G. F. A. Wendeborn thought that there was no place in the world 'where a man may live more according to his own mind, or even his whims, than in London'. 'Everyone may choose his company according to his liking,' he explained; and since everyone dressed similarly, it was difficult to guess people's ranks in life. By the new century, a German visitor found it 'impossible to discriminate the merchant from the lord and the scholar; the very shopkeeper and mechanic will occasionally baffle his observation', so far had 'fashion . . . subjugated all ranks and classes of society'. In London, James Boswell wrote, 'we may be in some degree whatever character we choose'.[7]

This hierarchical confusion was here massively overstated; yet such confusion as there was fruitful, so far as it was allowed to extend. It was in London that gossip flowed most freely, as patricians and gentry swanned in and out of their town mansions during the parliamentary season, there to pursue their ambitions, pleasures and amours. Well might Walter Scott the novelist lament the peculiar 'causticity' of Londoners' taste for 'persiflage and personal satire': for gossip spilled out from taverns, clubs, coffee-houses, salons and tea parties into scandal magazines, newspapers and printshops. No other city was so dynamic, free and uncensored, and nowhere else were the comedies of snobbery and emulation played out or ridiculed so determinedly. As the more louche of the male elite crossed social boundaries downwards into convivial, sexual or sporting arenas, vast social differences were softened slightly in territories where rich, middle and middling men laughed at and celebrated similarly low things. For countless high-born men, metropolitan clubs were venues for semi-ritualized bonding, the cementing of alliances and the plotting of political action; but rude laughter was also released by the booze and sexual gossip that flowed there. These men wielded immense power self-interestedly and oppressively. But at least they drank, gambled, swore and fornicated as frankly as their underlings did, and didn't commonly lecture or hector others, or impose new moral values at the cost of the ancient consolations of tavern and alehouse, or, as Byron put it, of fucking in the Park. Secure in their privileges and supported by self-serving libertine philosophies, they were seldom on the defensive, even against Jacobins or those they regarded as canting meddlers in the Almighty's name. And, despite a mounting swell of critical radical voices in the 1790s, many humbler people who lived off their patronage did not wish it otherwise, for their manners were similar. Such cross-fertilization was lubricated by a knowing, sardonic and mocking humour, and London living was its source and condition.

In the 1780s, Pastor Wendeborn noted how continental people thought the English less 'lively, merry and insinuating' than other nations were: they were 'no friends of mirth'. But Wendeborn insisted that the English had changed greatly over the past century, for they had 'grown more gay'. They laughed immoderately at trifles, and enjoyed harlequin plays. Even their House of Commons was sometimes convulsed in laughter, he noted; and of what other senate could that be said? All this expressed England's liberty, he thought: and in this he was right.[8] In its upper reaches, London was a rigidly stratified society in which form passed easily for substance. Yet it was in London that high-mindedness coexisted with low-mindedness most nakedly. Here, innumerable coteries of the literary and professional middle classes associated most closely; and here were concentrated *demi-mondes* of rakes, courtesans, struggling hacks and engravers, and sellers of libertine images and literature. Here, too, the politest of people gambled, fornicated and smelled more than a little, and lived with stinking privies, dung-laden streets, and illicitly tumbled beds – such low preoccupations and conditions part of their acknowledged and accommodated world.

## Satirical prints

The sources that best illuminate these indecorous mindsets are abundant but woefully under-explored. The 20,000 or so satirical and humorous prints that were published in London between 1770 and 1830, in the golden age of graphic satire, are a gold mine for the historian of cultural change, and one of this book's purposes is to make new sense of them. From the 1780s until the 1830s, when changing tastes, markets and publishing forms rendered them near-obsolete, they flourished with far less inhibition than they had in previous generations, as well as in increasing numbers and forms. Produced for elite and middle-class purchasers (not for plebeians), their commentaries became more pointed, personalized and varied than they had been, and watercolouring became standard. Discarding the congested, laboured or literal iconography of the mid-eighteenth century, they strengthened and simplified their designs or took flight into an often surreal expressionism. The engravings of James Gillray, Thomas Rowlandson and George Cruikshank count among the great creative works of their era.

Some half of the prints disseminated political news and commentary. Many of these are now familiar since they have been quarried to decorate conventional political histories. But the other half were what the British Museum catalogued as social and personal satires. Although thousands of these survive, few have been republished since their first appearance. Most commented on current gossip and scandal, manners, fashions and sexual relations with more or less acerbity. Some were joke-sheets rather than satires properly speaking – genially relishing life's comedies, the pleasures and vexations of London living, or the quiddities of personality, fashion, sex or class. Others were darker, crueller and more cynical images – malicious, misanthropic or misogynistic. Since its concern is with the history of manners, it is to these social as distinct from political satires that this book chiefly attends.

Historians' neglect of this immense archive is odd. The critic E. H. Gombrich once hoped that Dorothy George's great achievement in cataloguing and describing the British Museum's vast holdings of satirical prints (all who work on the subject depend on it) would dispel the theoretical or aesthetic scruples which had hitherto inhibited art historians' engagement with graphic satire. There have been many subsequent appeals to pull satirical print into the mainstream of social and cultural history,[9] but most of these appeals have fallen flat. Such studies of the satirical prints as there have been have had rather narrow ambitions. Most of the score or so of scholars who have worked on them (hardly more than that in the past half century) have concentrated on the political satires, or on particular engravers or motifs. With one notable exception (Diana Donald), few have had much to say about the lived metropolitan milieux in which they were generated. None has discussed why their numbers rose in the new century and then collapsed in the 1830s, and how this related to the history of manners.[10]

This neglect is easily explained. The simplest reason is that the print archive is very big, scattered and difficult to access and sample. A more significant reason is that satirical and comic art has been and remains undervalued. Just as Joshua Reynolds's *Discourses* dismissed Hogarth for addressing 'low subjects' suited only to 'vulgar minds', so a century later John Ruskin's *Modern Painters*, having applauded George Cruikshank's 'influence over the popular mind' and 'stern understanding of the nature of evil', still thought his work beneath any 'more dignified, or even more intrinsically meritorious, branch of art'. Artistic hierarchies remain jealously defended, and comic or satirical art is still generally excluded from them. A further reason for the prints' neglect is that most text-trained historians are uneasy about using visual evidence. To say that 'pictures form a point of peculiar friction and discomfort across a broad range of intellectual enquiry' is to put it mildly.[11] Visual rhetoric isn't easily reduced to the expository prose historians trade in. Moreover while texts usually explain themselves and tacitly or explicitly refer to each other, images don't always explain their existence. Satirical prints were often deliberately ambiguous, so that deciding on even so simple a question as whether they were 'satirical' may depend on how we choose to spin them. They constructed illusory reality-effects that were filtered through intentions, styles, or market interests remote from the initial observation, or from our easy understanding. On these and like grounds, most historians are wary of visual evidence like this, and feel that words are what they should live by.

It goes without saying that no historian can dispense with the verbal testimonies that put images into context. Yet squeamishness about using pictures as evidence is uncalled for. Images can distort information about the real world, but the written word does too: texts must also be interpreted with an eye on their hidden purposes, distortions and audiences. The fact remains that texts and images are both embedded in the world that produced them, and in that sense have comparable evidential standing.[12] More specifically, although the graphic satires' relation to reality was skewed by fantasy and illusion, they remain invaluable cultural barometers. Most were informal and quickly engraved commercial productions, so that their emotional impulses and purposes were lightly concealed, if concealed at all. (Words informed them anyway, in titles and subtexts.) They referred much more immediately than other artworks did to matters of topical concern to purchasers. And things could be expressed in images that words could not bear, and that if put into words the law wouldn't bear either. Prints were virtually immune to prosecution for personal, obscene, seditious or blasphemous libel, so that engravers could comment in terms that writers wouldn't dare to employ. So satirical prints convey much about the unspoken attitudes, fears or understandings of those silent majorities about whom contemporary books, pamphlets or newspapers tell us little.

An example of this is a small satirical print on the Prince of Wales's secret and illicit marriage to Mrs Fitzherbert in December 1785. He had wooed her by sobbing, pleading and stabbing himself with a penknife. It was one of a cluster of prints on the subject, but it expressed more forthrightly than most what was spoken among men rather than written in text or confessed in the salon; and it was published in full confidence about the market it aimed at. The prince's marriage was illicit both because Mrs Fitzherbert was a Catholic and because the king couldn't have sanctioned it even had he known of it (which he didn't): in due course the prince had to renounce her. News of the marriage leaked out very slowly, but then: 'Oh but the hubbub you are to hear and to talk of,' as Horace Walpole tittered in February 1786: 'they tell me the passengers in the streets, of all ranks, talk of it'. The first print on the subject was published on 13 March, selling so well that for several days 'the publisher's [Fores's] premises were crowded with the servants of the *beau monde* . . . demanding impressions faster than they could be printed'.[13] Our example capitalized on the sensation a fortnight later with one of the most wittily punning titles in the print repertoire. *His Highness in Fitz* shows the prince

**Fig. 3** Kingsbury *or* Stubbs, *His Highness in Fitz* (Fores, 1786)

literally inside 'Fitz', in an orgasmic 'fit', the title implies (though both are clothed and the penetration is concealed) [fig. 3].

This wasn't an aberrant production. It illuminates understandings that club- and tavern-loving men took for granted. One understanding was, as they would have put it, that princes and their women *fuck*: here a cheerfully materialist reductionism was at work, characteristic of libertine culture. Another turned on the licence that could be claimed for tacitly seditious graphic expression, and the scant respect for royalty that the print, like countless others, so insolently communicates even in that loyalist age. Importantly, this cheerfully equalizing declaration came from a respectable source. Though unsigned, the print was engraved either by the mezzotint artist H. Kingsbury or by George Townly Stubbs, the son of the artist, George Stubbs. The printshop doesn't announce itself either, but its address is given as 4 Piccadilly. This was next door to S. W. Fores's fashionable printshop at number 3, and Fores's responsibility for it is indisputable. He produced most of the prints exposing the marriage in these months. This one must have been one of his successes, because he followed it up a month later with a larger Kingsbury or Stubbs called *Out of Fits, or the Recovery to the Satisfaction of all Parties*, this one carrying his byline [fig. 4]. In it, the

OUT OF FITS,
*or THE RECOVERY* TO THE SATISFACTION OF *ALL PARTIES*.

**Fig. 4** Kingsbury *or* Stubbs, *Out of Fits, or the Recovery to the Satisfaction of all Parties* (Fores, 1786)

prince and Mrs Fitzherbert loll on a sofa in post-coital exhaustion. Two tired dogs sit at their feet, and a rough parody of Hogarth's *After* hangs on the wall behind them. The allusion to the indecencies of Hogarth's paired *Before* and *After* (1736) means that *His Highness in Fitz* stands for the missing '*During*'. In a further Fores print of the same month, Fores's shop-front features in the background, and both *His Highness in Fitz* and *Out of Fits* are displayed in its windows.[14] There's a lot going on here that the conventional histories of those years seldom accommodate. You'd have to dig deep and hard into texts to find comparably explicit evidence of the reflexive knowingness of libertine male culture in this era, or of the simple pleasure that could be extracted from an anti-royal joke so cheeringly offensive.

In the absence of hard information on print runs and circulation, it is often difficult to distinguish prints that were influential from those that were not, or to argue that one or another print spoke for an 'average' or a 'majority' opinion on this or that subject. But textual evidence presents the same difficulties. In any case, the historian of mentalities is concerned with what was thinkable and doable in the past, regardless of the assumed numbers of people involved or its assumed normative standing. In illuminating these questions the prints are unrivalled sources. To attempt to sample their contents 'systematically' would be futile. They covered nearly everything that moved and breathed in London, and were as diverse and idiosyncratic as life itself. As with all vastly rich sources, their reading must depend on the historian's insight and intuition, and will never be comprehensive. It helps, however, that their motifs tended to cluster chronologically. And since each cluster had its own external provocations, it can be read just as a cluster of written texts is read, that is, as a cue to the preoccupations of the moment. Follow these cues, and it becomes possible to think with and through images, and not merely about them.

The views of women – or of sex – in these prints remind us that theirs was chiefly a male humour. Women did collect and design satires, especially about fashion, and were participants in or critics of male humour as well as targets of it. But since most satires were engraved and bought by men, and since the men in question followed unapologetically 'manly' codes, and since again a very high proportion of the personal satires commented on relations between the sexes – this book led by the prints offers that rare thing for this period: a history of sexual and social politics above plebeian levels that is based on the evidence not of sermons, advice books, or female sensibilities, but of men's attitudes and practices – and not very earnest men, either.

Through the prints runs an ironic scepticism about power and high-minded affectation that was almost reflexive then, and that luckily still is, here and there. Peculiarly English, if metropolitan, products, they remind us where we've come from. In 1791, Pastor Wendeborn remarked that 'the respect paid to people of rank' was weaker in England than it was elsewhere: 'every one seems to know that those who, on account of their station or employment in life, wear a rich or a singular dress are and remain but men.' 'While gravity and imposture not only exist, but reign triumphant,' William Hazlitt snorted in 1829, 'while the proud, obstinate, sacred tumours rear their heads on high, and are trying to get a new lease for ever and a day; then oh! . . . to break the torpid spell, and reduce the bloated mass to its native insignificance!' A journalist in the *Literary Gazette* wrote a few years later that the English were 'the only true philosophers who thus turn all their political miseries into fun and laughter', since great satire could thrive only 'in a land of liberty'.[15] Expressing postures like these, graphic satires refused to shirk hidden truths and thus fuelled one of the nation's happier self-representations. In our own censoring age, deferential to corporate, managerial, religious and other forms of fashionably correct values, we should both celebrate and learn from their candour, and their refusal to put up with bullshit.

# Impoliteness

Many grand narratives attempt to tell the story of this era. The 'industrial revolution' and the growth of the state shape some of them; the spread of nationhood, empire and Protestantism shape others; and gender historians worry whether sexual differences were or were not sharpened by the century's end. All agree that Britain under George III (1760–1820) and George IV (1820–1830) was the richest and economically most dynamic state in the world. George III in later years went off his head and his son and heir was a despised and profligate rake. Britain's statesmen lost the American colonies and their political system protected elite interests and property; from the 1790s until the 1820s paranoid governments used censorship and prisons to silence their critics. Even so, with Britain's wealth built on impoverished labour at home and imperial conquest abroad, they consolidated Britain's national and Protestant identity, kept revolution at bay, and beat Napoleon. Until revolution in France silenced them, the Whigs, at least, favoured some kinds of reform. Both the younger Pitt (Tory prime minister for two decades after 1784) and Charles James Fox (the Whig opposition leader) enjoyed supra-European stature. By European standards, they reigned over a uniquely tolerant culture in which liberty of opinion and belief was more than a watchword, however deeply Pittite repression compromised it.

The narrative that matters most to this book addresses the dissemination of 'polite' values in the eighteenth century. It stresses that the privileged and the educated were high-minded and sober on the whole, and dedicated to virtue, profit, and progress. Many were enterprising and free-thinking polymaths who believed that reason should lead them and that life's greatest good was the urbane sociability that expressed reason. From Shaftesbury's *Characteristics* of 1711 and Addison's and Steele's *Spectator* shortly after, on through the works of many lesser writers, politeness was initially conceived as an oppositional and ethical creed: it was the chief bond of civil society and bore 'an idealized vision of human intercourse'.[16] In people of good breeding, Shaftesbury wrote, politeness induced an equal, just, and universal friendship; and benevolence, not Hobbesian self-interest, was its central principle.

As time passed, more and more people were touched by these values. The culturally renascent provincial town was one measure of their influence; the nation's associational and literary culture was another; while the mannered elegance of eighteenth-century portraiture expressed it artistically. Later in the century, politeness fused with 'gentility' and 'respectability' at lower social levels, while the deepening cult of 'sensibility' instructed both sexes to value emotion above reason and sympathy above self-interest. As both cause and effect of this movement, women became more influential cultural consumers and producers. Ever more audibly, too, they were told to be more chaste and domestic than their forebears, and men were advised to be more chivalrous towards women. These exhortations bred a gentler society. The rougher manners of the high and middle people were polished by them, and, in genteel if not in all arenas, behavioural distances between the polite and the vulgar widened.

But how far should we push this cheering story, and what does it conceal? Politeness's leading historian rightly notices how often polite manners came adrift from their ethical mooring, becoming what the likes of Lord Chesterfield regarded as mere 'external checks' to secure self-advancement.[17] But simpler versions of this narrative tend to forget this. Fixated on what was recommended rather than on what people actually did, they forget that the rising volume and energy of injunctions to act politely chiefly show how many people didn't. They particularly downplay the earthier behaviours and attitudes that ignored, competed with or coexisted with polite manners. These had always been embedded in the manly codes of clubroom, tavern and sporting arena, in the military codes of a recurrently warring nation, in the libertine codes that ruled freethinking men's (and some women's) sexual behaviour, not to mention in the vast numbers of gentlefolk who enjoyed lives of extraordinary sexual vividness or libertine brutality without the least self-consciousness. Nor does the simple narrative allow a place for the carnivalesque belly-laughter and farts-and-bums mockery that many fine people continued to relish, or for the scurrilous prints that undercut Sir Joshua Reynolds's idealized portraits. If these and similar behaviours are acknowledged, they tend to feature only as 'transgressions' against or as 'subversions' of dominant values, that is, as derivative or secondary reactions, which serve chiefly to highlight civility's deepening purchase.[18] This, though, won't do.

Some rude behaviours did consciously subvert polite norms: the excitement they offered originated from the act of defiance. Many low behaviours were unselfconscious, however, since they drew on norms with their own history and legitimacy. Indeed, some may be regarded as the primal historical subject, since they defined the baseline condition, rooted in past times, against which appeals to civility reacted. As French historians of mentality have pointed out, human action seldom discards the primal impulses of the old Adam or the imprint of past cultures, so that most people act in terms of 'ready-made ideas, commonplaces and intellectual bric-a-brac, the remnants of cultures and mentalities belonging to different times and different places'. 'Civilizing' discourses are constrained by these remnants. Braudel called them the prisons of the *longue durée*; Labrousse called them 'resistances', referring to the inertia embedded in habits, attitudes, feelings and carnivalesque ceremonies which new ideas can shift only slowly, if at all. These 'get in the way of history', Braudel wrote: 'as hindrances [they] stand as limits . . . beyond which man and his experiences cannot go'.[19] If all this is so, our conventional empahases need re-ordering. It's *im*politeness that becomes the baseline subject, and social disciplining that is the chronically challenged reaction.

Much academic ink has also been spilled on the need felt to defend the distance between the public and the private spheres of polite society. For the century's earlier decades, this has its point. Even the history of satire shows this. 'There is nothing that more betrays a base, ungenerous spirit, than the giving of secret stabs to a man's reputation,' Addison had ruled, and the satirists of Hogarth's era generally agreed. But, later in the century, the force of the public/private distinction weakened. When James Boswell planned Dr Johnson's biography in the 1780s, he knew better than to speculate on Johnson's sexual life; and his friends rebuked him for breaching the code of confidentiality when he betrayed Johnson's private comments. But breach that code Boswell did, when all is said and done, and in this he was far from alone. He wrote after all in the age that invented the novel of sentiment, the narrative of suffering, and the intimate biography and diary (his own), in all of which an increasing premium was placed on emotional authenticity and candour. At the same time, an expanding print culture was anticipating our own celebrity-obsessed media culture by disseminating the scurrilous details of private life more widely. Gossip became institutionalized in scandal magazines and in radical oppositional writing, while the satirical prints of the later eighteenth century blithely ignored the taboo that had constrained Hogarth. In the first decades of the nineteenth century, radical printshops could make political capital out of the Duke of York's infatuation with the courtesan Mary Anne Clarke, or out of the regent's funny way with mistresses – and this to radicalize or titillate shopkeepers, tradesmen, and similarly opinionated classes, none of whom gave a cuss for elite taboos. 'I know no distinction between public and private life,' the bookseller William Hone declared when tried for blasphemous libel in 1817: and his grounds were that 'men should be consistent in their conduct', and not shelter behind 'privacy' as the old elites were wont to.[20]

Our sense of the era greatly benefits from the information revealed by the unseemly disclosures that ensued. Drinking, gambling, predatory sex, female impropriety and rutting, the fudging of gendered or social boundaries – these were among the most familiar types of misbehaviour that polite moralists protested at. Rude humour in high places, and the low thoughts, habits and company that generated it, were others. Allow this rude language a more prominent place in our attentions, therefore – prioritize real behaviour and not the evidence of polite discourse, conduct books or sermons – and our view of the age is usefully reconfigured. It then matters deeply, for example, that the younger Pitt was a free-thinking drunkard (despite his being celibate and, as the quip went, stiff to everyone but a lady); that the young Charles James Fox confessed that 'fucking in cundums frigging etc. was my chief employment in Town'; and that when Fox died in 1806, he died, as debauchees do, of cirrhosis of the liver. For another narrative lurks in these stories, though not exactly a grand one. Over centuries past, the differentiation of high and low cultures had been steadily proselytized and continued to be so. In the salon, Fox and others could still count as 'polite'. Yet in their low behaviour outside the salon, and in the casts of humour that went with them, we glimpse the obstinate survival of a more unitary culture in which many elite and vulgar attitudes remained congruent.

# Change

If most of the book is concerned with resistances and continuities, Part IV addresses a history of change – a watershed, indeed, in the history of manners, to which the 1820s were crucial. The rules of 'politeness' have left little residue in modern behaviour; the taboos amplified in the 1820s have left many.

All manner of attitudes were affected by the shifts that occurred then, including some that may be unexpected. In the later Georgian years, for example, many of the great, the good and the not so good went to watch public executions with a candid curiosity. They observed the ghastly scaffold spectacle through understandings now lost to us, and without undue emotional disturbance. I have shown elsewhere that this changed in the first half of the nineteenth century, thanks partly to the mounting squeamishness of an increasingly fastidious and bourgeois people. The respectable classes' gradual retreat from the gallows was less a function of humanitarianism than it was part of that repudiation of the contaminating 'low' that is central to all civility.[21] The histories of public hanging and of humour could hardly differ more; yet both followed similar trajectories and expressed similar processes. Both bore witness to deep changes in publicly acceptable emotion, with squeamishness at their centre. By the 1820s and 1830s, 'indecencies' were being sanitized by analogous pressures, so that the old satirical bawdry, or Charles Fox's behaviour, or sexually exuberant women, would soon look as suspect as the scaffold. Economic improvement, political reform, evangelical meddling and intensified social policing all helped in this; nor should the cumulative impact of regency censorship be discounted. But as important as all these was the increasing audibility of the newly respectable classes who began to shun the more robust subjects and forms of humour, along with much else, as expressions of a ruder, crueller world. It took nearly 150 years for satire (and 'cartooning') to recover from this great silencing, just as it took as long for men and women publicly to reclaim their sensuality. Of course, ridicule, ribaldry and self-indulgence didn't die in the nineteenth century. Even now influential corners of British life retain the ironic, sardonic and cynical casts of mind that can call the bluffs of politicians, prudes and censors. Still, in the 1820s something happened to English manners that left a contrary legacy, and we'll see in chapter 14 that the word 'watershed' describes it as well as any.

# PART I

# THE SENSE
## *of* PLACE

CHAPTER ONE

# LONDON AND THE PLEASURE PRINCIPLE

## Traffic

In the later eighteenth century, London was growing so fast that contemporaries liked to think it beyond understanding. There would 'soon be one street from London to Brentford,' Horace Walpole worried, 'ay, and from London to every village ten miles round!'[1] But by modern standards it was still built to a human scale. Even in 1800, it offered virtually the same panorama that Hollar had engraved in the seventeenth century, apart from the expanding western suburbs. From the heights of Highgate or Hampstead, you would have seen a smoke-laden vista of steeples rising above grey brick and slate, with St Paul's Cathedral and the Tower dominating the ancient City to the east, and Westminster Abbey to the west. The City and Westminster and the parishes between them were linked by the Thames, but also by the ancient highway that ran from Cornhill, Cheapside and St Paul's Churchyard in the east, down Ludgate Hill into Fleet Street and the Strand to the west; then at the ancient junction of Charing Cross it swung south down Whitehall to Parliament and Westminster Abbey. It was parallelled to the north by the spinal route that led condemned felons from Newgate prison along High Holborn, via St Giles's High Street and Oxford Street, to execution at Tyburn, where Marble Arch is now. Tyburn marked the bounds of fashionable living in the north-west, but the area was growing so fast that public hangings were moved from there to the gate of Newgate prison in 1783 to spare fashionable inhabitants' feelings. The New (later Marylebone) Road, Somerstown and the City Road marked the same bounds further north, until Regent's Park was laid out in 1811.

From west to east you could walk across the metropolis in a couple of hours or so, and from south to north in one. The edges were so indeterminate that people debated where London turned into country. Go in any direction and you would soon enter a bedraggled countryside of smallholdings, market gardens and pastures for the livestock on its way to Smithfield market. Walk or ride a few miles north up the Great North Road, and you would have to cram yourself against muddy hedges when the tinkling of bells announced cattle, sheep or mule trains that would crowd you off the central causeway. Beyond Westminster Abbey and Parliament, housing quickly yielded to pastures and common lands. The Ranelagh pleasure gardens were a coach- or boat-ride away in rural Chelsea, and Vauxhall pleasure gardens were south of the Thames in Battersea. In the east, population pressure was contained by restrictions on house-building that extended back to the seventeenth century, so speculative builders filled every labyrinthine alley and courtyard with tenements. Whitechapel in 1800 still marked the limits of plebeian overcrowding, while Bethnal Green was circled by green, Shadwell was full of rope-walks to supply the dockland ships, and Stepney consisted largely of market gardens. South of the Thames, Battersea was covered in common lands interrupted only by Vauxhall gardens, and beyond the Elephant and Castle or down the Kent Road houses thinned quickly. In the 1770s, Southwark struck a visitor as comprising 'but two streets in its breadth, and almost entirely occupied by tanners and weavers'. The radical tailor Francis Place, that most compulsive recorder of London's daily life, recalled Lambeth as occupied by river fishermen. Even by 1800, only a minority of Londoners lived south of the Thames – and not the best of people, either. For most of his life, Walpole boasted that he was lucky never once to have had cause to cross the river.[2]

The square mile of the old Roman City was the beating heart of financial and mercantile London. It was full of merchants, agents, brokers and of the much-derided *nouveaux riches* 'cits', their cockney accents much mocked in satire. Craftsmen and artisans filled the City's backstreets and those of Clerkenwell to the north of it. They also filled the parishes centred on Covent Garden. The West End was where the fine people lived. The really poor were largely out of sight of the grander folk, except as beggars or street labourers. Silk-weavers sweated far away in the tenements of Spitalfields to the east of the City. Coalheavers, boatmen and casual labourers did the same along the eastern Thames. The very poorest were concentrated in the slums of Saffron Hill or of St Giles's, north of Covent Garden, or around Rosemary Lane and St Catherine's Lane in the East End, or in anciently derelict streets like the aptly named Thieving Lane and Little Sanctuary in Westminster. Better known than the eastern quarters (because it was in the heart of workaday London), St Giles's was to feature highly in the mounting anxieties about beggars and crime.

Streets were fog- and smoke-cursed, and the humbler houses noisome. A London visitor in 1777 reported an April smog so thick that he could see only four steps ahead. The park was 'impregnated with a sort of black stuff' left by winter smoke, and St Paul's Cathedral was so besooted that it seemed 'built of coal'. Streets began to improve in the next decade, but there was still much to do. Parliament Street, Charing Cross and Pall Mall had lately been paved with freestone; but in other streets even the richest coaches must jolt along muddy and uneven cobbles like so many farm carts, their occupants bemired if they left the windows open. Great streets like the Strand were in bad weather 'foul with a dirty puddle to the height of three or four inches', and shopfronts and coaches were caked with mud. Luckily, this foreign observer added, the English were unafraid of mud. Its effects were camouflaged 'by their wigs of a brownish curling hair, their black stockings, and their blue surtouts which are made in the form of a nightgown': women's clothes he didn't mention. West London was 'as much buried in dirt as the old' areas, he added, because the ground north of Piccadilly was too level for rainwater to drain away.[3] Nocturnal travel was risky, even if you were helped by the link-boys who for pennies would light your way with firebrands. A few streets were lit by oil lamps, but these did little more than 'warn the inhabitants to avoid the posts on which they were placed'.[4] Piccadilly was the first street to be lit by gas in 1809, the sensation of it meriting a comic commemoration in a print by Woodward, re-engraved by Rowlandson [fig. 5].

The fashionable squares were multiplying, their gardens closed to the common people. Hyde Park was also privileged territory. Deer were hunted there until 1768, and it remained the venue for gentlemanly duels and the horse- and carriage-riding *ton*. If the humble frequented it, it

**Fig. 5** Woodward and Rowlandson, *A Peep at the Gas Lights in Pall-Mall*
(Tegg, 1809)

The prostitute (r.) says that she may as well shut up shop if street lights aren't put a stop
to. 'True my dear,' replies her client, 'not a dark corner to be got for love or money.'

was usually to buy or sell what James Boswell called venereal pleasures.
Courtesans patrolled it in carriages, and Boswell in his many 'brutal
fevers' would go there to be 'relieved by dalliance' with poor girls and
then be smitten with anxiety about the pox.[5] St James's Park was 'a long
dirty field, intersected by a wide dirty ditch'; planted with rotten lime
trees, its rank grass was browsed by mangy sheep. The first effort to
improve it came in 1814, when a fete was held there for the Russian
emperor and the Prussian king.[6]

When poor people took the Sunday air or met to voice their views, they
had to walk to the ancient spaces on the city's edges: to Spa Fields above
Clerkenwell; to Tothill Fields between the Abbey and Millbank (where bulls
were baited as late as 1820); and to Goodman's Fields near the Tower. The
radical London Corresponding Society held one of its earliest public

meetings in Copenhagen Fields in Islington in 1795, and radicals and Chartists (later) continued to meet there until a new cattle market was erected in 1852. These places were indeed the fields that their names referred to, though overuse had worn them down to hardened earth or exhausted grass patches. South of the Thames, St George's Fields between Southwark and Lambeth, where the Gordon riots began in 1780, had only lately been obliterated by villas. Otherwise, plebeian festivity was crowded into such spaces as the medieval street patterns allowed. Eight times a year after 1783, in the most gruesome of spectacles, several people would be hanged at once in the narrow territory in the Old Bailey, outside Newgate prison; yet for famous executions, like those of the Cato Street conspirators, who in 1820 had tried to blow up the Cabinet at dinner, crowds of 100,000 people were claimed, mostly spilling down side streets remote from the gallows itself. Life and death were knowing neighbours in London. A couple of stones' throws from Newgate, Bartholomew Fair crammed itself into what was still a 'field' beyond St Bartholomew's hospital. Here, for five days a year in wonderfully carnivalesque disorder, portable theatres and sideshows swarmed with harlequins, columbines, mountebanks, fire-eaters, necromancers and rope-dancers, along with pickpockets, prostitutes and apprentices on the spree.[7]

Poorer people generally travelled on foot, richer people by horse, hackney carriage or coach, or by sedan chairs until around 1820, when they went out of fashion.[8] There were jams and accidents and many complaints about traffic. 'Chaise after chaise, coach after coach, cart after cart,' a German visitor complained of Cheapside and Fleet Street in the 1770s: 'all the world rushes headlong without looking'.[9] 'The foot-passengers run along as if they were pursued by bailiffs,' Smollett reported in *Humphrey Clinker*: 'The porters and chairmen trot with their burthens. People, who keep their own equipages, drive through the streets at full speed. . . . The hackney-coachmen make their horses smoke, and the pavement shakes under them; and I have actually seen a waggon pass through Piccadilly at the hand-gallop. In a word, the whole nation seems to be running out of their wits.' The press of people and traffic in Piccadilly twice caused Horace Walpole to stop his coach, 'thinking there was a mob': the 'tides of coaches, chariots, curricles, phaetons, &c. are endless'.[10] Yet commentators would always dramatize disorder. In fact, nothing normally moved faster than a horse's trot (horses were supposed not to gallop), and stopping twice while travelling down Piccadilly is nothing to us today. Contemporary paintings and drawings show streets with four-storey buildings and shops with fascia boards and small-panelled windows, with horses, haywagons, carriages and carts: but only Rowlandson's comic prints show the congestion. Depictions of Charing Cross from Canaletto's painting in 1755 on to Scharf's detailed drawings of 1825 show streetscapes hardly less peaceful. Yet Charing Cross was the antique junction, according to Dr Johnson, at which 'the full tide of human existence' flowed.[11] As it happens, we have an exact record of traffic there from observation. One morning in 1827, Francis Place gazed out of his Charing Cross bedroom and then in his diary froze this moment in the urban parade below:[12]

22 November 1827. 11 am
There are in the street between my house and Parliament Street, and consequently within sight in one direction:

*Horses / carriages*
  *8 — 2  stage coaches with 4 horses each}*
  *8 — 2  ditto } standing at the Ship*
  *4 — 1  ditto[standing] at the Silver Cross*
  *2 — 1  dray delivering ale*
  *6 — 1  wagon coming along loaded with Swedish turnips,*
       *drawn by 6 horses*
  *14 – 7  hackney coaches and cabriolets*
  *2 — 2  do. cabriolets*
  *3 — 3  do. private*
  *12 – 3  waggons with coals: several saddle horses*
  *4 — 1  do. [coal waggon] empty*
  *2 — 1  cart loaded with potatoes*
  *6 — 2  with bricks -*
  *2 — 1  - sand*
  *3 — 3  small carts with broken stones*
  *7 — 1  heavy truck with a block of stone drawn by 7 horses*
  *8 — 2  stages running*
  *3 — 1  cart with donkey [?]*
  *1 — 1  do. delivering boards*
  *2 — 1  mud cart loading*
  *1 — 1  do. waiting*
  ⎯⎯⎯⎯
*horses 102 — 37 carriages, not including several small carts...*

Those horses! – four for the stagecoaches and coal-wagon, six for the turnip wagon, seven to haul a block of stone: each horse depositing 22 lb of dung a day or over three and a half tons a year,[13] each leaving streets swilling in piss and in need of poor boys or beggars to sweep them, the stench so familiar that people didn't notice it, and each causing an incessant clatter and rumble of hoofs and iron-rimmed wheels on cobbles so that from a distance London sounded 'as if all the noises of all the wheels of all the carriages in creation were mingled and ground together in one subdued, hoarse, moaning hum'.[14] Accidents from 'furious driving' there were, and occasional inquests on poor souls caught under wheels, and on the uneven roads top-heavy coaches did overturn now and then. And yet, when all is said and done, those 101 horses and one donkey laboured on at little more than walking or trotting pace, and only two stagecoaches were 'running' when Place looked out, and this down a vista some half a mile long and thirty yards wide. So you could usually cross even Charing Cross at risk from little more than the filthy swill under your feet. And when crowds gathered to mock the miscreants put in the pillory there, it was the wagons that made way for the people, not the other way around.

## Happiness

What did people feel about London? How could comedy possibly reign in such a city, and how might it feed its satires? These are questions more easily asked than answered. If you put your trust in social historians, you would know London as a city of cruel deprivation. It saw the cruellest of public punishments at the Tyburn or Newgate gallows, and chronic disorder, social exploitation and crime. Disease, death and sweated labour ruled its backstreets, and its elegance was enjoyed by few. If you put your trust in historians of high culture, belly laughter is not what you'd expect to hear there. The canonical poets and moralists spoke of an alienated city in which, as Blake saw it, every face was written with marks of weakness, marks of woe: 'In every cry of every man / In every infant's cry of fear, / In every voice, in every ban, / The mind-forg'd manacles I hear.' Believe de Quincy, and you would expect a phantasmagoric city of 'faces never-ending without voice or utterance . . . like a mask of maniacs, or, oftentimes, a pageant of phantoms'. Follow Wordsworth and you would expect a city of 'Folly, vice, / Extravagance in gesture, mien, and dress' – of 'strangers, nor knowing each the other's name': 'How often, in the overflowing streets, / Have I gone forwards with the crowd, and said / Unto myself, "The face of every one / That passes by me is a mystery!"'; London was a world of alienated strangers for Dickens also, the fog that pervaded his city standing for people's inability to see each other, to connect.

Negative views of the city had so dominated the most self-conscious eighteenth-century texts that it would have needed a brave literary man to gainsay them. Viewing the world through classical filters and idealizing the harmony of ancient Rome or Athens, hardly a single writer failed to stress this modern Babylon's dangers.[15] John Gay's *Beggar's Opera* or Daniel Defoe's *Moll Flanders* might celebrate the energies of low life, but only to show the thinness of civility's veneer. For Alexander Pope, London had been the city of dullness, its literature the product of dunces, its very rivers symbolizing its putrefaction. Jonathan Swift saw horror in the effects of a London shower: 'Sweepings from Butchers' stalls, Dung, Guts, and Blood, / Drown'd puppies, stinking Sprats, all drench'd in mud, / Dead cats and Turnip-Tops come tumbling down the Flood.' Samuel Johnson deplored London's voice as it cried 'Get money, money still! / And then let virtue follow, if she will'. Defoe indicted a city awash with commercial wealth that was 'almost universally founded upon crime', 'a scene of rapine and danger', a breeding ground for plague, thieves and whores. The blind Bow Street magistrate, Sir John Fielding, saw crime as the consequence of London's luxury, while his half-brother Henry, the novelist, described the city as 'a vast wood or forest, in which a thief may harbour with as great security, as wild beasts do in the deserts of Africa or Arabia'. In Fielding's novels of the 1740s, *Joseph Andrews* and *Tom Jones*, the city was a place of artifice and seduction; only country life was wholesome. Smollett's *Humphrey Clinker* (1771) has Matt Bramble describe a populace 'actuated by the demons of profligacy and licentiousness . . . rambling, riding, rolling, rushing, justling, mixing, bouncing, cracking, and crashing, in one vile ferment of stupidity and corruption'; his London was 'an overgrown monster'. By the time Edward Gibbon published *Decline and Fall of the Roman Empire* in 1776, readers were conditioned to believe that great empires decline in luxury, vice and war, and that Britain was heading that way too. Evangelicals deepened the gloom towards the end of the century. From Greenwich, John Newton looked back one day at London's smoke and saw it as 'an emblem of the accumulated stock of misery, arising from all the trials and afflictions of individuals within my view': 'I thought it likewise an emblem of that cloud of sin which is continually ascending with a mighty cry in the ears of the Lord of hosts . . . In London the number and impunity of offenders, joined with the infidelity and dissipation of the times, make it a kind of hot-bed or nursery for wickedness. Sin is studied as a science, and there are professors and inventors of evil things in a variety of branches, who have an unhappy address in teaching others to sin with an *eclat*.'[16]

Descriptions like these determined the perceptions of earnest readers then and can shape our assumptions today. But how seriously should they be taken? The historian of mentality may feel that these representations reveal the cost of reading too much, their gloom a little too bookish. For London had many faces, and the face people saw depended on their experiences, temperaments and preoccupations, and what they felt about the city is, as like as not, illuminated by the things in it that they thought funny. There always prevailed a more celebratory and jollier view of the city, however seldom the poets revealed it. Turn to letters, diaries and prints across our period, and we encounter people who were attuned to the comic and who celebrated a London marked by something other than weakness and woe. Time after time we meet Londoners who knew how or who sought to be *happy*. These, not the poets, rule this story.

Nobody knew better than James Boswell, for example, that '*imaginary* London, gilded with all the brilliancy of warm fancy as I have viewed it, and London as a scene of real business, are quite different'. 'I have often amused myself with thinking how different a place London is to different people,' he wrote, then listing how differently a politician, a grazier, a merchant, a theatregoer and a man of pleasure would see the city, adding that 'the intellectual man' would be 'struck with it, as comprehending the whole of human life in all its variety, the contemplation of which is inexhaustible'.[17] Although a good part of Boswell's addiction to London was born of his venereal pleasures, there is no denying his intense joy in the city, or the comic vision that informed it. When he had first visited London in 1760, aged twenty-one, he had had a gloriously rakish time of it – with street girls mainly, so hard to come by in stony Edinburgh. Returning two years later, he found London's anonymity a source not of alienation but of delight. His well-primed expectations strike the note we're after:

> When we came upon Highgate hill and had a view of London, I was all life
> and joy. I repeated Cato's soliloquy on the immortality of the soul, and my
> soul bounded forth to a certain prospect of happy futurity. I sung all manner

of songs, and began to make one about an amorous meeting with a pretty girl, the burthen of which was as follows: 'She gave me *this*, I gave her *that*; / And tell me, had she not tit for tat?' I gave three huzzas, and we went briskly in.[18]

Arriving again five years later, he 'sallied forth like a roaring lion after girls, blending philosophy and raking'. And for many years thereafter he would still be 'in a flutter' at the prospect of returning to London, despite the gruelling five-day coach journey from the dour piety of Edinburgh.[19] Nor was sex the only draw. Even as his life darkened with the years, he would still erupt in delight at London's vivacity: 'I felt a completion of happiness. I just sat and hugged myself in my own mind. Here I am in London . . . and here is Mr Johnson, whose character is so vast; here is Dr Goldsmith, so distinguished in literature. Words cannot describe our feelings . . . the radiance of light cannot be painted.'[20] 'My mind *rusts* very soon in the country, especially in damp weather,' he wrote shortly before his death. Anticipating Dickens, though to different effect, he remained the prototypical *flâneur*, finding the bustle and human oddities of London streets 'a high entertainment of itself. I see a vast museum of all objects, and I think with a kind of wonder that I see it for nothing.'[21] 'I never knew any one who had such a *gust* for London as you have,' Dr Johnson told him, although it was Johnson who pronounced London a synonym for life itself: 'The happiness of London is not to be conceived but by those who have been in it.' His reasons for saying so were more sedate than Boswell's: 'there is more learning and science within the circumference of ten miles from where we now sit than in all the rest of the kingdom.' But, like Boswell's, Johnson's was a 'resolutely unsymbolic city' of ceaseless and pleasurable conversation.[22]

This Joswellian enthusiasm, this refusal to convert the city into a mere symbol of corruption, was too commonplace for us to think of it as a purposeful evasion of London's bleaker realities. For, even as Smollett's fictional Matt Bramble writes home peevishly about London's vices, Bramble's young niece Lydia observes of her uncle that 'people of experience and infirmity . . . see with very different eyes from those that such as you and I make use of'. There is no reason to call her bluff when she sees London through a young woman's eyes, and what a positive London it is! She describes its excitement and joy, her 'imagination . . . quite confounded with splendour and variety'. While her uncle had seen in Ranelagh's pleasure gardens 'a composition of baubles, overcharged with paltry ornaments, ill conceived, and poorly executed, without any unity of design or propriety of disposition', frequented by people more suited to Bedlam, she thought the gardens 'like the enchanted palace of a genie . . . crowded with the great, the rich, the gay, the happy, and the fair': 'I was dazzled and confounded with the variety of beauties that rushed all at once upon my eye.'[23]

If fictional artifice was at work here, the same can't be said for Charles Lamb's frank put-down of Wordsworth's rural and watery preferences in 1801: 'I have passed all my days in London,' Lamb told Wordsworth firmly, 'until I have formed as many and intense local attachments, as any of you mountaineers can have done with dead nature':

> The lighted shops of the Strand and Fleet Street, the innumerable trades, tradesmen and customers, coaches, waggons, play houses, all the bustle and wickedness round about Covent Garden, the very women of the town, the watchmen, drunken scenes, rattles; – life awake, if you awake, at all hours of the night, the impossibility of being dull in Fleet Street, the crowds, the very dirt & mud, the sun shining upon houses and pavements, the print shops, the old book stalls, parsons cheap'ning books, coffee houses, steams of soups from kitchens, the pantomimes, London itself a pantomime and a masquerade, – all these things work themselves into my mind and feed me without a power of satiating me. The wonder of these sights impells me into night-walks about her crowded streets, and I often shed tears in the motley Strand from fulness of joy at so much life. All these emotions must be strange to you. So are your rural emotions to me.[24]

'Streets, streets, streets,' Lamb wrote to another friend, 'markets, theatres, churches, Covent Gardens . . . noise of coaches, drowsy cry of mechanic watchmen at night, with bucks reeling home drunk if you happen to wake at midnight, cries of fire and stop thief . . . old book-stalls, Jeremy Taylors, Burtons on melancholy and Religio Medici's on every stall – . These are thy pleasures, O London with-the-many-sins. O city abounding in whores, for these may Keswick and her giant brood go hang.' Elsewhere he added that 'a mob of happy faces crowding up at the pit door of Drury Lane Theatre, just at the hour of six, gives me ten thousand sincerer pleasures, than I could ever receive from all the flocks of silly sheep that ever whitened the plains of Arcadia or Epsom Downs.'[25] Others were enchanted even by London's smoke: 'So far from the smoke of London being offensive to me,'

Haydon the artist said, 'it has always been to my imagination the sublime canopy that shrouds the city of the world. Drifted by the wind, or hanging in gloomy grandeur over the vastness of our Babylon, the sight of it always filled my mind with feelings of energy such as no other spectacle could inspire.'[26] And then there was Byron. Nominally studying at Cambridge in 1807 but in fact living it up in libertine London, he pityingly sent his friend Elizabeth Pigot, far north at Southwell, a catalogue of metropolitan titillations which she would never know:

> The intelligence of London cannot be interesting to you who *have rusticated* all your life, the annals of routs, riots, balls & boxing matches, dowagers & demireps, cards & crim-con [criminal conversation], parliamentary discussion, political details, masquerades, mechanics, Argyle Street Institution & aquatic races, love & lotteries, Brookes's & Buonaparte, exhibitions of pictures with drapes, & *women without*; statues with more *decent dresses*, than their *originals*, opera-singers & orators, wine, women, wax works, & weathercocks, cannot accord with your *insulated* ideas, of decorum & other *silly expressions*, not inserted in our *vocabulary*. – Oh Southwell, Southwell, how I rejoice to have left thee, & how I curse the heavy hours I have dragged along for so many months, amongst the *mohawks* who inhabit your *kraals*.[27]

Nor was it only the sophisticates who felt this delight. The self-taught Francis Place did too. One summer morning in 1827, a few months before he counted those horses, he gazed appreciatively from his bedroom window on to Charing Cross below, and again recorded what he saw with cinematic exactitude.[28] His description today reads almost as a sub-Dickensian chocolate-box pastiche, too good to be true: the coach-laden street as an arena of gaiety and good humour, the coach-buglers bugling, the working people picturesquely employed and grouped to sustain pictorial completeness, and not a blot on the landscape noted. Place must have been unusually exhilarated to achieve this effect. Most of his writing elsewhere is self-opinionated and pedestrian, but here he writes from conscientious observation, and for his own rather than posterity's benefit. His precision induces us to trust that matters *were* so disposed, that *this* happened, and that *that* happened also. He starts with the music of the streets, with what he could hear:

Thursday 25 July 1827. Half past 7 a.m.

Much pleased, not to say delighted just now. A most beautiful – a gloriously fine morning. My bedroom window projects into the street, and . . . both [windows] are open. At 7 came a coach from the Strand. 'Mathew Melton. Windsor' on the side. A good looking tall man in a scarlet frock coat and drab hat and white trousers as coachman – four as fine horses as ever I saw, the guard a well dressed man in an olive frock, was playing an air on a keyed bugle horn. The coach drew up at the Ship, nearly opposite to my window, and the guard played, in excellent tone and time the 'Death of the Stag' – and then one of our fashionable airs. Just as he finished, a coach drew up near the statue [of Charles I], and the guard a tall man in a scarlet coat, played on his bugle in excelling stile, 'The lass of Richmond Hill'. The guard of the Windsor coach as soon as the other commenced playing caught up his bugle and played the same tune in the same time, and tone and manner, both then played a waltz, and away galloped the horses with the coach from the statue. They were hardly off before another coach drew up and the guard a short man in a drab coat commenced a piece of music which he played exquisitely – this done he commenced a fashionable waltz, the Windsor guard accompanied him, and the two coaches started westward the guards of both playing the waltz.

What comes next alerts us to how (significantly for this book) Place could visualize London as a picture:

The fineness of the weather, the uncommon beauty of the horses in all the coaches, the sun shining on their well groomed skins, the hilarity they seemed to feel, the passengers on the outside gay and happy, the contrast of the colours of the cloaths worn by the well-dressed women outside the coach, large bonnets made of straw, or white silk and paper which at a distance has the appearance of white silk, all gaily trimmed with very broad ribbons woven in stripes of various bright colours running into one another like the colours in the spectrum, then white gowns and scarlet shawls, made the whole exceedingly lively and delightfully animating. The people in the street were variously grouped – market people with baskets of flowers on their heads, or on their donkeys, or in their small carts, numbers of others with vegetables, newsmen and boys running about to sell their papers to the coach passengers at least half a dozen of which leave the Golden Cross at about 7 o'clock, gave a coup d'oel [*sic*] which cannot be witnessed in any other country in the whole world, and perhaps at no other place in the world than at Charing Cross.

Guidebooks, comic books and panoramas peddled this delight in London equally. There was, for instance, a developing taste for panoramic views of the city that expressed a celebratory narcissism, if you like. These might be sold in engraved rolls pulled out from boxwood cylinders, or be written large in the Leicester Place rotunda of 1793, the St James's Street 'cosmorama', or Decimus Burton's 'colosseum' of the 1820s, the latter offering majestic views of London with the squalor and chaos of the streets below obliterated. As for guidebooks, it is true that by the turn of the century many were establishing a soberly informative neutrality about the metropolis, as were handsomely engraved works on the metropolitan picturesque or antique. Topographically fixated, excluding the human presence, and depicting an ordered and proudly imperial city, these were the textual counterparts of Rocque's or Horwood's great maps of 1746 and 1799. None the less, celebrate London's wonderfulness they still did, in effect, with scant concern for the underworlds hidden beneath it. They might attend to the most disreputable locations, but only to establish their picturesqueness rather than their terrors. Thus J. T. Smith's lavish collection of plates in the *Antiquities of Westminster* (1807) included fine engravings of unsalubrious places like Thieving Lane or the Little Sanctuary in Westminster, whose inhabitants 'of the lowest order . . . aggravate, by their numbers, that nuisance which the filthiness of their persons and the narrowness of the avenues had already created'; the Little Sanctuary was 'a harbour for wretchedness, filth, & contagion'. But Smith's plates withheld any visual representation of the filth, and he sold them for six expensive guineas to gentlemen who could afford indifference to both crime and public sanitation.[29]

Otherwise, many of the more popular guidebooks traded in a prurient facetiousness as they toured London's lowest haunts. As second cousins to the rogue and criminal literature that stretched back to the seventeenth century, they might bludgeon their readers with old-fashioned homilies on the follies and vices of town life or with reminders that London was no place for the gullible, but this moral content was neither intended nor taken seriously. The tastes of the readers they aimed at suggest otherwise. As these books took imagined tourists around London's low and high life (sometimes led by the devil), they catered to a frank curiosity about low life in general and ladies of the night in particular, their moralizing no more than a parodic alibi.[30] After the turn of the century an increasing number of guides abjured prurience and were comically illustrated by

G. M. Woodward, Thomas Rowlandson and others. Their images fed directly into George Cruikshank's comic vignettes of London life of 1818 and then into the work of his emulators. Among people hungry for images of the world they knew, it was London's positive or amused representation that tapped their pockets best. Throughout this period, we meet a taste for celebrating London in a more relaxed, expansive and humorous relationship to the streets than any poet or Hogarthian would attempt – an interest in real topographies, a pleasure in urban bustle and types for their own sake, a visual appreciation of the kaleidoscopic parade, with scant regard to moral meanings. Humour and pleasure determined the vocabularies of urban celebration in all these works, in some cases even in the 1830s.[31]

The metropolitan picaresque found its fullest expression in Pierce Egan's quasi-novel, *Life in London*, in 1821. Comically illustrated by Robert and George Cruikshank, the book followed the young swells Tom, Jerry and Logic around London's high life and low life, 'SEEING and not being seen' (as Egan put it in his characteristic capitals), in order to present a 'complete CYCLOPEDIA, each street a volume of intelligence'. In effect, it presented another urban diorama, though one full of actors. In view of its attention to the city's 'materiality', the book has been rather portentously interpreted as innovating 'a popular literary modernism' that led on, allegedly, to Dickens.[32] This downplays the book's relationship to the humorous and distinctly anti-intellectual tradition it emerged from. 'An accurate knowledge of the manners, habits, and feelings of a brave and free people is not to be acquired in the CLOSET,' Egan trumpeted, 'nor is it to be derived from the formal routine precepts of tutors.' London could be really understood 'only by means of a free and unrestrained intercourse with society'. This posture drew on the postures of the earlier works, as well as on the graphic art that sustained them. It suffused the behaviour also of the countless rakish gentlemen who crossed the social boundaries downwards in search of titillation. Their indifference to the anxieties about the 'low' that were mounting elsewhere, their refusal to judge or to worry, and their recurrent appeal to 'fun, frolic, fashion and flash', as Egan put it, caught one of the era's common styles just as accurately as moralizing reformers did. Shared by most of these works was a deepening, even tediously unrelenting and facetious *jollity*, as they celebrated London as the most interesting place on earth.

It goes without saying that vast numbers of more earnest texts than these were published, and that marks of weakness and woe were written into most of them. This was a period of revolutionary, wartime and post-war anxiety. By the 1820s, some comfortably-off people were responding to street-life with anxiety and disgust. The urge to regulate was deepening. All the same, it took a long time for London's sinister and befogged presence to taint all representations, and the celebratory motif continued to rule. Even in the 1820s, most sources continued to reflect people's experience as they were acted upon *by* the metropolis, rather than their interest in acting *upon* it.[33]

# Rowlandson's *Miseries*

The accommodation of print to this more genial vision was admittedly late in coming. For most of the eighteenth century, the artistic vision of the city was ordered either in Canaletto's terms or in Hogarth's. In the first case, it was seen as an ordered urban panorama, its street-life classically controlled or invisible. In the second, it was seen as the literary canon saw it, as a place of corruption, luxury and vice. The early satirical engravers followed Hogarth for the most part, so that, for many decades, doom-laden literary and visual representations were at one. Hogarth's vision was not panoramic like Canaletto's. It was grounded in the observation of street-life. He studied walls for their graffiti and signboards for their devices – 'with delight', he said, as he pursued that 'pleasing labour of the mind to unfold mystery allegory and riddles'. He would sketch people, incidents and places wherever he went – on his thumbnail, it was reported, if paper was lacking.[34] But, except in an unfinished painting of a smiling flower-girl, he conveyed no greater joy in the city than the poets did. Charles Baudelaire much later rightly wrote of Hogarth's 'cold, astringent, and funereal ingredient' and saw in him 'the death and burial of the comic spirit' – 'that indefinable breath of the sinister, the violent, and the ruthless which characterises almost every product of the land of spleen'.[35] This rings more true to modern tastes than do the repeated contemporary claims that Hogarth was comic.

For if Hogarth drew modern figures in realistic settings, it was either to make an aesthetic point about the right subject-matter of a modern English art, or it was to instruct. Nominally, his prints were realistically located. *Beer Street* and *Gin Lane* (1751) were recognizably in or near St Martin's-in-the-Fields and St Giles's, while his *Four Times of Day* (1738) were located in Covent Garden, Soho, Sadler's Wells and Charing Cross respectively, but in each print it was the didactic point that predominated and was emblematically underscored. In *Night*, for example, we may be led to believe that we are looking down an alley past the (real) Rummer tavern towards Charles I's (real) statue in Charing Cross. A barber's shop did exist there, just as the print shows. The bagnios advertised on the signboards were there too (they were public baths and brothels well known to young gentlemanly rakes like Boswell or Hickey) [fig. 6].[36] Even so, Hogarth was not recording London as a later generation might record it. He took great liberties with the topography, subordinating it to the

**Fig. 6** William Hogarth, *Night* (from *Four Times of Day*, 1738)

allegorical loading of a much older tradition. In *Night*, the figure of the drunken magistrate De Veil stood for Pluto and the woman ejected from her chariot for Proserpina. With every space in the engraving formally calculated and balanced, its every visual moment needed deciphering. Prints like these were full of moralizing conceits and puns, for Hogarth's was an intellectual wit, and his city 'a London of the mind'.[37] And so it long continued. When Paul Sandby, no friend of Hogarth's, turned his gaze upon street-people in his *Twelve London Cries Done from the Life* (1765), he saw them as uncaricatured types, but left the streets in which they sold their wares undepicted. Carington Bowles's mezzotints in ensuing decades repeatedly show metropolitan street-life both high and low; yet none convey much pleasure in it.

This changed utterly in the 1780s. Move on to Ramberg's *Humours of St Giles's* of 1788, re-engraved by Rowlandson in 1808, and the representation of the urban scene is suddenly transformed [fig. 7]. In ways unthinkable in Hogarth, pickpocketing and practical joking are the print's cheerful business. The boys play at dice; trades and occupations are deftly identified; and the central girl is drunk and (in Ramberg's original) bare-breasted. The dense reference and moral content of *Gin Lane* are discarded. Despite its squalor, this is a scene of *interesting*, cheerful, workaday bustle rather than of deplored licence.

Prints about London enter a different representational world around this point, and there they stay well into the nineteenth century. It is true that this change of mood and purpose didn't touch James Gillray. His prints seldom took notice of London's quotidian doings, and geniality was not one of his qualities. But Rowlandson's and George Cruikshank's sense of the comic was to be rooted in this non-judgemental vision of London. The shift had many causes. The main one was the expansion of print culture generally, and the growing demand and changing expectations of an expanding market that included not only West End sophisticates, but also lower professionals, upper shopkeepers, and skilled craftsmen to whom more and more income was accruing. These people's ability to consume fuelled a hunger for new kinds of image, for they were less haunted by classical analogies than the taste-makers of earlier generations and they were starved of images of their own lives and environs. To meet these expectations engravers began to allow themselves to be amused and titillated by London as Hogarth never could be. Striking in their images, consequently, is a flight from didacticism and an increasing engagement

**Fig. 7** Ramberg, *The Humours of St Giles's* (Harmer, 1788, re-engraved by Rowlandson, Fores, 1808)

with the comic for its own sake. They could address customers who wanted to, and sometimes did, feel good about life.

Some half of the 20,000 or more print titles published between 1770 and 1832 were about political or international affairs. They commented on elections, party manoeuvres and betrayals, ministerial changes in Parliament, the loss of the American colonies, or victories or disasters at sea and the pusillanimity of the French; and their numbers exploded with the revolutionary cataclysms in France. But the other half of the prints, in one way or another and with varying ambition, began from the late 1780s to comment on life as Londoners knew it, or on passing sensations of no earth-shaking moment. As commercial products they were rooted in the realities their purchasers recognized.

In ways unknown to Hogarth, in a huge range of formats, styles and competencies, and with greater or less geniality, they addressed anything from the inconvenience of traffic jams to the absurdities of royal levees, courtships and marriages; from the manners of Bond Street macaronis and fops, to the gender-play of dandies and dandyettes. They amused themselves with high-society adultery cases and scandals and with the oddity of female fashions as they varied from the City to St James's. They mocked female affectation and prudery, and the contradictions of female calculation and desire. They worried about the battle for the breeches, men's certainty of being cuckolded, and the fatal triangulation of old husbands, young wives and young lovers. They commented on the fashion for four-in-hand races, hobby-horses, or the new 'bazaars' in St James's. They reflected on women's displays of themselves in the Park, at receptions, or at faro clubs; on the ennui of drawing rooms and dances at Almack's; on drinking and gambling in clubs. They illustrate the wonder of false teeth and the miseries of gout and indigestion. They attend to Fox's scruffiness, Lady Archer's war paint, and the sad oglings of the ageing Duke of Queensberry in Piccadilly. They show Fores's and Humphrey's shopfronts, courtesans at the Pantheon, the masquerades and furtive delights of Vauxhall, and blue stockings raucous at tea. They ridiculed cockneys, Irishmen, Scots and foreigners, and titillated themselves over the London visit of the Persian ambassador's beautiful wife. They mocked parents' overindulgence of children, and the dreadfulness of untalented daughters whose parents made them sing when they couldn't. They lampooned doctors' quackery, clergymen's gluttony, lawyers' venality, the charlatanism of prophets, and the comical dress and speech of Quakers and Methodists. They recorded the unreliability of servants and the impudence of cab-drivers, the see-through dresses and bared breasts of ballet dancers, Grimaldi's comic songs, and exhibitions of giants, of fat men, or of the famous pig that could count, spell and read.

Approached in this spirit, the least promising of prints may contain worlds enough for those who are attentive. Take the learned pig that could count, for instance. In his early and more congested style, Thomas Rowlandson in 1785 engraved him for Fores's printshop as *The Wonderful Pig*, in which the prodigy busily exhibits his porcine erudition to a caricatured assemblage of genteel ladies and gentlemen. A notice on the wall announces '*The Surprising PIG well versed in all Languages. Perfect Arethmatician Mathematician & Composer of Musick*'. A ruffle neatly encircles his piggy neck, and with his snout he picks out alphabetical cards on the floor, to the gathering's astonishment [fig. 8]. The print is small, undistinguished, and about a trivial matter. But Rowlandson knew that exhibitions of this kind were the stuff of conversation in salon and parlour alike, so he catered to it to make his honest penny. The animal drew 'the attention of the beau monde,' a diarist reported; 'women of the first fashion waited four hours for their turn to see him.' When the poetess Anna Seward told Dr Johnson about him, she found that 'the subject amused him'. 'The pigs are a race unjustly calumniated,' he said: instead of killing a pig at a year old, we should 'allow time for his education'; for although it might be cruel to educate an intelligent pig, 'protracted existence is a good recompense for very considerable degrees of torture.' William Blake in 1800–3 mocked modern taste by versifying that the nation should 'Give pensions to the learned pig, / Or the hare playing on a tabor'. As late as 1807 Robert Southey could recall that 'the learned pig was in his day a far greater object of admiration to the English nation than ever was Sir Isaac Newton'.[38]

**Fig. 8** Rowlandson, *The Wonderful Pig* (Fores, 1785)

Or take as a second example the prints' relationship to ancestral jokes. Isaac Cruikshank's *The Origin of Cockney* (1798) shows a denaturalized family of prospering but vulgar cits on a country walk a mile from home. 'Loac father,' cries the little boy, 'what do you call that there noise this here horse is a making?' Father: 'Why I believe as how they calls it horse neighing.' Son: 'How vonderfull!! O my eye father look theres a cock neighing' [fig. 9]. Then go back two hundred years to John Minsheu's *Ductor in Linguas* (1617) for the definition of cockney that is the joke's source: 'A Cockney or Cockny, applied only to one borne within the sound of Bow-bell, that is, within the City of London, which tearme came first out of this tale: That a cittizens sonne riding with his father ... into the country ... asked, when he heard a horse neigh, what the horse did his father answered, the horse doth neigh; riding farther he heard a cocke crow, and said doth the cocke neigh too? and therfore Cockney or Cocknie, by inuersion thus: incock, q. incoctus i. raw or vnripe in country-mens affaires.'[39]

**Fig. 9** Isaac Cruikshank, *The Origin of Cockney* (Ackermann, 1798)

In prints like these, London had become the very frame, subject, source and *raison d'être* of comic and satirical commentary. In few of these images was the commentary exclusively satirical: the borders between satire and comedy had become hazy. Rather what intrudes is a genial amusement at life, along with a certain back-handed pride in London itself, and this despite, or because of, its difficulties – an affection for and pride in the city that was only lightly camouflaged in ironic vexation. In hundreds of prints, London became the central subject, and one to be celebrated. Underpinning all of them was a deepening refusal on the engravers' part to take the city, themselves, or anything very seriously.

---

Thomas Rowlandson was the artist best equipped to express the vision of London we are reaching for here. There were good reasons for this. The chief one was his unremitting fascination with the comic potential of disaster and disorder. For Rowlandson the moment when chaos descends is no time for pity, alarm or moralizing. Rather, it catapults people into a betrayal of their unveneered and common humanity, and thus becomes a moment for high comical observation.[40] Thanks to this quality, Rowlandson's art was never judgemental or satirical; it simply enlarged the viewer's sense of life's comic possibilities.

By the 1800s, Rowlandson's masterly watercolours of the rural picturesque had fallen out of fashion, and he had gambled away his small fortune. So he found employment as a book illustrator and single-sheet engraver for Ackermann's and Tegg's printshops. A fair amount of hack work ensued. Today, his best-known work from this period is his collaborative illustration with Pugin of *Microcosm of London* (1808–9), published by Ackermann. Pugin's topographical frames are descriptive, but the plates are full of Rowlandson's comically rotund figures massed as febrile crowds, arguing, gesticulating and flirting, their characters undifferentiated.[41] Similarly, his plates illustrating London cries depart markedly from Paul Sandby's earlier prints on the same subject, both in their vitality and in their identifiable locations (1811). But his most popular plates from this time are today all but forgotten. They were provoked by the success of James Beresford's *Miseries of Human Life* (1806–7), a book so much in tune with the popularizing market that it went into a dozen English and American editions, was translated into French and German, and was emulated in prints by Woodward and Isaac Cruikshank as well as Rowlandson. Beresford's text described a series of vexations that a gentleman might encounter in his social life, and these facetious and lightweight descriptions served wonderfully to fuel and inspire Rowlandson's ironic but life-affirming fascination with accident.

Two of Rowlandson's London *Miseries* exemplify this. One illustrates the misery of having to watch '*a brawling and scratching match, between two drunken drabs*' [fig. 10]. The central fight scatters fruit barrows and people, and cats and dogs fight. Rowlandson inserts himself as a witness on the right, his face the only face uncaricatured. The misery, the subscript tells us, ensues from 'the sudden influx of company by whom you are hemmed in, an hundred yards deep in every direction, leaving you no chance of escape until the difference of sentiment between the ladies is adjusted'. Rowlandson can't curb his verbal flow: 'Where you stand you are (that is I was) closely bounded in by a barrow of cats meat the unutterable contents of which employ your eyes and nose, while your ear is no less

MISERIES of LONDON.

*Being a compulsory spectator and auditor of a brawling and scratching match, between two drunken Drabs, in consequence of the sudden influx of company by whom you are hemmed in an hundred yards deep in every direction. leaving you no chance of escape till the difference of sentiment between the Ladies is adjusted. where you stand you are (that is I was) closely bounded in front by a barrow of cats meat the unutterable contents of which employ your eyes and nose. while your ear is no less fully engaged by the Tartarian yell of its driver.*

**Fig. 10** Rowlandson, *Miseries of London* [fight] (Rowlandson, 1807)

fully engaged by the yell of its driver.' The second example illustrates a
traffic jam [fig. 11]. Again Rowlandson turns congested streets into a
subject of ironic but also pleasurable vexation. 'Breast against breast with
ruinous assault / And deafening shock they come' – so the text goes: and
to illustrate it Rowlandson knocks off another high-voltage entanglement
of squabbling coachmen, rearing horses, barking dogs, tumbled orange-
sellers, screaming ladies, falling passengers and cascading bricks, all to
explain why it was so difficult in London to get to dinner in time. These
original plates were small and demure, but Rowlandson elaborated and re-
engraved some of them for Tegg's printshop as separate sheets later,
strengthening composition and line and making them more bawdily
explicit. Until 1814, he went on inventing further 'miseries' – 'of London',
'of travelling', 'of the country', etc., knitting chaotic tumbles of figures and
vehicles into brilliant compositional wholes [fig. 12].[42] Never before had
a major artist thus applied himself to street-life simply to celebrate its
vitality and not to judge it.

**Fig. 11** Rowlandson, *Miseries of London* [traffic](Ackermann, 1808)

**Fig. 12** Rowlandson, *Miseries of Travelling* (Ackermann, 1807)

These Rowlandsonian prototypes set a fashion that fuelled comic art for a quarter century to come. As Rowlandson turned out more and more of them over the next several years, other artists followed – attending to the huge varieties in the urban display in prints about anything from a balloon ascent at Hackney in 1811 to the frost fair on the frozen Thames in 1814. By 1818, Cruikshank was turning out vignettes on *The Art of Walking the Streets of London*, a motif which he and his emulators were to extend in comic vignettes into the 1820s and beyond, and which then entered George and Robert Cruikshank's and Thomas Hood's magazine and book illustrations during and after the 1830s [fig. 13].[43] In this spirit, particularly, George Cruikshank's *The Piccadilly Nuisance! Dedicated to the Worthy, Acting Magistrates of the District* (1818) was a virtual reprise of Rowlandson's traffic jam [fig. 14]. It, too, shows a street-life of unpoliced chaos: fast galloping coach, tumbling passengers, sprawling pedestrians, men fighting, an oafish countryman, pickpocketing boys, fruitseller, newsboy with his horn announcing 'great news from St Helena', with the mayhem overlooked by two dandies on the balcony of the White

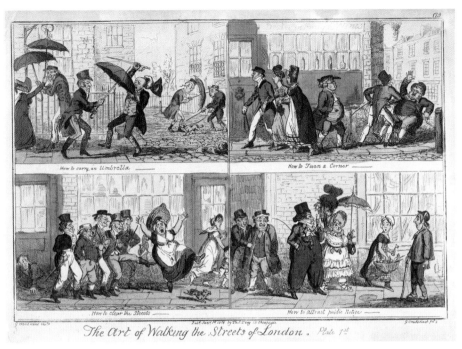

**Fig. 13** George Cruikshank (after Woodward), *The Art of Walking the Streets of London – Plate 1st* (Tegg, 1818)

**Fig. 14** George Cruikshank, *The Piccadilly Nuisance! Dedicated to the Worthy, Acting Magistrates of the District* (H. Humphrey, 1818)

Horse inn. This was not Cruikshank's only borrowing from Rowlandson's *Miseries*. Rowlandson's brawling drabs are the model for Cruikshank's illustration of a similar St Giles's fight in Dickens's *Sketches by Boz* nearly thirty years later.

Did such genial amusement soften the engravers' commentaries on manners also? Most modern accounts imply that 'satirical prints' peddled a critical view of high-born vices, and that geniality was absent from them. To see how wrong this is, we must first get closer to the elite, middle and 'middling' kinds of people who shaped their markets. We must explore how they experienced the city and what they knew of each other: first, in the metropolis's finer western quarters and then in the central artisan 'town', with Covent Garden at its centre. We'll find that the male denizens of these very different territories had many attitudes and habits in common and that, in specialized contexts, they could cross the boundaries between them with relative ease. These cross-fertilizations permitted as much geniality and amusement in the satires as they did moral judgement. Not for nothing did printshops advertise 'satirical and humorous prints'. By the 1780s, in all manner of prints, the linking of those terms had become axiomatic.

# CHAPTER TWO

# 'THE WEST OR WORST END'

## St James's and Piccadilly

George IV's coronation took place on 19 July 1821, and it passed off well enough, all things considered. Splendidly stage-managed and dressed in order to outdo Napoleon's, it was the most expensive coronation so far seen in England. Parliament had voted some quarter of a million pounds to subsidize it; the king's twenty-seven-foot long train cost £24,000, and its crimson velvet was bedecked with golden stars. The 12,313 diamonds in his new crown also cost a fortune, even if most were hired. Yet nothing that George did was unrisible, so there were a few comic hiccups in the order of things. For a start, he was having an emotional and a draining day of it. The country had been polarized by the return of his estranged wife Caroline from exile in June 1820; and now the Home Office received reports that at the coronation there would be an attempt to assassinate this least popular of kings. In the event most of the crowd stayed loyal when George arrived at the Abbey and despite hisses and angry cries of 'Queen!' Caroline herself turned up to claim the crown the king denied her, only to have bruisers disguised as royal flunkeys deny her entry at the Abbey door. But it was George himself that was the main problem. He sweated under his heavy robes, his head lolled, his eyes glazed, and he had to be revived with sal volatile during the ceremony. Worse, he had his mind on baser things:

The king behaved very indecently; he was continually nodding & winking at L[ad]y Conynham & sighing & making eyes at her. At one time in the abbey he took a diamond brooch from his breast &, looking at her, kissed it, on which she took off her glove & kissed a ring she had on!!! Any body who could have seen his disgusting figure, with a wig the curls of which hung down his back, & quite bending beneath the weight of his robes & his 60 years wd have been quite sick.[1]

What delivered the final humiliation brings us to the point of this story. It was the very strangeness of London itself. When George, exhausted, left the coronation banquet in Westminster Hall to return to Carlton House, his coach was blocked by two overturned carriages. So his cortège had to make a detour through some of the more noisome backstreets of Westminster, a 'maze of abominations' packed with brothels and lodging houses for beggars, thieves, and whores. 'Horribly nervous' at exposing himself in this frightful warren, George called to the guard to keep next to the carriage windows. Near Millbank, the procession jolted through a market garden on 'such a rough broken up old cart lane as was never trod by king before', where it was blocked by 'a broad deep canal, full of water and mud, over which lay an old wooden bridge, stopped up at its entrance by strong barricadoes'. The bridge was so dangerous that wheelbarrows weren't allowed to cross it. But it was thought unwise for the procession to go back the way it had come, so the guards removed the barricades and the coach clattered across precariously: 'the planks cracked, shook, bent and were all in great holes'. George did get to bed safely, but 'never was a monarch so lucky certainly', Lady Lyttelton wrote later: 'He must have been drowned if the bridge had given way.'[2]

We confront in this vignette a metropolis infinitely less ordered than the one we know now, and one in which social boundaries were fractured, when a king must enter a slum. London's districts were commonly thought of as socially segregated. 'A nobleman would not be found by any accident to live in that part which is properly called the City, unless he should be confined for treason or sedition in Newgate or the Tower,' Robert Southey noted. Someone else recalled that east and west Londoners were so different in clothing, pleasures and toils that when they met they contemplated each other with the curiosity they might give to an Esquimo in Regent Street: 'Each district was comparatively isolated; the state of isolation produced peculiarities, and the peculiarities corroborated the isolation, and thus the householders of Westminster . . . were as distinct from the householders of every sort of Bishopsgate Without, Shoreditch, and all those localities which stretch towards the Essex side of the city, as in these days they are from the inhabitants of Holland or Belgium.'[3] There was truth in these observations, but only broadly speaking. Had segregation been so strict, the pleasure principle that London stood for would have rung hollow. Most people experienced the metropolis as a dynamic, integrated and organic whole whose bizarre juxtapositions were of its essence. The classes couldn't be hermetically sealed off from each other, however much the higher ones wished they could be. 'Security' was minimal then, so that even the greatest in the land had to cope with London's promiscuous residential patterns, bizarre interminglings of high and low life, and uncomfortable encounters and intimacies. Even the king would come from the country to St James's Palace in 'a very plain equipage escorted by a few light horse', but 'coachmen and carmen never stop at his approach and take a pride in not bowing to him'. His palace, guarded only at the gate, was open to all well-dressed visitors. The Prince of Wales walked the pavements freely, and got bowed to if he was lucky.[4] Add to the conspicuous visibility of low tastes in high places the episodic violence of the lower orders, and we sense the city's demotic vitality, vexations and terrors – but the source of its comedy as well. In all that follows, as we explore the inhabitants of the West End in this chapter, and of Covent Garden in the next, the dominant motif is of meetings and cross-fertilization, not to mention the recurrent incursions of rioters into the most genteel of London's streets.

———•———

The great City merchants don't feature much in this book. Satires did comment on their roles in City politics, and self-made 'cits' and *nouveaux riches* were always fair game for the satirists, but the engravers largely ignored the commercial big-hitters, as if they were too boring to be worthy of attention, or too busy to buy their fripperies. The people who signified most for the engravers were those who lived in Byron's 'great world' in 'the west or worst end of a city':

> . . . about twice two thousand people bred
> By no means to be very wise or witty,
> But to sit up while others lie in bed,
> And look down on the universe with pity.[5]

These people inhabited the most handsome of London's territories. During the parliamentary season, nearly everybody who was anybody lived in the proudly fashionable streets and squares of the Portland, Portman, Grosvenor and Bedford estates – including 95 per cent of the House of Lords and 90 per cent of the Commons in the 1790s.[6] Patrician mansions dotted the streets eastwards from Portland Place to Bloomsbury Square and southwards through Mayfair to Piccadilly, St James's, and Pall Mall. Lesser gentry, higher professionals, and people of independent means inserted themselves into side streets as best they could afford, thickening in numbers as the distance from St James's increased. It wasn't difficult to navigate this territory.

Walk westwards from Charing Cross, and you would pass the Prince of Wales's Carlton House within minutes. The prince had employed the architect Henry Holland to refurbish it in 1783: 'the most perfect palace' in Europe, Horace Walpole called it; 'overdone with finery' said another. Walk on for another ten minutes down Pall Mall, and you'd come to the sooty brick façade and Tudor gateway of St James's Palace. This was where the king and queen lived, so the palace saw the levees, balls and birthday celebrations that none of the *ton* could afford to miss, tedious though they were. Here the Prince of Wales spent his fateful wedding night with Caroline, she so filthy, he said, and he so drunk, she said, that they never had sex again. Turn right from the palace and you walk north up the gentle slope of St James's Street to Piccadilly. Another ten minutes north up Bond Street takes you to Oxford Street, and beyond that to elegant squares and terraces then being fast erected. It was a mile and a half across these most elevated of all London's regions, with Piccadilly and St James's Street at their centre [fig. 15].[7]

Down Piccadilly fine town-houses had been multiplying since the 1760s. The street was dominated by Burlington House (now the Royal Academy) and Devonshire House (now demolished), where the Duchess Georgiana presided, much visited by Fox, Sheridan and the prince. The Melbournes lived on the site of what is now the Albany, until in 1791 they exchanged their mansion for the Duke of York's simpler one in Whitehall. From his Piccadilly mansion, the aged Duke of Queensberry ogled young women, his procuress enticing them inside to titillate him. Sir William and Emma Hamilton lived at no. 99 in 1800–3, Byron in no. 139 in 1815. On the corner of Hamilton Place, Lord Chancellor Eldon lived and died, to his last days counting the numbers of long and short petticoats as women passed

1.  S.W.Fores, 3 Piccadilly, 1783-
2.  S.W.Fores, 50 Piccadilly, 1795-
3.  Hannah Humphrey, 18 Old Bond St, 1779-
4.  Hannah Humphrey, 51 New Bond St, 1783-
5.  Hannah Humphrey, 27 St James's St, 1797-
6.  William Holland, 50 Oxford St, 1786-
7.  James Bretherton, 134 New Bond St
8.  Thomas Cornell, Bruton St
9.  Boydell's Shakespeare Gallery, 52 Pall Mall, 1789-
10. White's Club
11. Brooks's Club
12. Almack's Assembly Rooms
13. St James's Palace
14. The Pantheon
15. Burlington House
16. Devonshire House
17. Sir Francis Burdett, 80 Piccadilly

**Fig. 15** Map of Piccadilly and St James's, from Horwood, *Plan of the Cities of London and Westminster*, 1799

in the streets. Further south, in St James's Square, six dukes, seven earls, a countess, a baron and a baronet had had their town-houses in 1721. Later, the elder Pitt lived at no. 10, and in the 1800s Lord Castlereagh lived at no. 18. Queen Caroline stayed in no. 17 in 1820 while her case was being heard by the Lords, much incommoding the neighbourhood when the square was invaded by supportive crowds. The Prince of Wales's clandestine and illicit wife, Mrs Fitzherbert, lived at no. 105 Pall Mall. The talents who at one point or another lived or lodged around Pall Mall and St James's were stellar. They included Swift, Addison and Steele early in the century, and Sterne, Gibbon, Gainsborough and Byron later. In 1808 Byron lodged at no. 8 St James's Street, above Dollman's the hatter's, waking up one morning to find that *Childe Harold* had made him famous. Wits like Sidney Smith as well as the Pitts, Fox and Nelson lived or lodged there or around a corner or two. Spencer House was built in St James's Place in 1756, while in neighbouring houses Samuel Rogers later presided over his famous literary breakfast parties, and the bluestocking Mrs Delaney entertained Fanny Burney, Mrs Montagu, Hannah More, Horace Walpole and Lord North. Almack's Assembly Rooms, venue of masquerades and weekly balls for the *ton*, were opened in King Street in 1765, admission to it controlled by a committee of aristocratic ladies. St James's Street was dominated by the great clubs that had evolved from seventeenth-century coffee-houses. White's moved into nos. 37–8 in 1755. Rebuilt by James Wyatt in 1787, it had a bow-window added in 1811, within which Beau Brummell ruled on etiquette until gambling ruined him. Boodle's opened on the same side of the street in 1762, while Brooks's stood across from Boodle's at no. 60, having moved from Pall Mall into Henry Holland's fine new building in 1778. As party animosities intensified in the 1780s, Brooks's and White's became intensely partisan. When the younger Pitt was elected to White's in 1783, Fox and his Whig friends seceded to Brooks's, and thenceforth White's remained Pittite territory while Brooks's became the base of the opposition Whigs.[8]

To service aristocratic consumption, shopkeepers and craftsmen insinuated themselves into all these areas, however. Many were fashionable and prosperous, and knew themselves to be a cut above tradesmen elsewhere: 'A transit from the City to the West End of the Town is the last step of the successful trader, when he throws off his *exuviae* and emerges from his chrysalis state into the butterfly world of high life.'[9] St James's Street was lined by fashionable hatters, gilders, vintners and printshops, while the eastern half of Piccadilly was full of shops and taverns and of single-fronted four-storey houses from the later seventeenth century. These tradesmen's homes and premises were far more numerous than the mansions. Burlington House and the Albany were flanked by the shops and upper-floor dwellings of a toyman, a linen draper, a chemist, and a laceman, while other Piccadilly frontages were occupied by hairdressers, grocers, perfumers, ironmongers, Venetian blind-makers, butchers, eating-house keepers, chandlers, china shops, bootmakers, muffin bakers, gun-makers, upholsterers, confectioners, colour shops and cork-cutters. Some tradesmen were permitted a qualified familiarity with the great and the good. A fashionable silver and plated goods dealer listed in his memoirs scores of 'friendships' with his high clientele: duke this, lord that, or general the other would invite him to tavern dinners.[10] By 1800, booksellers included James Edwards and George Nicol in Pall Mall, and Hatchard, Stockdale and Debrett in Piccadilly. Hatchard's was part of the morning 'lounge' for idle Tories, Debrett's for idle Whigs.

An important index of West End consumption lay in its multiplying emporia for artworks. One of Wedgwood's porcelain showrooms opened at 8 St James's Square in 1796, and Christie's auction house flourished in Pall Mall until it moved to King Street in 1823. The most prominent force behind the developing commercial art market was Alderman John Boydell, who closed his City printshop in Cheapside to open his Shakespeare Gallery at 52 Pall Mall in 1789. The Prince of Wales, the Duke of York, Fox, Sheridan and the Duchess of Devonshire attended its opening exhibition. Boydell commissioned paintings on Shakespearian and similarly elevated subjects, having them engraved for wider sale. He was one of many, stretching from Hogarth on to Haydon and Barry a century later, who fought to free artists from aristocratic patronage and to win them more reliable incomes. His gallery folded in 1805 with the wartime collapse of continental markets for English engravings, and the premises were taken over by the British Institution for Promoting the Fine Arts – yet another effort to broaden artistic patronage. But this was not before his initiative had inspired the opening of Bowyer's Historic Gallery, Macklin's Gallery of the Poets, and Henry Fuseli's Milton Gallery.

The progress of these enterprises was watched beadily by the up-and-coming printshops to monitor the custom they attracted. In the 1780s, the satire business had drifted westward from the City and eastern Strand. Samuel W. Fores soon led the trade from Piccadilly. His standing was to be high enough for Nelson to act as godfather to one of his fourteen, possibly seventeen, children; Queensberry, Burdett and Nelson were among his customers; and Louis Philippe (as the exiled Duke of Orléans) later rented lodgings above his showroom. Hannah Humphrey had her shop first in Old Bond Street and then in New Bond Street before she moved to 27 St James's Street in 1797. There, thanks to her monopoly of the great caricaturist James Gillray, she too was soon on modestly familiar terms with the great. 'His highness of Clarence did me the honour of asking me how I did as we were walking on the Steine tho he had two noblemen with him,' she wrote to Gillray during a visit to Brighton. The printseller William Holland moved similarly from Drury Lane to 50 Oxford Street in 1786, and Ackermann opened his printshop on the Strand in 1795. Soon, these shops were knitted into the morning 'lounge' of the overdressed drones who would stroll into the shops to demand the latest caricatures before entering coffee-houses to peruse them.[11] It was the tastes and habits of these not necessarily bright people that inspired the innumerable prints on cuckoldry, gambling, fashion, or scandal in these years, and the scurrility and malice, we'll find, of much of their humour.

## What else to do?

Most aristocrats and gentlemen had serious estate and family business to attend to in London, and the serious-minded discussed philosophy, literature and science or agonized over what it meant to be 'polite'. The 1780s were a decade of vivifying debate about reform and reason, while the American colonists had to be fought between 1773 and 1776, and then the French between 1793 and 1815. Political tensions were high, and important parliamentary debates lasted through the night. Some tenth of men were under arms in the later war years; and, among those who weren't, the politically active had jockeyings for place and favour to occupy them, taxes to debate and an unruly populace to contain. Politics, place and favour made up the stuff of conversation – and of half the satires accordingly. These were also decades of great developments in the arts. The valuation of emotion refashioned taste, while more and more of the professional, mercantile and even autodidact classes – and women – engaged in cultural production and consumption. Their chief monuments were the mounting numbers of journals, newspapers and books published in these later eighteenth-century decades, and the accelerations of public debate and interest in science. In all of this the West End was a chief forcing ground, its patricians and gentlefolk leading participants or patrons, their lives earnest, busy and achieving.

Some aristocratic women also contrived escapes from the butterfly lives to which most were condemned. The consorts of the Devonshires, Melbournes, Hollands, etc., were women of wit and sophistication. Others wrote journals, novels, poems; learned to draw, paint, act and sing; studied the classics, philosophy and science; or did busily good works for charity. Again, West London was at the centre of these movements: the much-travelled Fanny Burney felt that the world beyond London and Paris was 'tame and insipid' by comparison.[12] In the 1750s, a handful of intellectually ambitious women had formed the 'petticoteries' (Horace Walpole's phrase) that came to be known as the Blue Stocking societies. Led by Elizabeth Montagu, Mary Delany and Mrs Elizabeth Vesey (Swift having once reminded her that 'a pernicious error prevails . . . that it is the duty of your sex to be fools'), the earliest of these gatherings was, Walpole proclaimed, 'the first public female club ever known'. In fact, they were neither exclusively female nor feminist in the modern sense. One of their purposes was to participate in conversation on equal terms with 'literary and ingenious men' (as Boswell noted); Walpole, Johnson, Samuel Richardson, Garrick and Reynolds attended them. 'These little societies have been sometimes misrepresented,' Hannah More prefaced the gushing verses she wrote in their praise: they met 'for the sole purpose of conversation, and were different in no respect from other parties, but that the company did not play at cards.' Actually, they were very different: their 'learning was as little disfigured by pedantry, good taste as little tinctured by affectation, and general conversation as little disgraced by calumny, levity and the other censurable errors with which it is too commonly tainted, as has perhaps been known in any society.' Though manners and dress were informal (whence 'bluestocking'), these circles remained polite: 'Hail, Conversation, heav'nly fair,' More versified: 'Thou bliss of life, and balm of care, / Still may thy gentle reign extend, / And taste with wit and science blend!'[13]

Yet even in these circles high-mindedness was not an unchallenged norm, nor was everyone tolerant of bluestocking pretensions. 'Chaste almost to a fault' and 'withered by time', the radical author of *The Female Jockey Club* wrote sourly of Mrs Montagu's circles in 1794. Byron soon tired of their swooning adulation:

The Blues, that tender tribe who sigh o'er sonnets,
And with the pages of the last Review
Line the interior of their heads or bonnets,
Advanced in all their azure's highest hue:
They talk'd bad French or Spanish, and upon its
Late authors ask'd him for a hint or two;
And which was softest, Russian or Castilian?
And whether in his travels he saw Ilion?[14]

Of the visual attacks, Thomas Rowlandson's was the strongest, if attack it really was. In the manic exaggeration of his *Breaking up of the Blue Stocking Club* (1815), polite masks are stripped off in another of his brilliant circular compositions. It turns the bluestockings into squabbling, screaming, scratching, fighting harridans; the tea-cups go flying, and the chamberpot on the floor reminds us of their corporality [fig. 16]. One might discern misogynist prejudices at work in these comments; yet they had their point. In May 1816 the *Lady's Magazine* reported without irony that at the bluestocking society 'the *conversationes* [were] enlivened by puns and *riddle-me-rees*, brought by the ladies in their ridicules, ready cut and dried. The following were sported at the last assembly near Berkeley-square with *éclat*:– Lady Elizabeth S— asked, "Why are Lord P—ts—m's dashing *pantaloons* like two foreign towns?" "Because," replied the Hon. Miss B—, "they are too long (Toulon) and too loose (Toulouse)!" The same lively Countess sported another, viz. "Why does a waiter resemble a *blood horse*?" General T—n instantly said, "Because he *runs for the plate*!"'[15] Bored and privileged minds were in dire need of stimulation, and there was a fair quota of desperate silliness and affectation.

Many found it difficult to escape the mannered tedium of their lives. In a society in which those who mattered knew everyone else who mattered, anxieties about reputation could be stifling. The idler men coped by cultivating that 'vacuity of thought and sensation' that was 'a necessary ingredient of the character of an accomplished gentleman', as a German visitor put it.[16] The clubs were their lifelines, along with drinking, gambling, wenching and sport. For women escape routes were fewer. Most women of quality, in Pastor Wendeborn's view, 'lead an idle life, useless, and tiresome even to themselves'; and Mary Wollstonecraft said much the same.[17] 'I am fatigued by a regular course of insignificant occupations,' the Duchess of Wellington's diary confessed in 1809. Within a typical week, her daily

**Fig. 16** Rowlandson, *Breaking up of the Blue Stocking Club* (Tegg, 1815)

entries were brief: 'Ill & idle. I have nothing to say to this languid day'; 'Much as yesterday, languid and dawdling'; 'Too late for church'; 'I am tired. This unvaried life fatigues but must be endured.'[18] Some were helped by sexual dalliances: 'Gallantry in this country scorns a mask,' Horace Walpole wrote: 'Maids only intrigue; wives elope. *C'est l'étiquette.*'[19] Others had babies to breed, often by the dozen. 'People of my stupid disposition who don't love the great world have nothing better to do than take care of their children,' Charles Fox's mother confessed. One of her sisters had nineteen children, some of whom she didn't recognize when she returned home from the London season. Childless women contrived a frantic activity. 'The hurry of this town is inconceivable, for I declare I have been only once to the play, opera and oratorio, to very few assemblies, and yet I cannot find a moment's time to myself,' wrote another of Fox's aunts after her arrival from the country.[20] Most female lives centred on fashion, shopping, scandal-mongering, marriage-plotting, tea-drinking, church-going, and the monitoring of precedence. Society leaders like Lady Archer, Lady Buckinghamshire, Mrs Sturt and Mrs Concannan ran notorious faro banks (a gambling card game), patronized by the prince, Fox and their cronies, but much mocked in satire. They took the air in carriages that were 'mostly filled with loungers of both sexes, who, to get rid of themselves ... look at each other in silence';[21] or they had themselves driven round Hyde Park to meet royalty and the *ton*.

There were royal levees and birthdays to attend at the palace, but the conversation in the monarch's company was stilted and wearing, to judge from Fanny Burney's reports of their infinite finesse. It was not always better in the great houses. Lady Lyttelton found the Prince of Wales's entertainments farcical: 'Two hundred lighted candles in the room, a bran new service of plate, the finest cut-glass lustres, bottles and glasses that ever sparkled, the twenty-five blue-ribboned gentry all in full dress and glee, and the prince doing the honours with due bustle. Altogether it was a glorious piece of – what shall I say? – grandeur or nonsense? For somehow it makes one laugh, as if it was a parcel of children playing at great people; so proud of their bits of blue ribbon, and their pretty shining playthings all about them.'[22] Salon entertainments could be just as lavish, their deportment refined and conversation vapid. The prince's estranged wife Caroline presided over boozy dinners that went on until dawn, and her husband's disaffected Whig cronies, so offensively dropped when he became regent, gravitated to them naturally. At other soirées, as at 'routs' and tea-parties, there was tedium, too. Here, as Hannah More wrote, 'Plain common sense was put to flight' and 'Each common phrase is an oration; / And cracking fans, and whisp'ring misses, / Compose their conversation blisses'. As Byron complained in 1814: 'Last night, *party* at Lansdowne House. To-night, *party* at Lady Charlotte Greville's – deplorable waste of time, and something of temper. Nothing imparted – nothing acquired – talking without ideas: if any thing like *thought* in my mind, it was not on the subjects on which we were gabbling. Heighho! – and in this way half London pass what is called life.'[23]

So what else was there for the idlers to do? They might now and then visit the mad in Bedlam or sit in on an Old Bailey trial if the felon was notorious, and Pastor Wendeborn was shocked at the pleasure ladies of quality took from watching executions. But few visited the City if they could help it. It was theatre and fashionable assemblies that distracted them mainly. Here, too, we shouldn't expect high-mindedness. The two licensed theatres of Drury Lane and Covent Garden and the theatre in the Haymarket offered few challenges. The Lord Chamberlain's power from

1737 to ban or censor plays meant that few risks were taken. 'Atrocious in content, absurd in form, objectionable in action, execrable English theatre,' the young Goethe lamented. Oliver Goldsmith observed in 1754 that even English comedy was dismal. When sentimental comedies began to multiply thereafter, 'in which the virtues of private life are exhibited, rather than the vices exposed' and 'almost all the characters are good, and exceedingly generous', Goldsmith dismissed them as meretricious things which could be hammered out as easily as novels.[24]

David Garrick, Drury Lane's actor-manager from 1747 to 1776, did revive Shakespeare, insist on rehearsals, get rid of inherited parts, and ban spectators from the stage, and under this regime leading actors and actresses were lionized; but people still came and went as they pleased during performances, and riots erupted when Garrick tried to abolish half-price admissions for those who liked to arrive after the interval. Most of the audience had the attention span of gnats, and went chiefly to see and be seen, as to a sexual marketplace. 'What an assemblage to *me*, who know all their histories,' Byron wrote of the mix of courtesans and ladies he surveyed in their Covent Garden boxes. The courtesans were '*understood* courtesans', he wrote, and these outnumbered the 'mercenaries'; but there was no difference between them except that the understoods might enter Carlton House while the professionals were confined to the opera and brothel. 'How do I delight in observing life as it really is!' he exclaimed in good cheer.[25]

Shakespeare unadulterated was thought too rough for refined tastes, so Garrick rewrote *Macbeth's* ending, allowing Macbeth to express remorse as hell opened for him. And when Goldsmith sought to restore 'laughing comedy' in *She Stoops to Conquer*, Garrick thought the play too advanced, and it was saved only when George Colman took it for Covent Garden. Its success did effect a comic renaissance in English theatre; it opened the way for Sheridan's comic satires. But for every *School for Scandal* or *Rivals*, hundreds of musical burlesques and sentimental comedies were staged that made no demands on the facial muscles whatsoever. Even when good plays were performed, they seldom stood alone. Open a random issue of the *Morning Post* – 3 January 1777, for example – and you find advertised *Semiramis* and a pantomime staged together at Drury Lane: boxes five shillings, upper gallery a shilling. *The Beggar's Opera* and *The Country Wife* were performed together at Covent Garden, but with a country dance and hornpipe thrown in ('no person to be admitted behind the scenes, nor any money to be returned after the curtain is drawn up'). The Haymarket had an Italian comedy *Gli Incantidi Circae et Atlante*, 'with beautiful transformations, and decorations, new songs, duets, and airs . . . Harlequin will be turned into an ass, and his mistress to a cow . . . Doors to be opened at six. To begin exactly at seven. Servants that keep places to be at the house at five.'

Balls and routs at Almack's also passed the time, as did masquerades. These were held at Vauxhall or Ranelagh pleasure gardens, in Carlile House in Soho, or in James Wyatt's Pantheon in Oxford Street. This last, built in 1772 as a winter alternative to Ranelagh, had a basilical hall and vast ceiling domed in emulation of its Roman prototype, and galleried aisles, apsidal ends, and tea and supper rooms. Horace Walpole thought it 'the most beautiful edifice in England', and Charles Burney saw in it 'the most elegant structure in Europe, if not on the globe'. Its opening was attended by 1,500 people, and during its first decade six guineas were charged for admission to its twelve seasonal assemblies. Concerts were frequent, though it was thought unnecessary to advertise the music that was to be performed there.[26] Until it burnt down in 1792, the great venue also served lower purposes. A powerful if morose mezzotint entitled *The Pantheon, in Oxford Street*, shortly after the Pantheon opened, shows two bewigged fops taking tea there with courtesans, and a little girl in their company bestriding one gentleman's phallicly angled sword which lifts her skirts meaningfully. All who bought the print knew that sex offered the most reliable escape from ennui; and in every public venue high-born lechers and loose-moralled ladies mingled to mutual profit and pleasure [fig. 17].

Attention to outward appearances took up a great deal of both sexes' time, though it took less time than that expended by the sweatshop seamstresses that catered to them for pennies. But if clothes were spectacular, the bodies underneath were less so. In a world still innocent of antibiotics and dentistry, nearly everyone had digestive ailments and bad teeth; some sported wooden false teeth that clacked like castanets. And before cotton and soap flooded the market, the bodily odours in every assembly, tavern and street would knock you backwards. The term 'the great unwashed' was first applied to the working classes by Bulwer Lytton in 1830, but in this earlier era it could hardly have been applied to them exclusively, for, if genteel clothing was clean, armpits, genitals and anuses were less so. Many fine people apparently washed little more than faces, hands and feet now and then. Soame Jenyns described a ball at which he was smitten by 'the balsamic effluvias from many sweet creatures who were dancing'; and Smollett's description of the 'compound of villainous smells'

**Fig. 17** Edwards and Humphrey, *The Pantheon, in Oxford Street* (Byron, 1772)

at fashionable Bath assemblies was probably not much overdrawn: 'Imagine to yourself a high exalted essence of mingled odours, arising from putrid gums, imposhumated lungs, sour flatulencies, rank armpits, sweating feet, running sores and issues, plasters, ointments, and embrocations, hungary-water, spirit of lavender, assafoetida drops, musk, hartshorn, and sal volatile, besides a thousand frousty streams which I could not analyze.'

Dr Johnson was famously grimy, and his friend Topham Beauclerk was said to be 'remarkably filthy in his person, which generated vermin'. Although William Byrd washed his feet every few weeks, it was only when he took a woman to a bagnio that he could be said to have bathed. Charles Pigott, the radical author, was known as 'Louse' for similar reasons. Fox would rise late in his St James's Street lodgings and walk the hundred or so yards to Brooks's club, careless of 'his bristly black person, and shagged breast quite open, and rarely purified by any ablutions ... wrapped in a foul linen night-gown, and his busy hair dishevelled'. The Duke of Norfolk was 'a vulgar, heavy, clumsy, dirty-looking mass of matter' who 'rarely

**Fig. 18** George Cruikshank, *A Brighton Hot Bath, or Preparations for the Wedding!!* (Sidebotham, 1816)

made use of water' or willingly changed his linen. His servants could sponge him down only when he was in his cups, though luckily that was often.[27] When in 1816 Prince Leopold married the regent's only daughter, Charlotte, he was so filthy and venereally diseased that on his wedding night he had to be forcibly bathed, if George Cruikshank's *A Brighton Hot Bath, or Preparations for the Wedding!!* is to be believed. Cruikshank has the regent complain that Leopold's condition reminds him of Caroline's on their wedding night: 'I recollect that I was served this way myself twenty years ago.' On the floor a dish of sausages, one pointing into the gaping hole of a boot, is labelled 'a German sausage for my intended wife newly dress'd & cook'd up in the best manner'. Next to it lie copies of Ovid's *Art of Love* and the sex manual, *Aristotle's Masterpiece*. Although the coming phallic penetrations are ubiquitously symbolized, these books imply that Leopold needs prior instruction in the necessary motions [fig. 18].

As for the over-painted ladies who led the best society, a large cluster of print commentaries appears to be cruelly *ad feminam*. Some, to be sure, bore an obvious relationship to the reminders in traditional memento mori that outward finery masked mortality and inner corruption: prints, for example, like Darly's *A Speedy and Effectual Preparation for the Next World* (1777), with the bluestocking Mrs Macaulay plastering her ageing face with cosmetics as a

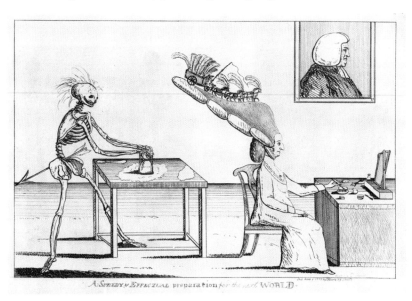

**Fig. 19** Darly, *A Speedy and Effectual Preparation for the Next World* (Darly, 1777)

**Fig. 20** Anon., *A Pig in a Poke* (Phillips, 1786)

grinning skeleton tips up its hourglass [fig. 19]. But from this tradition it was an easy step to move on to unchivalric inventions like the anonymous *Pig in a Poke* (1786) [fig. 20], with its lady fully dressed on the left, and on the right more truthfully revealed. Doubtless, some of these attacks spoke for an observed reality. Rowlandson's *Six Stages of Mending a Face* (1792) (Lady Archer at toilette transforms herself into a society belle: she puts on her wig, puts in her glass eye and false teeth, and rouges herself thickly) [fig. 21] was a vicious personal attack on a society lady infamous for the 'tawdry dress and prodigious quantity of rouge' (as Horace Walpole put it) with which she disguised her propensity to avoid washing.

In these cosmetic practices, Lady Archer was far from alone. Another Bath observer in the 1760s had written exaggeratedly: 'ladies without teeth, without eyes, with a foot and a half in the grave, ape youth, and dress themselves forth with the fantastick pride of eighteen or twenty'. Those who had their own hair 'do not comb their heads for three months together', he added, 'and whether they kill the lice with quicksilver, or Mr Coode's hammer, or by what other contrivance, is a secret; but they endeavour to conceal the stink of their filthy heads with perfumes, essences, etc. This is

**Fig. 21** Rowlandson, *Six Stages of Mending a Face* (Fores, 1792)

worse than painting an inch thick: but painting too is very necessary to a fine lady.'[28] Painting also hid the damage done by smallpox. While Wendeborn noted that English complexions improved only with the discovery of vaccination, he didn't add that thousands continued to be fatally damaged by the white lead upon which snowy complexions depended. Meanwhile, John Wilkes, who should have known, complained that women's 'nobler parts are never in this island washed ... they are left to be lathered by the men', while Mary Wollstonecraft lamented in 1792 that many respectable Englishwomen's 'regard to cleanliness ... is violated in a beastly manner'.[29] When Charles Greville took up with the young Emma Hamilton, it was, he announced, because she was 'the only woman he had slept with without offending his senses, and a cleaner, sweeter bed-fellow did not exist'. When the Prince of Wales was made to marry Caroline of Brunswick in 1795, her bodily odours soon got the better of him. On their wedding night, he was driven urgently to ask for brandy. Then he fell drunk into the bedroom fireplace, recovering enough to get into bed with his wife, managing intercourse with her only three times before abjuring sex with her altogether. The trouble was, he later explained, that she wore 'coarse petticoats, coarse

**Fig. 22** Isaac Cruikshank, *Oh! Che Boccone!* (Fores, 1795)

shifts, and thread stockings', and that she was 'never well washed, or changed often enough', and showed 'such marks of filth both in the fore and hind part of her ... that she turned my stomach and from that moment I made a vow never to touch her again'.[30] A whiff of this hit the public prints. In 1795, Isaac Cruikshank's *Oh! Che Boccone!* ('Oh! What a mouthful!') has the prince in his nightshirt standing by Caroline's bridal bed in dismay and terror; on the table a bottle labelled 'Cantharides' contains the aphrodisiac, Spanish fly [fig. 22]. The prince himself was usually fragrant, if we overlook the lice that Isaac Cruikshank's print, *A Sketch for a Viceroy!! The Royal J[er]a sey*, showed crawling from his new bob-wig (or 'jazey') [fig. 23].[31]

## The Piccadilly riots of 1810

Aristocrats could never be wholly insulated from lesser mortals. Privilege was recurrently and intimately exposed to its obverse – to those multiple contiguities, incursions and juxtapositions that were central to Londoners'

**Fig. 23** Isaac Cruikshank, *A Sketch for a Viceroy!! The Royal J[er]a sey!!* (Fores, 1797)

sense of their city, and to the unavoidable knowledge of the 'low other' that even the great must have. Some of these exposures were convivial and voluntary, but others were far from that. The riots that recurrently swept the West End were themselves elements in London's demotic vitality, part of the rich negotiation between the high people and low upon which much satire depended.

*Promis'd Horrors of the French INVASION, – or – Forcible Reasons for negociating a Regicide PEACE.*

**Fig. 24** Gillray, *Promis'd Horrors of the French Invasion, – or – Forcible Reasons for Negotiating a Regicide Peace* (H. Humphrey, 1796)

In 1796, James Gillray produced a famous print for Hannah Humphrey's shop, entitled *Promis'd Horrors of the French Invasion* [fig. 24]. It shows St James's Street invaded by grotesquely caricatured French troops. St James's Palace blazes in the background, and 'Jacobin' Fox, the Whig opposition leader, flogs a half-naked Pitt, the prime minister, at a stake topped by a cap of liberty, while aristocratic heads roll in baskets or in mud. In Brooks's club on the right, the gleeful opposition preside over a guillotine. On the left, French soldiers throw ministers and dukes from the balcony of White's club or hang them from a lamp-post outside it. Gillray produced many such prints tarring the Whig opposition with the Jacobin brush; and within a year of engraving this one he accepted a pension from the Tory minister, George Canning, to keep him doing so. With revolution blazing across the Channel, propaganda of this kind was a lucrative business. Yet despite real and recurrent invasion panics throughout these years, most of the peacock people of St James's who bought the print knew that Gillray's was an exaggerated fantasy and that Fox was no Jacobin. What really haunted them was the disposition of the lower people who lived within walking distance of St James's, in the poorer parishes to the east and the south. The prospect of *their* invasion seldom receded.

The most tumultuous disturbances London had known were the riots which ensued from the anti-Catholic fervour whipped up by Lord George Gordon in 1780. The Gordon riots had affected the City and the central town more than the West End, but they had caused the gravest damage to property and had humiliated great men. At one point, the rioters besieged Westminster itself, in the tumult seizing the Lord President's wig and relieving the Duke of Northumberland of his watch and a bishop of his carriage wheels; afterwards Lord Mansfield took his place on the woolsack quivering 'like an aspen'.[32] London would never again be as unprotected as it had been then. Even so, from then on, low Londoners' mud- and stone-throwing presence was never far distant from the aristocratic heartlands, and throughout the 1790s and early 1800s recurrent incursions made sure that 1780 was not forgotten. Even loyalist celebrations could turn nasty. When peace with France was signed in 1801, London erupted in a blaze of bonfires, illuminations and cheering crowds. But when the crowds surged into the West End streets, insisting that grand windows be lit to display the occupants' equal joy – 'Lights! Lights!' they cried – those who refused thus to signal their support had their windows smashed and their houses pelted with mud. Lord Camelford sallied forth from his Bond Street house to do contemptuous battle with the mob on this occasion, only to be floored by a brickbat and so violently kicked that he had to be rescued by his servants.[33]

The pro-Burdett riots of 1810 were among the most alarming of many such confrontations, and an index also of radicalism's revitalization after the 1790s. Sir Francis Burdett had long been a thorn in the government's side.[34] A delicately handsome man, he had lived in Paris in the first stages of the Revolution, sympathizing with its principles if not its excesses. Returning in 1793, he married into the Coutts family's banking fortune – and thus into their Piccadilly mansion. A Foxite MP since 1796, he had advocated parliamentary reform and denounced the war with France in years when this smacked of sedition. His popular following blossomed when in 1799 he compared the conditions in Cold Bath Fields prison to those in the Bastille and forced an enquiry into them. In 1802, he won the seat for Middlesex in one of London's most tumultuous elections since the 1760s: at the hustings a band played the revolutionary 'Ça ira!' and the crowd cried 'No Bastille'. In 1807, another turbulent election gave him the key constituency of Westminster. Two years later he supported the Cobbettite radicals in denouncing flogging in the army and the Duke of York's corrupt relationship with the courtesan Mary Anne Clarke. He then published a letter in William Cobbett's *Register* protesting at the Commons' imprisonment of the popular radical, Gale Jones, for criticizing the Commons' inquiry into the Walcheren naval disaster. It was this that tipped Parliament against him. An MP moved that Burdett's letter violated the House of Commons's privileges, so, on 5 April 1810, the House voted for a warrant for his arrest. Appealing to Magna Carta, Burdett refused to accept its legality and denied the sergeant-at-arms entry into his house. As news of the stand-off spread, crowds flowed in from the artisan and plebeian parishes to the east and the south to support him.[35]

On Friday, 6 April, several thousand gathered outside his house and began to stone the coaches of aristocrats. Some moved off to attack the houses of Burdett's parliamentary enemies. Windows were broken at Lord Chatham's house in Hill Street, the Duke of Montrose's and Lord Westminster's in Grosvenor Square, Wellesley's at Apsley House, Charles Yorke's and the much-hated minister Lord Castlereagh's in St James's Square, and Perceval's in Downing Street (prime ministers in those days didn't live in fortresses). Although the Life Guards and Horse Guards were called out, the crowd that night forced Piccadilly and St James's Street householders to show support by illuminating their windows; unilluminated windows were stoned. By two in the morning, the windows in these streets tactfully blazed with candles and lanterns. Lord Castlereagh, mingling incognito in the crowd attacking his own house, retired hastily when he was recognized and threatened with a ducking in St James's Square's fountain.[36] On Saturday, even bigger crowds assembled both before Burdett's house and at the Tower – for Burdett would be conveyed there once arrested. Burdett went for a defiant horse-ride amid cheers. The crowd compelled passers-by 'to do homage to them'. Those who refused to pull off their hats were pelted with mud. Now the ministry had the Riot Act read. Cavalry were stationed at every corner leading into Piccadilly, and the Life Guards began to clear the streets amid shooting, injury and panic.

On the third day, Sunday, while the law officers dithered about the legality of breaking down Burdett's front door to get at him, *The Times* reported that the crowd's active part consisted of 'idlers, pickpockets and boys'. All Lady Lyttelton saw was 'one continued mass of the blackest of blackguards, men, women, and boys!' But they were braver than idlers and blackguards. Defying the Riot Act, they hissed and pelted the soldiers and barricaded Piccadilly. There was more shooting and more heads were broken. With the military in position, the sergeant-at-arms at last broke into Burdett's house, arrested him while he was showily educating his son in the Magna Carta, and coached him off to the Tower with a large cavalry escort, taking circuitous routes to avoid the crowds. At the Tower several people were killed and wounded by soldiers, so that for months thereafter the Life Guards were taunted as the 'Piccadilly butchers'. The rest was anticlimax. Burdett was released from the Tower in June when Parliament prorogued. A year later Lord Chief Justice Ellenborough and other judges declared that the Speaker's warrant and the forcing of Burdett's door had been lawful – an unsurprising decision, from such judges. Lord Holland's was the better verdict. He regarded the government's actions as 'ill-timed executions of arbitrary power'.[37]

How dangerous had this eruption been? Tucked away in Spencer House, Lady Lyttelton watched the running crowds in Green Park and found them 'very shocking indeed': 'the look of the mob, black, sulky, and determined; their continual loud shouts; the horrid sight of the heavy Horse Guards riding in among them and over them, vainly trying to disperse them; the eager, anxious, frightened faces of every creature one saw in the streets at the increase of the tumult and noise'. 'The riot is not only in Piccadilly, but all over London,' she added, 'wherever there is a minister's house or that of any other unpopular man, a flying party of the mob attack it, shatter the windows, abuse the inhabitants, and often break open the door . . . The City mob, they say, is worse than ours . . . We are far from comfortable now, tho' the thing is done, for the people have threatened all sorts of horrors in revenge for their defeat. Well, Heaven keep the black gentry out of this quiet little nook!'[38]

She needn't have worried. By 1810, the government knew the wisdom of letting the people know their preparedness for insurrection. The cannons at the Tower were loaded with grapeshot and the Tower moat was flooded. Dragoons occupied Moorfields. Troops and artillery came from Woolwich and Hounslow, and cavalry occupied villages around London. Fifty thousand soldiers were ready for the revolution that for that very reason couldn't happen.[39] Well might Castlereagh declare five years later, when rioters again besieged St James's Square in protest at the Corn Laws, that 'the mob is not so dangerous as you think'. Dressed on that occasion 'in a blue coat buttoned up to the chin, a blue spenser, kerseymere breeches, long gaiters, shoes covered by galoshes, and white neckcloth', he was (we are told) 'not in the slightest degree ruffled by the popular excesses and the abuse which was liberally heaped upon him and his colleagues in the government'.[40]

All the same, Castlereagh had beaten that tactful retreat of his in 1810; and all those submissively candlelit windows prove the anxiety. Over the ensuing decade no aristocrat could feel wholly safe in his westerly mansion. Ten years after the Burdett riots, Lord Harrowby's Grosvenor Square mansion nearly witnessed what would have been an apocalyptic moment in British history. Conspirators planned to massacre half the Cabinet while it sat at dinner there. It would have been easy enough. No soldiers were on hand, there were no professional police, and the house was guarded only by servants. In the event, the conspirators were infiltrated by government spies and arrested in their Cato Street stable hours before they struck. They had planned to impale Castlereagh's and Sidmouth's heads on pikes and parade them around London. Three of the pike-heads, made from the arrowed tops of sawn-off iron railings, still rattle about in a box kept in the Treasury solicitor's papers: they were brought to the trial as exhibits against the traitors.[41] Instead it was the traitors' heads that were chopped off and held up to the crowd in the old-fashioned way after they had been publicly hanged at Newgate, just a year before George's IV's coronation.

— • —

The Piccadilly riots return us to that socially promiscuous intermingling, that insistent presence of the low other, even among the mansions. A spy report gives us rare details of this reality:

Spy report on the 'names etc of Inhabitants of Parts of Piccadilly', compiled during the Burdett riots, April 1810.[46]

CHURCH PASSAGE

| 7 | Edw. Bootham | greengrocer | quite respectable |
|---|---|---|---|
| 6 | Mary Mayland | umbrella shop | |
| 5 | Mary Snow | | old lady |
| 4 | Isaac Ward | chandlers shop | elderly man |
| 3 | Thos Baldwin | greengrocer | decent gentle people |

| 2 | Jos Hall | hairdresser | lately been very ill |
| 1 | Jno Bellow | publican | orderly house |

PICCADILLY

| 201 | Henry Escher | bookseller | foreigner. German. don't know him |
| 202 | Geo Jarratt | hatter | Volunteer |
| 201 | Jas Petton | wire worker [?] | resides chiefly at Chelsea; his business conducted by shopman |
| 203 | Jos Gordon | army . . .[?] | very respectable |
| 204 | Wm Gittins | ironmonger [?] | in Volunteers |
| 206 | Jno Bunner [?] | baker | very quiet decent people |

VILLIERS COURT FROM ST JAMES ST

| 1 | Jno. Lasson [?] | taylor [*sic*] | former of St James St |
| 2 | D . . . | [?] Morgan | plasterer and glazier |
| 3 | Wm Jarvis | hairdresser | very . . .? |
| 4 | Sophie Blake | laundress | lets the lower part of the house |

PICCADILLY NORTH

| 57 | Charles Webb | laceman | in Volunteers |
| 56 | Robert Hayward | Chemist | not young man and respectable |
| 53 | Mary Taylor | linen draper | don't know her |
| 52 | Rd Taylor | do. | very respectable |
| 51 | John Robinson | toyman | respectable in Volunteers |
| 50 | Susannah Brown | private house | old ladies |
| 49 | Walter Buckmaster | do. in Navy Office | latterly had a paralytic stroke |
| 48 | Sml. W. Fores | print seller | had his windows broken by the mob after he put out lights and was complaining to the . . . [?] of the mob |

CORNER OF SACKVILLE ST.

| 47 | was a large shop | now divided into two | |
| 46 | Geo Whithington | grocer | senior churchwarden |
| 47 | Jas Leuchard | perfumer | knows nothing of him . . . respectable |
| 44 | Cornelius Tongue | [?] ironmonger | respectable – in Volunteers |
| 42 | Mary Thompson | carver-gilder | ditto |
| 41 | John Peacock | sadler [*sic*] | very respectable |
| 40 | Jas Kendrick | menagerie of birds and beasts | |
| 39 | Peter Sanders | brace maker | lately come but apparently very quiet |

GEORGE COURT WEST SIDE

| 12 | Peter Sanders | carver and gilder | knows nothing of him |
| 11 | John Murray | Venetian blindmaker | do. |
| 10 | Geo Sullivan | bootmaker | low people – do. |
| 9 | Charles Gostling | butcher | pays well and appears [respectable?] |

| 8 | Jno Truslock [?] | china man | knows nothing |
| 7 | Francis Easter | eating house | good business and very quiet |

EAST SIDE

| 6 | – Rogers | chandler | lately come |
| 5 | Jas king | muffin baker | very steady |
| 4 | Joseph . . .? | ? | very decent respectable man |
| 3 | Jos Worhalls | carpenters | not known /tenants |
| 2 | Henry Isles | hairdresser | very decent |
| 1 | Wm – | | very respectable |

PICCADILLY CONTINUED

| 38 | Wm Brown | silver smith | |
| 37 | Jas Burnstead [?] | shoemaker | old man and old inhabitant but don't know much of him {part of the door blistered as supposed by a Ball [bullet]} |
| 36 | Jno Latchford | spurmaker | don't know anything of him |
| 35 | John Henry | cork maker | do. |
| 36 | Thos Hawson | gun maker | do. |
| 34 | – | upholsterer | just come in |
| 33 | – Clarke | bookseller | know nothing of him |
| 32 | Dominick Angiro | confectioner | foreigner – lived in the parish some time /had his hand cut by the Guards |
| 31 | Wm Stewart | tea man | very old inhabitant but don't know his sentiments |
| 30 | Wm Sanders | cork cutters | very respectable |
| 29 | Jno Ambridge | chemist | don't know him but has been here some years |
| 28 | Joseph Hurt | cardmaker | very old inhabitant very respectable |
| 27 | – Woolley | brazier | been there many years very respectable |
| 26 | – Brown | shoemaker | . . . respectable |
| 25 | Jno Turman [?] | silversmith | very respectable |
| 24 | Thos Williams | hair dresser | very respectable character |
| 23 | Edw Hall | card maker | very old – respectable |
| 24 | Hawkes and Co | Army . . . [?] | very respectable |
| 22 | empty and rebuilding | | |
| 22 | Dermer [Deard?] | colour shop | |

It lists each Piccadilly shopkeeper's name, address, occupation and political disposition, and it brings out both Piccadilly's heterogeneity and the watchfulness that was needed. Its main purpose was to forewarn the military of troublespots. These it identified in a 'sadler's shop near the corner of

Swallow Street', a 'house at the east side of Albany', an empty house, no. 22, from which a shot was fired, and in 'Albemarle St, last door on the right hand going to Piccadilly at the corner of Grafton St': here there was some 'firing from a house when the Light Horse men was clearing the mob away from the gentleman's door . . . pistol or blunderbuss fired from a upstairs window'. It also noted a 'quantity of brick bats collected at an ale house near the bottom of Bond St near Burlington House'. In the event, excepting unknown newcomers and the occasional bootmaker (the 'low people' at no. 10), the report chiefly exposed the loyalism of prospering, respectable and deferential shopkeepers. Most had every interest in keeping on the right side of genteel custom, for patron pressure was powerful.

In some grand houses, Burdett was loathed. A print of 1810, *Francis the First, Crowned, or the Dream Realized*, has him dreaming of his own coronation and awakening to find that he has crowned himself by tipping his chamberpot over his head; his head and nightgown are covered with its contents [fig. 25]. Yet some Piccadilly shopkeepers did stick cautious heads above their parapets. Foremost among them was the Piccadilly printseller, Samuel W. Fores, the print trade's leading light, his shop at nos. 48–50 next door to Devonshire House. We must tread carefully in decoding printsellers' politics. With the possible exception of the printshop proprietor William Holland (imprisoned in 1793 for selling Tom Paine's subversive works), none was deeply radical, least of all sympathetic to 'the mob'. The 1810 spy report noted that Fores 'had his windows broken by the mob after he put out lights' (i.e. his candle-lit windows), so he must have seemed opposed to the crowd. Later, the bookseller Stockdale's poll-book for the 1818 Westminster election lists Fores as voting not for Burdett but for the moderate Whig Romilly and the ministerialist Maxwell.[42] That said, there was always a liberal bias in Fores's prints. Throughout the 1790s and on until 1819, he commissioned some of the most biting satires against government restrictions on freedom of speech, and his prints were to be among the most effective in pleading the queen's case in 1820.[43] And, despite the mob's suspicions, he certainly supported Burdett during the 1810 crisis. He issued at least eight pro-Burdett prints, employing the veteran Isaac Cruikshank and the young William Heath to engrave them. Their titles hailed Burdett as, among other things, the '*Modern St George Attacking the Monster of Despotism*', or '*A Model for Patriots or an Independent Legislator*', depicting him in a heroic iconography that was reused in Burdett's favour for a decade to come. Isaac Cruikshank also provided

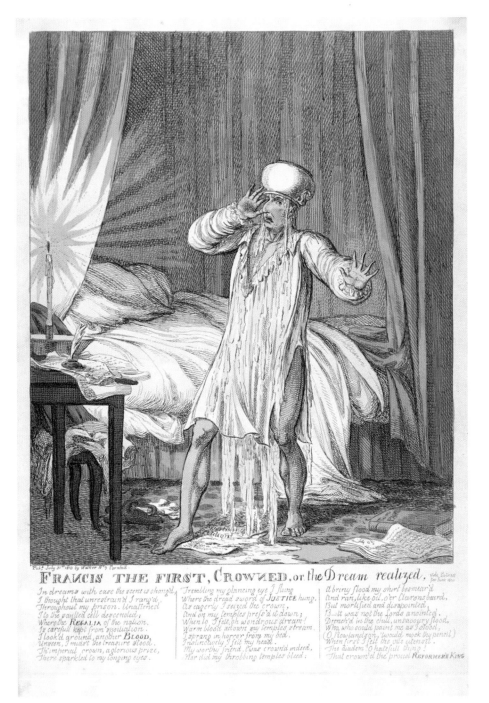

**Fig. 25** Anon., *Francis the First, Crowned, or the Dream Realized* (Walker, 1810)

Fores with '*The Last Grand Ministerial Expedition*', in which ministers and cutlass-wielding mounted soldiers ride down pedestrians while a constable smashes an upper window in Burdett's house to gain access.[44] In endorsing Burdett's cause Fores had nothing to lose. Hard-line West End loyalists would patronize Hannah Humphrey's St James's Street shop anyway, while there were liberal sympathies enough in many West End mansions: key newspapers were all pro-Burdett, and the City liverymen passed resolutions congratulating the hero.

The anxiety induced by these low incursions into great streets was proved two years after the riots. In 1812, John Nash unveiled his plan to construct an elegantly colonnaded royal mile between Regent's Park and Carlton House, where the Prince of Wales, now regent, lived just off the Mall. What became Regent Street had been mooted in 1766 and again in 1808, and it certainly made geographical sense. Between Bond Street to the west and Wardour Street to the east, the only direct route that led north was Swallow Street, and that was twisted and narrow. The regent's new street obliterated Swallow Street (along with 741 houses). Nash then laid out Regent's Park to the north as 'a garden city for an aristocracy'. It was meant to accommodate a pleasure house for the regent and villas for the wealthy, and Regent Street was to provide a processional route to Carlton House. The regent gave the great plan his blessing because, he said, 'it will quite eclipse Napoleon'. Yet it was no accident that the project was initiated while the Burdettite eruptions were fresh in mind. Nash admitted that its purposes were in some part strategic. He wanted to provide 'a boundary and a complete separation between the streets and squares occupied by the nobility and gentry, and the narrow streets and meaner houses occupied by mechanics and the trading part of the community'. So the street was carved out down the natural north–south boundary between the polite West London of the squares and fine terraces and the artisan London of Covent Garden, as if to dig a chasm between them. 'My purpose,' Nash added later, 'was that the new street should cross the eastern entrance to all the streets occupied by the higher classes and to leave out to the east all the bad streets.' In other words, access points from the directions of Soho and Leicester Square would be inhibitingly fewer and more difficult to negotiate than those from the upper-class streets to the west. So they still are.[45] What was it about those more easterly Covent Garden parishes, then, that the polite world had to keep at bay?

## CHAPTER THREE

# COVENT GARDEN AND THE MIDDLING SORTS

## The pleasures of the town

When the rude low people came to defend their hero, Sir Francis Burdett, by throwing mud at the gilded Piccadilly coaches in 1810, they hadn't had far to walk in order to do so. Some might have come from the backstreets of Westminster or the dense slums of St Giles's, but most probably came from the artisan and tradesman quarters in the seventeenth-century 'town' to the east where Burdettite radicalism burned most fiercely. This territory stretched eastwards from Leicester Fields (later Square) across St Martin's Lane to Covent Garden and Drury Lane, and from St Giles's southwards to the Strand and Charing Cross [fig. 26]. The heart of it, Covent Garden, is barely a mile from St James's Square as the crow flies. With its arcades laid out by Inigo Jones in 1631, its piazza had once been aristocratic, but by the early eighteenth century the grand people had moved westwards, leaving it to market stalls and itinerant shows. As coffee-houses, taverns and bagnios multiplied, it became the centre of a proto-Bohemia. The painters John Zoffany and Richard Wilson lived there; Fielding, Goldsmith and Hogarth had met in the Bedford tavern; Sheridan held court at the Piazza Hotel and coffee-house; and David Garrick's house in Southampton Street still stands. The rich still came here habitually, for Covent Garden and Drury Lane held London's two great theatres, and the surrounding streets and alleys were London's vice centres.

Nearly all London's satirical engravers lived in or near this area, and there they shared tastes for drink, sex and bawdry with the hacks, actors and artists who struggled alongside them for the great world's custom. They lived in odorous, workaday territories, full of struggling attorneys, surgeons, clerks, apothecaries, miniature portrait painters and preachers. In warrens of courts and workshops, in dank and decaying houses, in front premises or back, up stairs and down them, at ground level or in basements, not a street in these territories lacked its army of tradesmen. The 1818 poll-book of Westminster electors listed the businesses in Long Acre (just north of Covent Garden) as follows: tailor, bootmaker, victualler, saddler, fishmonger, locksmith, bitmaker, bookbinder, baker, china-warehouseman, currier, apothecary, grocer, toyman, wire worker, brazier, lapidary, smith, refiner, colourman, truss-maker, surgeon, draper, cutler, stablekeeper, artist, varnish-maker, butcher, ironmonger, button-maker, tobacconist, cabinet-maker, musical instrument-maker, coffee-house-keeper, porkman, silversmith, tallow

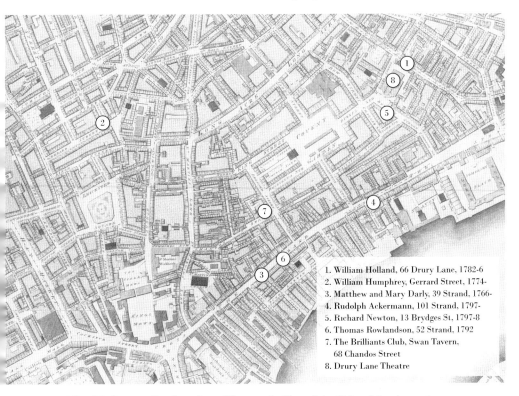

1. William Holland, 66 Drury Lane, 1782-6
2. William Humphrey, Gerrard Street, 1774-
3. Matthew and Mary Darly, 39 Strand, 1766-
4. Rudolph Ackermann, 101 Strand, 1797-
5. Richard Newton, 13 Brydges St, 1797-8
6. Thomas Rowlandson, 52 Strand, 1792
7. The Brilliants Club, Swan Tavern,
   68 Chandos Street
8. Drury Lane Theatre

**Fig. 26** Covent Garden, from Horwood, *Plan of the Cities of London and Westminster*, 1799

chandler.[1] The master tradesmen and craftsmen among these people were modestly prosperous. Together, they were thought of as the 'middling' sorts in the eighteenth century, and they are major actors in our story.

There were some 30,000 families of these 'middling' people in 1800 – or about one in seven of London's population.[2] The term encompassed many ranks and callings. Higher shopkeepers and master craftsmen were at their core, with lesser merchants above them and tradesmen below them 'who labour hard but feel no want', as Defoe had put it – people, altogether, who were 'within reach of those conveniences which the lower orders of mankind must necessarily want, and yet without embarrassment of greatness', as Johnson's *Dictionary* defined the 'middle station in life'. Across the second half of the eighteenth century, a significant minority saw their chances in life improve markedly:

> The substantial tradesman, who was wont to pass his evenings at the alehouse for fourpence half-penny, now spends three shillings at the tavern, while his wife keeps card-tables at home; she must likewise have fine clothes, her chaise, or pad, with country lodgings, and go three times a week to public diversions. Every clerk, apprentice, and even waiter of tavern or coffee-house, maintains a gelding by himself, or in partnership, and assumes the air and apparel of a *petit maître*. The gayest places of public entertainment are filled with fashionable figures; which, upon inquiry will be found to be journeymen taylors, serving-men, and abigails, disguised like their betters.[3]

Most such statements were exaggerated for rhetorical effect, since tradesmen's increasing pretensions and consumption blurred social distinctions. The truth was that craftsmen or shopkeepers had few chances of rising in the world; nor did the lowly attorneys, surgeons, teachers, and penurious journalists and artists who lived among them. Countless shopkeepers, journeymen, and employers in low trades like butchering were impoverished and semi-literate. Semi-skilled tradesmen like tailors, shoemakers, and furniture makers were under chronic pressure from the competition of cheap labour, and no craftsmen or shopkeepers had strong organizations to protect them. Nearly all had personal or neighbourhood knowledge of bankruptcies, illnesses or trade collapses, and knew that such misfortunes could propel them back into poverty. The chronic insecurity of many of these people is proved by their regular migrations from one grimy lodging to another. Before the tailor Francis Place was aged thirty, he and his growing family occupied sixteen different lodgings, mainly cramped single rooms in the dank courts of Drury Lane, the Strand, or Holborn. Born in 1771 in a tenement off Drury Lane, son of a spunging-house keeper and publican, he recalled the filth and decrepitude of most houses in the area. They were 'filled with rats mice and bugs', he remembered: 'circulation of air was out of the question, the putrid effluvia was a great inconvenience and a horrid nuisance, there was always a reservoir of putrid matter in the lower part of the house'. Many houses built of lath and plaster survived from the previous century; more recent ones were shoddily built, and let by the room.[4]

All the same, some were prospering. The better shopkeepers made up a powerful phalanx: all were literate, and some had modest capital. While the annual income thought to qualify one as a member of the middling kind was put at £50 to £80 a year in the middle of the eighteenth century, the incomes of such people in London rose to between £80 and £100 in the century's last quarter. Shopkeepers took out nearly a half of the capital's insurance policies in the 1770s and 1780s, made up over a third of the working Londoners who earned more than £75 a year, and headed 37 per cent of the London households that paid assessed taxes by the century's end. Over £100 outlay was needed to set up as a fashionable draper, mercer or hosier, and booksellers had to raise much more than that. The most comfortable lived off incomes of some £300 a year by the turn of the century.[5] Master craftsmen had similar standing. Just as the smarter shopkeepers were protected from price fluctuations by an affluent custom unaffected by them, so the mounting demand for craft skills offset the rising prices, taxation, and weakening apprenticeship controls of the war years. Middling-class demand for life's 'decencies' expanded accordingly. As William Blake noted in 1800, 'it is very extraordinary that London in so few years from a city of meer necessaries . . . should have become a city of elegance . . . & that its once stupid inhabitants should enter into an emulation of Grecian manners'. Booksellers and printsellers, he added, were now as numerous as butchers.[6]

— • —

The life that surrounded these Covent Garden people was vibrant. Artists, engravers, actors and well-born rakes took both their drink and their women there, while the theatres brought in the fashionable clientele for courtesans in chandeliered bordellos above the colonnades for those prepared to pay their fifty guineas a night. There was also the kind of bawd Boswell knew, who, in her white thread stockings, 'tramps along the Strand and will resign her engaging person . . . for a pint of wine and a shilling'. There were low dives, brothels and bagnios (or bathhouses) of vibrant squalor, but also grand bagnios like Mrs Welch's (or Wells's) in Cleveland Street, in which Casanova discovered that an evening's entertainment usually cost 'only' six guineas. He met the famous Kitty Fisher there, her body covered in diamonds; and he heard from her that she had eaten a 1000-guinea banknote that day on a slice of bread and butter. Either way, to these places well-heeled sparks came slumming it, spending youthful nights worrying how high or how low to go. With the 'whoring rage' upon him, for example, James Boswell in 1776 thought he 'would devote a night to it': 'I went to Charing Cross bagnio with a wholesome-looking, bouncing wench, stripped, and went to bed with her. But after my desires were satiated by repeated indulgence, I could not rest . . . and went home cold and disturbed and dreary and vexed, with remorse rising like a black cloud without any distinct form.'[7] Likewise young William Hickey. He was the son of an affluent lawyer living off Pall Mall who knew Burke's and Johnson's circles and was himself painted by Reynolds; but this didn't stop young Hickey from taking 'the most hackneyed and common' women to the lowest bagnios, preferring them to politer company. Outside the Charing Cross bagnio his brother was once involved in a killing affray. One night some years later, at a noisome dive in Little Russell Street, William watched two half-naked women wrestle on the floor as onlookers cheered them on. Escaping to Murphy's in the same street, he found it full of pickpockets and prostitutes. Next, he and his friends visited three bawdy houses in Bow Street 'in rotation'. One was 'under the very nose' of the magistrate, Sir John Fielding, and it puzzled Hickey that Fielding was not only literally blind but also metaphorically deaf to the riotous mayhem next door.[8]

This, too, was Grub Street territory: a cut-throat bohemia of hack writers and actors, artists and printmen, all competing for the pennies and shillings of new reading and theatre-going publics. It was the centre (with the City) of the 600 tradesmen listed in Pendred's 1785 guide to London's publishing firms, so it is no surprise that although some of the leading printshops were gravitating towards the West End to pick up elite custom, many of the earlier prints reproduced in this book were engraved and sold in this region. William

Humphrey's printshop was in St Martin's Lane and Gerrard Street between 1772 and 1777, and then at 227 Strand in 1777, until his business failed ten years later. William Holland ran his first printshop of 1782 in Drury Lane before he moved to Oxford Street in 1786. In Drury Lane he traded alongside a publisher of flagellation literature, George Peacock, possibly as a partner. The precocious and prolific Richard Newton was an apprentice in Holland's shop and sold his first work through it. Then Newton opened his own shop in Brydges Street ('opposite the pit door, Drury Lane', his later prints advertised), and he traded there until he died aged twenty-one in 1798. In the 1790s Robert Dighton was publishing his own prints from 12 Charing Cross. Isaac Cruikshank and his family lived in a four-storeyed terrace in Dorset Street, off Fleet Street, his sons George and Robert remaining there after Isaac died in 1811; the printseller Rudolph Ackermann lived in Little Russell Street in 1792 before moving to the Strand; and Thomas Rowlandson sold prints on his own account from his house in the Strand and later in the Adelphi.

The lower niches of the print trade were occupied by fly-by-night dealers and stationers. Around Westminster Hall, a French visitor noted in 1772, 'a prodigious number of little shops . . . are every day lined with prints, in which the chief persons, both in the ministry and in parliament, are handled without mercy, by emblematical representations'.[9] The Covent Garden area had many small shops of this kind, some of them trading in erotica as well as satires. As Francis Place reported, 'obscene Prints were sold at all the principal print shops and at most others. At Roach's in Russell Court, where play books and school books and stationery were sold, Mrs Roach used to open a portfolio to any boy and to any maid servant, who came to buy a penny or other book or a sheet of paper, the portfolio contained a multitude of obscene prints – some coloured, some not, and asked them if they wanted some pretty pictures, and she encouraged them to look at them. And this was done by many others.' Roach's and several other shops were prosecuted at King's Bench in 1794 for selling indelicacies like *Harris's List of Covent Garden Ladies*. Holland himself ran pornographic or flagellatory sidelines, perhaps under Peacock's influence, and in early prints for Holland the young James Gillray catered to those tastes. In 1793 Holland was sent to Newgate prison for selling the radical works of Tom Paine. A taste for erotica cohabited easily with infidel and radical inclinations in these cultures.[10] And the pleasures of booze and sex suffused them all.

# Drink, sex and the engravers

In January 1801, Ackermann's printshop in the Strand published one of Rowlandson's largest prints (21 by 16 inches). It depicted the boozily convivial members of a Covent Garden club, *The Brilliants*, as they cavorted at table in a chandelier-lit tavern clubroom [fig. 27]. As ever, Rowlandson's line flows exuberantly, and the figures are dynamically realized. Empty bottles litter the floor, and waiters open more. Three of the well-dressed members are vomiting, one is about to vomit, and another has collapsed on the floor. The club's rules are displayed on the wall:

1st    That each member shall fill a half pint bumper to the first toast.

2nd    That after twenty four bumper toasts are gone round, every [member] may fill as he pleases.

3    That any member refusing to comply with the above regulations to be fine[d] a bumper of salt & water.

*The Brilliants* was a reprise of and probably inspired by two duller and smaller drolls engraved by Isaac Cruikshank and published by Robert Laurie and James Whittle a week earlier: one, *Son's* [sic] *of Friendship – Scene, Chandois Street*, showed the Brilliants roused to drunken fisticuffs, while *Son's* [sic] *of Harmony – Scene, Chandois Street* showed its members sunk in drunken torpor [fig. 28]. Along with Gillray's *Union-Club*, published a week after Rowlandson's print, these were core images in an important cluster of 'debauchery prints' that multiplied in and after the 1790s.[11] They might be read as moral satires on alcoholic vice were they not so comic. They are better understood as celebrations of the boozy conviviality that was as common to the engravers as it was to the great in the land. For it is very much to the point that the Brilliants was Rowlandson's personal club, as well as Isaac Cruikshank's and the printsellers, Laurie's and Whittle's: Whittle, indeed, was the club's 'perpetual president'. Despite the Brilliants' propensity to vomit, therefore, Rowlandson had no reason to castigate their festive pleasures. This louche and boozy territory was his own, shared sociably with downmarket bohemians just like himself.

The Brilliants was a real club, then, and the rules on the wall were probably real as well. It might have originated in the 1760s, and it allegedly survived into the 1820s, renamed 'The Finish'. At that later date it still catered to theatrical and after-theatre custom, though in Robert

**Fig. 27** Rowlandson, *The Brilliants* (Ackermann, 1801)
This large print depicts Rowlandson's own club of that name as they enjoy a drunken and vomiting debauch in the club chamber of the Swan tavern, Chandos St.

**Fig. 28** Isaac Cruikshank, *Son's of Friendship – Scene, Chandos Street* (Laurie and Whittle, 1801)

Cruikshank's illustration of it in 1825 the room is humbler than the one Rowlandson shows; the top-hatted members disport themselves with women and thieves, and two Bow Street officers lurk in the doorway [fig. 29]. In Rowlandson's day the Brilliants met at the Swan tavern in Chandos Street, just off the Covent Garden piazza, five minutes from the shop in which the print was sold. The club's hours were long: 'the chair was seldom taken till the theatres were over, and rarely vacated till 4 or 5 a.m.'[12] All its members were press or theatre men. This was a significant association. Theatre was one of the few arenas in which all classes mingled, and few engravers escaped its influence, most living minutes away from the Drury Lane and Haymarket theatres. In titles, quotations and subject-matter, theatrical allusions inform several hundred prints, Gillray's included, each assuming their purchasers' understanding. The actor Jack Bannister had been Rowlandson's closest friend since they had both studied at the Royal Academy. Many of Isaac Cruikshank's drolls for Laurie and Whittle illustrated current stage sensations or theatrical gossip. Isaac's son, George, had wanted in boyhood to be an actor or stage designer, and both George and Robert had been 'stagestruck almost from birth'. They grew up with the actor Edmund Kean as a boyhood friend, and Grimaldi the clown was

**Fig. 29** Robert Cruikshank, *Peep o' Day Boys and Family Men at the Finish a Scene near Covent Garden* (in C. Westmacott, *The English Spy*, 1824)

also one of George's intimates.[13] Theo Lane, who engraved many anti-Caroline and loyalist satires for Humphrey's shop in 1820–21, was himself an impoverished actor.

Since the engravers were nearly all born into the rough, struggling world of London's middling class, these tastes were predictable. The only caricaturist who was comfortably born was Henry Bunbury. He was the son of a gentleman connected to the Holland House circle; Horace Walpole regarded him as 'the new Hogarth' but his work was bland by comparison with that of our rougher diamonds (although not without its scatological moments).[14] G. M. Woodward was the son of a landowner's steward who was affluent enough to allow him a £100 annuity when he went to London. An untrained artist, he seldom engraved his own designs (Isaac Cruikshank, Newton and Rowlandson, Woodward's drinking companion, did that for him). But he could achieve a bawdy vigour, and his strip cartoons and middling-life jokes (well over 500 are catalogued) were so popular that it was his, not Rowlandson's, name that dominated the advertising for and contents of Tegg's *Caricature Magazine* in 1807–9. It was, however, virtually a condition of Woodward's talent that he led as dissipated a life as any of his rivals. He haunted taverns to study and sketch 'those peculiar species of low characters, the inhabitants of the round house [the Bow Street lock-up], and the myrmidons of the police'; and when he died in 1809, it was 'with a glass of brandy in his hand' in the Brown Bear tavern in Bow Street, whose landlord had to bury him.[15]

Most engravers' origins were much humbler. Hogarth's father had been a coffee-house keeper, Gillray's a soldier, Thomas Rowlandson's a bankrupted Spitalfields silk manufacturer, Dighton's a printseller, Newton's a modestly prospering Drury Lane haberdasher, James Sayer's a Yarmouth ship-master, and Isaac Cruikshank's an immigrant Scot. Only Gillray, Rowlandson, and Woodward (and Sayer perhaps) were formally educated. Misspellings abound in the others' print titles, speech bubbles and subtexts, especially in Isaac Cruikshank's. Admittedly, Rowlandson's artistic and social talents at first guaranteed him good connections. In the 1770s he lived with his wealthy aunt at Wardour Street and Poland Street in Soho, consorting with great people whom he met through his lifelong friend, the fashionable fencing master, Henry Angelo. But when the aunt died in 1789, he gambled away her legacy and in 1791 had to set up printselling on his own account at 52 Strand.

Thereafter he lived in a basement at 2 Robert Street in the Adelphi (the rate collector described it as 'dismal'); next, in rooms adjoining his friend George Morland's above a printshop near Carlton House; and last in an attic with its own printing press in 1 James Street, Adelphi, where he died in 1827. Throughout these years he moved in and out of satire-engraving, publishing for himself or for others as prosperity or penury dictated; in the new century he had to turn his huge talents to book illustration for Ackermann's printshop and later to hasty hack-work for Thomas Tegg. By 1804 he was complaining with the rest of them about the niggardly patronage of 'the long pursed gentry'.[16]

Other engravers led even more precarious lives. Obscure to all but their tavern companions, women and employers, they moved their lodgings as luck and employment dictated, and took such jobs as they could. The young William Blake, for example, after a seven-year apprenticeship with the leading antiquarian engraver in London, made his living by producing stipple engravings after Morland or Watteau or line engravings after Hogarth, and from hack-work for journals like *The Wit's Magazine*. Dighton supplemented his artistic income by singing at theatres and pleasure gardens and by stealing prints from the British Museum; in 1812 he tried to put his daughters on the stage to assist his 'present pecuniary embarasment [*sic*]'. At his best, Isaac Cruikshank was a significant caricaturist, but he had to turn out lottery tickets and theatrical portraits to help make a living, and his wife had to watercolour his satires at home. His first son, Robert, for a while led a midshipman's life at sea, while his second son, George, was 'too busy' for an education because at the age of twelve he had to work on lottery tickets also.[17] Newton had no more than a drawing-master's training before he was apprenticed to William Holland at the age of fourteen. His work had a violent clarity of line and attack that would have evolved importantly had he not died young in 1798, aged twenty-one, leaving 300 prints altogether.[18] Although Newton and Robert Cruikshank tried their hands at miniature portrait-painting, only Gillray, Rowlandson and Dighton had Academy training and sought recognition as serious artists, in Gillray's case in vain.

Like most pressmen, engravers were poorly paid. The printshops that lived off their labour got the best of the deal, it seems. Among the lesser shops bankruptcies were common, and proprietors justified low piece-rates by claiming that their profits were slim. But 'this was too bad', one of George Cruikshank's friends wrote ironically, 'considering [that] the unfortunate publishers drank wine, and had their gigs to keep'. Certainly, when Carington Bowles's father died in 1779, he left Carington only a token legacy on the grounds that 'he is not only in a very flourishing business but possessed of a plentiful fortune out of trade'. On Hannah Humphrey's death in 1818, her bequests to her many relatives and her servant Betty Marshall show substantial affluence. The fact that both Fores and Hannah's nephew, George, were still prospering in the 1820s speaks for long profitability at the top of the business. This was no surprise when the retail mark-up on the payments made to engraver and watercolourer was some 100 per cent or more.[19]

By the turn of the century, demand for the engraver's skills was increasing and prospects were improving. 'Every engraver turns away work that he cannot execute from his superabundant employment,' William Blake noted. But it was in fine art rather than satirical engraving that the best employment lay, and few of our rougher diamonds hoped for that. One estimate put the payment for an engraved satire at twenty-five to thirty shillings, though the quality, size or sales of the prints concerned are unspecified, and all such payments had to cover the cost of the copper, design, etching and coloured example. In his early if not later years George Cruikshank made a guinea a time from a large etching, and then he provided the copper. Most artists engraved satires as sidelines when opportunity offered; trade cards and advertisements provided steadier income; and some score or so of engravers are known now by mere handfuls of satires. After Gillray's death, Robert and George Cruikshank were said to be the only artists able to dictate to printshops the content of their work and to demand three guineas per plate; George's *Bank Restriction Note* of 1819 allegedly netted him and his publisher Hone £700 [fig. 87]. At the bottom end of the trade, the fortunes of watercolourers were bleak. Engravers usually provided coloured templates for their prints; but the fact that many of Gillray's are variously coloured suggests a small army of women and girls doing piece-work in their own lodgings away from supervision. Few did well; but in the 1790s (according to Francis Place) the radical Thomas Evans and his wife lived by colouring bawdy prints, though Evans also advertised himself as a 'map, chart and print colourer'. Arrested in 1798, Evans claimed that he made £100 profit annually from business, sufficient to rent the substantial premises off Fetter Lane in which he met his English Jacobin friends.[20]

The engravers left scant recollections of their younger days. George Cruikshank sanitized his in his respectable middle years. But it is clear that their pretensions were as modest as their status. None of them theorized about or explained his own or others' work. Rather they lived for liquor, enjoyed the easy ways of the girls of their class, and found much of their material in the city's lively streets and casual violence. Although they had to keep their eyes on their markets' expectations, it was in the 'people' and in their own struggling backgrounds that their humour was hatched. When their engravings moved from low-life to high-life motifs, as in some of the Cruikshank brothers' plates for Egan's *Life in London* in 1820–21, their energy and conviction fell off noticeably. An analogy with Dickens's relish for low life suggests itself here. Dickens was never debauched and avoided bawdry, but he was born into the same middling cultures as the engravers were. He too loved penny theatres and street-life, and his cast of humour was as boisterous, ironic and sentimental as theirs. No surprise, then, that Cruikshank and Dickens in 1836 began their collaboration in Dickens's *Sketches by Boz*. At that point, it was a measure of Cruikshank's stature that he wasn't called 'Dickensian'; it was Dickens who was dubbed 'the CRUIKSHANK of writers'.[21]

'Respectable' before the 1820s the engravers were not. Nor were they religious. Although both Gillray's father and the Cruikshanks' mother were devout Dissenters, the sons rejected this legacy. Most ridiculed Methodists and Quakers as zealously as they did churchmen, and they all castigated religious pronouncements as 'cant' and clergymen as 'canting'. George Cruikshank's *Interior View of the House of God* (1811), for instance, shows the Bermondsey papermaker Elias Carpenter conducting one of his fire-and-brimstone services in his meeting house [fig. 30]. His congregation consists of rough or sanctimonious hypocrites overlooked by the devil. One man shows a young woman a copy of *Fanny Hill* while another has a copy of 'Capt Morris Hymns – Hymn 1st Great Plenipo', the dirtiest song of its day.[22] What moral views the engravers shared turned on the virtues of candour, directness, good fellowship and the pursuit of manly pleasure. None was protected from London's fleshier or more liquid pleasures. None failed to depict street women with sympathy, and they all knew 'loose women'. It was not from ignorance that both Richard Newton and Robert Cruikshank produced plates depicting the aptly named cock and hen clubs that met in innumerable tavern back-parlours. Such places, too, were their territory.

**Fig. 30** George Cruikshank, *Interior View of the House of God* (1811)

Francis Place later remembered some fourteen or fifteen cock and hen clubs along the river between Blackfriars and Scotland Yard in the 1780s. Apprentices and their girls passed their evenings in them, 'drinking – smoking [*sic*] – swearing – and singing flash songs' until the sexes paired off and 'by 12 o clock none remained'.[23] Recording this in respectable middle age, Place denied that he ever 'in even a single instance' paired off himself, but you'd believe anything if you believed that. A German visitor reported of one such club, meeting on Tuesdays in Wych Street, that 'it consisted of servants, journeymen and apprentices. Every member laid down fourpence, for which he had music and a female gratis, everything else to be paid for separately.' When the club was raided and twenty of the girls were brought before the magistrate Sir John Fielding, their beauty 'roused general admiration'.[24] In his 1798 *A Row at a Cock and Hen Club*, Richard Newton shows constables breaking up just such a gathering. Fisticuffs erupt as sticks and chairs are brandished, noses bleed, pistols are drawn, and the girls' breasts are drawn with amiable attentiveness [fig. 31].[25] A murder was committed in a club like this at the King's Arms in St Giles's just a year later. It was (an Old Bailey witness said) 'a club,

**Fig. 31** Newton, *A Row at a Cock and Hen Club* (Newton, 1798)

consisting of a mixture of men and women, with dancing and music, and that sort of disorder, a meeting that never could have been licensed upon an application'. 'What is the name of your club?' the publican was asked: 'I know of no name for it, only people that behave friendly together.' 'It is extraordinary,' the judge summed up in heavy irony, 'that all these prisoners should have had the character of being sober, honest, and quiet, quiet in particular, when they are found ... collected together in the form of a club, forty or fifty of them, a cock and hen club, with dancing, and singing, and fiddling, and doing what you have heard done.'[26] In Robert Cruikshank's much later *Tom, Jerry and Logic* (1824), behaviour seems more demure, but the company is mixed in sex, colour, and class, and jollity reigns still [fig. 32].

None of our engravers could have been innocent of such places. Every London tavern had its clubroom: and, just as a clubbish sociability knitted together the men of the high elites, so any number of Old Bailey trial interrogations during the 1790s and 1800s show that it bonded middling men likewise:

Was there a club that night at Wood's house? [at the White-horse, Aldgate] –
I believe there was a club, for I heard the people singing up stairs myself . . .
What had they for supper? – A piece of boiled beef, I think they had some
punch, I do not sell wine, I am sure they had no wine . . . So there were a
hundred of you? – Yes, there were a hundred and thirty odd. All in one room? –
Yes. What might be the expenses of the evening? – Only sixpence apiece, the
supper I paid for myself . . . Had you any ladies among you? – There were
several women. Any dancing? – Yes, and music. What music? – A piper.

I work at the lead mill at Islington; I was at the club that morning till near
two o'clock . . . How many hours had you been drinking? – About two hours
and a half; it was rather late before I left work, when I went down; I do not
know rightly what time; the club meet about seven in the evening.

**Fig. 32** Robert Cruikshank, '*A Bit of Good Truth*' – *Tom, Jerry and Logic
Enjoying the Lark, Song, Fun and Frisk at a Cock and Hen Club* (in P. Egan, *Finish to
the Adventures of Tom, Jerry, and Logic*, 1829)

You had a club at your house? – A shoe-club. What is a shoe-club? – A club for people that want shoes cheap, to pay sixpence a week, and spend twopence. Did not the prisoner apply to you respecting this club? – He asked me if there was a club, and said he wished to be a member of it. What was he to pay to be a member? – Two shillings . . . What sort of people composed this club? – Creditable people in the neighbourhood.

I had been at a benefit club at Doctor's-commons, and had had two or three pipes of tobacco, which I am not used to, and drinking beer and punch, till I was so intoxicated, that I did not know where I went, or what I did, till I waked, and found myself in the watch-house in the morning.

I was drinking with Dodson at a free and easy club that is held at Mr. Gibson's, he was very drunk, and I took off his clothes, and put him to bed; he desired me to take his watch and other things to take care of them.[27]

Not all tavern clubs were as dissolute as the cock-and-hens and free-and-easies were. Many catered to more specialized tastes – in pugilism, say, or sport. They could still be as jolly as Collings's parodic *A Pugilistick Club* implied, with its black-eyed and raucous members [fig. 33]. But in their maturer years, like most comfortable tradesmen, the artists would have frequented clubs smarter than the worst of the dives. A good example of the middling sociability to which more prosperous printmen might have gravitated is that of a shopkeeper of 'the better sort', Joseph Brasbridge. He sold silver and plated goods in Fleet Street to a fashionable clientele, with some of whom he consorted socially. He was 'one of those loyal jolly souls whose moral notions all centre in their bellies', Francis Place recalled primly. Like Rowlandson, he was a friend of Jack Bannister, the actor. He belonged variously to a club in the Globe in Fleet Street (its members including surgeons, printers, booksellers, actors and the keeper of Newgate); a sixpenny card-club of twenty members at the Queen's Arms in St Paul's Churchyard; a free-and-easy at the Queen's Arms which boasted some thousand members; a political debating society at the Cider Cellar, Maiden Lane; and a club at the Spread Eagle in the Strand, which was famous as the resort of young sparks after the theatres closed, its landlord observing that he had 'an uncommon sort of customers, for what with hanging, drowning, and natural death, he had a change every six months'. These were all gatherings (Place sniffed as he looked back from his own improving

**Fig. 33** Collings, *A Pugilistick Club* (Bentley [*Attic Miscellany*, i, 81], 1789)

1820s) of 'jolly or facetious fellows who talked nonsense and anathematized all who were not as sottish and as ignorant as themselves'. Brasbridge confessed that he divided his time 'between the tavern-club, the card-party, the hunt, and the fight', but he gave a more sedate account than Place did of the goings-on there. Richard Tattersall's Highflyer Club, to which he also belonged, met not for gambling, he wrote, but 'purely for social intercourse' and for 'stories of wit and good-humour'. This was probably true, but only so far as generous lubrication allowed. Not for nothing was one of Brasbridge's friends known as 'T. B'. or 'Two Bottles'.

As like as not there would have been lewder goings-on than story-telling in these places: rude singing for a start. Place recalled that in the 1780s songs like 'Sandman Joe' were sung in a Crown and Anchor club in the Strand 'by gentlemen'. If so, this was an appropriation from low culture: for the song was most familiar from the female street-singers in the Strand who 'amidst roars of laughter' bucked their pelvises and shammed orgasm at its key moments:

He star'd a while then turn'd his quid,
Why blast you, Sall, I loves you!
And for to prove what I have said,
This night I'll soundly fuck you.
Why then says Sall, my heart's at rest
If what you say you'll stand to;
His brawny hands, her bubbies prest,
And roaring cried, 'White sand O'.[28]

Place insisted that low ballads like these were appreciated not only by 'the lower orders but by the middling classes also'. Although they were sung by 'flash and fancy men with the peculiar dress – rollers at the cheeks, striped silk stockings, numerous knee strings, long quartered shoes and all en suite', they were also sung by master tradesmen at the Dog and Duck or the Temple of Flora, where the tradesmen mixed with the flash set promiscuously. During the 1780s, Place's father was a publican on the Strand, 'a resolute, daring, straightforward sort of a man, governed almost wholly by his passions and animal sensations', famous for 'drinking, whoring, gaming, fishing and fighting'. Place remembered rowdy parties of tradesmen in his father's parlour, and also in a house in the Strand when he was ten years old. They sang songs that were 'very gross', with doors left open so that every word could be heard. George Cruikshank, significantly, let slip a childhood memory just like Place's. It was of 'gentlemen coming to dine occasionally at his father's house, and he was often surprised on coming downstairs of a morning to find some of them rolled up in the carpet in an extraordinary manner'.[29]

In lives in which work was unremitting, sex was the leading pleasure. By Place's account there was plenty of it to be had in the craft and shopkeeper cultures of the 1780s – along with a candour about it that would be unthinkable by the time he recalled it in the 1820s. Conversation on 'the union of the sexes' had been 'much less reserved' than it was now, he noted; and 'books relating to the subject were much more within the reach of boys and girls': 'I had little to learn on any part of the subject.' Aged thirteen, he had pored over the sexual advice manual, *Aristotle's Masterpiece*, 'at that time openly sold, on every stall'. Comparing its 'badly drawn cuts explanatory of the mystery of generation' with New Testament accounts of the miraculous conception, he was convinced by the science and dismissed Christian belief once and for all. No doubt the middle-aged

Place dramatized the youthful immoralities from which he had distanced himself, but his account of the relative fluidity of moral boundaries in the lightly policed 1780s rings true. Even middling people then thought that thieving was more acceptable than their equivalents did a half-century later (his own sister married the son of a receiver of stolen goods; whose siblings were thieves and whores); whereas by 1824 only the 'lowest class' were thieves, Place noted. The borders between whoring and respectability had been just as hazy. The girls of his youth were 'under comparatively little restraint', he wrote; and their early loss of virginity didn't make them worse wives when they married later. 'Want of chastity' was 'not by any means considered so disreputable in master tradesmen's families as it is now in journeymen mechanics' families'; and female lewdness was encouraged by 'the songs which were ordinarily sung by their relatives and by young men and women and the lewd plays and interludes they occasionally saw'. Nor were the girls too wholesome, if he is to be believed (he had some difficulties with women). The leather stays of 'wives and daughters of journeymen, tradesmen, and shopkeepers' were 'worn day by day for years', while the girls he knew discarded their camblet petticoats, quilted with wool or horsehair and 'standing in their filth', only when they had rotted.

> [They] wore long quartered shoes and large buckles, most of them had clean stockings and shoes, because it was then the fashion to be flashy about the heels, but many had ragged dirty shoes and stockings and some no stockings at all . . . their gowns were low round the neck and open in the front, those who wore handkerchiefs had them always open in front to expose their breasts this was a fashion which the best dressed among them followed, but numbers wore no handkerchiefs at all in warm weather, and the breasts of many hung down in a most disgusting manner, their hair among the generality was straight and 'hung in rats tails' over their eyes, and was filled with lice, at least was inhabited by considerable colonies of these insects . . . Fighting among themselves as well as with the men was common and black eyes might be seen on a great many.

Among the engravers, the deepening cult of the artistic temperament imposed its own raffish obligations. Artists should be 'noted for being dissipated & wild', William Blake wrote: 'he who has nothing to dissipate cannot dissipate; the weak man may be virtuous enough but will never be an artist.'[30] Dissipated, therefore, the engravers were to a man. Rowlandson left a rich graphic record of his models and doxies, one of them his housekeeper, with whom he lived for years. He also gambled and drank. His tavern scene, *A Brace of Blackguards* (1789) [fig. 34], depicts two aggressive-looking men, with prints of pugilists on the wall behind. The sparring man was said to be a self-portrait; the other, with the cudgel, was allegedly his friend, the artist George Morland.[31] Gillray drank compulsively too, even in his heyday resorting to 'dishonest shifts', it was said, to get money to feed his thirst. The Cruikshanks were heavy topers as well. Their favoured ambience is nicely conveyed in a pencil sketch from the late 1790s by Isaac Cruikshank

**Fig. 34** Rowlandson, *A Brace of Blackguards* (Mrs Lay, Brighthelmstone, 1789)

depicting himself and his young sons in a tavern room. Isaac sits with arms folded, Robert has a girl on his lap, and George looks drunkenly miserable [fig. 35]. Isaac died in 1811, having 'shortened his life by the fashion of the day', as George later put it: he had accepted a challenge to a drinking match that sent him into an irreversible coma at the age of forty-eight.[32]

George himself was certainly a tavern kind of man. He later boasted that his only academy had been the 'tap-room of a low public house, in one of the dark, dirty, narrow lanes which branch off from one of the great thoroughfares towards the Thames... just the place in which to witness the lowest of low life in all its grotesqueries and drollery'. What he didn't later boast about was his knowledge of obscene songs, several times cited in his prints.[33] Notorious for his all-night drinking and fondness for cockpits and brothels, he complained of chronic hangovers and poverty. He lived on gin and water, he told William Hone in 1821, because his mouth let the gin in, and his boots the water. Hone would take him in despite his oafish behaviour, urging him to 'forswear late hours, blue ruin, and dollies'. But Cruikshank's reply that Hone should teach his granny to suck eggs ended the hitherto hugely fruitful Hone–Cruikshank friendship. He sobered up a bit on his marriage in 1824, but not for long.

**Fig. 35** Isaac Cruikshank, *The Cruikshanks in a Tavern* (pencil and ink) (*c.*1800)

Dickens later described him as 'turning up at his friends' houses at unseasonable hours in the morning, unkempt and unwashed and smelling of tobacco, beer, and sawdust'. He was 'pretty constantly in police custody during the small hours of the morning; having . . . been found in the street in an insensible condition, full length on the pavement'. Yet this was the culture that sustained Cruikshank's art. In one tavern full of fiddling and dancing coal-heavers, he was impressed to see a bust of Shakespeare on the chimneypiece, a pipe stuck in its mouth – a meeting, he thought, 'of the sublime and the ridiculous; the world of intellect and poetry seemed thrown open to the meanest capacity; extremes had met; the highest and the lowest had united in harmonious fellowship . . . What a picture of life was there! It was *all life*!' As was later said of his art, his field of observation 'stretched from the foot of the gallows to Greenwich fair; through coal-holes, cider-cellars, cribs, and prize-fighters' taverns, Petticoat Lane, and Smithfield . . . [to] Covent Garden market, where the young bloods drank and sang and fought under the piazzas, something more than sixty years ago'. Only in 1847 did he take the teetotal pledge and turn himself into a respectable Victorian. Even then he lived secretly for years in a quasi-bigamous relationship with his wife and embarrassingly fertile mistress.[34]

In view of all this, it is not surprising that the comedies of drunkenness, sex and prostitution are written deeply into these men's engravings; nor that, in a culture in which it was as yet only the moral minority who thought of prostitution as an evil symbolic of the *whole* of society's failings, their visual commentaries on prostitution were comically upbeat rather than judgemental. Admittedly, there had been change in this representation. In Hogarth's *Harlot's Progress* (1732), the moral narrative that brought Moll Hackabout to her miserable end had left purchasers in no doubt what to think about her choices. And those who worked in Hogarth's shadow felt obliged to moralize also.[35] But later eighteenth-century prints on the subject refused to direct meanings so didactically. Their moral alibis were exiguous or self-parodic, and their attack aimed less at the whore than at the punter's gullibility – establishing cousinhood in this with guidebooks that warned of the tricks of the town in Carington Bowles's *An Evenings Invitation* [sic]; *with a Wink from the Bagnio* (1773), for example [fig. 36]. Prostitution was otherwise invariably presented as an amusing or titillatory subject. Only Gillray's extraordinary *The Whore's Last Shift* (1779) seems momentarily to raise the curtain on the bleakness of the prostitute's life [fig. 37]. In her garret, the

An EVENINGS INVITATION; with a WINK from the BAGNIO.

Printed for Carington Bowles Map & Printseller, N° 69 in St Pauls Church Yard, London. Published as the Act directs

**Fig. 36** Carington Bowles, *An Evenings Invitation; with a Wink from the Bagnio* (Carington Bowles, 1773)

naked whore concludes her night's business by washing her last shift in her chamberpot (the pun on 'shift'), the incongruous finery of her hairpiece belied by her tattered stockings, both indicating that she'd come down in the world. Hogarthian symbols are present too: the cat arches its back and the pot is cracked. The broadside in the window proclaims 'The comforts of a single life. An old song'. The wall-print is 'Ariadne forsaken'. The print might intend no more than a conventional if eroticized comment on the contrast between the outward presentation of the self and the corrupted inner reality,

THE WHORE'S LAST SHIFT.

**Fig. 37** Gillray, *The Whore's Last Shift* (W. Humphrey, 1779)

echoing Swift's poetic satire to that effect, *Beautiful Young Nymph Going to Bed*. But is it contemptuous of the poor woman, or does it seek to disclose the poignancy of her plight? The answer is left to the viewer. The fact that it was produced for William Humphrey's shop during Gillray's erotic period, its cousin being his prurient *Female Curiosity* of the year before [fig. 111], may suggest a less generous answer – that it strove for no more than titillation.

No other print dealing with prostitution gives cause for similar reflection. By the late 1780s, even the tricks-of-the-town alibi was discarded in favour of a titillatory prurience that probably reflected the engravers' own attitudes and experiences. This is true of the many prints by Dent, Newton and Rowlandson. The best of them touch brilliance. Newton's *Male Carriage or New Evening Dilly* (1798) shows the prostitute dressed to kill as she sets out demurely on her business, its energy depending on a subtext (probably by

**Fig. 38** Newton, *The Male Carriage or New Evening Dilly* (Holland, 1798)

its publisher, Holland) that compares her purposes and bodily parts with those of a carriage ('dilly'), in a series of elaborate sexual puns [fig. 38]:

> The Male Carriage or New Evening Dilly sets out for Soho at 8 o'clock every evening: stops at Drury Lane and Covent Garden to take in [passengers], or if desired, will receive in the Yard [penis] of St George, and go easy over the Stones [testicles], and for the accommodation of the Public will also take up and let down in any part of the Town – Inside Passengers to pay £1.1.0 allow'd to carry two Stone – The Carriage fresh painted, lined with Crimson velvet; fine hair seat, of remarkable pleasant pace, well guarded and kept in good order – The Axle-Tree warranted from taking fire let the motion be ever so quick. The standing rule to pay before entrance. None permitted to get up behind. Performed by Derriere Harris and Co.

**Fig. 39** Rowlandson, *Launching a Frigate* (Tegg, 1809)

Eleven years later, Rowlandson drew on Newton's image for his *Launching a Frigate* [fig. 39], the background chimney on fire hinting at male ejaculation. And when in the same year Rowlandson engraved *Cattle Not Insurable*, a wonderful boatload of whores being ferried to service the sailors on the ships berthed at Portsmouth, the girls stand for a part of male life's rich feast and, hopefully, for the girls' own exuberant happiness also [fig. 40]. It took a later generation to challenge the cheeriness of this form of representation. A naval memoirist publishing in 1844 remembered the ferrying out to ships of 'boat loads of defiled and defiling women . . . some of them not without pretensions of beauty'. Another thought them 'most pitiable; the ill-usage and the degradation they are driven to submit to, are indescribable, but from that habit they become callous, indifferent as to the delicacy of speech and behaviour, and so totally lost to all sense of shame, that they seem to retain no quality which properly belongs to woman but the same shape and name'. 'Thus these poor unfortunates are taken to market like cattle,' he added, 'and while this system is observed it cannot with truth be said that the slave-trade is abolished in England.'[36] We are nowadays conditioned to acquiesce in these verdicts. But the tone of the satires obliges us to ask whether the girls themselves would have voted this way, in an era when life expectations were modest and the stigma attached to prostitution weaker than it became. Rowlandson, Newton and others had a better sense than historians now dare allow themselves that countless whores might have been *happy*.

Cheerful obscenities, *doubles entendres*, genital symbols and allusions, lavatorial jokes, the farts beloved of the Cruikshanks, the breasts bared ubiquitously – these we may see now as the common stuff of tavern badinage, jest and chatter. But their origin and their drift raise important questions. Relishing booze and easy women and enjoying so much more artistic licence than their predecessors, how could such men affect to be *satirists*? How did the dispositions revealed here influence their commentary on the vices and tastes of their betters? What did they know about vice at higher social levels anyway?

CATTLE NOT INSURABLE.

**Fig. 40** Rowlandson, *Cattle Not Insurable* (Ackermann, 1809)

# CHAPTER FOUR

# CROSSING THE BOUNDARIES

## Manliness

Although St James's and Covent Garden were worlds apart in wealth, privilege and manners, the more louche of their young males had low tastes in common. Leaving aside the admitted legions of the godly, clean, thoughtful and ageing, it is not difficult to uncover practices among many high-born men that matched those of their inferiors. If men of our engravers' kind relished sexual adventure unapologetically, the gently-born young did too. If the girls the engravers knew were free with their bodies, so were innumerable high-born women. If cock and hen clubs occupied the low end of metropolitan sociability, West End clubs occupied the high end, and their alcoholic enthusiasms were identical. While Rowlandson's Brilliants Club ruled on the size of the bumpers to be downed at each toast, Lord Barrymore's Warble Club ruled 'that any member who has two ideas shall be obliged to give one to his neighbour' and 'that if any member has more sense than another he be kicked out of the club'. If the journeyman settled disputes with punches, the gentleman settled his with duels. In the sexual or sporting *demi-monde* high and low met promiscuously. And both found the comedies of booze, sex and body funny. These congruences explain two things in the satirical prints: a good deal of their subject-matter first, and the compromised nature of their representations of aristocratic vice second. They were 'laughing' not 'savage' satires – or less satires than *celebrations*.

Two sets of codes shaped the mentality of the money-laden and cultivated young rake, and the manners of the salon had nothing to do with either of them. One was broadly 'libertine' and was sanctioned by Enlightenment assumptions that sensory indulgence and sexual pleasure were 'natural'. The other code, of much older provenance, valued 'manliness'. It took male superiority and privileges for granted, it valued sincerity, candour and the honour of men, while execrating cant, affectation and effeminacy, and its casts of humour were bawdy, ironic, and satirical.[1] These postures were intensified during wartime. On the one hand, the years of the American war saw a deepening hostility to transgressive plays with sexual identity: men must be men, and women must be women. On the other, male cultures between 1793 and 1815 seem both to have defied moralists' and women's determination to nudge men towards a more domesticated civility, and to have repudiated male foppishness ever more determinedly. Male clothing was freed from colour, satin and lace in these years, and sober country styles became the very mark of English manliness. The cluster of 'debauchery prints' that appeared in the 1790s and 1800s bore the same masculinist subtext, as did the near-fetishization of pugilism. Satire itself came to be thought of as a 'manly' form, deeply opposed to gushing female sensibility.

Polite critics had their difficulties with both libertine and manly codes, as did people of sensibility later. But Lord Shaftesbury's rule that a man of good breeding was 'incapable of doing a rude or brutal action' fell on deaf ears in these circles, while hopes for a chivalric rather than a predatory masculinity were, as they always are, chronically thwarted. Full manhood was defined as it had been defined for centuries. Gravitas came with marriage, inheritance and maturity. Before marriage, however, the well-born male was expected to sow wild oats and explore his identity. It was understood that he might move in and out of polite venues and postures as he chose, affecting contempt for their over-refinement even while retaining his social investment in them. Courtly to ladies in salon or in family life, outside those arenas he might prove himself in clubbishness, sporting wagers, sexual conquest, the defence of honour and martial skill. Publicly aloof to inferiors, he might hobnob in licensed venues with publicans, pugilists and sporting swells. Highly mannered among ladies, in tavern and club he could laugh and lech with the lowest. 'They break through no laws, or conscientious restraints,' Charles Lamb wrote of these aristocratic playboys: 'They know of none. They have got out of

Christendom into . . . the Utopia of gallantry, where pleasure is duty, and the manners perfect freedom.'[2]

The 'half-mad' Lord Camelford provides one example of this. Worth £30,000 a year (£1.25 million in today's values), and related to the Pitts, Grenvilles and Stanhopes, he 'never forgot his rank even in the lowest society' and demanded the respect due to his station. He also knew how to be *polite*: 'in good society, with his sister Lady Grenville, his mother and his friends, he was the best-bred and finest gentleman you could imagine'. Yet he flirted with low life habitually, and his enthusiasm for duelling, boxing, fisticuffs and nocturnal adventures was infamous. He 'despised the customs, advantages and luxuries of the great world as mere fripperies, *unworthy of what ranked as a man* in his estimation'. His bachelor drawing-room in Bond Street was full of prints of pugilists, racehorses and fighting cocks, not to mention boxing gloves, pistols, foils, cudgels and horsewhips: 'manliness' was proved in aggression.[3]

Much the same duality characterized the manners of the princes. Byron, who had expected to find the Prince of Wales a debauched vulgarian, was disconcerted to find otherwise when introduced to him in 1812: 'for more than $\frac{1}{2}$ an hour HRH conversed on poetry and poets, with which he displayed an intimacy & critical taste, which at once surprised & delighted Lord B. . . . He quoted Homer & some of the obscure Greek poets even, & appeared as Lord B supposes to have read more than any prince in Europe.' When George Canning first met the prince, he was 'charmed beyond measure' and found 'the elegance of his address and the gentlemanliness of his manner' far beyond his expectations. 'In intellectual endowments he very far surpassed his father and his brothers,' it was said of the prince later, but also: 'his tastes were sensual, and though he was ambitious of being considered the most polished gentleman in Europe, there was little real refinement and little delicacy in his behaviour. He could *play* the fine gentleman, as Louis XIV is said to have played the monarch.'[4] Despite the tutting of moralists, the sniping of radicals, and women's efforts to impose a more chivalrous manhood, young elite males, supported by wealth, privilege and near-total unaccountability, had no cause to be defensive about these alternate dispositions until the 1820s, and in many cases not even then.

Masculine and libertine codes fused so easily in the male cultures that concern us that it is artificial to separate them. But because libertinism raises its own questions, it needs separate discussion. It had its own intellectual pretensions, practices and humour; and its view of women and women's of it were distinctive. For these reasons the relationship between manliness and libertinism is left for the discussion of the sexes in Part III. Although manly codes subsumed libertine practices in obvious ways, they had older and rougher origins, and were less class-specific. They were nurtured in the rural and sporting cultures in which well-born males were raised on family estates, often rather rudely. As one clergyman recalled of the later eighteenth-century Cheshire gentry, 'making noises to imitate beasts, singing bawdy songs, telling bawdy tales, boasting of their exploits with women, relating filthy stories, drinking disgusting toasts, and getting throughly drunk made up the sum of their amusements whenever they met'. They enjoyed farting at passing women, he added; and 'fox-hunting, drinking, bawling out obscene songs and whoring was the employment, the delight and the boast of these people'. Rowlandson's *Miseries of the Country* leaves a plausible record of one form of these manly occasions [fig. 41], while George Cruikshank nicely caught the alcoholic enthusiasms of aristocratic sporting clubs like Lord Barrymore's Four in Hand Club in

**Fig. 41** Rowlandson, *Miseries of the Country* (1807)

DINNER of the FOUR IN HAND CLUB at SALTHILL.

**Fig. 42** George Cruikshank, *Dinner of the Four in Hand Club at Salthill* (from *The Scourge*, 1811)

his print of its tavern dinner in 1811 [fig. 42].[5] The Cheshire clergyman might have added gambling to his list. Byron recalled Cambridge undergraduates enjoying 'a villainous chaos of dice and drunkenness, nothing but hazard and burgundy, hunting, mathematics and Newmarket, riot and racing'.[6] As for the military frame: during a war in which one in ten men saw service in camp or at sea, few young men would have escaped the lesson that women were their sexual servicers. The anonymous *Wags of Windsor or Love in a Camp* (1800) makes the point deftly [fig. 43]. This chapter faces young manliness at its most unreconstructed, rampant and worst, as these manners were transplanted into London.

———•———

London, for young men especially, was a place of lascivious temptation, 'a sort of hot-bed', as Pastor Wendeborn put it mildly, 'where all natural instincts, and all vices . . . vegetate very powerfully'. Not the least of its delights were sensual. Hence Boswell's arriving from Edinburgh 'all life and

The *WAGS of WINDSOR or LOVE in a CAMP.*

**Fig. 43** Anon. *The Wags of Windsor or Love in a Camp* (Hixon, 1800)

joy' and giving three huzzas as his coach 'went briskly in', or the happy release that Byron felt in London from the 'insulated ideas, of decorum & other silly expressions' of his mother's home at Southwell.[7] For young and frisky men arriving there from their estates or business elsewhere, country living was dull, and the ladies duller. Compliant women were hard to come by in the country, but in town most married men, Wendeborn noted, were 'at the expense of double housekeeping'.[8] 'Women and wine were the joys of life,' a Guards officer recalled; no officer thought it disreputable to visit St James's bawdy houses in daytime since 'every body went to them'.[9]

Distaste for married domesticity was the norm in male company. Not for nothing is the print archive peppered by well-worn jokes about the toils of matrimony, the battle of the breeches, or hen-pecking wives, that extended back to the seventeenth century. Rowlandson's paired *At Home and Abroad* and *Abroad and at Home* (1807) contrasted domestic tedium and the wife that went with it with the pleasures of dalliance with the mistress. Richard Newton gave a nineteen-year-old's view of *The Four Stages of*

**Fig. 44** Gillray, *Harmony before Matrimony* (H. Humphrey, 1805)
The raptures of courtship are reflected in the cooing doves at whom Cupid aims
in the wall-picture; the kittens play; the goldfish gaze fondly at each other. Ovid's
*Art of Love* is open on the table.

**Fig. 45** Gillray, *Matrimonial-Harmonics* (H. Humphrey, 1805)
The baby cries, the cat hisses at the dog; the caged love-birds quarrel; Cupid sleeps
on the mantlepiece; the thermometer is at freezing-point; the wife sings 'Torture –
fury – rage – despair – I cannot bear.' On the floor lies 'Seperation: a Finale for two
voices' and 'The wedding ring a dirge'. 'The art of tormenting' lies open on the
chair. The husband tries to read 'The Sporting Calendar'.

*Matrimony* (Holland, 1796) as it descended from initial bliss to violence and acrimony. And Gillray showed that *Matrimonial-Harmonics* [fig. 45] could never regain the *Harmony before Matrimony* (1805) [fig. 44]. In print after print, mistresses were willowy and doting while wives were fat, scowling or scolding. And if men's venues were noted for 'noise, inebriety and wrangling', Rowlandson's subtext noted in his debauchery parody, *The Harmonic Society* (1811), 'the assemblies of women are too frequently marked by malice to each other, and slander to the absent' [fig. 46]. Women hated 'every thing which strips off the tinsel of *sentiment*', Byron lamented; they were too decorous by far.[10] So although the female sex were necessary for all sorts of reasons, the urbane gentleman's preferred world was homosocial. Boswell's diary records his almost daily dependence on club meetings and dinings-out. Alongside these, domestic bliss paled by comparison. It is, he wrote, 'the mark of a brutish disposition to feed alone, or even to eat perpetually with one's family, which is comparatively unsocial and makes one figure a group of beasts in the same den day after day'.[11] Only in fiction was the domestic illusion sustained. Even so, when in Jane Austen's *Emma* young Frank Churchill deserts the ladies on the excuse that he has to go to London to have his hair cut (in fact to buy a gift for his secret fiancée),

**Fig. 46** Rowlandson, *The Harmonic Society* (Rowlandson, 1811)

knowing male readers, if they read the novel at all, might have at once assumed that, hair once cut and away from those chaste and watchful females, Frank would have drifted towards club, brothel or bagnio, and had a bit on the side, as everyone else did.

Clubs offered well-born men their chief escape route from female scrutiny, just as they did men of the middling sorts. Their latest historian, Peter Clark, estimates that there were 25,000 clubs in the eighteenth-century English-speaking world, the vast majority in London: some 20,000 men were said to have spent nearly every night in them. In fact, London's innumerable tavern clubs make these figures certain underestimates. Moreover, the clubs he attends to were mainly dedicated to philosophical, scientific or religious discussion, or to the sociability that made business sense: and of course these preoccupations were important. Enlightenment flourished there, while politicians talked politics earnestly, and commercial men talked business. The artist Joseph Farington's diaries list innumerable convivial occasions of which nothing more noxious is recorded than art-world gossip, and the main subjects of Boswell's diaries and *Life of Johnson* are the pleasures of philosophical or literary conversation.[12]

Yet Clark makes nothing of the drink that lubricated even these high-minded gatherings. By the 1780s, he soberly notes, 'public drunkenness both inside and outside the club was increasingly condemned'. Condemnation isn't the same as practice, however; and the number of debauchery prints published in and after the 1790s alone suggests a different story. That Dr Johnson's Literary Club was copiously watered, Boswell's sore head on the mornings afterwards only too often attested. Johnson's club's membership was stellar: it included Joshua Reynolds, Fox, Burke, Goldsmith, Garrick, Boswell, Edward Gibbon, Adam Smith, Sheridan, Joseph Banks, George Steevens, Charles Burney, and Sir William Hamilton. But that didn't check its boozy indulgence. We get some sense of its ambience from an astonishing wax model of one of its meetings in the Turks' Head tavern. Made from life between 1783 and 1790, and apparently rescued from a Soho coffee-shop in the early nineteenth century (it's now in the Museum of London), its size (50 by 85 by 200 cm) allows it to achieve exceptional detailing. There on the left Johnson presides from his 'throne' as he converses with Reynolds and his ear-trumpet. From left to right are ranged Gainsborough the artist, Topham Beauclerk, Boswell (standing on the bench), Fox (in portly dishevelment), the tavern owner, Joseph Wharton and the sculptor Joseph Nollekens. Not for nothing does

**Fig. 47** Anon., *Samuel Johnson's Literary Club* (wax model *c*.1783–90, Museum of London)

the model feature prominently the decanters, tankards and wine-glasses that no decent club would think of meeting without [fig. 47].

Was high-mindedness the norm in most club gatherings? Johnson's *Dictionary* defined a club as 'an assembly of good fellows, meeting under certain conditions'. This was not (as Clark thinks) 'untypically vague' of the great lexicographer. The phrasing was deliberate and apt, since 'club' covered all manner of assemblies, and by far the majority of them had not the least interest in pursuing truth and beauty except in female form. The *Attic Miscellany* in 1789, for example, listed fifty 'convivial societies' frequented by affluent men in the City and Westminster, and drink, sport and lewd song were as much their business as they were that of tradesmen's, engravers', and actors' clubs – their membership, indeed, often including these professions. Their names alone make for a dazzling comic display. With chairmen, mock initiation ceremonies and self-parodic rules, they included the Beef-eating Barons, the Johns, the Druids, the Learned Brothers, the Old Codgers, the Independent Codgers, the Fumblers, the Kiddies, the Black Friars, the Blues, the Starecaps, the Nose Club, the Knights of the Moon, the

Sons of Momus and the Anacreontic Society (this last a singing society, named after an ancient Greek poet, which met fortnightly for a singing concert and dinner). The club historian mentions not one of these. Bunbury's *Smoaking Club* [sic] (1792) almost certainly had its real-life counterparts [fig. 48]; and while the Farting Club referred to by Ned Ward early in the century was probably fictive, it is thinkable that that skill was catered to also.[13]

Men went to clubs like these to get drunk and to talk dirty – and to talk *about* women, not with them. As that indefatigable commentator on his generation's manners, Francis Place, observed, the polite and urbane clubbishness recommended by Addison and Steele at the beginning of the century expressed no more than a 'delightful ideal'. In real life clubs were full of men 'without understanding', he wrote, who 'substituted brutality and drunkenness for exhilaration and pleasant enjoyment'. It was 'largely to these clubs,' the French visitor La Rochefoucauld wrote primly in 1784, 'that one attributes the lack of society in London and the ruin of many people': gentlemen spent 'part of the day and all the night' in them. Entry fees were between five and nine guineas a year, he found; gambling was rife, and liquor flowed freely. Englishmen, he thought, 'need, more than we

**Fig. 48** Bunbury, *The Smoaking Club* (1792)

[French] do, to come together in order to discuss their common interests . . . but I couldn't help being astonished that people who have had a good education, and are capable of doing almost anything else, find pleasure – and a pleasure renewed daily – in rejoining other men in order to eat and drink'. London clubs, he added, were 'nothing more than associations for debauchery and expense' in which 'the most miserable of men' devoted themselves 'to wine and gaming and women'. (By contrast, clubs in provincial towns were 'most sensible institutions'.) Fielding had described London bucks as men who 'slept all day and drank all night: fellows who might rather be said to consume time than to live. Their best conversation was nothing but noise: singing, hollowing, wrangling, drinking, toasting, spewing, smoking.'[21] Other critics deplored them as centres 'for public irreligion... obscene talk, noise, nonsense and ribaldry ... fumes of tobacco, belchings and other foul breaking of wind'. Contemporaries had no doubt that gatherings like these were more typical than those that measured out philosophy, politeness and progress.[14]

If drink lubricated club-life, it lubricated dinner company too. Few apologized about this:

> There are two reasons for drinking: one is, when you are thirsty, to cure it; the other, when you are not thirsty, to prevent it. The first is obvious, mechanical and plebeian; the second is most refined, abstract, prospicient and canonical. I drink by anticipation of thirst that may be. Prevention is better than cure. Wine is the elixir of life . . . What is death? Dust and ashes. There is nothing so dry. What is life? Spirit. What is spirit? Wine.

So proclaimed the cheerful Reverend Mr Portpipe in Thomas Love Peacock's *Melincourt* (1817). 'Drinking was the fashion of the day,' Captain Gronow recalled: 'a three-bottle man was not an unusual guest at a fashionable table': at dinner, 'a perpetual thirst seemed to come over people, both men and women, as soon as they had tasted their soups; as from that moment everybody was taking wine with everybody else till the close of the dinner; and such wine as produced that class of cordiality which frequently wanders into stupefaction. How all this sort of eating and drinking ended was obvious, from the prevalence of gout, and the necessity of every one making the pillbox their constant bedroom companion.' 'Many others, who gave the tone to society,' Gronow added, 'would, if they now appeared at an evening party... be pronounced fit for nothing but bed.' What was usually drunk, Wendeborn recorded, was port, sherry, and hock – claret and burgundy then being 'poor, thin, wishy stuff'. Tastes were unrefined: 'many will drink anything for [as] port-wine that is red, and will praise it the more as it is mixed with brandy to make it fiery'.[15]

French visitors again found all this hard to take. 'The drinking is sometime quite alarming,' La Rochefoucauld wrote of London dinner-parties. Men relaxed best when, in the English fashion, the ladies retired:

> There is not an Englishman who does not feel contented at that moment. The drinking is sometime quite alarming, and every man has to drink in turn, for the bottles go continually round the table, and the master of the house makes sure that no one misses a turn. When one has been drinking for some time . . . the drinking of 'toasts' is begun. The master of the house begins by naming a lady and drinking to her health: everyone does likewise. Another 'toast' follows, and everyone drinks to the health of everyone's lady. Then everyone names a man, and the ceremony is repeated . . . The conversation could hardly be freer; everyone gives his political opinions with the same ease as his opinions on personal matters. Sometimes the conversation becomes equally free on indecent matters, for one is allowed to speak of everything . . . I have heard things said here in good company that would be the worst breach of decent manners in France.[16]

Another Frenchman, Faujas de Saint-Fond, had something else to be shocked about. 'If the lively champagne should make its diuretic influence felt, the case is foreseen, and in the pretty corners of the room the necessary convenience is to be found. This is applied to with so little ceremony that the person who has occasion to use it does not even interrupt his talk during the operation.' Eighteenth-century English sideboards had cupboards to hold the chamberpots which good drinking gentlemen so urgently needed. And there the chamberpot rightly sits – in, for example, Rowlandson's *Miseries of the Country* [fig. 41] – as it does in the corners of most debauchery prints of this era, when it's not hurtling through the air. A French satire of 1814 on Englishmen's post-prandial and urinary habits conveyed the French view of them. Echoing Hogarth's *Midnight Modern Conversation* [fig. 132], it has five men loll drunkenly at table, one prone on the floor, and another misdirecting his aim at the chamberpot in the cupboard [fig. 49]. Its companion print has the ladies at tea, bored and neglected [fig. 50].[17]

L'APRÈS-DINÉE DES ANGLAIS
*Scènes Anglaises dessinées à Londres*
*par un françois prisonnier de Guerre*
*A Paris chez Martinet, Libraire, Rue du Coq St Honoré*

**Fig. 49** Anon., *L'Après-Dinée des Anglais* (French, *c*.1810 or 1816)

LES DAMES ANGLAISES APRÈS-DINÉ.
*Scènes Anglaises dessinées à Londres,*
*par un françois prisonnier de Guerre*
*A Paris chez Martinet, Libraire, Rue du Coq St Honoré*

**Fig. 50** Anon., *Les Dames Anglaises Après-Diné* (French, *c*.1810 or 1816)

Actually, three bottles at dinner was nothing. The younger Pitt might be cold, celibate and hence 'stiff to everybody but a lady' as the quip had it, but he had no trouble in knocking back six bottles of wine a day. Once he told the Commons that he was so 'oppressed by indisposition' that he must postpone a reply to Fox: the night before he had drunk himself silly at a ball given by the Duchess of Gordon, at which 'no minister ever cast a more pitiable figure'. Coming to the Commons after downing a bottle of port at his own house, he would afterwards 'go into Bellamy's with Dundas, and help finish a couple more'. His and Dundas's jollity feature in Gillray's *God Save the King – in a Bumper; – or – an Evening Scene, Three Times a Week at Wimbleton* [sic] (1795) [fig. 51]. The Duke of York was remembered as such a toper that 'six bottles of claret after dinner scarcely made a perceptible change in his countenance'. Byron and friends would drink from six in the evening until five the next morning in the Cocoa Tree club in St James's Street: 'we clareted and champagned till two – then supped, and finished with a kind of regency punch composed of madeira, brandy, and green tea,

**Fig. 51** Gillray, *God Save the King – in a Bumper; or – an Evening Scene, Three Times a Week at Wimbleton* (H. Humphrey, 1795)

no real water being admitted therein. There was a night for you!' Sheridan, the Prince of Wales's friend and playwright, knocked back just as much. In caricature, his rubicund face and boozer's nose were turned into instantly recognizable icons. Fox's autopsy revealed a liver that was 'preternaturally hard' and 'almost entirely schirrhous'.[18]

In these conditions, the chief concern of male conversation is easily predicted. As one writer noted, men's impatience for the women to withdraw after dinner was 'a certain indication, that they either want to debauch themselves with liquor, or indulge in those decencies of discourse, which the company of women always restrains'.[19] Risqué talk had always been commonplace in male company. Sir Nicholas Le Strange's manuscript jest-book from the previous century is full of sexual and scatological jokes, the fine people he heard them from carefully noted. Pepys's diary contains mannish axioms by the score – like Lord Sandwich's, that a man who gets a girl with child and marries her 'is as if a man should shit in his hat and then clap it upon his head'; or like Lord Crew's that 'you can't argue with a standing cock'.[20] Such idioms weren't forgotten in our period, and countless more were invented. While in Venice, Byron told his friends at home that he was lucky there to be untroubled by inconveniently clingy liaisons, and could luckily enjoy 'only *fuff-fuff* and passades – & fair fucking'. Lord Barrymore was remembered as more 'proficient in slang and vulgar phraseology' than a costermonger: 'the way he blackguarded his servants for the misadjustment of a [horse's] strap was horrifying.'[22] The Englishman's humour chiefly consisted in 'swearing and talking bawdy', Horace Walpole lamented, and as for 'the history of our private life God knows it won't bear description'.[23] Fox's private life wouldn't have borne description either. He confessed that dining, gambling and 'fucking' were the chief business of his youth,[24] and Gillray's was no fantasy when he caricatured Fox in *Homer Singing his Verses to the Greeks* (1797) calling on Captain Morris for a bawdy song [fig. 132], or with Hanger, Courtenay and Sheridan in '*The Feast of Reason, & the Flow of Soul' i.e. – the Wits of the Age Setting the Table in a Roar* (1797), as they enjoyed obscenities over the bottle [fig. 52].

The Prince of Wales set no better example. The king complained that he and the Duke of Cumberland, his uncle, frequented 'the lowest places of debauchery' from which were they often carried home dead drunk. Cultivated and well read he might be; but his taste for low venues, low jokes and low songs was notorious. Caroline, just married to him in 1798,

**Fig. 52** Gillray, *'The Feast of Reason, & the Flow of Soul', i.e. – the Wits of the Age, Setting the Table in a Roar* (H. Humphrey, 1797)

was astonished by the prince's 'blackguard companions'. They were 'constantly drunk and filthy', she reported, and 'sleeping and snoring in boots on the sofas'; her husband 'was more like the Prince of Wales at Eastcheap in Shakespeare than like any notions she had acquired of a Prince or a Gentleman'. Walpole believed that 'nothing was coarser than his conversation and phrases ... it made men smile to find that in [his father's] palace of piety and pride his Royal Highness had learnt nothing but the dialect of footmen and grooms'.[25] He could 'drink, wench, and swear like a man who at all times would prefer a girl and a bottle to politics and a sermon',[26] and his humour and conversation matched these talents. 'The Prince of Wales was so amusing that I and the other guests could not contain our mirth,' the Persian ambassador wrote appreciatively on his visit to London in 1809:

> One of his stories was about the huge size of the penis of one of his royal
> brothers – a fact which he had discovered one night while riding with him
> in a carriage. His brother had felt the need to relieve himself: when he did
> so out of the carriage window, the water flowed as from a fountain ...! 'That
> is how I found out,' said the prince, 'and I am letting you into his secret too!'

Then the conversation turned to affairs of the heart. The prince asked: 'Thin women or fat – which do you prefer?' 'I like a woman as plump and as tall as a cypress tree,' I answered. 'Thin women do not attract me at all.' The prince was greatly pleased by my poetic allusion and congratulated me; it seems our tastes are similar. He wanted to know if I had found a woman in England, but I had to reply that, though I wished it were otherwise, none desired me because of my beard. The prince replied: 'If indeed they flee from your hairy face, you may at least be thankful to be spared their hairy intellects!' We could not help laughing at his joke! Then the prince decided he wanted to go to the opera. He stood up and all the guests rose, mounted into golden carriages and left for the opera.[27]

Finally, there can be added to all this the profligate spending and the gambling, the Prince of Wales's indulgences being the most notorious. In 1783, parliament had to give him £30,000 to pay off his debts, and he was granted a further annual £50,000 from the king. It wasn't enough. Setting himself up at Carlton House, he spent lavishly on it, turning it into 'a perpetual scene of excess' when he entertained his Whig friends and hangers-on there.[28] A year later, he embarked on building the Brighton Pavilion, and parliament had to grant him another £161,000 to pay for it, thanks to Fox's and Sheridan's lobbying. He still owed £400,000 a decade later, and it was to have this settled that he agreed to marry Caroline of Brunswick in 1795, thus paying the price for profligacy. As Thackeray put it, the prince would not have cost more had he been 'a manufacturing town, or a populous rural district, or an army of five thousand men'.[29]

The prince's extravagance was widely attacked in Parliament, press and the prints, but it wasn't exceptional. Aristocratic overspending was another vice of the age, and the estates crippled by it were legion. Gambling had the same effects. The prince's friend Lord Barrymore once won £25,000 on a fight between Hooper 'the Tinman' and Watson, but lost ten times that amount at Newmarket races in his lifetime and left his estates in bankruptcy. Every man who counted went to gamble at Almack's, Brooks's or White's, the prince included. By the 1780s the last two clubs were politically partisan and played key roles in parliamentary manoeuvrings. But they were chiefly famous for the fortunes made or lost at their tables. 'Dinner say at seven o'clock, play all night, one man unable to sit in his chair at three o'clock, break up at six the next morning and the winner going away drunk with a thousand guineas': yet, actually, a thousand guineas hardly hits the mark. Walpole in 1770 observed that at Brooks's 'the young men of the age lose five, ten, fifteen thousand pounds in an evening', and that 'a thousand meadows and corn-fields were staked at every throw'. One evening in 1755 Sir John Bland lost £32,000 and shot himself. Beau Brummell's £50,000 gambling debts at Watier's club forced him to leave England. At White's, Lord Arlington bet £30,000 on which one of two raindrops trickling down a window would reach the bottom first. When a man collapsed outside Brooks's in 1750 and was carried inside, Walpole recorded, members rushed outside to bet whether he was dead or alive: 'when they were going to bleed him the wagerers for his death interposed, and said that doing so would affect the fairness of the bet.' None of this was exceptional in a club in which Fox was challenged in 1783 to write an *Essay upon Wind* (farting), or in which his friends once bet (puzzlingly) on who it was who had defecated in Fox's trousers. This wondrous entry still survives in Brooks's betting book: 'Ld. Cholmondeley has given two guineas to Ld. Derby, to receive 500 g[uinea]s whenever his lordship fucks a woman in a balloon one thousand yards from the earth.'[30]

Fox's heroic gambling featured often in these stories. Walpole described him as arriving 'to speak in the House of Commons after playing hazard at Almack's for more than twenty-four hours at a stretch'. For a whole night before one debate he sat up gambling, and by five o'clock the next afternoon had lost £11,000. Next day he again spoke in the Commons, went to dinner at half past eleven at night; from thence to White's, where he drank until seven the next morning; thence to Almack's where he won £6,000. Later, in three consecutive nights, he and his brother lost £32,000 between them.[31] In the 1770s his father had to pay off £120,000 of his gambling debts, in the 1780s he was bankrupted by them twice, and in 1793 his friends agreed to raise a subscription to relieve his desperate plight. He let them know that £70,000 would 'pay all my debts that are in any degree burdensome, and give me an income upon which I can live comfortably'.[32] *Blue and Buff Charity*, Gillray called this negotiation, after the Whigs' party colours, in a print showing Fox and his equally needy followers (Sheridan, Burke, Horne Tooke, Hanger Priestley, Stanhope) as Jacobin sans-culottes holding out a *bonnet rouge* to receive contributions from the devil. Profligacy of this order had always been disreputable, and Jonathan Swift had shaken his fist at

White's whenever he passed it. Disapproval grew more vocal in the 1790s and again in the 1820s, when the Bow Street magistrate Birnie began to raid the more common gambling hells, sending transgressors to the treadmill. But the great clubs were untouched by this. More moral times did nothing to stop Crockford setting up his gambling club in St James's Street in 1828, with a frontage nearly as big as Brooks's and White's put together.

## Slumming it

Privileged young bucks consorted with rough low people habitually. This practice was so common that it was fairly (though critically) said that 'the two extremes of *very high* and *very low* border close on each other; and the manners, language &c. of the ragged rabble differ in [only] a few instances (and those merely circumstantial) from the vulgar in lace and fringe'.[33] Some of their encounters with low life were violent, for example in the street fights between swells and young roughs, but most were convivial or sporting. Some, in backhanded ways, were oddly democratic, as when the Duke of Norfolk summoned Francis Place's father, his publican tenant, to drink with him at the Crown and Anchor whenever the duke got bored. Ill-clothed, unwashed and a great belcher, Britain's premier duke was happy to eat in a chophouse with the humblest.[34] Others who went downmarket were moved by that simple curiosity about low life that past generations had known too. In the seventeenth century, Pepys had found Southwark Fair 'very dirty', but he had visited it all the same. The puppet show he saw there was an 'idle thing'; nonetheless he watched it. Christmas theatres were full of 'mean people', he wrote, but he went to them even so. And although he catalogued his own collection of jest-books, chapbooks, and ballads as 'vulgaria', collect them he still did.[35] For most young men, the voyeuristic foray into low life served more necessary functions. So long as the venues were spatially confined and unthreatening, they surrendered to their titillations relaxedly, relishing a controlled emancipation from whose *frissons* they could safely return when they chose. For they permitted a play with danger and identity and opened a passage to maturity. There was liberation in these migrations and, away from salon and polite female constraints, much of that liberation was sexual.

When young Boswell arrived in London from Scotland in 1762, he discovered to his delight that in the metropolis 'we may be in some degree whatever character we choose'. And so, as the spirit moved him, he quite deliberately crossed social boundaries in the guises of rake, mock-highwayman, or man of letters, with sex his usual goal:

> I resolved to be a blackguard and to see all that was to be seen. I dressed myself in my second-mourning suit, in which I had been powdered many months, dirty buckskin breeches and black stockings, a shirt of Lord Eglington's which I had worn two days, and little round hat with tarnished silver lace belonging to a disbanded officer of the Royal Volunteers. I had in my hand an old oaken stick battered against the pavement. And was I not a complete blackguard? I went to the Park, picked up a low brimstone, called myself a barber, and agreed with her for sixpence, went to the bottom of the Park arm in arm, and dipped my machine in the canal and performed most manfully.

In the Strand, he bought a 'little profligate wretch' for sixpence, only to have her allow him 'entrance' but refuse him 'performance', despite his abusive threats. Walking next to Whitehall, 'I picked up another girl to whom I called myself a highwayman and told her I had no money and begged she would trust me. But she would not. My vanity was somewhat gratified tonight that, notwithstanding of my dress, I was always taken for a gentleman in disguise. I came home about two o'clock, much fatigued.'[36] Boswell's games with identity were also experimental. He sought 'to fulfil the charge of beef-eating' by swallowing a solitary steak at Dolly's steak-house, or 'to fulfil the charge of cruelty' by frequenting the royal cockpit in St James's Park (which he didn't enjoy at all). He tried on the persona of the polite gentleman, modelling himself on Addison and Steele in order 'to attain some degree of propriety'. In this he met some difficulty, since 'I had accustomed myself so much to laugh at everything that it required time to render my imagination solid and give me just notions of real life and religion' – politeness, clearly, not much of a laugh. The young buck-about-town William Hickey also had legions of low encounters in Drury Lane dives, clubs and bagnios, his experiences, like Boswell's, uncommon only in the way he lavishly recorded them. On at least one occasion a drunken 'frolic' brought him before the watchmen; there must have been many more.[37]

Sex wasn't all that these adventures offered. Privileged young playboys' nocturnal slumming expeditions, infamous for their violence, had been familiar to Londoners for centuries. Just as Elizabethan London had been terrorized by its gangs of 'roaring boys', so Queen Anne's London had its Mohocks (named, Richard Steele believed in 1712, after 'a sort of cannibals in India': the American Mohawks unknown to him). The Mohock Club caused much public alarm, for as Steele described its members in the *Spectator*, they were moved only by the 'outrageous ambition of doing all possible hurt to their fellow-creatures' and took care 'to drink themselves to a pitch, that is, beyond the possibility of attending to any notions of reason or humanity; then make a general sally, and attack all that are so unfortunate as to walk the streets through which they patrol'. Steele spelled out their excesses in detail, and they were widely publicized. The accuracy of his and others' charges has been disputed; yet in ensuing decades references to the riotous misdeeds of high-born gangs are many.[38] And although the more violent behaviour of rakish youth was being curbed across the eighteenth century (and duelling was technically outlawed and increasingly deplored), these 'savage nobles' were still having their merry way in nocturnal streets right to the century's end, the law usually turning blind eyes to it.[39]

So, after heavy drinking, Fox, Lord Derby and other young men roamed the streets to egg on layabouts to break their political opponents' windows,[40] while the memoirist Henry Angelo recalled the slumming expeditions of the Prince of Wales's crony, Lord Barrymore. Barrymore 'at that time was seeking life in all its grades', Angelo wrote, 'even from the palace at Carlton-House, down to the Finish in Covent Garden. With this eccentric nobleman I was on the free and easy list, and many a frolic have I . . . been betrayed into, by his irresistible manners.' Once Barrymore took Angelo, incognito and disguised, to the notorious Jacob's Island, later infamous as the 'capital of cholera' and as the site of Bill Sikes's death in *Oliver Twist*. In one bedizened den there, Angelo found the bustle and clatter and songs 'quite exhilarating'. After such nocturnal revels, Barrymore would career home through the darkened streets, breaking shop windows with his whip, 'delighted with the noise as he heard them crack'.[41] Lord Camelford was another such practitioner, though some of his forays claimed charitable motives. Late at night he would 'dress himself in an old brown coat and slouched hat, in order to visit some poor family in the crowded courts between Drury Lane and Charing Cross', allegedly dispensing thousands of pounds a year in this way. Perhaps so, but this didn't curb his nocturnal pranks – cudgel fights by the score and, 'flown with insolence and wine', the overturning of a watchman's box to trap the wretched man inside. One of his punch-ups earned a print from Gillray.[42] The memory of such practices echoed a quarter-century later in the rakish pranks of the young swells, Tom, Jerry and Logic, that Pierce Egan chronicled in his *Life in London* in 1821. As late as 1826 a Robert Cruikshank plate could still play on the fantasized memory of the prince and the long-dead Barrymore and Fox slumming it in a beggars' den in St Giles's [fig. 281].

Adventures like these often led young men to the magistrate's court, though as like as not only to laughable reprimands or fines: Cawse's *Birds of a Feather Flock Together – or Bond Street Loungers Attending the Examination of thier* [sic] *Fellow Scarecrows!!!* (1800) has two fashionably tousle-haired 'loungers' in the dock, 'quizzed' through eyeglasses by their equally unprepossessing friends [fig. 53]. The consequences of larger mistakes were usually easily evaded. One summer evening in 1797, Sir John Riddle went to Astley's circus to meet two 'ladies'. They didn't turn up, so at ten o'clock he went to Green Park to meet some other women he 'knew'. There he exchanged some bawdy banter with a sentry, asking him whether his penis didn't 'stand' at the thought of fucking them. According to the soldier, the baronet then 'opened the slap of my breeches, and took hold of my t[esticle]-s in his

**Fig. 53** Cawse, *Birds of a Feather Flock Together – or Bond Street Loungers attending the Examination of thier Fellow Scarecrows!!!* (Fores, 1800)

hand'. The soldier had the baronet arrested. In court, Riddle denied the accusation and retaliated by charging the soldier with robbing him of several shillings. The soldier was convicted of highway robbery at the Old Bailey and sentenced to death. As Garrow, the prosecuting counsel, put it, Riddle had 'done a silly thing', but his unctuous expatiations upon Riddle's good birth and gentlemanly standing meant that the baronet's rather than the soldier's version of events was believed, and Riddle's honour was saved.[43]

The thirst for gambling could also take the well-born downmarket. If great men confined themselves to the great clubs' tables, the more venturesome went lower. A King's Bench prosecution of 1799 reported five common gaming houses in Oxenden Street, off Leicester Fields, two or three in Panton Street, and 'many others' in Lisle Street, Orange Street and Covent Garden. When constables raided the Oxenden Street house, this was the mixed bag they arrested: 'a notorious highwayman, some gentlemen of character, two merchants, a banker's clerk, an attorney, a hairdresser, several valets, a captain of dragoons, and a black musician in the same regiment, an ambassador's secretary, some apprentices, a shoemaker, a breeches-maker, and two immigrant priests'. The house, incidentally, was equipped with escape hatches, and entry was guarded by an iron swing-gate, then by a barred gate and a porter, next by a thick deal door; the entrance to the den then followed, through a door disguised as brickwork.[44]

The greatest leveller was a shared enthusiasm for pugilism. The sport boomed in this era as never before, and was as central to the great affirmation of manly as opposed to effeminized values as was the boom in clubbish debauchery. Massively boosted in the late 1780s by the popularity of fighters like Humphries and Mendoza, the sport grew unchecked for thirty years. The patronage of the great was indispensable to it. The Prince of Wales instigated Mendoza's first significant fight (against Sam Martin, the Bath Butcher) in 1787. Lord Camelford arranged scores of later fights. To avoid magistrates' beady eyes, most fights were organized secretly or on private land. In 1808, for example, Sir John Sebright arranged a great fight on his Hertfordshire estate between Gully and Gregson, the Lancashire Giant. The men did battle in white breeches, silk stockings and without shoes for twenty-seven rounds over one and a half hours. Gully retired from the ring soon after, set himself up as a country gentleman, and became MP for Pontefract and thrice winner of the Derby.[45] Only in the 1820s did the sport's aristocratic patronage wane and its appeal decline as criminal associations tainted it.

**Fig. 54** Ramberg, *The Triumph* (Hamar, 1788)

Meanwhile, at the ringside, as at the cockpit or at Newmarket races, male mixing was socially promiscuous. Ramberg caught this in *The Triumph* (1788): the victorious Humphries is chaired by the Prince of Wales and a butcher, the latter with an arm around the prince's waist, while the bleeding Mendoza is comforted by his fellow Jews on the left [fig. 54]. The great pugilists counted among aristocrats' most respected associates. When Jemmy Belcher retired from the ring after losing an eye while playing rackets in 1803, he took over the Jolly Brewers tavern in Wardour Street, and there his aristocratic admirers spent nights reminiscing with him, Lord Camelford among them. When Camelford died in 1804, he bequeathed Belcher his bulldog, Trusty. On his Wargrave estate, Barrymore employed the pugilist Hooper to sort out 'difficulties', while Byron took lessons from Gentleman Jackson, thinking him 'the greatest man in England'; his fire-screen was pasted with prints of the great fighters. Cambridge undergraduates were told to take time off their studies to welcome a visiting boxer and learn from his skill. Moreover, the ring also created its own market interests, over and above the betting. Between 1812 and 1824, Pierce Egan's *Boxiana; or, Sketches of Modern Pugilism...by One of the Fancy* went into several editions in five expensive volumes. Through it, Egan began the relationship with the Cruikshank brothers that later flowered in Egan's *Life in London* in 1820–21: they contributed etchings to *Boxiana's* early issues. In 1819, Robert Cruikshank designed a continuous strip-panorama 6.5 metres long, *Going to a Fight* [fig. 55]; you have to uncoil it from a small boxwood cylinder. Full of comic incident and detail, it depicts a winding procession of carriages, barouches and common carts, and a medley of urban types, rich and poor, making their way from Hyde Park Corner, past country taverns, to the ringside in a field at Moulsey Hurst in Surrey, venue of many famous fights.[46]

**Fig. 55** Robert Cruikshank, *Going to a Fight* [detail] (1819)

At the ringside, too, young bloods learned new fashions like the 'Belcher' neckcloth and slouched hats of 1802–3. There they also cultivated the canting slang, to the profit of many opportunists who published expensive dictionaries to explain it.

The soldier-actor George Parker explained that his knowledge of the slang resulted from his 'happy knack of conversation . . . as likewise a talent of easily and naturally accommodating myself to the manners of every rank in life'. And when Captain Francis Grose, fellow of the Society of Antiquaries and 'greatest antiquary, joker, and porter-drinker of his day', published his *Classical Dictionary of the Vulgar Tongue* in 1785, he got many of his 3,000 examples from the boys of Westminster School, but claimed that he himself collected most of them during his many visits to the boozing dens of St Giles's. Between 1785 and 1823 his book went through five editions. Cant thus became the humorous argot not only of the underworld in which it originated, but of the fast set also, soon cohabiting easily with 'those burlesque phrases, quaint allusions, and nicknames for persons, things, and places, which, from long uninterrupted usage, are made classical by prescription'. A generation later, Cambridge swells were plagiarizing Grose for their own *Dictionary of Buckish Slang, University Wit, and Pickpocket Eloquence*; Tom Moore published a comic canting poem advising the congress of Aix-la-Chapelle on the history and skills of pugilism; and Pierce Egan's slang-loving gentlemen-Corinthians in his *Life in London* made for the greatest publishing success of the 1820s.[47] Many gentlemen's understanding of cant doubtless drew less on the fast and accented dialogues of the streets than on this long print record. The fact remains that these fascinated visitors to the *risqué* worlds of gaming dens, cockpits, ringsides and bagnios felt no need to repudiate vulgar cultures. In their licensed and episodic forays they crossed the boundaries unapologetically, considering it the manly thing to do.

## Satires or celebrations?

So what of the higher classes' vices did humbler mortals see? What did they think of them, and how frankly could they comment? The last question is the easiest to answer. By the late eighteenth century, the borders defending the private realm were much less efficiently patrolled than they had been. Biographies, scandal-magazines and caricatures had been breaching them for decades. The satirical engraver himself had come to be regarded as something of a licensed jester. His vulgarity might be deplored and some dismissed him as 'a caterpillar on the green leaf of reputation . . . a sort of public and private spy' (as Gillray was later called).[48] But provided he didn't betray elite confidences to the common people and confined his comments on their elite transgressions to respectable markets, he could get away with visual outrages that in texts might be deemed libellous or seditious.

The engravers were as well informed as any about their superiors' habits. Their craft required that they should be. Most of their information they got from tavern, newspaper and magazine gossip. Gillray in his prime got some of his from the Tory Canningites; they paid him to besmirch the opposition and the Prince of Wales. Thomas Rowlandson for a time even had sociable access to grandees, on controlled terms. In the 1780s, he was fashionably known as a penman and watercolourist, his work prolific, picturesque and charming. His famous watercolour of *Vaux-Hall* [fig. 56], exhibited at the Academy in 1784 and engraved a year later, was only one of many great drawings in which incident and character were exuberantly combined. This one included the figures of the prince, his mistress Mrs Robinson, and the

**Fig. 56** Rowlandson, aquatinted by F. Jukes, engraved by R. Pollard, *Vaux-Hall* (1785)

Duchess of Devonshire; and the prince duly bought it. Four years later, when the king went briefly mad, the prince was negotiating to have Rowlandson produce prints against the Pittites to support his bid for the regency.[49] Rowlandson did cruelly caricature the duchess's role in the 1784 Westminster election, but his transgression was apparently forgiven. His pen and watercolour drawings of her (at, for example, *A Gaming Table at Devonshire House*, 1791) can only have been taken from life. It was at the gaming table or through mutual acquaintance with Henry Angelo that he was on some terms with the Barrymores, the prince's dissolute cronies.[50] These connections explain why Rowlandson generally abstained from the mockery of powerful people. Alone among the major caricaturists, he never once lampooned the prince; and it was probably only penury that drove him to attack the Duke of York during the Mary Anne Clarke scandal of 1809.

Engravers were not only paid to have opinions about the social and political world; they could hardly fail to have opinions about it, given the vibrant political cultures they lived in. Among London's middling sorts, disaffected views were fuelled by all manner of resentments. In that city of vast indulgences and inequalities, the engravers would seem to have had many grounds for sharing them. How 'radically' inclined were they, therefore?

Middling people had grievances enough to feed on. Most were engaged in a chronic struggle for a living, and even those who prospered knew how easily their comforts could collapse under illness or trade depression. Only a tiny minority could hope to wield a modicum of political influence, and when they did they were made to pay for it. When Francis Place, the tailor, organized Sir Francis Burdett's Westminster electoral victory in 1807, 'so inveterate was the hatred produced by my conduct . . . that nearly one and all of my customers left me'. Fashionable tradesmen like him also had to cope with the condescension of fine customers and their funny ways with bills. When Place opened his genteel Charing Cross tailor's shop in 1799, he knew that 'the most profitable part for me to follow, was dancing attendance on silly people, to make myself acceptable to coxcombs'. 'To make money,' he added, 'I must consent to submit to much indignity, and insolence, to tyranny and injustice; I can imagine nothing except being a footman or a common soldier as more degrading than being either a barber or a tailor.' If the tradesman didn't stand in the presence of a lord without 'a curve in his back', he would be ostracized, Place recorded.[51] There was also endemic snobbery. The best way to insult the Pall Mall bookseller Stockdale, for example, was to remind him that his father had begged his way on foot to London from the north, and had worked as a shoeblack while his mother took in washing.[52] John Boydell, the great printseller, had to endure similar insults:

> Boydell was originally – God knows what! but his first appearance in public life was at an unsheltered stall, selling common prints, sometimes with the ballads, odes, &c. thereunto belonging. He gradually became acquainted with distressed engravers and printers, and by a sort of brutal instinct, like that which enables a wild boar to find truffles, discovered what was and what was not saleable. At length he became opulent enough to contract for the productions of the best artists. What a humiliation of genius to be the instrument of gain to a mere trading patron![53]

Needless to say, satirical engravers were beyond the social pale also. 'A Grub Street print not void of humour,' Horace Walpole wrote aloofly of an early Gillray. 'The mere life of a caricaturist can neither be interesting nor instructive,' a review of Gillray after his death proclaimed: 'for who would wish to know of the haunts and habits of a sort of public and private spy? – and who can desire to learn the secrets of so disreputable a profession? . . .

Of a life thus employed little is known, and still less can be related: neither his mode of study nor his mode of life, can be disclosed with propriety.'[54]

Tradesmen and craftsmen might, however, take electoral revenge on those responsible for their tribulations and humiliations. Although they were excluded from the highest office and power, their political views could never be ignored. Even in the 1760s, wholesalers and retailers had made up some 40 to 45 per cent of the City of London's Common Council, and craftsmen between 10 and 15 per cent (although these were the elites of their trades and the merchants dominated them). Furthermore, London's parliamentary constituencies were far more exposed to tradesmen's and artisans' pressure than other English constituencies could be. The City had over 7,000 freeman electors in the late eighteenth century, rising to 10,000 in the early nineteenth century; and Middlesex and Southwark were almost as open. Westminster, of which the Covent Garden parishes were part, was the largest and most democratic constituency in England, with some 12,000 'scot and lot' (in effect ratepayer) electors in the late eighteenth century, and 18,000 by 1818. In these conditions, middling men, even the meaner among them – smiths, carters, poorer watchmakers, butchers – had evolved into an 'informal political nation' ever since John Wilkes had galvanized them in the 1760s. Committed to voter independence and electoral reform, such people could swing elections.[55] This explains why the satirists could show Fox and the Duchess of Devonshire wooing butchers' votes in the 1784 election, and why Westminster was represented by Fox's radical Whiggism from 1780 until his death in 1806, and by the Foxite radical, Sir Francis Burdett, from 1807 to 1837. Burdett's radicalism made him a popular hero, as the 1810 Piccadilly riots in his support showed. He had won Middlesex in 1802 by appealing directly to the interests of shopkeepers, artisans and lesser merchants, and he contested that seat again in a by-election in 1804. When Gillray depicted this election in one of his best crowd scenes, he showed the Whig friends who drew Burdett to the hustings as a turbulent rabble appropriately surrounded by flying vegetables, noose-hanged rats, squashed dogs and the turbulent hat-waving crowd [fig. 57].

The democratic thrust of London's radicalism was not unqualified. Voters' self-interest, piety or other convictions compromised it. Ministerialist and loyalist votes were numerous, and radical votes far from universal. Yet the Westminster voters in and around Covent Garden were more independent than those in the constituency's western and court-dominated parishes. So the majorities Burdett got in St Martin's Lane or Covent

**Fig. 57** Gillray, *Middlesex-Election. 1804 – a Long-pull, a Strong-pull, and a Pull-All-Together* (H. Humphrey, 1804)

Garden were far higher than those he got in Piccadilly. The 1818 voters' poll-book shows that over a half of the 117 tradesmen in St Martin's Lane voted for Burdett in one or another combination. Well over a half of the 108 tradesmen in Long Acre did the same: victuallers, pastry-cooks, truss-makers, cheesemongers, saddlers, grocers, stationers, and the like. While the master coachmakers of Long Acre nearly all went for the ministerialist candidate, the subsidiary coach trades – carvers, varnishers, platers, joiners – were Burdettite almost to a man.[56] In all these quarters, political exclusion combined with an acute sense of self-worth to generate a sour self-esteem. 'The *rabble* in high life, and the *rabble* in low life differ only in dress,' Wooler's radical newspaper, *The Black Dwarf*, announced in 1817: 'The *people* are distinct from both; that title should unite the thinking and honest portion of all classes . . . In this body should be found all the middling classes, as in their natural sphere.'[57]

Raised in this uneasy and politicized culture, the engravers and printshop proprietors must surely have been critically opinionated; theirs, surely, must have been among the more audibly disaffected voices; for they are called satirists, after all. In the large sense, this has to be true. Admittedly, few prints had fixed political meanings, and their wilfully parodic distortions would always inhibit simple binary interpretations as either 'for' or 'against' the established order. But it was precisely thanks to that multivalence that they could cut free from control of their content. This meant that, when read below their surfaces, they denied easy acquiescence in the established order – almost despite themselves and the artist's conscious intentions. Whatever their spirit, whether genial or savage, their ceaseless wry commentaries on abuses of power and on double standards, their incessant lampooning of princes and statesmen, their repetitive equation of Foxites with Jacobins, their lip-smacking exposures of high-born vices – all these could not but subvert the dignity of established hierarchies and even the sacrality of royalty. In their constant barrage, it's not difficult to discern that notion of the public good that many continentals thought of as essentially English: sceptical of high pretensions and habitually disrespectful – the inherited cast of mind many of us, to the bemusement of others, still live by, largely for the better, though politicians and celebrities disagree.

The time arrives for caution, however. To represent the case thus is different from agreeing with the more literal gloss that is commonly put upon the satires, by the leading print historian Diana Donald among others. She states several times that the prints of the 1790s were 'anti-aristocratic', 'radical' or 'subversive'. She claims further that their representations of a lewd, drunken and reckless nobility were influenced by 'attempts by the Tory evangelicals to reform upper-class morals', and then announces her 'unmistakable sense' that in the satires as elsewhere 'for the first time, the aristocracy as a caste was under concerted attack'.[58] If we must reach for either/or polarities, the print satires don't by and large fit this one. We must beware of too simple a view of moral and class polarization even in that highly politicized decade, and remember, anyway, how printshop commentaries were constrained by their markets. The prints' postures certainly shouldn't be associated with overt radical attacks like those delivered by Pigott's scurrilous *The Jockey Club*, for example – let alone with evangelical critiques.

Of course, the mockery of privilege and its duplicities had a central place in engravers' repertoires, as we've just acknowledged. They all knew where they stood in relation to repressive government ministers, and none failed to defend free expression against governments' extending controls.[59] The Piccadilly printseller S. W. Fores was consistently liberal-minded, while William Holland sold Tom Paine's pamphlets until he was imprisoned in 1793 for doing so. The young Richard Newton, who worked for Holland, trembled once or twice on the edge of sedition. Few missed a chance of castigating the prince for his marriages, amours, debts, debauches and patronage of the Whigs. None had time for the deity and his servants, either. When they ridiculed these things, attack was fully intended. And in the 1810s, with popular radicalism resurgent, George Cruikshank led the pack against the despised regent.

What best indicated an egalitarian inclination among later eighteenth-century printmen was their appropriation of one of the great motifs of past satire. Triggered early in the century by Sir Robert Walpole's dominance and political corruption, it turned on the recognition, as Gay's *Beggar's Opera* had put it, that there was 'such a similitude of manners in high and low life, that it is difficult to determine whether (in the fashionable vices) the fine gentlemen imitate the gentlemen of the road, or the gentlemen of the road the fine gentlemen'. Or as Fielding had written, 'Great whores in coaches gang, / Smaller misses, / For their kisses, / Are in Bridewell hang'd; / Whilst in vogue / Lives the great rogue, / Small rogues are by dozens hang'd.' Or, as Defoe had asked, 'How many honest gentlemen have we in England, of good estates and noble circumstances, that would be highway men, and come to the gallows, if they were poor?' This deepest of folk-realizations stretched back to seventeenth-century joke-books and boghouse graffiti (not to mention Shakespeare). Moreover, it endured. In Europe, Pastor Wendeborn wrote in 1791, it was only the English who knew that 'those, who, on account of their station, or employment in life, wear a rich, or a singular dress, are and remain but men'.[60] It is no surprise, then, that in our period the ironic equivalences between princes, statesmen and aristocrats on the one hand, and beggars and thieves on the other, came easily to engravers' imaginations. More overtly, the manners of aristocratic St James's and the depravities of mendicant St Giles's were many times compared, and always to St Giles's advantage. With its sexually suggestive symbols, Carington Bowles's smiling young *St Giles's Beauty* (1784) alludes to Hogarth's harlot [fig. 58]; but its central point of reference was established in its companion print, *St James's Beauty*, in which the fashionably dressed girl betrays her kinship with the whore by simpering with her own seductive intent [fig. 59].

A St GILES'S BEAUTY.    A St JAMES'S BEAUTY.

**Fig. 58** *(left)* Carington Bowles, *A St Giles's Beauty* (Carington Bowles, 1784)
**Fig. 59** *(right)* Carington Bowles, *A St James's Beauty* (Carington Bowles, 1784)

In Rowlandson's contrast between the jolly *St Giles's Courtship* and the miserable *St James's Courtship* (1799), the falsity and hypocrisy of the fashionable is exposed while the 'naturalness' of the poor is lauded. The subtexts tell us that in the St Giles's girl, wooed by a handsome fellow, 'vulgar nature plays her coarser part. / And eyes speak out the language of the heart, / While health and vigour swell the youthful vein / to die with rapture, but to live again.' In the wiles of the St James's beauty, by contrast, wooed by a grotesque monied old man, 'Here, like the fly, vice flirts the painted wing / . . . While withered age surveys the tempting bait, / Takes what he can't enjoy, & meets its fate.'

But that's about the limit of it. Look more closely at the repertoire, and 'radicalism' is hard to find.[61] Until the 1810s, no leading satirical engraver or printshop proprietor could risk advanced political views. By selling Paine's works and publishing Richard Newton's more daring satires, Holland made for a fleeting exception, but he recanted after his imprisonment. Most did defend free expression, but largely because their livelihoods depended on it. Otherwise, no engraver was moved to depict London's popular radicals with respect. Indeed, for the most part they ignored them. The artisan London Corresponding Society earned only two prints from Gillray, and each grotesquely caricatured its members and refused to dignify them with names. To constitution and hierarchy the printshops were steadfastly loyal. They ridiculed the royal princes, but pulled their punches on the king.

They mocked the Prince of Wales for his profligacy, mistresses and Foxite friends, but it was his comic potential that they exploited mainly: and nothing was said about him that Tory loyalists would have deplored. They lampooned gluttonous clergymen, canting pietists, and overenthusiastic dissenters, but never faith itself. If they worried about the Jacobin threat, they located it among the Whigs. They satirized greedy lawyers, but rarely gallows justice or the judicial bigots who delivered it. They addressed politicians' duplicities, but not their right to rule. And if they joked about London living, to its inequalities they turned blind eyes. No print overtly challenged privilege or (outside Gillray's panic-prints) conceded that the established order was threatened seriously. Turning common Frenchmen into emaciated froggies and common Englishmen into well-fed John Bulls, they were indifferent to the function of both as cannon-fodder, and commented on their families' hunger only when the king invited the nation to support the war by fasting. In short, a gentleman could convince himself that however scurrilous the satires he bought, however feared their sting, their ironies would be politically palatable, and probably match his own. These limitations give the lie to the

**Fig. 60** Isaac Cruikshank, *Breaking Up of the Union Club* (Hixon, 1001).

**Fig. 61** Woodward, *The Humours of Belvoir Castle – or the Morning After*
(Fores, 1799).

notion that satirical print was characteristically subversive. It was in loyalism
that printshop profits lay.

Many motifs underscore this view of the satires, but those that depicted
aristocratic vices do so particularly. When Gillray's great *Union-Club*
[fig. 131] showed the prince and the Whigs in drunken debauch, it was as
much in the spirit of a comic print as it was in the spirit of satire. And
when, a few days later, Isaac Cruikshank produced his *Breaking Up of the
Union Club*, showing the same Whigs fighting drunk and pouring into Pall
Mall through the club doors – one Whig in a sedan chair quietly vomiting –
that print, too, conveys more amusement than condemnation [fig. 60].
Similarly, G. M. Woodward's *The Humours of Belvoir Castle – or the Morning
After* offers a double strip of comic vignettes to illustrate the nocturnal
goings-on after a party celebrating the Duke of Rutland's coming-of-age
in 1799 [fig. 61]. As members of the company pursue their assignations at

**Fig. 62** Dighton, *Keep Within Compass* [male] (Bowles and Carver, *c*.1765, reissued by Carington Bowles *c*.1785)

night or greet each other's befuddled hangovers next morning, some of the men wear women's garters or nightgowns by mistake. The print is bedroom-farce comic and not judgemental. In short, most of that quarter or so of the social satires which depict aristocratic vices are too cheery to be explained in terms of the austerely satirical purposes commonly ascribed to them. Satire was not the engravers' only business: humour was as well. So if the prints must be called satires, most again were 'smiling' not 'savage' satires. They spoke from (and to) men who were familiar with, amused by, and guiltless about their own and others' excesses.

Fashions in the print repertoire changed after Hogarth's death. Overt didacticism was all but discarded. Few if any of the prints published by

**Fig. 63** Dighton, *Keep Within Compass* [female] (Bowles and Carver, *c*.1765, reissued by Carington Bowles *c*.1785)

Holland, Fores or Humphrey were of the kind that a sober parent or employer might buy to warn an errant son or apprentice to mend his ways. For that purpose, he would have to go back to earlier prints – to Hogarth's *Rake's Progress* or *Industry and Idleness*, often re-engraved and never out of print, in which the costs of profligacy were rubbed home in unambiguous narratives. Or he might turn to the catalogues of older firms like Carington Bowles or Bowles and Carver. Known for their old-fashioned prints,[62] they continued to turn out *memento mori* or text-laden admonitory plates like Dighton's 1785 pairing, *Keep Within Compass*, instructing men that 'industry produceth wealth' and women that 'prudence produceth esteem' [figs. 62 and 63]. Or the parent might buy something like Dighton's *The Drunkard's*

**Fig. 64** Anon., *The Drunkard's Arms* (Carington Bowles, 1785)

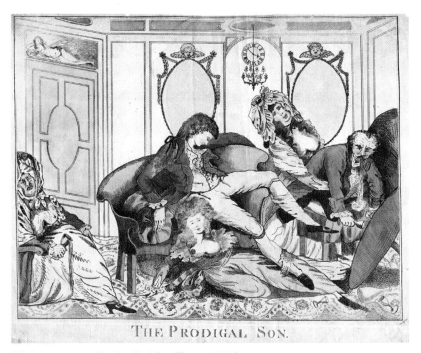

**Fig. 65** Anon., *The Prodigal Son* (Fores, 1785)

**Fig. 66** Carington Bowles, *Two Bloods of Humour, Returning from the Bagnio, after Having Kept it Up* (Carington Bowles, 1771)

*Arms* of the same date, with its emblematic castigation of a drunken couple and forewarning of their fate [fig. 64]. But, whatever else he did, the anxious parent or employer would not go to Rowlandson to advance his charge's moral education. Nor was he likely to go to the unpleasant 1785 Fores print, *The Prodigal Son*, with its men and breast-exposed women lolling in vomiting drunkenness [fig. 65]. Still less would he go to Carington Bowles's bagnio prints, like his *Two Bloods of Humour, Returning from the Bagnio, after Having Kept it Up* [fig. 66], or to the anonymous paired plates, attributed to

**Fig. 67** *(left)* Dighton(?) *Twelve at Night* (*c.* 1795–1800)
**Fig. 68** *(right)* Dighton(?) *Five in the Morning* (*c.* 1795–1800)

Dighton, which gruesomely depict a young rake's violent progress through his nocturnal Covent Garden pleasures, the first at *Twelve at Night* and the second at *Five in the Morning* [figs. 67 and 68].[63]

These last are vicious images, enhanced by garish watercolour. In the first, the drunken rake in torn clothes bludgeons Covent Garden watchmen. In the second, incapacitated, his head lolling and thigh bloodied, he has to be helped into a sedan chair. A thin moral alibi is provided in the playbill at the youth's feet that advertises 'The Road to Ruin'. But one senses that prints like these would be sold and bought as mementos of the purchaser's own boisterous errancy rather than as didactic satires. It was the young rake-about-town who would have bought prints like these, not a prudent parent. William Hickey, indeed, expressly reported just such a jolly night on the tiles, and he did so with some pride and glee. During it, he sang 'Let poor priggish parsons' at the Shakespeare tavern, had his pocket picked, woke in a tenement, and was taken home in a coach, vomiting. He would have relished just such a record of his adventures.[64]

Prints about upper-class gambling point the same way. Spectacular aristocratic bets were reported in awe rather than disapproval.[65] One cluster published in 1796–7 seems to attack gambling. Look closer, though, and one sees that it satirized the hypocritical laws that targeted humble gamblers and ignored their high-born equivalents, rather than the gamblers' habits *per se*. The cluster was provoked by the evangelically inclined Lord Chief Justice Kenyon's promise that he would punish even 'the first ladies in the land' and 'the highest ranks of society' if they were convicted of illicit gambling. Gillray, Newton and Isaac Cruikshank

**Fig. 69** West(?), *Cocking the Greeks* (Fores, 1796)

promptly snorted in disbelief. Several prints show the female keepers of the most notorious of the high-society faro banks – Lady Buckinghamshire, Lady Archer, Mrs Sturt and Mrs Concannan – variously pilloried or whipped bareback at a cart's tail for their misdemeanours [fig. 69]. In the cruellest prints, buttocks or backs are naked, fat flesh unpityingly exposed: but the point is heavily ironic. Isaac Cruikshank's *St James's / St Giles's: Dividing the*

**Fig. 70** Isaac Cruikshank, *St James's / St Giles's: Dividing the Spoil!!* (Fores, 1796)

*Spoil!* (1796) shows in its top half the four grand ladies sharing the profits of a faro bank, while the bottom half shows four St Giles's prostitutes sharing out their night's plunder, the equivalence underscored by the revealing necklines of the former and the exposed breasts of the latter [fig. 70]. If you believed Kenyon's promise, you would believe anything – the prints were saying. Sure enough, when a case was brought against Lady Buckingham for running her faro table in 1797, she was neither pilloried nor flogged, only fined.

Least of all should Rowlandson's many gambling prints and drawings be seen as remorse-laden satires on that vice. Rowlandson embarked on an alcohol-sodden and gambling life after his aunt's restraining influence was lifted on her death, sharing his dissipations with his artist friend, George Morland. He lost £2,000 at fashionable gaming houses, gambling 'without emotion', we are told, 'throughout a night and the next day, and once continuing at the gaming table for nearly thirty-six hours'.[66] But, like *The Brilliants*, his *Kick-up at a Hazard Table!* (1790) is too comic to be received as a judgement on his own or others' folly [fig. 71]. And it is only the title, not

A KICK-UP AT A HAZARD TABLE!

**Fig. 71** Rowlandson, *A Kick-up at a Hazard Table!* (Holland, 1790)

**Fig. 72** Rowlandson, *Gaming House Where a Parcell of Sharks Meet to Bite One Anothers Heads Off!!* (Rowlandson, 1808)

the representation, of his *Gaming House Where a Parcell* [sic] *of Sharks Meet to Bite One Anothers* [sic] *Heads Off!!* (1808) that comments negatively on the same excess [fig. 72]. There seems no necessarily higher content in prints like these than delight in the gaming table's excitements and disorder. Time after time, as prints thus slide into comedy, they celebrate as much as satirize. If you were one of the growing army of the respectable, you could say that the subject of celebration was vice itself. If, on the other hand, you were a Covent Garden engraver, you'd reply that, in that hard world, louche pleasures were well worth celebrating, and a fig for the moralists and radicals.

Several explanations for the constraints on the satirists' aggression are implicit here. Censorship and the threat of prosecution had some effect; but what signified far more was the market they depended upon, combined with the congruence between aristocratic vices and the engravers' own. We're not to overdo their 'radicalism', therefore. To repeat, there's no denying their cynicism-inducing and sceptical subtexts, nor the messages their repeated exposures delivered subliminally. That said, little more than a sardonic disaffection ruled most of the engravers at least until the regency years. It was booze, women and pleasure that gave their lives most meaning. So, on surface readings, their prints reflected their own amusement at and backhanded respect for their clients' excesses – so much so that, far from endorsing a 'moral' agenda, most engravers lined up *against* the moral reformers in order to defend the old manners; and when at last they did get upset, in the 1810s, it wasn't aristocratic *manners* that upset them, but aristocratic political corruption.

Not surprisingly, therefore, the publicity the engravers gave to the misdemeanours of the elite caused their targets little anxiety. Some prints did wound individuals, particularly the prince. And caricature does discomfort its targets. But it is wrong to argue that they put the aristocratic caste under 'concerted attack', or that it would have mattered much to aristocrats even if they had. In those revolutionary and war-torn years the elites had much to worry about. They wouldn't have defended the established order so repressively if they hadn't. When critics overstepped the mark, prosecution, fines and prison could silence them, and most great people thought nothing of that. Yet it's easy to overestimate the apocalyptic nature of the patricians' fears, and to forget the quotidian routines that allayed them. Thackeray saw this only too well much later. He recalled of these decades that 'the patricians were yet at the height of their good fortune. Society recognized their superiority, which they themselves pretty calmly took for granted . . . Small blame to them if they took and enjoyed, and over-enjoyed, the prizes of politics, the pleasures of social life . . . One almost hears the voice of the dead past; the laughter and the chorus; the toast called over the brimming cups; the shout at the racecourse or the gaming table. How fine those ladies were, those ladies who heard and spoke such coarse jokes!'[67] These patricians were the very people who bought the prints – and we must believe that they bought them, not in the interests of self-flagellation, but as mirrors of their own magnitude and self-imaging, and even out of amused self-regard. To be sure, one could always read more into them than they did. The images which exposed the excesses of the prince and his circle would have confirmed every view of aristocratic profligacy held by the pious or the radical. But the sober people who would have been really shocked or gratified by such prints' exposures – by their functioning as *corrective* satires – would also have kept their distance from them.

This reading undercuts a common interpretation of graphic satire. Just as it becomes impossible to assume axiomatically that the muse at work in it was invariably savage, so it becomes impossible to agree that the prints' repertoires were 'contingent on . . . the agenda of moral reformers', as if satirical engravers must by definition be on the side of virtue and decorum.[68] The 1810s did see the rise of a more popular and radical satire. But until then both the engravers' own dispositions and their market dependence upon a dominant, secure, and unapologetic elite suggest a quite contrary conclusion.

# PART II

# HOW THEY LAUGHED

CHAPTER FIVE

# LAUGHING POLITELY

## Controlling laughter

In 1759, in one of his most genial fictions, Samuel Johnson commented wryly on prevailing prescriptions about how polite people should laugh. A newcomer to London, he wrote, struggled earnestly to be accepted as a fine gentleman. He frequented the polite coffee-houses, grew acquainted with the men of humour, and gained the right of bowing familiarly to half the nobility. His efforts were fruitless, however, until he realized that his first 'great labour was to learn to laugh' – to laugh not out of merriment, but as 'one of the arts of adulation'. So 'from laughing only to shew that I was pleased, I now began to laugh when I wished to please':

> This was at first very difficult. I sometimes heard the story with dull indifference, and exalting myself to merriment by due gradations, burst out suddenly into an awkward noise which was not always favourably interpreted. Sometimes I was behind the rest of the company, and lost the grace of laughing by delay, and sometimes when I began at the right time [I] was deficient in loudness or in length. But by diligent imitation of the best models, I attained at last such flexibility of muscles, that I was always a welcome auditor of a story, and got the reputation of a good-natured fellow.[1]

Johnson's own laughter was either immoderately hearty or else 'a good-humoured growl' (like a rhinoceros's, someone said), and since his *Dictionary* acknowledged laughter's spontaneity as 'an inarticulate expression of sudden merriment', Johnson's irony here was pointed. He wasn't alone in ridiculing the best models; but others dismissed polite advice less amiably. In 1788, William Blake bought and read Lavater's *Aphorisms on Man*, published that year, and his many marginal inscriptions show that he pondered it closely. One of Lavater's aphorisms was that 'frequent laughing has been long called a sign of a little mind – whilst the scarcer smile of harmless quiet has been complimented as the mark of a noble heart'. Lavater's own response to this was sardonic: 'But to abstain from laughing, and [from] exciting laughter, merely not to offend, or to risk giving offence, or not to debase the inward dignity of character, is a power unknown to many a vigorous mind.' Next to this, Blake, who did have a vigorous mind, wrote in agreement: 'I hate scarce smiles; I love laughing.'[2]

Johnson and Blake were in effect objecting to what we might now call laughter's 'codification'. No writers before or since have worried as much about how, whether, when, and at what one might laugh as writers did in the eighteenth century. Admittedly, some part of their concern was to understand laughter's physiological and psychological sources, for these puzzled them deeply. The philosopher Frances Hutcheson was bewildered by this 'sensation, action, passion, or affectation, I know not which of them a philosopher would call it'. In France, *L'Encyclopédie* thought it 'impossible to explain how this movement is produced on the lips and the rest of the face when an idea strikes the mind; it is impossible even to hope to understand it'. And James Boswell saw in laughter 'that distinguishing faculty of man, which has puzzled philosophers so much to explain'.[3] Much effort went into solving the puzzle, and we touch on some of it shortly. But eighteenth-century writers' larger concern was with how laughter bore on good manners. They denied that unseemly laughter had any place in polite company, and for satirical humour they laid down the strictest conditions. Social and moral standing depended on a poised self-comportment, while a genially inoffensive sociability was regarded as civil society's chief condition and bond. As a result, the mockery of individuals was generally deplored, while people who enjoyed boisterous or bawdy humour knew that in polite company they shouldn't. Although these strictures loosened towards the end of the century, lampoons on private reputation were still deplored in earnestly principled circles, and taboos on untoward laughter continued to constrain both the elite salon and the middle-class parlour, as, in displaced senses, they still do.

We always simplify life's complexities when we analyse the world in terms of binary oppositions – between theory and practice, say, or between high culture and low, or (here) between politeness and impoliteness. The well-born eighteenth-century man, if not woman, had access to venues in which many alternative codes applied; and the likes of Johnson and Blake – not to mention our prints – connect us to earthier realities. The manners and the humour that we've noticed so far were unmitigatedly 'low' by polite standards; and the chapters ahead will be plumbing depths that were very much lower. The prints we explore were largely for elite consumption; and indicators of low manners in high places multiply as this book progresses. On the other hand, most people organize their sense of the world in binary terms, and eighteenth-century people did so especially. Clarifying antitheses characterized prose from the time of Locke until that of Jane Austen's entitling of *Sense and Sensibility*. There is no reason to deny their influence on opinion and manners. Indeed, engage with the eighteenth century's great debate about laughter, and you might fairly think that if any age was taboo-laden, it was that age, quite as much as the Victorian.

There is no doubt what the central worry was. Unrestrained laughter was characteristic of the lower orders from whom the elites and those aspiring to polite status sought to dissociate themselves. More important, it was both cacophonous and physically unseemly. There was nothing new in this perception. Laughter's unseemliness had been explored as part of the 'civilizing' debate that stretched back over centuries. Plato and Aristotle had both deplored immoderate laughter, and Cicero had advised against the ugly facial distortions that unchecked passion elicited. Renaissance etiquette had followed their lead. In Castiglione's *Cortegiano* (1528) or Erasmus's *De Civilitate* (1530), unregulated laughter was deplored as much as spitting, farting, belching, nose-picking, nudity and other bodily improprieties were. Erasmus had advised that 'if something so funny should occur that it produces uncontrolled laughter . . ., the face should be covered with a napkin or with the hand'. 'Wrinckle not thy face with too much laughter, lest thou become ridiculous,' Francis Quarles warned a century later. 'Laugh not aloud and to the disfiguring of thy countenance,' Francis Hawkins instructed in *Youth's Behaviour, or, Decency in Conversation amongst Men* (1641), while Obadiah Walker's *Of Education* (1673) permitted 'a little laughter' but much preferred 'moderate smiling'. And Lord Halifax in *The Lady's New Year's Gift* (1688) deplored female laughter as 'an unnatural sound', than which there were 'few things . . . more offensive'.[4]

Post-Renaissance anxiety about laughter's bodily consequences was sharpened by the lessons delivered by anatomical science. Gazing on the body as on a machine newly revealed, the early-modern anatomy schools had provided a disconcerting way of unravelling its mystery. What they exposed about its effects on the body helps explain why so many thought that laughter was no laughing matter and sorely needed taming.

The physiological vision extended back to Laurent Joubert's *Traité des causes du ris et tous ses accidents* (1579). In this most influential of all early analyses of the comic, Joubert had argued that laughter ensued from the tension between the 'sadness' felt for another person's defect, error or ugliness, and the 'joy' released when compassion for those things was withheld: as these dilated the heart in joy and then contracted it in sadness, the diaphragm was forced to expel breath in laughter.[5] Descartes agreed with this in 1649, and described the outcome physiologically, too: 'Laughter results when the blood coming from the right-hand cavity of the heart through the arterial vein causes the lungs to swell up suddenly and repeatedly, forcing the air they contain to rush out through the windpipe, where it forms an inarticulate, exploding sound.'[6] Automotive models continued to be favoured in the eighteenth century (indeed, on to Charles Darwin).[7] They even helped construct a new risible subject. After describing laughter's grimaces, the *Encyclopaedia Britannica* illustrated them by reprinting Le Brun's caricature of a laughing face. Anatomical study offered the coming art of caricature both inspiration and authority. Even so, the shocking implications of anatomical revelation were best conveyed in the meticulous observation of Cureau de la Chambre in 1640. Writing in French, he tacitly equated laughter's effects with those of orgasm:

> The fore-head expands itself, the eye-brows are depressed, the eye-lids narrow themselves near the corner of the eyes, and all the neighbouring skin becomes wrinkled and unequal. The eye being thus compressed, and half shut, owes its lustre to a forced-out moisture with which it is suffused . . . The nose is contracted, and terminated more or less in a point; the lips are drawn backwards and lengthened; the teeth are displayed; the cheeks are elevated, and tending to overstretch their muscles, which by the interstitial hollows caused by the resistance or retraction of their fibres, cause those dimples so pleasing in the cheeks of some, so disagreeable in those of others unfavoured by nature.

The mouth now obliged to be open, shews the tongue in a suspended state, and continually agitated by forcible vibrations. The voice is no longer articulate, and renders only broken sounds, now loud and piercing, now low and plaintive. The neck swells and becomes short, all the veins are full and distended; from the blood's being hurried in a tumultuous manner into the smallest vessels of the epidermis or scarfskin, spreads over the countenance the hue of a violet red, which is the neighbouring symptom of suffocation. Yet all these effects are moderate, when compared to the violent exertion felt in other parts. The breast is so violently actuated, as to labour under the greatest difficulty, nay, of an almost impossibility of letting an articulate word be uttered; a violent pain is felt in the sides, the bowels feel as if they were torn, and the ribs as if rent asunder.

During this outrageous crisis, the whole body is bent, twisted in a manner, and as it were crumpled together; the hands throw themselves upon the sides, and there closely fasten; the face is soon dewed over with sweat; the voice is converted into groans, and breathing into smoothered [*sic*] sighs.

Sometimes the over violence of this agitation produceth the kindred effects to those of a mortal beverage, such as bolting bones out of their joints, dreadful swoonings, and sometimes death. While this kind of torture lasts, the head and shoulders undergo the same fatiguing emotions, which the breasts and sides do. Their agitation at first is perceptible and irregular; then all on a sudden, as if exhausted by their vigour, they drop nerveless into quiet. The hands hang listless, the legs have no power to move, and the whole machine languisheth in a state of inaction.[8]

With these legacies in mind, it is no surprise that eighteenth-century writers amplified early-modern strictures. Lord Shaftesbury thought that loud laughter should be left to porters, carmen, clowns, jail-birds and the denizens of Bedlam. Steele in *The Tatler* insisted that laughter required art and restraint, not noise and facial distortion. An anonymous satire observed that 'bursts of mirth are looked upon as marks of savage manners'; only 'a governed smile' was graceful. The most notorious because extreme expression of these notions was Lord Chesterfield's. In letters written to his natural son in the 1740s, he gave that instruction in which Dr Johnson famously discerned the morals of a whore and the manners of a dancing master. Chesterfield advised young Philip to advance his own interests by adopting a decorous opportunism in personal relationships, by deceiving and dissimulating before women, and by comporting his body with 'that propriety and *decorum* which Cicero lays so great stress upon'. Despite its self-serving purposes, what he advised in this last connection we moderns may find bearable in detail. We, too, might tell our young not to scratch themselves, bite their nails, or pick their noses; to wash regularly; to walk, sit and stand gracefully; to avoid false English, bad pronunciation, old sayings and common proverbs, along with sottish drinking, indiscriminate gluttony and rustic sports. It would no longer be advisable to tell them to be be-laced, be-powdered, and be-feathered like other fellows, but we might agree that they should blow their noses in their handkerchiefs 'without looking at it afterwards'.[9] The one thing we wouldn't do is tell our young, as Chesterfield told young Philip, that, since the noise and grimaces of laughter were objectionable, it was acceptable to 'be seen to smile, but never [to be] heard to laugh'. This passage has understandably been much quoted:

> Frequent and loud laughter is the characteristic of folly and ill manners: it is the manner in which the mob express their silly joy at silly things; and they call it being merry. In my mind there is nothing so illiberal, and so ill-bred, as audible laughter. True wit, or sense, never yet made anybody laugh; they are above it: they please the mind, and give a cheerfulness to the countenance. But it is low buffoonery, or silly accidents, that always excite laughter; and that is what people of sense and breeding should show themselves above. A man's going to sit down, in the supposition that he has a chair behind him, and falling down upon his breech for want of one, sets a whole company a laughing, when all the wit in the world would not do it; a plain proof, in my mind, how low and unbecoming a thing laughter is: not to mention the disagreeable noise that it makes, and the shocking distortions of the face that it occasions. Laughter is easily restrained by a very little reflection; but as it is generally connected with the idea of gaiety, people do not enough attend to its absurdity. I am neither of a melancholy nor a cynical disposition, and am as willing and apt to be pleased as anybody; but I am sure that since I have had the full use of my reason, nobody has ever heard me laugh.[10]

Chesterfield's advice was mocked when it was published posthumously in 1774, but more for its cynical opportunism than for its advice on manners. This was because he was far from alone in advancing these views. The elder Pitt in 1754 similarly warned his nephew to control all 'peculiar . . . movements of the muscles of the face', on the grounds that 'it is rare to see in any one a graceful laughter; it is generally better to smile than laugh out, especially to contract a habit of laughing at small or no jokes. Sometimes it would be affectation, or worse, mere moroseness, not to laugh heartily, when the truly ridiculous circumstances of an incident, or the true pleasantry and wit of a thing call for and justify it; but the trick of laughing frivolously is by all means to be avoided.' This advice the humourless younger Pitt was to observe scrupulously.[11] Apparently Pope, Swift and Voltaire never laughed either. The Scottish philosopher-poet James Beattie was still deferring to these models as late as the 1770s. The 'art of pleasing those with whom we converse,' he wrote, 'lays many restraints upon laughter, and upon all other emotions that display themselves externally': for 'we cannot please others, if we either show them what is displeasing in ourselves, or give them reason to think that we perceive what is unpleasing in them.' For this reason:

> A man of breeding will be careful not to laugh much longer, or much oftener, than others; nor to laugh at all, except where it is probable, that the jest may be equally relished by the company . . . [These constraints] render society comfortable, and, by suppressing the outward energy of intemperate passions, tend not a little to suppress those passions themselves: while the unbridled liberty of savage life gives full play to every turbulent emotion, keeps the mind in continual uproar, and disqualifies it for those improvements and calm delights, that result from the exercise of the rational and moral faculties.[12]

The point need not be laboured that, long before Chesterfield, and after him too, Western notions of civility were in good part constructed around the deepest suspicion of laughter's propriety.

---

What *is* laughter? we may ask next. Not all eighteenth-century writers were satisfied with a physiological answer; nor should we be. 'Those who are aware that laughter draws the zigometrical muscle backwards towards the ears, are doubtless very learned,' as Voltaire dismissively noted, but every sensible person, he thought, knew that laughter was born of *joy*. In short, eighteenth-century writers were increasingly interested in laughter's *psychological* sources; and these still perplex us. How can we explain the strange disproportion between the complexity of risible stimuli and the response's simplicity? Only weeping displays anything like it. Worse, as Arthur Koestler put it, 'the involuntary contraction of fifteen facial muscles, associated with certain irrepressible noises, strikes one as an activity without any utilitarian value, quite unrelated to the struggle for survival. Laughter is a reflex, but unique in that it has no obvious purpose. One might call it a luxury reflex. Its only function seems to be to provide relief from tension.'[13]

We need not detain ourselves with the great range of modern laughter theories. If we did, we should expire of something other than laughter.[14] In any case, most have focused on specialized forms of laughter. None has tried to accommodate all laughter's repertoires in a single theory. This is understandable in view of laughter's many provocations. We can laugh at others in ridicule and derision, or from malice. We can laugh in triumph, joy, sympathy, surprise or satisfaction, or sardonically in misery and pain. We may laugh at incongruity or transgression, or at the 'verbal ambushes' of wit or pun. And 'laughter' includes its more muted preliminary, the smile (the 'sub-laugh' or *sourire* in French). Because none of these has a common cognitive basis, theories on the subject divide into several kinds. One stresses the laughter that expresses aggression, contempt, superiority and self-glory, so important to past rhetorical practice (Hobbes). Another stresses the sudden realization of incongruity (Hutcheson and other critics of Hobbes). A third notes how laughter releases tension (Descartes, Hartley, Kant, Herbert Spencer, Koestler). A fourth follows Freud and his successors, notably Kris, who stressed the regressively infantile elements within laughter, and its source in the saving of 'psychic expenditure'. 'Under the influence of the comic,' as Kris put it, 'we return to the happiness of childhood. We can throw off the fetters of logical thought and revel in a long-forgotten freedom.'[15]

Yet most of these theories have one thing in common, and that brings us to the understanding that underlies this book: laughter depends on the sudden and surprised recognition of *incongruity* between two mutually exclusive codes or contexts, when these are unexpectedly yoked together in verbal play, images or behaviour. As Koestler put it, when this unanticipated clash compels us to see a situation in two incompatible frames of reference at once, we experience a bodily tension which has to find an outlet. The laughter reflex fulfils this function by disposing of these pointless excitements 'along physiological channels of least resistance'.[16] Or, to paraphrase Aristotle again, if mankind is the only animal that laughs (and weeps), it is because humans alone can surprise themselves with the difference between how things are and how they ought to be.[17] If you laugh or smile at any of this book's pictures or jokes, you will be responding to the unexpected revelation of incongruity that humour always trades in.

## Laughter and geniality

If laughter had been allowed any justification from classical until early-modern times, it had been as a rhetorically aggressive weapon whose purpose in argument was to establish superiority by deploying ridicule and contempt. In this tradition, as Quentin Skinner has put it, 'to laugh [was] almost always to laugh *at* someone'. It aimed to score a point off another, at his or her expense. Thus Quintilian had claimed that 'mirth is never very far removed from derision'; and such was classical authority that most Renaissance rhetoricians and poets, when not deploring laughter's unseemliness, followed this view. With Sir Philip Sidney, 'we laugh at deformed creatures'; with Bacon, 'absurdity be the subject of laughter'; and, according to an Elizabethan proverb, 'they laugh that win'.[18]

When Thomas Hobbes turned to the question, therefore, it was disingenuous of him to imply that his thoughts were original: 'There is a passion which hath no name, but the sign of it is that distortion of the countenance we call LAUGHTER, which is always joy; but what joy, what we think, and wherein we triumph when we laugh, hath not hitherto been declared by any.' In fact, Hobbes remained indebted to classical and Renaissance precepts, and to them added only two points. One was the recognition that mirth depended on the shock of the 'new and unexpected'. The other was his denial that laughter was chiefly provoked by wit or by jokes against ourselves: 'for men laugh at mischances and indecencies, wherein there lieth no wit or jest at all'. For Hobbes, laughter was self-congratulatory. It was best elicited by our own unexpected successes and by our own jests at 'the infirmities of others, by comparison of which [our] own abilities are set off and illustrated'. These cases made it 'manifest, that the passion of laughter proceedeth from a sudden conception of some ability in himself that laugheth', or 'from the sudden imagination of our own odds and eminence . . . by comparison with another man's infirmities or absurdity'. From this he famously concluded 'that the passion of laughter is nothing else but a sudden glory arising from sudden conception of some eminency in ourselves, by comparison with the infirmities of others, or with our own formerly'. This view infiltrated several later theories, including those that otherwise kept their distance from Hobbes; and it continues to be much cited.[19]

Hobbes did mute the harshness of his formula. A passing observation in *Leviathan* (1651) noted that those who laugh most are those 'conscious of the fewest abilities in themselves; who are forced to keep themselves in their own favour, by observing the imperfections of other men'. He elsewhere thought that 'much laughter at the defects of others is a sign of pusillanimity'. And his famous conclusion allowed laughter some geniality, for it continued: 'It is no wonder ... that men take it heinously to be laughed at or derided, that is, triumphed over. Laughter without offence, must be at absurdities and infirmities abstracted from persons, and where all the company may laugh together.' In other words, he had some sense of laughter's relationship to manners. All the same, the narcissistic core of his argument didn't go down well with most eighteenth-century writers, and this brings us back both to the point and to our era. From Shaftesbury, Addison and Steele in the early eighteenth century and for many decades subsequently, those who sought to advance civility recommended the socialization of the reflex of laughter whose expressions could be otherwise unseemly, antisocial and cruel. Accordingly, the rhetorical and forensic uses of ridicule which had been validated from classical times onwards began to be displaced by a much stronger emphasis on the relationship between laughter, self-control and a genial sociability.

The first salvo against Hobbes's view that laughter expressed self-glory was delivered when Addison perfunctorily summarized it in the *Spectator* in 1711. James Beattie later thought that Hobbes's views 'would hardly have deserved notice' had not Addison brought them to attention.[20] As it was, there, sounding cramped and mean, they seemed to confirm Lord Shaftesbury's charge that Hobbes was blind to human benevolence, and that his principles were inimical to a civil order based on a 'sense of the public weal and of the common interest, love of the community or society, natural affection, humanity, [and] obligingness'. Shaftesbury himself wrote little on laughter directly, but his *Characteristics of Men, Manners, Opinions, Times* (1711) included the view that, since 'it is the height of sociableness to be ... friendly and communicative', humour must stop short of gratuitous offence. He acknowledged laughter's cathartic purposes: 'If you would have the wise, the grave, the serious, always to rule and have sway, the fool would grow so peevish and troublesome, that he would put the wise man out of order, and make him fit for nothing: he must have his times of being let loose to follow his fancies, and play his gambols, if you would have your business go on smoothly.' But the chief purpose of humour, he insisted, is to enable us to 'polish one another and rub off our corners and rough sides by a sort of amiable collision'. Not only must laughter be moderate, it must also steer clear of ridicule and mockery: for 'there is a great difference between seeking how to raise a laugh from everything and seeking in everything what may justly be laughed at. For nothing is ridiculous except what is deformed, nor is anything proof against raillery except what is handsome and just.'[21]

Subsequent British texts addressed laughter's proper subjects and purposes with this advice in mind. The key texts were few in number but influential. Frances Hutcheson's *Thoughts on Laughter* first appeared as a series of letters in the *Dublin Journal* in 1725, but its fifty-five pages of airy typography were many times republished. Fielding discussed laughter in the preface to *Joseph Andrews* (1742) and in his 'Essay on Conversation' (1743). Mark Akenside's didactic poem, *The Pleasures of Imagination* (1744), contained thoughts on ridicule in its third book and its footnotes; it, too, was many times reprinted up to the mid-nineteenth century. The anonymous *Essay on Laughter, wherein are Displayed, its Natural and Moral Causes, with the Arts of Exciting it* (1769) made only one edition, but it was a rich and thoughtful work, in fact a translation of Poinsinet de Sivry's *Traité des causes . . . du rire* (1768). Beattie's *Essay on Laughter, and Ludicrous Composition* followed. This ponderous essay was saturated in classical citations, and was notable for its inability to tell jokes. But it offered the most widely read and ambitious English discussion of laughter in the eighteenth century. It was republished in five separate Edinburgh and London editions of Beattie's collected works between 1776 and 1779; and the *Encyclopaedia Britannica* appropriated chunks of it for its article on 'Laughter' right up to its seventh edition of 1842. Francis Grose in 1788 ventured a few thoughts which drew on these predecessors.[22] Then there was near-silence on the subject until Hazlitt's *Lectures on English Comic Writers* (1819) and Basil Montagu's anonymous *Thoughts on Laughter* (1830) (the silence expressing a declining interest in politeness punditry in the later eighteenth century). Most of these authors found the Hobbesian argument unacceptable and elaborated on the Shaftesburian position.

Their leading positions were threefold. The first we have already noted. It turned on the sense that when laughter was 'too profuse or too obstreperous', as Beattie put it, it was physically unseemly. It should accordingly be checked by men of breeding in the interests of rendering society 'comfortable' and of exercising the more 'rational and moral faculties'. Chesterfield's celebration of the fact that nobody had ever heard him laugh was the *reductio ad absurdam* of this position.

The second position turned on laughter's potential for geniality and generosity. As Hutcheson wrote, laughter was better inspired by benevolence than by vainglory over others. Indeed, Hutcheson thought that Hobbes should be dismissed for his 'ill-natured nonsense' in deducing 'all human actions from self-love' at the expense of 'every thing which is generous or kind in mankind'. Superior people were those least likely to laugh, he added, for 'if we observe an object in pain while we are at ease, we are in greater danger of weeping than laughing'. So ridicule was obviously undesirable. This didn't mean that parody and burlesque should be avoided. Parody might 'move laughter in those who may have the highest veneration for the writing alluded to'. Hutcheson also agreed that we might laugh at ourselves, or at quite uncruel things, as when verbal 'likenesses' are 'forced', as in puns. Altogether, he concluded, laughter depended on the surprise and shock delivered by a perception of incongruity, when images were yoked, that is, which have 'contrary additional ideas': 'This contrast between ideas of grandeur, dignity, sanctity, perfection and ideas of meanness, baseness, profanity, seems to be the very spirit of burlesque, and the greatest part of our raillery and jest are founded upon it.'[23] Yet when Hutcheson considered why laughter was implanted in our nature, he saw it chiefly as a polite theorist would, as 'an easy remedy for discontent and sorrow', and as a source of the good fellowship that bound people together.

The third motif was quite new to the eighteenth century. It turned on a sense of laughter's historical and cultural relativism. It was Dryden who first inferred from his study of the Roman satirists the notion that culture witnessed a progress towards refinement and harmony. Shaftesbury also implied as much when he claimed that politeness and sociable good humour flourished better under British liberty than under despotism. The Italians, he noted, specialized in buffoonery and burlesque because it was 'the only manner in which the poor cramped wretches can discharge a free thought'.[24] Beattie then generalized the point. First, he asserted that the politeness of nations could be judged 'from their turn of humour, from their favourite jokes and stories, and from the very sound, duration, and frequency of their laughter'. Then he asked why moderns were more adept than the ancients in 'ludicrous writing'. He answered that, because modern people inhabited societies in which manners, fashions and commercial, sexual and social relationships were more diverse and complex than those of the ancients, they had more matters to laugh about. Even monarchy had improved modern humour, he thought, as courtly wit became more refined (for instance, by discarding the court jester). That humour improved over time was witnessed universally. Just as Horace's wit had been more refined than Plautus's a century and a half before him, so the humour of modern people was more refined than Shakespeare's or than that of the Restoration dramatists. The history of humour was a history of progress, he concluded; it improved alongside, and indicated, the improvement in manners.[25] Beattie was a man of his time, and not the best of them either. A 'bigoted silly fellow', David Hume called him, and he was the most po-faced of all laughter theorists.[26] Even so, he knew as well as we do that laughter has a history, and that the history of manners is its most interesting frame.

## Politeness and the problem of satire

Satire occupied a central place in polite eighteenth-century culture. All art had to be morally useful, and of all arts, in principle, satire was the one that was most judgementally grounded. Dryden had been the first to affirm satire's status in these terms. 'The principal end of satyr, is to instruct the people by discrediting vice,' he declared; it must teach 'the noblest ethicks to reform mankind'. For Defoe similarly, 'the end of satyr is reformation'; while Swift discerned 'two ends that men propose in writing satyr, one of them less noble than the other, as regarding nothing further than personal satisfaction, and pleasure of the writer . . . ; the other is a publick spirit, prompting men of genius and virtue, to mend the world as far as they are able'. Even Johnson, who loathed Swift's subject-matter and deplored the 'general lampooners of mankind', accepted that 'a man should pass a part of his time with *the laughers*, by which means any thing ridiculous or particular about him might be presented to his view, and corrected'.[27] Although increasingly challenged by the novel as the premier literary form, morally corrective satire retained an honoured place in the literary pantheon from the Restoration until the 1820s – so long as it conducted itself politely.

For suspicion of satire was of long standing also: so much so that, for every reflection on laughter in general, a barrage was published on the dangers of satire. Wrongly handled, ridicule's collision with its subject would hardly enhance the 'good fellowship' that laughter was supposed chiefly to be good for. As a result, the reconciliation of satire with politeness was a matter for anxious negotiation. If anything, suspicion deepened as the century wore on, not least as 'sensibility' began that long battle with the satirical muse by which the muse was eventually all but silenced.

Satire's enemies began by questioning its reformative power. By pretending to chastise vice, Charles Abbott claimed in 1786, satire merely publicized it, even as it diminished the standing of 'illustrious characters'.[28] It could correct only the most trivial failings, William Cowper declared in *The Task* (1782–5): 'It may correct a foible, may chastise / The freaks of fashion, regulate the dress, / Retrench a sword-blade, or displace a patch; / But where are its sublimer trophies found? / What vice has it subdued?' 'Wit and satire are transitory and perishable,' Thomas Warton announced grandly in 1756; only 'nature and passion are eternal'.[29] More to the point, critics charged satirists, and when it suited them satirists charged each other, with a lack of good nature and candour, and with the basest of motives – slander, envy and malice. William Combe in 1778 thought satire 'a proof of a discontented mind'. Vicesimus Knox listed among its ill effects the traducing of 'all the useful and amiable qualities, which sweeten private and domestic life . . . conjugal attachment and fidelity, filial regard, regular industry, prudent oeconomy, sincerity in friendship, delicate scruples, benevolence and beneficence'.[30] The satirist 'too often rails to gratify his spleen', Cowper wrote. Mary Wollstonecraft in 1789 believed that ridicule was incompatible with female sensibility, modesty, and virtue.[31]

To modern tastes, many of the debates on the subject are tedious. Buckets of critical ink were spilled on the differences between ridicule, raillery, slander, libel and lampoon, for example, and yet more on the differences between humour, wit and satire. Although this was part of the great eighteenth-century project of classifying species, it also proves how seriously laughter's many repertoires were taken. What signify more for present purposes are three elements in the eighteenth-century critique that identified the risks of satirical practice more directly.

The first turned on the impropriety of satirizing individuals. Addison had ruled definitively that 'there is nothing that more betrays a base, ungenerous spirit, than the giving of secret stabs to a man's reputation.

Lampoons and satires, that are written with wit and spirit, are like poison'd darts, which not only inflict a wound, but make it incurable . . . If, besides the accomplishments of being witty and ill-natured, a man is vicious into the bargain, he is one of the most mischievous creatures that can enter into a civil society. His satyr will then chiefly fall upon those who ought to be most exempt from it.'[32] So when Hogarth paraphrased Swift in the subtitle of his *Midnight Modern Conversation* (1732) [fig. 132], 'Think not to find one meant resemblance there / We lash the vices but the persons spare', or when Fielding announced in *Joseph Andrews* that he described 'not men, but manners, not an individual, but a species', and added that there was a difference between the satirist and the libeller ('for the former privately corrects the fault for the benefit of the person, like a parent; the latter publicly exposes the person himself, as an example to others, like an executioner'), or when George Crabbe observed in 1818 that 'Man's vice and crime I combat as I can, / But to his God and conscience leave the man' – they were all deferring to Addison's ruling.[33]

On this score, there were some contrary opinions, however. They suggested that satire's legitimacy depended on the public standing of its targets. From Dryden onwards, some agreed that personalized satire was justified when it sought to expose *public* enemies who were otherwise unassailable. Satire must 'direct its shafts to known persons and characters, by whom general [i.e. lesser] severities would be scarcely felt', Combe argued in 1777; this 'holds them forth to the immediate and certain odium of their fellow creatures'. According to T. J. Mathias in 1794, 'all publick men, however distinguished, must in their turns submit to [satire], if necessary to the welfare of the state'. He added that 'satire can never have effect, without a personal application', since 'it must come home to the bosoms, and often to the offences of particular men'. Even in 'smiling' satires, Abbott thought, 'the occasional introduction of known characters gives particular force, as they both interest the passions by their familiarity, and convince the judgment by their truth'.[34]

The second element in the critique rather contradicted the foregoing exceptions. It turned on the view that 'smiling' satire was to be preferred to 'savage' satire (or, in classical terms, it should be Horatian rather than Juvenalian).[35] The trouble with savage satire was that it was properly the province of tragedy, since it showed how great vices resulted in great falls. Moreover, some matters were too grave to be satirized – 'crimes too daring and too horrid', as Congreve had defined them. For Hutcheson, 'the enormous crime or grievous calamity of another, is not of itself a subject which can be naturally turned into ridicule: the former raises horror in us, and hatred; and the latter pity'. Fielding agreed that 'all great vices . . . misfortunes, and notorious blemishes of mind or body' roused only disgust, so that 'no object is risible but what appears slight, little, or trifling'. Nearly every critic of satire made these points, from Dryden and Congreve on to Johnson and Sheridan, including men, these strictures notwithstanding, who produced savage satires themselves.

It followed from this, thirdly, that smiling satire should never attack 'a great being, character, or sentiments', as Hutcheson put it, but only the comical mishaps of people who were possessed of 'false grandeur': 'thus the strange contortions of the body in a fall, the dirtying of a decent dress, the natural functions which we study to conceal from sight, are matter of laughter, when they occur to observation in persons of whom we have high ideas . . . it is this contrast, or opposition of ideas of dignity and meanness, which is the occasion of laughter.'[36] Since 'good breeding' was literature's goal, Fielding agreed, satire should confine itself to 'a gentle animadversion on some foible' (like vanity, avarice or hypocrisy), rather than expose named victims to shame and contempt. Mirth was most appropriately raised 'when ugliness aims at the applause of beauty, or lameness endeavours to display agility'. Even so, 'the jest should be so delicate, that the object of it should be capable of joining in the mirth it occasions'.[37] For Beattie, similarly, satire should attack only the lesser vices and foibles if it was to serve as 'an instrument of moral culture'. Laughter best arose 'from the view of dignity and meanness united in the same object' or from the juxtaposition of 'inconsistent, unsuitable, or incongruous parts or circumstances'.[38]

These thoughts gave rise to numberless catalogues of modestly foibled targets. Akenfield gave his list as follows: 'ignorant pretenders to learning, boastful soldiers, and lying travellers, hypocritical churchmen, conceited politicians, old women that talk of their charms and virtue, ragged philosophers who rail at riches, virtuosi intent upon trifles, romantic lovers, wits wantonly satirical, fops that out of vanity appear to be diseased and profligate, dastards who are ashamed or afraid without reason, and fools who are ignorant of what they ought to know'.[39] Francis Grose also believed that the best route to comic effect was to represent individuals 'in that office or business, for which by age, size, profession, construction, or some other accident, they are totally unfit'. Hence, from him, another catalogue of 'ludicrous objects': 'a cowardly soldier, a deaf musician, a bandy-legged dancing-master, a corpulent or gouty running-footman, an antiquated fop or coquet, a methodist in a brothel, a drunken justice making a riot, or a tailor on a managed horse'. He instructed amateur caricaturists that 'if the methodist has his pocket picked, or is stripped, the justice is drawn with a broken head, and the tailor appears just falling off into the kennel, we consider it as a kind of poetical justice, or due punishment, for their acting out of their proper spheres'.[40]

All these were highly restrictive principles for satire, but they did influence subsequent assumptions. It is true that Augustan manners were those of a small elite, and that a wider reading and print-perusing public were far less awed by classical or polite precepts than these writers were. In the new century the comic savagery of Byron's or Shelley's satires gave the lie to all these precepts, as did vast numbers of satirical prints. Moreover, many textual satirists were indifferent to Shaftesbury's concern to diffuse 'natural affection, humanity, [and] obligingness'. If anything, satire became more scabrously personalized as the century wore on. Indeed, most jobbing satirists, visual and literary, were becoming so blatantly indifferent to advice on how they should pursue their calling that one senses a deepening unreality in the critical commentaries.

On the other hand, Augustan precepts were never wholly discarded. Smiling satires in our later period were countless. Many prints were so genial that they may be said to have celebrated rather than castigated the errors they exposed, while visual and verbal jokes by the score continued to trade on the comical mismatches that Akenfield, Grose and others recommended as ridicule's proper subjects. Further, most Augustan restrictions continued to be formally endorsed. In his *Thoughts on Laughter*, as late as 1830, for example, Basil Montagu believed that ridicule was useful in refuting error and inciting 'to the practice of what is right'; but he too insisted with his Augustan forebears that ridicule should cause no more offence than this example: 'the Bill in the House of Commons for taxing dogs, was rejected by a proposal from a country member to introduce a clause extending it to cats'. Laughter could offend if freely unleashed, he argued, for 'the passion of laughter' had a great regard for itself, as Hobbes had taught. Its aggression and contempt must be muzzled. At this point Montagu cited Bacon: 'As for jest, there are certain things which ought to be privileged [excluded] from it: namely, religion, matters of state, great persons, any man's present business of importance, and any case that deserveth pity.' He also cited Addison: 'Laughter where things sacred are transacted has not excuse, breaking through all the rules of order and decency.' Finally he cited Sir Thomas West: '1. He never played upon a man's unhappiness or deformity, it being inhuman. 2. Not on superiors, for that is saucy and undutiful. 3. Not on serious or holy matters, for that's irreligious.' Montagu did once briefly refer to indecent humour towards the end of his book, but only to note that it excited 'lascivious sensations' in 'gross minds'. The story of Lady Godiva's naked ride through the streets of Coventry, for example, 'interests or disgusts according to the mind to which it is presented'. Montagu, playing safe, counted himself among the disgusted.[41]

## Practice versus theory

But now we approach the moment of redemption that returns us to the real world, which is where we stay henceforth. Redemption lay in the truth that normative prescriptions were contested or ignored, so much so that prescription may itself be regarded as a 'reaction' against behaviours that relaxed people regarded as 'normal'. Hearing the tautly mannered voices of Chesterfield, the Pitts and those who thought like them, we think they defined the norm. Doubtless some over-regulated people did follow Chesterfield's precepts, just as many of the godly and devout did, for their own puritanical reasons. But far more people subscribed to an earthier humour than those who respected polite taboos. Moreover, the public/private distinction was itself losing its force and clarity in the later years of this period. Textual satires observed the boundary more than graphic satires did, because they were more easily prosecuted for libel. But Hogarth had already produced personalized prints ridiculing Wilkes's squint and Charles Churchill's vulgarity. And in the later generation Gillray was not alone in naming private adulterers, adulteresses, faro gamblers or fashion victims. In short, chasmic discrepancies yawned between the polite anxieties about ridicule on the one hand, and its impolite practice on the other.

As is often true of historical silences, it is what the eighteenth-century texts did *not* say about laughter that claims attention now, along with what this omission implied about practice. For the striking thing is that eighteenth-century writers ignored everything that Joubert, Rabelais and many of their English counterparts in the sixteenth century had thought funny. They had nothing affirmative to say about laughter's scatological or bawdy repertoires, and they gave 'the people's laughter', the belly-laughter of carnival, no attention whatever. And if it is the task of satire to comfort the afflicted and afflict the comfortable (H. L. Mencken), this levelling notion was not admitted in laughter theory either. Yet each of these forms flourished in this period.

Nothing in what follows denies the importance of polite manners among those who wished to appear polished. Augustan precepts might well look old-fashioned to new reading publics by the end of the century; but even then, as 'polite' values were subsumed within 'respectable' values (a shift in nomenclature that spoke for a broadening in the social locations of aspiration), a German visitor could note of the English that 'the epithet "genteel" is applied to every thing, which conveys the idea of beauty and propriety in manners and externals. Among all ranks of society, the mob only excepted, a general emulation to appear "genteel" is conspicuous . . . The theory of polite manners is nowhere so universal.'[42] All the same, everything that follows reveals huge distances between the socialized humour which polite ideology sanctioned, and that raucous laughter of elite as well as of humble people that suffused mens' convivial associations, many womens' private ones, and both sexes' tastes in visual satire – and suffused not only these, but the era's highest literary achievements also – Smollett's or Fielding's work, for example, not to mention Laurence Sterne's dirt-swilling and *double entendre*-laden 'sewer of fiddlesticks, sausages, noses, whiskers, buttered buns, yards, spouts, asses, cabbage-planters, whim-whams, pipes, organs, holes, crevices, breaches, wind, battering-rams and horn-works', as Roy Porter catalogued *Tristram Shandy*'s subject-matter unforgettably.[43]

Since this was the great age of English scatology and *ad hominem* caricature, these omissions in polite theorization reveal a great deal about the paradox at this book's centre – if, in view of the obliteratively contrary evidence in this book, 'paradox' it need still be called. This was an age when gentle and would-be gentle people learnt their good manners resolutely. How, whether, or at what one laughed helped define politeness. Never before nor since have these questions been matters of such debate, suspicion and anxiety. Yet most of the humour we encounter henceforth betrayed their strictures shamelessly. Despite Chesterfield, despite Beattie, in well-heeled metropolitan circles, and in country houses also, elite as well as middle- and middling-class laughter drew on a long, vigorous and unseemly tradition that still had the most raucous of futures.

# CHAPTER SIX

# BUMS, FARTS AND OTHER TRANSGRESSIONS

## Laughter below the belt

It was said in the 1790s that there were confidential places in London where 'truth herself may be sported without the breach of veracity, and where well-imagined nonsense is not only superior to, but is the very index to wit and wisdom'. In such places 'the spirit of a gentleman . . . either shuts men's ears against what should not be heard, or closes their lips with the sacred seal of honour'; the very 'happiness and security of social life' depended on the liberties enjoyed there.[1] The speaker was referring to the private places in which men should be allowed to talk freely without fear of disclosure. He could as well have been referring to the clubs, taverns and sporting arenas in which well-born men celebrated two modes of humour that lay well outside laughter theorists' sense of the permissible. The well-born and polite were meant to withhold unseemly laughter. Humour must serve amiable sociability, and low idioms were for plebeians. Yet among men in the highest of circles these forms of immodest humour flourished. Sanctioned by older, manly codes, one mode was the libertine-erotic: it was concerned with sexual comedy and its intellectualization. The other was scatological: the humour of defecation, urination, farting and the parts used in those functions. The taste for the scatological had long been apparent in Jonathan Swift, in

**Fig. 73** Hogarth, *The Punishment Inflicted on Lemuel Gulliver by Applying a Lilypucian Fire Engine to his Posteriors for his Urinal Profanation of the Royal Pallace at Mildendo…* (1726)

joke-books, and in certain hidden texts, but by our period it was most visible in satirical prints. From Hogarth's *Punishment Inflicted on Lemuel Gulliver by Applying a Lilypucian Fire Engine to his Posteriors for his Urinal Profanation of the Royal Pallace* [sic] *at Mildendo…* (1726) (the punishment is an enema syringe shoved up Gulliver's backside) [fig. 73], and on until the 1810s, engravers deployed buttocks, chamberpots, enemas, farts, urine and turds as recurrent elements in their symbolic language. How can we understand the taste for such material in this nominally politest of eras?

We could close the subject at once by saying that most eighteenth-century men – and many women – were simply unsqueamish about Anglo-Saxon words and the parts and uses they referred to. They inherited a bawdy humour from past times. Puns on 'cocks', pissing and copulation had filled seventeenth-century jest-books matter-of-factly. As late as 1803 the 'carefully corrected and improved' twenty-third edition of the nation's standard French–English dictionary, Abel Boyer's *Royal Dictionary* ('specially designed to afford help to young students'), unselfconsciously provided the French equivalents for phrases like 'to hang an arse', 'a short-arse', 'his arse make buttons', 'a shitten girl', 'he came off very shittenly', 'he is the crack-fart of the nation', 'turdy', 'to piss upon one'. And why shouldn't such terms be tolerated among a gentry who spent half its time in muddy shires overseeing animals and the labourers who tended them? When they came to London, furthermore, they entered a city innocent of sewers and full of cesspit odours, that wasn't far short of a public lavatory. Newly arrived in London, Casanova was shocked in St James's Park to see the 'hinder parts of persons relieving nature in the bushes', and found that 'when an Englishman wants to ease his sluices in the street he doesn't turn up an alley or turn to the wall', but turned 'towards the middle of the street where they are seen by everybody who is driving in a carriage'.[2]

We could just as well say, beyond that, that the titillation of bodily and sexual functions has timeless psychosocial roots, and hence is no more mystifying than school-playground or locker-room bawdry is today. Can we psychoanalyse dead people? Jonathan Swift once wisely advised his readers not to believe 'certain fortune-tellers in Northern America, who have a way of reading a man's destiny, by peeping in his breech'. With this we may sympathize. Most historians believe that what's in a man's breeches is none of their business. Yet it is difficult to deny that one source of the scatological or sexual joke was the same in the eighteenth century as it is today. It either expressed a primal, infantile curiosity, or it reactivated in the adult the infant's frustration at parental taboos on excretion and the lower parts as untouchable and shameful. Adults who tell dirty jokes in effect protest at those remembered prohibitions, turning their infantile frustration into hostility against the joke's audience (by offending them), or against the joke's subject-matter (the opposite sex), or against both. The joke may provoke anger in return, if it is received as offensive. It may evoke the surprised sense of incongruity that provokes laughter. Or it may elicit laughter to defuse the harm the joker intended. In whatever case, the strongest reactions will be elicited in those most inhibited by parental vetoes. If most of those taboos (and jokes) are generalized from infant prohibitions, the deepest impulse behind them cannot be time- or culture-specific. Anthropological evidence shows that scatological humour crosses all cultures and eras. From ancient times to modern, it has always both expressed and rebelled against the shame of the 'civilized' and repressed.[3]

The trouble with these approaches, however, is that they obliterate dirty jokes as historical subjects. The truth is that history has indispensably determined their contents. The intensity of excremental taboos has varied with time and culture – along with the child-raising practices which have endorsed them. As a result, how or whether the primal curiosity will have its way, or how far adults will rebel against or ignore those remembered taboos, have correspondingly varied. In some circumstances the dirty joke will be unselfconscious, in others, defiant; or it may lose its purchase when manners change.

For example, some thirty years after the death of the Elizabethan dramatist George Peele, a jest-book included an account of his revenge on an ill-mannered old woman who had vexed him at table:

> As she put out her arme to take the capon, George sitting by her, yerks me
> out a huge fart, which made all the company in a maze, one looking upon the
> other, yet they knew it came that way. Peace, quoth George, and jogs her on
> the elbow, I will say it was I. At which all the company fell into a huge
> laughter, shee into a fretting fury, vowing never she should sleepe quietly till
> she was revenged of George his wrong done unto her.

The book containing this was unproblematically republished in 1809, but lifting thresholds of tolerance ensured that it was never published thereafter.[1] Or take the plausibly genuine graffiti collected in *The Merry-thought: or, the Glass-window and Bog-house Miscellany* (1731–) – a valuable source, since we have for obvious reasons lost sight of the graffiti of past times. Those recorded from bog-house walls included a levelling motif that we no longer see. They repeatedly declared that the act of defecation was socially levelling. 'Good lord, who could think / That such fine folks should stink,' proclaimed a scratching in the bog-house of 'a person of quality' in the 1720s. The Temple bog-house reminded its vistors that 'No hero looks so fierce in fight / As does the man who strains to sh-te'. And a graffito in Hoxton asked, 'What difference between the king's turds and mine? / One may be costive, one be full of slime; / Yet equally will any hog that feeds, / Produce good pork by feeding on our needs.'[5] Scholarship has not been favoured by an equivalent Victorian or modern collection. In short, changing conventions or political frames permit particular forms of joke to be acceptable in one era or community but not in others. Their content and meaning shift with period, class and sex. This makes eighteenth-century scatology as much a historical as a psychoanalytical subject, and this chapter explores some of its sources, expressions and meanings.

The language of popular satire and ridicule was saturated in scatological allusion throughout early-modern times.[6] That it survived into the elite English cultures of the later eighteenth century the graphic satires show incontestably. First, it was deployed against the overmighty, as in Dent's *Public*

**Fig. 74** Dent, *Public Credit, or, the State Idol* (Aitken, 1791)

*Credit, or, the State Idol* (1791), in which the farting buttocks imply a view both of the younger Pitt's grandiosity and of the MPs at whom he aimed his contempt [fig. 74].[7] Secondly, it communicated aggression. Gillray's *The French Invasion; – or – John Bull Bombarding the Bum-Boats* (1793) maps Britain in the form of George III defecating on France [fig. 75]. Among innumerable

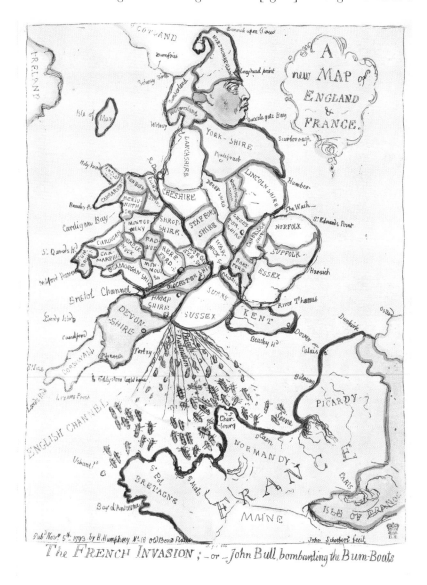

**Fig. 75** Gillray, *The French Invasion; – or – John Bull, Bombarding the Bum-Boats* (H. Humphrey, 1793)

**Fig. 76** George Cruikshank, *Loyal Address's Radical Petitions, or the R—t's most Gracious Answer to Both Sides of the Question at Once* (Tegg, 1819)

other examples are Richard Newton's *Treason* (1798), in which a defiant John Bull farts at a poster of the king [fig. 235], and George Cruikshank's *Loyal Address's Radical Petitions* (1819), in which the Prince Regent farts contempt at radical petitioners [fig. 76].[8] Thirdly, defecation indicated cowardice or delivered shame by association. In Gillray's *Evacuation of Malta*, Napoleon terrifies Prime Minister Addington into the literal evacuation of Guadeloupe, Martinique, St Domingo, the Cape of Good Hope, Egypt and Malta during the peace negotiations of 1803. A French officer holds his nose as he catches Addington's offerings in his cocked hat, and advises Napoleon not to purge Addington too hard lest Addington, weakened, be replaced by a minister less easily humbugged [fig. 77].[9] And fourthly, it offered taunting social commentary, as in Gillray's comments on the primitive lavatorial habits of the Scots, French and Dutch as compared with the sophistication of the English in his *National Conveniences* (1796) [fig. 78].[10]

In grand houses, material objects sustained the lewd commentary also. Glazed tiles were sold which showed John Bull urinating on the French,[11] and there was a fashion for chamberpots into whose bases were glazed either portraits of national enemies like Napoleon, or grotesque faces, or

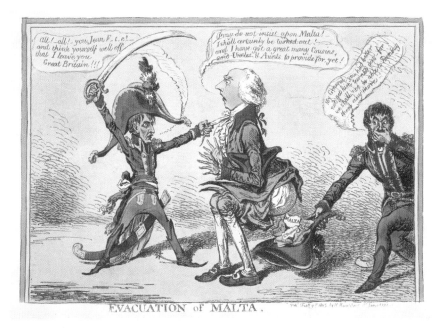

**Fig. 77** Gillray, *Evacuation of Malta* (H. Humphrey, 1803)

all-seeing eyes with the ominous motto, *video omnia* – 'I see all'. In a bawdy satire on the marriage in 1816 of the Prince of Wales's daughter Charlotte, George Cruikshank inserts under the bed a chamberpot with a grinning face inscribed 'what do I see?'[12] A 'chamber-pot room' in Newby Hall, Yorkshire, tastefully displays just such a collection, some of them early-modern, some European, some made in China for the English market. The motif was common on children's pots as well as adults'. We can't guess at the consequences for infant psyches, but mothers and nursemaids connived in the joke, clearly.

The literary counterparts of this material were also abundant, although they cluster within an earlier and briefer timespan. Between the 1720s and 1750s something odd happened in the history of English publication. Bookshops were hit then by a small boom in excretion-obsessed pamphlets and verses; thereafter they mysteriously died out. It was Swift's scatology – in *Gulliver's Travels* particularly (1726) – that activated this taste, though a few of the texts predated *Gulliver* and might even have influenced it. In eighteenth-century terms, Swift was a modern, his irony highly developed. He was often compared to Rabelais, whose *Gargantua and Pantagruel* (1532–52) had been the first major work to give the people's bawdry a

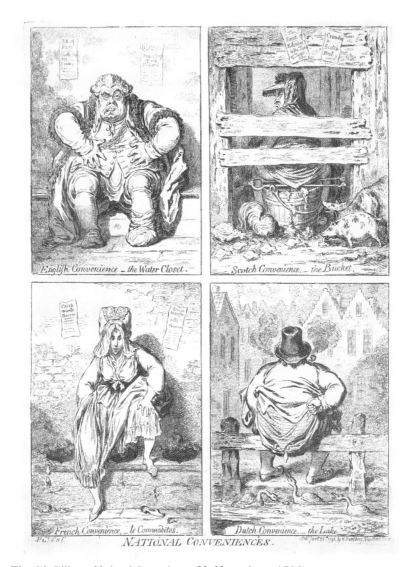

**Fig. 78** Gillray, *National Conveniences* (H. Humphrey, 1796)

literary voice. But when urine and turds had flowed in Rabelais, they had not flowed ironically; they had stood for life's munificence and fertility. In Swift, by contrast, urine and turds were so many 'satiric daubs and missiles' which forced the shamed reader to recognize his kinship with the disgusting Yahoos rather than with the noble Houyhnhnms. Swift aimed not to celebrate life but to assail human pretension, pride and self-respect by exposing the conflict between the animal body and its functions and human pretensions and repressions. 'Civilized' behaviour was a fiction; only the body's lower enactments conveyed humanity's grimmest truth: 'Nor wonder how I lost my wits, / Oh! *Caelia, Caelia* shits.'[13] If Swift's excremental preoccupations were never gratuitous, the same can't be said of the other works, however. These often lengthy effusions were aimed by well-known publishers at gentlemen with fat purses. A few of this small boom's masterworks may be listed in chronological order and with commentary enough to convey their tone:

> *The Benefit of Farting Explained, &c.; or, The Fundament-all Cause of the Distempers incident to the Fair Sex inquir'd into: Proving a posteriori most of the Disordures in-tail'd on 'em are owing to Flatulences not Seasonably Vented*: by Don Fart-in-hand-o Puff-in-dorst (1722). This was the pioneer text, predating *Gulliver*. Six editions appeared in 1722 alone; 13 had appeared five years later, 25 by 1810 (the text by then was 33 pages long). The text was translated into German in 1737. The publisher Curll had included it in Swift's *Miscellanies* in 1722, along with *The wonderful wonder of wonders* and *Serious meditations* (below), but Swift insisted that these 'slovenly pages' were written 'by one Dobbs a surgeon'. The title poem conveys the book's ambition: 'A fart, though wholesome does not fail, / If barr'd of passage by the tail, / To fly back to the head again, / And by its fumes disturb the brain. / Thus gun-powder confin'd, you know sir, / Grows stronger as 'tis rammed the closer; / But if in open air it fires, / In harmless smoke its force expires.' Elsewhere, conceits like this: 'It is a question greatly controverted among the learned, whether a fart be a spiritual or a material substance . . . The famous Mr Boyle brings it in as an example to prove the vast subtlility of matter, since a fart, which in the hydrostatical balance does not weight the thousandth part of a grain, shall, in one minute expand itself so far, as to occupy the whole atmosphere of a large drawing room.'

> *Arse Musica; or, the Lady's Back Report to Don Fart-in-hand-o Puff-in-dorst . . . on the benefit of Farting* (11 pp., 1722).

> *The Wonderful Wonder of Wonders, being an Accurate Description of . . . Mine a-[r]se* (1722): almost certainly by Swift, this was a punning life-story of a backside whose purpose was satirically to attack the Bank of England (excrement representing money); it elicited an equally scatological riposte in *The Blunderful Blunder of Blunders* (anonymous, 1722).

*The Sixpenny Miscellany; or, a Dissertation upon Pissing . . . by the Author of the Wonderful Wonder, etc.* (1726).

*Meditations on a T[ur]d, Wrote in a Place of Ease* (in 1727 edition of *Benefits of Farting*, as above): its egalitarian point thus summarized: 'All human titles, soon or later / Contribute to the jakes of nature.'

*A Hymn to a Chair . . . The Beauties and Advantages of Other Necessary Utensils to Rest the Bum Upon, and Ease the Mind, the Body, and the Breeches* (32 pp., in verse, 1732).

*Human Ordure, Botanically Considered. The First Essay, of the Kind, ever Published in the World. By Dr S . . . t* (Dublin, reprinted in London 1733 for 6d): a study of the 'wonderful variety in all productions of this nature'. Some critics accept this as Swift's work, though it is witless.

Jeffrey Broadbottom [William Guthrie], *Serious and Cleanly Meditations upon an House-of-Office (a Bog-House), etc.*, and *The bog-house, a Poem, in Imitation of Milton* (both in 1744 edition of *Benefits of farting*, above).

[Rolleston, Samuel], *A Philosophical Dialogue Concerning Decency. To which is added a Critical and Historical Dissertation on Places of Retirement for Necessary Occasions* (1751) (discussed in chapter 10 below).

*Bum-Fodder for the Ladies: a Poem upon Soft Paper* (single folio poem, 1753).

A full list might add the tales from Chaucer that were 'modernized' in these decades, their lavatorial content made even more explicit than it was in the original,[14] or Ned Ward's *Compleat and Humorous Account of the Remarkable Clubs and Societies in the Cities of London and Westminster*, predating Swift and first published in 1709. This last went into its seventh edition in 1756 at two shillings sewn and two shillings and sixpence bound: it, too, targeted gentlemanly purses. What gentlemen got was a satirical account of members of a series of real or fictitious London clubs suited to their humours. Ward got his lowest laughs from the tension between his confident prose and the crudity of its subject-matter. Here he introduces the Farting Club:

> Of all the fantastical clubs that ever took pains to make themselves stink in the nostrils of the public, sure no ridiculous community ever came up to this windy society, which was certainly establish'd by a parcel of empty sparks, about thirty years since, at a public house in Cripplegate parish, where they used to meet once a week to poison the neighbouring air with their unsavory crepitations, and were so vain in their ambition to out fart one another, that they used to diet themselves against their club nights with cabbage, onions and pease-porridge, that every one's bumfiddle might be the better qualified to sound forth its emulation.[15]

The text then takes a turn for the considerably worse as it describes the old dame whose task it was on club nights to inspect members' breeches to ensure that they had not perpetrated in their exertions what Ward delicately called a brewer's miscarriage.

Apart from a few bog-house meditations and later editions of these works, these titles pretty well exhaust the list for the eighteenth century. The British Library catalogue yields no results whatever for the relevant keywords after 1753. Tastes, in short, were changing. Cloacal literature didn't expire in the later eighteenth century; its titles merely advertised themselves less visibly. Charles James Fox wrote an *Essay upon Wind* – not of the meteorological sort – in 1783, and lavatorial jokes continued to be recycled in jest-books like *The Covent Garden Jester* of 1785.[16] But while the first edition of Smollett's *Peregrine Pickle* (1751) was littered with excremental references and knockabout jokes about drilling chamberpots with holes, etc., they were so poorly received that Smollett had to delete most of them in the second edition six years later. After mid-century the *relative* decorum of the written text is striking, not least because it throws the continuing scatology of graphic satires into much sharper relief. Clearly, things could be said in images that in texts were tabooed. This was because prints could be perused in exclusively male venues. It was probably the growth of a female readership that explains the silencing of the text.

From early-modern times onwards in the West, excremental taboos had been intensified as part of the so-called 'civilizing process'. Behaviour manuals from the fifteenth century on had earnestly taught readers how to manage bodily products, along with nose-pickings, table manners and correct behaviour towards others. Decorum depended increasingly on arousing disgust, embarrassment and shame when taboos organized around such things were violated.[17] Since this process obviously didn't lag in the eighteenth century, we may be tempted to think of eighteenth-century scatology in one of two ways. Most simply, it may present itself as an ironic counter-cultural form that offered an escape route from an excess of behavioural restriction. Alternatively, we may recognize with the critic Frye that 'genius seems to have led practically every great satirist to become what the world calls obscene' – or with the critic Paulson that the satirist rubs our noses in the dirt he seeks to alert us to, forcing us to suffer such revulsion that the truth embedded in that 'central symbol of violence' cannot be evaded.[18] Both views downplay what we may still wish to regard as the infantile impulses within this humour; but the bigger problem is that, if subversion or genius were all there was to it, we should expect scatology to flourish in the nineteenth century also, when the pressures to regulate the self and others were even deeper. Yet in public Victorian cultures, scatological modes were relegated to the free-and-easies of the louche and the low, and overt scatology was removed from the print record. No Victorian produced an image of Queen Victoria farting or of a duke defecating, for example, as the Prince Regent or Lord Stanhope were depicted in our earlier era. Does one ever encounter a reference to a fart in the Victorian novel or in *Punch*? A language relished by Smollett, Sterne or Gillray had been wholly repudiated or forgotten, it seems.

So to understand the prevalence of scatological irony in the eighteenth century, we should look for a cultural frame to which the Victorians lost access, a holistic understanding that bypassed modern distinctions between sacred and profane, high and low, and that stretched far back in time and crossed the classes; in other words, the scatology that was the accepted language of early-modern humour, and the enduring hold of what we now call the 'carnivalesque'. 'What is it, I ask you,' the great humanist Erasmus wrote in his *In Praise of Folly* in 1509, 'which begets gods or men – the head, the face, the breast, hand, or ear, all thought of as respectable parts of the body? No, it's not. The propagator of the human race is that part which is so foolish and absurd that it can't be named without raising a laugh.' The early-modern language of popular ridicule lived by this understanding. By projecting the shame associated with the lower bodily parts and functions on to the person or group selected for shaming, it achieved, in the collective laughter of the people's carnival or festival, dizzy heights of parodic bawdry and obscenity. If, except in sanitized survivals, the Victorians lost sight of the carnivalesque, the more robust of our Georgian male elites were neither forgetful of its legacy nor uneasy about it.

# 'The people's laughter'

It was taken for granted in the eighteenth century that common people and higher-class people had different senses of humour. As James Beattie put it, if the commoners' humour was crude, it was at least direct: they 'speak and look what they think, bluster and threaten when they are angry, affect no sympathies which they do not feel, and when offended are at no pains to conceal their dissatisfaction. They laugh when they perceive anything ludicrous, without much deference to the sentiments of their company; and, having little relish for delicate humour, because they have been so little used to it, they amuse themselves with such pleasantry as in the higher ranks of life would offend by its homeliness.'[19] Another writer noted that London laughter had its own social geography. 'What is [accepted as] high humour at Wapping, is rejected as nauseous in the City. What is [regarded as] delicate raillery in the City, grows coarse and intolerable as you approach St. James's.'[20]

In formal terms these demarcations were valid. The refined obviously dissociated themselves from the rough humour of Wapping, as they did from the old grotesqueries and comic inversions of the people's fair, bonfire night or charivari. Many literary men found Swift's scatology unbearable, too. Samuel Richardson, Edward Young, and many others abhorred it, while Dr Johnson wondered at a man who took 'delight in revolting ideas, from which almost every other mind shrinks in disgust'.[21] Swift was often compared with Rabelais, but not as a compliment. Rabelais 'offends our pride, as men, and our unaffected taste, as judges of composition', Young declared in 1728, placing him well below Cervantes as master of the comic. Not for the politest people, either, the notion advanced by one sixteenth-century theorist, that laughter was best provoked by the 'laughable in word' (word-plays, puns and comic anecdotes) or by the 'laughable in deed', when this last entailed accidental falls, practical jokes, parodic mimicry and accidental glimpses of 'the shameful parts' and buttocks.[22]

In this as in other contexts, however, the refined part never spoke for the whole. If refined critics rejected Swift, most readers worried less: *Gulliver* went into many editions. If moralists drew boundaries, the majority refused to, and more holistic views stayed resilient. The hold of the crudest humour even on high people needs to be positively affirmed. It drew precisely on those 'ready-made ideas, commonplaces and intellectual bric-à-brac, the remnants of cultures and mentalities belonging to different times and different places' that historians of mentalities attend to. The result was that Rabelais's scatology and the sixteenth-century notions about the 'laughable in deed' remained close to what many still thought of – and still think of – as comic. Thus Hogarth once saw a man's head split open by a quart pot in a tavern fight: 'The blood running down the man's face, together with the agony of the wound, which had distorted his features into a most hideous grin, presented Hogarth . . . with too laughable a subject to be overlooked. He drew out his pencil, and produced on the spot one of the most ludicrous figures that ever was seen.'[23]

In early-modern times the most familiar location of rude humour was in the levelling belly-laughter of the common people. This included the ancient uses of ritual inversion and the reference to the bodily parts and functions as weapons of insult, mockery, and shaming. There can be few more explicit visual examples of these usages than the taunting joke in a sixteenth-century Flemish satirical triptych which parodied the devotional format [fig. 79]. The figure in the first panel points to a scroll advising us not to open the triptych. Open it, and we see a mooning backside, anus alarmingly exposed [fig. 80]. 'You can't say I didn't warn you,' its scroll declares. In the third panel a man pulls a mocking face and cites the proverb: 'the more you are warned not to, the more you will wish to jump out the window'. These images might have been defiant, or didactic (the

**Fig. 79** Flemish satirical triptych (*c.*1520): panels 1 and 3

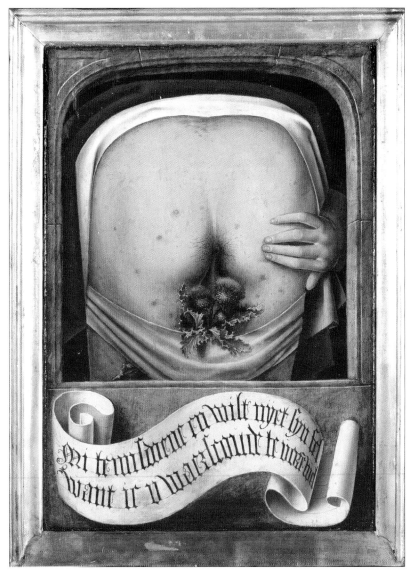

**Fig. 80** Flemish satirical triptych (*c.*1520): middle panel

thistle at the anus a warning against buggery?), or just comically proverbial. In whatever case, most people today would construe the triptych as shockingly and gratuitously offensive or unintelligibly rude. This, however, testifies precisely to our lost sense of the body's symbolic vocabularies in early-modern and earlier times. Elaborate bodily rituals, ceremonies, gestures and punishments were central to the display of power, respect or submission.

It was natural for this language to be parodied and subverted or inverted. The significance of urination, defecation and eructation was self-evident, their 'transcripts' by no means hidden. By contrast, in the more bureaucratically disciplined cultures of the nineteenth century, the intelligibility of this symbolic language faded. Although the derisive 'mooning' of the backside is still universally understood, modernity has by and large rendered the resort to somatic symbolism obsolete and beyond comprehension.

What the triptych certainly opposed was an 'official life' in the medieval and post-medieval world that was 'monolithically serious and gloomy, subjugated to a strict hierarchical order, full of terror, dogmatism, reverence and piety'.[24] As the Russian critic Bakhtin famously argued, works like these expressed the 'peculiar folk humour' that had been centred in 'the life of the carnival square' for centuries past. This humour was 'free and unrestricted, full of ambivalent laughter, blasphemy, the profanation of everything sacred, full of debasing obscenities, [and delighting in] familiar contact with everyone and everything'. Giving a 'temporary liberation from the prevailing truth and from the established order', it 'marked the suspension of all hierarchical rank, privileges, norms, and prohibitions'. Like Rabelais's, it imagined a world in which all people and things were connected, the body not individualized but subsumed within the collectivity. In this spirit, the 'carnivalesque' delivered its comic and satirical effects through the inverson of conventional hierarchies, the parodic deployment of animalistic and other masks and disguises, the obscenity of the grotesque body and the private parts, and the celebration of the tumultuous crowd. The whole encapsulated both a popular relationship to hierarchical control and a temporary relief from it.

How many of these forms survived in eighteenth-century England? And how did the elite experience and understand them? The answers to these questions are tricky. First, in post-Reformation England, the clarity of the carnivalesque shouldn't be overstated. In its many forms it never matched Bakhtin's ideal type. Festivals of misrule usually affirmed the hiearchical norms they ostensibly mocked, and their 'rough play' was always finite and relatively safe, embedded as it was in the rhythms of work and of the church calendar. This explains why elites patronized them. Moreover, local and central authority had controlled or reshaped these rituals for centuries. They had either curtailed them or (after 1660) permitted their expansion as shifting norms dictated. Far from surviving from an antique past, they were endlessly reinvented. Indeed, in relatively static rural hierarchies, the waxing and waning of festive ritual was conditioned more directly by political regulation than by economic or social change.[25]

Because of this, secondly, most historians assume that by the eighteenth century the old popular rituals in England had become gravely attenuated and by the end of it all but obliterated. Local regulation of urban and village space was closing down many market-place bonfires, bull-baitings and processions, and local elites' patronage of such occasions is assumed to have been declining. This is thought to have been particularly true of London. Historians of popular festivals generally ignore London, on the grounds that its size undercut the communal intimacy upon which the carnivalesque fed, and because regulations were tighter. Official enemies of London's popular pleasures were vocal throughout the century. 'In this town,' the magistrate Sir John Fielding complained, 'diversions calculated to slacken the industry of the useful hands are innumerable': 'Bull-baitings bear-baitings, cock-matches, and such races as are contrary to law, are in the numbers of out-door diversions that call for redress . . . These are the thieves that rob the journeymen and labourers of their precious time, their little prosperity, and their less morals.'[26]

Thanks to this disapproval, it is not surprising that metropolitan evidence of popular festivals at first seems quite thin. Little is recorded in eighteenth-century London to compare with the vibrant May games described in John Stow's *Survey of London* in 1598. Organized parish by parish, with maypoles, 'warlike shows', morris dancing, stage-plays and bonfires, these had been presided over by 'the governors and masters of the City'. Parish football and brawling at Shrovetide continued, but according to J. Strutt in 1801 the more elaborate forms of Shrovetide festivity – the bringing of 'twisted trees' into great houses, for example – were forgotten. There is no metropolitan record of 'thrashing the fat hen' – the bird tied to the back of a man with bells on his arms, for blindfolded participants to thrash with sticks when they heard the man move. Cock throwing (throwing stones at tied-up cocks to kill them) was prohibited in the City in 1752, earlier than in most provincial centres. (In both sports, cocks were allegedly ancient emblems of impiety and parricide, their killing a relic of the practice of delivering capital sentences on animals.) Of Christmas itself, 'all persons say how differently this season was observed in their fathers' days', Southey wrote in 1807, 'and speak of old ceremonies and old festivities as things which are obsolete'. When the format of old processions was revived in London, they often had a quality of self-conscious antiquarianism about them. When the freemasons were mocked in a charivari in 1742 (carts drawn by asses, and men riding donkeys with cow-horns in their hands), the episode was later recalled as almost 'the last remnant' of mocking public spectacles in the capital. The carnival atmosphere of the annual Lord Mayor's pageant was also waning. The adornment of houses along the Lord Mayor's route was long gone, along with the seventeenth-century tableaux of nymphs, fauns, satyrs, gods, angels and devils, and accompanying giants, savages, dragons, knights, buffoons and dwarfs. Strutt recalled 'some faint traces' of these displays in the 1770s, but the show was now 'so much contracted, that it is in reality altogether unworthy of such an appellation'.[27]

Yet, as always in this context, we are at the mercy of what antiquarians or law enforcers recorded, and most of these observers were ignorant of or hostile to popular customs, or they were nostalgic for imagined and merrier times past. Even as he claimed to be compiling their histories, Strutt thought lords of misrule were 'puerile and ridiculous' and 'adapted to the ages of ignorance, when more rational amusements were not known' – and so he almost wanted not to see them. Wakes and fairs had 'dwindled into mere markets for petty traffic, or else they are confined to the purposes of drinking, or the displayment of vulgar pastimes' (this observation rather missing their main point). In 1817, similarly, Leigh Hunt claimed that 'merry Old England died in the country a great while ago; and the sports, the pastimes, the holidays, the Christmas greens and gambles, the archeries, the May mornings, the may-poles, the country dances, the masks, the harvest homes, the new-year's-gifts, the gallantries, the golden means, the poetries, the pleasures, the leisures, the real treasures – were all buried with her'. As for London, 'Nothing . . . remains but the dancing of the chimney-sweepers on May Day, as if in mockery . . . An air of constraint, and business, is thrown over every thing.' Strutt's work fed off nostalgia for a golden past (his sources after the sixteenth century are thin), while Hunt's lament was fuelled by his distaste for 'the commercial and jobbing spirit' and for the evangelical regulation which seemed set to change the world as he wrote. Both authors forgot that the upper classes had almost always feasted separately and indoors, 'withdrawing' from low festivals with a fair amount of distaste even as they tolerated them. There might have been an acceleration of this distancing from *c.*1600 onwards, but their detachment was apparent in late medieval Europe also.[28]

There is, then, still room to reassess carnivalesque survivals in England. Recent research has excavated a plethora of localized and still vital 'petty carnivals' surviving in the provinces into the early nineteenth century and later. Timed by the church calendar, though increasingly secularized in spirit and content, outbreaks of tolerated sexual and gender play continued to flourish, along with masks and disguises, dancing, eating, drinking and violence, celebrations of misrule, and mock elections of and mock lords, ladies, bishops and mayors. In these episodes, hierarchy continued to be parodically inverted, authority lampooned, and laughter released in the grotesque and obscene.[29] Thus 'wakes' endured in the north and horn-dances in the south, and May Day festivals, Guy Fawkes bonfires, and Christmas wassailing and mumming continued everywhere, the mummers' plays that country people brought into great houses enacting mythological or legendary subjects in coarse buffoonery and burlesque. As late as the 1890s in the north, the 'wassail cup' was still being carried by carol singers from house to house before Christmas; from it the singers gave a twig in return for a gratuity. Pagan survivals like this were ubiquitous. Sprigs of holly or mistletoe were at that late date still given out by country girls when they went 'mumping' or 'a-gooding' to collect money on St Thomas's Day to help them lay in good things against Christmas.[30]

'Skimmingtons' survived throughout England too. The word is first cited from 1609 (possibly adapting a personal name, as in 'simpleton'). They were sometimes called 'charivari', to refer to parodically clothed processions or serenades of 'rough music' (banged kettles, pots, pans and the like). They mocked cuckolded spouses or henpecked husbands by forcing the errant couples to ride back-to-back on donkeys, the men wearing horns, the women wielding wooden spoons or brooms as emblems of their improper dominance, while villagers banged drums and kettles in derision. When Thomas Rowlandson in 1820 depicted his Dr Syntax encountering a village skimmington, he took it for granted that his well-heeled customers knew what he referred to [fig. 81]. In the 1830s, broadside woodcuts continued to depict skimmingtons or devils come to take sinners, confident that purchasers understood their symbolism. Village skimmingtons were still being reported in 1865; and Hardy's readers knew what he meant when he described one in *The Mayor of Casterbridge* (1886).[31] Similarly, from his early nineteenth-century boyhood in the industrializing Lancashire community of Middleton, Samuel Bamford recalled stang-riding at Shrovetide, mock mayors and 'mischief-neets' at Easter, morris bells at Whitsun, all lubricated by eating, drinking and sexual dalliance. Stang-riding required a derided man to straddle a pole or 'stang', or a derided woman to sit in a basket, to

DR SYNTAX WITH THE SKIMMINGTON RIDERS.

**Fig. 81** Rowlandson, *Dr Syntax with the Skimmington Riders* (Ackermann, 1820)

be carried through the streets until he or she paid drink-money. The practice was still being reported in the 1890s.[32] Wakes in early nineteenth-century Birmingham continued to be moments of sexual release and cruelty to animals: it took three prosecutions in 1809 to put a stop both to 'boys in a nude state, and females almost in a similar condition' racing in Birmingham streets, and to the men who publicly competed for prizes while 'nude, bedaubed with treacle, and sometimes feathered'.[33]

Much of this survived in eighteenth-century London, some of it into the early nineteenth century. Since most Londoners were rural immigrants, it would be surprising if it were otherwise; nor did you have to walk far to enter an older countryside. In the towns and villages of Surrey or Middlesex, shops shut for the annual street football matches on Shrove Tuesday. In the hamlet of Garrett, between Wandsworth and Tooting, a mock mayor was elected annually amidst accompanying charivari from 1747 to 1796, attracting crowds of up to 100,000. In London itself, Wilkesite crowds in the 1760s mocked the authorities through rituals and symbols, while election campaigns were accompanied by charivari of their own. Mock trials conducted in their cells by Newgate prisoners parodically turned the hierarchies of their narrow world upside down.[34] Francis Place remembered bull-running in London streets in the 1780s, and on May Day, right into the 1820s, London chimney-sweeps paraded the streets dressed as 'green men'. May Day had once belonged to the milkmaids, thanks to the rural custom of returning maypoles overnight 'by a yoke of oxen adorned with flowers, attended by boys blowing cows' horns or hollow canes, and milkmaids wearing garlands, which they afterwards hung up in the churches'. The garlands migrated with the milkmaids into London, the horn-blowers once accompanying them replaced by fiddlers and clarinet players; and the girls shared the chimney-sweeps' festivities. By 1807, Southey was describing May Day as the chimney-sweeps' 'saturnalia', and his account conveys wonderfully the antique fantasies that popular memory still sustained:

> The sweeps' sooty clothes were bedecked with pieces of foil, and with ribbons of all gay colours, flying like streamers in every direction as they whisked round. Their sooty faces were reddened with rose-pink, and in the middle of each cheek was a patch of gold-leaf, the hair was frizzed out, and as white as powder could make it, and they wore an old hat cocked for the occasion, and in like manner ornamented with ribbons, and foil, and flowers. In this array were they dancing through the streets, clapping a wooden plate, frightening the horses by their noise, and still more by their strange appearance, and soliciting money from all whom they met . . . A more extraordinary figure is sometimes in company, whom they call Jack-in-the-Bush; as the name indicates, nothing but bush is to be seen, except the feet which dance under it. The man stands in a frame-work which is supported upon his shoulders, and is completely covered with the boughs of a thick and short-branched shrub; the heat must be intolerable, but he gets paid for his day's purgatory, and the English will do any thing for money.[35]

Then there were London's fairs: here the carnivalesque reigned too, though under increasing pressure. They had long been attacked as venues for riot and vice, and because of its turbulence, the duration of the greatest of them, Bartholomew Fair, held at Smithfield near Newgate, was shortened from a fortnight to three or four days in 1735, while Southwark Fair was abolished in 1762. By the 1820s William Hone was sure that Bartholomew Fair was 'going out like the lottery, by force of public opinion'. Side-shows were fewer and tawdrier than they had been, he noted, and it was an indication of more moral times that a 'religious agent' was seen distributing leaflets among the stalls, asking 'Are you prepared to die?' 'Bartholomew Fair must and will be put down', Hone wrote, for it was 'an annual congregation of ignorance and depravity.'[36] Put down it was, though not until 1855. Otherwise, Bartholomew Fair sustained its carnivalesque chaos throughout this period, the microcosm of a happier and a freer world order:

> Here are drolls, hornpipe dancing, and shewing of postures;
> Plum-porridge, black puddings, and op'ning of oysters.
> . . . Pimps, pick-pockets, strollers, fat ladies, sailors.
> Bawds, bullies, jilts, jockeys, thieves, tumblers and taylors
> . . . The world's a wide fair, where we ramble 'mong gay things;
> Our passions, like children, are tempted by play-things.[37]

As late as 1817 the Fair was explicitly represented as 'the City carnival – the delight of apprentices, the abomination of their masters – the solace of maid servants, the dread of their mistresses – the encouragement of thieves, the terror of the constables'. And again, in 1826, it was described as a 'saturnalia of nondescript noise and nonconformity'. Its official opening saw inversion and parody: 'The Lord Mayor changes his sword of state into a sixpenny trumpet and becomes the lord of misrule and patron of pickpockets', and his opening proclamation was travestied by the so-called 'Lady Holland's mob', licensed jesters in effect, whose origins Hone traced back to the Commonwealth. All these accounts were self-censoring; but we are entitled to imagine the enduring deployment on these occasions of derisive farts, mooning buttocks and like obscenities.[38]

Finally, the plebeian carnivalesque colonized new territories, migrating into the bawdy knockabout inversions of Punch and Judy shows, harlequin pantomimes and circuses. There they were consumed by customers educated in carnival's subtexts. Punch, for example, came from the traditions of the mumming play and the seventeenth-century Italian Pulcinella. His dress, appearance and squeaky voice seem to have been established by the 1730s, the symbolism of his long hooked (phallic) nose and the ambiguity of his effeminized voice not lost on audiences practised in reading every sexual pun they encountered. Punch carried into the nineteenth century the anarchic, randy and profane voice of a Rabelaisian mockery that turned the world upside down. As a Punch man told Henry Mayhew as late as 1851, Punch was 'like the rest of the world, he has got bad morals, but very few of them'. 'Bad morals' were at least free of cant, he implied. They were 'true, just, right, and sound; [even though] he does kill his wife and baby, knock down the Beadle, Jack Ketch [the hangman], and the Grand Signor, and puts an end to the very devil himself'. Punch had one irresistible message, the Punch man added. It was that, once he had outwitted and killed the devil, 'we can now all do as we like!'[39]

# Masquerade

So carnivalesque idioms echoed ubiquitously in the cultures of our period. And, again, the visual satires carry the point – not only in their taunting scatology, but in their innumerable inversion metaphors too: in repeated prints showing wives ruling or riding husbands; in their deployment of animal masks to indicate human character or individuals; in the representation of the prince and his cronies as beggars in the fairgrounds that stand for the world's stage; in the cuckolds who are always antiquely horned; in the worlds that are turned upside down (the mule driving the packman, he carrying the baggage); and in horsemen of the Apocalypse, dances of death and *memento mori* by the dozen. However self-conscious these motifs might have become, each drew not only on a popular demotic still enacted in England, but also on a graphic tradition which stretched back over centuries. The wife riding the horned (i.e. cuckolded) husband in the anonymous *Petticoat Government or the Scriptures Fulfilled* (1778) [fig. 82] goes right back to German Reformation imagery; the other motifs do too.[40]

It would be silly to say that these legacies invariably drew on the elite's direct experience of popular enactments. Yet that experience was widely available in the eighteenth century, and understanding could be taken for granted. Most young males from the country houses visited fairs, saw pantomimes, watched skimmingtons, or entertained mummers. Lord Barrymore on his estate employed the mummer Delphini to entertain him and his guests with 'low ribaldry and lewd buffoonery', like an updated court jester.[41] Gentry and clergy attended cock-throws, cock-fights, and bear- and bull-baitings, even as they knew that these pleasures were uncouth (as like as not breeding the bulls or supplying the cocks that were needed).[42] In London itself, cultural boundaries were repeatedly crossed by rakish young gentlemen or patricians, so that 'an adulterous intercourse in low life is an unfortunate partiality in high life,' it was noted in 1819,

**Fig. 82** Anon., *Petticoat Government or the Scriptures Fulfilled* (1778)

when self-consciousness about this was increasing.[43] On May Day in the 1780s, Mrs Montagu of the Blue Stocking Club treated chimney-sweeps to a dinner of roast beef and plum pudding and a present of a new shilling on the lawn of her house in Hill Street, Portman Square. Just as those who perused Rowlandson's Dr Syntax illustrations were presumed to know about skimmingtons, so Humphrey's printshop in 1820 knew that its customers would take the point of Lane's mocking *Grand Entrance to Bamboozl'em*, in which Queen Caroline processes into London seated on a donkey, accompanied by a carnivalesque crowd in a charivari [fig. 83]. Engravers knew, too, that in satires on domestic or international politics the people's fairground was an apt visual metaphor for the world's stage: Woodward's and Williams's *A Political Fair* of 1807 is one example [fig. 84]. Time after time we notice that, although the high classical culture was closed to low people in our period, the low culture was emphatically accessible to the high.

**Fig. 83** Lane, *Grand Entrance to Bamboozl'em* (G. Humphrey, 1820)

**Fig. 84** Woodward and Williams, *A Political Fair* (Tegg, 1807)

Direct personal experience of low-life inversions was not essential in order to secure this legacy. That cultural memory went deeper than that, nothing shows better than the cult of masquerade. The masquerade craze originated in the court masques of the previous century and in the carnivals and masked balls which gentlemen encountered on the Grand Tour, particularly in Venice. The first public masquerades in England were organized by 'Count' Heidegger in the Haymarket in 1717. Thereafter hundreds of such gatherings were held at fashionable venues like Almack's in St James's, the Pantheon on Oxford Street, the pleasure gardens of Vauxhall or Ranelagh, and at Carlisle House in Soho Square. In this last, Theresa Cornelys, herself Venice-born and brought up amidst the licentious carnivals of her birthplace, served as masquerade's entrepreneur-in-chief. Opera-singer, adventuress and promiscuous (Casanova began his sexual career with her and implanted in her one of his children), she found a patron in Miss Chudleigh, the queen's maid-of-honour who was later tried for bigamy as the Duchess of Kingston. She drew to her Soho soirées the great, the good and the bad of all Europe.

The craze didn't go down well with moralists, needless to say. They knew that masquerades encouraged social and sexual promiscuities and liaisons 'against nature'. Masquerades fed every anxiety about the vice and luxury of the times. After the shock delivered in 1751 by the divine judgement on Lisbon, when that city was demolished by earthquake, English masquerade fell out of fashion for a year. In any case, masquerades made no *sense* in the age of Enlightenment. Fielding, Johnson, Goldsmith and countless churchmen assailed them as feasts of unreason, and Hogarth did too. Count Heidegger appears in Hogarth's mock *Masquerade Ticket* (1727) [fig. 85], a vehement print surmounted by a clock embellished by Heidegger's famously ugly face. The clock is flanked by a reclining (near-masturbating) lion and unicorn. The clock's pendulum is marked 'Nonsense' – and 'Impertinence' and 'Wit' are inscribed on the minute and hour hand respectively to indicate their relative frequency. Flanking the masked figures, 'lecherometers' measure the degree of lustful heat released. One lecherometer is inscribed 'Expectation', 'Hope', 'Hot Desire', 'Extreem Hot', 'Moist', 'Sudden Cold'; the other is inscribed 'Dry', 'Changeable', 'Hot', 'Moist' and 'Fixt'. Placards meaningfully advertise 'Supper Below'. On the left of the plate is an altar to Priapus, on the right a statue to Venus, and a bacchanalian debauch is painted on the rear wall. The print probably inspired Fielding to write *The Masquerade* a year later:

**Fig. 85** Hogarth, *Masquerade Ticket* (1727)

> Cardinals, quakers, judges dance;
> Grim Turks are coy, and nuns advance,
> Grave churchmen here at hazard play;
> So for his ugliness more fell,
> Was H–d–g–r toss'd out of hell,
> And in return by Satan made
> First minister of masquerade.

At masquerade, Fielding added, 'Fortune sends the gamesters luck, / Venus her votary a — [fuck]': the deceits practised at masquerade were always associated with the duplicitous identities and unconfessed diseases of courtesans and prostitutes. Eliza Haywood advised her readers that 'women of honour' should avoid masquerades, as should the 'gentlemen who were so depraved as to offer them tickets'.[44] But counter-urges would have their way, and the hunger for the release that masquerade offered was irresistible. Even Horace Walpole was a devotee.

So how 'carnivalesque' were masquerades? The fact that they merely transformed the elaborate inversions of popular festival into highly commercialized and frivolously erotic and ironic celebration might tilt the vote against their 'authenticity'. Still, the elements within masquerade that drew on the carnival tradition were too explicit to be dismissed. As the leading scholar of the subject, Terry Castle, has put it, masquerade was a form of 'erotic theatre' and a place of 'carnival metamorphosis'. It permitted the 'merging of self and other', establishing those 'magical continuities between disparate bodies' which carnival had always celebrated. 'Like the world of satire,' she adds, 'the masquerade projected an anti-nature, a world upside-down, an intoxicating reversal of ordinary sexual, social and metaphysical hierarchies. Its hallucinatory reversals were both a voluptuous release from ordinary cultural prescriptions and a stylized comment upon them.' The association with satire is suggestive. Masquerade was a form of living satire; in their many disguises, Castle notes, 'masqueraders sometimes resembled walking political cartoons'.[45]

Masquerade's festive roots were witnessed in its timing. Indoor masquerades clustered around Christmas and New Year; outdoor masquerades around May Day and Midsummer's Eve. Like their market-place counterparts, devotees wore transvestite or animal disguises and masks, ate, drank and gambled without restraint, and mixed promiscuously if not always willingly with those of the middling people who could afford tickets. Above all, masquerade turned the world upside-down. 'Everyone here wears a habit which speaks him the reverse of what he is,' someone reported in 1729. 'I found nature turned topsy-turvy,' another wrote, 'women changed into men, and men into women, children in leading-strings, seven-foot high, courtiers transformed into clowns, ladies of the night into saints, people of the first quality into beasts or birds, gods or goddesses.' People could discard their identity there, say and do what they pleased, touch whom they pleased. One gentleman went to masquerade naked under his domino, and in 1770 a Captain Watson appeared dressed, or undressed, as 'Adam'. You could dress as a goat and communicate in animal noises, if you chose.[46] Cross-dressing was commonplace. William Hickey went to a Haymarket masquerade dressed as a nun, his female companion as a man, and in 1808 Lord Hartington and William Ponsonby went 'as two tall young ladies, dressed in the last fashion, with diamonds, spotted muslin, and silver turbans and feathers'.[47] In Fielding's *The Female Husband* (1746) a masquerade woman dresses as a man in order to woo women to satisfy her lesbian desire.

Thanks to their masked anonymity, these were places of unique licence for women. Dryden's play, *Marriage à la Mode* (1673), in which masquerade made its first literary appearance, opens with Doralice's song in praise of adultery, its frankness accepted as a licensed element at the masquerade itself. Thereafter masquerade was to be endlessly deployed in literature, for with its disguises, deceptions, licence and questions of identity no other location could so effectively advance a plot or justify a moral commentary. The presence of unescorted women was taken for granted on these occasions: only at church was it otherwise sanctioned. While virtuous women went so that they could 'pretend to be bad', a Mrs Egerton went 'as Curiosity, all eyes and ears, knew everybody, and attacked them with so keen a wit, as to make her company both coveted and dreaded'.[48] The erotic charge could be intense, and male predators had field-days: 'Fishes are caught with hooks, birds are ensnared with nets, but virgins with masquerades.' The queen's maid-of-honour, Miss Chudleigh, went bare-breasted as Iphigenia to the Venetian ambassador's masquerade at Ranelagh gardens in 1749. According to Charles Churchill, her costume 'showed at once the graces of her person and the disposition of her mind'; Horace Walpole reported that she was 'so naked that you would have taken her for Andromeda'; and Mrs Montagu wrote that her 'dress, or rather undress, was remarkable; she was Iphigenia for the sacrifice, but so naked the high priest might easily inspect the entrails of the victim. The maids of honour (not of maids the strictest) were so offended they would not speak to her.' Satirical prints depicting her near-nudity (and dalliance with the king) seem not to have been exaggerated [fig. 86], and gossipy David Garrick sent them to the countess of Burlington to amuse her.[49]

At Almack's fashionable assembly rooms off St James's Street, or at Vauxhall pleasure gardens on the south bank of the Thames, masquerades trickled on into the 1820s. In 1790, Rowlandson could still produce an uncritical plate like his *Dressing for a Masquerade*, a reprise of Hogarth's *Strolling Actresses Dressing in a Barn* (1738), while a quarter-century later Byron's *Beppo* (1818) took his readers' continued tolerance of carnival for granted. Sensibilities, though, were changing. Most of Carlisle House had burned down in 1788, and four years later the Pantheon burned down also, while Vauxhall and Ranelagh turned seedy. In an era which increasingly valued sincerity and stricter sexual demarcations, the disguises, cross-dressing and sexual play of masquerade began to look *passé*. By the turn of the century, masquerade imagery began to symbolize morbidity rather than a collective and promiscuous joy. Just as Goya in 1799 produced a dark masquerade plate in *Los Caprichos* (entitled 'Nobody knows himself'),

**Fig. 86** Anon., *Iphigenia* (1749)

so even Rowlandson showed that self-indulgence must meet its comeuppance in a plate in his *The English Dance of Death* (1816) [fig. 87], in which
Death as a grinning skeleton haunts a masquerade in pursuit of his victim.
These images portended a shift in values that was to affect much more
than laughter's history.

There is an obvious risk of overinterpreting the more infantile images
or texts referred to in this chapter. There is also a risk of explaining the
durability of scatological forms by appealing to 'collective memory', always
an easy way out. All the same, the inversion motifs of most of the
enactments and prints mentioned above do seem to connect them to rather
ancient understandings. Whether they reacted 'transgressively' against

Such is the power, & such the strife,
That ends the Masquerade of Life.

**Fig. 87** Rowlandson, *Dance of Death: The Masquerade* (in *The English Dance of Death*, Ackermann, 1816)

dominant norms when they were so reflexively and widely accepted is debatable. If playfulness is a primal force, it was playfulness's critics that did the 'reacting'. Yet reaction might in turn provoke defiance; and, once that happened, these expressions may be regarded as examples of resistances to the civility otherwise recommended.

The philosopher David Hume once opined that 'the skin, pores, muscles and nerves of a day labourer are different from those of a man of quality', and that 'his sentiments, actions and manners' were also. Faint proof of that in this material, however. The quest for a more chivalric manhood was being pursued energetically in the late eighteenth century, and, as the middle people invested in 'respectability', bawdy manners would one day be tamed. Yet we note here the distance that this socializing enterprise had still to travel. The advice of Beattie, Chesterfield and like theorists of laughter was easily evaded in London's pleasure-seeking world. At licensed moments and in licensed venues, laughter in St James's remained as lewd, violent and mocking as any laughter in Wapping.

## CHAPTER SEVEN

# IMAGE MAGIC

What does it mean to say that satirical prints were knitted deeply into metropolitan cultures in the later eighteenth and early nineteenth centuries? Looking back from the 1890s, a Victorian observer might well be puzzled at the 'immense effect' they had once had on the public mind. Their effects had been 'extraordinary', he wrote; there had always been 'a rush and a crush to get them'. And it was true that crowds of the idle rich and their servants would storm Humphrey's shop to get the latest Gillray, their enthusiasm 'indescribable': 'it is a veritable madness; you have to make your way in through the crowd with your fists.' 'The English, of high and low birth alike,' the German journal *London und Paris* noted in 1806, 'are so enamoured of these satires, that all of them – good or bad – find a buyer'; 'caricature shops are always besieged by the public.'[1]

The Victorian commentator would have been less puzzled about this had he recalled the image-hunger of a people who lacked the great image-multipliers of later times – lithography, steel-engraving and photography. Beyond the paintings in affluent houses or art exhibitions, or the woodcuts in chapbooks or broadsides, or such painted signboards as survived in London (most had been removed after 1762), there was little imagery for people to look at. It's this that explains why crowds so often gathered to gawp into printshop windows [fig. 88]. People 'of all ranks', for example, had gazed at the window displays of Hogarth's *Industry and Idleness* when it was first published. Later, Oliver Goldsmith complained that outside printshops 'the brick-dust man took up as much room as the truncheoned hero, and the judge was elbowed by the thief-taker; quacks, pimps, and buffoons increased the group, and noted stallions only made room for more noted strumpets'. Sophie von la Roche looked out from Boydell's fine-art printshop one day in 1786 at 'a great many reflective faces, interestedly pointing out this or that object to the rest'. She later reported a crowd elsewhere transfixed by caricatures on the Prince of Wales's illicit marriage. When William Hone displayed George Cruikshank's *Bank Restriction Note* in his window in 1819, it caused such a sensation that police had to disperse the crowd.[2] Many decades later, Thackeray recalled the printshop windows of his schooldays, *c*.1820, as follows:

> Knight's, in Sweeting's Alley; Fairburn's in a court off Ludgate Hill; Hone's, in Fleet Street – bright, enchanted palaces . . . How we used to believe in them! to stray miles out of the way on holidays, in order to ponder for an hour before that delightful window in Sweeting's Alley! in walks through Fleet Street, to vanish abruptly down Fairburn's passage, and there make one at his charming 'gratis' exhibition. There used to be a crowd round the window in those days of grinning, good-natured mechanics, who spelt the songs, and spoke them out for the benefit of the company, and who received the points of humour with a general sympathizing roar.[3]

**Fig. 88** Anon., *Caricature Shop* (Roberts, 1801)

As a memoirist recalled of the 1830s, 'The shop-windows of the London printsellers were the people's real picture galleries at this period, and always had their gaping crowds before them. The caricatures of the day, representations of famous prize-fights, and Cruikshank's and Seymour's comic scetches [*sic*] were most to the taste of the *cognoscenti* of the pavement . . . Most of the book illustrations were copperplates – the annuals were then in their hey-day – and odd collections of these used to be hawked in the principal thoroughfares, arranged in umbrellas spread open on the ground, and were the only cheap prints people then had an opportunity of purchasing.' As late as the 1850s it was still being reported that 'a well known source of gratis recreation to the unemployed is what is called "a picture-fuddle", when a party of idle hands will hunt up all the printshops and picture-shops of a whole district, and spend perhaps the whole day in the contemplation of this gratuitous gallery'.[4] By then, however, advances in print technology had long brought down the cost of image reproduction, so that graphic art flourished not in the single sheet, but in bound magazines allied to the printed word.

As all this implies, we should discard the notion that the satirical prints of this period were regarded as disposable fripperies, as newspaper cartoons are today. Indeed, in reference to a satirical or comic sketch, the word 'cartoon' is anachronistic to our period: we deal with 'caricatures', not cartoons. 'Cartoon' was first coined by *Punch* only in June 1843 in parodic reference to the fresco designs for the new Houses of Parliament exhibited in Westminster Hall: the magazine then published its 'cartoon no.1' by John Leech on 15 July.[5] Thereafter, 'cartoon' came to refer to a genre that was blander, more speedily produced, and less ambitious than the prints we're concerned with, and 'cartoonist' (first recorded as late as 1880) to an artist whose work was evanescent. Moreover, people who spent expensively on prints valued them more than our association of them with cartoons can possibly convey. Over 20,000 print titles were issued in this period, each etched or engraved on copper and pressed onto handmade paper, coloured by hand, and selling expensively in scores, hundreds or thousands of copies. Princes and connoisseurs bought them, as well as tradesmen and spinsters. There exists no other artefact that reveals so graphically how their purchasers thought about and imagined their world.

There is always something otiose in efforts to measure the 'impact' of an art-form, and perhaps a temptation to overstate it. Our claims shouldn't be overdone. It is unlikely, for example, that the likes of Gillray or Rowlandson cared a fig whether their caricatures 'reformed' their contemporaries or whether posterity would remember them. Making a living was what mattered. Satirical engravers were too low a breed to be much noticed anyway. Hardly anyone mentioned Gillray's death in 1815, and few discussed his work in the century after it. Beyond that, it was argument that changed the world, not imagery: the sedition that mattered to the law was textual, not visual. Also, educated people were readers first and print perusers only secondarily; and prints more often fed off newspapers than vice versa. Diary- or letter-writers referred often to newspapers, but seldom to prints.[6] Read Hazlitt's closely recorded conversations over half a lifetime with the artist Northcote, and you'll find no reference to the graphic satires of their day; instead, their breadth of cultured reference makes caricature look trivial.

That said, scarcity of comment is no index of a commodity's cultural consequence. References to engraved artworks and topographical or scientific illustrations were also infrequent in diaries, but their multiplication in the eighteenth century was part of the shift from a text-based culture to the image-saturated one of ensuing times.[7] And, if graphic satires came second to newspapers as communicators, it was a close second. No image caught the fleeting moment or transient sensation as they did. If a sensation was to be commented on, a point quickly made, it was to the copperplate as much as to newspapers that people turned. People even saw their world in terms of caricature: 'What a subject for caricature!', John Wilkes exclaimed in 1786, as he described an unseemly punch-up in Carlton House over the Prince of Wales's debts.[8] No wonder that the aesthetic Horace Walpole's letters fairly bubble with comments on this or that print on the latest scandal or political sensation. Sending one of George Townshend's caricatures to his friend Horace Mann in Tuscany, he wrote that it so captured the characters that it 'made me laugh till I cried'; and Mann replied that it was 'the most extraordinary caricature I ever saw', and it 'made me laugh most inordinately'.[9]

When visual satire's influence is compared with that of textual satire, it won hands down on several counts. Not only did it circulate more widely; it was also longer and more easily remembered. It spoke to senses that lay beyond reason too, so that, as Hogarth put it, pictures 'shadow forth what cannot be conveyed to the mind with such precision and truth by any words whatsoever . . . Ocular demonstration will carry more conviction to the mind of a sensible man, than all he would find in a thousand volumes.'[10] Ocular demonstration was better imprinted on memory, moreover. When in 1860 Thackeray recalled Pierce Egan's picaresque quasi-novel, *Life in London* of 1821 (the greatest publishing sensation of his youth), all he remembered of the text was that it was 'a little vulgar'. What he fully recalled were the Cruikshank brothers' illustrations for it: 'But the pictures! – oh! the pictures are noble still!'[11] The power of the print was deepened by its exploitation of long iconographic traditions. Visual references to anthropomorphized beasts and bugaboos (or scarebabies), to the dance of death, to *memento mori*, to a hell with flaming jaws, or to the character of 'nobody' as a bodiless head and limbs, remained almost as common as they had been in 1600 and much earlier. When modernized, prints' iconography remained just as accessible. Many recycled the familiar imagery of advertisements, chapbooks, children's books, nursery rhymes, games, songs, dying confessions, playbills, showman's notices, or offered visual puzzles, rebuses, or mock coats of arms.[12] Others drew on the Bible, *Aesop's Fables, Pilgrim's Progress, Robinson Crusoe*, or *Gulliver's Travels*. And when they simply joked, their humour replicated a familiar world in which Scotsmen were mean, wives disobedient, and mothers-in-law unbearable – all easily remembered.

The simpler and more familiar the icons, indeed, the more potent their effects. Long after the event, in a letter of 1875 vaingloriously headed 'How I put a stop to hanging', the ageing George Cruikshank recalled how on the morning of 16 December 1818 he had walked down Ludgate Hill and seen several bodies hanging on the Newgate gallows. Two were women's, hanged for passing forged pound notes. 'The fact that a poor woman could be put to death for such a minor offence had a great effect upon me,' he wrote; he went home to design his mock *Bank Restriction Note*, and had it published by William Hone [fig. 89]. Signed by 'J. Ketch', the hangman, it was decorated with shackles and skulls, with the £-sign formed by a rope into a noose framing a prison. A line of eleven men and women, heads hooded and necks twisted, dangled in line from a scaffold. Of course, it wasn't the print that curbed hanging; Cruikshank had a sharp eye for a market in which hanging for forgery was being debated anyway. He also overstated the print's originality, for mock banknotes were common in the satirical print repertoire well before this [see fig. 220 for an example]. But

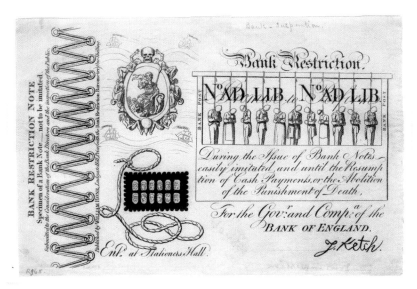

**Fig. 89** George Cruikshank, *The Bank Restriction Note* (Hone, 1819)

there is no reason to doubt its impact on as well as its reflection of opinion. A second plate had to be engraved after two or three thousand impressions had been taken from the first, and, at a shilling a sheet, the print allegedly netted Cruikshank and Hone some £700, two or three times most craftsmen's annual income. And when, far away in Italy in 1819, Shelley wrote *Oedipus Tyrannus, or Swellfoot the Tyrant*, his dramatic satire at the regent's expense, it included, in direct reference to the print, the character 'Banknotina', Mammon's daughter, who was married to the gallows.[13]

Another example is one of Gillray's most powerful exercises in truth-telling, his representation of the Prince of Wales in *A Voluptuary under the Horrors of Digestion* of 1792. This itself soon became iconic [fig. 90]. Before this, even as engravers registered the prince's extravagance, debauchery and illicit marriage and affairs, their portrayal of his appearance had been rather flattering. The *Voluptuary* marked the turning-point in his public representation, not least as it fed into ensuing depictions that had far wider circulation than any formal portrait could hope for, even when engraved. While John Hoppner in 1792 was painting an official portrait of a handsome young man framed by a romantically stormy sky (his seventeen-stone weight well camouflaged), it was Gillray who exposed the swelling truth of the matter. The shock the *Voluptuary* must have delivered is difficult now to recapture, but no preceding print had so economically embodied

**Fig. 90** Gillray, *A Voluptuary under the Horrors of Digestion* (H. Humphrey, 1792)

the prince's many vices: in the empty wine bottles, gnawed bones, purgatives and pills for venereal disease behind him, in the vomit- or shit-brimming chamberpot, the dice, unpaid bills, and record of gambling debts on the floor, in the extravagant columns of Carlton House outside the window – the whole dominated by that indolent and aloofly indifferent figure picking his teeth with a fork: the final commentary on the wall laconic and understated, in the parodic coat of arms and the portrait of the famously long-lived and abstemious sage Cornaro, and (as always in Gillray) in the print's sardonic titling. This was one of the several Gillrays that were cited as proof of a bookseller's seditious views in a prosecution a year later. Not surprisingly, the image was never forgotten. George Cruikshank reconstructed the prince's icon just as devastatingly in the 1810s, but he still paid court to the Gillray in the corpulent posturing peacock he produced in woodcut for Hone's pamphlet, *The Political House that Jack Built* [fig. 91], and in the lolling woodcut voluptuary he produced for Hone's *The Queen's Matrimonial Ladder* in 1820 [fig. 92].

Textual satire played some part in these constructions. It was probably no accident that *Voluptuary* appeared in the same year as Charles Pigott's scurrilous exposures of the prince's decadence in his *The Jockey Club* (though there is no proven connection between them). Similarly, one of Cruikshank's most damaging images of the prince, in 1812, was shaped by Lamb's doggerel on the 'prince of whales', while Shelley's *The Devil's Walk*

"Great offices will have
Great talents."

This is THE MAN—all shaven and shorn,
All cover'd with Orders—and all forlorn ;

Give not thy strength unto women, nor thy ways to that which destroyeth kings.
*Solomon.*

### QUALIFICATION.

In love, and in drink, and o'ertoppled by debt ;
With women, with wine, and with duns on the fret.

**Fig. 91** *(left)* George Cruikshank, *The Dandy of Sixty* (in Hone, *The Political House that Jack Built*, 1819)

**Fig. 92** *(right)* George Cruikshank, [*George IV*] (in Hone, *The Queen's Matrimonial Ladder*, 1820)

of the same year also left its deposit: 'Fat as that prince's maudlin brain / Which, addled by some gilded toy, / Tired, gives his sweetment, and again / Cries for it, like a humoured boy.' But it was the image that was always best remembered, and the image could just as well shape texts as be shaped by them. A talented caricaturist himself, Thackeray, for example, certainly remembered Gillray's *Voluptuary*, even though it had appeared nearly twenty years before he was born. In 1855, he recalled how Gillray's prince had picked his teeth with his fork: 'Fancy the first young gentleman living employing such a weapon in such a way! The most elegant prince of Europe engaged with a two-pronged fork – the heir of Britannia with a *bident*!' And when he recalled George as 'a fribble dancing in lace and spangles', 'a worn out voluptuary', 'nothing but a coat and a wig and a mask smiling below it – nothing but a great simulacrum . . . we cannot get at the character; no doubt never shall' – it was on the satirical iconography that he drew. 'His natural companions were dandies and parasites,' Thackeray continued: 'French ballet-dancers, French cooks, horse-jockeys, buffoons, procurers, tailors, boxers, fencing masters, china, jewel and gimcrack merchants.' 'Swaddled in feather-beds all his life, lazy, obese, perpetually eating and drinking . . . Here was one who never resisted any temptation; never had a desire but he coddled and pampered it . . . What muscle would not grow flaccid in such a life.' No account betrays the impact of satirical iconography on memory and hence on verbal caricature more obviously than Thackeray's. Even now Gillray's and Cruikshank's prints more deeply influence our sense of the prince than any contemporary textual description. Modern attempts to rehabilitate George IV's reputation as connoisseur or statesman in effect still do battle with the caricatures.[14]

The prints also left gentler legacies. By representing political, social or sexual relationships visually, by disseminating news and gossip, or by turning life's vexations into jokes, the prints endorsed, but also shaped, how people saw and recalled the city around them. Indeed, the pleasure they took in London life fed the comic vision of the generation or two that followed. However crudely knocked out, Rowlandson's *A Midwife Going to a Labour* (1811) [fig. 93] is a prototype of Dickens's Mrs Gamp, for example. As Dorothy George wrote of it: 'the streets before dawn, the sleeping watchman, the little chimney sweep "crying the streets", and the mountainous but indomitable woman who makes her way over the cobbles on her pattens, in the teeth of driving rain, form a picture which today has a historical significance transcending the comedy of Rowlandson's design.'[15] In one incarnation Dickens was a verbal caricaturist, and the congruence between his vision and that of the engravers of his boyhood days is recurrently in evidence.

Fig 93 Rowlandson, *A Midwife Going to a Labour* (Tegg, 1811)

What about the satires' impact on their targets? Very light, some might reply. Even the most loathed politicians today collect caricatures of themselves. Provided they are bland enough, they affirm their subject's importance and flatter their narcissism. It was no different in this period. Canning wanted to advance his career by featuring in a Gillray, and as Dr Johnson said when informed about a Gillray caricature of him in 1783: 'I hope the day will never arrive when I shall neither be the object of calumny or ridicule, for then I shall be neglected and forgotten. Sir I am very glad to hear this.'[16] Beyond that, many of those targeted in prints about aristocratic vices could use them as the genially flattering mirrors that engravers sometimes intended, while more vicious attacks might simply bounce off the hides of people who were too proud either to care or to be seen to care. 'The ministers and their friends . . . mind no abuse, when they remain in possession of the good things which they enjoy under government,' Pastor Wendeborn noted.[17] The likes of Lady Worsley with her well publicized bottom [fig. 1], or the Countess of Strathmore with her well publicized breasts (another woman calumniated by Gillray) [fig. 149], would maintain a contemptuous silence rather than stoop to challenge gutter products. Most grandees were insulated within circles of admiring friends and dependants and could afford indifference to attacks from outside them. Fox affected not to care in the slightest about his public reputation: 'He became so callous to what was said of him, as never to repress a single thought, or even temper a single expression when he was before the public.'[18] In any case, few could deny the critic T. J. Mathias's principle that satire had public utility: 'All publick men, however distinguished, must in their turns submit to it, if necessary to the welfare of the state' – the agonized debates about whom exactly the satirist might aim at being pretty well swept aside by this date.[19] So, however personal the prints against him, Pitt was bound to admire their audacity, thinking them 'congenial to the national feeling' and 'one of the harmless popguns of a free press'.[20]

Indifference, however, was more often affected in public than it was privately felt. Those mocked in print were more commonly wounded than they admitted, for the satires operated within a shame-culture in which the public demolition of reputation was the most feared of social sanctions. Satires on the Prince of Wales so damaged his self-esteem that his 'one fear' was of ridicule, the Duke of Wellington said; and Cruikshank's repeated attacks on him in effect drove him from public view between 1812 and 1820. As king, he wanted prints like these prosecuted for seditious libel; failing in that, he bribed Cruikshank and others into silence. William Cobbett, similarly, was repeatedly lampooned as a political turncoat after he reneged on his earlier Tory loyalism and associated himself with Burdettite radicals in 1805. For some years he affected not to care about the graphic attack on him. Caricatures broke no bones, he wrote in his *Political Register* in 1808; they were only 'things to laugh at':

> I, for instance, have been represented as a bull-dog, as a porcupine, as a wolf, as a sansculotte, as a nightmare, as a bear, as a kite, as a cur, and, in America, as hanging upon a gallows. Yet, here I am, just as sound as if no misrepresentation of me had ever been made. The fact is, that caricatures are nothing more than figures of rhetoric proceeding from the pencil; and as the inimitable Gillray is not in the habit of making sentences, I see no reason why he should not ridicule what he deems to be the follies and vices of the times, or of particular persons, with his pencil.

A year later he had second thoughts about these brave words, however, for Gillray had wounded him severely. In 1809 London was beset by one of the great corruption scandals of the age when it was alleged that the courtesan Mary Anne Clarke had persuaded her besotted lover, the Duke of York, to grant promotions in the armed forces on her say-so. Cobbett exploited the allegations to launch his attack on 'old corruption', thus helping to regalvanize the metropolitan radical cause. Gillray's riposte to Cobbett's initiative took the form of eight plates entitled *The Life of William-Cobbett, – Written by Himself* (1809). Each plate drew on episodes in Cobbett's published accounts of his career to portray him as a vain, boastful and cowardly renegade whose own words condemned him. 'Father kept the sign of the Jolly Farmer at Farnham.' Gillray's opening salvo reports in the first plate: 'I was his pot boy and thought an ornament to the profession. – at seven years old my natural genius began to expand and display'd itself in a taste for plunder and oppression! – I robbed orchards, set father's bull-dog at the cats – quarrelled with all the poor boys, and beat all the little girls of the town – to the great admiration of the inhabitants' [fig. 94]. Since each plate continued in this vein [see fig. 245], it was not surprising, then, that when Cobbett next referred to Gillray (in 1818) his phlegmatism about caricature had evaporated. Gillray, no longer 'inimitable', had become a 'wretch' who propagated falsehood.[21]

**Fig. 94** Gillray, *The Life of William Cobbett, – Written by Himself*: 1st plate
(H. Humphrey, 1809)

Humbler victims of the satirists had occasional recourse to prosecutions for personal libel. The Piccadilly printshop proprietor S. W. Fores, for example, was charged in 1800 for 'publishing and exposing to view' a lampoon on an 'eminent surgeon', one Long, by one of Long's pupils. Thomas Erskine, prosecuting, lamented on Long's behalf that 'this system of libelling by caricature prints, was becoming but too prevalent, and was too seldom made the subject of legal animadversion'. He argued that visual libels were far more damaging than textual libels, because texts had to argue their case and so might be rebutted. Caricatures on the other hand were 'the most dangerous of all libels' since they might be had for next to nothing, and were 'considered as matter of amusement'. 'Libellers of this description could lay hold of little infirmities, that had nothing to do with a man's moral character.' This case collapsed; however, private prosecutions against graphic satires were usually counterproductive.[22]

Examples of the damage that personalized caricature could do are innumerable. That Townshend caricature that Horace Walpole sent to Mann so 'diverted the town', Walpole wrote, that a pamphlet had to be published to denounce it. When James Sayer caricatured George Steevens, the Shakespearian annotator, Steevens threatened to cane him.[23] Politicians so well understood the power of caricature that they bought engravers to work for them. A Foxite pamphlet of 1784 referred to a 'secret service ledger' with the items: 'To several print shops £2,000' and 'To Mr. — for his indecent engravings £500'. The reference was to W. Dent, whose calumnies on the Duchess of Devonshire's role in the Westminster election, in prints like *The Dutchess Canvassing for her Favourite Member*, were coarsely sexualized. This print has the great lady inserting her hand under a butcher's apron in 'Cockspur Street' as she prepares to kiss him in exchange for his vote, declaring, 'I'll leave no stone [testicle] unturned to serve the cause' [fig. 95].[24] Print and press mockery of the duchess in 1784 curtailed her political activities thereafter. Indeed, one print's implication that her politicking made her a neglectful mother was so wounding that she got Joshua Reynolds to refute it by painting her holding her child lovingly [fig. 96].[25]

Even Fox, normally above caring, thought that James Sayers's caricature attacks on him in the 1780s delivered 'more mischief' than any parliamentary debate or press attack. Sayers's comment on Fox's India Bill, *Carlo Khan's Triumphal Entry into Leadenhall Street*, was arguably 'one of the most influential political caricatures ever published'. Fox later also deeply resented his representation in the 1790s as a bloodthirsty Jacobin sans-culotte, and

**Fig. 95** Dent, *The Dutchess Canvassing for her Favourite Member* (Carter, 1784)

**Fig. 96** 'J. M. W.', *The Devonshire Amusement* (Wallis, 1784)

was said to be especially hurt by Gillray's *A Democrat, – or – Reason and Philosophy* (1793) [fig. 97], in which, farting, he features trouserless, hairy-legged, and bloody-handed, and crying the revolutionary 'Ça ira!'. When Holland's printshop sold Gillray's *The Loyal Toast* (1798), an influential satire

**Fig. 97** Gillray, *A Democrat, – or – Reason and Philosophy* (H. Humphrey, 1793)

on Norfolk's and Fox's eviction from the Privy Council for toasting 'Our sovereign, the majesty of the people', the Duke of Norfolk withdrew his patronage from the shop in high dudgeon.[26] Gillray's *New Morality* (1798) [fig. 222] was also highly influential. Its mockery of the Jacobin sympathies of Coleridge, Southey and Wordsworth allegedly hastened the poets towards their recantations of French principles. That print was certainly closely monitored. 'Pray, Mr Lamb, are you toad or frog?', Godwin teased Charles Lamb when they first met, referring to the print's depiction of Lamb as one or the other animal.[27] Canning and his circle had no doubt about the utility of employing Gillray against the radical Whigs, while Fox was convinced that the best way 'to lower' Pitt 'personally' was to ridicule him.[28] Nor did printshops and engravers have any compunction in resorting to caricature to damage personal enemies when it suited them.[29]

Fiction took caricature's power for granted too. 'I shall be laughed at over the whole town. I shall be stuck up in caricatura in all the printshops [as] the DULLISIMO MACCARONI,' Marlow exclaims in horror in Goldsmith's *She Stoops to Conquer*. And when, in Maria Edgeworth's novel *Belinda* (1811), Lady Delacour retreats from the fashionable world, she worries that she will be the target of 'witticisms, epigrams, caricatures without end': 'we should have *Lord and Lady D—, or the domestic tête-à-tête, or the reformed Amazon* stuck up in a printshop window! Oh, my dear! think of seeing such a thing! I should die with vexation, and of all deaths that is the death I should like the least.' Elsewhere, Lady Delacour described her own caricatures of an electoral opponent: 'I took out my pencil, and drew a caricature of *the ass and her panniers*; wrote an epigram at the bottom of it; and the epigram and the caricature were soon in the hands of half *****shire.'

What clinches these claims for caricature's effect goes beyond particular examples. The pervasive fear of ridicule was betrayed in the contempt marshalled against Grub Street satire in eighteenth-century theories of laughter. The lampooner who delivered 'secret stabs to a man's reputation' was 'one of the most mischievous creatures that can enter into a civil society', Addison had declared. 'Maggots' or 'bugs', 'unknown to all, but when they stink or bite' and fit only for 'common sewers': this was what the antiquarian Richard Payne Knight thought about the low 'sketchers and reviewers' who bit him cruelly at the century's end.[30]

It has been plausibly suggested that caricature delivered these effects because it was a modernized form of an ancient effigy magic delivered against otherwise unassailable enemies. As the critics Gombrich, Kris and others have argued, it was related to the act of symbolic defilement anciently embedded in ritual destructions of the defamatory image (hanging in effigy, for instance): the pre-modern image was thought of as the subject's reincarnation, so that to mutilate it was to mutilate its living equivalent. Although the visual and literary grotesque had been deployed by very early scribes and stonemasons, free play with the image could be experienced as *funny* only in the seventeenth century, when this magical resonance had all but evaporated. Caricature was first developed as a form of ludic virtuosity in Carracci's studios in Italy, but the art took time to catch on in England. As late as 1690, Sir Thomas Browne still had to explain the term: 'when men's faces are drawn with resemblance to some other animals, the Italians call it, to be drawn in caricatura.' In 1712 the *Spectator* had to refer informatively to 'those burlesque pictures, which the Italians call caricaturas; where the art consists in preserving, amidst distorted proportions and aggravated features, some distinguishing likeness of the person'. Hogarth deplored caricatures (though he produced some). They were chiefly imported into England by gentlemen from the Grand Tour, notably by George Townshend in the 1750s. At first the art was received as nothing more noxious than the establishing of a witty equivalence between reality and its grotesque exaggeration to elicit the surprised recognition of incongruity that is the source of laughter. But Townshend soon applied it to aggressive political purposes, and thereafter it fused with the more elaborate parodic, witty or ironically punning forms of representation that fill this book, with ridicule a purpose and antique sacral meanings quite forgotten.[31]

Yet this demystification of the mocking image didn't (and doesn't) deprive it of its primal sting. As caricature was ever more closely married to parody, wit, irony, innuendo or allegory, it became more intriguing to sophisticated viewers, but its aggressiveness was also sharpened. 'Abuse is not so dangerous,' as Dr Johnson put it, 'when there is no vehicle of wit or delicacy, no subtle conveyance.' Moreover, the grotesque image remained beyond the control of language and was opposed to reason. Hence, although the caricature's target might defend him or herself by affecting to appreciate its wit or to be flattered by its attention, the childish self was likely to be less confident. A primordial offence is delivered when caricature reveals a likeness in a 'perfect deformity', while it diminishes, shames and hurts us to see ourselves parodically imitated in gesture or speech, just as it does to have our nakedness exposed. Such exposures may be more painful because their humorous alibis make it difficult to object to (or prosecute) them without inviting further ridicule. And, since the greatest satires are created by the best haters, the contempt or anger they bear are menacing – all the more so for being public and unanswerable. 'Such is the vanity of human nature,' Byron observed, 'that men would prefer being defamed to being ridiculed, and would much sooner pardon the first than the second.'[32]

The claims for the satirical image mount higher as we add in another factor – that we commonly read an attack on a part as an attack on the whole. As the critic Elliott has put it, 'an attack by a powerful satirist on a local phenomenon seems to be capable of indefinite extension in the reader's mind into an attack on the whole structure of which that phenomenon is part.' This imaginative process depends on what grammarians call synecdoche, which itself is a foundation of magic:

> In 'mythico-linguistic thought' . . . the part does not merely represent the whole, it *is* the whole; by the magical process of identification the nail paring or the lock of hair from an enemy *is* the enemy, and whoever controls the part has dominion also over the whole. This process is by no means confined to a mythically bound society . . . it is the way of the imagination when it is bound, in its own way, by the spell of the creative artist. The judge who has been ridiculed by a powerful satirist comes to stand for – to be – lawyers in general and even the law itself. What starts as local attack ends by calling the whole institution into question . . . Let the conscious intent of the artist be what it will, the local attack cannot be contained: the ironic language eats its way in implication through the most powerful-seeming structures.[33]

So monarchy is impugned by jokes about a prince, just as a family is impugned by the exposure to public mockery of one of its women's bottoms or breasts.

In view of this associative power, it is no mystery that there were recurrent if rare and vain moves to prosecute prints for personal or seditious libel, or that loyalist propagandists, commissioning and subsidizing them in the 1790s, put so much faith in their power. 'Such prints make stronger impressions on the minds of comon [*sic*] people than many times reading accounts of the subject,' one loyalist wrote (echoing views fully understood in revolutionary Paris also).[34] Gillray's satires on the 'weary knife-grinder' or on the government of 'broad bottoms', Sir Walter Scott wrote, 'did more upon the public mind than a hundred grave arguments could do'.[35] It is equally clear why it was no comfort to Sheridan, for example, who saw himself as a great orator and statesman, to have Gillray represent him as a red-nosed alcoholic harlequin climbing up a greasy pole; or to the prince's Lady Hertford to be repeatedly represented by George Cruikshank as a huge-breasted dominatrix; or to the prince himself to be transformed from the good-looking libertine profligate of Gillray's early prints into that voluptuary lolling under the horrors of digestion, and then into Cruikshank's obese, chop-whiskered 'prince of whales'.

*Ad hominem* caricature was and still is an offence against dignity, and images like these did deeper damage than most textual squibs ever could. 'If satirical prints could dispatch them,' Walpole wrote of the new administration in 1783, 'they would be dead in their cradle.'[36] 'You have been of infinite service in lowering [the opposition] and making them ridiculous,' Lord Bateman wrote to Gillray in 1798: 'nothing mortifies them so much as being ridiculed and exposed in every window. That ridicule is clear to every capacity of the high and low . . . Thank God, they are so lowered that the meanest of the people despise them.' A few months later, he wrote that 'the opposition people . . . are very angry with you for some of your late performances'.[37]

Meanwhile, Gillray's correspondence swelled with proposals from strangers for graphic attacks on their enemies. 'What do you know, you bitch? every one knows I am a whore & a thief & setting that aside who can say black to my eye': so proclaims the speech accompanying a sketch sent *c.*1795 to Gillray as a suggestion for a satire on Lady Cecilia Johnston. To correspondents like these, caricature still functioned as the modern equivalent of the public defamations of early-modern times, or of the waxen effigies of witchcraft.[38]

## CHAPTER EIGHT

# SEEING THE JOKES

## The range and numbers of satires

The satirical and humorous prints of this era are as central to an understanding of literate Londoners' views of their world as their newspapers are. They speak volumes about attitudes and prejudices that were so taken for granted that they were otherwise rarely expressed, or that lay well below the levels of what could be publicly admitted. Yet, despite their importance, very little has been written about their numbers and diversity or how they were sold and received. So, before returning to the manners they illuminate, we should tackle key questions about them in some detail. Who sold the satires, and where and at what prices? Who bought and perused them, and did purchasers include women? How were they collected, and how did they vary across time? The prints' status as sources depends on our answers.

The prints published between 1770 and 1830 are so diverse in subject-matter that one might almost say that all London life is there. Just over a half of them addressed party and parliamentary upheavals, revolution in and war with America and France and, later, the iniquities of the hated Regency. The other half illuminate their engravers' and purchasers' shifting attitudes to sex, scandal, sentiment and fashion or the pleasure of living in London. To note their numerical increase and diversifying styles is to be reminded that their middle- and middling-class as well as elite purchasers multiplied after 1780 as widening constituencies were yoked into consumption and debate. They remind us, too, that this era saw the real heyday of satire, not the early Augustan decades with which satire is normally associated.[1]

The prints had their limitations. They held up their mirrors to Londoners primarily, and then to the minority of Londoners who could afford them. This was because it was in London that they were conceived, engraved, sold and mainly bought. The result was that they had little or nothing to say about matters that weren't the common currency of coffee-house, tavern-club or drawing-room discussion. Until the late 1820s, they hardly registered the impact of what we would now call 'social change'. They were silent on factories, entrepreneurs and mass immiseration in the north, and until the 1810s they said little about plebeian lives or radicals that was not condescending or hostile. They commented on the French wars incessantly, but never on their cost in torn limbs and lost lives. They reflected little upon the thought or literature of the day thanks to the mild philistinism of engravers and purchasers alike. Sterne's *Tristram Shandy* is referred to a dozen times, but Johnson and Boswell more rarely – even though Boswell was one of the most laughed-at men in literary London.[2] The more sophisticated prints, Gillray's especially, might cite Milton and Shakespeare or make classical allusions and all engravers had views on the writings of Tom Paine and Edmund Burke, while even the meanest could parody Fuseli's *Night Mare*. But on Coleridge's German philosophers, for example, they were silent, while on advances in the sciences none commented except, occasionally, Gillray. The Prince of Wales's connoisseur-ship and patronage of the arts was invariably mocked, as were the vast cohorts of the sober, benevolent and pious. Reflecting the subjects of everyday observation and conversation, they remind us that the views of most comfortable Londoners were then as unexamined and as bound by daily preoccupations as they are now.

That said, there were thousands of these prints, far more than we now commonly realize, and it was within the period covered by this book that their numbers exploded. The British Museum catalogues 17,391 satirical or humorous titles published from earliest times to 1832. Only 5,848 of these predate 1771, while 12,543 were published in the sixty years thereafter. Moreover, output accelerated in the early nineteenth century. Just as we talk loosely of 'English' or 'British' satires when we really mean metropolitan ones, so we talk loosely of 'eighteenth-century' satires when nearly two thirds (7,698) of those 12,543 catalogued for 1771–1832 were issued *after* 1800; and the purposes, varieties and quality of those later prints were more diverse than those of their predecessors.[3] Furthermore, the British Museum catalogues understate the total output. The Museum has purchased 1,500 prints since the catalogues were published; but it still lacks copies of some 2,000 of the 9,900 titles in George IV's collection, now in the Library of Congress. Holdings in other American libraries may double that number of British Museum omissions. Many hundreds more are more obscurely preserved, and we'll never know how many have been completely lost to posterity. It is probable that between 1771 and 1832 well over 20,000 satirical and humorous print titles were published altogether.[4]

Prints were not of equal standing; nor did they work to identical effect. Some made jokes merely, drawing on the traditions of jest-books or children's books. Others were 'smiling' rather than savage satires, if satires at all. The British Museum's catalogue distinguished between the 'political' satires that were the printshops' bread-and-butter during the parliamentary season, and the 'personal and social' satires and humorous prints largely produced outside that season. But the division is a loose one and its categories overlap. For what it's worth, 46.5 per cent of all satires for 1771–1830 were catalogued as 'personal and social' (though in the 1780s these included many portrait caricatures in so-called macaroni prints and têtes-à-têtes). Political satires far exceeded the personal and social satires in politically tense years; overall numbers would boom then as well. The feud between George IV and Queen Caroline in 1820 generated the highest production of prints in the whole period: 601 titles are catalogued then, of which 553 are 'political'. The year of the Westminster election, 1784, came next: 315 political prints and 94 personal and social are catalogued then. Yet in twenty-nine of the sixty years 1770–1830 there were more personal and social prints than political, sometimes many times more. These twenty-nine years – the mid-1770s, the mid-1780s, and the early- to mid-1820s – were years of relative political calm.

Prints differed enormously in size, technique, quality and ambition. Modern reproductions obscure this variety. The impact of a small reproduction, even in colour, simply can't match that of the original hand-coloured print on handmade textured paper, with the imprint of the pressed copperplate apparent to sight and touch. Nor can it convey the splendour of finely engraved prints on imperial folio sheets sized 15 by 22 inches (Gillray's *Apotheosis of Hoche* [fig. 129] and *Lady Termagant Flaybum* [fig. 148] and Rowlandson's *Brilliants* [fig. 27] are examples), or sized 12 by 18½ inches (like George Cruikshank's *New Union Club* [fig. 234]). Least of all can it do justice to the several three-sheet satires that William Holland published: these joined up into six-foot lengths. Reproduction further obscures the relationship between prints of these sizes and quality and cheaper prints on paper a half or a quarter of those sizes. It particularly camoflages the prints' technical variety. Most were line engravings executed by gouging burins into copper plates. Mezzotints were favoured by Carington Bowles and other firms from mid-century to the 1780s. Executed by scraping white highlights from roughened copper plates to produce the soft effects of oil painting, these plates wore away so speedily that they weren't used for print satire after that. Aquatints displaced them: these were achieved by allowing acid to penetrate a resin ground to form a network of small dots in the plate, to convey some of the qualities of wash drawings; they became popular in the early nineteenth century. Stipple engraving combined etching, drypoint and engraving, and was executed with a roulette and spiked tools to produce a softer effect akin to drawings and watercolour: these impressions also quickly wore down. Stipple and aquatint were time-consuming techniques much favoured for fine-art prints; but for satire they never fully displaced etching and line engraving. Altogether, although reproductions may convey the contents of images (with loss of detail), handling the originals is indispensable to a sense of them as material artefacts with a tactility as distinctive as that of porcelain, silver or canvas – and to knowing, therefore, why they were valued.

Because no records of print runs survive other than for very occasional prints, it is difficult to be certain about prints' relative success. Some shops (like Holland's) produced expensive titles in short runs for specialized markets; others produced cheaper prints in many copies for wider sales. Weaker or amateur satires might sell poorly. The more successful prints could be published in runs of between five hundred and a couple of thousand sheets before the engraving on the soft copper deteriorated.[5] A print on the repeal of the Stamp Act in 1766 allegedly sold 2,000 copies in four days at a shilling a sheet, with an eventual sale of 16,000.[6] Likewise, the first print to appear on the Prince of Wales's secret marriage to Mrs Fitzherbert sold so well that Fores's printshop was 'crowded with the servants of the *beau monde*, for several days, demanding impressions faster than they could be printed'. Being first with the news enabled Fores to sell it at the high price of two shillings and sixpence, despite its amateurish quality.[7] Gillray's *Political-dreamings!* of 1801 was so sensational that it sold out in days. For prints in high demand like these, re-engraving was common. Hogarth was constantly re-engraved and reissued, and, as the market expanded, lesser images were also. In the 1810s, the printseller Thomas Tegg had old plates by Rowlandson, Woodward and others reworked and their defects camouflaged in heavy watercolouring.

By the later 1820s, the output of comic vignettes and images accelerated further. This reflected demand, but also advances in print technology. By 1800, print's capacities had hardly changed since the Renaissance. The wooden hand-press could produce only 200 sheets an hour, at the cost of very hard labour [fig. 98]. But the Stanhope iron-press at the turn of the century (costing £30 after 1815), the wider application of steam power after 1814, and the Albion Press of 1822 meant that over 4,000 sheets an hour could be printed by 1830. Paper, made by hand in 1800, could now be made mechanically. In the eighteenth century, furthermore, all detailed illustrations had to be engraved or etched on copper and be printed separately from the text. Boxwood engraving helped speed up image reproduction in the new century, thanks to Thomas Bewick's influence. But the real advance came with the invention of lithography: that is, engraving on stone. Since stone never wore out, very big print runs became possible. Lithographic satires first appeared in 1817–18; a dozen years later they filled numbered weekly sheets or quasi-magazines.[8] Thomas McLean's

**Fig. 98** Rowlandson, *Copper Plate Printers at Work* (1785)

printshop in the Haymarket led the way in capitalizing on the new technology. His imprint first appeared in 1821; half a dozen years later he was leading the market, relying on the work of lightly humorous artists like William Heath, Robert Seymour, John 'HB' Doyle, and Henry Alken; the weekly sheets of *McLean's Looking Glass* were the forerunners of bound journals like *Punch*. By the 1840s, steel-engraving further opened the way to the mass circulation of images – in the *Illustrated London News* as well as *Punch*, for example. With the demise of the watercoloured single-sheet satire in the 1830s, visual humour stayed monochrome until the 1960s (when *Playboy*, of all things, pioneered the return of the coloured cartoon).

Meanwhile, most prints, like newspapers, were perused by many more people than their purchasers. Fewer of the earlier prints were pinned to coffee-shop and tavern walls than we nowadays assume. They were too costly for that, though the practice might have spread as prints got cheaper. But printshop windows always had their gawpers; morning West End 'loungers' bought and then perused them in coffee-shops; printshops hired out portfolios for the evening; private portfolios were shown sociably; and people pasted screens with caricatures (as Byron did, with prints of boxers on one side and of actors and actresses on the other). A room is dedicated to framed caricatures in Calke Abbey, Derbyshire; caricatures hang in a dressing-room at Wimpole Hall, Cambridgeshire; a print-plastered room survives in Rokeby Park, Durham; and a room in the Queen's Cottage at Kew was pasted with Hogarths.[9]

Although sometimes the higher classes bought prints on impulse and in person, they usually sent servants out to purchase the latest or had standing orders with printshops for regular deliveries. The Duke of Norfolk had the printseller Holland send him political prints 'as they came out'; his portfolios were 'filled with all the graphic satires and scurrilities, private as well as public, of which the press was then so prolific'.[10] Fox was also a collector, as well he might be. In the 1780s and 1790s he was by far the most caricatured figure in politics, featuring nearly twice as often in the satires as Pitt or George III, and two-and-a-half times as often as the Prince of Wales.[11] He would invite visitors to 'lounge over' his collection, he 'being the principal figure in each': and visitors noticed that he was equable about all but the cruellest depictions of himself as a bloodthirsty sans-culotte and Jacobin. Hearing of Gillray's *Loyal Toast*, Fox went to see it in Hannah Humphrey's window and bought it for one shilling and sixpence, even though the print damaged him. Mrs Humphrey was impressed by his courtesy.[12] Doubtless many people discarded their more casually purchased prints, especially those about passing sensations. Otherwise we owe their survival to the fact that they were preserved in portfolios, pasted into albums, and sometimes finely bound. Horace Walpole's portfolios of Hogarths and Bunburys survive in the Lewis Walpole and the New York Public Libraries, while Sir Robert Peel's collection of 3,300 political caricatures, broadsides and engraved portraits is in the Pierpont Morgan Library. The Cambridge University Library holds two sets of beautifully bound volumes of satires and ephemera on the Queen Caroline case in 1820–1 (collected respectively by Charles Fox's nephew, Lord Holland, and by one Minto Wilson). Twenty folio volumes (largely of Fores's prints) are in the De Rothschild collection at Ascott, Buckinghamshire.[13]

Print consumers were neither all of the high or political elites, nor all male, however. Women doubtless kept their distance from the harsher and more scurrilous satires. But women ran shops at the top of the trade (Mary Darly and Hannah Humphrey), and female customers found plenty of prints to amuse them. John Wilkes regularly posted satires to his daughter in Paris in 1786–9. They included 'two most extraordinary prints,' as he wrote to her in 1788 'for which the prince's solicitor is prosecuting Fores'. A year later he sent her 'with the prints . . . the most daring pamphlet ever published in this country': and since Wilkes here took it for granted that his daughter was tough-minded enough to cope with Paine's *Rights of Man*, we may assume that she was unlikely to have been troubled by visual scurrilities.[14] The Lennox sisters were regular print purchasers,[15] as was the wealthy Mrs Judith Baker of Elemore Hall in County Durham. Her husband had been a prominent county Tory whose mining businesses and estate she continued to run after his death, and she was related to Annabella Milbanke, briefly Byron's wife, who was born at Elemore in 1792. One hundred and seventy-one prints published between 1774 and 1810 survive from her personal collection, pasted into a portfolio bound in marbled boards with leather trimmings. Most seem to have been bought on her seasonal visits to London; some were sent by her sisters to communicate metropolitan gossip. They included prints on fashion or on female frivolities, prints about the prince's illicit marriage and affairs, and the Gillrays that calumniated Lady Worsley and the Countess of Strathmore, whose marital sagas she followed avidly (the countess was her neighbour). She pasted Gillray's *Sir Richard Worse-than-sly, Exposing his Wifes* [sic] *Bottom – O Fye!* into her portfolio [fig. 1].[16] The outrageous breasts and semi-nudity of fashion satires in the 1790s didn't trouble her either – nor other women, it seems. Thomas Bewick's aunt's house in Yorkshire *c*.1800 was covered 'from the ceiling to the walls' with engravings, including caricatures 'of every grade and allusion', some of them salacious. The most avid female collector we can now identify was Sarah Sophia Banks. Her collection of printed ephemera came to the British Museum after her death in 1818: it included 1,044 fashion and political satires, some scurrilous. She would get Gillray to mark up on her copies of his plates the names of the protagonists.[17] Women were also always included in depictions of those perusing printshop windows, and they feature prominently in Newton's watercolour of Holland's Oxford Street showroom *c*.1794 [fig. 99]. A Rowlandson pen and watercolour drawing depicts a caricatured family group perusing *The Caricature Port Folio*, men, women, young, and old equally amused.[18] Well into the new century, with many daughters now taught by peripatetic drawing masters, women designed their own satires for professional engraving. They provided good opportunities to score points off men's absurdities. 'Queer my sconce,' says the ridiculous homuncule of the pretty girl in Maria

**Fig. 99** Newton, *Holland's Caricature Exhibition* (ink and watercolour, *c*.1794)

Carolina Temple's *Pupils of Nature* (Fores, 1798), 'but that's a d—d fine woman, now if she has got any shiners [money], I've a great mind to noose: and tip her the go by when I'm tired of her' [fig. 100].

The biggest collection to survive is George IV's. For years, as Prince of Wales and regent, he kept standing orders at printshops in order to monitor how little he was loved. He bought 121 prints from Humphrey's shop in 1806–7, for example. Robert Cruikshank's son, Percy, recalled how proofs of the next day's print would be taken by command to Carlton House at night, as like as not to induce indigestion at the royal breakfast table next morning. His collection could easily have joined other lost collections. In a fit of witless vandalism in 1913, George V, his queen and his secretary one evening sat in a parlour at Windsor and systematically burned the contents of thirty-seven

**Fig. 100** Temple, *Pupils of Nature* (Fores, 1798)

boxes of George IV's love letters, including 'masses' to and from Mrs Fitzherbert, on the grounds that George was 'the meanest and vilest of reprobates'. The royal collection of satires might have gone the same way had it not seemed safely obscure. In the event, 9,900 of them were sold in 1921 to the Library of Congress to help pay for George V's stamp collection.[19]

Did the facts that the overwhelming majority of satires were engraved in and were about London limit their countrywide or international appeal and circulation? There are grounds for thinking so. Jonathan Swift had noted long before that Alexander Pope's barbs in *The Dunciad* were obscure to distant readers: 'twenty miles from London no body understands hints, initial letters, or town-facts and passages; and in a few years not even those who live in London.'[20] Moreover, despite a few provincial publishers and satirists and some pirating of London prints, especially in Dublin, the provincial town's sociability was too intimate for local satire to be accommodated comfortably. So satirical prints (as against art or portrait engravings) were virtually absent from Edinburgh inventories in the later eighteenth century, and from provincial English inventories before then.[21] Even Hogarth might have suffered from this constraint. During Hogarth's lifetime, the abbé Le Blanc thought that 'the whole nation has been infected' with Hogarth's prints; he had not seen 'a house of note' without them. Yet houses of little note might have been another matter. By the mid-nineteenth century, Hogarths were said to be 'unknown in the cottages and villages of the country'.[22]

These inhibitions were offset, however, by unremitting provincial curiosity about the metropolitan manners and fashions that so many prints illuminated. 'Is there a creature in the whole country but ourselves, that does not take a trip to town now and then, to rub off the rust a little?' Mrs Hardcastle complains in *She Stoops to Conquer*. 'Ay,' her husband replies, 'and bring back vanity and affectation to last them the whole year . . . In my time, the follies of the town crept slowly among us, but now they travel faster than a stage-coach.' Intense political partisanship in the 1780s followed by revolution and war also fuelled the provincial hunger for commentary. So, along with other fripperies, country gentlemen took prints home with them at the end of the season, or left orders with printshops to have the latest posted on, while visitors would take back the *têtes-à-têtes* provoked by illicit liaisons in high society, along with the fashion and social satires that were less esoteric than political sheets.[23] In 1802, for example, the Piccadilly printseller Fores brought a case at King's Bench against Thomas Johnes, MP for Cardiganshire, on the grounds that he had not paid the £137. 10s due to Fores for a collection of satires ordered and delivered a couple of years before. As the prosecuting counsel (Erskine) put it, Johnes had ordered 'a complete collection of caricature prints . . . to amuse his idle hours, and give him an opportunity of being acquainted, though at a distance, with those who are in this great town called by the names of giggs, odd fish, and quizzes'. Erskine added that 'it was natural to suppose that a gentleman residing in a remote part of the country should wish to be acquainted with the fools that inhabit the metropolis'.[24] In 1821, similarly, the journalist John Hunt urged William Hone and George Cruikshank to take advantage of the 'golden opportunity' offered by the king's divorce case: 'there will perhaps be 50 or 60,000 people in town from the country, all wanting something to carry back with them of the droll kind'.[25] The country-house habit of perusing portfolios continued well into the nineteenth century:

> Shy girls and silent young men generally get on pretty well by means of such a medium – in truth, grave and reverend seignors and ancient tabbies . . . grow quite amiable, as well as cheerful, as the more equivocal prints were turned over. It was the custom before my day, and in my youth, to get all the novelties of this kind from London as regularly as the fashionable novel or the last new ballad; and notwithstanding that they were coarsely drawn and still more coarsely coloured, it is impossible to exaggerate the amusement they afforded – especially if at the expense of any particular friend.[26]

There was also a strong continental demand for English satires. Censorship meant that the continent could produce nothing like them (until the burst of French pornographic and scatological satire during the Revolution).[27] When the German pastor Wendeborn arrived in London in 1770, he had been puzzled both by the number of printshops and by the fact that, although people looked in their windows, few went in to buy. A printseller explained that this was because his chief markets lay abroad. He 'sold great quantities of goods to the country . . . to Scotland, Ireland, the East and West Indies, to America, and other parts of the world, disposing on an average, weekly, five hundred pounds worth'. Wendeborn noted that 'caricature prints go likewise in great quantities over to Germany, and from thence to the adjacent countries'. He thought this odd, since 'very few of those who pay dearly for them, know anything of the characters and transactions' upon which the satires commented: yet 'they laugh at them, and become merry' even though 'the wit and satire of such prints . . . are entirely lost on them'. Sayer and Bennett advertised their satires to 'merchants for exportation', while William Holland advertised that his shilling admission charge bought access to the largest exhibition of humorous prints in Europe. Holland had a regular purchaser in Count Starhemberg, the Austrian envoy who arrived in London in 1792; Starhemberg also bought up all available Gillrays.[28] The German taste for Gillray is attested in the elaborate commentaries on his work in the Weimar journal *London und Paris* between 1798 and 1806.[29] Spain's greatest private print collector, Sebastián Martínez of Cadiz, collected Hogarth and probably Gillray and others as well. It was through friendship with Martínez that Goya was exposed to the English tradition; both Hogarth and Gillray influenced his *Los Caprichos*. Later in Spain, English caricatures against Napoleon were widely copied.[30] In 1802 Gillray's satires were being pasted up in the Calais passport office to taunt English travellers with their mockeries of British ministers.[31] After the Peace of Amiens, Fores announced that he was 'caricaturist to the first consul', Napoleon. Gillray's comment on George III and Napoleon, *King of Brobdingnag & Gulliver*, was pirated in German, Spanish and Italian versions, and at critical wartime junctures there was a fair amount of cross-fertilization between continental and English satirists, not all of it one way.[32] Expatriates also hungered for the London prints. 'I thank you for the print,' Horace Walpole's friend Mann wrote in 1757: '. . . I should be much obliged to you if you would now and then make up a bundle of these sorts of papers or anything new, and bid my brother James send it to me by sea.'[33] In his satirical verse play *Oedipus Tyrannus, or Swellfoot the Tyrant*, written in Italy, Shelley could only have drawn his caricatured representations of the regent and his ministers and mistresses from satires collected in the houses of the English in Leghorn.

## The elite printshops

No detailed records on print buyers survive, but their diversity is indicated in the range in printshop locations and specialisms. Until the 1780s, the print and book trades had been concentrated in or near St Paul's Churchyard and the eastern end of Fleet Street. Boydell's in the City was at the top of the fine-art print trade even before he opened his Shakespeare Gallery (though humour and satire were beneath his interests). The humorous printshops in the 1770s were led by the Bowles family, Sayer and Bennet, and Matthew Darly in the Strand and Mary Darly (his wife) in Leicester Fields, where she sold prints on her own account before joining her husband. All these produced humorous mezzotint posture-prints or drolls rather than satires overtly (they seldom touched politics).[34] In the lower reaches, businesses were hand to mouth. No eighteenth-century printshop (and, later, only Humphrey's, it seems) sold prints exclusively. Sayer and Bennet advertised more maps, portraits, topographical, sporting, military and genre prints than satires, and most sold books, pamphlets and stationery also (Fores included). Many were small family concerns (the family above the shop), anchored in what market niches they could find. Women, many of them widows, ran several. For years, such shops continued to sell only occasional satires, while jobbing engravers and hand-presses remained at work in cramped backrooms, and lesser imprints came and went.

In the 1780s and 1790s, however, the print business was expanding, fed both by the growth in purchasing power and by mounting political excitements. The print and book trades were jointly revitalized, and the ambition and range of graphic satire increased correspondingly. Caricature-drawing was by now a fashionable practice. In Mary Darly's *A Book of Caricaturas on 59 Copper Plates, with the Principles of Designing in that Droll and Pleasing Manner* (1779), she advertised her services to amateur 'gentlemen and ladies' anxious to have their designs engraved on copper for 'their own private amusement' or for publication (if the latter, she promised that the originators would be shown 'due honor').[35] In ensuing decades many small as well as large printshops exploited amateurs' urge to have their witty ideas engraved. In 1783, Horace Walpole learned from 'the woman who keeps the print-shop in Bruton Street' that 'she has engraved all the drawings that are sent her, and that she gets by them, one with another, ten pounds apiece'. One of Walpole's scrapbooks is full of designs by his well-born friends, women included. 'NB,' a Fores print announces in 1786, 'Gentlemen's designs executed without any expence [*sic*].' Gillray fed off dozens of designs sent to him by amateurs.[36]

This revitalization enticed some of the most enterprising printshops and booksellers away from the City into the aristocratic heartlands and nearer to court and Parliament. The older firms continued to trade from

St Paul's, eastern Fleet Street, and the Strand, and by the 1810s several new shops were tapping middle- and middling-class pockets in the City. But the centre of London's high cultural and material consumption had already shifted westwards, and printshop proprietors like Fores, Humphrey, Holland and Ackermann followed it cannily. Fores opened in 3 Piccadilly in January 1784, and quickly dominated the trade with just over 200 known print titles for the 1780s. He profited enough to move to 50 Piccadilly (next door to Devonshire House) in 1795 and to run a branch at 312 Oxford Street; and although in 1806 *London und Paris* reported that he struggled in vain 'to conjure up works which would stand any kind of comparison with those of Gillray', he retained his lead into the 1820s. (In fact the firm flourished into the twentieth century.) William Holland in 1786 also moved upmarket, from Drury Lane to 50 Oxford Street, a couple of blocks from the Pantheon, a good place to snare fashionable custom. In 1797 Hannah Humphrey repositioned herself by moving from New Bond Street to 27 St James's Street, with Gillray in tow. She couldn't have been better placed to pull in the courtiers, aristocrats and gentry passing by outside, since Brooks's club stood opposite and Boodle's and White's clubs were just up the street. Even when her nephew George took over the business in 1818, it retained its elegant shopfront [fig. 101]. James Bretherton sold prints in New Bond Street in the 1780s. Ackermann opened his Repository of Arts

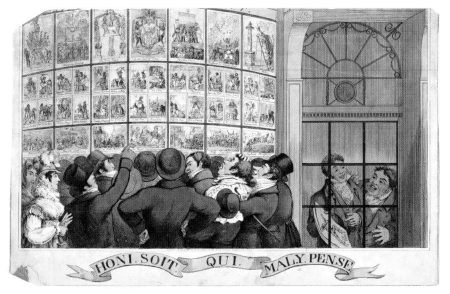

**Fig. 101** Lane, *Honi Soit qui Mal y Pense* (G. Humphrey, 1821)

at 96 Strand in 1795 before he opened a larger shop at no. 101 two years later because he found the first one 'too confined, from a continued encouragement by the nobility, the gentry, and the public in general for several years'.[37]

Feeding off the affluent purchasers of the high political world, these shops' products grew in sophistication. By the turn of the century, visitors noted the differences between the City and the West End prints, the former catering to the 'cits', the latter to the 'court'.[38] Ackermann's grew into a splendidly overfurnished emporium, producing publicity images of its interiors, windows and gaslighting to advertise its profitability and standing.[39] Competition was high and self-advertisement innovative. Holland opened an exhibition of satires at his 'Museum of genius' in 1788, charging a shilling admission in pointed parody of the Royal Academy's identical charge 'to prevent the room being filled with improper persons'. His market aspirations were conveyed in the elegant if caricatured visitors depicted in Richard Newton's watercolour of *Holland's Caricature Exhibition* (*c*.1794), itself a parody of a watercolour by Francis Wheatley of the *Interior of the Shakespeare Gallery, Pall Mall* (1790) [fig. 99]. Fores ran a rival exhibition for the same entrance fee between 1789 and 1794, 'the whole forming an entire caricature history, political and domestic, of past and present times'. Knowing that taste among the higher classes was to a degree negotiable, Fores added to the exhibitions the cast head and hand of Count Struenzee, lately executed by the King of Denmark, along with 'a correct model of the guillotine, 6 feet high'. In 1794 his prints advertised the lending-out of print portfolios for the evening, a practice widely adopted thereafter.[40]

That the market's upper reaches were dominated by the London elites and prospering professional and mercantile people is also indicated by the peaking of print production during the parliamentary season, while pointers to the standing of their real or hoped-for customers litter their advertisements.[41] Their clientele is further indicated by the high cost of many if not all prints, not to mention their bindings. To measure the prices that follow, recall that a prosperous tradesman's family could live very comfortably off £300 a year, and that an everyday coat cost five shillings (£0.25), a woman's plain gown only a shilling or so more. In the 1770s, a large Sayer and Bennet print could cost five shillings, while an unbound set of twelve of Austin's prints, *Nature Display'd Both Serious and Comic*, was sold at a guinea (i.e. £1 1s. 0d, or 21 shillings or £1.05 today). Mary Darly in

1776 sold bound volumes of *Darly's Comic-prints of Characters Caricatures Macaronies &c* at four guineas. Holland sold a long print, Nixon's *A Country Dance*, for a guinea, Gillray's elaborate *Lady Termagant Flaybum* (1786) [fig. 149] for 7s. 6d, Newton's larger prints for four shillings (one for half a guinea); and for a three-sheet satire which joined up into a composition six feet long he charged 13s. 6d. In 1789, his prints announced: 'Caricature collectors may now be supplied with the greatest variety in London of political and other humorous prints, bound in volumes and ornamented with an engraved title and a characteristic vignette: one hundred prints in a volume, five guineas plain or seven guineas coloured.'[42] In 1799, £210 was paid to J. Sayers for 'a collection of Hogarth's works, consisting of 407 prints in the 1st and 2d state'; nine and a half guineas were added to pay for their portfolios and gilded lettering.[43] In 1816, Hone sold Cruikshank's *The Royal Shambles* [fig. 261] at four shillings. Prices like these obviously excluded most tradesmen or shopkeepers from the market. That said, there were many cheaper prints than these, and the average price fell in the new century as middling-class demand expanded. Moreover, satires were far cheaper than fine-art engravings. For these last, prices of a guinea or more were usual if the print was fresh-minted, as against the five shillings for the larger Gillrays and the shilling or so for lesser prints.[44] Mockery and humour cost less than sentiment or sublimity.

## The rise of Thomas Tegg

Impressed by these prices or by the complex parliamentary references in some political prints, historians have implied that visual satires were closed to less educated viewers.[45] But the truth of this depends both on the kinds of print and on the period one refers to. Prices obviously excluded plebeian buyers, but not necessarily tradesmen or craftsmen. In his teens in the 1790s, William Hone, then a clerk, bought current satires as well as old master prints and Lutheran woodcuts, the combing of second-hand bookshops a common pursuit for one of his class.[46] Hogarth had aimed at just such people in the 1740s when he sold the twelve plates of *Industry and Idleness* at a shilling each, so that, as he wrote, 'the purchase of them became within the reach of those for whom they were chiefly intended'. Sayers's or Carington Bowles's drolls, uncoloured, were still aiming at such people in the 1770s, as were prints sold by Laurie and Whittle (Sayers's successors) and by Fores in the 1790s and 1800s. For this market, printshops generally avoided the humour of fart, bum, vomit or genital symbol, and politically radical postures likewise. Instead, for the most part they peddled innocent jokes about metropolitan sensations, domestic comedies and the humbler leisure venues. Isaac Cruikshank's *Paddy Whack' s First Ride in a Sedan* (for Laurie and Whittle, 1800) typically lampoons the Irish newcomer to London whom the sedan-chairmen trick by cutting out the chair's base and making him walk while inside the box: 'Arrah! My dear Honey,' he cries, '– to be sure I'd rather walk, if it wasn't for the fashion of the thing.' G. M. Woodward was the master of this form of genial comedy. He hatched inspired puns like his *Union between England and Ireland* (1801) [fig. 102], or mirrored the foibles of comfortable tradesmen and their families in vignette-sheets with indicative titles like *Ourselves*, or joked at marriage in prints like his *Symptoms of Crim. Con..!!* (1796), in one vignette of which the anxious husband is moved to

**Fig. 102** Woodward, *Union between England and Ireland* (1801)

intervene when his visitor a little too lasciviously embraces his too compliant wife: 'Come come this is carrying the joke a little too far,' he expostulates, as the lover's leg lifts in a symbol of rising desire that remains intelligible across centuries [fig. 103].

By the 1810s, however, the expanding middling market combined with publishers' enterprise quite radically to shift the ways in which graphic satire was sold. With radicalism itself resurgent, the virulence of the satirical attack on the regent and his repressive ministers also intensified. Behind this process lay the rise of a group of new City printshops that sought both to capitalize on the angry political climate and to aim more explicitly downmarket. Fores, Holland, Humphrey and Ackermann continued to enjoy fashionable standing, to be sure, but Ackermann had given up caricature some years before (it had never been a main part of his business), while Holland died in 1816 and Hannah Humphrey's output diminished

**Fig. 103** Woodward, *Symptoms of Crim Con !!* [detail] (Fores, 1796)

with Gillray's madness and then death in 1815. Fores and Humphrey still produced substantial numbers of sheets; but their supremacy was now undercut by a transformative force that knocked their comfortable West End assumptions sideways. It arrived in the person of Thomas Tegg.

Tegg was born in 1776, the son of a Wimbledon grocer. Orphaned in his ninth year, he was brought up by a landlady in Scotland, there enduring one of those unimaginably harsh childhoods that peppered the annals of craftsmen and tradesmen in this era, and that left many who survived them determined to climb as far distant from them as possible. Apprenticed to a tyrannical bookseller in Dalkeith, he absconded with ten shillings, a crooked halfpenny, and Benjamin Franklin's essays in his pocket, and worked his way south over several years, reaching London in 1796. There, inspired by Franklin's 'The Way to Wealth', he resolved 'to visit a place of worship every Sabbath-day . . . to read no loose or infidel books . . . to frequent no public-houses . . . [to] form no friendships till I knew the parties well, and . . . not [to] go to any theatre till my reason fortified me against my passions'. In later life he boasted that everything he gained was 'by industry, patience and privation'; his ruling maxim was that 'method is the soul of business'. For eight years he worked in other men's bookshops or in shaky partnerships. Then he opened his own cheap book and printshop at 111 Cheapside in 1804, and proceeded to build his fortune on it.[47]

Tegg capitalized on the revolution in the later eighteenth-century book trades. By 1780 a quarter of all English households had income enough to buy books; book titles escalated from the annual 21,000 titles published in the 1710s to the 56,000 of the 1790s, while book prices fell by a half in the 1780s and by three-quarters at the turn of the century; and editions of the classics tripled and light reading material increased spectacularly – a boom that owed much to a Lords' decision in 1774 that prohibited publishers from claiming legal support for their insistence on perpetual copyright. Importantly, print-selling was borne along by the same tide. 'There are now, I believe, as many booksellers as there are butchers & and as many printshops as of any trade,' William Blake wrote in 1800: 'We remember when a print shop was a rare bird in London.'[48]

Tegg's forerunners in cheap bookselling were John Bell and James Lackington, the last of whom was advertising himself by 1792 as the 'cheapest bookseller in the world' and claiming to be selling over a hundred thousand volumes annually thanks to his remaindering policy and catalogues. This was the example Tegg followed a dozen years later. Profiting from a sixpenny *Life of Nelson* (selling 5,000 copies, he said), Tegg began to turn out scores of cookery and conjuring books and the like, along with cheap out-of-copyright editions, reprints or abridgements, helped by his buying up and rebinding of booksellers' or printers' bankrupt stock. He disposed of these volumes at evening auctions which became one of the sights of London – 'puns, bon mots, and repartees [flying] about like crackers'. He had a short way with the classics. If they contained too many pages for the size he was prepared to bind and the price he wished to charge, the last pages might be omitted. Thomas Hood satirized Tegg's philistinism in his 'Tylney Hall', while Wordsworth denounced him as a wretch who would 'murder the authors for the sake of getting sooner at his prey'. But his butchery made money. In the early 1820s, he reported, 'I took a country house at Norwood, and set up my carriage . . . I had a beautiful garden, though . . . scarcely knowing a rose from a rhodedendron.' Eventually he became the richest bookseller and most prolific publisher in England to date, having published or republished 4,000 titles by 1840, and leaving nearly £90,000 when he died six years later. The 'ingenious and opulent Mr Tegg of Cheapside', Thackeray later called him. 'He desired wealth and gained it by honourable labour,' the newspaper summarizing his autobiography said of him. Doubtless his rivals would have put it more harshly.

From 1806 onwards Tegg set about transforming the print trade just as he had the book trade, by cutting costs and prices. He bought up the plates of defunct firms, had worn Rowlandsons, Woodwards and Isaac Cruikshanks re-engraved and reprinted on cheap paper, and sold them for sixpence plain or for a shilling brashly watercoloured, thus achieving as near mass production as the hand-pressing and colouring of copperplates permitted. He also sold his prints ready-bound in *Tegg's Caricature Magazine*, aiming at tradesmen and lesser professionals, even if his advertising pretended otherwise.[49] He employed Rowlandson as his chief artist between 1809 and 1812 and George Cruikshank shortly thereafter. All this quickly put him at the head of the trade, quantitatively speaking. Whereas in 1811–19 Fores published some 165 catalogued prints and Humphrey 110, Tegg beat both together with 368. He got Rowlandson to attack the Duke of York in 1809 and Cruikshank to attack the regent and Napoleon, but generally avoided parliamentary commentary. Most of his output continued the tradition of genial commentaries on the quiddities of his self-improving customers, the mishaps of London living, or the battle of the sexes. Charles Williams's *Bobbin about to the Fiddle – A Familly Rehersal* [sic] *of Quadrille*

*Dancing, or Polishing for a Trip to Margate* (1817) is one of the better examples of his output [fig. 104]. In a parlour whose gilded mirrors and portrait display the *nouveau riche* family's pretensions, father, mother, grown-up daughters and children practise their dancing with their French dancing master before they go to Margate (the favoured resort of the City's self-made 'cits'). 'I say, Mounseer Caper!' the father declares: 'Don't I come it prime? Ecod, I shall cut a figor!!' 'Law, Pa,' cries a daughter, 'that's just as when you was drilling for the Whitechaple Volunteers – only look how Ma and I & sister Clementina does it!!'[50]

If Tegg swum with the tide of opportunity unleashed by a mounting thirst for commentary in that fast-radicalizing and regent-hating decade, his example was followed by the opening of several new City printshops, often by more radical or radically inclined booksellers who acknowledged the image's propagandist power in an increasingly disaffected middling market. They included John Johnson, John Fairburn, William Hone, Thomas Dolby, J. Sidebotham, John Marshall, William Benbow and

**Fig. 104** Williams, *Bobbin about to the Fiddle – A Familly Rehersal of Quadrille Dancing, or Polishing for a Trip to Margate* (Tegg, 1817)

J. L. Marks. By radicalizing and cheapening prints, these 'low' firms were to redirect the thrust of graphic satire in the regency years. Until the king's bribes closed it down in 1821, a truly radical and popular satire was now on offer, in ways the West End shops of the 1790s hadn't anticipated. But we shall come back to this in chapter 16. We should now return to the satires of the 1780s and 1790s, and think harder, finally, about how the elites received them.

## The connoisseur collector

Some time towards the end of the 1780s, in the library of his gothic extravaganza at Strawberry Hill in Surrey, Horace Walpole – prime minister's son, bachelor, gossip, aesthete and connoisseur (his boyhood spent under the looming canvases of the family's great art collection at Houghton) – put his collection of caricatures and satirical prints into good order. He did this now and then. 'I pass my time in clipping and pasting prints,' he wrote in 1769; and in 1776, 'I am pasting Henry Bunbury's prints into a volume.'[51] On this occasion, he carefully stored his Hogarths in boxes (together with two of Hogarth's cherished copper plates), and pasted 200 further Bunbury and other satires into large portfolios, snobbishly believing Bunbury, as we may not, to be 'the new Hogarth' (for Bunbury was a gentleman, related by marriage to the Fox and Holland clan). He then selected 'from a vast number' 139 of the 'best prints' of other engravers. The rest he either left loose, sold or threw away.[52] Naturally most of those he selected on this occasion were from the 1780s. They included satires on the American war and peace; a large group which he labelled 'on the changes of administration in 1782, 1783, and 1784, on the coalition between Mr Fox and Lord North, on Mr Fox's East India Bill in 1783, and on the Westminster election in 1784'; a dozen or so caricatures of fashionable ladies and town characters; and some three dozen political and gossip prints dated between 1785 and 1789. Mixed into them was a handful of fashion satires, a few on the 1760s and 1770s, and, added later, a print from 1791. On most prints, Walpole identified the protagonists in his neat, taut handwriting. On a handful he wrote brief explanations. His selection was fairly representative of the more sophisticated reaches of the print repertoire, and it throws light on what a man of taste thought about them.

Walpole of course valued his fine art prints infinitely more than his satires, but it is obvious that he cared for these rude things too. Why he did so is a puzzle. Like most of his contemporaries, he believed that the history of wit over his lifetime had been a history of improvement, but he would have found scant evidence of that in these prints, and he was not uncritical of them. 'Parties vent themselves in deluges of satiric prints,' he wrote of the satires on the 1784 Westminster election, 'though with no more wit than there is in a case-knife.'[53] A few of those he kept were strongly designed: *The Horse America, Throwing his Master* (George III) of 1779, for example, still much admired by Americans, since it flatters them [fig. 105].[54] But most in his selection were execrable by comparison with those published a decade or two later. Caring little about proportion or perspective, they were ill composed and cramped in line and design. Portraits could be simple grotesques, figures wooden and uncomical, emblems and symbols laboured or infantile, and surroundings drawn with the literalness of the schoolroom. James Sayers's famous attack on Fox's India Bill, *Carlo Khan's Triumphal Entry into Leadenhall Street*, for example, shows Fox as an Indian potentate riding an elephant which has Lord North's face: the elephant-face is witlessly designed, the elephant's trunk the merest apology for a trunk, and the whole is over-engraved. Early Rowlandsons in the selection also descend from the accomplished (on the 1784 Westminster election) to the terrible – rushed, ill composed, finickily drawn, and nervously overworked, without the fluent line of his maturity. Three early Gillrays, dated 1783, are

THE HORSE AMERICA, *throwing his Master*.

**Fig. 105** Anon., *The Horse America, Throwing his Master* (White, 1779)

cramped little political satires which give no indication of the flowering to come. Nearly all Walpole's Gillrays employ the punning emblems of earlier generations, with Lord North represented as an ill-drawn badger (more like a bear) whose head is inscribed with compass lines of which one is helpfully labelled 'north'; and with Fox, of course, as a fox.[55] So the bulk of Walpole's prints fell far short of the bravura of the more carefully composed, engraved, and watercoloured satires that were to fill the printshops in and after the 1790s.

Walpole's selection did filter out a lot of material that was gratuitously crude or libellous. Lady Worsley's bottom found no place in it, for instance, nor did Gillray's lubricious libels on Lady Strathmore (though that doesn't mean that Walpole didn't know or at some point own them).[56] Even so, the biggest surprise lies in the scatological and sexual improprieties of some of the prints he kept. A Gillray satire on North and Fox has the fox defecating copiously outside the badger's lair. An earlier Gillray has Shelburne as a kettle with a phallic spout.[57] Sayers shows the speaker of the Commons as Gulliver urinating on a fleet of ships.[58] In *The General P—s, or Peace* (1783) figures representing England, Holland, America, Spain and France piss amicably into a brimming pot to celebrate the Peace of Paris with the subtext 'Come all who love friendship, and wonder and see, / The belligerent powers, like good neighbours agree, / A little time past Sirs, who would have thought this, / That they'd so soon come to a general P—s?' [fig. 106].[59] Elsewhere a Dutchman urinates on a 'British memorial',[60] while in a Gillray of 1788, Prince William, returning from Jamaica, lies in a hammock caressing his bare-breasted black paramour as she reclines between his legs: Walpole conscientiously inscribes it, 'Prince William and his squaw'.[61] In the anonymous *Signor Piozzi ravishing Mrs Thrale*, Dr Johnson looks on disapprovingly ('she has quitted literature for a fiddlestick') as Piozzi woos her with his violin, and she responds: 'Your music has ravished me, and your instrument is large and delightful.'

Now, these and like prints were preserved by a celibate aesthete who kept a determined distance from his own and others' lower bodily parts. They were selected by a gentleman connoisseur, one of nature's snobs, whose friends were high-born and who disdained the vulgar; by a man, moreover, who took a very high view of art, believing that 'pictures cannot adapt themselves to the meanest capacities, as unhappily the tongue can'.[62] What place could prints like these possibly occupy in Walpole's aesthetic pantheon? Yet they obviously had a place. One way of explaining this is to

**Fig. 106** Anon., *The General P—s, or Peace* (Barrow, 1783)

note that they provided mementos of political or national sensations, along with handy likenesses of politicians who would be otherwise unknown. Another is that Walpole inhabited a world in which the privileged felt safe enough to play with dangerous ambivalences, certain, until the revolutionary 1790s at least, that the established order wouldn't snap. So what we today might read as 'subversive' in the prints (satires on clerical gluttony or princely debauchery, for example) could then be read as playful. Walpole also knew the value of satire which elsewhere would be suppressed. Mocking pretension, vice and the corruption of principle, visual satires were 'of great utility' to the English, a German visitor in 1802 noted. Through them political factions communicated the grounds of their opposition, even as they acted as 'conductors, by preventing a conflagration' of political passion. They were 'salutary mementos to the nobility that their motions are watched'.[63] Walpole would have understood this argument.

Beyond this, the prints were constituents of Walpole's sociability. He knew personally or by repute several amateurs who designed prints, and in letters he sent or referred to prints to illustrate his own news and gossip. Thus the much-lampooned Lady Archer, over-fond of cosmetics, appears twice in his selection, as she often does in his letters. His collection also commemorated great sensations like the Prince of Wales's secret marriage to Mrs Fitzherbert: 'they tell me the passengers in the streets, of all ranks, talk about it.'[64] Or they referred to this or that 'buzz of the day', as he put it. Thus, when the adventures of the beautiful Miss Gunning filled the scandal sheets, they filled Walpole's letters too. He clucked in disapproval at a family which 'dragged themselves through all the kennels of the newspapers', but there is no mistaking his delight as the Gunning adventuress pestered and blackmailed her way into the favours of aristocrats: 'one has heard of nothing else for these seven months; and it requires some ingenuity to keep up the attention of such a capital as London for above half a year together.' When she was accused of forging love letters from the Marquis of Blandford (scion of Blenheim) in order to publicize them and thus make the Marquis of Lorne jealous enough to propose to her, Gillray produced the first of many satires on the scandal. It wasn't a very finished one, or a polite one. *The Siege of Blenheim – or the New System of GUNNING, Discover'd* (1791) shows Lord Blandford's bared buttocks protruding from a window of Blenheim Palace the better to project a fusillade of turds at Miss Gunning below. She receives the aristocratic volley while sitting indecorously astride an unambiguously phallic cannon, legs cocked in the air; and from the cannon she fires back a fusillade of her forged letters [fig. 107]. Walpole was unsqueamish about this cheerful image even as he measured its triteness. It was, he wrote, 'a Grub Street print not void of humour' – Gillray, its artist, beneath the dignity of naming. All the same, he kept it.[65]

The widest frame in which to locate Walpole's attitude to these indecorous images relates to the distances that were understood to exist between the public and the private, the polite and the 'manly'. Like most

**Fig. 107** Gillray, *The Siege of* BLENHEIM – *or* – *the New System of* GUNNING, *Discover'd* (H. Humphrey, 1791)

of his male contemporaries, Walpole saw no inconsistency in altering his postures as company or location permitted. Just as men who affected the greatest refinement in female company or in the salon were allowed among other men to drink themselves silly or tell rude jokes in the tavern, so even aesthetes like Walpole knew that the high-minded theories that ruled public art could be bent a little in private.

On the face of it, artistic theory was awesome and restricting. Arbiters of taste from Shaftesbury on to Reynolds taught that public, academic, or 'fine' art must unify taste, virtue and moral tone in dignified composition. It should, as Shaftesbury put it, celebrate 'order, harmony and proportion' – ideals that were 'naturally improving to the temper, advantageous to social affection, and highly assistant to virtue'. These ideals were best expressed in classical subjects, historical narratives or allegories of civic or national virtue: the supreme art being allegorized history painting. Art which merely described the particular – landscapes or portraits – must be held in lower esteem (although their capacity to represent the sublime was valued). The lowest form was humorous art, if it could be deemed art at all. Addressing low subjects, it spoke for a low Dutch taste, the taste of Dutch genre painting. Merchants put it on their walls, as the money-grubbing merchant did in Hogarth's *Marriage à la Mode*. Engravings were merely artisanal, imitative and mechanical products, and so were excluded from Royal Academy exhibitions.

In private, however, these austere values were relaxed. As John Barrell puts it, once they were in their libraries or studies, and with women excluded except by invitation, gentlemen could lay aside their aesthetic obligations as easily as they laid aside their wigs and formal clothing. Out would come their portfolios, in which they might then appreciate the comical, the frolicsome, the indecent. 'The greatest men . . . will not scruple adorning their private closets with nudities,' wrote Cleland, author of *Fanny Hill*, 'though, in compliance with vulgar prejudice, they may not think them decent decorations of the staircase, or saloon.'[66]

In such settings, print satires would be forgiven their vulgarity, especially if they could seem to serve satire's most legitimate function of correcting vice and folly. Most prints in Walpole's collection bore some such didactic point, however thinly. On the other hand, even that alibi was by now pretty elastic. By Walpole's later years, the constraining norms of Augustan satire were obsolescent, just as distinctions between public and private were hazier. People still paid them lip-service, and they still mattered to many, but graphic satire had become much more personalized than it had been at the beginning of the century, and Addison's contempt for satirists' 'secret stabs to a man's reputation' sounded old-fashioned and prim. Most engravers had long ago discarded Hogarth's high didactic ambitions. What now mattered more was their prints' teasing cut against the didactic grain, their ironic flippancy, and their relationship to gossip and scandal. Society was full of people who cared not a fig for Shaftesbury or the *Spectator* ideologues or for the sanctity of the private realm. 'Politeness' for many entailed less a commitment to virtue and the public good than a social veneer. It was mere 'embroidery, guilding, colouring, daubing', as Shaftesbury had himself lamented. Most of those who bought satirical sheets after the 1770s were sufficiently loose in principle, secure in status and eclectic in taste to accept the prints' vulgarities without anxiety, and yet still, as public beings, to deem themselves 'polite'.

# CHAPTER NINE

# GILLRAY'S DREAMSCAPES

## The innovator

Many of the caricatures that Horace Walpole collected in the 1770s would have struck the next generation as naïve if not incoherent. They inherited an old-fashioned emblematic literalism from the seventeenth century. Laboriously explaining their 'hieroglyphicks' with subtexts or speech bubbles, they were by later standards overinformative, congested and 'wretchedly executed', as a French visitor wrote in the 1770s: 'The engraver thinks he has attained his end, if he can but hit off a few features, to make the persons known.'[1] The only engraver exempted from criticism of this kind was Hogarth, who died in 1764. But his works had had different ambitions; the most famous of them started their lives as paintings anyway. They were elaborately composed, meticulously engraved and detailed and squared antique emblems with realistic conventions and moralizing narratives. They were 'books', Charles Lamb later wrote, full of 'the teeming, fruitful, suggestive meaning of words. Other pictures we look at – his prints we read': and since his 'modern moral progresses' told stories across six or eight plates, Lamb's point was well put.[2] Until the 1770s, few satirical engravers would escape Hogarth's shadow. He influenced immigrant engravers like L.-P. Boitard and home-grown artists like his enemy Paul Sandby, and Carington Bowles also; and for decades yet he would be respectfully cited or paid the compliment of parody. Still, neither

Hogarth nor these successors prepared purchasers for what lay ahead in the 1780s and 1790s.

In the last decades of the century, as war in America and then with France increased the hunger for commentary, the character, vehemence and ambition of the West End satires were transformed, to achieve an unprecedented, undidactic and often self-indulgent freedom. Speech bubbles and emblems survived, but Hogarth's narrative didacticism was discarded, along with the Augustan principle that satire shouldn't be 'personal'. Earlier critics like Dr Johnson had defined 'proper satire' in terms of 'the generality of the reflections' on 'wickedness or folly'. Proper satire differed from a 'lampoon', his *Dictionary* had pronounced: a lampoon was only 'a personal satire' that aimed 'not to reform but to vex'. By this standard, most later eighteenth-century prints, when not humorous, were lampoons rather than satires, and they regularly breached the boundaries between the public and the private. Speedily produced, often self-parodically flippant in composition and line, and accepting their own evanescence as Hogarth's prints never would, they reached for a more frankly journalistic relationship between situation and commentary. In the 1780s, increasing numbers of prints were watercoloured (only James Sayers's prints resisted this, along with sixpenny drolls), and new forms appeared, like Henry Bunbury's strip designs or G. M. Woodward's vignette rows of expressive figures. As the social base of the market broadened, genial and 'celebratory' prints, along with simple jokes for simple tastes, multiplied right to the end of this period. But the biggest shift was apparent in the fact that the more ambitious satires in and after the 1780s catapult us into a crueller, more freely expressive and aggressively personalized iconographic world. The biggest single influence on all this was James Gillray.

The organizers of the Tate Gallery's Gillray exhibition in 2000 hailed Gillray as the producer of some of the greatest prints of the eighteenth century. This may be pushing it somewhat in view of Gillray's academic failures; but another scholar, Ernst Gombrich, has claimed that the inventiveness of Gillray's graphic satire outstripped nearly everything produced by the 'official' art of the period, and this can hardly be disputed.[3] Gillray was certainly the most daring and innovative engraver of his era. He often cited Hogarth, and in prints like *Promis'd Horrors of the French Invasion* drew on Hogarth's spatial conventions [fig. 24]. He also learned from Hogarth's capacity to remain true to the spirit of a familiar text while extracting imaginary emblems from it in order to address a topical situation

(Hogarth's *The Punishment Inflicted on Lemuel Gulliver* (1726) is a good example [fig. 73]).[4] But Gillray shunned Hogarth's overt didacticism as well as his narrative 'progresses', integrated the political and the emblematic more frequently and deftly than Hogarth, and added much that was new. In particular, no other artist so confidently subverted the classical principles that Joshua Reynolds and the Academy stood for. By burlesquing high art's sublimity and by harnessing the free associations and 'Romantic' dream imagery that began to imbue art in the 1780s, he set new imaginative, compositional and technical standards which were major elements in the ending of that classical tradition. Internationally recognized, he influenced Goya in Spain and David in France; and his stature in his own terrain beat William Blake's in his.

Gillray was an enigmatic fellow, and we're not going to *like* him. In appearance he seems to have been rather daunting [fig. 108], so it comes as no surprise to learn that, with his 'slouching gait and careless habits', he was too taciturn to have intimate friends. As the artist-journalist W. H. Pyne remembered, he was 'meanly mischievous' to other people and as lazy in his personal relationships as in his art, and 'a stranger to the feelings of friendship'. But although he was 'a careless sort of cynic, one who neither loved, nor hated society', 'his aberrations were more the results of low habits and the want of self-esteem, than from malignity, envy, or meanness'. He certainly lacked pretensions. 'He probably never enquired further into motives than as there was a necessity for doing something to live . . . He accomplish[ed] what he undertook without scientific parade, and even

without the appearance of rule, or pre-concerted plan. His best designs were *off-hand* compositions.'

Gillray occasionally shared a tavern drink with Rowlandson, Pyne tells us, but no characters could be more different, and the two men's relationship was detached. They would 'exchange half-a-dozen questions and answers upon the affairs of copper and aquafortis; swear all the world was one vast masquerade; and then enter into the common

**Fig. 108** Anon., *James Gillray. The Caricaturist* (*c.*1800)

chat of the room, smoke their cigars, drink their punch, and sometimes early, sometimes late, shake hands at the door, look up at the stars, say "It is a frosty night", and depart, one for the Adelphi, the other to St James's Street, each to his bachelor's bed'.[5] Johan Huttner, correspondent of the Weimar journal *London und Paris*, also found Gillray a man who 'doesn't talk very much about things' or 'explain himself about anything'. He 'rarely gives anything away. Outwardly, indeed, in his manners and conversation, he gives the appearance of such everyday simplicity, such a straightforward, unassuming character, that no one would guess this gaunt, bespectacled figure, this dry man, was a great artist.'[6] While Rowlandson was a cheerful libertine and gambler and the Cruikshanks were emphatically tavern kinds of men, Gillray's closest relationship was with the spinster Hannah Humphrey, his patron and protector. From 1793 onwards, he lodged with her above her shops in Old Bond Street and St James's Street, and she profitably monopolized the sale of his prints. There is no hint of a sexual relationship between them (she was some twenty years older), but she blessed him with a pleasantly mothering domesticity. 'Don't forget the pigeon pye,' one of her letters tells him. And in 1804, from Brighton, she tells 'Dear Gilly' about her coach journey and lodgings and supper there: 'a boiled chicken with parsley and butter which I assure you went down very sweet'. And then: 'P.S. I hope you take care of the cat.'[7]

Gillray was born in 1756, in the same year as Thomas Rowlandson and (probably) Isaac Cruikshank, and a year before Blake. His soldier father was a Lanarkshire kirk member who converted to the Moravian creed. Having lost an arm at the battle of Fontenoy in 1745, he became a Chelsea pensioner, and served as sexton for the Moravian religious community in Chelsea. As a boy, Gillray was briefly educated in a Moravian academy in Bedford. There he would have been exposed to the joyless beliefs that mankind was depraved and life worthless, and that release would be delivered, gloriously, only in death. The alleged last words of Gillray's six-year-old brother, who died as a pupil at the school in 1762, show how deeply these principles could penetrate: the boy supposedly affirmed that 'he had fixed his mind upon going over to the Saviour' and that he would prefer that destination to going home with his mother. 'He begged his coffin might be brought and soon after said "Pray don't keep me. O let me go, I must go . . ."' – which he then did. A surviving letter from an uncle to Gillray's father ends, '. . . and may God the father Jesus Christ his son and the Holy Spirit thy comforter be with you all hence forth and for ever Amen'.[8]

Gillray must have rebelled against this austere upbringing. Neither his later letters nor reports of him suggest any religious belief whatsoever. Instead, he developed the most saturnine view of human affairs and principles, along with the manic-depressive nature that led to the insanity of his last years. He was indifferent to the pleasurably erotic. Several prints of the mid-1780s suggest that his sexual inclinations were flagellatory. He was contemptuous of heroes and pessimistic about human folly even as he exposed it. Except in a few depictions of St James's characters from life, his works lack warmth or affection. And, although comedy and wit abundantly inform many of his prints, none was charming or mischievous as Rowlandson's could be. Many are moved by a dark, even-handed misanthropy – by something approaching hatred, mixed with sadism. His early prints are scatological as well as flagellatory, and his later ones betray a fair relish for decapitated and blood-spouting corpses. Yet even in these supercharged images, the figures and faces are too burlesqued to convey real feeling.

In his well-known and blood-curdling *Petit Souper, a la Parisienne; – or – a Family of Sans-culotts Refreshing, after the Fatigues of the Day* (1792), he harnessed the composition of a sixteenth-century print after Pieter Brueghel to show bare-bottomed sans-culottes feasting greedily off naked aristocratic bodies, eating their eyes and roasting their bodies [fig. 109]. The horror is relieved only in the title's heavy irony. His *High German Method of Destroying Vermin at Rat-stadt*, commenting on an Austrian atrocity at the Rastadt Congress in 1799 (its theme suggested to him by an anonymous amateur),[9] depicts the decapitation of two French envoys by a pair of ferocious Austrian hussars [fig. 110]. The print depicts the massacre at the very moment at which it happens. In this frozen instant, one of the headless victims is still standing, his hands raised in shocked incredulity even as his neck spouts blood and his head is impaled on the Austrian sword. One hussar holds the other body upside down as he jams the spouting head between the corpse's legs. In the background, a battle rages, and a soldier's lopped-off nose gushes blood. These obscenely explicit images coolly transgressed against all artistic norms. In high art, horrific situations were conventionally depicted immediately *before* their climax, the protagonists as yet allowed their decorum and composure and the coming horror only implied. But in Gillray euphemism is repudiated and truth fully named. There is nothing else like these depictions in their time. Their effect must have been electrifying.

Gillray was first apprenticed to a writing engraver before allegedly spending some obscure years as a wandering player.[10] Then in 1778 he

**Fig. 109** Gillray, *Un Petit Souper, a la Parisienne; – or – A family of Sans-Culottes Refreshing, after the Fatigues of the Day* (H. Humphrey, 1792)

**Fig. 110** Gillray, *The High German Method of destroying Vermin at Rat-stadt* (H. Humphrey, 1799)

entered the Royal Academy schools for a couple of years to study engraving under Francesco Bartolozzi. This was shortly after Thomas Rowlandson's period there, and overlapped with William Blake's; but there is no evidence that at this stage the men knew each other. Under Bartolozzi he was required to cultivate a style 'of super-Italian softness and elegance, verging on beautiful insipidity', as Pyne put it. Success eluded him. Those of Gillray's academic engravings that survive are conventionally sentimental. What was intended as a commercial portrait of Pitt teeters on the edge of

**Fig. 111** Gillray, *Female Curiosity* (W. Humphrey, 1778)

caricature (Fores, who commissioned it, had to withdraw it). His women wilt sensitively, and his shipwreck scenes are melodramatically overblown. He hoped for recognition as a serious engraver for some years yet, but, since commissions were few, he turned his hand to producing satires. He had already dabbled in these. The earliest attributed to him is dated 1775. In his first year at the Academy, he produced a couple of mildly indecent satires for William Humphrey, notably *Female Curiosity* (the girl gazing in a mirror at her bared buttocks was a familiar erotic trope) [fig. 111]; and in his second year these multiplied to thirteen attributed titles. Only in the 1780s does he seem to have capitulated to his destiny as a satirist. He began then to work regularly for Holland, Fores and lesser printshops, until Hannah Humphrey took him under her wing in 1791.

Gillray never fully recovered from his academic defeat and reacted to it with characteristic sourness. On the back of a pen-and-wash sketch, he listed 'a series of subjects quite new and never attempted by the ancients in the year 1805, worthy of the talents of British artists': it included the promise of a print on the 'Somerset House triumph of the arts polite' in which he might have vented his contempt for Reynolds's principles had he fulfilled it.[11] He was still complaining of 'a life made up of hardships and disappointments' when he was at the height of his fame.[12] Nursing his resentments as every good hater should, he took revenge on his academic mentors. His large *Titianus Redivivus – or – the Seven-Wise-Men Consulting the New Venetian Oracle, – a Scene in ye Academic Grove* (1797) [fig. 112] ridiculed the gullible Academicians who had paid ten guineas to a young female charlatan for the alleged secret of Titian's colouring. In the background the Royal Academy splits apart as if in an earthquake, and in the foreground a simian youth pisses on the portfolios of leading Academicians, including Bartolozzi's. In similar spirit, he travestied Reynolds in 1783 and Benjamin West in 1795. And when Boydell refused to employ him as an engraver for his Shakespeare Gallery in 1789, he produced his five-shilling aquatint, *Shakespeare Sacrificed* (1789), to mock Boydell for his commercial opportunism.[13] His *Sin, Death, and the Devil* (1792) parodied Fuseli's Miltonic *Satan, Sin and Death*, itself appropriated from Hogarth's and earlier images [fig. 113]. Vexed by the news that Boydell was to employ Fuseli to illustrate Milton, he sourly recommended the print to 'Messrs Boydell, Fuzelli & the rest of the proprietors of the three hundred & sixty five editions of Milton now publishing'. The print was a brilliantly offensive representation of the political feuds between the ministers Pitt and Thurlow in which Queen

**Fig. 112** Gillray, *Titianus Redivivus – or the Seven-Wise-Men Consulting the New Venetian Oracle, – a Scene in ye Academic Grove* (H. Humphrey, 1797)

Charlotte is depicted as the naked and hang-breasted mediator. It offended the royals mightily.[14]

In his lifetime, Gillray produced well over a thousand satires altogether, at a rate of one or two a week in peak years. Many were hack works in a diversity of styles, but the best of his earliest work married his academic training to an eye for parodic exaggeration. Elaborately and meticulously composed, they deploy skilful figure-drawing and ambitious mixtures of stipple and line engraving (his *Lady Termagant Flaybum* [fig. 148] is a good example). His greatest and most prolific years began under Hannah

**Fig. 113** Gillray, *Sin, Death, and the Devil* (H. Humphrey, 1792)

Humphrey's aegis in the 1790s. He began then to make influential contacts and to be taken seriously. He was well qualified to deal with high people – 'extremely well-informed and widely read', Huttner found in 1798. His surviving letters are polished and literate, and knowledgeable about political affairs. Literary quotations fill his subtexts and his range of interests was panoramic; no other engraver monitored the West End's cultural venues so comprehensively. He also had manners enough to hobnob with the artistic establishment when it suited him. His only visit abroad was to Holland with the artist Loutherbourg. He knew the artist Northcote and went to occasional dinners at the Academician Joseph Farington's. The engraver John Landseer (the painter's father) recalled a dinner at which Gillray, drunk, leapt on a table to propose a toast to the French painter David.[15] Some prints are inscribed '*ad vivam*' to indicate that they were drawn from life, and these suggest access to the Foxites' tavern chambers, for example (unless the phrase was ironic. By now he was acknowledged as a powerful propagandist that great men needed to know. In 1795, he befriended the amateur caricaturist

John Sneyd, and Sneyd introduced him to the up-and-coming Tory minister, George Canning, so that between 1797 and Pitt's resignation in 1801 he worked as a loyalist propagandist for Canning's 'Anti-Jacobin' circle, and was secretly paid an annual 'pension' of £200. In 1798, politically Gillray's most productive year, forty-eight out of his year's total of fifty-seven prints assailed Francophile Foxites, the prince and sundry parliamentary or international statesmen, invariably with unashamed partisanship.[16]

Decline set in as his eyesight began to fail in 1807 and as depression eroded his manic inventiveness. George Cruikshank, who knew him in his last years, then found it painful to watch the energy with which he covered his copper with intricate compositions and inventions: 'His natural temperament was excitable. Sometimes he would at once etch a subject on the prepared copper plate . . . unable even to submit to the process of drawing it upon paper. When [engraving] he worked furiously, without stopping to remove the burr thrown up by the [graver]; consequently his fingers often bled from being cut by it.' As his health declined, his hand would 'pulsate electrically' across a surface, always 'moving as if in the act of painting'.[17] After the publication of his last plate in 1811, the obverse of the mania set in, and Gillray was almost permanently 'insane' and recurrently suicidal. He once tried to throw himself out of Hannah Humphrey's upper window, and was saved because he jammed his head and was spotted from White's club across the street. He believed that young Cruikshank was Joseph Addison and that he himself was Rubens. His death in 1815 went all but unnoticed. His coffin was accompanied to St James's churchyard by Hannah Humphrey and Cruikshank, now Gillray's undisputed heir, from whom the canny Mrs Humphrey had been commissioning work for two years past. Yet even in his insanity Gillray's drawing can still astonish. A pen, brush and black ink drawing of Hannah Humphrey's nephew is inscribed: 'this portrait of George Humphrey junr was drawn by James Gillray on the 1st July 1811 he being at that time insane' [fig. 114]. It hardly justifies one critic's view that, in its 'incoherence', 'not a trace of the artist's skill remains'. It brings us to the edge of nightmare.[18]

In 1797, the prospectus for George Canning's *Poetry of the Anti-Jacobin* advertised Gillray's accompanying plates as the works of 'the first moral satirist since the days of Hogarth'. The comparison was somewhat

**Fig. 114** Gillray, *Portrait of George Humphrey junr . . . He being at that time insane* (ink drawing) (1811)

overdone. All satire rests on some moral standard, but Gillray wasn't what you'd call a principled man, and his prints were never didactic. What one meets in them, rather, is a lack of moral fixity, an ambivalence of tone and feeling – this, indeed, being a condition of their power. If there is a moral centre in his prints (his best modern commentator has noted), it lies in the victim figure of John Bull, but even he is stupid.[19] Otherwise, his contempt for his characters was unremitting. He rendered all plebeian faces as simian, lumpen and grotesque, and the common people as deluded radicals or as gullibles who exist only to be conned. Heroes (including Nelson) were mocked as ambitious or corrupt. Gillray did produce a few early prints celebrating the fall of the Bastille, but he hated Jacobins and was no friend of democracy, and Whigs and radicals were as viciously attacked as the French. Until his pension checked him, he attacked the Tories too. If the Foxites were shown as so many shabby sans-culottes, 'fat, drunken, and speechifying', Pitt was variously 'a huckster, a vulture, a drunkard, a toadstool, a sleepwalker, an alchemist, a glutton, a highwayman, and Death on the white horse of Hanover'.[20] The king and queen were misers, or, in the king's case, a bumbling 'farmer George'. The Prince of Wales was a fornicating layabout and voluptuary. Those who wielded power, or preened themselves, or were driven by delusions of grandeur or folly, or who were idealists about anything, including revolution – upon all their houses Gillray wished the plague.

All this his contemporaries seem to have let pass. What caused them most difficulty was his apparent political volte-face in 1797. Having hitherto attacked Pitt as mercilessly as Fox, he seemed suddenly to toe the Tory-loyalist line. This he cynically explained as a response to the fact that the Foxites 'are poor' and 'do not buy my prints, so I must trade them on the stock exchange of the great parties'.[21] But that comment concealed the effects of Canning's pension. When the pension's existence was disclosed by the bookseller and printseller William Hone in 1817 (he had learned about it 'from the relations of that gentleman', he reported, and Cobbett confirmed the truth of it: 'Gillray told me,' he said),[22] Gillray's reputation was greatly damaged. 'Gillray was a great man in his way,' Northcote the artist told Hazlitt, '. . . yet it was against his conscience, for he had been on the other side, and was bought over.' Many years later Thackeray thought that Gillray lacked 'Hogarth's honesty of purpose': he 'would have been far more successful and more powerful but for that unhappy bribe, which turned the whole course of his humour into an unnatural channel'.[23]

These verdicts are too high-minded to worry us much today. No engraver of Gillray's time was expected to have the manners and honour of a gentleman. Most took any commission that paid, regardless of its source. In any case, as *London und Paris* observed in 1806 when it doubted rumours of the pension, Gillray's patriotism and hostility to the French were his own, not imposed upon him; and he remained loyal to the Tories after Pitt's resignation and death.[24] Nor did he sacrifice his independence. The propagandist prints whose subjects the Canningites dictated to him were bland productions, and Gillray repeatedly vexed his paymasters by embroidering their suggestions, and by his sly hits at their own side as well as the opposition. If Gillray's moral virtue has to be at issue, it stands judged less by his political volte-face than by his vicious calumnies of women like Lady Worsley or the Countess of Strathmore.

Meanwhile, there is no harm in best remembering him for his wit and brilliant composition. Many of his simplest conceits are unforgettable, their impact enhanced by their inspired titling. In 1791–2, he turns Pitt literally into *An Excrescence; – a Fungus; – alias – a Toadstool upon a Dunghill* [fig. 115]. Pitt's elongated and fleshless figure becomes *The Bottomless-Pitt* or, in *A Sphere, Projecting against a Plane*, a vertical rod juxtaposed against his friend

An Excrescence – a Fungus; – alias – a Toadstool upon a Dunghill.

The BOTTOMLESS-PITT.

**Fig. 115** *(left)* Gillray, *An Excrescence; – a Fungus; – alias – a Toadstool upon a Dunghill* (H. Humphrey, 1791)

**Fig. 116** *(right)* Gillray, *The Bottomless-Pitt* (H. Humphrey, 1792)

Mrs Hobart's spherical rotundity. In *Lubber's-hole; – alias – The Crack'd Jordan*, the Duke of Clarence's actress mistress and common-law wife, Mrs Jordan, becomes a cracked chamberpot (or 'jordan'), her welcoming genitals symbolized in the pot's gaping crack through which the duke dives head-first [fig. 117]. In *Fashionable Contrasts; – or – The Duchess's Little Shoe Yielding to the Magnitude of the Duke's Foot*, the union of the newly married Duke and Duchess of York is summarized in the opposing positions of their shoes in bed [fig. 118]. In *The Orangerie; – or – the Dutch Cupid Reposing, after the Fatigues of Planting* (1796), Gillray satirizes William of Orange's antics while exiled at Hampton Court,

**Fig. 117** Gillray, *Lubber's-Hole, – alias  The Crack'd Jordan* (H. Humphrey, 1791)

LUBBER'S HOLE. alias  The Crack'd JORDAN.

where 'his amours with the servant-maids were supposed to be very numerous'. The prince is portrayed in this as a comically rotund and naked cupid, pleasantly dreaming of the pregnant servant-girls with whom the print surrounds him, while baby 'Oranges' sprout meaningfully from potted orange trees in the foreground [fig. 119]. And his satire on the fate delivered

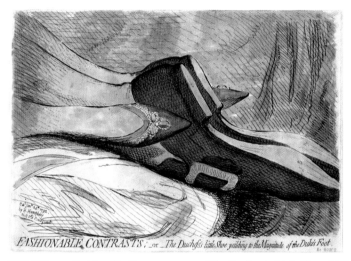

**Fig. 118** Gillray, *Fashionable Contrasts; – or – The Duchess's Little Shoe yielding to the Magnitude of the Duke's Foot* (H. Humphrey, 1792)

**Fig. 119** Gillray, *The Orangerie; – or – the Dutch Cupid Reposing, after the Fatigues of Planting* (H. Humphrey, 1796)

to the overambitious embezzler Lord Temple, *The Fall of Icarus* (1807), even now provokes the viewer's anticipatory somatic reflex as, wings melting from exposure to George III as the sun, the fat, naked Temple descends bare-buttocks-first towards the pointed stake that awaits their arrival in the street below [fig. 120].

The FALL of ICARUS.

In former days the Poet sings,
    An Artist skill'd and rare
Of Wax and Feathers form'd his Wings
    And made a famous pair.

With which from Precipice or Tower
    From Hill or highest Trees.
When work'd by his mechanic power
    He could descend with ease.

Why T-p-e then wants such a store
    You surely ask in vain ?
A moment of reflection more
    Will make the matter plain.

With Plumes & Wax . & such like things
    In quantities not small
He tries to make a pair of wings
    To ease his sudden Fall !

**Fig. 120** Gillray, *The Fall of Icarus* (H. Humphrey, 1807)

# Visions and dreams

Gillray hatched his prints out of three inheritances: his academic training, the new artistic fashions exhibited in the West End's commercial art establishments, and the work of his fellow jobbing satirists. These cross-fertilizations enabled him to transform the very nature and ambition of satirical print. What mattered most was the artistic shift that rebelled against academic models and permitted the image to bear new meanings. Gillray was well placed to be influenced by this great movement. He was alone among the satirists in monitoring artistic fashions with a beady eye, not least those on view around the corner from Humphrey's shop, in John Boydell's Shakespeare Gallery and Henri Fuseli's Milton Gallery which opened in Pall Mall in 1789 and 1799 respectively. Gillray alone had seriously studied the masters: some of his strongest parodies drew on Raphael, Brueghel and Michelangelo. And since his contempt for the Academy was unremitting, the stylistic revolution in the art of and after the 1780s was for him a liberation.

Artists had long been striving both for a new professional standing and for a fuller recognition of an intrinsically 'English' art rooted in English life and manners. Hogarth had led the way in his attack on 'the eternal blazonry, and tedious repetition of hackneyed, beaten subjects, either from the Scriptures, or the old ridiculous stories of heathen gods'. He had mocked connoisseurs, 'none daring to think for themselves', and laughed at young men who 'by studying in Italy have seldom learnt much more than the names of the painters'.[25] The Royal Academy was established in 1768, four years after Hogarth's death, but he would have hated what it came to stand for. Joshua Reynolds became the Academy's first president, reigning from 1769 until 1790; and Reynolds had no more time for the likes of Hogarth than Hogarth had had for the likes of Reynolds. In his *Discourses*, Reynolds dismissed 'the painters who express with precision the various shades of passion, as they are exhibited by vulgar minds (such as we see in the works of Hogarth)'. Such artists might deserve praise, he grudgingly admitted, 'but as their genius has been employed on low and confined subjects, the praise which we give must be as limited as its object'. Indeed, 'Hogarth's method of exposing meanness, deformity and vice is rather a dangerous or, at least, a worthless pursuit.' Reynolds accordingly posited a rigid hierarchy of genres from which Hogarth and his emulators were excluded. Grand history painting was at the top, portraits and landscapes followed, and genre and comic painting – 'the Dutch taste' – were at the bottom. Engraving was a mere artisanal product, while caricature and low satirical creations were beneath consideration. Reynolds followed Shaftesbury and Burke in teaching that art must communicate universal ideals and allow good to triumph over evil. It must also emulate classical models and the old European masters, so that the artist's best training lay in respectful imitation. Since between the 1720s and 1770s Britain had emptied Europe of some 50,000 master paintings, half a million engravings and countless antiquities, it was no wonder that these emulative principles ruled English art under Reynolds's presidency. Those of Hogarth's successors who tried to fight free of academic classicism were to feel ostracized for near on thirty years.

This regime stifled free spirits like Gillray, Rowlandson and Blake, and their contempt for it was withering. As Blake put it: 'Having spent the vigour of my youth & genius under the oppression of Sir Joshua & his gang of cunning hired knaves without employment & as much as could possibly be without bread, the reader must expect to read in all my remarks on these books nothing but indignation & resentment. While Sir Joshua was rolling in riches Barry was poor & unemployed except by his own energy, Mortimer was calld a madman & only portrait painting applauded & rewarded by the rich & great. Reynolds & Gainsborough plotted & blurred one against the other & divided all the English world between them. Fuseli indignant almost hid himself – [as] I am hid.' At the opening of the new century, Blake was still complaining that 'the enquiry in England is not whether a man has talents and genius, but whether he is passive and polite and a virtuous ass: and obedient to noblemens opinions in art and science. If he is, he is a good man: if not he must be starved.' 'Such artists as Reynolds are at all times hired by the Satans, for the depression of art,' he fumed, adding this optimistic prophecy: 'When Sir Joshua Reynolds died / All nature was degraded: / The king drop'd a tear into the queens ear: / And all his pictures faded.'[26]

Blake needn't have despaired, however. By 1800 academic classicism was visibly retreating. In the first place, the strangleholds of the Academy and of aristocratic patronage were yielding to the increasing commercialization of the art market. Boydell's Shakespeare Gallery exhibited commissioned paintings of Shakespearean scenes (admittedly sublime in style, and some by Reynolds), and sold engravings of them to non-aristocratic subscribers. Boydell's enterprise collapsed within half a dozen years, as did Fuseli's imitative Milton Gallery, not least thanks to the wartime contraction of European demand for English engravings. All the same, it was a sign of rising commercial expectations that in this new climate the engraver's business boomed. Blake admitted in 1803 that 'art in London flourishes': 'engravers in particular are wanted. Every engraver turns away work that he cannot execute from his superabundant employment.' Even the caricature shops of William Holland and Fores were beneficiaries, as they joined (and might have anticipated) Boydell in advertising exhibitions of prints, charging a shilling admission to keep out the vulgar, just like the Royal Academy.

More important was the shift in the very function of the artistic image. There was, after all, an alternate tradition to draw on. The disordered nature accommodated in the notion of the 'sublime' had long opposed the 'beauty' of the classical model. The gothic novel, with its taste for the macabre, exotic and supernatural, had flowered decades before, in Horace Walpole's *Castle of Otranto* (1764), for example. By the turn of the century, the stage melodrama and the 'phantasmagoria' had brought its language to popular audiences.[27] But the chief force to drive a hole through classical academicism was personified in the Swiss émigré in London, Henry Fuseli.

In his early years, Fuseli had subscribed to neo-classical theory. His early mannerist figures reflected his studies of Michelangelo in Rome, he owed much to Reynolds's patronage, and he was himself an Academician. But with his most famous and knowingly original work, *The Night Mare*, exhibited at the Academy in 1782 and repainted in 1790, he broke new ground. Hitherto, so far as classical rules permitted, artworks had pretended to represent an intelligibly observed and usually a narrative reality. *The Night Mare*, however, discarded realism and narrative and conveyed meanings beyond reason and words alike [fig. 121]. What happened before or after the nightmare is not the picture's concern. Rather, it portrays what a young woman might *feel* in dreaming – her emotion is its central point. The squatting incubus on her breast hints at a mystic incubation to whose erotic force she yields swooningly. The horse peering from behind the curtain is a figure of dread but is unexplained also. Nothing like this had been attempted before, and it created a sensation in art-viewing London, alerting even the Academy to the notion that art might 'make philosophical ideas intuitive' rather than aspire chiefly to moral elevation.[28] Along with similar pictures that Fuseli painted for the Milton and Shakespeare Galleries, *The Night Mare* opened the way to a

**Fig. 121** Fuseli, *The Night Mare* (stipple engraving, Thomas Burke; Smith, 1783)

new expressionism among younger artists. Exposed to it in paint or in engraving, they, too, began to draw on their inward associations and emotional impulses, not least to harness the imagery of dreams or to address the erotic (in which Fuseli was a past master). Soon, the cult of 'enthusiasm' was colonizing art as well as faith, and the notion that the artist was an inspired genius (rather than Reynolds's emulative craftsman) marked the end of classical academicism. Where Reynolds thought that enthusiasm would carry the artist 'but a little way', Blake retorted that inspiration was 'the first principle of knowledge and its last' and that 'meer [*sic*] enthusiasm is the all in all!': 'What,' he asked himself, 'has reasoning to do with the art of painting?'

Since the authorized engraving of *The Night Mare* cost only five shillings, its sensation touched common engravers as well as the cognoscenti. Rowlandson, Newton, Sayers, George Cruikshank and lesser satirists each exploited the *Night Mare* motif many times in ensuing years, making it the most travestied of all major paintings.[29] Most of their parodies were easily read, their comic effect depending on the incongruities of replacing the sleeping girl by John Bull, Pitt, Fox, etc. Gillray never used the motif in this way. It was dream language itself that he appropriated, aware of its potential for satire since dreams could speak of hidden truths.

So Gillray drew on Fuseli in at least seven prints in the decade 1789–98,[30] most directly in his aquatint on the regency crisis, *Wierd-Sisters; Ministers of Darkness; Minions of the Moon* (1791). Based on Fuseli's 1783 depiction of the witches in *Macbeth*, Gillray's dedication of this print was probably sincere: 'To H: Fuzelli Esqr this attempt in the caricatura-sublime, is respectfully dedicated.' The two men were on good terms. When Fuseli prepared the English edition of Lavater's *Essays on Physiognomy*, he got Gillray to engrave one of the examples. And as Gillray negotiated the shift from his simpler emblematic style of the 1780s to his maturer expressionism, he well understood how Fuseli's gothic imagination might be harnessed to visual satire. He told Sneyd in 1800 that Fuseli's 'mock sublime "mad taste"' was 'very necessary' to his engravings for the *Anti-Jacobin*; and Sneyd agreed. A much later reviewer aptly noted of Gillray's work that 'the ludicrous is not divided by a step from the sublime': it 'blended with it and twined around it'.[31]

In Gillray's best prints in this mode, the outcomes are as condensed as dreams themselves, carrying visionary associations and meanings that lie beyond words, and eliciting an unease in the viewer which their 'manifest' content hardly warrants. They deliver the shock once achieved by the medieval iconography which must have influenced him – by the nightmare figures of purgatory and hell. In these qualities he betrayed unconscious affinities both with Goya in Spain and Blake at home, each of whom were influenced by Gillray. In these artists, too, one finds the dream-grotesque that cut determinedly free from academic models and, in Goya particularly, the cruel tortured imaginings which bore close kinship to Gillray's.[32]

Fuseli's psychological penetration was beyond Gillray's talents, but as he began to marry dream imagery to the grotesque he achieved an art of free association that transformed graphic satire's potential. The critic Ronald Paulson has argued that classicism was as surely silenced by Gillray as it was by Fuseli and Blake: through Gillray, excess became the watchword, 'not the restraint of classicism'. He achieved 'abbreviation, not careful finish; physical imperfection, not graceful form; and distortion, not controlled and idealized forms'.[33] In these ways, Gillray began to claim a new licence that helped him to shift from the reportorial fantasy of his earlier work to the representation of extreme bodily distortion.

Hitherto, caricature had exaggerated facial expressions and features. Gillray now caricatured the body itself. Surreally elongated, distorted or abbreviated figures populate several of his prints in and after 1786.[34] In *A March on the Bank* (1787), an officer of the Guards struts balletically across strewn pedestrian bodies, his impossibly wasp-like waist the essence of

**Fig. 122** Gillray, *A March on the Bank* [detail] (Fores, 1787)

popinjay arrogance [fig. 122]. In *The Giant-Factotum Amusing Himself* (1797), Pitt is turned into a surreal Gulliver among pygmies [fig. 123], and in *Midas, Transmuting all into ~~Gold~~ Paper* (1797) Pitt becomes a monster made of money, straddling the Bank of England and defecating notes as if into a privy [fig. 124]. Faces elsewhere are reduced to the barest icons. In *Smelling out a Rat; – or – the Atheistical-Revolutionist Disturbed in his Midnight 'Calculations'* (1790), a ghastly spectre of Edmund Burke rises from smoke to terrify Dr Price. Price sympathized with the French Revolution; Burke wrote his *Reflections on the Revolution in France* to reply to one of Price's sermons. Burke is identified by no more than a grotesquely elongated nose and spectacles, the rest of his face lost in clouds [fig. 125].

The key shift lay in Gillray's adoption of a dreaming protagonist. Examples are many,[35] but among the most famous in its time was his *Political-Dreamings!* (1801) [fig. 126]. This was a response to the MP Windham's attack on the British concessions required by Pitt's peace terms with France. 'Are these idle dreams the phantoms of my disordered imagination?' Windham had asked: and this was just the kind of leading question Gillray could never ignore. So, in a composition which *London und Paris* aptly termed 'a phantasmagoric apparition',[36] Windham is made to

**Fig. 123** *(left)* Gillray, *The Giant-Factotum Amusing Himself* (H. Humphrey, 1797)
**Fig. 124** *(right)* Gillray, *Midas, Transmuting all into ~~Gold~~ Paper* (H. Humphrey, 1797)

**Fig. 125** Gillray, *Smelling out a Rat; – or – the Atheistical-Revolutionist disturbed in his Midnight 'Calculations'* (H. Humphrey, 1790)

**Fig. 126** Gillray, *Political-Dreamings! – Visions of Peace! – Perspective Horrors!* (H. Humphrey, 1801)

dream. While Pitt presides over the signing of Britannia's death warrant, Windham lies in bed tormented by images of the decapitated royalty and nobility of France and England, their headless necks bloodied, while Napoleon directs a broken-sceptred Britannia towards a bloodied guillotine. At the foot of the bed, Fox is a corpulently evil demon singing the Revolutionary 'Ça' ira!', while the opposition in the guise of rats – each recognizable – rifle a casket in the foreground labelled 'Treasury'. Justice sits on a chamberpot, her head bowed in mourning and her sword broken. In the background, St Paul's burns and the French tricolour flies over the Tower. The guillotine's rope is held by a grim red skeleton on stilts, capped by a *bonnet rouge*. This most astonishing figure bestraddles the crown jewels and plate, a mitre, John Bull's barrel of stout and side of roast beef, and a list of British conquests. According to *London und Paris* the print was so sensational that it sold out in a few days. Gillray did not deliberately allude to Fuseli here, but the print could not have been imagined or produced before Fuseli.

**Fig. 127** Gillray, *Presages of the Millenium; with The Destruction of the Faithful, as revealed to R. Brothers, the Prophet* (H. Humphrey, 1795)

The red skeleton in *Political-Dreamings!* is not the only example of Gillray's nightmare creations. Other such figures of the 1790s include the naked and gaunt figure of Pitt as a horseman of the apocalyse in his *Presages of the Millenium* [sic] (1795) [fig. 127], and the blood-dripping and guillotine-wielding monster bestriding the Mediterranean in *Destruction of the French Collossus* (1798) [fig. 128]. In this last, Louis XVI's decapitated head hangs from the monster's neck; its own snake-entwined skull is decapitated, and

**Fig. 128** Gillray, *Destruction of the French Collossus* (H. Humphrey, 1798)

its limbs are fragmented by British thunderbolts (the whole celebrating Nelson's victory on the Nile).[37] Gillray's most fantastic extravaganza depicted *The Apotheosis of Hoche* (1798) – the French revolutionary general who had planned to invade Ireland in 1796 [fig. 129]. Engraved in response to a suggestion by J. H. Frere of the anti-Jacobin circle, this must be among the most elaborate satirical plates ever engraved (and among the largest). On Hoche's death, he was given a magnificent funeral on the Champs de

**Fig. 129** Gillray, *The Apotheosis of Hoche* (H. Humphrey, 1798)

**Fig. 130** Gillray, *The Apotheosis of Hoche* [detail] (H. Humphrey, 1798)

Mars in Paris. Choirs in classical costume sang his praises before his effigy; words and music were by Chenier and Cherubini. Frere suggested the funeral to Gillray as a subject, and also wrote a descriptive leaflet to accompany the print, as was commonly done for conventional historical paintings. Gillray rose to the challenge spectacularly. In a parody of Christ's figure in Michelangelo's *Last Judgement*, he shows Hoche, holding a guillotine and with a noose around his neck, ascending to a secular heaven presided over by winged monsters who guard the commandments of 'Equality'. On the clouds in the background stand little baby sans-culottes and blood-spouting decapitatees; disconcertingly, they are comically drawn, as if Gillray couldn't sustain the print's epic ambition. But it is the detailing that always matters in Gillray's grand set-pieces; and if you enlarge one landscape at the foot of the print [fig. 130], you are not far short of one of Callot's seventeenth-century nightmare engravings of the horrors of war, which Gillray must have known.[38]

285

as he did from his academic training, and in his work cross-references to others were many. Gillray's *The Union-Club*, engraved in 1801, finely illustrates these mutual dependencies, as well as the engravers' inside knowledge and the fantasies they could turn it to [fig. 131].

A now all-but-forgotten masterpiece (bizarrely excluded, for example, from the Tate Gallery's great Gillray exhibition of 2001), *The Union-Club* is an elaborate comic fantasy on the debauchery of the Prince of Wales and his friends, the Foxite Whig grandees. In their newly founded Union Club in Pall Mall, they and their hangers-on celebrate the queen's birthday, presided over by the Prince of Wales. The prince's ceremonial chair dominates the scene, its decorative emblems referring to the just-enacted Irish Union. 'Presided' is too strong a word, however, since the heir apparent lies in drunken stupor under the table, his white-stockinged legs extending towards us. While he relaxes there, the great men of state disport themselves around or under the table as their conditions permit, each

**Fig. 131** Gillray, *The Union-Club* (H. Humphrey, 1801) (279 x 435)

identifiable to purchasers. Fox sleeps off his drink on the left, an overflowing pisspot-cum-tankard under his chair. To the left, Tierney vomits gently on to the Duke of Bedford's hat. At the table, clockwise, sit Erskine the lawyer, Sheridan, the politician-playwright well schooled in the arts of scandal, his boozer's face bloated and nose bulbous and a bottle raised in his right hand. Then follow Clermont, Lansdowne, Dr Parr, the Duke of Queensberry with his quizzical lecher's face, and Lord Derby in profile, his baby-like head not wholly caricatured. The inseparable dandies Skeffington and Mathew skip jovially together on the right, while Moira on the table and Lord Cholmondeley behind it toast the Union zealously. Collapsed on the floor are Lord Stanhope, the Duke of Norfolk and Nicholls, each much the worse for wear. As two waiters bring in another barrel of whisky punch to spur the party to yet greater jollity, fights erupt in the background. They are led by Colonel George Hanger, the prince's rough-mannered dogsbody, with hooked nose, slouched hat and blackened eye. Chairs, candlesticks, pokers and an overflowing chamberpot fly through the distant air, as musicians in the background try to play 'God Save the King'. The wall-clock, showing ten to two in the morning, is adorned with the figures of Bacchus and Time, the latter trampling his hourglass and brandishing a goblet. 'W. Pitt' is its maker, as he was of the Union. Cobbett's loyalist newsheet, *The Porcupine*, lies on the foreground floor. It lists the 'benefits of the Union' and declares 'Fear God Honor the king' – which is not what the Whigs were thought to do.

There is no surviving textual record that these grandees ever conducted themselves quite as spectacularly as this, so it is tempting to read the print as just another of Gillray's attacks on the prince and his opposition cronies. On the other, hand, it is one of the rare prints in which, for once, Gillray let comedy rip. In this respect, the timing of its production is significant. The Union Club celebrated the queen's birthday on 19 January; yet Gillray's print was published a mere three days later. Slighter prints were sometimes produced as fast as this to catch a passing sensation. But this one is too ambitious to have been knocked out so speedily. It must have taken days to plan, engrave, print and watercolour. In other words, it had a prehistory that enabled Gillray to prepare for the occasion.

First, Gillray must have been forewarned about the opposition's imminent celebration. If its excess was fantasy, it was of an informed kind, and Gillray lived in high gossip's vortex. Humphrey's shop in St James's Street was a stone's throw away from the great clubs, the Union Club included; and the street was awash with gossiping 'courtiers, aristocrats, guards, spies and informers', as *London und Paris* put it. As information flowed in this environment, engravers' responses had to be speedy if turnover was to be maintained and purchasers guaranteed.

Secondly, there can be no doubt that Gillray was prepared for the engraving by earlier models. The grandfathers of all 'debauchery prints' (seventeenth-century Dutch prototypes apart) were two of Hogarth's: *Midnight Modern Conversation* (1733) [fig. 132] and *Election Entertainment* (1755), their candid representation of convivial drunkenness sensational for their time. But, oddly, Hogarth's motifs were all but neglected over the following decades, until they were picked up again in the 1790s – when the number of debauchery prints virtually exploded. Prints were sensitive cultural barometers, and this explosion had meaning. An immediate provocation lay in the Prince of Wales's and the Whigs' bacchanalian tastes (many of these prints were about them). What operated in more complex ways, however, was the 'great masculinist assertion' that became apparent in these years, when one in ten men were being exposed to the manners and assumptions of the warship or military camp. The assertion was witnessed in the simplification in male fashion in these years, in what appears to be the growing fashion for the gratuitously dirty joke at women's expense, and in

**Fig. 132** Hogarth, *Midnight Modern Conversation* (1733)

**THE ROYAL SOCIETY.**

Published 1st April 1786 by S. W. Fores, at the Caricature Warehouse, Nº 3, Piccadilly.

**Fig. 133** Kingsbury *or* Stubbs, *The Royal Society* (Fores, 1786)

men's near fetishization of pugilism. For whatever reason, images of princely and Whig debauchery now began to multiply, their tropes passed on from one engraver to another – arms raised in toast, drunken figures on the floor, the fighting in the background, and the vomit. Kingsbury's (or Stubbs's) ironically entitled *The Royal Society* (1786) opened the cluster by showing the prince's Carlton House set in drunken conviviality [fig. 133]. Then Rowlandson took up the theme, both in *A Kick-up at a Hazard Table!* (1790) and in his watercolour sketch *Hunt Supper* of the same year (from which derived his *Miseries of the Country* (1807) [fig. 41]). Then Gillray chipped in, both with his *Loyal Souls; – or – a Peep into the Mess Room, at St James* (1797), and with his *Loyal Toast* (1798) in which the *The Union-Club*'s bodily postures were anticipated. Finally, on 8 January 1801, Isaac Cruikshank published two weak plates of his drunken companions in his own club, the Brilliants, *Son's of Harmony* and *Son's of Friendship*, and a week later Rowlandson produced his own *The Brilliants*, in which again the vomit flows as freely as the wine [fig. 27]. Since Gillray's *Union-Club* was published only six days after *The Brilliants*, the greater print's indebtedness to these predecessors is certain.[45]

But Gillray took up this idea and ran with it, of course, as no other engraver could. This ensured that 1801 was not the end of the motif's several migrations, for *The Union-Club*'s fame guaranteed its longevity thereafter. Within days the Gillray was being plagiarized by Williams for Fores's shop, and then it was amplified in Isaac Cruikshank's *Breaking Up of the Union Club* (in which the Whigs pour from the club into Pall Mall fighting drunk, the prince in a sedan chair, vomiting) [fig. 60]. Rowlandson unleashed several later prints depicting similar mayhem. Samuel de Wilde produced a clever parody of the Gillray in his anti-radical *The Reformers' Dinner* in 1809 [fig. 246]. And George Cruikshank paid tribute to the masterwork both in his *Dinner of the Four in Hand Club at Salthill* (1811) and in his *The New Union Club* (1819) [figs. 42 and fig. 234]. Several of the Cruikshank brothers' plates paid homage to the Gillray in the 1820s; and even into the 1840s, it echoed in Henry Alken's work as well.[46]

It is, then, not only the conception of Gillray's print that needs explaining, but also its lasting impact. The critic Northrop Frye noted that the irony of great satire is consistent both with complete realism of content and with the author's suppression of his own attitude. This can be said of *The Union-Club*. Gillray's scene is only quasi-realistic; but his attitude to it is ambivalent, or difficult to read; and it is in this that its power resides. He disliked the prince's extravagance, love affairs and louche Whig friends. But in this case he also seems half in love with what he mocks. As so often in the satires of this era, there is so much relish for and vicarious participation in the scene that one might be tempted to say that the Whigs' manic enthusiasms are close to his own. As a result, the print may chastise the prince and the Whigs for their indulgence, but it doesn't invite us into full-blown disgust. We are permitted both to condemn *and* to enjoy, which is a luxurious position seldom permitted since. To be sure, satire cannot thrive where there is too much geniality: hatred is needed, or fierce indignation. On the other hand, when the hatred is excessive, the satire teeters over into misanthropic horror.[47] The balance is a fine one, and in many prints Gillray lost it. In this great print, the balance is achieved.

# PART III

# THE SEXES

## CHAPTER TEN

# THE TREE OF LIFE

## The promptings of nature

In several of the prints depicting the boozy conviviality of the Prince of Wales and his circle in the 1780s and 1790s, you might glimpse among the great carousers a marginal and dilapidated figure who is obscure to us now but who was very familiar to print purchasers then. He appears in the ironically entitled *The Royal Society* (1786), for example, as the man on the left who rests his head drunkenly on the back of his chair with a sheet of music before him [fig. 133]. He also appears in Gillray's *Homer Singing his Verses to the Greeks* (1797), drinking claret with Fox and Sheridan. His shabby clothes suggest disreputability, and from his pocket peeks a booklet inscribed *Captain Morris's Songs*. 'Come sing me a bawdy song to make me merry,' Fox instructs him; so sing he does, from a sheet entitled 'A New Song to the Tune of the Plenipotentiary' [fig. 134]. This man was Captain Charles Morris (1744–1838), and everyone knew that he was the prince's, the Duke of Norfolk's and Fox's favoured bard: the prince paid him a £200 annuity, and his appearance in many more prints proves his fame. Once a man of fortune, but unaware of his own strength when it came to liquor (he would say), Morris admitted that his face was dyed a permanent red thanks to 'internal applications of that fluid'; later he was the associate of gamblers and prize-fighters. His roistering drinking and patriotic songs and their scores were widely published (by William Holland among others), and they were sung in clubs like the Beef-Steak, the Humbug, the Harmonic, and the Anacreontic Society. This last, named after an ancient Greek poet, met fortnightly for a singing concert and dinner, the Prince of Wales (allegedly)

**Fig. 134** Gillray, *Homer Singing his Verses to the Greeks* (H. Humphrey, 1797)

occasionally attending: Gillray engraved its musical jollifications also [fig. 135].[1] But if everyone knew Morris, they knew his 'The Plenipotentiary' better. Much prosecuted for indecency, it is referred to in prints all the way into the 1810s. It celebrated the Algerian ambassador's allegedly gigantic penis, and was the rudest song of its day:

> The Dey of Algiers, when afraid of his ears,
> A messenger sent to our court, sir,
> As he knew in our state that the women had weight,
> He chose one well hung for the sport, sir;
> He searched the divan, till he found out a man,
> Whose bollocks were heavy and hairy,
> And he lately came o'er, from the Barbary shore,
> As the great plenipotentiary.
>
> When to England he came, with his prick in a flame,
> He shewed it his hostess on landing,
> Who spread its renown thro' all parts of the town,
> As a pintle past all understanding;
> So much there was said of its snout and its head,

**Fig. 135** Gillray, *Anacreontick's in Full Song* (H. Humphrey, 1801)

That they called it the great janissary,
Not a lady could sleep, till she got a sly peep,
At the great plenipotentiary . . .

When his name was announc'd, how the women all bounc'd,
And their blood hurry'd up in their faces;
He made them all itch, from the nave to the breech,
And their bubbies burst out all their laces;
There was such damn'd work to be f—k'd by the Turk
That nothing their passion could vary . . . [2]

The fact that clubbish gentlemen had always sung bawdy songs of this kind returns us to the 'manliness' we've discussed earlier.[3] But the manliness in question in this part of the book was of a more specialized kind (not just about boozy conviviality, for example), and it sets the frame for what follows. Put simply, it turned on some very particular understandings about sex that should quite technically be called *libertine*. They turned on three assumptions. The first was that the pursuit of sexual pleasure was justified by the urgent promptings of 'Nature'. The second was that because women were beings as 'natural' as men, the sexes' desires and pleasures were identical. The third assumption followed, that women hungered for the penis, and that the penis was the tree of life.

Examples of these understandings in the songs are legion. On the compelling powers of 'Nature', in the first instance, the song known as 'The Black Joke' was typical. Its title referring to the female pudenda, it was lewdly known to every tavern frequenter from the 1730s to the 1810s, and it featured in print culture as well, for it was alluded to from plate 3 of Hogarth's *Rake's Progress* all the way through to George Cruikshank's prints in the 1810s:

> No mortal sure can blame the man,
> Who prompted by *Nature* will act as he can,
>> With a black joke, and belly so white:
> For he the Platonist must gainsay,
> That will not human *Nature* obey,
>> [chorus] *in working a joke, as will lather like soap,*
>> *and the hair of her joke, will draw more than a rope,*
>>> *with a black joke, and belly so white.*[4]

There are further examples. As 'Lady Worsley' was made to sing in the 1780s (she of the naked bottom that Gillray celebrated in 1782): ''Tis *Nature* prompts, what harm can there be in this, / To give and take from each the balmy bliss! / . . . To bounteous *Nature* I my song will tune, / And make my whole life long a honey-moon!'[5] Or as Robert Burns affirmed (these not just metropolitan fancies): 'Say, puritan, can it be wrong / To dress plain truth in witty song: / What honest *Nature* says we should do, / What every lady does, or would do?'[6] 'No enthusiasm is so strong, so stimulous, as that of copulation,' *Harris's List of Covent Garden Ladies* declared: 'It brings its warrant from *Nature's* closest cabinet.' As for the belief, secondly, that women were both lusting for and unfailingly satisfied by sex, the songs written by men in the female voice were just as eloquent:

> Now lustful nature eager grew,
>> And longer could not wanton toy,
> So rushing up the path of joy,
>> Quick from the fount love's liquor flew!
> At morn, she cried, 'full three times three,
>> 'The vivid stream I've felt from thee!

'O how I'm eas'd! O how I'm pleas'd! Gods how I'm charm'd!
  'I'm charm'd, with rapt'rous three times three!'[7]

– or as 'Lady Worsley' exclaimed again, 'I strok'd the marble pillar with my hand, / And, as it grew, I found my bliss expand; / . . . And let the prudent wives say all they can, / A woman's chiefest bliss must flow from man!'

Finally, an unabashed phallic narcissism underpinned all these male-composed songs, as it did male culture in general. 'Nine inch will please a lady', Burns lyrically affirmed – this from the man who boasted elsewhere that his own inches did just that: 'O, what a peacemaker is a guid weel-willy p—le [pizzle]! It is the mediator, the guarantee, the umpire, the bond of union, the solemn league and covenant, the plenipotentiary, the Aaron's rod, the Jacob's staff, the prophet Elisah's pot of oil, the Ahasuerus's sceptre, the sword of mercy, the philosopher's stone, the horn of plenty, the Tree of Life between man and woman.' 'I have f—d her till she rejoiced with joy unspeakable and full of glory,' Burns added bathetically, referring in 1788 to an inconveniently demanding girl.[8] Reference to the Tree of Life returns us to Morris, since one of his best songs, parodically hyperbolic, had the same title and worked to the same effect:

Come prick up your ears, and attend Sirs, a while;
I'll sing ye a song that shall make ye to smile:
'Tis a faithful description of the Tree of Life,
So pleasing to ev'ry maid, widow, and wife!
        Tol de rol &c.


. . . This tree universal most countries produce,
But till eighteen years growth 'tis not much fit for use,
Then nine or ten inches, for it seldom grows higher,
And that's sure as much as the heart can desire.
        Tol de rol &c.


. . . Like a stalk in the autumn if it should seem dead
Or like the willow, hang drooping its head,
If a female's the gardener its nature is such
That it shoots up its length at her delicate touch.
        Tol de rol &c.

> . . . Ye ladies who long for a sight of this tree,
> Take this invitation – come hither to me;
> I have it just now in the height of perfection,
> Adapted for handling, and fit for injection.
>                   Tol de rol &c.[9]

Although these and similar effusions cocked their snooks both at salon convention and at those advising more chivalrous and less predatory sexual relations, they cohabited too easily with the cultures of excess that 'manliness' relished (and were also too commonly sung in tavern and club-room) for us to think of them as consciously or purposefully transgressive. We may safely trust that each one of the carousing men in our pictures took their phallocentricity for granted, along with their assumptions about Nature's promptings and women's shared pleasure in those promptings. In due course, therefore, we'll see that these assumptions suffused a great deal of male behaviour, and some women's as well. Their prevalence further undercuts any illusions we may retain that among elite young bucks a prudential morality was hegemonic in this era, or that they were tightly 'polite', or that the satire that celebrated their lifestyles necessarily endorsed moral reform. Moreover, their light-hearted scurrility and self-parodic bravado had kinship with the anti-authoritarianism of carnivalesque humour and satire alike: in that sense they cut across the classes.

But let libertine practice await the next chapters. What's needed here – since much depends on it, not least a sense of what women might have tolerated in and taken from this culture, and eventually a sense of the cultural shifts that obliterated it – is a fuller understanding of what libertine values taught our protagonists about sex.

———•———

Libertine values might not have been consciously transgressive, but there's no denying that they were very seriously contested, or that most respectable eighteenth- let alone nineteenth-century people would have denied them any legitimacy. This was so much the case that it has been common for gender historians to construct a narrative about eighteenth-century gender politics that either bypasses libertinism altogether or sees it simply as a deviant or marginal expression. This is the currently dominant narrative; and it empahasises (and, so far as it goes, reasonably) so the enduring purchase of a morality of sexual restraint, monogamy and female submission that stretched back over centuries.

Men and women had long been told to occupy separate spheres, public and active for men, maternal and domestic for women. In law, religion and social organization, the wife's fidelity, the daughter's submission to the father, and the provision of unchallenged heirs had always been paramount principles. Increasingly in the eighteenth century science weighed in to this effect too. Medical texts and their discursive spin-offs could only endorse separate-spheres thinking in an era when the microscope was revealing the physiological bases of sexual difference by showing that woman possessed, not an active 'seed', but a passive ovum that awaited the male seed (or 'active principle') to bring it to life. Since, clearly, female pleasure wasn't necessary for conception to occur, this realization in principle steadily eroded all notions about sexual equalism and the necessary legitimacy of the pleasure-taking woman. The stereotype of the desexualized Victorian woman was already being prefigured in the medical advice given to her forebears.[10]

We should add to this the obvious truth that conventional moralists took a dim view of libertine arguments and manners. Since libertine materialism required moral questions to be settled by reason rather than by dogma or by reference to spirit, libertine casts of mind were equated with the early-modern Antinomian sects that held that, under the Law of Grace, moral law was not binding upon Christians. No surprise, then, that Dean Jonathan Swift had linked 'persons of libertine and atheistical tenets' axiomatically. Whether in the novel or in Hogarth's engravings, accordingly, libertine rakes, like whores, were required to meet sticky ends. Moreover, although the policing of libertine expression was relatively light (the pre-publication censorship of texts ceased with the suspension of the Licensing Act in 1695; the first Society for the Reformation of Manners collapsed in the 1730s; and the power of the ecclesiastical courts faded), there were key prosecutions. That of the bookseller Edmund Curll in 1727 (for publishing *Venus in a Cloyster, or, The Nun in her Smock*) inserted the notion of obscene libel into the common law that was embedded shortly after in an obscenity statute against anything 'tending to corrupt the morals of the king's subjects' or that was 'destructive of morality in general': henceforth libertine writers had to tread more carefully. Altogether, it is clear that we shouldn't think of the eighteenth century as a simply hedonistic age in which, as used to be said, 'the libido was liberated'.[11] Most people were sexually reticent by modern standards; and those who had free sexual lives were minorities and disproportionately male. In any case, the numbers of women who knew from bitter experience that conception had nothing to do with whether or not they felt sexual pleasure must have been legion. Moreover, as evangelical propaganda ever more noisily reaffirmed separate-spheres principles in the early nineteenth century, and as increasing cohorts of respectable people bought into them, it is fair to say that these views of sex were dominant by the 1820s, and almost impossible to contest.

That, however, lay in the future. Meanwhile, and until then, a quite different narrative should still be allowed to coexist with this prudential one, and it must allow plenty of room in high circles for libertine manners to flourish. Laying aside the fact that no man or woman cared a jot about theory once they got down to business in the bedroom, the truth is that no single discourse on sex has ever ruled unchallenged, and it certainly didn't in the long eighteenth century. First, among elites there had always been two rules on right sexual conduct: one conjugal, to provide heirs; the other extramarital, for love or pleasure. If anything, this dualism was accentuated in the early eighteenth century. Hitherto, adultery in either sex had been condemned regardless of the protagonists' social station. But the deepening valuation of male 'gallantry' and 'intrigue' seems to have softened hostility to the extramarital sex of men at least.[12] Furthermore, whatever was true of the prudential middle-class or provincial women (or of those who read advice books, medical texts or sermons), the assumptions about and practices of sophisticated metropolitan women show that older sexual models lived on. Even at the end of the century, articles in the fashionable *Bon Ton Magazine* still took it for granted, in the early-modern way, that women were the more voracious and passionate sex; and visual satires and erotica implied this as well.[13] The prints here as elsewhere are always eloquent cues to the unspoken, and it wasn't for nothing that Richard Newton's *Too Much of One Thing Good for Nothing* (1797), for example, has its post-coital couple on a settee, the man lolling in exhaustion while the complacently smiling and bare-breasted woman waits for more. In the wall-picture above them, a cock and hen spar meaningfully; the cock falls flat on its back, the pun fully intended [fig. 136].[14] Much the same understanding of female sexual capacity is implied in the anonymous *The Rivals, or a Dumpling in Danger* (1805). In blunt negation of female modesty, two young women compete for the eligible man, one pulling at his legs while the other swallows his head [fig. 137].

**Fig. 136** Newton, *Too Much of One Thing Good For Nothing* (Holland, 1795)

**Fig. 137** Anon., *The Rivals, or a Dumpling in Danger* (1805)

Further subverting the prudential sexual narrative were the numbers of people who continued to deny that men and women experienced sexual pleasure differently. For this there was good reason. Libertine values rested on what may be called a 'one-sex' model of male and female equivalence that retained its own 'scientific' justification. As Margaret Jacob has argued, the scientific revolution of the sixteenth and seventeenth centuries had made the body knowable less by its owner's moral qualities than by its size, shape, motion and weight. Lockeian psychology, additionally, had taught that the senses, written in 'nature', were the primary drives behind behaviour, ruling the body as the laws of mechanics ruled the machine. The senses' power was such that they compelled the individual to pursue pleasure and avoid pain: it was irrational, futile and unhealthy to deny their dictates. In nature, therefore, women's as well as men's bodies were propelled by identical urges and needs, so that in both sexes the indulgence of desire was a natural obligation. This 'materialism' – accordingly thus called – denied the rule of spirit, equated God and 'nature', and made matter and spirit one.

Sexual equalism was finally endorsed by cultural 'resistance' or 'inertia'. The lessons of the microscope weren't wholly or widely accepted. Many still believed – as Greek science had taught – that men and women were mirror-equivalents whose genitals differed only in their internalized or externalized expressions. They also believed, consistently with that, that each sex harboured 'seeds' that must be simultaneously ejaculated if conception was to occur. On these grounds, again, women must be assumed to enjoy the grand sexual quest as naturally as men. Here again examples are legion. Libertine texts like *The Battle of Venus*, sold by John Morgan of Hanover Square and prosecuted for obscene libel in 1788, insisted that in sex the woman experienced a 'paroxysm of fainting' and that her ejaculation was 'a precious effusion' that she 'discharged' upon the man's 'instrument of her joy'. In *Dialogue between a Married Man and a Maid*, for which Morgan was also prosecuted, the maid declares that 'he made me emit so pleasantly such a quantity of the delicious nectar that it flew about his hand and wetted him'. Another obscene libel – as late as 1830 – had a woman attributing her daughter's birth to the 'excess of pleasure' that she remembered enjoying exactly nine months before.[15] Among early nineteenth-century sexual nonconformists these understandings remained unshaken. The infidel bookseller, Richard Carlile, had no doubt (he told Francis Place) that women 'had an almost constant desire for copulation': 'the customs of society alone, I think, deter them from it'.[16] And in its early- to mid-nineteenth-century editions, the most popular of all sexual advice manuals, *Aristotle's Masterpiece*, was still leaving its readers to decide on the validity of 'one-sex' and 'two-sex' models respectively, but knew which it would choose. Women 'both have, and emit seed in the act of copulation', it asserted, adding that women 'take it ill to be thought merely passive in the act wherein they make such vigorous exertions; and positively affirm, that they are sensible of the emission of their seed in that action, and that in it a great part of the delight which they take in that act, consists'.[17] Until the 1820s these notions survived even in the common law. The law had always ruled that a prosecution for rape must fail if the act impregnated the woman, since the ejaculatory model indicated that she must in that case have consented pleasurably. The first legal text to contest this was published in 1803; but other legal authorities continued to endorse it into the 1820s.[18]

Altogether, views like these, though challenged, were prevalent enough to provide convenient justifications for those secure enough in status and wealth to indulge themselves. In licensing the equivalence of male and female desire, they tacitly licensed the extramarital adventures of both. What ensued was a good deal of male and some female sexual adventurism, a high degree of sexual candour, and a flourishing erotica as well – and this continued into the 1810s. There was, to be sure, crudity too. The word 'libertine' had been first coined pejoratively in the seventeenth century to describe the sexually incontinent, but it soon extended to many forms of free thought, and not all of them were sober or solemn. On both sides of the Channel, it was libertinism's wondrously flippant expression that caused most offence, along with its sexual reductionism. 'However weak and slender is the string, / Bait it with CUNT, and it will hold a king,' the Earl of Rochester had announced in the previous century. 'There is a bit of testicle at the bottom of our most sublime feeling and our purest tenderness,' as the French *philosophe* Diderot more amiably put it, while, as someone else opined, 'When one says, the gentleman . . . is in love with the lady, it is the same as saying . . . [that] the sight of her excited his desire, and [that] he is dying to put his prick into her cunt. That's truly what it means.'[19] 'Life can little else supply / But a few good fucks and then we die,' declared John Wilkes in *Essay on Woman* (1763) (if the text was his).[20] Or as the freethinker Richard Carlile wrote from prison in 1824, 'There is nothing in sexual intercourse . . . that has any relation to morals, more than in eating or drinking together.'[21] All the same, libertine texts occupied their own high ground. Scientific materialism became, in Jacob's words, 'the natural philosophy of choice among those narrators seeking to write in a voice that would now be described as fictional realism'; and since the erotic celebrated 'nature' and challenged artifice, it gave the writer and artist an alibi to write about sex. Indeed, some historians nowadays seek to extend the term 'libertine' to embrace nearly every cultural expression in the eighteenth century that gave the lie to all that was conventionally polite or religious. In its innumerable forms of 'sexual action and talk', they see libertinism as emblematic of Enlightenment itself, for it was centrally an Enlightened creation.[22] If flippant irreverence was one libertine tone, lofty speculation was another, for materialism encouraged people to see, think, and express purposes clearly and without cant: 'how I delight in observing life as it really is!' as Byron exclaimed.[23] In one form or another, the drift of libertine materialism was critical. For if nature ruled human compulsions, it followed that culture and its conventions were *artificial*: and this, too, was a liberating realization.

## How cultures differed

Two very different kinds of text may take us to the core of libertine understanding about the artificiality of culture and the relativism of morals. The first was *A Philosophical Dialogue concerning Decency: To Which is Added a Critical and Historical Dissertation on Places of Retirement for Necessary Occasions* (1751). Its author was probably Samuel Rolleston, a canon of Salisbury cathedral: if so, he was one of those advanced-thinking churchmen who later so vexed evangelical reformers.[24] In the next century, Francis Place included Rolleston's work in his list of the 'gross' books that wouldn't be tolerated in his later, much improved times. And the book does pose difficulties, not least in its cloacal concerns and its Swiftian obsession with the fetid materiality of women. Even so, as it enquires whether notions of decency are 'natural' or merely cultivated, it connects with Enlightened reasoning both about the physical body and about the relativism of manners. In the event, it doesn't resolve the tensions between materialist and conventional norms, but its purposes can be glossed generously. As it reminded its readers that women's lower bodily obligations were, after all, the same as men's, it was in effect rejecting the idealization of women and stressing the sexes' common humanity:

> Is it not a great absurdity, for a creature [woman] to be proud who produces
> such monstrous filth and nastiness? . . . If a lady was extremely proud and
> insolent on account of the beauty and form of her body, or the exquisite
> firmness of her flesh and skin, she could not but see the absurdity of being
> so, if a philosopher should say to her, Madam, what you are so proud of is
> made of no better materials than my chamber-pot or close stool pan: and has
> the same kind of nastiness in it.

Or, as Pope had realized years before, 'Celia, Celia, Celia shits'.

At the book's centre is its protagonists' argument about whether decency
is 'natural'. The author is walking in the country with two friends when he
is taken short. Hating 'to do such a thing in public', he retires to a field,
observing that he could not pass water if anyone watched him. While he
relieves himself, one friend, 'P.', is provoked to ask the other, 'E.':

> Don't you think that decency is founded in nature? And don't you observe
> that there is a desire in almost everyone of retiring from company to do
> several things, which are not only lawful, but necessary? which desire seems
> to me a natural instinct or (perhaps to speak more properly) a dictate of
> nature, and the shame of doing such things in publick, or before other
> persons is a *natural* shame, what nature and reason produce in us.

'E.' disagrees. Decency is defined not by nature, he says, but by 'customs
and manners'. He reminds his friend that in some societies people copulate
in public 'without any manner of ceremony'. Christian Adamites once
went naked, as some races still do. In Venice, people defecate and urinate
publicly against the pillars of St Mark's. In England women have hidden
their breasts in one century and exposed them in another. And while 'our
ladies in England are asham'd of being seen even in going to, or returning
from the most necessary parts of our houses, as if it was in itself shameful
to do even in private, what nature absolutely requires at certain seasons
to be done', he cites 'an old woman in Holland [who] set herself on the
next hole to a gentleman, and civilly offer him her muscle [mussel] shell
by way of scraper after she had done with it herself'. In England, men
urinate in the streets but women never do: 'if this shame or modesty be
founded in nature, why should not a man be asham'd of such a thing as
well as a woman?' If there was some *natural* shame in mankind, it was
only because food becomes 'filthy and nasty' when it passes through the

body: 'Such filth and ordure proceeding from our lower parts is the reason why St Paul in one of his epistles calls them, I think, uncomely parts, and less honourable', even though 'surely they are to sight as comely as any other'.

'P.' won't have any of this. A sense of decency is 'natural', he insists. The ancient names of the private parts (*pudenda*, etc.) 'show the sense most nations have of modesty and decency'. If men and women were not to conceal their parts from each other, 'rapes, fornication, adultery, and all uncleanness would appear at noon day, and be common in our public streets'. In the end, Rolleston lets it rest here by announcing bathetically that 'Nature dictates the decency . . . of all the polite and well-bred people in the world'. Churchman though he is, however, one feels that he votes with 'E.'[25]

— • —

The second example, Richard Payne Knight's *Worship of Priapus*, had much greater impact in its time. As the century wore on, multiplying encounters with distant or past cultures enhanced all manner of speculation about the cultural relativism of manners and values, along with the desire to return to first, or 'natural', principles. Some of these encounters elicited risky recommendations of polygamy or polyandry,[26] but the most important for our purposes was with the antique Roman past in the excavations at Pompeii and Herculaneum. For English readers this was mediated through Sir William Hamilton's anthropological and archaeological explorations while serving as plenipotentiary at Naples. The priapic fertility cults he discovered not only challenged prevalent assumptions about the chasteness of antique Roman culture; they also bore a fair responsibility for the phallocentrism of ensuing libertine values.

Dutiful, self-contained, and austere, Hamilton was no practising libertine (despite his implausible love of and marriage to the low-born but beautiful Emma Hart, thirty-one years his junior). Yet he was certainly a man of the freethinking Enlightenment. He was fascinated by what he saw as the equivalence between the phallic Roman amulets excavated at Herculaneum, the similar amulets still worn by the women of the Neapolitan poor, and the surviving phallic votive offerings and fertility practices discovered in the remote churches of the Abruzzi and Calabria. During the festival of St Cosmas ('the modern Priapus', he noted), country women would still sleep overnight in front of the saint's altar, nursing waxen phalluses in pursuit of magical fertilization, and sometimes emerging pregnant (with priestly help). Hamilton sent examples of these phalluses to the British Museum, praising the 'naturalness' of the local people above the affectations of the Neapolitan nobility: 'I am one of those who think the animal man in its nude state is by no means bad.' He believed that his researches exposed the pagan elements in Catholicism, which in the anti-Catholic 1780s was a useful point to score. More pertinently they revealed in both ancient and contemporary worship the enduring power of a 'natural' religion.

In 1781, Hamilton described his discoveries in a letter to Sir Joseph Banks, president of the Royal Society. In 1786 Payne Knight published Hamilton's letter to Banks and elaborated on his discoveries in his *Account of the Remains of the Worship of Priapus, Lately Existing at Isernia, in the Kingdom of Naples...to which is Added a Discourse on the Worship of Priapus, and its Connexion with the Mystic Theology of the Ancients.*[27] Knight had himself travelled in Sicily, collecting bronzes which he bequeathed to the British Museum. A Whig-radical MP, he was vice-president of the Society of Antiquaries and a member of the Society of Dilettanti, this last including high-minded men like Hamilton, Banks, Horace Walpole, politicians like Dundas, and the less high-minded Sir Francis Dashwood and Duke of Norfolk – many of them fellows of the Royal Society also. It was to the Dilettanti that Knight circulated his *Account*, and it became a manifesto of the anthropologically and historically informed materialism of that decade.

The book insisted that 'there is naturally no impurity or licentiousness in the moderate and regular gratification of any natural appetite; the turpitude consisting wholly in the excess or perversion'. It appealed to the rule of 'nature' over human behaviour, as against the mere 'artifice' that ruled manners. And it explained why the representation of the phallus, far from being 'ludicrous or licentious', should be regarded as 'a very natural symbol of a very natural and philosophical system of religion'. In his recurrent appeal to the natural, Knight spoke directly to the materialism that these circles took for granted: 'Men, considered collectively, are at all times the same animals, employing the same organs, and endowed with the same faculties: their passions, prejudices, or conceptions, will of course be formed upon the same internal principles, although directed to various ends, and modified in various ways, by the variety of external circumstances operating upon them.' Manners and customs, therefore, must be considered 'relative to the natural causes which produced them':

the senses' promptings, taking it for granted that it was better to indulge them than to suffer in 'misery supreme' from ungratified desire. 'The nakedness of woman is the work of God,' his *Marriage of Heaven and Hell* declared (*c.*1789), and he illustrated that truth by depicting naked couples embracing, not what the Academy would have approved of. 'Those who restrain desire,' he wrote, 'do so because theirs is weak enough to be restrained. And being restrained it by degrees becomes passive till it is only the shadow of desire.' (Seventy years later, the poem was thought unsuitable for 'every drawing room in England'; republication was refused in 1863.)[33] In the new century, Shelley, though advocating 'natural temperance', believed that chastity was a 'monkish and evangelical superstition', and his 'Queen Mab' (1813) protested at 'religious, political, and domestic oppression'. Privately issued, the poem was castigated as an exercise in freethinking libertinism, and its printer's name was cut out of copies to avoid prosecution.

Quacks and charlatans fed off bastardized versions of these notions. From 1780 to 1782 Dr James Graham offered fashionable customers the revitalizing experience of his 'grand celestial state bed' in his Temple of Health and Hymen in Adelphi Terrace, off the Strand, and later in Pall Mall. Twelve feet wide and nine feet long, filled with stallions' hair, the bed was supported by forty glass pillars and linked to fifteen hundredweight of magnets. Intended to cure jaded sexual appetites and infertility, couples were allowed to buy a night on it for £50 to help them conceive perfect babies. This profitable fantasy drew on a notion of the efficacy of inseminatory 'effluvia' that was not far distant from what was believed in Sir William Hamilton's Abruzzi. The magnets were 'continually pouring forth in an everflowing circle . . . inconceivable and irresistably powerful tides of the majestic effluvium, which every philosophical gentleman knows, has very strong affinities with the electrical fire'. They delivered their cure without active copulation as soothing music carried 'the happy couples into the arms of Morpheus'. 'The most impudent puppet-show of imposition I ever saw,' Horace Walpole scoffed; and a half-dozen ribald prints show how many agreed with him. Within a couple of years Graham was bankrupt. A taste for sexual speculation didn't mean that gullibility was limitless.[34]

Libertine practice was here and there purposively organized and enacted across the country. The allegedly orgiastic goings-on among Sir Francis Dashwood's 'Monks' (later erroneously called the Hellfire Club) at

Medmenham Abbey *c*.1750–76 – its members including the fourth Earl of Sandwich and John Wilkes – never ceased to be cited by the libertine's enemies, even if largely on hearsay.[35] Kindred ideas and practices spread widely. Their best recorded and least expected rooting-place was the small town of Anstruther in Scotland. There, a group of merchants and libertine gentlemen, all Enlightened, publicly polite, and convinced that their practices were sanctioned by reason and nature, in the 1730s formed a club called the Beggar's Benison. It survived for a century. They entertained themselves biennially with lectures on sex, much drink, collective masturbation, and half-naked posture girls dancing on a table. In 1783 the club extended honorary membership to the Prince of Wales. On the great man's Scottish visit as king in 1822, he allegedly gave the club a snuff-box full of his mistresses' pubic hair. The club spawned branches in Edinburgh and Glasgow. How many other such clubs flourished we'll never know; we know about this one thanks only to the chance survival of its records and relics: these including the prince's pubic snuff-box, utensils engraved with genital emblems, and a glass drinking cup in the shape of a penis and testicles.[36] The club's genial 'benison' or blessing was 'May prick nor purse [testicles] ne'er fail you'. Back in London, the same blessing was familiar to the cognoscenti. 'That your *great toe* & your purse may never fail you is the wish of . . . y.ʳ most faithful humble servant William Hamilton' – so that sedate antiquarian signed his letters to Joseph Banks, president of the Royal Society, 'great toe' referring to the Roman phalluses and votive equivalents that had so intrigued him in Naples.[37]

## CHAPTER ELEVEN

# PHILOSOPHY AND RAKING

## Practices

When the young James Boswell 'sallied forth like a roaring lion after girls', he claimed that he was 'blending philosophy and raking'. 'Swear solemn with drawn sword not to be with women *sine* condom *nisi* Swiss lass,' he instructed himself in his continental diary: and then, also, 'chase libertine fancies'. But it was the raking, not the philosophy, that mattered most to him. Undeluded, Boswell knew very well that his urges originated in bodily parts that lay a good deal lower than his head. By the age of twenty-nine he had tried to seduce over a dozen high-born ladies, had made mistresses out of three wives, four actresses, Rousseau's paramour, and three middling-class women, and had had sex with over sixty street-girls. Even though he guarded himself in 'armour complete', he was infected by gonorrhoea at least seventeen times in his lifetime. His diaries carefully recorded his conquests as they multiplied virtually until his death.[1]

Boswell wasn't unusual in these enthusiasms. The wealthy lawyer's son, William Hickey, spent even more of his youth than Boswell did in and out of London's bagnios and brothels, there accumulating a knowledge of courtesans, whores and venereal infections as extensive as Boswell's; not once do his candid memoirs examine his compulsions. Aristocrats and princes had no cause to think hard about their sexual lives either. England's seldom-washed but premier Duke of Norfolk had amours 'without delicacy and without number'. His 'intemperate indulgence of animal impulse'

Fig. 138 Gillray, *Le Cochon et ses Deux Petits, – or – Rich Pickings for a Noble Appetite* (H. Humphrey, 1792)

lasted into his very old age, even as he lived publicly with his mistress, Mary Gibbon. Libertinage of this kind was highly visible to the print-buying public, for printshops publicized it frequently. Gillray's depiction of Norfolk hobnobbing with two fat prostitutes in *Le Cochon et ses Deux Petits* (1792) would have caused little offence [fig. 138]. In the spirit of *Harris's List of Covent Garden Ladies*, its subtext explains who the women and their clients were: 'Nell H—t—n, weighs rather under thirty stone; & in the absence of the great man, his place is agreeably filled by T— W—d, the celebrated collector on the highway.' Yet the joke was about their fatness, not the duke's behaviour. Everyone knew that masculine identity was constructed around what most men, to each other, called fucking. This was what manliness was about, even more than drinking, clubbing, gambling and duelling.[2]

Clearly, most gentle young bloods who acted out libertine principles could do so without having to ponder their rationale very deeply. Materialist theories gave them excuses for their sexual incontinence should they need them, but their sideways slippage from philosophy to self-indulgence was usually unselfconsciously achieved. Again, the era's libidinousness shouldn't

Armitstead at the time and that she would swear to it. His candour was much admired. When he did marry Mrs Armitstead (they became a very happy couple, sharing a taste for gardening), it was eight years before he announced it, 'the odd thing' then being that 'people who were shock'd at the immorality of his having a mistress are still more so at that mistress having been his wife for so long'.[7] Despite his priapic enthusiasms, Fox was still 'polite'. By the age of twenty-five, he was a member of Johnson's literary club, the Society of Dilettanti, and friends with Johnson, Burke and Goldsmith.

'Let not the joy she proffers be essay'd, without the well-try'd cundum's friendly aid': given the company these men kept, this was sensible advice, though, since catgut 'armour' didn't always work, neither illegitimate offspring nor venereal disease could be stigmatized unduly. Boswell, Fox, Byron and their like would detail their venereal symptoms to friends with sardonic frankness if not relish. About their predatoriness they were just as open. Most affected to believe that their female targets were equal and willing participants. Sometimes this was justifiable, but there was sexual savagery also. Poor girls were especially fair game. Polite women never moved in the nocturnal streets unescorted, but poor women had to; and young bloods used the streets as hunting grounds. Lord Barrymore would drive through London 'fancy free', sending his minion to run after fanciable girls to arrange 'interviews' later.[8] Although the violence delivered upon them is seldom recorded, we occasionally glimpse it. When one 'little profligate wretch' refused Boswell 'performance', he 'pushed her up against the wall', and when people came to help her, he made his escape after abusing her 'in blackguard style'.[9] Wordsworth liked telling tales about Hazlitt's 'licentious conduct to the girls of the Lake' during his 1803 visit. Rejected by one girl, he 'lifted up her petticoats & smote her on the bottom' or (in another version) 'whipped her *more puerorum* [in the way of boys]'. Hazlitt narrowly escaped being ducked by the local people by retreating to Wordsworth's house.[10]

Once hooked, poor girls, if pretty and clean, might be passed around like commodities. '*Try her*,' Byron wrote to a friend of one girl in 1818: 'you will find her a good one to go . . . uncommonly *firm* of *flesh* . . . sufficiently expert in all the motions . . . though a little too full in her person.' In just such a spirit, Sir Harry Featherstonehaugh got the beautiful Emma Hart to pose for his friends as a half-naked posture girl (the tale that she served as one of the votaries at Dr Graham's Temple of Health and Hymen was probably apocryphal) before passing her on to Charles Greville. Greville proclaimed that she was 'the only woman he had slept with without offending his senses, and a cleaner, sweeter bed-fellow did not exist', and had her painted by Romney (who himself became obsessed by her). Then Greville passed her on to his uncle, that compulsive collector of beautiful objects, Sir William Hamilton. Hamilton married Emma while he was in Naples, and then in turn tolerated her liaison with the much younger Nelson. From 1798 all three then lived in a more or less amicable ménage.

All this was publicly known, and it provoked much ribaldry from Gillray, Rowlandson and Isaac Cruikshank – their commentaries, incidentally, as well informed about Hamilton's priapic discoveries as they were about his private life.[11] Cruikshank's *A Mansion House Treat – or Smoking Attitudes!* (1800) has Hamilton, Emma and Nelson smoking pipes (with the Lord Mayor of London and Pitt). The conversation is full of heavy *doubles entendres.* Hamilton's pipe is being relit by a sailor who tells him that his 'pipe is too

**Fig. 139** Isaac Cruikshank, *A Mansion House Treat – or Smoking Attitudes!* (Fores, 1800)

Ah where, & ah where, is my gallant Sailor gone?—  
He's gone to Fight the Frenchmen, for George upon the Throne.  

*DIDO, in Despair!*  
*Lady ―――*

He's gone to fight ye Frenchmen, t'loose t'other Arm & Eye.  
And left me with the old Antiques, to lay me down & Cry.

**Fig. 140** Gillray, *Dido, in Despair!* (H. Humphrey 1801)

short, 'tis quite worn out, it wants a new life', while Emma sits next to Nelson in one of the 'attitudes' (or classical postures) for which she was famous. 'Pho,' she says of Hamilton, 'the old man's pipe is allways out but yours burns with full vigour.' 'Yes yes,' Nelson complacently replies, 'I'll give you such a smoke I'll pour a whole broadside into you.' His pipe is the longest, and its bowl resembles one of Hamilton's phallic ex-votos [fig. 139]. In 1801, similarly, Gillray's *Dido, in Despair!* [fig. 140] has Emma, barefoot in her nightgown and now very fat, theatrically lamenting Nelson's departure to battle, his ships visible through her window. The floor is scattered with vaguely phallic antique statuettes, while an open book on the windowseat has a picture of her in a naked 'attitude'. 'Ah where & ah where, is my gallant sailor gone?' she exclaims in the print: 'He's gone to fight ye Frenchmen, t'loose t'other arm and eye / And left me with the old antiques, to lay me down and cry.'[12] The story echoed on long after Nelson's death – in Rowlandson's *Modern Antiques* of 1811, for instance, in which a buxom young woman opens an Egyptian mummy-case to embrace the handsome young officer hidden inside, while an old man (Hamilton) glares at them malevolently in a room littered with antique vases and figures [fig. 141].

Marrying beneath one was always laughed at, but Hamilton wasn't the only man to do so. Poor girls and actresses made good mistresses and wives because they were pliable, unthreatening, and thus more easily loved. Lord Chancellor Thurlow when young offered his hand to Polly

**Fig. 141** Rowlandson, *Modern Antiques* (Rowlandson, 1811)

Humphries, the daughter of the keeper of Nando's coffee-house at Temple Bar, as several prints cheerfully advertised. Unmarried, he had three daughters by her. The Duke of Bedford lived with 'an antiquated demirep'. The Earl of Derby's beloved was the actress Miss Farren, once shown naked in a Sayers print; physically ill-matched, he married her in 1797, and was then much lampooned in the prints.[13] When Byron went down-market, which was usual, it was because he deplored 'that dangerous thing a female wit': 'I despise the sex too much to squabble with them.' 'I am still living with my Dalilah, who has only two faults, unpardonable in a woman,' he wrote in 1808, '– she can read and write.' 'She is the prettiest bacchanti in the world – & a piece to perish *in*,' he wrote of one of the 200 women he claimed to have bedded in Venice in 1818–19, both his creative energy and his organ much refreshed in that tolerant city: 'there is no *liaison* only *fuff-fuff* and passades – & fair fucking.' Or, as he quipped jauntily to his publisher John Murray when he sent him the fourth canto of *Childe Harold*:

> Now I'll put out my taper
> (I've finished my paper
> For these stanzas you see on the *brink* stand);
> There's a whore on my right
> For I rhyme best at night
> When a c—[un]t is tied close to my *inkstand*.[14]

Although the king himself was chaste, blue blood had similar standards. The Duke of Clarence, sent to Hanover to polish his manners, lamented his separation from 'the pretty girls of Westminster; at least such as would not clap or pox me every time I fucked'. Later he took the actress Mrs Jordan as mistress, discarding her and their children when he became William IV in 1830.[15] The Duke of York when young took as his mistress Letitia Smith (among many others, the venturesome Mary Anne Clarke included). Elevated by royal favours and painted by Reynolds and Stubbs, Letitia was soon known to have lived 'in the style of mistress' to a half of the prince's cronies; later she married Sir John Lade, who was one of them.[16] When the princes did justify their infidelities (not often), the appeal to 'nature' served well enough. 'Our inclinations are not in our power,' the Prince of Wales wrote to his rejected wife Caroline in 1796, 'nor should either of us be held answerable to the other because *nature* has not made us suitable to each other.'[17] For the most part, however, the princes felt accountable to no one, their licentiousness even more reflexive than Boswell's or Byron's.

## Mocking the prince

Princely and aristocratic profligacy was not new to this era. What was new, thanks to expanding print cultures and markets, was its high visibility and hence risibility. No sexual adventurer suffered more from this exposure than the Prince of Wales. Satirists let his very youngest affairs pass – with his sisters' governess Mary Hamilton, for example, and then with the actress Perdita Robinson, when he was seventeen. It was his illicit and initially secret marriage in December 1785 to Mrs Fitzherbert, a Roman Catholic widow of twenty-eight, six years older than himself, that put him irretrievably in their sightlines. The marriage defied the insistence of the Royal Marriages Act of 1772 that royal marriages should be invalid without the king's consent; in any case, those married to Catholics were excluded from the succession by the Act of Settlement of 1701. So, to Mrs Fitzherbert's distress, the prince was forced in due course to deny the marriage, not least to persuade Parliament to settle his debts as a *quid pro quo*. From then on, his amours, debts and debauches were compulsively monitored.

On these subjects prints were less discreet than newspapers were, both because they translated textual hints and allusions into literally represented scenes and because it was more difficult to prosecute them for seditious libel. The prince's several efforts to curb them were in vain. A reference in John Wilkes's letters in 1788, to 'two most extraordinary prints, for which the prince's solicitor is prosecuting Fores', indicates the prince's initial response to the exposure of his 'marriage'; and he later tried to have Gillray's *Voluptuary under the Horrors of Digestion* (1792) prosecuted too [fig. 90].[18] Neither attempt succeeded; as a result, many scores of prints addressed his errancies from 1786 all the way through to the 1820s, and none of them pulled their punches. In the 1780s and 1790s satires on George came fifth in frequency to those on Fox, Pitt, the king and Lord North, in that order (from 1778 to 1797, 294 catalogued prints were about the prince, just ahead of Burke); but he dominated the print repertoire thereafter.[19] (Not that the prince's victimization stopped him from resorting to satire on his own behalf. When his father went mad in autumn 1788, his advisers asked Thomas Rowlandson's friend, Henry Wigstead, to get Rowlandson to provide prints against the Pittites to support the prince's bid for the regency.[20]) Until the 1820s, not a move was missed in his sexual meanderings – from his secret marriage to Mrs Fitzherbert, on to his paternally imposed and disastrous marriage to Caroline of Brunswick in 1795; on via his affairs with Lady Jersey, the Duchess of Manchester, Miss Gubbins, Mrs Taylor, Mrs Billington, Lady Hertford, the Duchess of Richmond (among many others), to his efforts to divorce Caroline in 1820; and finally on to Lady Conyngham, upon whose capacious bosom he found peace as king. In the 1780s, prints had been on the edge of respectful, depicting George's still handsome visage flatteringly. But their tone darkened as patience and deference wore thin. The indecent exposure of Kingsbury's or George Townly Stubbs's *His Highness in Fitz* (1786) [fig. 3] was the first to break one great taboo by venturing right into the princely bedroom. Gillray wasn't far behind: in his wholly ficticious *The Morning after Marriage – or – a Scene on the Continent* (1788), the prince and Mrs Fitzherbert wake up in the bedroom of a French inn after their 'marriage';

**Fig. 142** Gillray, *The Morning after Marriage – or – a Scene on the Continent* (Holland, 1788)

the prince's posture recalls the yawning wife in Hogarth's *Marriage à la Mode* and the whole recalls Hogarth's indecent cabinet engravings, *Before* and *After* [fig. 142]. Henceforth, Gillray (for Humphrey) and Isaac Cruikshank (for Fores) all but captured this prurient market in what looks like an amiable competition, the latter usually lifting ideas from the former. Skim even a brief sample of their 1790s prints, and you must wonder how much any prince could bear. No heir apparent had been so contemptuously treated before; none has been so treated since, not even the present one.[21]

If the prince's marriage to Mrs Fitzherbert had been sensational, it was as nothing compared to his ensuing dalliance with Lady Jersey. Fores employed Isaac Cruikshank to produce the first of many satires on this new liaison, the separation between the prince and Fitzherbert now public knowledge. In *My Grandmother, alias the Jersey Jig, alias the Rival Widows* (1794), Mrs Fitzherbert (left) clutches the £6,000 annuity that paid her off, as she laments: 'Was it for this paltry consideration I sacrificed my – my – my – ? for this only I submitted to – to – to – oh shame for ever on my ruin'd greatness!!!' – while the haglike Lady Jersey sits on the prince's knee as he

**Fig. 143** Isaac Cruikshank, *My Grandmother, alias the Jersey Jig, alias the Rival Widows* (Fores, 1794)

declares, 'I've kissed and I've prattled with fifty grand dames / And changed them as oft, d'you see, / But of all the grand mammys that dance on the Stein [in Brighton] / The widow of Jersey gave me &c &c.' A portrait of Solomon on the wall announces that he had 300 wives and 700 concubines [fig. 143]. In 1796, as the Jersey affair resumed, Gillray's *Fashionable-Jockeyship* has Lord Jersey piggy-backing the prince towards Lady Jersey in bed, the prince holding up two fingers to represent the cuckold's horns and asking

**Fig. 144** Gillray, *Fashionable-Jockeyship* (H. Humphrey, 1796)

'Buck! Buck! how many horns do I hold up?' – to which the cuckold replies, 'E'en as many as you please!' [fig. 144]. Cruikshank's *Future Prospects, or Symptoms of Love in High Life* (1796) has the prince kick over the tea-table as he shouts at Caroline, 'Marriage has no restraints on me! No legal tie can bind the will – tis free & shall be so!' Caroline replies: 'Obey, alass the task's seviere [*sic*] how can the female mind with pleasure yield when every look's a frown!!! Alass poor babe!!!'. On the wall Gillray's earlier print, *The Constant Couple*, underscores a pointed contrast with the contented marriage of the George III and the queen; papers on the floor include *Marriage à la Mode*. Peering around the door as the couple quarrel, Lord Jersey, horned, announces that his wife awaits the prince in the next room, and there, on a sofa, you can glimpse her, bare-breasted, with her legs obscenely open [fig. 145]. I. Cruikshank's *A Cure for the Heart Ache!! – A New Scotch Reel Altered from the Brunswic* [sic] *Minuet & the old Jersey Jig* (1797), brings Lady Jersey to her own tribulations. Her rival for the prince's favours is briefly the Duchess of Manchester, here escorting him drunk to bed and snapping

**Fig. 145** Isaac Cruikshank, *Future Prospects, or Symptoms of Love in High Life* (Fores, 1796)

**Fig. 146** Isaac Cruikshank, *A Cure for the Heart Ache!! – A New Scotch Reel altered from the Brunswic Minuet & the Old Jersey Jig* (Fores, 1797)

her fingers at Jersey. George carries a phallic candle, broken; Lord Jersey under the bed complains of his own and his wife's usage [fig. 146]. Visual humiliations like these multiplied and continued, to Fores's and Humphrey's profit. They added to the large corpus of prints that were simultaneously publicizing his debts, debaucheries, increasing corpulence and association with the Foxite opposition.

As events proved, these exposures of the 1790s were by no means the cruellest that the prince had to endure. It was when George Cruikshank took over Gillray's and his father's mantles in the 1810s that the real vitriol flowed. Sharpened by the iniquities of the regency years, prints then were to bear much more overtly radical subtexts. Meanwhile, what do these earlier images tell us?

It would be foolish to deny their critical tinge, but it would be just as foolish to associate them with the 'jacobin' textual attacks on the prince and other grandees that were multiplying more or less audibly in the 1790s (in Pigott's *Jockey Club*, say). Their exposures of princely transgressions were for elite or sophisticates' consumption. They didn't aim to influence the common people, still less to subvert the monarchical principle. They had their formal alibi in the notion that satire was publicly useful, and that 'all publick men, however distinguished, must in their turns submit to it, if necessary to the welfare of the state'. Earlier critics of satire had deplored the ridicule of great men, and mocking royalty was sedition in common law. But even Hutcheson had agreed that 'the very spirit of burlesque' resided in the contrast between ideas of 'grandeur' and of 'baseness'; and this principle tacitly sanctioned the mockery of the Prince of Wales also.

George was not the only victim of the celebrity voyeurism that ruled the printshops. From the 1780s onwards, prints increasingly defied the barriers between private and public, so that many besides the prince were mocked. The satires variously targeted Lord Derby's inappropriate liaison, for example, or Captain Bissett's spying on Lady Worsley's nakedness, or the fattening Emma Hamilton's comical yearning for Nelson, or Lord Barrymore's sporting habits. The Duchess of Gordon's compulsive matchmaking featured in print, along with Miss Gunning's adventures, Sir John Bowes's flirtations with Lady Tyrconnel, the celibate Pitt's ('stiff to everybody but a lady') comical efforts to woo Eleanor Eden, and Lord Thurlow's fury at his illegimate daughter's elopement. In high circles most of these exposures were complacently received. They breached the codes of privacy, but only in the interest of the upper class's own titillation: they were acceptable so long as the lower classes didn't get titillated as well. Reputation amongst the high-born was not necessarily eroded by private disreputability: to that extent, public and private borders held firm. As one commentator put it:

> Our ministers may constantly be carried to bed in a state of complete intoxication without being reproved by me, when they do not reel or stutter in the senate; they may every night drown their intellects in a sea of spirits and water at White's, if they attend to the national business in the morning; they may ruin themselves at play, if they faithfully administer the laws; they may be mean and parsimonious, if they do not defraud the public, and seize on pensions and sinecures beyond all bounds of decency and justice; or they may betray and calumniate private friends, if they do not renounce and vilify public principles.

Or, as one of Fox's supporters wrote, 'The friends of the present ministers are fond of contrasting the virtues of Mr Pitt's private character with the excesses of Mr Fox . . . [But] it is rather problematical whether a man will make the better minister for having uniformly kept the ten commandments.'[22]

Under these conditions, those who were *not* targeted could regard the personalized attack upon others as funny. Stories in this spirit – about all manner of sexual jinks in high places – filled the multiplying scandal sheets that catered to middle- and upper-class readers from the 1770s onwards. This readership was not interested in reforming the world; nor were they 'radically' critical: it was celebrity voyeurism that fuelled them. The *Town and Country Magazine* and the *Bon Ton Magazine: or, Microcosm of Fashion and Folly* of 1791–5 were hugely popular sources of gossip, but the juicier stories also appeared in costly volumes like *Trials for Adultery, or the History of Divorces* (published in seven volumes in 1779–80 and explicitly illustrated), or *Crim. Con. Biography: or Celebrated Trials in the Ecclesiastical and Civil Courts for Adultery*, which appeared in twelve volumes in 1789. The even more salacious *Cuckold's Chronicle* in 1793 helpfully omitted tedious legal details in order to highlight the rude bits. Affording much titillatory amusement, they added to London's gaiety, as such things still do. Thus when Lord Grosvenor brought a divorce action against his wife, interested readers could learn that her several lovers had included the Duke of Cumberland, George III's libertine brother. Grosvenor's servants, they would read, had tracked the couple to an inn in St Albans, broken down the bedroom door, and 'found the D of C sitting at the bedside along with Lady G . . . the lady with . . . her breasts wholly exposed'. In due course, the offended Grosvenor was exposed in his turn when *Trials for Adultery* published a plate entitled 'Miss Roberts sitting naked in Ld. Grosvenor's lap at the hotel in Leicester Fields'.[23]

Where scandal sheets led in exposing these and like stories, satirical print secured them in memory. Just as Isaac Cruikshank's *Sketches from Nature!!!* of 1796 could remind its purchasers of Gillray's exposure of Lady Worsley's bottom fourteen years earlier, so prints by Gillray, Cruikshank and Williams in 1799 would ironically remind their purchasers of Cumberland's long-past misdeeds by having the duke's overfleshed ghost appear to warn his nephew to shun profligacy. In Williams's *The Ghost*, the duke visits the Prince of Wales while the prince is in bed with one Miss Gubbins. As the ghost urges the prince to 'shake off the traitorous crew that lurk around thy table; expose their treacherous schemes . . . and thus by

The Ghost.

**Fig. 147** Williams, *The Ghost* (Fores, 1799)

one bold patriotic deed restore Britannia's darling son', Miss Gubbins exclaims in understandable alarm: 'Oh dear, if this is the amusements of high life I wish I was in the Crescent [at Bath] again.' 'Hush Gub,' the prince replies: 'dont be alarmed the old boy is only come for some more burgundy' [fig. 147].

## Lady Termagant Flaybum

The cruelty of this culture is undeniable, although it was no more cruel than ours is, in its media-led fixation on the errancies of celebrity. But the cruelty then was compounded by the fact that the attack was usually men's upon errant women. Male violence upon women is thought to have been curbed in the eighteenth century, but that referred to violence in public.[24] Men who for their own convenience might assume an equality in the passions of courtesan or mistress didn't necessarily think of wives in the same spirit.

Domestic aggression was endemic, and wives could be legally chastised. In 1782, Judge Buller ruled that a husband could thrash his wife provided the stick was no thicker than his thumb. Distinctive also was the cruelty that male culture could deliver to the wealthiest as well as the poorest of women, and the near indifference with which it was regarded. So we turn finally in this chapter to a gothic melodrama about a wife's sadistic victimization by her wicked husband, and to how it was thought about and publicized. It illuminates the cramping of an Enlightened woman's ambition in that age, the part Gillray's caricatures played in advertising her misfortunes, and the public indifference to her fate.

In May 1786, William Holland's shop published an extraordinary print by the then up-and-coming Gillray. It was entitled *Lady Termagant Flaybum Going to Give her Step Son a Taste of her Desert after Dinner, A Scene Performed Every Day near Grosvenor Square, to the Annoyance of the Neighbourhood* [fig. 148]. Gillray didn't sign it, though not because he was ashamed of its lubricity (he signed few of his satires before 1789). He was almost certainly commissioned to produce it, and he did so without compunction, along with other calumnies, as we'll see. The print was unusually large (16 by 21 inches) and expensive: Holland sold it at 7s. 6d. coloured. John Wilkes wrote to his daughter in Paris that he would have sent her a copy had the price not been so 'extravagant'; but it must have sold well, because Holland was still advertising it three years after publication.[25] Gillray at this date continued to be tortured by his flagging career as an art engraver, and this helps explain the print's ambition. Carefully composed, the uncaricatured faces of its three protagonists are deftly rendered in stipple, and their figures display Gillray's most fluent line. The sardonic but concrete titling is pure Gillray, and so is the subject. In *déshabille* and elaborate hair styling, Lady Flaybum leans back in her chair languidly. One breast is bared and her legs are crossed, then an indecorous posture for a woman. Holding a birch-rod in her right hand, she gestures with her left towards a crying boy. A servant girl unbuttons his breeches to prepare him for chastisement.

The print carried its own pornographic shadow. Holland at this date shared his Drury Lane premises with the publisher of flagellation literature, George Peacock. Some who bought Gillray's print would have recognized its provenance in Peacock's *Sublime of Flagellation: or Letters from Lady Termagant Flaybum to Lady Harriet Tickletail, of Bumfiddle Hall* (*c*.1777–85) and in his *Exhibition of Female Flagellants in the Modest and Incontinent World* (1777).[26] The

LADY TERMAGANT FLAYBUM *going to give her* STEP SON *a taste of her* DESERT *after Dinner*,
*a Scene performed every day near Grosvenor Square, to the annoyance of the neighbourhood.*

**Fig. 148** Gillray, *Lady Termagant Flaybum Going to Give her Step Son a Taste of her Desert after Dinner, A Scene Performed Every Day near Grosvenor Square, to the Annoyance of the Neighbourhood* (Holland, 1786)

second of these cost a guinea (a guinea and a half if its six plates were coloured): it aimed at affluent buyers. Its subtitle announced that it was based on the 'indubitable facts, that a number of ladies take a secret pleasure, in whipping their own, and [other] children committed to their care', and that their passion for the birch-rod was 'as predominant, as that of mankind' (i.e. men). Gillray knew the book. In the same year as *Flaybum*, he engraved for Holland *A Sale of English Beauties in the East Indies*, showing newly arrived English courtesans being auctioned off at Madras. Would-be purchasers pinch their breasts and lift their dresses speculatively. The quayside is littered with crates of birch-rods, anti-VD pills and books. The books include Cleland's erotic prostitute novel, *Fanny Hill*, and Peacock's

*Female Flagellants*.[27] So it might have been Holland that encouraged Gillray in these flagellatory fantasies, although Gillray's tastes pointed that way as well. Flagellation motifs recur in his later work. In 1795, he recalled *Lady Termagant Flaybum* by inventing *Lady Termagant Tinglebum: the Lovely Flagellation*. This showed another lady of the birch-rod about to chastise a young girl. The subtitle is again pure Gillray, though it reads like the invention of a man in alcoholic or other delirium: '*Vide Monthly Recorder June the 1st 1792. The Pupils of Birch or the Severe Aunt a Scholastic Scene Frequently performed by Lady Eliza W\*\*\*\*\*\*. The Beauty of Worcester upon her Juvinile* [sic] *Offenders her Usual Recept for the Cure of Idleness, Carelessness. &c.&c.&c. . . . The Pupils of Birch the Severe Aunt and Governess and the Lovely Flagellation*'.[28]

What matters here is Lady Termagant Flaybum's real identity and Gillray's relation to it.[29] She was Mary Eleanor Bowes (1749–1800). On her father's death in 1760, she had inherited one of the greatest fortunes ever made in the Newcastle coal trade, and thus became one of the richest women in England. She owned Durham estates at Streatlam Castle and at Gibside, and had some £600,000 in trust. Her mother brought her another estate in Hertfordshire and the Grosvenor Square house to which the title of Gillray's *Flaybum* refers. She was also 'Enlightened': as she recorded in her later *Confessions*, her doting father had been a libertine rake, but he had brought her up to be a cultivated and freethinking young woman with 'an insatiable thirst' for knowledge. Moral teaching he had neglected: 'I never heard him once say . . . that chastity, patience and forgiveness of injuries were virtues; and he was very passionate.' As a child she had read the Bible, but 'equal or greater pains were taken to instruct me in the mythology of every heathen nation that ever existed'. Religious commitment she discarded early, for characteristically rational reasons: 'my mind was so puzzled with such a variety of religions, that, except the firm belief of a God, I knew not which of all the modes of worship to adopt from real conviction, as to the weak judgement of a child, all appeared equally supported by tradition.' Fluent in languages, she later privately published a poetic drama, and, until her first husband forced her to break off the relationship ('telling me she was a wild, light, silly woman of bad character'), she befriended the bluestocking Mrs Montagu. She was also a woman of rare botanical curiosity. She built experimental hothouses and conservatories in Chelsea to raise exotic plants, and she patronized the great botanist Linnaeus's pupil, Daniel Solander, who accompanied Captain Cook and Joseph Banks on the *Endeavour*.

In 1767, aged eighteen, she married the ninth Earl of Strathmore. Although she bore him five children, the marriage was miserable. Strathmore had no intellectual tastes to match hers, while the countess, in his eyes, had bizarre ones. He complained of her sharp tongue and malice, her friendship with Mrs Montagu, her whimsical fondness for cats and dogs, and her inclination to favour her daughters over her sons, the eldest of whom she virtually rejected. He did not, oddly, complain of her many flirtations. 'No woman piqued herself more upon her principles, or allowed love to be made to her more profusely': so Thackeray later wrote of her in *Barry Lyndon* (1844), his novel based on her story. She became pregnant by the most serious of her lovers, George Gray. This may explain why, despite her enlightenment, she consulted gypsy fortune-tellers at her Hertfordshire estate and 'conjurors' in bedizened dives in London. She confessed to trying (vainly) to abort Gray's child with 'a black inky kind of medicine' and a mixture of pepper and brandy. Once with three confidantes, she marvellously migrated across social boundaries incognito to seek guidance on whether she should extricate herself from her marriage:

> we walked to the Old Bailey, where we met a little boy, who came up to us and asked if we wanted the gentleman who so many people came after, and that he would conduct us to him? We said yes, and he carried us through blind alleys to Pear-Street . . . There was such a number of people in the room we waited in . . . that it was almost six o'clock before they began with us . . . Capt Magra, who went down in perfect unbelief, came up convinced of the man's knowledge from what he told him . . . [In] the coldest room I ever was in, and which had no other furniture than two (or three at most) rotten chairs and a wooden trunk[,] I went by the name of the widow Smith . . . I passed myself . . . for a grocer's widow, and was come to consult the conjuror whether I should marry a brewer, who proposed to me amongst others.[30]

In the event her relationship with Gray collapsed, and with it her reputation. The *Morning Post* traduced her for betraying her husband: 'Who has not seen her since [her marriage] in the Mall gracing the hymenial throng?' The paper recycled gossip about her fondness for cats and her aversion to her son. It told how the little boy wept when he saw a young lady stroking a cat, and wished he were a cat himself, for then 'my mama would love me!' (These stories were the sources of Gillray's *Flaybum* print and of another we shall come to shortly.) But the countess's future looked brighter when the earl died of consumption in 1776. Widowed at the age of thirty, with an income of some £20,000 a year and a cultivated intelligence on which to rebuild her life, she had everything to look forward to. Jesse Foot, later the family's surgeon, whose account is a major source, described her at this point as glowing 'with all the warmth of a gay widow'. She had a clear complexion, graceful neck and shoulders, and a 'very pleasing embonpoint'. The one sign of unease was a nervous tic. Her jaw moved from side to side when she was agitated. It had increasing cause to do so, for she had poor taste in men, and her misfortune was next to meet and fall for the villain of this piece, Andrew Robinson Stoney.

Stoney was the anti-hero protagonist of Thackeray's *Barry Lyndon*. (Thackeray had been at school with the countess's grandson, and drew on Jesse Foot's *Lives* of the benighted couple.) A bankrupt Irish lieutenant on half-pay, Stoney lived at the St James's coffee-house. He was the libertine adventurer incarnate. His associates, Foot wrote, were 'all of that sort, which idle and uneducated men of pleasure pick up at the gaming table, clubs, horse races, watering places, &c'. Having already got through a previous wife's fortune, he now sought another and harassed the countess for her favours. In 1777 he impressed her by fighting a duel on her behalf with 'Parson' Bate, the calumnious editor of the *Post*. Rumour had it that the duel was shammed, but within days the couple were married.[31] Stoney changed his surname to Stoney-Bowes, or Bowes for short (the countess's father's will required this), and then, the quarry snared, revealed himself in his true colours.

The countess had had the wit before the marriage to execute a deed securing her estates to herself, but Bowes brutally forced her to make a deed of revocation to put her wealth at his disposal. That done, he resumed his rakish ways. 'Hymen's torch burnt not clear,' as Foot discreetly put it, 'and the countess from henceforth may truly be pronounced to be DEAD ALIVE.' The divorce trial a decade later heard evidence about Bowes's foul language and physical abuse, the black eyes he gave her, and her tears – a list of abuses so offensive to the 'tender and delicate eye of chastity' that Foot withheld its details. The countess bore children by Bowes, but his illicit amours were resumed, and his illegitimate children multiplied. With the female house-servants permanently imperilled by his wandering hands, he forced the countess to dine with his mistresses. He sold her Chelsea house and greenhouses and cut down her timber at Gibside to pay for his gambling losses. He controlled her every movement, supervised her letter-writing and discharged her servants. One servant testified that his wife trembled whenever she heard him approaching, and wept continuously. She went to every length to appease him. She used her local influence to secure his election as MP for Newcastle. And in 1778 she abased herself in her lengthy *Confessions*, written at his command. In them she acknowledged her many past sins. These included her 'unnatural dislike' of her eldest son, past flirtations at Almack's, adultery with Gray, the attempt to abort Gray's child, the breaking of her promise to marry Gray, and her irreligion. She hoped Bowes would now stop abusing her, 'for indeed I fear that you are of an unforgiving and, in this respect, unforgetting temper; else you could not, for so many months together, have behaved so uniformly cruel to one whose whole wish and study was to please you'. Bowes locked away the *Confessions* for future use.

Then in February 1785 she snapped, unable to take more. Decamping from the Grosvenor Square house, she brought articles of the peace at the Court of King's Bench to restrain Bowes from abusing her further. Bowes was bound over for a year on his own sureties (and it indicates Bowes's rakish but elevated connections that the Duke of Norfolk provided sureties also). Next, she brought a suit at the Consistory Court to obtain a separation on grounds of cruelty. She moved to an apartment in Oxford Street, but Bowes moved in nearby, so she moved again to Bloomsbury Square. In the Consistory Court in May 1786 Bowes was found guilty of cruelty and ordered to pay £300 in annual alimony. He appealed against the verdict to the Court of Arches, at this point releasing the countess's *Confessions* as evidence against her. He stalked her obsessionally, a deepening madness upon him. 'A more pitiable object I never beheld than Bowes,' Foot recalled. 'His mind was every moment upon some new device; and although he had more than a dozen engines at work, I am confident not one of them knew what the other was about . . . He laid all his plans over the bottle. He sat up all night, drinking very hard . . . Castles and rents melted away like the baseless vision of a dream.' It was in this condition that Bowes must have turned to Gillray.

Excepting the internal references in the three, perhaps four prints that Gillray produced on the saga in 1786, there is no evidence that Gillray and Bowes were acquainted. But his *Lady Termagant Flaybum* in May can only be explained as Bowes's lunatic commission – a resort to image magic against his wife in a culture highly respectful of the image's power. Its inaccuracies betray Bowes's bizarre projections (who was the flagellant really?), but also Gillray's ready compliance. Perhaps Gillray had been incoherently instructed. The boy about to be chastised should have been Lady Strathmore's eldest son, not stepson. Of her interest in flagellation there is no evidence whatsoever outside Bowes's say-so.

Bowes's fingerprints also mark Gillray's second comment on the saga, *The Injured Count..*[*es*]*s* — (undated, but probably also 1786) [fig. 149]. An innovative print of technical interest to print historians (its texture was achieved by printing on a gauzed ground),[32] it is even more bizarre than *Flaybum.* It fastens on the gossip of nearly a decade past about Lady Strathmore's dislike of her son and fondness for cats. The countess sits below-stairs drinking with her gin-swilling servants. She suckles two cats at her bared and exaggeratedly bulbous breasts. A little boy beside her cries (as had been reported in 1777), 'I wish I was a cat my mama would love me then.' A footman holds a candle and says pointedly, 'My lady it is time to come to bed'. Behind her, a man gazes at a wall map of the Bowes

**Fig. 149** Gillray, *The Injured Count..*[*es*]*s*— ('C. Morgan', 1786)

estates: 'we'll have it far'er or nearer,' he says, the phrase indicating that he was her current lover, the East India Captain Farrer, brother of her solicitor (a detail that Gillray might have had from Bowes). On the wall hangs an obscene picture of Messalina. Also at the table is an extraordinary figure identified by a paper in her lap, entitled 'Duty of a ladies maid. by M. Morgan see Old Baly Chron[le]'. This was Mrs Morgan, who had helped Strathmore escape from Bowes in February. In a print in which the other figures are conventionally drawn, her torso is grotesquely figured. It tapers down to the merest point at the waist.

This surreal device links the print, next, to a mysterious Holland-published aquatint by Gillray, *The Miser's Feast* of March 1786 [fig. 150]. It contains the prototype of Mrs Morgan's figure. In it, a fashionably dressed woman enters a room followed by her servant. She carries a book entitled *W[oma]n of Ple[as]sure* (the subtitle of *Fanny Hill*). She is greeted by a bizarrely wasp-waisted female representing Famine. She wears a hat and lower petticoat and holds a cup: her top is bare, her breasts pointed. A miserly figure in patched gown and cap sits at the central table dining on a rind of cheese. On the right, the naked figure of Death holds an arrow

**Fig. 150** Gillray, *The Miser's Feast* (Holland, 1786)

behind his back with one hand and with the other holds out a plate bearing a bone. An emaciated cat miaows for it. The room is bleakly furnished; a window is blocked to avoid the window tax; the fireplace is blocked by a crucifix. But locked cupboards, chests and money-bags indicate the miser's wealth. 'What else can follow, but destructive fate, / When Famine holds the cup, & Death the plate?' the subtext asks. This puzzling print has usually been read as an eccentric allegory on miserliness. Yet the manuscript note with which the Victorian collector Edward Hawkins described his copy (now in the British Museum) reads, 'Lady Strathmore'.[33] And the parallel between Famine's tapering torso in *The Miser's Feast* and Mrs Morgan's in *The Injured Count..[es]s—* does suggest that *The Miser's Feast* was another Bowes-commissioned print. The fashionable lady entering the room and associated with prostitution makes a plausible countess, while Famine may be Mrs Morgan. The print either predicts the miserable company awaiting the countess should she desert Bowes, or it was meant to depict her consultation with the conjuror, its point then refashioned for better sales.

Gillray's engagement with the tragedy wasn't yet concluded; but the story had yet to move to its climax. By late 1786, a few months after *Flaybum*, the long-suffering countess had every reason to fear Bowes's further plots against her. In November, having lost his appeal to the Court of Arches against the separation, he appealed to the High Court of Delegates, thus extending proceedings for another three years. Meanwhile, 'suspicious persons' were seen haunting Bloomsbury Square and following the countess whenever she drove out.[34] When she employed a constable to watch her house, Bowes bribed the constable to help him. On the afternoon of Friday, 10 November, she went to visit someone in Oxford Street, taking Mrs Morgan and her lover Farrer for protection. The treacherous constable and several men burst into her host's or hostess's house, claiming to hold an arrest warrant from Lord Chief Justice Mansfield. She and Farrer were forced into her coach, ostensibly to drive to Mansfield's house. At Highgate Hill they were stopped by armed ruffians, Bowes among them. Farrer was ejected from the coach, Bowes and other men climbed in, and off they drove with the captive countess up the Great North Road. Though the carriage windows were broken, and cries of 'Murder!' were heard, and a turnpike keeper glimpsed a woman inside struggling and gagged, nobody intervened. Farrer, however, had hastened back to London to raise the alarm. On Monday, Mansfield sent his tipstaffs in pursuit, while the Court of King's Bench granted a writ of *habeas corpus* and warrants against the abductors.

On the Saturday, the fleeing coach changed horses at Doncaster, and was later spotted at Branby Moor and Ferrybridge. Bowes was taking her to the family seat at Streatlam Castle. Both on their journey and on arrival there, he abused her cruelly, pressing her to stop the separation process and live as his wife. Over the eleven days she was in his power, he punched her, whipped her breasts with his watch-chain, beat her with sticks, and put a pistol to her head. The abduction had by now been reported nationwide. The tipstaffs arrived at last, and the castle was besieged by angry locals. Bowes bundled the countess out of a hidden door and on a single horse rode off with her (as the newspapers had it) 'over dismal heaths and trackless wilds covered in snow'. Lodging in Darlington, he threatened her with a red-hot poker to her breast, swearing that he'd get a mad-doctor and straitjacket to bring her to her senses. Next morning, 21 November, they rode off early over fields and hedges to shake off their pursuers. The countess cried out to some countrymen, and luckily they went for help. Bowes was cornered in a field and knocked to the ground with a stick, and Lady Strathmore was freed. 'In a kind of womanish exaltation', the countess bade him farewell as he lay bleeding, and 'with the whole country in her favour' returned to London in exhaustion.

A week later Bowes was arraigned before King's Bench for breaching the articles of peace and ignoring the writ of *habeas corpus*. Hissed as he entered Westminster Hall, he stood before the court with his head bandaged, two men supporting him, close to real or shammed collapse from his wounds. It was at this point that Gillray returned to the subject with one last print (unsigned and unfinished), showing the tottering figure of *Andrew Robinson Bowes Esqr. as he appeared in the Court of Kings Bench . . . to Answer the Articles Exhibited Against Him, by his Wife, the Countess of Strathmore* [fig. 151]. He depicts the countess and Mrs Morgan among the spectators. In fact, the countess didn't attend the trial. Returning to London after her ordeal, she was unable to stand or walk for a month. One might have hoped that this print was Gillray's effort to make amends for his earlier calumnies – were it not that in the background, in a mad and an impossible conceit, the countess is shown bare-breasted.

So far as Bowes was concerned, the rest was diminuendo. Renewed articles of peace kept him in King's Bench prison for the last twenty-two years of his life. He spent his time there waging complex legal battles and (according to Foot) in heavy drinking, seductions and cruel jokes on fellow prisoners. For the abduction, in 1787, he was fined £300, required to

**Fig. 151** Gillray, *Andrew Robinson Bowes Esqr. as he Appeared in the Court of Kings Bench . . . to Answer the Articles Exhibited Against Him, by his Wife, the Countess of Strathmore* (Jackson, 1786)

provide fourteen years' surety of £10,000, and sentenced to prison for three years. A year later, the Court of Common Pleas ruled that the deed of revocation which had given Bowes control of the countess's estate was invalid because it had been made under duress. A decade later again, he was still appealing unsuccessfully to have that decision reversed in the House of Lords. Futile litigation occupied him until he died. In 1789 the High Court of Delegates ruled in favour of the countess's suit for divorce. When this was announced, the countess sent him a triumphant epitaph: 'He was the enemy of mankind, deceitful to his friends, ungrateful to his benefactors, cringing to his superiors, and tyrannical to his dependants.' 'A villain to the backbone,' Foot called him.

The countess might well now have recovered some equilibrium; nevertheless her reputation was in tatters. For a dozen years, newspaper coverage and gossip about her had been unremitting, and her erratic behaviour in the first years of the Bowes marriage had lost her her friends. Only her attorney and General Lambton, MP for Durham, stayed loyal to her. Nor did the several court cases help in her rehabilitation, for Bowes's defence rested on the *Confessions* of her immorality that he had extorted in 1778. In 1793, she had to bear the *Confessions'* open publication (they sold expensively for 2s. 6d.). It was also repeatedly said that she slept with her manservants, as Gillray's *Injured Count..[es]s*— hinted, while in 1788 Captain Farrer's wife published a pamphlet to publicize her husband's affair with the countess. Probably written by Bowes, it denounced her taste for 'the meretricious impurities of a libidinous and adulterous passion'.[35] For at least three years, moreover, Gillray's *Flaybum* had been selling well. Four years after her liberation, the countess's reputation was still being besmirched in satire. In 1790, the Duke of York displaced the countess's eldest son, the tenth earl, as Lady Tyrconnel's lover. An Isaac Cruikshank satire at once showed Tyrconnel in bed bare-breasted, with Strathmore crawling under the bed to hide as the duke enters the bedroom. 'My mither did sa before me,' he says in his northern accent, in case purchasers had forgotten his mother's adulteries [fig. 152].

**Fig. 152** Isaac Cruikshank, *A Strath Spey or New Highland Reel as Danced at Seaton D—l* [Delaval] (Fores, 1790)

In this melodrama we measure what some women had to bear in that libertine world. There was no contemporary pity for the countess's victimhood, let alone interest in Gillray's small part in her story. When Horace Walpole wrote to Lady Ossory about her in 1785, he conveyed his indifference to her plight: 'the news of my coffee-house . . . is that Lady Strathmore eloped last night, taking her two maids with her – but no swain is talked of. The town, they say, is empty – it certainly does not produce its usual complement of extravagances, when one solitary elopement of a veteran madwoman is all that is at market.' Wilkes told his daughter in Paris of four new prints 'on the old subject', including 'a family scene or two [Gillray's *Flaybum*], in Grosvenor Square' (the Wilkeses were planning to buy a house in the Square); but he said no more than that about the scandal. 'That strange and eccentric woman', William Hickey's memoirs noted briefly in passing.[36] Thackeray's *Barry Lyndon* did her no posthumous favours either. 'She had as much love of admiration, as strong, uneasy a vanity, and as little heart as any woman I ever knew': thus Thackeray allows her wicked husband to define her in the novel, and no contrary view is given. Far north in Durham, Mrs Judith Baker's interest in her neighbour's miseries is attested in the prints, songs, verses and press-cuttings that she kept on the case; but her interest apparently stopped short of support. In sum, for most people this was a celebrity tale of passing and merely gossipy significance. It was fit stuff for newspapers and printshops, but no more than a part of the pageant of others' misfortunes that fed the pleasures of voyeurism and malice.

# CHAPTER TWELVE

# WHAT COULD WOMEN BEAR?

## The female libertine

One day in 1819 the poet Tom Moore remarked to a Mrs Methuen ('very pretty & very agreeable,' he noted in his diary) 'what odd things women's hearts were (in reference to matters of love & gallantry)'. 'Not odder than men's,' she niftily replied. But Moore ignored this riposte and ploughed on:

> I asked her didn't she think the restraints with which women had to struggle produced more inconsistencies in their conduct & more fantastical fancies in their minds than were usually observable in men. – The course of the latter is like a free, unresisted current, whereas the continued pressure under which the feelings of women lie, and the narrow channels of duty through which they are forced, produce all those multiform shoots and unexpected gushes which arise from similar causes in artificial water-works.[1]

Moore failed to record her response to this inventive thought, but his puzzlement about how the constraints imposed on the women of his class affected their attitudes matches ours now. It isn't easy to answer the questions tackled in this chapter. How did women bear the many condescending, cruel, parodic or fantasy-laden representations of themselves that were peddled by men? What did they think of men's farts-and-bums humour when (or if) they met it? And did they recognize 'misogyny' when it hit them? Although the word was first recorded in 1656 to signify hatred of or contempt for women, it is unlikely to have passed their lips. Yet by modern standards practically the whole body of jokes and satires that addressed relations between the sexes can seem to have been woman-fearing, woman-hating, or woman-patronizing. Women's novels and diaries reveal the range of female wit and their appreciation of men's wit in the salon; but evidence of their responses to men's humour outside the salon is muted. Add to that our tendency to project on to past women present-day notions of what they *should* have found intolerable, and the trickiness of the task is clear. What women laughed at, how unrestrainedly they laughed, whether they laughed at all, and how many of them laughed, are among the murkiest of our subjects.

Commonly met with nowadays is the notion that women's attitudes to body-centred ribaldry differs 'naturally' from men's. Menstruation, childbirth and mothering are said to induce in women a commonsensical relationship to the body that precludes the obsessional curiosity that plagues the male. They are also said to be more at ease with the sexual body because they are free of the growing boy's obligation to detach himself from the mother – from which flows men's supposed battle against the feminine in themselves and in others, and the peculiarly male pathologies that ensue.[2] All this may or may not be so; but biologically grounded explanations carry less weight than the more obvious historical truths that, over centuries, the male policing of female decorum has been unremitting, and that women have policed themselves just as vigorously. This induced in many women in the period, if not Moore's hydraulic turbulences, then as great a 'learned ignorance' and hence anxiety about bodily matters as any attested among the Victorians.[3] What room was left, then, for the expressions of female bawdry?

Dr Johnson once wryly explained why there were 'ten genteel women' for every genteel man: 'A man without some degree of restraint is insufferable; but we are less restrained than women. Were a woman sitting in company to put out her legs before her as most men do, we should be tempted to kick them in.' Few genteel girls escaped the conditioning that Johnson parodied here, not to mention volumes of manly advice to the effect (say) that 'one of the chief beauties in a female character is that modest reserve, that retiring delicacy, which avoids the public eye, and is disconcerted even at the gaze of admiration'. A 1798 conduct book managed in a single paragraph to commend woman's 'feminine reserve', 'delicacy of manners', 'delicacy of sentiment', 'duty and affection', 'unwearied circumspection', 'habits of privacy', 'useful and methodical employment', 'diffidence', 'purity of heart' and 'enjoyment of domestic happiness'. Just as efficiently, male pundits were setting women on their way to chronic invalidism. John Gregory, for example, reminded them of the 'timidity, arising from the natural weakness and delicacy of your frame; the numerous diseases, to which you are liable; [and] that exquisite sensibility, which, in many of you, vibrates to the slightest touch of joy or sorrow'. 'The sedentariness of your life,' he continued, 'naturally followed with low spirits or *ennui*, whilst we [men] are seeking health and pleasure in the field; and the many, lonely hours, which in almost every situation, are likely to be your lot, will expose you to a number of *peculiar* sorrows, which you cannot, like the men, either drown in wine, or divert by dissipation.'[4] Familiarly, the sexual double standard operated too. A husband could divorce a wife for adultery, for example, but she could divorce him only for cruelty. High-born wives might be allowed discreet affairs once the male heir was born, but full sexual licence was for men. Some men saw the injustice in all this, but Dr Johnson's was the more common response: 'the woman's a whore, and there's an end on't'. When Boswell wondered why a woman should be thought more culpable than her partner in sin, Johnson explained that chastity was 'the great principle which she is taught. When she has given up that principle, she has given up every notion of female honour and virtue.' As he put it on another occasion, all the property in the world depended on the chastity of women: for 'confusion of progeny constitutes the essence of the crime; and therefore a woman who breaks her marriage vows is much more criminal than a man who does it. A man, to be sure, is criminal in the sight of GOD; but he does not do his wife a very material injury if he does not insult her; if, for instance, from mere wantonness of appetite, he steals privately to her chambermaid. Sir, a wife ought not greatly to resent this . . . A wife should study to reclaim her husband by more attention to please him.'[5]

Most polite women colluded in this subjugation because they internalized and amplified the stereotypes it rested on. Long subjection to volumes of high-minded exhortation delivered crippling effects. If a handful did challenge patriarchal values, they still castigated female transgression in patriarchal terms. When Helen Maria Williams informed her readers that 'my political creed is entirely an affair of the heart, for I have not been so absurd as to consult my head upon matters of which it is so incapable of judging', she mandatorily denied the very real power of her political opinions. The evangelical Hannah More was not alone in insisting that 'an early habitual restraint is peculiarly important to the future character and happiness of women' and that a 'curb on their tempers and passions can alone ensure their peace'.[6] 'Men,' the *Lady's Magazine* opined in 1803, 'are formed to stand firmer and behave braver in dangers than women. In those distresses and misfortunes which reduce women to tears and bewailing, men . . . exert their stronger mental powers' to remedy them. Time after time as a result, we encounter in women's public if not private writings such self-consciously and prissily inflected prose, such anxiety about convention, such a disciplining and denial of the self, such buttoned-up rectitude – that the modern reader is tempted anachronistically to cry out, 'get real!': though it is also true that these stylistic postures had male equivalents in abundance.

It is no surprise that female anxiety about 'reputation' could be stifling. When Charles Fox's unhappily married aunt ran off for love, her sisters unleashed a chorus of panic-stricken and prissy clucking, ostracizing her until she left her lover in penitence, and then closeting her like contaminated goods.[7] Or take Fanny Burney. When one day in 1792 she and some friends visited Boydell's Shakespeare Gallery, they were harassed there by a seeming madwoman. Excruciatingly embarrassed, Burney's party were set to 'run for their lives' until the woman was recognized as an actress 'performing vagaries to try effect, which she was quite famous for doing'. When one of the party suggested that they report the woman to Boydell, Burney cried 'O no!' in a 'horrid fright': 'I beseech I may not be named! – and indeed, Ma'am, it may be better to let it all alone. It will do no good: and it may all get into the news-papers.' Burney devotes a letter of several excited pages to this minuscule adventure. Though a natural novelist, she was convention-ruled to the core. Meeting a young woman who professed belief in 'dissipation' and who had discarded belief in the afterlife after reading Hume's essays, she was first '*horror'd*' and then disgusted. 'A young and agreeable *infidel* is ever a shocking sight,' she thought. 'She is in a very dangerous situation with ideas so loose of religion, and so enthusiastic of love.'[8] This was one woman who would not have patronized printshops. Her self-censoring journals and letters are free of sexual tittle-tattle or scandal-mongering and, although the queen's intimate, she doesn't once hint at the Prince of Wales's dissipations. So we are not to overdo our sense of female liberty in this era, even in high social circles. A numbing concern for propriety was woman's lot, and most deferred to it in pained anxiety.

All that said, however, female culture was not monolithic, so that we can and now should have it both ways. Here and there, women could express themselves with relative freedom – relative at least to the arid volumes of moralized advice aimed at them. 'Pictures of perfection, as you know, make me sick and wicked,' as Jane Austen wrote cheeringly. Restrictive advice affected pious, or provincial, or upwardly striving middle-class women more than it did the elites, but, even among these, individual personality allowed for huge variance, and cussedly independent-minded women were many. Increasing numbers of women were active in the public world, despite evangelical and other advice not to be. The arenas in which they engaged had to be appropriate to female delicacy and could never be overtly political. Even so, we are now aware of a 'female Enlightenment', for example, and that female mobilization in associational, civic and national duties (and in the anti-slavery movement also) was impressive.[9] In any case, we should repeat that the historian of mentalities looks not for an impossibly 'averaged' opinion in this or that age, but for what was thinkable and do-able, regardless of its assumed normative status or the imagined percentages of people involved. There are, then, many grounds for allowing the ostensibly 'transgressive' woman of our period the autonomy she claimed for herself; and there is no particular need to regard her defiance as 'dangerous' either.[10] Furthermore, if libertine materialism sanctioned the passions and pleasures of men, we shouldn't forget that it licensed women's also. Among many of the female elites and metropolitan sophisticates, we discern a lack of coyness, a knowing worldliness, and a fair indifference to the taboos that constrained their more anxious sisters. Despite the deepening insistence on male and female differences, 'one-sex' assumptions still found their voice in these circles, and were not punished unduly.

In 1776 James Boswell heard this in a conversation with an unnamed lady. She talked about marriage with what struck him as a man's clear-sightedness, even if her point that conventional norms were negotiable disconcerted him mightily:

> [She] argued with me that marriage was certainly no more but [than] a political institution, as we see it has subsisted in so many different forms in different parts of the world. 'Therefore,' said she, 'it is merely a mutual contract which if one party breaks, the other is free. Now,' said she, 'my husband I know has been unfaithful to me a thousand times. I should therefore have no scruple of conscience, I do declare, to have an intrigue, and

I am restrained only by my pride, because I would not do what is thought
dishonourable in this century, and would not put myself in the power of a
gallant.' I argued that the chastity of women was of much more consequence
than that of men, as the property and rights of families depend upon it.
'Surely', said she, 'that is easily answered, for the objection is removed if a
woman does not intrigue but when she is with child.' I really could not answer
her. Yet I thought she was wrong, and I was uneasy, partly from my own
weakness as a reasoner, partly from the pain which one feels on perceiving
established principles sapped.[11]

Ironic, self-valuing, careless of convention and informed about the larger
world too, this lady had a mind to speak with, and spoke it openly.
Conventional moralists would have called her libertine. Most of her
sisterhood would have reacted to her as Fanny Burney did to the young
lady who read David Hume. Yet her candour and self-control were at one
with the spirit of rational enquiry which the Enlightenment demanded.
And there were hundreds of women like her. The freethinking Lady
Strathmore was another of Enlightenment's daughters (never once taught
'that chastity, patience and forgiveness of injuries were virtues', and a friend
of the bluestocking Mrs Montagu). She was certainly punished for her
indiscretions, but her grief was delivered by her wicked husband, not
'society'. 'I am no woman,' the free-living Teresia Phillips ironically
proclaimed as she flaunted her 'female masculinity' as courtesan-rake and
defied what she called 'female supineness'.[12] Lady Hester Stanhope, niece
of William Pitt and daughter of the third Earl of Stanhope, likewise
consorted with the 'half-mad' Lord Camelford unchaperoned. She coined
her own word 'primosity' as a synonym for 'cant', declaring that she cared
no more for genteel gossips 'than if they were to spit at the sun': 'They are
like the flies upon an artillery-horse's tail – there they ride, and ride, and
buz [sic] about, and then there comes a great explosion; bom! And off they
fly.' 'I hate affectation of all kinds,' she added. 'I never could bear those
ridiculous women who cannot step over a straw without expecting the man
who is walking with them to offer his hand. I always said to the men, when
they offered me their hand, "No, no; I have got legs of my own".'[13]
G. M. Woodward's print, *A Repartee* (1801) [fig. 153], would have appealed
to her. 'Upon my soul my dear! I have seen you before,' the man quizzes
her through his monocle. She turns on her heel: 'Have you, sir? Then now
you may see me behind.'

**Fig. 153** Woodward, *A Repartee* (Fores, 1801)

Lower down the social scale, the freest women, as like as not, were the daughters of rational dissenters. Mary Hays, for example, friend of Mary Wollstonecraft and Godwin, wrote frankly about her own sexual passion in her novel, *The Memoirs of Emma Courtney* (1796), while her second novel, *The Victim of Prejudice* (1799), advertised itself as exposing 'the mischiefs that have ensued from the too great stress laid on the reputation for chastity in women'. Wollstonecraft also acknowledged that female desire was 'natural'. She might lament that women were 'subjected by ignorance to their sensations, and only taught to look for happiness in love'; and in some of her recommendations Horace Walpole's 'hyena in petticoats' could be numbingly demure. But she knew that she could not live 'without some particular affection'; and when a Frenchwoman boasted to her that she was innocent of lust, her reply was '*Tant pis pour vous, madame, c'est un défaut de la nature*'. Women must be allowed 'free scope to grand passions', she declared; amorousness was the foundation of that 'loving flame of universal love' that could alone redeem mankind. Girls, she said, should refer to the 'organs of generation' with the same freedom with which they spoke of their hands and eyes. Woman was not created 'to be the toy of man', or a 'rattle' that 'must jingle in his ears whenever, dismissing reason, he chooses to be amused'. It is true that Wollstonecraft was made to pay for her boldness. Richard Polwhele's poem 'The Unsex'd Female' (1798) charged her with giving 'instructions in priapism'. And when, after her death in 1797, William Godwin's *Memoirs* of her revealed how determinedly she had sought extramarital happiness (first with Fuseli the artist before he rejected her, then with Gilbert Imlay, and at last, fulfillingly, with Godwin himself), she was attacked by Polwhele for her 'licentious indecorum' and by the *Anti-Jacobin Review* as writing 'scriptures . . . for propagating w[hore]s'.[14] In his elaborate print for that journal, the *New Morality*, Gillray included her *Vindication of the Rights of Woman* among the papers pouring forth from a 'Cornucopia of ignorance' [fig. 222]. Even so, the fact that in the whole body of graphic satires this last is the only catalogued reference to Wollstonecraft hardly suggests that everyone thought her views earthshaking or worthy of satire.

In London's great world, the notion that each sex must inhabit separate spheres was easily fractured. The playful inversion of sexual roles was more or less tolerated, and sexual boundaries were commonly crossed. At masquerades women dressed as men and men dressed as women, while salon society accepted both the female 'amazon' and the effeminized fop, not to mention the chevalier D'Éon, so practised in transvestism that in later years people couldn't remember and took bets on what sex he belonged to; a post-mortem print of his naked corpse had to be engraved to prove his manhood.[15] Effete male 'macaronis' ruled the coffee-shops while great ladies like Devonshire engaged in politics. Theatre played with gender inversions, and (to judge from prints) lovers did also. '*See here presented to your view, / A Scene most frolicksome* [sic] *& true, / A Lady – but a Rakish one, / Her lover's breeches putting on*', proclaims a print of 1750, and it shows a military captain in *déshabille* reclining effetely on his bed as his open-breasted lady pulls on his breeches [fig. 154]. Thirty years later, in Carington Bowles's extraordinary *A Morning Frolic, or the Transmutation of the Sexes* (1780), the man dons his lady's headdress as she poses bravely in his military clothes [fig. 155]. Thirty years on again, and Caroline Lamb played cross-dressing and probably sado-masochistic games with Byron – even if her enthusiastic dalliances with the poet said more about her own febrile masochism than it did about common behaviour: 'I lov'd you as no woman ever could love,'

*See here presented to your view.*
*A Scene both frolicksome and true.*
*A Lady – but a Rakish one,*
*Her Lovers Breeches putting on,*

*The Captain too seems highly Blest*
*At seeing her so smartly Drest*
*But who will e'er commend his Taste;*
*Or who can think the Lady's Chaste.*

Printed & Sold by HENRY BRYER Engraver & Printseller, Fleet Street ?

**Fig. 154** Anon., *'See here presented to your view / A Scene both frolicksome &
true . . .'* (Bryer, 1750)

she told him, 'because I am not like them but more like a beast who sees
no crime in loving & following its master.'[16]

Naturally, moralists deplored these inversions of right order; and the
1750 print just cited was formally disapproving. 'Who will e'er commend
his taste / Or who can think the lady's chaste?' it asks. As the Revd James

A MORNING FROLIC, or the TRANSMUTATION of SEXES.
*From the Original Picture by John Collet, in the possession of Carington Bowles.*

**Fig. 155** Carington Bowles, *A Morning Frolic, or the Transmutation of the Sexes* (Carington Bowles, 1780)

Fordyce expatiated in 1766, 'a masculine woman must be naturally an unamiable creature. I confess myself shocked, whenever I see the sexes confounded.'[17] Disapproval of this kind usually peaked in periods of military danger, when male effeminacy was linked to martial failure. This was especially true in the late 1770s and 1780s, when the American war exposed the English officer class's incompetence. A 'rather sudden' shift

**Fig. 156** Carington Bowles, *An Officer of the Light Infantry, Driven by his Lady to Cox's Heath* (Carington Bowles, 1778)

in attitude and behaviour is said to have got under way then, as tolerance or begrudging acceptance of transgressive gender play was replaced by 'profound alarm' in the course of what has been called a 'gender panic'.[18] A cluster of prints certainly suggests that differentiated sexual roles were then more loudly insisted upon. Carington Bowles's *An Officer of the Light Infantry, Driven by his Lady to Cox Heath* (1778) has the stout and torpid officer

if not wit by appearing at the Venetian ambassador's ball bare-breasted, her body scantily veiled in transparent gauze.

Still, loose morals continued to be tolerated later in the century also. In a close-knit world in which everyone who mattered knew or was related to everyone else and in which cousinhood knitted aristocracy to gentry, marriages continued to be contracted for land and title as much as for love. Since the wife might deem herself fancy-free once the heir was provided, faithful couples were treated with some incredulity, while predatory men could assume a fair degree of female compliance. Indeed, the traditional notion that women, not men, were the naturally voracious sex was confirmed by adventuresses in plenty. The actress Mary 'Perdita' Robinson ensnared the Prince of Wales in 1779 by addressing her love orations directly at him in his theatre box. Lady Letitia Lade, wife of one of the prince's libertine cronies, was said to be able to 'withstand the fiercest assault and renew the charge with renovated ardour, even when her victim sinks drooping and crestfallen before her'; she never 'turned her back against the most vigorous assailant'. The ladies at masquerades or soirees described in Hickey's *Memoirs* were as thick-skinned about ribaldry and as discreetly promiscuous as their mothers.[22]

Anxieties about reputation never faded; yet many high-born women were enmeshed in networks of intrigue and liaison that were semi-public right to the end of this period. As Lord Egremont wrote to Lord Holland: 'There was hardly a young lady of fashion, who did not think it almost a stain upon her reputation if she was not known as having cuckolded her husband; and the only doubt was who was to assist her in the operation.'[23] Lady Tyrconnel's husband and father were so proud of her affair with the Duke of York that they felt it as 'an affront and an indignity put on them and the family' when the duke threw her over in 1780.[24] Fox's mistress and later wife, the widowed courtesan Mrs Armitstead, had earlier pleasured Viscount Bolingbroke, the Duke of Dorset, the earl of Derby, Lord George Cavendish, the Prince of Wales and the Earl of Cholmondeley – at least. The Countess of Oxford's six illegitimate children were allegedly by different men: after the family name, Harley, they were called the Harleian Miscellany. A cultured and sophisticated lady with a compliant husband, she had been Sir Francis Burdett's mistress, among others, and her forty 'autumnal' years did not stop her bedding the young Byron, sixteen years her junior. Georgiana of Devonshire tolerated her husband's several bastards in her own household, and had her own bastard by Lord Grey, and acknowledged it without difficulty. Georgiana's close friend, Lady Melbourne, had affairs with the Prince of Wales, the Duke of York, Lord Coleraine, Lord Egremont and the Duke of Bedford. Only the first of her six children were by her husband. Her niece, Caroline Lamb, though married, consoled herself for Byron's rejection by moving on to Wellington. Wellington was himself married, but was currently entangled with Lady Frances Wedderburn Webster, another of Byron's earlier conquests. And although the queen ostracized Lady Holland for remarrying two days after her first husband divorced her, this didn't abash Lady Holland in the slightest. In her Holland House salon, she presided over Whig and literary high-mindedness until 1840. Many of these women, moreover, were as active in the political world as she was.

Finally, bawdy wit remained acceptable in urbane female cultures even as decorum descended upon others. It was commented upon as unfortunate but not unbearable that when her son joked that if he were a tradesman he would make and fit ladies' garters, the Duchess of Gordon blithely observed, 'Ah, George! You would soon be above your trade.' Another lady embroidered passages from the scriptures on her clothing, including the motto on her garters, 'set your affection on things above'. Fox's mother and aunts relished his father's ribald teasing. Mixing easily with freethinking wits and sexual adventurers, they spoke comfortably about sexual matters and gossiped about scurrilities.[25] These tastes were also fed by bound accounts of divorce and adultery trials 'printed without expurgation'. In 1800 these were said to have comprised 'the most scandalous literature in London'; yet 'no book is asked for so frequently in the lending library, and the editions, reprints and extracts from them prove their popularity'.[26] Immured in their country houses, countless women hungered for salacious metropolitan gossip. Mrs Judith Baker, far north in Durham, had her sisters send her 'scandalous' prints and letters, along with the *Herald* newspaper with 'all the scandale and chit chat in it'. The Prince of Wales's misdeeds featured prominently in her collection of scandal and fashion prints; she also kept a copy of Gillray's exposure of the Worsleys in *Sir Richard Worse-than-sly, Exposing his Wifes Bottom – O Fye!* [fig. 1][27]

Joke-books suggest similar tolerance. The female readers of *The Rambler's Magazine; or the Annals of Gallantry, Glee, Pleasure, and the Bon Ton, etc.* (1783–90) would not have been grandees. Still, the publisher took it for granted that there were women enough who would be amused by risqué jokes, however dire:[28]

Lord D—n told Betty Careless upon shewing her legs, that they were very handsome, and so much alike that they must needs be twins: 'but indeed, said she, you are mistaken, for I have had more than two or three between them.'

The late Duke of York asking a young lady, one day, what it was o'clock; she told him her watch stood at ten o'clock. 'I don't wonder at that, madam, replied His Highness, when it is so near your what-do-you-call it.'

A beautiful young lady, but extremely fanciful and humorous, being on the point of resigning herself into the arms of her lover, began to enter on the conditions that she expected should be observed after the articles were signed and executed. 'Among the rest, says she, positively, I will lye in bed as long as I please in the morning.' 'With all my heart, madam,' says he, 'provided I may get up when I please.'

A fellow having his breeches torn between his legs, [so] that something hung out, which being spied by a young lass, she asked him, 'what it was?' 'he told her it was his purse.' 'Your purse, says she, if that be your purse, then I am sure my purse is cut.'

Although written by Grub Street hacks, the fact that some of these jokes appropriated the female voice at men's expense implies both a masculinity that didn't take itself too seriously and female readers for whom such jests were palatable and plausible:

A gentleman happening to make water against a house, did not see two young ladies looking out of a window close by, till hearing them giggling, when looking towards them, he asked, what made them so merry. 'O lord, said one of them, a very little thing will make us laugh.'

An old gentleman made his addresses to a young lady. She, neither liking him nor his love epistles, wrote him the following lines, in answer to a letter of his: 'As I sat sh—g, I received your letter; / The more I read, I thought I sh—t better; / The place being bare for want of grass, / Your letter serv'd to wipe my a—se.'

The female market for this kind of thing was wider than women's public presentations of themselves suggested. Their private bawdry is now difficult to access except in chance survivals, but the rude anecdotes which Ellen Weeton (genteel and highly literate, though driven to governessing by penury) unselfconsciously shared with her aunt and her brother hint at its ubiquity. One of her female friends, her journal tells us, primly abhorred all coarse remarks but simply couldn't help laughing at farts, particularly her father's: so 'sometimes', Ellen reported, 'her father, to tease her, knowing her peculiar delicacy, indulges her in a little perfume not such as costs him money, nor such as is gifted with scent alone, but such as ushers itself into the world with some noise.' Next time this happened and her friend screwed up her mouth to stop herself laughing, Ellen vowed to taunt her with 'a great *cow* laugh, mo-o-o-o-o!' Again, in 1810, she told her aunt of a foot-race at the local regatta in which two men raced without shirts and another only in drawers: 'very thin calico, without gallaces [braces]'. When the drawers 'burst' during the race, the man cried out, 'O Lord! O Lord! I cannot keep my tackle in, G–d d–n it! I cannot keep my tackle in.' Although the watching ladies were disgusted and left the ground, Ellen thought the scene funny. In 1808 she was so bored in church, she told her brother, that when the clerk announced a public meeting for 'certain purposes' (undeclared), she busied herself during the service in 'making [imagining] a *caricature* of the subject instead of being as sedate as I ought to have been':

> Tom! I *am* wicked, for instead of praying or singing &c., I was setting the old clerk in the midst of *all* the inhabitants of the township . . . every one in the attitude of *doing business* . . . I made a circular platform for them to stand upon, with their backs towards the centre; some saying 'I am ready,' others 'I can stop no longer,' &c . . . Then when Banks [the clerk] was ready, he gave the word Sh—e, and behold! an effusion of matter flowed forth till it formed a hill as high as the platform.

The ways in which long exposure to 'caricature' might direct a woman's subversive imaginings here couldn't be clearer.[29]

## Interpreting the fashion satires

Women's capacity for ribald self-mockery was nowhere more apparent than in their amusement at their own sartorial excesses. What was tolerated here is often surprising. In 1786 an anonymous print was published entitled

A Modern Venus,
or a Lady of the PRESENT Fashion in the state of Nature, 1786.
This is the Form, if we believe the Fair,
Of which our Ladies are, or wish they were.

**Fig. 159** 'Miss Hoare', *A Modern Venus or a Lady of the Present Fashion in the State of Nature* (1786)

*A Modern Venus or a Lady of the Present Fashion in the State of Nature.* It shows a naked woman viewed sideways, her curves grotesquely exaggerated. Her breasts balloon out implausibly, and vast buttocks project from behind. The print satirized the current female fashion for hugely padded breasts and buttocks, and it implied that the female body must be thus if its clothed profile was to be credited [fig. 159]. Though it was one of several prints in the 1780s that made the same point more decorously, it is the one out of hundreds that history students are most inclined to think of as 'misogynist'. They are wrong. Both a copy of the print and the original sketch from which it was engraved are preserved in Horace Walpole's personal collection of satires, and that connoisseur was unsqueamish about it. On the original, his own hand proposed the motto that was engraved on the finished version: 'This is the form, if we believe the fair, / Of which our ladies are, or wish they were.' And to this he added the information, carefully inscribed, that it was designed 'By Miss Hoare of Bath' (presumably no pun was intended). Thinking that his friend Lady Ossory would be amused by it, he sent her the original, explaining its female provenance matter-of-factly. It was a drawing of 'a Venus of the present hour in her "*puris non naturabilis*"', he wrote, '. . . by a young lady at Bath . . . given to me by her sister'. It 'diverted me so much', he added, 'that I gave it to Kirkgate [his printer and secretary], with leave to have it engraved for his own benefit, and I should think he would sell hundreds of them'. Lady Ossory was not disconcerted by the image either. On top of the original drawing she pencilled in clothing to show what the figure would look like in public. Then, amused, she returned it to Walpole.[30]

Fashion satire was a flourishing genre, and most of it, however startling, must have been bought by or for women. Over a hundred fashion satires are listed in the British Museum catalogues for each of the last three decades of the century (and that count is far from complete). In the 1770s, the extravagance of ostrich-feathered hairstyles was the favoured target. Great towering edifices of hair recur in dozens of Darly drolls. Hairdressers climb ladders to attend to them; gardens, or furniture, or coaches-and-horses are embedded in them; others need lids in sedan chairs to protrude through; heads have to be bent to enter doorways. A few are as startling as Miss Hoare's; yet women bought them. One pair, *Top and Tail* and *The Dowry, or Top and Tail Turn'd About* (1777 and 1778), unflatteringly shows a naked lady from the back and the front, her bare buttocks and stockinged legs topped comically by her monstrous hairstyle [figs. 160 and 161]. (The first announced that it was 'engraved by *Miss* Heed', though perhaps in jest.) A decade later, the corked padding of the female backside was the standard subject. 'There were protuberances on the hips called bustlers, another behind which was called in plain language a rump, and a merry-thought of wire on the breast to puff out the handkerchief like a pouting pigeon,' as Robert Southey remembered, never failing to find female

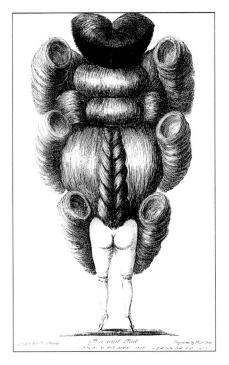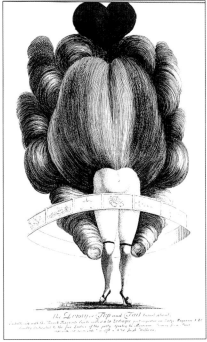

**Fig. 160** *(left)* Anon., *Top and Tail* (1777)
**Fig. 161** *(right)* Anon., *The Dowry, or Top and Tail Turn'd About* (1778)

fashions comical: 'Women were obliged to sip their tea with the corner of their mouths, and to eat sideways.'[31]

Many satires on these fashions are included in the 1,044 prints collected by Sophia Banks; Judith Baker's interest in them has already been noted. Mrs Baker dressed expensively, and on her London visits her towering hairstyles must have been like those lampooned in her portfolios. For three sessions at her London hairdresser's in the 1770s, she paid 7 shillings for a cushion of hair, 6 shillings for a pad with curls, 6 shillings for a 'bow', 4 shillings for two curls, and 6 shillings for three dressings. Not for nothing did Southey recall this as 'the golden age of hairdressers': 'On important occasions . . . it was not unusual to submit to the operation overnight, and sit up all night in consequence, – for to have lain down would have disordered the whole furniture of the upper story.'[32] There is no mystery why women found even outrageous fashion satires tolerable. Those excluded from the society of the extravagantly fashionable were consoled by parodic images of their betters, while the fashionable themselves saw in them that wry self-mirroring we have noted in other contexts. Just as rakish men bought debauchery prints in amused self-regard, so women bought fashion satires likewise, self-knowingly amused by, if uneasy about, their own excesses.

Could tolerance extend equally to the lip-smacking male prurience that was unleashed by the body- and breast-revealing fashions of the 1790s? In most cases, probably yes. For, even as a new decorum was said to be descending on the sex, fashionable women were themselves responsible for their own unprecedented bodily exposure. 'When the ladies began to strip themselves they did not know where to stop,' Southey wryly observed: 'The dress of Englishwomen is perfect, as far as it goes; it leaves nothing to be wished, – except that there should be a little more of it.'[33] For centuries hitherto the female body had been padded, corsetted, bodiced and concealed in broad petticoated or hooped dresses. But between 1793 and 1796, a historic and extraordinary transformation took place that paralleled the great male renunciation of lace, silk and colour. High fashion ceased to conceal the female form generally and the breasts particularly. As we are informed by Marilyn Yalom, the historian of those organs, breasts which had hitherto been separated into breasts for nursing and breasts for sexual gratification were now 'reunited into one multi-purpose bosom'; 'even lactating breasts became sexy'.[34] Isaac Cruikshank's *Too Much and Too Little – or, Summer Cloathing* [sic] *for 1556 and 1796* (Fores, 1796) [fig. 162] conveys the shift deftly.

**Fig. 162** Isaac Cruikshank, *Too Much and Too Little – or, Summer Cloathing for 1556 and 1796* (Fores, 1796)

'Perhaps you do not believe this fashion, but it is quite literally true,' the astonished Sir Gilbert Elliot recorded of a ball at Lady Anstruther's in 1793: 'The original idea seems to have been an imitation of the drapery of statues and pictures, which fastens the dress immediately below the bosom, and leaves no waist . . . This dress is accompanied by a complete display of the bosom – which is uncovered, and supported and stuck out by the sash immediately below it. I am giving you a faithful description of

Lady C[harlotte] C[ampbell] as she was at the ball last night.' As Lady Malmesbury confirmed, 'Lady A— [Archer] and Lady C— C— actually wear false stomachs; and the former literally goes so naked, that at a ball the other day all the men swore that she had on nothing but a thin calico dress over her shift, and the whole clung like wet drapery.'[35] Young ladies were 'covered with nothing more than transparent shawls that float and flutter over their breasts, which are clearly seen through them', the *Lady's Magazine* later reported. By 1801, even Jane Austen was reporting from rural Hampshire that at dinner 'Mrs Powlett was at once expensively and nakedly dressed; we have had the satisfaction of estimating her lace and muslins; and she said too little to afford us much other amusement.'[36] Two years later, the *Lady's Magazine* noticed 'a party of high-bred young ladies, who were dressed or rather undressed in all the nakedness of the mode': it was 'as much of hazard of health as it was trespass against modesty, to come into public *en chemise*, as if they were just out of their beds'. Mary Anne Clarke, the Duke of York's mistress and no friend of the princess, recollected that Princess Caroline dressed day and night with particular 'indecency'. So did the Duke of Leinster's daughters, who 'wore a thin dress, slit up from bottom to the top, with only one article of under-dress'. 'Feminine dress of the present fashion is, perhaps, the most indecent ever worn in this country,' the *Sporting Magazine* declared in 1794: 'The breast is altogether displayed; and the whole drapery, by the wanton management of the wearer in throwing it behind her, is made to cling so to the figure, that nothing can be said to be completely concealed. Well may it be necessary [soon] to veil the face.'[37] Even in July 1816, the *Lady's Magazine* felt obliged to warn readers who in public wore summer dresses 'extremely low in the back and bosom, or off the shoulders' to watch out for one male obsessive. He was a respectable elderly gentleman who 'almost imperceptibly' stamped in caustic the words 'Naked, but not ashamed' upon women's bare backs. It became visible after exposure to air, and couldn't be removed by washing.

Although this body-revealing fashion owed much to artistic classicism, its immediate debt – like male fashion at the same time – was to Paris under the Directory. As French revolutionary iconography turned the exposed breast into a patriotic emblem, the translucent silhouette of the chemise dress and the rejection of the corset affirmed a new female freedom and the old order's end. In his *La Belle Espagnole* (1795), Gillray showed the wife of one of the Directors, Madame Tallien, wearing a silk tunic slit to the thigh,

**Fig. 163** Gillray, *La Belle Espagnole, – ou – la Doublure de Madame Tallien* (H. Humphrey, 1796)

and without sleeves, corsetting or underwear [fig. 163]. On the other hand, this revolutionary subtext would hardly go down well in London; the real key to the fashion's acceptability, therefore, was the deepening vogue for a 'natural' femininity. The increasing insistence on sexual differentiation in these years had many sources, but if it owed anything to a single text, it was to Rousseau's approval of motherhood and breast-feeding in *Emile* (1782). 'Once women become mothers again men would . . . become fathers and husbands,' he proposed. One response to this fantasy was that the practice of breast-feeding spread steadily: while in 1700 under a half of English babies were breast-fed, probably two-thirds were a century later. By 1793, motherhood had become so idealized that it was fashionable for society women to pad out their bellies to simulate the different months of pregnancy.[38] Gillray's comment on the cult is famous. *The Fashionable Mamma; – or – the Convenience of Modern Dress* (1796) shows a kindly nursemaid holding a baby to a slit in the gown of a head-feathered society lady, who breast-feeds it aloofly and touches it not, her eye on the coach waiting outside to take her to her pleasures. A wall-picture entitled 'Maternal Love' depicts the ideal of the simple breast-feeding country mother. Gillray's double-edged satire conveys the futility of imposing the Rousseauan principle on society women, but mocks the principle also [fig. 164].

In fact, women's fashions in public or by daytime were never as revealing as high fashion dictated. Draperies *à la grec* were for the delectation only of salon circles – of 'balls etc.', as Elliot observed, and although the idea of exposed nipples was much salivated over, the overwhelming majority of the nation's nipples in fact remained demurely hidden. If bodices were low and loose and breast outlines newly visible, kerchiefs usually covered them. And if one newspaper lamented that Lady

**Fig. 164** Gillray, *The Fashionable Mamma; – or – the Convenience of Modern Dress* (H. Humphrey, 1796)

Charlotte Campbell's 'excusable vanity in displaying a beautiful figure to the greatest advantage' had unfortunately 'incurred the offensive imitation of all the City fussocks' (i.e. *arriviste* 'cits'), the fashions were rarely seen in full splendour outside London.[39]

    All the same, in so far as breasts did come into their own as well as into view, fashion satires made what can only be called a meal of them. The list

**Fig. 165** Isaac Cruikshank, *Symptoms of Lewdness or a Peep into the* BOXES (Fores, 1794)

of breast and near-nudity prints of these years is extensive, and fantasies about fashionably revealed nipples flourished parodically. Isaac Cruikshank's *Symptoms of Lewdness* (1794) has Lady Buckinghamshire and Mrs Fitzherbert seated in an opera box brazenly bare-breasted: 'instead of being shocked at the sight of each others naked body they [strive] who shall shew most of their own,' the subtitle reads [fig. 165]. Newton's *Peep into Brest* [sic] *with a Navel Review* (1794) has a gentleman 'quizzing' two fashionable ladies whose necklines plunge to the navel to expose their breasts fully [fig. 166]. Gillray's *Ladies Dress, as it soon will be* (1796) shows a lady, probably Charlotte Campbell, in a loose tunic split high up thighs that are as bared as her breasts. There was, too, a significant cluster of prints on the near-transparent and abbreviated dresses of the French ballet dancers now exiled in London. Both Cruikshank and Newton produced prints on the lightly-clad Mademoiselle Parisot on her

**Fig. 166** Newton, *A Peep into Brest with a Navel Review* (Newton, 1794)

Covent Garden debut in 1796 [figs. 167 and 168]. Cruikshank's has Queensberry, Fox, Pitt, Sheridan, Burke, Bedford and Erskine leering appreciatively as her leg extends and raises her dress, their viewpoint helped by that 'positively magical' balance which the *Morning Chronicle* noted, her body 'almost horizontal while turning as on a pivot on her toe' (the recent invention of the blocked ballet shoe making the pirouette possible). In the same year the great Charles Didelot and his wife Rose danced at Covent Garden. He had studied in Paris under the founder of dramatic ballet, J.-G. Noverre, and was later the founding father of Russian classical ballet; and when he danced both with Mme Parisot and her famously exposed breast, and with Mme Rose and her famously transparent dress, Gillray honoured the threesome in a print that, rarely for Gillray, was generously unsatirical [fig. 169].

Among virtuous if not red-blooded males these balletic displays provoked predictable hostility. When in the same year the Lords discussed a bill to simplify divorce, the evangelical bishop Barrington denounced

**Fig. 167** Isaac Cruikshank, *A Peep at the Parisot! with Q[ueensberry] in the Corner!* (Fores, 1796)

**Fig. 168** Newton, *Madamoiselle Parisot* (Holland, 1796)

**Fig. 169** Gillray, *Modern Grace, – or – the Operatical Finale to the Ballet of Alonzo e Caro* (Humphrey, 1796)

French dancers as the secret emissaries of the enemy 'who by the allurement of the most indecent attitudes, and most wanton theatrical exhibitions, corrupted the people'. Since the dancers were obviously aiming to undermine English marriages, he asked the king to prohibit their indecencies: so the bill for divorce reform was rejected as being better suited to Paris. The engravers made gleeful fun of this prudery. Woodward's *A Minute Regulation of the Opera Step – or an Episcopal Examination* (1796) has the bishop and the Lord Chamberlain peeping up Mlle Parisot's dress as she dances with one leg raised high, instructing her not to raise her foot a quarter-inch higher if she valued her licence. 'No! No! No! Not a hair's breadth higher for the world,' the Lord Chamberlain cries: 'such sights as these is the cause of so many divorces.' In a picture on the wall, a courtesan tempts St Anthony with fire [fig. 170]. Williams's *Ecclesiastical Scrutiny* (Fores, 1798) has Bishops Barrington of Durham and Porteous of London measuring and adjusting the flimsy petticoats and bodices of four young women to ensure that they are decent, while Porteus says, 'What! I suppose you'd like to have nothing but a fig leaf on': he was currently giving lectures on 'the growing relaxation of public manners'. Isaac Cruikshank's

**Fig. 170** Woodward, *A Minute Regulation of the Opera Step – or an Episcopal Examination* (Fores, 1796)

*Durham Mustard too Powerfull for Italian Capers, or the Opera in an Uproar* (1798) has Barrington spring on to a stage on which four dancers taunt him with short skirts, their legs raised and exposed; on the wall a playbill advertises 'Peeping Tom'. In Gillray's *Operatical Reform; – or – La Dance a l'Eveque* [fig. 171], Rose Didelot and two others dance in transparent dresses on a stage flanked by statues of a laughing satyr and an alarmed-looking Venus. The subtext proclaims: "Tis hard for such new fangled orthodox rules, / That our opera-troop should be blam'd, / Since like our first parents, they only, poor fools, / Danc'd naked, & were not asham'd!'

Efforts at a sartorial remoralization soon came, though it wasn't particularly successful. In Rowlandson's prints of these years, not a woman tumbles over who fails to reveal her bare buttocks. When Dr John Trusler (author of *Hogarth Moralized*) recommended drawers and prototype brassieres for decency's as well as warmth's sake, he was mocked in Williams's *The Virgin Shape Warehouse* (1799) [fig. 172]: drawers were generally adopted only around 1812, following Princess Charlotte's lead, it seems. Perhaps women mocked Trusler also. A Williams satire, *A Naked Truth, or Nipping Frost* (1803) [fig. 173], has a grotesque Jack Frost nipping

**Fig. 171** Gillray, *Operatical Reform; – or – La Dance a l'Eveque* (H. Humphrey, 1798)

**Fig. 172** Williams, *The Virgin Shape Warehouse* (Fores, 1799)

**Fig. 173** Williams, *A Naked Truth, or Nipping Frost* (Fores, 1803)

at the bodies of lightly clad women in the Park. They are watched by an amused and heavily overcoated gentleman – but why should women not have acquiesced in its point just as amusedly? As one moralist worried reasonably in 1798: 'when we observe the loose and indecent attire, in which only half-dressed females present themselves, without a blush, to the public eye, it is impossible not to conclude that shame, the last barrier of virtue, is taking its leave even of that part of the fair sex, who would scorn any imputation on their character.'[40] That the 'fair sex' was as relaxed as this about exposing fashionable breasts and thighs suggests that women were not as suppressed as we tend to consider them in this era.

## The question of misogyny

In 1745, in an essay entitled 'Advice to a young man on the choice of a mistress', Benjamin Franklin offered several reasons why a young man should go for a mistress much older than himself. One was that older women were '*so grateful*'. Another was that since women age, helpfully, from the head downwards, an older woman's lower parts could, in the right conditions (if her top half be hidden), be as much enjoyed as if she were young:

> The face first grows lank and wrinkled; then the neck; then the breast and arms; the lower parts continuing to the last as plump as ever: so that covering all above with a basket, and regarding only what is below the girdle, it is impossible of two women to know an old from a young one. And as in the dark all cats are grey, the pleasure of corporal enjoyment with an old woman is at least equal, and frequently superior, every knack being by practice capable of improvement.

However equipped some women might be to cope with the more robust forms of male humour, the question will probably never be settled what they made of sallies like this, should they by mischance encounter them. Men's verbal wit was appreciated, along with their political satire. Even the more salivating fashion satires were bearable, as was the gossip. But men's jokes about women's bodies and absurdities were surely other things altogether, their aggression palpable. Freud's explanation of the misogynist joke turned on the notion that when the male finds his libidinal impulse inhibited by the woman, he develops a 'hostile trend' against her and calls on a male ally to share the joke at her expense. As male thus talks to male over the woman's body, the hostility and anger embedded in the verbal or visual obscenity reduces her.

It is always easy to score points off past generations' misogyny, and (on first view) these graphic satires provide plenty of ammunition for doing so. Women were repeatedly represented as vain, pretentious, unfaithful and predatory. Their sexual transgressions were castigated while men's were excused. And female bodies were titillatory or comical subjects. Moreover, around and after the turn of the century, some nasty stuff began to be published. Since few equivalents survive from before this era, we may be faced here with the unprecedented rise of the gratuitously dirty joke. Visual jokes at female expense seem to have become more voyeuristic and prurient than hitherto, their clustering and greater frequency in these years suggesting that witless woman-hatred was one of several reactions to women's increasing cultural visibility and idealization. Thus in Kingsbury's *The Inside of the Lady's Garden at Vauxhall*

**Fig. 174** Kingsbury(?), *The Inside of the Lady's Garden at Vauxhall* (Fores, 1788)

(1788) we are required for no clear satirical reason to peer at Lady Archer and others on their communal lavatories [fig. 174]. Nelson squats on the sleeping Emma Hamilton's breast while pulling up her flimsy nightgown to peer at *The Source of the Nile* (*c.*1798). Isaac Cruikshank's *Indecency* (1799) pointlessly shows a St Giles's woman urinating in the street [fig. 175].

Rowlandson's urinating *Family on a Journey Laying the Dust*, one of his under-the-counter prints *c.*1800, has the young women's and man's organs on spectacular display, their streams vast and copious, and horse and dog participating in the general relief [fig. 176]. In 1803 we gaze for no obvious reason at the *Backside and Front View of a Modern Fine Lady* as she swims naked at Ramsgate [fig. 177]. From his declining years, Rowlandson's *The Little Mouser* (*c.*1821) shows a cat about to creep up a girl's dress. Not dirty, but as meaningful (and several times recycled

**Fig. 175** Isaac Cruikshank, *Indecency* (Fores, 1799)

**Fig. 176** Rowlandson, *Family on a Journey Laying the Dust* (*c*.1800)

**Fig. 177** Anon., *A Backside and Front View of a Modern Fine Lady . . . or the Swimming Venus of Ramsgate* (Fores, 1803)

subsequently), is Rowlandson's cruel exercise in the grotesque, *The Cobler's* [sic] *Cure for a Scolding Wife* (1809) [fig.178]: the old man ties his old wife to a chair as he sews up her mouth, with an expectant younger woman watching .[41]

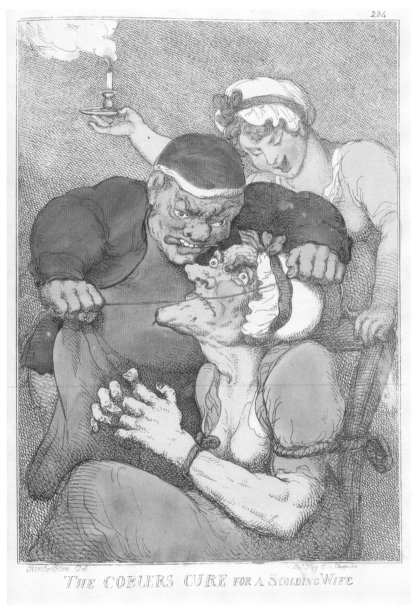

**Fig. 178** Rowlandson, *The Cobler's Cure for a Scolding Wife* (Tegg, 1809)

Textual jokes in *The Covent Garden Jester* betray the same troubled proclivities:

> A young married woman, in the morning being a bed, was trying to put her heel over her neck; which being done, she could not get it back again but with striving tumbled off the bed. Her husband being in the shop, and hearing a great noise, sent up his apprentice, a raw country boy, to see what was the matter; who came down and told his master, 'that his mistress was bewitch'd, or turn'd into an owl; and that she had fallen off the bed, and with her fall had got a great gash in her shoulder'.

> A forward girl being in company of two or three with her mother, must needs whip her hand up her petticoats and scratch her ——. 'Lord, child,' says the mother in a pet, 'what are you about?' 'Only laying the itch of that which you have often plagued my poor father to do for you.'

Others achieve a chilly detachment from their subject-matter:

> A man being tried for a rape made this defence, 'that the prosecutrix having frequently come into his garden to steal beans, he told her, if ever she came again, she should not return without a green gown [i.e. without having sex with him],' and this he proved by a witness. On being acquitted, Mr Harward, a barrister remarkable for his humour, said to him – 'My friend, you have taken a very good method to save your bacon, but a very bad method to save your beans.'

Yet others betray a defensive transition from thwarted desire to amused contempt:

> A husbandman going to his master, told him the news of his wife's being brought to bed: 'and what has she got,' replies the master, 'a girl, I warrant you?' 'better, sir,' replies the husbandman: 'has she a boy then,' continues the master? 'better still,' replies the husband, 'for she's brought to-bed of a dead female child.'

This last joke, with its play on class, gender and inheritance, invites readers to laugh at the husbandman's insensitivity, but its subtext is that, although all children were expensive, female children were dispensably so.

How can we find redemption in all this? Well, when all is said and done, these dismal jokes were few in number. Get beyond them to the mainstream repertoires, and matters become more complex, for most risqué prints worked on several and much more interesting levels. For a start, although few brought good news to women, they didn't bring good news to men either.[42] Men are just as often represented as vain and pretentious, while their bodies become comic if not titillatory subjects. Most importantly, when female uppityness was castigated it was usually in order to expose the weakness of men. In such cases, women were less often patronized than allowed their sexual power – indeed, as compared with most historians' assumptions nowadays, extraordinarily so. Just as the battle of the breeches was always lamented because women invariably won it, so women continued to be thought of as sexually insatiable, in total indifference to 'two-sex' theory to the contrary. 'Yet what is a man tho' he martial appears / Compar'd to the female volunteers?' – as the popular ballad asked (playing on the eroticizing fantasy and occasional reality of women dressing as men in order to go to war):

> In love's soft seige they show their sport,
> Let hero on hero attack their fort,
> We may open their trenches and batter on
> Till our guns are burst and our powders gone;
> Be we ever so stout, we're put to the rout,
> Our magazines empty'd and matches out,
> No more employ'd as engineer,
> Such force has Female Volunteers.
>
> For alas! What are we but outside shew,
> When we boast what feats with women we do.
> If, after a fight girls cry encore
> We ground our arms, and we give it o'er.
> Alas poor men not one in ten
> Are soldiers so stout to rally again,
> But sneak like curs with hanging ears
> Such force has female volunteers . . .

The image of the sexually initiating, predatory, even emasculating woman is common in the satires. It is particularly visible in the commentaries in 1809 on the courtesan Mary Anne Clarke's manipulation of the Duke of York. In the scandal's early stages, Mary Anne was represented as the empowered, not to say emasculating woman, the duke at her mercy. In *Raising the Wind* (1809), Isaac Cruikshank has her bend over with other courtesans to fart defiance at the establishment of Church, State, Army and Navy. 'This is not the first time I have employed my bottom to raise the wind,' says one; 'Aye and no bad way to raise an army also,' replies Mary Anne [fig. 179]. In Rowlandson's *Sampson Asleep on the Lap of Dalilah*, she cuts off and holds up the duke's pigtail, and declares that, with his 'tail' cut off, 'his strength is now gone and there is no danger' [fig. 180]. In *A General Discharge, or the Darling Angel's Finishing Stroke* Rowlandson has her bestraddle a phallic canon as she spikes it with a peg. 'Alas! Alas,' the duke cries: 'for ever ruined and undone See see she has spiked my great gun' [fig. 181].[43]

Beyond that, other ostensibly misogynist images allow for varied readings. In *Nymphs Bathing* (1810) [fig. 182], is the male gaze on sagging female bodies too cruel to be witty, or too witty to be cruel? Does it mock women, or

**Fig. 179** Isaac Cruikshank, George Cruikshank(?), *Raising the Wind* (Fores, 1809)

**Fig. 180** Rowlandson, *Sampson Asleep on the Lap of Dalilah* (Tegg, 1809)

**Fig. 181** Rowlandson, *A General Discharge, or the Darling Angel's Finishing Stroke* (Tegg, 1809)

**Fig. 182** Anon., *Nymphs Bathing* (Sidebotham, 1810)

merely lampoon a standard motif in academic art – or both? It was popular enough to be recycled several times, so it caused little unease.[44] How, similarly, would women have received Rowlandson's tumultuous excoriation of feminist mayhem, *Breaking up of the Blue Stocking Club*, of 1815 [fig. 16]? It lampoons opinionated women, but we know enough about Rowlandson to sense that he was moved more by the comic exuberance of his conception than by what we might now call its misogynist point. (Anyway, the print's reference back to the classic representations of male mayhem in Gillray's *Union-Club* and Isaac Cruikshank's *Breaking up of the Union Club* softens the clarity of its attack.) But then, to modern taste, there is the most disturbing of all prints, Williams's *Tameing* [sic] *a Shrew, or Petruchio's Patent Family Bedstead, Gags & Thumscrews* (1815) [fig.183]. In this, a bed with pillory holes at top and bottom confines the wife by hands and feet while her husband menaces her with a whip and a metal thumbscrew. Over the bed a plaque reads 'Love Honour and Obey'. The books on the floor include Fletcher's comedy, *Rule a Wife and Have a Wife*, and Kenrick's advice manual, *The Whole Duty of Woman*. Was this meant to endorse female submission? Or is it a brutal satire

**Fig. 183** Williams, *Tameing a Shrew, or Petruchio's Patent Family Bedstead, Gags and Thumscrews* (Tegg, 1815)

on the sheer excess of the man's effort at domination – a plea, in effect, for the easier relations between men and women that would prevail if the new separate-spheres moralists were silenced? My sense is that the latter is more likely. In these and similar cases, the male gaze upon the female body was layered and complex rather than single- or simple-minded; and women's responses would vary too. What was seen in such satires would depend on the beholder's eye, as it still does.

From the crudest prints most women must have kept their distance (as would many men). But we have seen otherwise that women like Sophia Banks and Mrs Baker collected prints almost as avidly as men, and perused them unsqueamishly. Two principles help to explain their tolerance of them. The first operates universally to ease the acceptability of any generalized satire. As Jonathan Swift once put it, satire is 'a sort of *glass*, wherein beholders do generally discover every body's face but their own; which is the chief reason for that kind of reception it meets in the world,

**Fig. 184** Woodward, *A Bill of Fare for Bond Street Epicures* (Tegg, 1808)

and [why] so very few are offended with it'.[45] In other words, consumers of satire usually exempt themselves from its aggression, thinking it attacks others more foolish, ridiculous or culpable than themselves. This principle suggests a more nuanced range of female responses to 'anti-woman' satires than those that we might project on to them today. Woodward's *A Bill of Fare for Bond Street Epicures* (1808), for example, offers what now looks like an offensive commodification of female flesh. Six women, in terms of bodily shape and clothing, are labelled respectively 'à la mode beef', 'rump of beef', 'breast of veal', 'veal cutlets', 'baron of beef', and 'pork sausage'. But female perusers might easily assume that the satire was aimed at others, and let it pass [fig. 184].

The second principle invokes malice. Malice is rarely acknowledged as a social force, but since it subverts collectivity, it should be. Sisterly solidarities were fractured by it. By the later eighteenth century, sentimental novels were bonding women into an increasing familiarity with how other women felt and thought, and therefore with how they should feel and think likewise. Many knew that men should be chivalric, and when they weren't, they could be sardonic. ''Tis an animal quite incapable of leading a rational life,' as one of the Lennox sisters put it: ' . . . It must always be running after a fox, a hare, a blue ribbon, a place or some such thing, or given up to play. I do think nature has given us women the best lot in this queer jumble of life.'[46] Many also recognized the double standards that men imposed (some men did, too). All the same, we may puzzle nowadays that educated women then put up with so much – that they were innocent of critiques that would ally them axiomatically in sisterhood, and that they accepted the patriarchal hierarchy and so often ostracized those who defied it. One of many reasons for their acquiescence lay in their simple curiosity about the scandals that flowed around people known to them, and in the fact that many would find the most vicious slanders of other women gratifying.

# CHAPTER THIRTEEN

# THE LIBERTINE'S LAST FLING

## Rowlandson's erotica

It is to Thomas Rowlandson's erotic engravings that we should turn for the most explicit and last visual offshoot of the libertine spirit. Engraved at different times between *c.*1790 and 1810, their like was never produced again; the erotic lost touch with humour thereafter. How representative they were of similar works is now unfathomable, since so much was later destroyed. From chance survivals we know that all manner of late eighteenth- and early nineteenth-century artists produced erotic images, Fuseli, Blake and Turner included. Even George Cruikshank has four such engravings attributed to him; and two mezzotints *à la* Carington Bowles of copulatory scenes in *Fanny Hill* survive too. Fuseli's erotic drawings number many hundreds, mostly from the 1790s; some survive, but his widow burned most of them on his death. The vulvas and flying phalluses that Blake sketched in his *The Four Zoas* were posthumously erased from the manuscript, but are now revealed through infra-red photography. Turner's erotic sketches and watercolours were mainly *c.*1805–10, though he continued to produce them to the end of his life. John Ruskin found them when he sorted the Turner bequest to the Tate Gallery in 1858. Deeply shocked, he could think of them only as 'drawn under a certain condition of insanity'. He declared (falsely, as we now know) that he burned most of them, keeping a handful 'as evidence of a failure of mind only'.[1]

Rowlandson's plates survived the Victorian bonfire in unique abundance because they were engraved in multiple copies and bound and preserved in private collections beyond the censors' reach. A few are signed, but publication details are omitted (though this was true of many of the 'public' prints that he published himself). How were prints like these sold? They were probably easy enough to get hold of. A correspondent writing to *The Scourge* magazine in 1811 wrote that 'half a dozen opulent book and print-sellers have several hundreds of pounds invested in this sort of property, the great profit upon which, from the secrecy of the sale, induces them to run the hazard' (of the law). 'A noted picture-shop under the nose of the magistracy in the neighbourhood of York-street, Covent Garden,' he added, 'sells an abundance of these articles by the vehicle of women of the town, whose nightly attendance at taverns and the play-houses enables them to deal in this way with gentlemen.' At least one of Fores's family shops sold copulatory prints on the quiet, though later it was prosecuted for it.[2] Rowlandson's market was probably a cut above this kind of thing, however. Its affluence is indicated by the expensively bound copies of his *Twelve Plates of Amorous Scenes* and of thirty-seven *Erotiques*, both now in the Victoria and Albert Museum, one volume is bound in brown Morocco leather, the other in vellum. The museum dates them 'probably post 1812'. In fact, their stylistic diversity and the allusion in one plate (*Lord Barr...re's Great Bottle Club* [fig. 200]) suggests earlier dates than that. About 120 single sheets are held in the British Museum and the Victoria and Albert Museum. Barely fifty have been republished in modern times, and then furtively.[3] Not one has been seriously commented upon. Art historians and biographers who have fulsomely praised Rowlandson's drawings and watercolours have dismissed even his caricatures as reprehensible hack-work, an index of failing powers. His erotic images they have passed by aloofly – as 'accumulations of pictured filth, incredible elaborations chalked by gutter-snipes on street walls or worse', as one has put it – though what could be worse than street walls is not explained.[4]

Some recent historians have put a sympathetic gloss on erotica of this quality. They note that it is anachronistic to call it 'pornography', a word coined only after the mid-nineteenth century as print culture and image reproduction threatened to open the erotic to the masses. Obscenity was thenceforth more sedulously policed and prosecuted than hitherto lest it corrupt the servants and lower classes. In any case, at its best, though only at its best, the eighteenth-century erotic offered more wit and humour than the joyless pornotopian fantasies of Victorian and subsequent times. 'Pornography does not lead to laughter,' Margaret Mead once wrote; 'it leads to deadly serious pursuit of sexual satisfaction divorced from personality and from every other meaning.'[5] In fact, much eighteenth-century erotica did lead to laughter. It seldom aimed exclusively to arouse, although arousal it was meant to achieve. A great deal of it also subverted hierarchical and gendered orders, as like as not through parodic inversion or overstatement. In France it was a powerful weapon against the priesthood and absolutism. In England, naming the parts in defiance of 'cant', it spoke up for reason against superstition, sensuality against control, equality against hierarchy.[6] Most notably, it rarely turned women into the passive victims of male desire. Men and women were imagined as equally capable of erotic passion, and women as consenting participants or as sexual initiators. In Cleland's *Memoirs of a Woman of Pleasure* (1748–9), Fanny Hill might be 'seduced' (the common trigger for a woman's fall); but she controlled her own destiny thereafter, and told her own story too. Although imagined by male writers or artists, female erotic narratives spoke for a desire to advocate 'a commonplace, domesticated sexuality that could be experienced by everyone'.[7] All these qualities are apparent in Rowlandson's plates. For all his fantasies about implausibly well-endowed couples copulating in ambitious positions, the naked body and genitals are downplayed as the exclusive sources of titillation. Titillatory they remain, but his prints never lack a satirical or humorous point also.

We shouldn't overdo this affirmative way of thinking about eighteenth-century erotica. Beyond the jollier examples, one does meet compulsions and anxieties that had nothing to do with liberation – in the flourishing taste for flagellatory motifs, for example. And, although the fantasy of the equally participating female might be fed by materialist assumptions or even by real experiences of easy-loving courtesans or society ladies, it was still the wishful fantasy of men. To judge from citations in indictments for obscene libel, male fantasizing about the female body could be just as congested – coy, prurient, needy, puerile, obsessional – as any later equivalent: 'to see the curly tuft that arches over the delicious chink to receive the staff of your manhood stiffly thrusted into the tender vermilion fissure . . .' is one example.[8] Much of it disclosed the wish for fusion or conquest to overcome anxieties about female sexuality or phallic incompetence; the wish turned to aggression when thwarted. Rowlandson himself acknowledged one of these anxious subtexts. In his *The Hairy*

THE HAIRY PROSPECT OR THE DEVIL IN A FRIGHT.

Once on a time the Sire of evil
In plainer English call'd the devil
Some new experiment to try.
At Chloe cast a roguish eye
But she who all his arts defied
Pull'd up and shew'd her sexes pride
A thing all shagg'd about with hair
So much it made old Satan stare
Who frightend at the grim display
Takes to his heels and runs away

**Fig. 185** Rowlandson, *The Hairy Prospect or the Devil in a Fright* (*c*.1800)

*Prospect or the Devil in a Fright*, a young woman pulls up her dress to show the devil 'her sexes pride' – 'A thing all shagged about with hair / So much it made old Satan stare / Who frightend at the grim display / Takes to his heels and runs away' [fig. 185]. And in *The Curious Wanton*, a girl gazes at her genitals in a mirror and asks, 'Is this the thing that day and night / Make men fall out and madly fight / . . . How grim it looks yet enter in / You'll find a fund of sweets begin' [fig. 186]. Talismanic vaginas confronting

**Fig. 186** Rowlandson, *The Curious Wanton* (*c*.1800)

devils were sometimes engraved on seventeenth-century drinking mugs,[9] while the latter trope goes back at least to Matthew Prior's poem on 'The Curious Maid' who straddles a mirror to gaze upon her reflected pudenda: 'And is this all, is this all, she cry'd, / Man's great desire and woman's pride / The spring whence flows the lover's pain, / The ocean where 'tis lost again?' Nonetheless, Rowlandson's reworkings of these intuitions are surprising in a culture that had lost faith in talismans and that predated Freud.

Be that as it may, in Rowlandson too we encounter as much obsession as 'philosophy'. The most notorious of his fixations focused on the relationship between the aged lecher or husband and the cuckolding young mistress or wife – a familiar trope in his 'public' as well as erotic caricature. Yet not only does he usually treat the relationship sympathetically or comically; his heart is also invariably on the side of the young.[10] He had it in for old men on the whole, and never fails to imply that they deserved their sexual comeuppance. His cruellest grotesques were of ageing and vicious-faced judges or of drooling brewers and cooks, while in public plates like *The Detection* (1785) old men feature repeatedly as being cuckolded behind their backs, or as voyeurs upon youthful flirtations, or as inappropriate husbands or seducers [fig. 187]. In *Gratification of the Senses a la Mode Francois* (1800), old men fawn over a young woman, feeling, smelling, tasting, hearing her [fig. 188]. If the men are grotesques, the young women are uniformly buxom, fleshy and curved. They are always the same; but although never individualized, they are never caricatured either. In the erotic images produced when he was in his fifties, these motifs explode repetitively. Print after print shows more or less identically curvaceous young women copulating graphically with young lovers behind ageing husbands' backs, or young couples' love-making spied upon by ageing voyeurs [fig. 189].

The critic Ronald Paulson sees in Rowlandson's fixation on the triumph of youth over age and in his delight in disorder an approval of revolution

**Fig. 187** Wigstead, Rowlandson, *The Detection* (Smith, 1785)

**Fig. 188** Rowlandson, *Gratification of the Senses a la Mode Francois*
(Ackermann, 1800)

**Fig. 189** Rowlandson, *The Old Husband* (*c*.1800)

and renewal. Rowlandson was not a political animal, however, and his
personal proclivities provide the better explanations. We know too little of
his upbringing or sexual life to do more than guess why he projected on to
the ageing his loathing of his father or uncle – if that's what was at work.
His merchant father was bankrupted in 1759 when Thomas was aged two,
and seems then to have deserted his children. Thomas and his sister were
raised kindly by his childless aunt and uncle (he was a well-off Spitalfields
silk manufacturer), who cossetted his artistic ambitions by paying for his
academic training and several trips to France; he inherited his aunt's fortune
when she died in 1789. He doesn't seem to have been socially or sexually
crippled by this upbringing. He was as promiscuous as most artists were, to
judge from early drawings of himself surrounded by his standardized
beauties, some having sex with him; and, although he never married, he

long cohabited with one Betsy Winter, sometimes described as his housekeeper.[11] He had several close friendships with other artists like Henry Wigstead and John Hamilton Mortimer, whose romantic style influenced him deeply. Nonetheless, something had hurt him. Despite gambling and drinking, he was never other than a detached if amused voyeur upon life's feast and disasters. Sex for Rowlandson seems to have been simply another subject in life's disordered pageant, albeit the most comic and life-affirming subject. Did he ever notice that he was as much a gawper as the aged connoisseurs he caricatured? Is *that* what his triangles were about?

His own voyeurism on life was promiscuous. Few other artists could or can boast so immense an output. Daily, it seems, he drew any and everything that confronted him, from executions and gibbet scenes to deathbeds, as well as sex, with total lack of emotional involvement. He delighted in images of anarchy and disorder; and when he engraved his fantasy of a collapsing theatre auditorium, *Chaos is Come Again* (1791), there was no engagement with the screaming and crushed victims [fig. 190].

**Fig. 190** Rowlandson, *Chaos is Come Again* (Fores, 1791)

Admittedly, that print was a satire on the imminent demolition of the Drury Lane theatre for rebuilding; even so, for whatever reason, he had callousness in him, though perhaps only that of his times.[12] Robbed by a footpad, he was 'mightily pleased' when he later procured the conviction and execution of another robber: 'Though I got knocked down, and lost my watch and money, and did not find the thief, I have been the means of hanging *one* man. Come, that's doing something.' When in 1794 he and his friend Angelo visited Portsmouth to view the return of Lord Howe's battle-battered fleet, Angelo found the scenes on board of carnage and suffering 'too much for me': yet Rowlandson insisted on lingering longer (Angelo noted in puzzlement) in order to draw a French prisoner dying in agony, immune to both pathos and stench. Angelo thought that the misfortune of this 'eccentric genius' was 'that of possessing too ready an invention' – which is to say that he drew too much, too often, and nothing seriously.[13]

Some of his engraved compositions are breathtaking. They present confidently constructed pyramids of jostling figures, exuberantly drawn and relished (as his London prints have shown: figs. 10, 11, 12 and 16), and human appetite – sex, eating, drinking – fascinated him. But all this energy can also flatten his effects. There is an absence of highs and lows in his work, a universal reduction to the comic. 'The one perhaps relevant biographical fact about Rowlandson,' Paulson observes, is that he was a compulsive gambler, so that 'much of his world seems to be predictable not in terms of human folly or evil so much as odds and probabilities based on steepness of hill, size of body, amount of food or drink intake, goutiness of legs, etc.' As Wark puts it, Rowlandson was an immensely gifted genre artist and a brilliant draughtsman, 'probably the finest that England has produced'. Yet, Wark adds, the sheer quantity of his work is 'rather depressing'; for what seems at first an extraordinary versatility becomes repetitious in the end, and 'one is left with the impression that Rowlandson does not feel, or think, very deeply'. 'Rowlandson saw everything in the same way; everything he touched became Rowlandsonian,' is how Paulson puts it.[14]

Yet there is feeling and attitude in Rowlandson if you look hard enough. Like Gillray, he had scores to settle, for a start. The one that weighed heaviest with him seems to have been against the moral and academic constraints that had vexed him during his student days at the Academy between 1772 and 1778. There he had had to cope with Joshua Reynolds's looming influence, the Academy's president who excoriated the comic and affirmed the aesthetic and moral primacy of history painting. There had also been prudishness to cope with. Rowlandson was at the Academy when it censured Barry's *Adam and Eve* for its 'insufficiency of drapery'. In 1780, similarly, a copy of the Apollo Belvedere was set up in the Academy and then condemned for being so well endowed that it would offend female modesty. And when a copy of the Venus Callipudia was displayed there, some worried that its 'indecent posture cannot but fully [rouse] the imagination of every beholder'. Like Gillray and William Blake, his exact contemporaries as students, Rowlandson found all this stifling and hypocritical. Angelo reported that he was nearly expelled for shooting his drawing class's nude model with a pea-shooter, thus interrupting 'the gravity of the study for a whole evening'.[15]

His resentments died hard, it seems, for there is a fully intended subversion of moral and academic principles in many of his later prints. A public satire like his *Chamber of Genius* (1812) was one projectile against his one-time mentors and tormentors. In it, the artist labours to paint an impossibly wild Romantic head, ignoring the 'real' subject of the disordered but vital family life behind him, young wife enticingly abed and children playing happily [fig. 191]. His erotic *The Modern Pygmalion* is a projectile of

**Fig. 191** Rowlandson, *The Chamber of Genius* (Rowlandson, 1812)

the same sort [fig. 192]. It parodies a room very like the Academy's plaster-cast room. It is crowded with classical nude statues, and on a pedimented urn is sculpted a fearsomely erect male figure swooping up a conspicuously vulvaed young woman. Dominating the scene, the naked female statue into whom Pygmalion's desire has breathed life crouches over the sculptor to guide his spectacular penis into herself. This affirmation of life and vigour can only be called a pointed mockery of academic sterility. The classical erudition travestied here was the same as that lately galvanized by the Pompeiian and Herculanean excavations.

**Fig. 192** Rowlandson, *The Modern Pygmalion* (*c*.1800)

Rowlandson had little time for current emotional or intellectual fashions. As an artist, he was most at home in the rural picturesque, and he allowed high-tide Romanticism to pass him by, except in his parodies; and he was contemptuous of 'sensibility'. His hostility to connoisseurs and cognoscenti was unremitting. Raddled *Connoisseurs* (1799) gawp at a painted reclining nude in a public print of that title [fig. 193], just as in several erotic plates the same archetypes gawp at genitally self-exposing models [fig. 194 and 195]. Sir William Hamilton's implausible love of the beautiful but vulgar Emma was an unavoidably ribald target, both when he married her in 1791, and then when her and Nelson's mutual infatuation and Hamilton's status as cuckold became public. The backgrounds of several Rowlandson prints on this subject are littered with phallic citations from Hamilton's antiquarian collection and with comic references to Emma's famous *tableaux vivants*, or

**Fig. 193** Rowlandson, *Connoisseurs* (Fores, 1799)

**Fig. 194** *(left)* Rowlandson, *The Examination* (*c*.1800)
**Fig. 195** *(right)* Rowlandson, *The Congregation* (*c*.1800)

'attitudes'. Rowlandson shows her in her pre-Nelsonian prime in his *Lady H\*\*\*\*\*\*\* Attitudes*, probably published shortly after the Hamiltons married when she was modelling for Romney and Lawrence. In this she poses naked in an 'attitude' while an old man (implying Hamilton) points out her charms to the young artist drawing her (the triangle again); classical nude statues embrace lasciviously in the background.[16]

Despite their obsessiveness, however, Rowlandson's erotic plates are usually redeemed by self-parodic delight in their own comic excess. Exhibiting in this the undifferentiated amusement that he brought to all his subjects, it is through this quality that Rowlandson undermines any temptation to regard his erotic conceits as 'misogynist'. To the contrary, like so many engravers, he unfailingly allows the woman her power. Sex is the game of the young and the full-blooded; crabbed old age must cope as it can; and, above all, the most sympathetic figures in the game are female. It is the old husband that is mocked, never the young wife; it is she who taunts the gawping male or who actively betrays the failed lover. In Rowlandson's more comical sexual conceits, she is active in her own pleasure as well. In *The Farewell* [fig. 196] Rowlandson celebrates her exuberant betrayal of her departing sailor, to whom she waves duplicitously even as she receives the her new lover's shafting. She's just as zealous a participant in Rowlandson's *New Feats of Horsemanship* and in *Rural Felicity or Love in a Chaise* [fig. 197], in which young couples inventively make love

**Fig. 196** Rowlandson, *The Farewell* (*c.*1800)

as together they straddle a trotting horse or bump along in their chaise. In each case the act is energized by the movement of horse or vehicle, and the accompanying verses are as amused as the images. In the second of these, Rowlandson may recall (though he doesn't cite) the contemporary street song in which the earth really does move for both parties: 'Thus down in the waggon this damsel I laid / But still I kept driving for driving's my trade / As her bubbies went up her plump buttock went down / And the wheels seemed to stand and the waggon go round.'[17]

What relationship did the overtly erotic bear to Rowlandson's and others' publicly sold engravings? Quite a close one is the answer, for there is a case for regarding the pornographic gaze and the satirical gaze as sprung from similar sources. Each expresses a form of frustration projected either on to the unattainable female or unassailable but power-wielding targets. On this view, it is not surprising that much eighteenth-century erotica hovered on the edge of satire, or that so much satire hovered on the edge of the erotic. Many publicly sold satires carried a very distinct pornographic shadow – that is, sanitized references to secret images which knowledgeable purchasers might recognize or guess at, or tacit references to familiar erotic genres.

RURAL FELICITY or LOVE IN A CHAISE

The Winds were hush'd the evening clear.
The Prospect fair no creature near.
When the fond couple in the chaise.
Resolved each mutual wish to please
The kneeling youth his vigour tries
While o'er his back she lifts her thighs.
The trotting horse the bliss increases
And all is shoving Love and kisses
What couple would not take the air
To taste such joys beyond compare.

**Fig. 197** Rowlandson, *Rural Felicity or Love in a Chaise* (*c.*1800)

A typical example of this crops up in prints that were excited by the arrival in London in 1819 of the Persian ambassador with his beautiful wife. This unleashed in the newspapers all manner of fantasies about the sexual utopia of the harem. While they slavered over 'the Circassian beauty's' many charms, the 'lower' printshops – Sidebotham's or Marks's – depicted her imagined nudity and intimate servicing by eunuchs in a series of prints crowded with pointed symbols and innuendos [fig. 247]. For many purchasers, these prints would be framed by the Turkomanic imaginings fashionable in these years, which Rowlandson had made explicit in his *The Harem* [fig. 198], in which a score of naked and conspicuously vulvaed women line up before a sultan who sports one of Rowlandson's monumental erections.

**Fig. 198** Rowlandson, *The Harem*
(*c*.1800)

The shadow effect is even more obvious in one of Rowlandson's public comments on the scandalous relationship between the Duke of York and the courtesan Mary Anne Clarke in 1809. (She exploited his infatuation to get him to promote military officers who had paid her to do so.) Rowlandson's *Days of Prosperity in Gloucester Place, or a Kept Mistress in High Feather* [fig. 199] is one of that cluster of 'debauchery prints' discussed elsewhere. It depicts a drunken debauch in Gloucester Place (Mary Anne's home, paid for by the duke before he threw her over in 1806). She is on the far side of the table with her arm around the duke. A paper on the wall explains (from Cobbett's *Political Register*) that 'Money was expended upon her footmen chariots, musicians, singers, players, dancers, parasites, pimps & bawds. – But in the

**Fig. 199** Rowlandson, *Days of Prosperity in Gloucester Place, or a Kept Mistress in High Feather* (Tegg, 1809)

end the money of the people – vide Cobbet *An Reg.*' The other revellers echo the debauchery themes of Gillray's *Union Club*: the vomit, the glasses raised in toasts, etc. The print was one of fifty-six that the now necessitous Rowlandson knocked out on the scandal for Thomas Tegg's printshop in Cheapside. It would not in itself be remarkable were that all there was to it. But around this date Rowlandson also engraved one of his most energetic copulatory prints, and both in composition and spirit it paralleled the sanitized version quite precisely. It recalls Hogarth's orgy scene in *The Rake's Progress*, although it lacks the complexity of Hogarth's no less obscene references.[18] It depicts a joyous orgy at *Lord Barr...re's Great Bottle Club* [fig. 200]. 'With women and wine I defy every care. For life without these is a volume of care,' the subtext reads. Six near-naked couples sit entwined (or vomiting) around a table in much the same composition as in the public print, except that breasts, buttocks and genitals are graphically emphasized, and the couples copulate energetically while a naked posture-girl dances on the table above them. In all Rowlandson's erotica, this print is unique in naming a protagonist. Rowlandson knew the Barrymores through his friend Angelo; and their reputations were such that it is quite possible that they

**Fig. 200** Rowlandson, *Lord Barr...re's Great Bottle Club* (*c.*1800–10)

presided over occasions of this kind. Barrymore, the memoirist Captain Gronow wrote, 'assisted at the orgies that used to take place at [the Prince of Wales's] Carlton House, where he was a constant visitor . . . I have heard a host of crimes attributed to his Lordship.'[19] But we cannot say for what profit, or out of what malice, or for whom, Rowlandson betrayed his confidential knowledge – if confidential knowledge is what it was, and not fantasy.

## Byron's farewell

In 1800, Fores's Piccadilly printshop published a sheet entitled *He has Locked up all my Treasure*, engraved by one John Cawse. Like many such, it was knocked out speedily by an obscure and infrequent artist to make an opportunistic pound or so. Yet it spoke with some precision of changing times. A thin, short man (the Duke of Queensberry) stands between two hefty courtesans. His hands are muffled and his genitals are padlocked in a capacious metal chastity belt. A parson walks off with the key, saying:

**Fig. 201** Cawse, *He has Locked up all my Treasure* (Fores, 1800)

'Aye the rutting season is over now.' As the ageing lecher pleads to be unlocked, the woman on the left taunts him, 'Time was, my Tup'; the other woman, the notorious bawd Mrs Windsor, says, 'No, not even a fumble allow'd' [fig. 201].

The print's implication is that libertinism was falling out of fashion. The likes of Queensberry, the Duke of Norfolk, Lord Sandwich, the Barrymores, the Hertfords, and Sir John Lade still pursued their priapic pleasures shamelessly into the new century. But outside their circles libertinism was now being associated with the nation's political corruption or the moral collapse of revolutionary France. Female decorum was being more noisily recommended, and protests against the old mores were mounting. New and female readers were becoming more influential, and their sensibility could have no truck with libertinism. Charles Pigott's scurrilous exposures in *The Jockey Club: or a Sketch of the Manners of the Age* (1792) fastened on great men's vices unprecedentedly, and the fact that he aimed the book at a humbler public than the closed circles in which gossip had hitherto circulated exposed those who sold it to prosecution for seditious libel. Moreover, by the turn of the century the most notorious libertines like Queensberry were pretty palpably past it, and Cawse was not the only one to mock them. Libertines *qua* libertines (as distinct from young rakes) had rarely featured as satirical subjects before the 1790s. Now they became conspicuous targets. Mostly, the satires made clear, they could rise to little more than the 'quizzing' of girls in the street. 'Poor Sir J. L. grows old very fast,' the Prince of Wales wrote of Lade: 'Her ladyship was the first to make the discovery, but was not believed till the cook maid and the hostler's wife very imprudently said the same thing.' Not much was missed in this gossiping world.[20]

Queensberry was by now the saddest of these figures. Before he died, aged eighty-six in 1810, he was infamous for the female menagerie he ran in his Piccadilly mansion. His procuress was an elderly lady skilled at combing inns, lodging houses, servant-hirings and girls' boarding schools for talent. He would view his victims from behind a lattice while smoking his pipe, and then ring a bell to have them brought before him if he approved. He and his procuress are illustrated at their work in a 1793 Fores print, *Introduction* [fig. 202]. By the end of his life, memoirs about him were unforgiving: 'a greedy gamester, a heartless voluptuary, and a profligate *débauché* . . . with the effrontery of a court libertine of the days of Charles II'. He did his best to keep it up to the end of his days, though

INTRODUCTION.

**Fig. 202** Anon., *Introduction* (Fores, 1793)

none too successfully, it seems. He hired young women to undress for him at ten guineas a time – to watch, not touch, them. He applied veal cutlets to his cheeks to keep them plump, then fed them to his dogs. He put all London off drinking milk when news spread that he took milk-baths to rejuvenate himself and then resold the milk. His failing powers were advertised in sixpenny pamphlets: 'An impotent pretender is perhaps, of all things, the most ridiculous and contemptible,' one of his women proclaimed; with him she went to bed a maid, she said, and so she left it.[21] Dighton's *Old Q-uiz, the Old Goat of Piccadilly* (1796) [fig. 203] has Queensberry with bottles of 'renovating balsam' and vegetable cordial in his

OLD Q-UIZ
the old GOAT of Piccadilly.
A Shining Star in the British Peerage
And a usefull Ornament to Society——Fudge

**Fig. 203** Dighton, *Old Q-uiz, the Old Goat of Piccadilly* (Dighton, 1796)

PUSH-PIN.

**Fig. 204** Gillray, *Push Pin* (H. Humphrey, 1797)

pocket as he pinches a young woman's bottom, the subtext declaring the notion that he was a shining star in the British peerage as so much 'fudge'. A year later, stick-legged and ageing, Queensberry plays the game of 'push-pin' in Gillray's print of that name, with the bawd, Mother Windsor, as his partner and the young girl watching as the prize at stake [fig. 204]. Gillray's depiction of Queensberry's contemporary, Lord Sandwich, was no more flattering. In his *Sandwich Carrots!* (1796), a copy of *The Rules of the Order of St Francis* in the bookshop window in the background refers to Dashwoods's libertine club at Medmenham Abbey, of which Sandwich's father (who died in 1792) had been a member. How times have changed, the print implies: Sandwich, however, hand pointedly in pocket, can merely make a pass at a girl selling carrots [fig. 205].

But, although attitudes were changing, these exequies were premature. In some of its expressions, the now fashionable Romantic sensibility could encourage its own forms of self-exploratory excess. Predatory young bloods were still numerous, and continued their old ways. The drinking and

**Fig. 205** Gillray, *Sandwich Carrots! – Dainty Sandwich-Carrots* (H. Humphrey, 1797)

gambling continued, along with the voracious sex and extravagant carnality. 'Let us have wine and women, mirth and laughter, / Sermons and soda-water the day after,' proclaimed Byron in *Don Juan* in 1819 – as well he might, for this was a poet who in his giddy days a decade earlier cheerfully described his life as 'buried in an abyss of sensuality', 'given to harlots', and 'in a state of concubinage'. Indeed, Byron is the unavoidable exemplar of how the old ways endured and then were vanquished, nobody more libertine in his heyday. 'I have this moment received a prescription from Pearson, not for any *complaint* but from *debility*, and literally *too much love*,' he wrote to a friend in 1808; and later, 'I am at this moment under a course of restoration by Pearson's prescription, for a debility occasioned by too frequent connection.' 'Laudanum is my sole support,' he added elsewhere; 'on disclosing [to him] the mode of my life for these last two years . . . my chirugeon [surgeon] pronounced another quarter would have settled my earthly accounts, and left the worms but a scanty repast.' Byron's malaise was hardly surprising. In 1808 his letters are littered with titbits like these:

> Last night at the opera masquerade, we supped with seven whores, a *bawd* and a *ballet-master*, in Madame Catalani's apartment behind the scenes, (of course Catalani was *not* there) I have some thoughts of purchasing D'Egville's [the ballet master's] pupils, they would fill a glorious harem . . .

> I am still in or rather near town residing with a nymph, who is now on the sofa *vis-a-vis*, whilst I am scribbling . . . I have three females (attendants included) in my custody . . .

> I have given up the Casta . . . You have heard of one *nymph*. Rumour has been kind in this respect, for alas! I must confess that *two* are my *property* . . .

> I saw Mahon last night, he made one of a party of ten at a house of fornication.

Not long after this erotic *annus mirabilis*, Byron was travelling in Greece and Turkey in pursuit of sexual adventures with young boys, boasting to his old Cambridge friends that he there managed over two hundred '*pl and opt Cs*' – his circle's code for full sexual congress (*coitum plenum et optabilem*). None of these one would think adequate gratifications stopped Byron continuing to long to 'reestablish Medmenham Abbey, or some similar temple of Venus, of which I shall be pontifex maximus'. Throughout all this, Byron affected an olympian disdain for conventional virtue, dramatizing himself as 'the votary of licentiousness, and the disciple of infidelity', and holding 'virtue in general, or the virtues severally, to be only in the disposition, each of *feeling* not a principle'. 'The great object of life is sensation,' he wrote, ' – to feel that we exist – even though in pain – it is this "craving void" which drives us to faming – to battle – to travel – to intemperate but keenly felt pursuits of every description whose principal attraction is the agitation inseparable from their accomplishment.'[22]

It couldn't last. Lionized in Whig society after the publication of *Childe Harold* in 1812, feted by the Melbournes, Jerseys and Hollands and adored by female admirers, his affairs were now so visible that scandal soon erupted. To consort with nymphs was one thing. To have affairs with the dangerous Lady Caroline Lamb and then to drop Caroline for Lady Oxford were other things entirely. It was still worse to be suspected (rightly) of sleeping with his half-sister Augusta Leigh, she soon mysteriously with child. Well-founded rumours of sodomy spread too: this was a capital offence. Byron tried to establish a respectable front by marrying the implausibly virtuous Annabella Milbanke ('a woman who went to church punctually, understood statistics, and had a bad figure', Caroline Lamb described her spitefully). But rumours of his past and continuing sexual misdeeds and of violence to his wife still circulated. Byron was increasingly ostracized, and his wife sought a separation. Plagued by debt, drink-sodden, hinting wildly at past sins, and fancying himself as 'the stag at bay who betakes him to the waters', he deserted his wife and left England forever in April 1816.

Two self-dramatizing poems which he circulated privately found their way into a Sunday newspaper. They read like English libertinism's swan-song. 'All my faults perchance thou knowest – / All my madness – none can know; / Fare thee well! – thus disunited – / torn from every nearer tic, / Seared in heart – & lone – & blighted – / More than this I scarce can die!!!' Few were impressed. 'I do not understand this kind of whimpering,' one enemy proclaimed: 'here is a man who first weeps over his wife, and then wipes his eyes with the public'. 'Wretched doggerel, disgusting in sentiment, and in execution contemptible,' sneered Wordsworth.[23] A George Cruikshank satire, one of several such, showed Byron being rowed out to the ship that was to take him to exile. Uttering the same verses, he waves to his wife and

**Fig. 206** George Cruikshank, *Fare Thee Well* (Johnston, 1816)

infant left on the Dover cliffs. His arm is around his latest actress-paramour, and two adoring women sit at his feet [fig. 206].

In Italy, Byron recovered his poetic as well as his priapic energies. There, fuelled by an unremitting contempt for English 'envy, jealousy, and all uncharitableness', and inveighing repeatedly against 'cant political, cant poetical, cant religious, cant moral; but always *cant*, multiplied through all the varieties of life,'[24] he wrote his scathingly satirical indictment of the mad king and his repressive Tory ministers in his *Vision of Judgement*, and embarked on the great comic-libertine epic, *Don Juan*. But the outcry continued. *Don Juan* was castigated in *Blackwood's Magazine* as 'a filthy and impious poem', and his old publisher John Murray had to plead with him to water down its later cantos. The stanzas in which the female protagonists took the sexual initiative, he explained, prevented the book 'from being shown at ladies' work tables', so that it could be read only between plain covers. For the impieties of his verse epic *Cain* two years later, Byron was denounced from the pulpit as 'a denaturalized being' who, 'having exhausted every species of sensual gratification', now showed 'that he is no longer human, even in his frailties, but a cool, unconcerned fiend'; for Bishop Heber, reviewing *Cain* in the *Quarterly Review*, he was 'the professed and systematic poet of seduction, adultery and incest'.[25] This chorus of vilification only made Byron more defiant. In *Cain*, he refused to make 'Lucifer talk like the bishop of Lincoln', saying that that would be out of character. And to his friend Lady Blessington he staked out his own moral ground. Acknowledging his past misdeeds, he insisted: 'it is my respect for morals that makes me so indignant against its vile substitute cant, with which I wage war, and this the good-natured world chooses to consider as a sign of my wickedness'.[26] His most impassioned protest had come in a letter to his friend Kinnaird, commenting on *Blackwood's* attack on *Don Juan*. In its swooping prose and breathtaking lament that the age of 'cant' had displaced the happier age of 'cunt', it, too, reads like the swan-song of a culture with nowhere now to go:

> As to 'Don Juan' – confess – confess – you dog – and be candid that it is the sublime of *that there* sort of writing – it may be bawdy – but is it not good English? – it may be profligate – but is it not *life*, is it not *the thing*? – Could any man have written it – who has not lived in the world – tooled [had sex] in a post-chaise? in a hackney coach? in a gondola? against a wall? in a court carriage? in a *vis a vis*? – on a table? – and under it? . . . [B]ut the outcry has frightened me. – I had such projects for the Don – but the *Cant* is so much stronger than *Cunt* – now a days, – that the benefit of experience in a man who had well weighed the worth of both monosyllables – must be lost to despairing posterity.[27]

It was in discussing Byron's comeuppance that Macaulay in 1831 famously opined that there was 'no spectacle so ridiculous as the British public in one of its periodic fits of morality'. Yet Byron and his ilk were laid low by something deeper than a passing spasm of moralizing. A cultural revolution was more like it, and Byron's lament for the shift from cunt to cant was no bad way of describing what had happened. Only after his self-sacrificial death from fever at Missolonghi in 1824, aged thirty-seven, would his reputation be romantically rehabilitated. None would have been more scathing about that hypocrisy than Byron himself. As it was, the Dean of

Westminster prohibited Byron's burial in the poets' corner in the Abbey; but as the poet John Clare put it, after watching Byron's funeral cortege on its way to his burial at Newstead Abbey, 'the reverend the moral and fastidious may say what they please about Lord Byrons fame and damn it as they list – he has gained the path of its eterni[t]y without them and lives above the blight of their mildewing censure to do him damage – the common people felt his merits and his power and the common people of a country are the best feelings of a prophecy of futurity.'[28] Clare's confidence in the 'common people's' aversion to cant was, Part IV of this book will show, misguided.

In the 1820s, aristocratic self-indulgence still had a future. Prime Ministers Wellington and Melbourne were both sexually incontinent; Palmerston was too, though he was the last nineteenth-century premier whose mistresses were publicly declared. Nor did sex die with the Victorians, any more than gambling, drinking and debauchery did. Masculine predatoriness continued in the nineteenth century, along with much other behaviour that gives the lie to simple trajectories of 'change'. Even so, in the second quarter of the century the libertinism of the old order had become the next best thing to a joke among middle- and middling-class people. When in 1827, Moncrieff's play, *Giovanni in London: the Libertine Reclaimed*, was performed at Drury Lane and at Covent Garden, it was a measure of its subject's emasculation (and of how Mozart's *Don Giovanni* was parodied) that Giovanni's part was played by a woman, and that the tone was unremittingly jaunty:

> Giovanni is leading his usual life
> Hey randy dandy, O!
> He's come here to make love to another man's wife,
> With his galloping randy dandy, O!
> Three bottles he drank at a tavern today,
> Hey randy dandy, O!
> So it's odds, but there'll soon be the devil to pay,
> With his galloping randy dandy, O!

The play ends bathetically. Leporello tricks the Don into thinking that Charles I's statue at Charing Cross speaks to warn him to mend his ways. A few lines on, mend his ways Giovanni duly does, and the play closes abruptly in cheerful ensemble celebration.

PART IV

# THE ENEMIES
# *of* LAUGHTER

## CHAPTER FOURTEEN

# TAMING THE MUSE: THE LONG VIEW

## Watersheds

In 1827, Thomas McLean's Haymarket printshop bought the rights to Gillray's copperplates from George Humphrey when that great business closed after leading the trade for half a century. McLean issued a prospectus which advertised that *The Genuine Works of James Gillray: Engraved by Himself* would be sold at a price of a guinea and a half for twenty-five parts of six or seven sheets each, aiming at comfortable purchasers as usual. But the prospectus acknowledged the coming of more squeamish times by proposing a separate supplement for those plates in which 'the humour will be considered too broad for general inspection'. His anxiety about offending purchasers' sensibilities anticipated the publisher Henry Bohn's twenty years later. When Bohn heroically rescued Gillray's discarded copperplates from the scrapyard and reprinted them in large folio volumes, he found it wise to bind the master's lewder satires separately and to omit the lewdest altogether. Each man understood that Gillray had spoken to, and of, a ruder age.

A watershed was reached in the public history of English humour in the second quarter of the nineteenth century, as in so much else. The bawdy carnivalesque of the old laughter was replaced by a humour that was domesticated and tamer. And some of the wiser Victorians knew it. When Thackeray reviewed John Leech's genial prints for *Punch* in 1854, he saw in them a comic muse that had been 'washed, combed, clothed, and taught . . . good manners'. Indeed, the muse had taught himself good manners, Thackeray added: 'for he is of nature soft and kindly, and he has put aside his mad pranks and tipsy habits; and, frolicsome always, has become gentle and harmless, smitten into shame by the pure presence of our women and the sweet confiding smiles of our children'. Thackeray dismissed what now passed as 'satirical' (John Doyle's political sketches, for instance) as no more than 'polite points of wit, which cause one to smile in a quiet gentlemanlike kind of way'. In his boyhood, by contrast, children had often had grandfathers who kept portfolios full of Gillrays, Rowlandsons and early Cruikshanks. Many of those prints had been beyond their comprehension; others, 'very odd indeed', were never to be shown to sisters, and there were some that boys shouldn't see either. But 'how savage the satire was – how fierce the assault – what garbage hurled at opponents – what foul blows were hit – what language of Billingsgate flung!' That past humour he now thought 'wild, coarse, reckless, ribald'. But he also recalled it as '*generous*', a value now forgotten. 'We cannot afford to lose Satyr with his pipe and dances and gambols,' he declared. Then, alas, he changed the subject.[1]

Thackeray was not alone in registering English humour's softening. 'We have plenty of satire in our literature,' a mid-century critic wrote: 'but, for the most part, satire does not bloom independently as a plant . . . We have not the satiric laurel . . . We have novelists, and essayists, and journalists, who are satirical; but where is our satirist?' Thirty years later, the writer Andrew Lang exclaimed: 'How very singular has been the history of the decline of humour!' Was there, he shrewdly wondered, 'any profound psychological truth . . . to be gathered from consideration of the fact that humour has gone out with cruelty?' Not long ago 'we had bull-baitings, and badger-drawings, and hustings, and prize-fights, and cock-fights; we went to see men hanged; the pillory and the stocks were no empty "terrors unto evil-doers," for there was commonly a malefactor occupying each of these institutions. With all this we had a broad-blown comic sense.' Now, however, that 'naughty, fox-hunting, badger-baiting old England' was 'improved out of existence', and the old humour had gone with it.[2]

Broad-blown comedy and the harsher manners that had hatched it were not the only casualties of the new forms of 'correctness'. A watershed was reached in the history of civility and manners also; and the change had the widest expression. Thoughtful people began to look back on their forebears' open sensuality and cruelties with the complacency of the morally reborn. As early as 1807 Robert Southey was announcing that 'no kingdom ever experienced so great a change in so short a course of time, without some violent state convulsion, as England has done during the present reign . . . This alteration extends to the minutest things, even to the dress and manners of every class in society.' By the 1820s this claim had become axiomatic. 'In no period of our domestic history has so universal a change in the manners and habits of the people generally taken place, as within the last half-century,' Henry Angelo wrote: the manners of his younger days had been 'of a cast and character so dissimilar to modern habits, that . . . we may be said to be no longer the same people'.[3] In 1824, the evangelical William Wilberforce wrote to Hannah More about 'the greatly improved state of society in this country since I came into life', while More herself asked in 1833, 'Where is the world in which I was born?' – never doubting that she and her fellow revivalists were the chief agents of its eclipse.[4] 'We are a much better people now than we were,' affirmed Francis Place, the self-improving tailor of Charing Cross: we are 'better instructed, more sincere and kind hearted, less gross and brutal, and have fewer of the concomitant vices of a less civilized state.' 'If we have not become more virtuous,' the *London Literary Gazette* agreed in 1824, 'we have become more decorous, in language and outward appearance . . . We cannot help wondering to see the wits and beauties of what is called the Augustan period of our literature, using expressions and making allusions, which would almost shock the delicacy of Billingsgate, and certainly offend the moral sentiments of St Giles's.' By mid-century, Thackeray could look back to exclaim, 'In this quarter century, what a silent revolution has been working! How it has separated us from old times and manners! How it has changed men themselves!'; while the memoirist R. J. Richardson insisted that 'a good deal that was formerly brutal' was now 'humanized'. There was 'less open vice, less flagrant indecorum, and less obtrusive profligacy' than hitherto, and 'external decency of behaviour' was 'more generally assumed': 'Amongst the higher classes, the barefaced profligacy which displayed itself towards the conclusion of the last century, and to a great extent flaunted in defiance of a better sense of feeling within the first quarter of the present, has been scouted by all but universal reprehension; and though a very vitiated practice may or rather does exist in the privacy of many great and many little people, the requirements of society, as now constituted, force the most abandoned to be upon their guard, and to "assume a virtue, if they have it not".'[5]

This sense of root-and-branch change was unprecedented. To be sure, the taming of popular cultures had been timelessly prosecuted; and Puritans had reformed manners in the seventeenth century. But neither they nor the people of the eighteenth century thought of 'change' as an all-embracing force as their descendants did by the 1820s. The eighteenth century might well have believed in progress, but, even as revolution and regicide across the Channel catalysed a sense that a new world was stirring, governments so successfully defended the old order that the first issues of magazines like the *Gentleman's* in the new century contained none of the compulsive speculation about the shape of things to come that were to blight the first journalistic weeks of ensuing centuries. By the late 1820s, the faith in long continuity implicit in this omission had evaporated.

The processes that induced this sense of rupture were vast and deep, and political shifts were essential to it. Under the despised regent and in worsening economic conditions, the 1810s had seen the most vehement mobilization of opinion against oppressive government since the 1760s. Censorship and the chronic threat of prosecution accentuated disaffection. Led by new City printshops, and particularly by George Cruikshank, even the satirical attack on the state was radicalized in those years. To escape ridicule, the regent-cum-king became a virtual recluse, and public anger only sharpened when on his accession he tried to divorce his wronged wife Caroline. But then, suddenly and extraordinarily, hostilities ceased with the coronation, and the anger that had sustained the short burst of radical action and satire in the regency years virtually evaporated.

The ceaseless threat of prosecution might have helped in this, though in 1820–1 the king's buying off of the caricaturists helped much more. The revelation of Caroline's own infidelities caused great disillusion; then George IV was crowned and Caroline died, as did the old enemy Napoleon: and the world seemed suddenly changed. What really signified was that the repressive policies that had kept the lid on free expression since the 1790s yielded at last to talk of reform. As the revenues swelled, taxes were lowered and sinecures and Crown appointments began to be dismantled; and the Whigs' long vendetta with the regent faded. Castlereagh's suicide and Sidmouth's departure from the Cabinet disposed of the most hated of the regency ministers; and Peel, Huskisson and Canning replaced them with the promise of a more liberal Toryism. A new earnestness also descended, opinion-mongers so multiplying that England soon seemed divided into 'a dichotomy of exhorters and exhorted'. Mounting anxieties about population and urban growth, vagrancy and crime encouraged interventionists to campaign for a more disciplined urban order: 'improvement' became the watchword. Controls on dissenters' rights were withdrawn, and in due course the 1832 Reform Act expanded the urban male franchise. By 1833, the novelist Bulwer-Lytton was noting the growth of that 'strong attachment to the practical, which became so visible a little time after the death of Byron': 'we grew to identify ourselves, our feelings, and our cause, with statesmen and economists, instead of with poets and refiners.'[6]

The change, however, expressed much more than a merely political optimism. It also reflected the modestly growing prosperity, confidence and articulacy of middle-ranking people. A world in which a tradesman like Francis Place could castigate that icon of Augustan politeness, Addison, for his low 'tavern propensities' was a world whose manners were seriously shifting.[7] The middle classes have never not been 'rising', but the professional, commercial, and trading classes had been steadily swelling the number of cultural players since the later eighteenth century. These people had more leisure to dispose of now, and an increasing inclination to identify themselves with respectability, virtue and progress. England wasn't the only Western country in which bourgeois identity was affirmed and remoralised; but it might have been the first in which 'the middle class' was rhetorically identified as such, and as the real source of improvement.[8] 'Respectability' became their emblem. The word was first recorded in 1785 to refer to a more interiorized virtue than the 'politeness' recommended in Augustan codes, and in a culture ruled by a decadent aristocracy it even had a radical ring to it. Their growing consumer power was accompanied by the affectation of softer sensibilities and new pieties that repudiated the old values. London's cultural stranglehold was also weakening, so that provincial opinion mattered more. The iron-framed press led to such a proliferation of provincial printers that by the 1820s most provincial towns were producing their own literature, news and broadside commentaries. This expanded the circulation of the printed exhortation by which the principles of order and virtue were disseminated. With moral revivalism in the air, one enters a world in the 1820s in which more noise was being made about the need for personal and social discipline than had ever been raised hitherto.

The single-sheet satire flourished for a decade yet, and something of its old vehemence resurfaced in 1830–2. But Diana Donald rightly notes how 'the stereotyped vocabulary of eighteenth-century satire simply could not accommodate the political realities of the reform era. Its habitual cynicism excluded any affirmation of faith in the possibility of political progress, [while] its public excoriation of statesmen was inimical to the desire for political goodwill and consensus among the educated classes.' Dorothy George observed that between 1822 and 1827 the clamour for reform and allusions to corruption all but disappeared from the print repertoire.[9] What replaced them was excitement about 'improvement'. By the late 1820s, humorous prints were celebrating the 'march of intellect', the 'march of morality', even the march of bricks and house-building to the north of Islington. They ironically envisaged futures in which dustmen attended improving lectures, read Byron, or played harps, in which people travelled by airship or by pneumatic tube, and in which the horses that would be displaced by steam-carriages would be literally 'going to the dogs' [figs. 207, 208, and 209]. A year before the Reform Act, John Stuart Mill

**Fig. 207** Seymour, *The March of Intellect* (McLean, 1829)

**Fig. 208** George Cruikshank, *London Going Out of Town* (from *Scraps & Sketches*, 1829)

**Fig. 209** George Cruikshank, *The Horses Going to the Dogs* (from *Scraps & Sketches*, 1829)

was able to announce, as a novel revelation, that this was 'an age of transition'. Change was 'the first of the leading peculiarities of the present age', he insisted. He was right to add that the term contained a truth that was 'obvious a few years ago only to the more discerning'.[10]

# Bodies

Historians are always rightly suspicious of 'watersheds'. The term obliterates continuity. So let it be said at once that deep continuities across the 1820s were apparent in nearly every attitude and practice this book discusses. Next to nothing was said in the early nineteenth century about right moral, social or sexual order that had not been said a century and more earlier. Nor would relations between the sexes shift overnight merely on the evangelicals' say-so. Middle-class and high-born women continued to act in the public sphere, despite advice that they shouldn't. In the 1830s, someone could still tick off the known adulteries in *Burke's Peerage* to reveal 'nearly universal immorality' and a 'regular transfer of husband and wife'. The predatory habits of young males endured well into the period of classic Victorianism, and men continued to pursue low convivial, sporting and sexual pleasures as keenly as their ancestors did, even if more discreetly. Pornography and prostitution continued to flourish in the Victorian city, and healthily sensual couples abounded. Moreover, a people that loved Dickens was a people that still laughed. One could say that what mainly differed in and after the 1820s was little more than the volume and printed circulation of exhortation, the sharpened anxieties about change that underpinned exhortation, and the widening of the social groups that did the worrying.

On these grounds, many historians would vote with the contemporaries who regarded the behavioural changes of the 1820s and 1830s as superficial. There were plenty of people who claimed this. Sir Walter Scott, for example, admitted in 1827 that men could no longer 'insult decency in the public manner' of his youthful days; but all that meant was that 'modern vice pays a tax to appearances, and is content to wear a mask of decorum'. William Cobbett believed that the supposed 'delicacy of the present age' merely combined 'modesty in the word and grossness in the thought'.[11] Francis Place acknowledged the common belief (he disagreed with it) that 'we have refined away all our simplicity and have become artificial, hypocritical and upon the whole worse than we were half a century ago'.[12] John Wade wrote in 1829 that there were 'fewer conscientious scruples entertained respecting sexual intercourse than at any former period', and that kept mistresses were still 'among the phenomena of nature'. A decade later, Fennimore Cooper found that, although upper-class English girls were more restrained before marriage than hitherto, a more 'exuberant mode' was common in castes just below them.[13] In mid-century, R. J. Richardson felt that 'the simulated sanctity of saintly counterfeits, the noisy vociferations of professional patriots, the petulant volubility of mendacious statesmen, have suffered no diminution within the scope of my experience'. There was simply 'more hypocrisy, more cant, and more pretence to propriety than formerly'.[14] All this reminds us that the old Adam isn't easily tamed, and that resistance to social discipline was and always is powerful.

On the other hand, regulation and expression *can* change very quickly, and historians who stress continuity shouldn't deny this. Reiterated exhortation has effects. What begins as lip-service to newly insistent exhortation gets internalized and becomes reflexive, so that ways of thinking about manners, the body and others may shift profoundly. One historian argues that the linguistic euphemisms often cited as proof of Victorian prudery were too few really to suggest a deepening Victorian anxiety about sex. Well, that repertoire of euphemisms is massively expanded once we look to the taboos on sexual or scatological reference in jokes, satire and humour.[15] So we should reaffirm that in the 1820s the subjects of permissible laughter were being limited. Squeamishness about unseemliness and disorder combined with a deepened fastidiousness about those sights and functions of the lower bodily parts in which eighteenth-century humour had delighted. The excesses of eighteenth-century satire went out of fashion, and the old carnivalesque idioms went with them. The Gillray tradition became 'socially unacceptable, even shocking'; and this happened (as Dorothy George noted) 'almost suddenly'.[16] In private male discussion you would still have heard frank references to the illicit couplings of princes, aristocrats and gentlefolk, or the scatological ridicule which Gillray and contemporaries inherited from past times. But humour otherwise – as Thackeray implied – was now quite literally being domesticated by 'the pure presence of our women and the sweet confiding smiles of our children'. As a Victorian edition of the *Encyclopaedia Britannica* observed, 'the satirical grotesque' of the eighteenth century had been characterized by 'a sort of grandiose brutality, by a certain vigorous obscenity, by a violence of expression and intention' which 'in these days of reserve and restraint' seemed 'monstrous'.[17] The aggressive symbolism of farts and bums which had sustained the satirical carnivalesque for centuries, along with the humorous celebration of manliness, sex and drink, were displaced by the harmless geniality of the domestic joke and pun, and sexual or bodily vulgarities were relegated to the *doubles entendres* of music-hall or saloon bar.

A few popular satirical miscellanies in the 1830s and 1840s mute the sharpness of this shift. The work of Robert Seymour and C. J. Grant had its acerbic moments, and periodicals like *Asmodeus*, *Fool's-Cap* and *Figaro in*

**Fig. 210** Isaac Cruikshank, *The Renunciation of an Ex Noble now become a Republican Sans-culotte Citizen* (Fores, 1794)

*London* could rise to occasional vituperation. These journals didn't last long, however, and *Punch*, first published in 1841, dominated the field thereafter. Compare *Punch's* jokes with those from half a century earlier, and the change needn't be laboured further. In 1794, for instance, Fores published a small Isaac Cruikshank print, *The Renunciation of an Ex Noble now become a Republican Sans-culotte Citizen*, that did the dirt on Lord Stanhope, one of the Whig aristocrats most sympathetic to republican principles [fig. 210]. His contempt for constitution, monarchy, and church is conveyed as, half squatting, he defecates into his coronet and urinates into an inverted mitre while holding a picture of George III with which to wipe his bottom.[18] Contrast this with one of John Leech's visual jokes for *Punch* sixty years later [fig. 211]. Leech's vast output aimed at safe targets – at the amusing quiddities of children or servants, at the gaucheries of the *nouveaux riches*, the charming innocence of nice young women, or the pleasures of the fox-hunt – never at the vices, let alone lower bodily parts, of princes, dukes or statesmen. Towards people of influence his work paid 'almost unbounded

ENTER MR. BOTTLES, THE BUTLER.

*Master Fred.* "THERE! THAT'S CAPITAL! STAND STILL, BOTTLES, AND I'LL SHOW YOU HOW THE CHINESE DO THE KNIFE TRICK AT THE PLAY"                                                                    [BOTTLES *is much interested.*

**Fig. 211** Leech, *Enter Mr. Bottles the Butler,* from *Pictures of Life and Character* (1854)

homage' (as was later said of du Maurier's *Punch* cartoons).[19] If laughter is provoked by surprise at the difference between how things are and how they ought to be, there is no doubt which of these prints has the greater energy and purpose, or which is the more risible.

The history of the pun also illuminates this great movement. Polite critics had long deplored puns for their triviality, and it is true that much eighteenth-century punning was as vacuous as any that followed. Yet in the earlier tradition the pun could also function as a powerful satirical tool when it went beyond a mere play with words to heavily ironic reference. It was by this means that many satires delivered their damage. Thus when the national signatories of the 'general' Peace of Paris of 1783 are shown participating in *The General P—s* [*Piss*], or when Gillray comments on the 1803 peace agreements by depicting the prime minister literally 'evacuating' Malta, the comments on international affairs are pointedly sardonic [see figs. 106 and 77]. When Gillray depicts Pitt as *The Bottomless-Pitt*, the comment is on the depths of Pitt's deviousness as well as on his scanty

**Fig. 212** Rowlandson, *The Road to Preferment through Clarke's Passage* (Tegg, 1809)

buttocks [fig. 116]. When he parodies West's heroic *The Death of Wolfe* by imagining Pitt's death in place of the hero's, his punning title, *The Great Wolf*, carries its pointed judgement on Pitt. When George Cruikshank turns the Prince of Wales into *The Prince of Whales*, the fat regent's degradation was happily achieved [fig. 251]. When Rowlandson shows *The Man of Feeling* fumbling a country girl's breasts, his contempt for the sentimental novel of that name becomes explicit [fig. 216]. Or when, in Rowlandson's *Road to Preferment through Clarke's Passage* (1809), the 'passage' of the title is geographically identified, the title also refers to the vaginal passage upon which Mary Anne Clarke's profits depended [fig. 212].

In the 1820s, this satirical reference to truth outside the pun was largely dispensed with. Instead, the punster presented himself as morally neutral and harmless, and his pun's effect depended on the incongruity of linguistic accident alone. This obliterated the pun's relationship to the truth-telling of satire. Humorous publications to this effect multiplied apace throughout the 1820s and 1830s. Thomas Hood's were representative of many. A man of liberal instincts and friend of Hazlitt, de Quincey and Lamb, Hood knew exactly what he was surrendering to. 'I am born out of time,' he lamented when attacked for mocking middle-class domesticity: 'I have no conjecture about what the world calls delicacy.' Yet, with a living to make, to the new delicacy he profitably yielded. As the critic Gary Dyer points out, his *Odes and Addresses to Great People* (1825), *Whims and Oddities* (1826–7), and *Comic Annuals* and *Hood's Magazines* of the 1830s and 1840s led readers to anticipate a satirical attack by appearing to draw on the old satiric convention. In the event, the thwarting of that anticipation became the point of the joke itself and was harmless. So when Dickens reviewed *Hood's Comic Annual* in 1839, he could approvingly declare that Hood's works were 'all smiles and sunshine'.[20]

In graphic culture, Hogarth continued to be adored. His moral didacticism suited Victorians' taste, despite their unease about its ruder bits. But in images otherwise, the excretory, phallic and other low symbols which suffused eighteenth- and early nineteenth-century prints were eradicated, while the satirists had either to reinvent themselves as George Cruikshank did, or have their achievements posthumously forgotten or excoriated. George Cruikshank's caricatures, for example, had been the chief scourge of the regent in the 1810s; but on the regent's accession to the throne in 1820 he was paid off by the king and agreed never again to depict him in an 'immoral situation'. So Cruikshank, too, turned to comic

A Gentleman. intended for the Bar—          "Practising at the Bar—"

**Fig. 213** George Cruikshank, *A Gentleman Intended for the Bar* and *Practising at the Bar* (from *Scraps & Sketches*, 1828)

magazine and book illustration. The vignettes in his *Scraps & Sketches* (1828–9) or later comic annuals could be brilliantly and economically witty [fig. 213], but they, too, discarded the truth-claims of satire. In due course Cruikshank reinvented himself as an eminent Victorian. Long a drunk, he became teetotal in 1847, and propagandized that cause in his pseudo-Hogarthian 'progresses', *The Bottle* and *The Drunkard's Daughter*. Their social commentary was superficial (Dickens rightly castigated their evasion of the social conditions that caused alcoholism), but these were among the best-selling prints of the century. In France, Baudelaire praised Cruikshank for 'his inexhaustible abundance in the grotesque', but it was Cruikshank's humorous vignettes and comic albums that Baudelaire knew, not his violent images of the 1810s.[21] Gillray's posthumous fate has already been indicated. Despite Bohn's censored reprinting from the scrapyard plates, the master was all but forgotten. Although he was rehabilitated somewhat in the 1870s in T. Wright's and Joseph Grego's *Works of James Gillray, the Caricaturist* (1873), which hailed him as 'our first great master in comic grotesque invention', the editors still regarded Gillray as a curiosity who belonged to rougher times. Gillray had 'very great artistic powers, the drawing being often very able and even learned', but since his work was 'offensive and ungainly', they admitted to suppressing those prints 'which, from their vulgarity, have injuriously reflected their coarseness upon the choice examples of graphic humour by which they are accompanied'. Rowlandson's reputation was obliterated even more thoroughly. By 1869, the Birmingham collector

William Bates believed that 'even among artists and professed "picture-men", few in London, none out, have ever heard of his name' (though Grego issued a two-volume collection of his works in 1880). Richard Newton was more predictably forgotten. One extremely rare reference to him, in Redgrave's *Dictionary of Artists* (1878), dismissed his work as 'convivial and licentious'.[22]

Literary satire suffered a similar fate. It had been the dominant literary genre from the days of Pope and Swift and retained its vigour into those of Byron and Shelley. But it all but vanished from publishers' lists in the late 1820s and 1830s, as publishers turned to the broadening market for light verse, lectures, tracts and fiction. And although Dickens's, Eliot's, or Thackeray's novels retained satirical elements, none attempted 'pure', let alone bawdy, satire in the manner, say, of *Gulliver's Travels*. Even the broad-minded Thackeray found *Gulliver* so shameful, horrible, blasphemous, obscene and unmanly that he advised against reading it.[23]

In the new order, it was John Leech's work that won the plaudits. Just as Thackeray did, Dickens praised Leech's 'improving' tone and 'good-natured' wit – 'the wit of a true gentleman', he thought. Leech was an artist, Dickens bizarrely added, who considered 'beauty as being perfectly compatible with art'. And although Dickens's own satire rose to savagery, he announced his satisfaction that the violence of earlier artists was now unacceptable. Gillray's and Rowlandson's work he found 'wearisome and unpleasant', he wrote; their characters were 'ugly'.[24] Others agreed. John Ruskin thought Leech's 'kind' and 'pretty jests' preferable to the older, 'loathesome' satires.[25] At the very end of the century, the old *Dictionary of National Biography* lauded Leech for his delight 'in domestic respectabilities; in handsome, healthy womankind; in the captivating caprices and make-believes of childhood'. He had 'a compassionate eye for eccentricities which are pardonable, and vanities that injure no one'. His raillery was 'good-humoured' and 'exceptionally pure in tone'. Above all, it was free of 'dubious equivocations'.

What were the costs of this vast process? Not many, some readers will think: for what we respectable moderns are able to tolerate has been conditioned by the selfsame cultural shift outlined here. As a result we (or some of us) have learned new ways of feeling about cruelty, the sexes and ourselves that we can't repudiate now. We may be as hedonistic, celebrity-fixated and other-sex-commodifying as eighteenth-century people were, but publicly we have learned to be more democratically sympathetic, and so can hardly regret the softening of the manners that once sustained blatant masculinism, sensuality and malice, any more than we could wish for the return of public executions. And if the repudiation of public cruelty ended broad-blown comedy also, so much the better, some will say. A good deal of the old satire now seems infantile, fart-obsessed and gross, and as cynical and cruel as the hierarchical society that hatched it. It was unchivalric or worse to women, and reflects by modern standards the pervasive misogyny of a world ruled by men. At least one historian sees the taming of libertine values by Victorian anti-sensualism as 'bold, progressive and refreshing' – a view that accords cosily and fashionably with modern critiques of over-testosteroned masculinity.[26] To moderns of his ilk, the demise of the culture that fostered the old humour will look like civility's gain.

Yet the angels can't be allowed to score all the points. What sustained the cleansing process was a deepening wish to control, moralize and pathologize those who defied that process, along with that mounting fastidiousness about aggression, desire and the body that now helps to define moral respectability. What often ensues are elaborate ways of containing primal impulses by projection or repression, and that 'learnt ignorance' about sex and the body that Peter Gay has analysed in Victorian bourgeois culture: an ignorance 'unconsciously desired, informally imparted, and assiduously fostered' which served as an 'unplanned, if highly adaptive defence' against dangerous feelings.[27] Even Thomas Carlyle protested at this pusillanimity: 'How delicate, decent is English biography, bless its mealy mouth! A Damocles's sword of respectability hangs forever over the poor English life-writer (as it does over poor English life in general), and reduces him to the verge of paralysis.'[28] Many contemporaries recognized a deepening hypocrisy in this vast process: for 'cant' is what the 'civilizing process' characteristically elicits, and the greater the pressure for instinctual denial, the more needed cant becomes. 'Civilization is built upon a renunciation of instinct,' Freud affirmed – then warning that 'serious disorders will ensue' if the renunciation is inefficient: whence the denials, neuroses and conflicts that make up civilization's discontents. We should take care 'not to concur with the prejudice that civilization is synonymous with a trend towards perfection', he added laconically.[29]

The last things the old graphic satires were guilty of was the politically correct and sentimental posturing that followed them. At least their baser instincts were openly displayed. Cruelty, contempt and 'dubious equivocation' were parts of their language; but without that language satire cannot flourish, and self-righteousness and pusillanimity win. William Hazlitt once declared his respect for 'great haters'. Only they, he wrote, could muster the 'sacred vehemence' that was opposed to the 'grovelling servility' and 'petulant egotism' of convention's time-servers. 'Power and prejudice, armed with force and cunning' were creativity's primary engines, he wrote; when combined with anger, they were also liberty's friends. Hazlitt was writing about the energies that informed great oratory and prose, but he could have been writing about the most vehement of the visual satires also. There was a lot of rubbish among the prints. But while the old laughter flourished, their frankness, the forms of release they achieved, and the taste for satire itself were redemptively life-affirming. Just as there was an unapologetic candour in eighteenth-century 'curiosity' about others' pains (on the scaffold or in Bedlam), so there was candour in its laughter – an *incorrectness*, by modern standards, that couldn't be mealy-mouthed if it tried. The best satires in this tradition achieved a complexity of effect, an incisiveness and vehemence, unequalled since. They took an unabashed pleasure in the primal engines of human happiness – sex, drink, low bodily crepitations, the lot. It is this dangerous mixture of a primal male humour, playing with tabooed bodily parts and hovering on the edge of indecency, combined sometimes with an astonishing inventiveness, that explains why the old visual satires today still speak to us vivifyingly – and why Leech's 'purity of tone' is forgotten.

Both satire in general and what came to be called 'cartooning' took a century and a half to recover from the sanitizing process. Wit there remained in plenty, but the Victorian and twentieth-century cartoon, unlike the satirical caricature, was invariably fit for family consumption and underwritten by respect for the great. With some French or German exceptions,[30] the extreme forms of the comic grotesque and the ancient bodily symbols of ridicule were all but completely erased in visual commentary. Twentieth-century let alone nineteenth-century commentators couldn't cope with the old tradition's indecencies. Rowlandson's 1949 biographer drew an apologetic veil over that artist's erotic or satirical tastes, as do the many art historians who still safely fixate themselves on his pretty watercolours. It's a measure of taboo that the best modern publication of

Rowlandson's erotica is held by neither the Bodleian Library nor the Cambridge University Library; the one copy in all Cambridge seems to be my own.[31] Even now, the most recent and valuable study of the old caricatures, Diana Donald's, downplays the unseemly subtexts that informed them. More largely, it was only in and after the 1960s that English satire and cartooning recovered some of their bawdy and angry irreverence. In the United States, however, despite the once-surreal obscenities of underground comics, newspaper and magazine cartooning remains cautious, inoffensive and deferential to political and moneyed power even now. Neither the corporate marketplace nor a polity and media in thrall to patriotic, evangelical or gendered correctness can provide satire with grounds intelligent or secure enough to sustain it.

This discussion shows that historians can never fully discard hindsight. All the same, it's time we returned to what contemporaries knew and experienced in their own time, and especially to the ways in which change was *resisted*. For in the culture wars of the first quarter of the nineteenth century, powerful constituencies did contest the transformations this chapter refers to. Even as (or because) evangelical, Benthamite and similarly disciplinary exhortations were escalating, and even as (or because) censorship threatened free expression, the satiric muse for a time retained his old vitality. Indeed, as the old laughter's enemies multiplied in these decades, graphic and verse satire raised a near-universal voice in protest. Printshops mocked women's idealization and growing cultural clout, as well as gushing sentiment and canting virtue. During the regency, new and more vulgar City shops even seemed set to turn satire into a popular-radical language, which would have done po-faced Victorian radicals no end of good had their efforts lasted. The polarization of opinion on the radical threat, on free expression and on the royal divorce battle inspired graphic satires more virulent even than Gillray's, and aimed at lower audiences. In short, notwithstanding their eventual capitulation, large numbers of those who engraved for and who patronized printshops flatly refused for many years to buy into the respectability that was offered them.

## CHAPTER FIFTEEN

# THE AGE OF CANT

## The trouble with women

> He on all occasions professes a detestation of what he calls *cant*; says it will banish from England all that is pure and good . . . he says, that the best mode left for conquering it, is to expose it to *ridicule*, the only *weapon*, added he, that the English climate cannot rust.

Byron was persecuted and in exile for his past excesses when he said this in 1823, so he had his own good reason to denounce what he saw as the age's multiplying hypocrisies – its 'cant political, cant poetical, cant religious, cant moral', as he put it.[1] But he wasn't alone in using the word 'cant' to castigate them, in seeing its deepening anti-sensualism as a threat to the manners of his class, or in reaching for satire to fight it. In the changing climate, satire did rust eventually, but it developed unprecedented energy before succumbing to that fate. Between the 1790s and the 1830s, 'cant' became one of satire's main targets (just as 'luxury' had been hitherto). The word had been a synonym for modish or religious hypocrisy since the very early eighteenth century: 'a whining pretension to goodness', Johnson's *Dictionary* called it. Now it was almost exclusively applied to those who paraded an excess of feminized sensibility or impassioned piety – or of both, since those postures were related.

These were tense decades in cultural as well as political history. The French regicide and terrors of 1792–3 and the virtually uninterrupted twenty-two years of war that followed unleashed floods of loyalist and patriotic writing in defence of church, king and constitution, with Burke's *Reflections on the Revolution in France* (1790) galvanizing a renascent conservativism. Debate was dominated by these crises, and they rightly determine our sense of those times. But a quieter struggle was also under way that is less often attended to than the great ideological battle, but that had its own importance. One might call it a culture war, for contrary ways of contemplating the personal and the social world squared up against each other in these decades, and the outcome generated one of those great attitudinal swings that move nations episodically. The coming voices argued that in turbulent times faith should be revitalized, morals reformed, and the underclasses disciplined. They recommended a faith that drew on the language of the 'heart', and their rhetoric was impassioned. Against them were ranged the cooler voices of men brought up on Enlightened principles, many of them deists or freethinkers who had no time for gushing enthusiasm. At issue for them was the continued rule of the rational, freethinking and pleasure-taking masculine self. Their resistance to the new sensibility crossed party divides, and it had good reason to do so. Not all cultural expression in the later eighteenth century shifted 'from a reptilian classicism, all cold and dry reason, to a mammalian romanticism, all warm and wet feeling'.[2] But the deepening cult of sensibility was proving to be a transformative force that was set to dethrone classical, rationalist and materialist values.

'Sensibility' was a word as much bandied about as 'cant' in these years. It had initially referred to structures of feeling and thought originating in seventeenth-century science, and it rested on the notion that thought was driven by the nervous system and by bodily sensation. This led to an associational psychology that put feeling and appetite at consciousness's centre. It insisted that 'sympathy' was society's securest bond, and that the test of authenticity lay in truth to emotion rather than reason. These ideas appealed strongly to cultivated professional and mercantile families, since they were both illuminating and also socially useful. Elites not of birth but of virtuous attainment (as the philosopher David Hume put it), these middle-class people had a mounting interest in proclaiming their own cultural postures and consumption patterns, and 'sensibility' gave them new vocabularies with which to do this. Among their women, particularly, the ability to feel spontaneous emotion, to sympathize, and to communicate through 'exclamations, tender tones, fond tears, / And all the graceful drapery' of pity and feeling (as the evangelical Hannah More put it), became marks of moral authority. And since sensibility entailed a *dis*sociation from aristocracy and gentry, it acquired a critical edge also. People of sensibility were in effect rejecting aristocratic mores as energetically as they rejected plebeian mores. They thus generated a hostility to the *ancien régime*'s values which, fused with commercial interest, shaped middle-class cultures deep into the nineteenth century. By the 1780s, sensibility was colonizing new Romantic art-forms; while new forms of 'humanitarian' endeavour, against slavery, for example, were moved by fashionable 'sympathy' also.[3]

For our purposes, what mattered most was that sensibility challenged existing relations between the sexes, and between respectable people and the Almighty also. Let the Almighty wait a moment: it's to women that we attend first – to how sensibility affected their behaviour, and how male attitudes to them were affected in turn.

It may be overstating it to say that English cultural life was being 'feminized' in these decades; yet it is true that cultivated middle-class women were joining their better-born sisters as cultural producers and consumers in the second half of the eighteenth century, and as opinion-makers too. One reason for this was that new literary models were combining with rising material expectations, reading skills and leisure opportunities to give women an unprecedented cultural confidence. Nothing helped in this more than the novel. Authorizing a freer emotional expression and with 'sensibility' at their centre, novels like Samuel Richardson's *Clarissa* (1747), Rousseau's *Nouvelle Héloïse* (1761), Laurence Sterne's *Tristram Shandy* (1759–67) and Henry Mackenzie's *The Man of Feeling* (1771) touched female cultures so deeply that it was women, chiefly, who sustained the novel's extraordinary rise in the decades that followed. It was in good part thanks to female readers and authors that the novel was to supplant poetry and satire as the leading literary form by the 1820s – the days by then long past when young Fanny Burney (in the 1760s) had worried about her female presumption even in writing a journal, or when people took seriously Sheridan's quip that 'a lady should not write verses, till she is past receiving them'. Between 1750 and 1770 six of the twenty most popular novelists in England were women, and by the end of the century women might have been writing as many novels as men, some of them selling better than any male novelist except Walter Scott. Sentiment also drove women to poetry: at least 339 poetesses published under their own names between 1760 and 1830, and a further 82 anonymous ones can be identified.[4] Alongside this literary efflorescence went an increasingly confident female engagement in the world. By the end of the century and into the new one, women were ever more active in charities, philanthropy and war-work. Their periodicals and circulating libraries were multiplying, and they dominated theatre and concert audiences and attendance at art galleries and lectures. At the Royal Institution off Piccadilly, where 'the arts and sciences are now taught in lectures to fashionable audiences of both sexes', Robert Southey in 1807 noticed that the women paid much more attention to the lessons than the men did: 'part of the men were taking snuff to keep their eyes open, others [were] more honestly asleep, while the ladies were all upon the watch, and some score of them had their tablets and pencils, busily noting down what they heard, as topics for the next conversation party'.[5]

Men might have tolerated this female renaissance better were it not for three undesirable consequences – apart, that is, from the challenge it offered to men's cultural dominance. First, if Jane Austen's Marianne Dashwood occupied the more appealing end of the axis of female sensibility, a fair amount of emotional posturing and wallowing occupied the other, and this many men couldn't bear. For, as has been well put, sensibility only too often 'signified revolution, promised freedom, threatened subversion, and became convention'. 'There is a sort of luxury in giving way to the feelings!' the young Elizabeth Fry gushed in her diary: 'I love to feel for the sorrows of others, to pour wine and oil into the wounds of the afflicted; there is a luxury in feeling the heart glow, whether it be with joy or sorrow . . . I love to feel good – I do what I can to be kind to everybody.' No sentimental heroine could have put it better. As Mary Wollstonecraft admitted, sensibility invited women to become 'the prey of their senses' and to be 'blown about by every momentary gust of feeling'. Or else it provoked in women those 'shoots and unexpected gushes' that reminded the poet Tom Moore of artificial waterworks.[6]

With the wallowing, secondly, came an intensified female prudishness. Female delicacy wasn't peculiar to this era. Fielding's *Joseph Andrews* had long before commented sourly on English ladies' 'violent modesty and virtue' and 'rampant passion for chastity'. Conversely, society ladies continued to fornicate well into the nineteenth century; independent-minded and quirky women were, as ever, innumerable; many women still relished bawdy jokes and satires; and the semi-nudities of female fashion in the 1790s suggests a sex not at all shy about signalling its desires and intentions. All the same, in many if not all middle-class circles by the turn of the century the thresholds of polite female decorum appear to have been lifting. This process was accelerated by the mounting torrent of conduct books and sermons aimed at women that told them to stay within that domestic sphere to which their anatomies fitted them (even if this advice betrayed anxiety that they weren't in fact staying there). Even women who had established their own independence were now earnestly advising younger women not to emulate them. 'The bold, independent, enterprising spirit, which is so much admired in boys, should not, when it happens to discover itself in the other sex, be encouraged, but suppressed,' the indubitably independent and enterprising Hannah More declared in 1799. At the other end of the political spectrum, Mary Wollstonecraft insisted that 'chastity must more universally prevail' and that woman's 'first wish should be to make herself respectable'.[7] Under these and like pressures, it began to be noted that younger women were nowadays holding fans to their faces when middle-aged ladies told rude jokes; old Lady Townshend was thought to be 'singular' in her taste for bawdry. French exiles during the revolutionary years found genteel Englishwomen peculiarly prudish and frigid. They noted that women refused men access to their bedrooms, that they had raised blushing to a fine art, and that their conversation in mixed company had become constrained both by French and by earlier English standards. They neither kissed in public nor urinated together, and went to extraordinary lengths to conceal the fact that they used lavatories.[8] None of this went down well with men who liked to think that women were as lascivious as they were.

What the manly world got most upset about, thirdly, was that in these conditions women were ever more audibly claiming an entitlement to civilize and tame male manners also – to police male manners as well as their own. It was increasingly the male that was being defined as the fickle and dangerous sex, rather than passion-led, reason-less womankind, as hitherto. For Hannah More, woman's moral influence was 'one of the great hinges upon which the great machine of human society turns', while Mary Wollstonecraft dismissed the immoral influence of 'idle superficial young men whose only occupation is gallantry and whose polished manners render vice more dangerous by concealing its deformity under gay drapery'.[9] During the 'delicate investigation' into Princess Caroline's suspected adulteries, Lady Anne Hamilton's *Epics of the Ton* (1807) set up Caroline as the virtuous wife of a cruel and faithless husband, in terms that would be sustained until Caroline's own spectacular infidelities were exposed in late 1820:

> He who vow'd thy weakness to defend,
>
> In joy thy partner, and in grief thy friend.
>
> To other cares, to other pleasures fled,
>
> Deserting thine to share another's bed,
>
> Mock'd at thy woes, and scoffing at thy pain,
>
> Had joy'd to hear thy heart had burst in twain.

'How blind are princes,' Hamilton trilled on the question of princes' inclination to take mistresses, 'how criminal, when they endanger their own destruction, and the good order, virtue, and happiness of their people, for such sensual gratifications as would appear despicable in the lowest debauchee!'[10] 'Poor woman,' Jane Austen wrote of Caroline as the princess's saga dragged on: 'I shall support her as long as I can, because she is a woman, & because I hate her husband . . . She would have been respectable, if the prince had behaved only tolerably by her at first.'[11]

The quest for a tamer and more disciplined manhood wasn't women's alone. Countless men led or colluded in it for all manner of motives. Some would have agreed with the *Gentleman's Magazine* (in 1798) that women were 'more sensible than men to all *moral* distinctions', and that society depended 'more for its happiness on the quiet apprehension and strong abhorrence of the woman of every trespass on female modesty, than on all the boasted *manly* virtues'. And in the long term the quest had effects. The novel had long discarded the indecencies relished by Smollett and Fielding, and, in the new century, scatological imagery faded in graphic satire. The Prince Regent's sexual manners were universally scorned, while the big sexual scandals were more likely to involve male dalliances with courtesans than with society ladies. The Duke of York's affair with Mary Anne Clarke was one example; the courtesan Harriette Wilson's memoirs betrayed many others. Publishing in 1825, Harriette let it be known that she had been the mistress of the Dukes of Wellington, Argyll and Beaufort, the Marquesses of Worcester, Anglesey, Bath and Hertford, and many lesser aristocrats beside. Men who sowed their wild oats among women of their own class seem to have been more censured than hitherto. Deep into the nineteenth century, many of the more extravagant or at least visible practices of a rampantly testosteroned masculinity were curbed.

But what now of the masculinist counter-attack that most concerns us? The fact is that little in this cultural shift went uncontested, so that men's socialization was very gradual. In the first place, the civilizing task wasn't easy, for much of their resistance was passive. 'The gentleman [her husband] came home near 12 at noon and sans ceremony went snoring to clean bed – where he farted and stunk like a pole cat': so lamented the sorely tried Elizabeth Shackleton in her Lancashire diary in the late 1770s. 'Most exceedingly beastly so to a degree never saw him worse – he had made water into the fire,' she recorded on one occasion, and 'he shits in bed with drinking so continually' on another. 'Mr S like a brute. No man,' she complained; and 'Hottentots not men when assembled together' – this on his drinking bouts with his cronies.[12] Provincially isolated, Mrs Shackleton's civilizing mission failed lamentably, as it would in countless other bedrooms subsequently.

Beyond that, the task of civilizing men might even have got tougher in these years as the pleasures of homosociability were reactively affirmed. The trouble with men's socializing excessively with polite women, it was being argued in the 1780s, lay in the risks of effeminate contamination. Female company might well help to polish 'roughness of behaviour, and slovenliness of person'; but if men were to 'retain the firmness and constancy of the male' and to cultivate manly forthrightness and sincerity, it was desirable for them to mix more with men.[13] On this principle, male resistance to their own taming escalated into a great reaffirmation of manly values during the war years of 1793–1815. The friend who had accompanied Southey to the Royal Institution, for example, thought that the female pretension displayed there was a poor thing altogether: 'The days of tapestry hangings and worked chair bottoms were better days than these! – I will go and buy for Harriet [his wife] the *Whole duty of women*, containing the complete *Art of cookery*.' Gratuitously dirty jokes might have multiplied in these years. Pugilism reached the heights of its popularity; club life appears to have boomed; while 'debauchery prints', rarely produced after Hogarth's *Modern Midnight Conversation* (1732) and *Election Entertainment* (1755), were significantly reinvented. Satire itself came to be thought of as an intrinsically manly form in its resolute opposition to gushing sensibility.[14] So successful were these masculinist affirmations that Robert Burns could reach for his heaviest irony as he reflected in his 'The Rights of Woman' (1792) on the long battle to subdue the male sex, knowing very well that its rampancy would be far less easily vanquished than the other sex hoped:

> There was, indeed, in far less polish'd days,
> A time, when rough rude man had naughty ways,
> Would swagger, swear, get drunk, kick up a riot,
> Nay even thus invade a lady's quiet.
>
> Now, thank our stars! those gothic times are fled;
> Now, well-bred men – and you are all well-bred –
> Most justly think (and we are much the gainers)
> Such conduct neither spirit, wit, nor manners.

The most visible affirmation of manly values was apparent in men's adoption of 'natural' fashions in the 1790s. This movement was quite as revolutionary as the simultaneous simplification of women's fashion discussed earlier, and its meaning is as poorly understood. Colour, lace, silk and surface decoration yielded to the dark-toned sobriety that men's clothes have never since formally discarded. Knee-breeches ('culottes') gave way to pantaloons on the *sans-culotte* model while, encouraged by the 1798 powder tax, younger men gave up wigs, and unaffected country styles became the mark of a 'sincere' English masculinity. By 1803 the *Lady's Magazine* could fairly note that 'with the ladies, it is the object to shew how little will do for a dress; with the gentlemen, how much they can carry without fatigue. Hence the total disuse of silk, linen and cambric, and the substitution of broadcloth and leather.' The change is sometimes seen as entailing a rejection of aristocratic fopperies in a revolutionary era and hence as a form of bourgeois self-affirmation. The raffish Parisian fashions of the male *incroyables* (carefully bedraggled hair, 'jacobin' trousers), along with those of their female equivalents, *les merveilleuses*, were widely illustrated in the English satires and fashion plates of 1797.[15] The trouble with this *embourgeoisement* argument, however, is that aristocrats and princes appropriated the new fashion with alacrity. A better way of reading it may be to see it as a capitulation to the notion, now fashionable in some quarters, that the sexes were emotionally as well as functionally distinct. But even this claim is blunted on the fact that male self-interest lay in defending the libertine idea that men and women were sexually pleasure-pursuing equivalents. The best answer, therefore, may be to see the new male fashions as a form of masculine self-affirmation, which reacted *against* the chivalric principle while also being appropriate to wartime conditions. With one in ten men obliged to experience voluntary military or naval service between

**Fig. 214** George Cruikshank, *A Dandy Fainting or – An Exquisite in Fits. Scene a Private Box . . . [at the] Opera* (H. Humphrey, 1818)

1793 and 1815 (one in six if militia service is included), the very possibility of the effeminized male seems to have been denied or evaded. The anxieties audible during the American war about cross-dressing and foppishness were silenced, to re-emerge (in the Cruikshank brothers' prints especially [fig. 214]) only during the dandy-mania of 1818–19.

To such forms of resistance should be added the frank male disbelief in the authenticity of the new female delicacy, and hence the mockery of its hypocrisies and pretensions. Enlightened men remained convinced that, underneath female posturing, passions lurked that were as indecorous as their own. Byron wasn't alone in loathing women's 'cant of *sentiment*' – '*cant*' being 'so much stronger than *cunt* now a days', as he put it in that usefully memorable phrase. Women who read too many novels were those guiltiest of it, he thought. The sex couldn't bear his *Don Juan*, he complained, because it so '*took off the veil*', and 'showed that all their d—d sentiment was only an excuse to cover passions of grosser nature'. They wished 'to exalt the *sentiment* of the passions, – & to keep up the illusion which is their empire'.[16]

A knowing familiarity with female sensuality and hence deep suspicion about the hypocrisy of female decorum was affected by the engravers too. In 1822, the grateful ladies of England subscribed £22,000 to raise Westmacott's twenty-foot high statue of Achilles in Hyde Park in order to celebrate Wellington's victories. When asked whether it 'should preserve its antique nudity or be garnished with a fig-leaf', the ladies voted, of course, for the fig leaf. George Cruikshank guffawed in incredulity. In *This Brazen Image* (Tegg, 1822), he has ladies gaze at Achilles's naked magnitude with prurient appreciation. 'See what we ladies can raise'; 'My eyes what a size!!', they cry; and 'what is that, Mama?' a little girl asks, pointing at the fig leaf. The print is topped by verses from 'Paddy Carey, the lady's joy': 'His brawny shoulders 4ft square / His cheeks like thumping kidney tatees / His legs would make a chairman stare / And Pat was loved by all the ladies.' In Marks's *The Wish* (*c*.1821), a demure young woman fantasizes: 'I wish I had (I know what) / And I know who [it] could give me / I wish I was (I know where) / And I know who was with me' – the nature of her hopes indicated in some half dozen phallic and vaginal symbols [fig. 215].

What finally advanced the masculinist backlash was satire's reinvigoration as an explicitly masculine muse. The equation of satire and manliness became almost axiomatic. Vicesimus Knox believed that satire

**Fig. 215** J. L. Marks, *The Wish* (Marks, *c*.1821)

proved that the national spirit was 'of the *manly* and rough kind', while the *Anti-Jacobin Review* thought satire was sustained by 'the *manly* warmth of contemptuous indignation'. Resisting enthusiasm, emotional pieties and Frenchified sensibility, the journal declared its morality to be 'commonsensical', 'English' and '*manly*'. The 'New Morality' of the present times, George Canning's satirical poem of that title announced, was contaminated, *inter alia*, by sensibility's 'shrinking softness'.[17] The prints carried the same message, more violently. Rowlandson's *The Man of Feeling* (1788) punned contemptuously on the title of Mackenzie's novel in a joke at sensibility's expense, versions of which he repeated until 1811 [fig. 216]: the true man of feeling felt women's breasts. Rowlandson's eroticized pun

THE MAN OF FEELING.

*Pub.d Feb.y 29 1788 by Wm. Holland, N.o 50, Oxford Street.*

**Fig. 216** Rowlandson, *The Man of Feeling* (Holland, 1788)

on *Sympathy* reduced 'sympathy', sensibility's central principle, to an exclusively genital compulsion, witnessed in the enthusiasm of animals and humans alike for fucking. In its reductionist denial of spirit, no print was more rooted in Enlightened materialism than this one [fig. 217].

But if satire was opposed to sensibility and the more ostentatious forms of female delicacy, both of these were reciprocally opposed to satire. Even

**Fig. 217** Rowlandson, *Sympathy* (*c*.1800–10)

Wollstonecraft, in her *The Female Reader; Or Miscellaneous Pieces in Prose and Verse: . . . for the Improvement of Young Women* (1789), advised that 'persons of true and finished taste seldom affect ridicule, because they are conscious of their own superior merit'. It was incompatible with modesty and other feminine virtues, she added; only women who lacked 'native charms' practised it. In her poem 'Written in Condemnation of Satire' (1806), Elizabeth Bath thought that ridicule destroyed amiable sociability. Among the few women who did attempt satire, Eliza Thompson, in her 'Retaliation; or The Reviewers Review'd' (1791), apologized that the form was 'by no means the province of a woman', and Sarah Green prefaced her satirical 'The Reformist!!!' (1810) by acknowledging that 'politics is too large a field for one of my sex to venture on; to submit without meanness, not to rule, is woman's province'. The evangelical Jane Taylor worried about women's writing for adults at all: in her *Essays in Rhyme, on Morals and Manners* (1816) she, too, deplored the arrogance of satire. Only Jane Austen's demure satirical touch refused to falter. In *Sense and Sensibility* (1811), Lady Middleton's bawdily candid mother stands for the more relaxed female manners of past times; Marianne, the novel's model of sensibility, thinks the older woman crude; while, because they were fond of reading, the tautly self-restrained Lady Middleton dislikes Elinor and Marianne Dashwood for being 'satirical' – 'perhaps without exactly knowing what it was to be satirical; but that did not signify. It was censure in common use, and easily given.'

As these ladylike notions were endorsed in evangelical and like propaganda, it can only be said that women's increasing cultural and literary presence and deference to convention blew an ill wind for satire. All the same, it was not as ill a wind as that blown by religious revivalism.

## The trouble with piety

In 1825, Thomas Hood etched for McLean's Haymarket printshop a large and ambitious print entitled *The Progress of Cant* [fig. 218]. It was bylined as being by 'One of the authors of "Odes and addresses to great people"'. The fact that this referred to one of Hood's lightly humorous works might have raised false expectations. Because if Hood's comic works by this date were capitulating to the new decorum, this print indicates his reluctance about doing so. Admittedly, it's too conscientiously and densely drawn to

**Fig. 218** Hood, *The Progress of Cant* [detail] (McLean, 1825)

achieve the bravado of earlier satires. Its bite is blunted by something of the earnestness it mocks, for the eye is caught not by boldness of design but by a flood of information, most of it too carefully drawn. A sea of banners, slogans and advertisements meticulously identifies the do-gooders who parade their causes against a backdrop of too accurately drawn houses: the British Museum catalogue takes 2,000 words to explain them. As Charles Lamb described it:

> Priests, anti-priests, architects, politicians, reformers, flaming loyalty-men, high and low, rich and poor, one with another, all go on 'progressing,' as the Americans say . . . There is . . . a barber's shop, with 'Nobody to be s[-]aved during divine service,' the *h* worn out . . . Among the crowd is a jolly, but vehement, reverend person holding a flag, inscribed, 'The Church in [-]anger,' the *D* for danger being hidden by another flag, inscribed 'Converted Jews.' Then there is the Caledonian Chap[-] (*el* being obstructed in the same way), who holds a pennon, crying out, 'No Theatre!', [and] Purity of Election, with a bludgeon, very drunk . . .

Still, no print offered a more ambitious or ironic synopsis of the coming virtues, and none targeted their hypocrisies so explicitly. It achieved mild fame in its time.[18] It parades a rich sample of those whom virtuous people were now scapegoating. They include the beggars, street-women, vagrants and pickpockets – all living off or parodying the holy ranters and philanthropists who march across the picture with them: people who want to suppress beggars, St Bartholomew's Fair, pugilists, climbing boys, state lotteries, bubble companies, slavery and even Egan's comic book, *Tom and Jerry*. They include people who want Mind to march onwards, Jews to be converted, savings banks to be multiplied, and the sabbath to be observed. A paper publicizes anti-vice prosecutions: *H. Rickets & Sarah Grumpage the former for Shaving & the latter for selling fruit on the Lords Day were convicted on the oath of the notorious Johnson & fined 10s each* (Johnson an anti-vice society informer). A sectary flaunts the names 'Whitfield and Wesley', while the hellfire Presbyterian ranter Edward Irving proclaims 'No Theatre'. Hobhouse champions the cause of Greece, O'Connell that of Catholics, 'Humanity' Martin that of animals. The one-legged black beggar Billy Waters hopes for 'No Treadmill', the joke being that he had too few legs to work it. Elizabeth Fry is lampooned for profiting from the female prisoners of Newgate. Improving and bowdlerized books litter the foreground. Fighting ruffians trample the banner 'Peace to the World', and pugilists square up to the rear. From the windows of neighbouring schools, a schoolgirl and boy leer at each other promisingly, the boy's school advertising 'Morals Church of England Principles Knife & Fork'.

A second, more pointed and smaller print for McLean's shop followed a year later, an anonymous aquatint that put the knife satisfyingly into *A Missionary Society Meeting* [fig. 219]. No more contemptuous image is available to us of laughter's enemies in full swing. A 'sour, sly, and sanctimonious' audience (as Dorothy George described it) is ranted at by an ugly speaker whose windy verbosity causes the candles in front of him to gutter. Three pictures on the wall show savages being preached at by missionaries, a tropical seascape and a grotesque cleric, possibly the speaker. This last tells the gathering that, thanks to their subscriptions, the Word is being preached in all 'uninhabited' parts of the earth after translation into 500 'unknown' languages, and that it will soon be translated into as many more (the phrasing cited from a pietistic newspaper). The unnamed society was probably the evangelical British and Foreign Bible Society.[19] Both prints convey the hostility with which evangelical virtues could be represented even in the 1820s; and both took for granted a market that agreed with them.

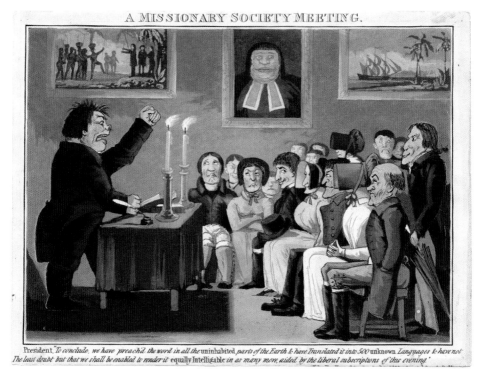

A MISSIONARY SOCIETY MEETING.

President "To conclude, we have preach'd the word in all the uninhabited parts of the Earth & have Translated it into 500 unknown Languages & have not The least doubt but that we shall be enabled to render it equally Intelligable in as many more, aided by the liberal subscriptions of 'this evening.'

**Fig. 219** Anon., *A Missionary Society Meeting* (McLean, 1826)

The early revivalists were in fact quite jolly men, with the sociability of their era. William Wilberforce (their leader) and his cronies were good-humoured enjoyers of wine, and Wilberforce was very partial to opium. A nice observer like Jane Austen could even wonder whether 'we ought not all to be evangelicals', since evangelicals 'from reason & feeling, must be the happiest and safest' of people. She allowed for their 'goodness' too, in some cases. The real killjoys in the eighteenth century had been the Dissenters – men like William Godwin's father, who rebuked his son for picking up the family cat on a Sunday, or the Methodists who lie rather outside our orbit, too lowly for more than a handful of our prints to attend to.[20] The Methodists were lampooned in the new century. One of Fores's mock banknotes (*c*.1811) [fig. 220], for example, assailed them for 'ignorance, hypocrisy & fanaticism and for scaring John Bull with tales of the Devil'; like so many prints, it advised 'No Cant'. But the people who played the larger part in the culture war were those sour, sly and sanctimonious faces that filled the evangelical societies. 'Fat and drowsy dowagers, and other

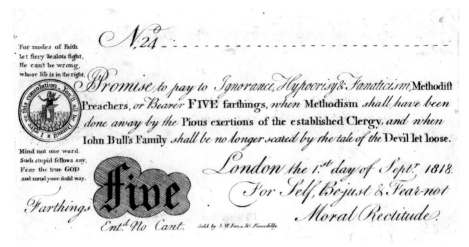

For modes of Faith
Let fiery Zealots fight,
He can't be wrong,
whose life is in the right.

*No. 24*

*Promise* to pay to *Ignorance, Hypocrisy & Fanaticism,* Methodist Preachers, *or Bearer* FIVE farthings, *when* Methodism *shall have been done away by the* Pious exertions of the established Clergy, *and when* Iohn Bull's Family *shall be no longer scared by the tale of the* Devil let loose.

Mind not one word
Such stupid fellows say,
Fear the true GOD
and mend your sinful way.

*Farthings*

**five**

*London the 1st day of Sept.r 1818.*

*For Self, Be-just & Fear-not*

*Moral Rectitude*

Ent.d No Cant.    Sold by S. W. Fores, 50. Piccadilly.

**Fig. 220** Anon., *Imitation Bank-Note* (Fores, *c*.1811)

elderly females in small-clothes and petticoats; hypochondriacs of all ages; half a dozen crazy lords; an odd bishop or so; and some few straggling, decayed foxhunters': that's how one set of moral rearmers was described in the 1820s.[21]

The McLean print foreshadowed the innumerable missionary and temperance bigots who multiplied alarmingly in ensuing decades – the forebears of people like John Ruskin's mother, who, as great a zealot as Godwin's father, turned pictures to the wall on Sundays, or of the joyless religious pedants later immortalized by Dickens, George Eliot and Samuel Butler. Countless Mrs Jellybys, Mrs Pardiggles and Revd Mr Chadbands were to subscribe for bibles and tracts for benighted foreigners or the poor; none sent them food or clothing. The newspaper *Figaro in London* in 1832 calculated that 'twenty times as much money' went to giving bibles to the poor 'as would clothe and feed some thousands of starving families'. Expecting their rewards in the afterlife, *Figaro* added, subscribers were 'actuated by the most interested motives'. They 'put down so much per annum in this manner, and look to their heavenly Father as they would do to the bank for the interest.'[22]

By the 1830s, evangelical doctrines are said to have shaped 'the "official mind" of the period',[23] as well as the real or affected piety of multiplying thousands of the middle classes. Self-interest, social pressure and deft organization achieved this, helped by awesome gullibility. As the Whig divine Robert Fellowes sourly noted in 1801, the English were 'pre-disposed to lend a willing ear to the instructions of any religious juggler who endeavours to persuade them, that faith without holiness, grace without exertion, or righteousness by imputation will supersede the necessity of personal goodness'. In 1809 Sydney Smith, the Whig wit, agreed: 'The loudest and noisiest . . . will always carry it against the more prudent part of the community. The most violent will be considered as the most moral, and those who see the absurdity will, from the fear of being thought to encourage vice, be reluctant to oppose it.'[24]

With its faith 'written in the feelings of the human heart', the evangelical revival was one of sensibility's outcrops. It remained loyal to the established church but had no truck with the relaxed Anglicanism of the Enlightenment. Whereas conventional Anglicanism believed in the redemptive power of good works, evangelical justification came from faith in atonement alone. Man's chief business in this world was to prepare himself for the next by impassioned belief rather than by applying his powers of reason. This was a creed attuned to the needs of self-affirming middle-class people, as well as to women practised in Hannah More's 'exclamations, tender tones, fond tears' that were the new tokens of moral authority. Although the revival was far from the only force that refashioned manners in these decades, it was the most publicized and self-publicizing, and is one undeniable marker of the 'watershed' that this part of the book discusses. It was the movement that most upset people of Enlightened mores, and the charge of 'cant' was deployed with deadliest intent against it.

When Wilberforce was converted to vital Christianity in 1785, he trumpeted forth the news that God had set before him 'the reformation of manners'. And he meant it. Over the ensuing half-century he set about changing his world with the complacent egoism characteristic of all who convince themselves that they have been reborn and saved. Political life was soon dominated by anxieties about the contagion of French principles, by war until 1815, by the battle between Pittite reactionaries and Foxite reformers, and by the fight for free expression; and popular radicalism was recurrently resurgent. All this made for a world ripe for remoralization. 'That a great and general increase of moral corruption has taken place within a century, and, more particularly, within the last ten years, is too obvious to need any proof,' the anti-vice pamphleteer John Bowles intoned in 1802: 'luxurious habits, dissipated manners, and shameless profligacy, are the characteristics of the age.' As floods of pietistic journalism and pamphleteering played on fears of these looming dangers, evangelical belief, like sensibility, provided increasing numbers of upper- and middle-class people with a reinvigorated moral language and identity, or with the appearance of the same.

The movement prospered because it harnessed the associational instincts of the urban middle classes and tapped into their social ambitions. This was 'the age of societies', Macaulay announced in 1823: 'There is scarcely one Englishman in ten who has not belonged to some association for distributing books, or for prosecuting them; for sending invalids to the hospital, or beggars to the treadmill; for giving plate to the rich, or blankets to the poor.' Women were particularly active, their experiences of charitable committees having increased during wartime. As the historian F. K. Brown has elaborated, there were 'societies to improve, to enforce, to reform, to benefit, to prevent, to relieve, to educate, to reclaim, to encourage, to propagate, to maintain, to promote, to provide for, to support, to effect, to better, to instruct, to protect, to supersede, to employ, to civilize, to visit, to preserve, to convert, to mitigate, to abolish, to investigate, to publish, to aid, to extinguish. Above all there were societies to suppress.' Brown then lists over 150 societies established to achieve these ends between Wilberforce's conversion in 1785 and his death in 1833. Most of them were evangelical, the others messianic in spirit. Wilberforce cultivated the king's ear, befriended the irreligous Pitt, and toadied to the dissolute prince; and through all this the evangelicals' parliamentary presence expanded satisfactorily, not least since evangelicals turned blind eyes to aristocratic vices. They voted consistently for the repressive legislation of the 1790s and 1810s, yoking faith to loyalism axiomatically, and irreligion to sedition and to illicit pleasure. Good works were marginal to the evangelical mission because they weren't essential to salvation. Believers need not be moved by the worldly compassion of 'democrats', Wilberforce made clear: instead, they 'should always prefer suffering to sin'. But good works usefully spread the word, facilitated conversions, and captured the moral high ground. Even the crusade against slavery had this propagandist purpose for many. When the slave trade was abolished in 1807, Wilberforce turned 'playfully' to Henry Thornton 'and [said] exultingly, "What shall we abolish next?" The answer fell with characteristic seriousness from the lips of his graver friend: "The lottery, I think."' Through all these projects, Wilberforce came to preside over 'a moral directorate that [was] not figurative but literal'.[25]

# Anti-vice

After anti-slavery, it was the evangelical attack on 'vice' that attracted most attention in the movement's early decades. Within two years of his conversion Wilberforce got the king to issue a proclamation 'for the encouragement of piety and virtue, and for preventing and punishing of vice, profaneness, and immorality'. Then he set up the Proclamation Society to enforce its principles. Some 150 Pittite aristocrats, bishops, MPs, lawyers and county grandees were persuaded to exercise their minds on how best to regulate vagrancy, gin and beer shops, subversive publications, indecent prints, and the baking of bread on Sundays. Although their successes were few and their membership flagged, events across the Channel kept them earnestly at it.[26] They brought prosecutions against booksellers who sold subversive authors like Tom Paine. They tried to check great ladies' gambling in faro banks (a rare attack on the vices of the great). Bishop Porteus of London lectured on 'the growing relaxation of public manners' and got heated about the selling of indecent prints to Westminster schoolboys. And Bishop Barrington worried about the revealing dress of French ballet dancers and their noxious effects on English marriages. None of this was the stuff of radical remoralization. It said nothing about poverty or privilege. And the society justly attracted mockery and opprobrium.

In 1802 the Society for the Suppression of Vice was formed to reactivate the sanitizing mission. The society's founder membership was socially broader, more female and more exclusively evangelical than its predecessor's, and in London it drew on City merchants rather than on West End elites. London membership increased from some 200 in 1802 to 1,200 in 1804, while provincial offshoots attracted professionals, lesser gentry and women similarly.[27] Although it included powerful evangelical names like Wilberforce and Hannah More, most members were nobodies in particular. All had the most conservative views. An early member was John Bowles, for example, the barrister son of John Bowles and brother of Carington Bowles, the printseller. An energetic loyalist pamphleteer in receipt of secret government pay, Bowles was the most active of all anti-vice members between 1803 and 1809 (when a fraud case happily disgraced him). The elevated windbaggery of his *Reflections on the Political and Moral State of Society at the Close of the Eighteenth Century* (1800) provided the anti-vice society with its manifesto.[28] Another of the same ilk was John Reeves: in 1792 he had helped establish the Association for the Preservation of Liberty and Property against Republicans and Levellers. There was an inexpungable odour of the upward-thrusting and aspirant classes about the anti-vice society, not to say an odour of personalities more pathologically driven.

The society's methods were as dubious as its political interests were transparent. Exceptional among evangelical societies in furthering its ends through prosecutions, its bestselling publication was *The Constable's Assistant*. Giving instruction in 'the apprehending of offenders, and the laying of informations before magistrates', this reached a third edition in 1818 and another in 1831. The society began its operations by informing against Italian itinerants who sold obscene prints outside young ladies' boarding schools. Thereafter its prosecutions for the sale of indecent prints, toys and snuff-boxes (and once of an indecent toothpick, of all things) pepper the King's Bench papers. Those who sold Captain Morris's rude song 'The Plenipotentiary' were prosecuted, as were sellers of Cleland's *Fanny Hill*, several times. The society employed agents provocateurs to advance its prosecutions, and got away with this in court. One victim was sentenced by Lord Chief Justice Ellenborough to six months in prison, despite the fact that the indecent prints for which he was prosecuted had been sold to him by a society agent. Ellenborough admitted that entrapment was a 'crime of the highest enormity', but in this case he thought it 'no crime but a beneficial service to the community'.[29] The society's prosecution of one John Harris before the Westminster sessions in 1802 shows how these attacks were conducted. 'The prisoner is a man with only one arm,' a newspaper reported, 'and usually took his stand at the Privy Garden wall, where under pretence of exposing ballads for sale, he took the opportunity of inveigling men, women, and even boys, to purchase his prints, which he used to exhibit to them behind the wall. They were of such a nature, as none but the most depraved and abandoned mind could have invented.' The chairman of the sessions had no doubt what to think about this. Vice had many fifth columnists, he said, but sellers of obscenity were the worst:

> When a robber commits his depredations on the property of people on the highway, there is an end to it . . . Here, however, is a constant course of life, a regular profession of debauching the minds and morals of youth of every description. God only knows how many may grow up to be men and women, having their principles and habits corrupted and tainted by these seeds of

vice, so early implanted in them! Women who have nothing so great as virtue to recommend and adorn them, and who would otherwise retain it unsullied, being thus early debauched, are liable to be led into every species of iniquity.

And so the unfortunate Harris was sentenced to stand for an hour in the Charing Cross pillory, followed by two years in the house of correction.[30] Between 1817 and 1825, the society claimed to have secured the convictions of fourteen publishers or sellers of such works, especially of those who sold Tom Paine. To this list of targets it added the prosecutions of those who ran private theatricals, fairs, brothels, dram shops, gaming houses or illegal lotteries, and fortune-tellers and sabbath-breakers. It ended its first two decades by prosecuting Shelley's 'Queen Mab' for infidelism, and by burning every accessible copy of Shelley's verse drama, *Swellfoot the Tyrant*, which had defended Queen Caroline by ridiculing George IV's sexual antics.

What did this sanitizing endeavour achieve? Not as much as was hoped for, luckily, since no moral campaigners were more hated than this lot, and resistance to them was concerted. In time, even its sympathizers had to admit that much of their attack on dirty publications was tokenist, aiming, as one lamented in 1811, only at 'poor wretches whom their agents had suborned by the lure of money', so that the agents could enjoy 'the credit of doing *something*'. The big bookshops and printshops that sold the really serious stuff were beyond their reach, he added.[31] Moreover, puritan values stood a good distance from supremacy, as these further three cases show.

In 1814, a Thames Police Act was passed in order to deprive the common people of their rights to bathe in the Thames in daylight, on pain of a fine. To correct this needless injustice, a Thames Bathing Bill was introduced in the following year on the liberal grounds that the new restriction 'was a most injurious encroachment on the comfort of the lower classes'. Common law provided 'sufficient remedy against public indecency', the proposer said, 'if any such were complained of'. In any case, if decent females were annoyed, better that they should stay at home 'than that the health of all the lower classes of the metropolis should suffer for the accommodation of their delicacy'. Wilberforce and his friends would have none of this sane advice. They insisted that, if the bill passed, no decent person would be able to live along the river 'from the number of persons undressing themselves, and exposing their naked bodies to view'.

The banning was also justified by 'the want of deference in the lower classes towards the higher, which had increased so much of late years'. In the event, an MP who lived along the river pointed out that in twenty-five years he had never once seen an act of indecency, and sometimes hadn't seen six persons bathing in a year. Another denounced Wilberforce as a 'pious fraud' and deplored that 'itch for legislating which prevailed in the subordinate offices of the State'. The more generous amending bill was passed accordingly.[32]

A second defeat occurred in 1820 when Sir John Jervis declared in a letter to the Home Secretary that Sunday newspapers were vile publications that broke the sabbath, peddled sedition and villainy, and 'violated with a face of brass the Constitution and laws of the land': no wonder the country was full of crimes and conspiracies. Drawing the idle to places of vile resort where, in drink, treason was hatched, they 'should not be suffered in a Christian country', and should, of course, be banned. But again, in the event they weren't.[33] And when, thirdly, the hellfire preacher Edward Irving ranted against the immoralities of the theatre, George IV pointedly commanded a performance of Bickerstaffe's *The Hypocrite*. This pleasant rebuke was visually commemorated both in Hood's *Progress of Cant* [fig. 218] and in Robert Cruikshank's *Taste and Common Sense, Refuting Cant and Hypocrisy* (1824), which attacked Irving's rant against Shakespeare ('Ye followers of Shakespeare you'll all be damn'd!!') by surrounding him with clouds labelled 'hypocricy [*sic*], fanaticism, hatred', as George IV defends Shakespeare.[34]

On the other hand, these rebuffs didn't mean that anti-vice campaigns were ineffectual. Francis Place recorded their impact on bawdy street ballads, for example. 'There were probably a hundred ballad singers then [in the 1780s] for [every] one now,' he noted in 1819. Now, 'if any one was found singing any but loyal songs, he or she was carried before the magistrate' who instructed them to sing only loyal songs if they wished not to be molested: 'Thus the bawdy songs, and those in favour of thieving and getting drunk, were pushed out of existence . . . The old blackguard songs were in a few years unknown to the youths of the rising generation, thus the taste for them subsided. I have no doubt at all that if the ballad singers were now to be left at liberty by the police to sing these songs . . . the public in the streets would not permit the singing of them. Such songs as even 35 years ago produced applause would now cause the singers to be rolled in the mud.'[35]

Other effects were less direct. The Aldgate stationer, Richard Fores (almost certainly related to S. W. Fores of Piccadilly), had published three of ninety-one satirical prints against the king that the Treasury Solicitor bought up to consider for prosecution in 1820. Fores was left alone on that occasion, but he got his comeuppance in 1822 when the anti-vice society had him imprisoned in Cold Bath Fields for nine months for publishing a print they found 'offensive'. His two mercy petitions to the Home Secretary show his terror about what would follow. Young and inexperienced in the trade, he declared, he had immediately submitted to the anti-vice vigilantes by destroying the offending plate; then he had given up 'premises, place, and neighbourhood' and pleaded guilty to the charge. Now in prison, in 'sickness nigh unto death', he was suffering far more than the court intended him to. His life was ruined, and he and his wife survived only on friends' charity. Robert Peel refused the petition, as he invariably did in such cases. And we never hear of young Fores again.[36]

A similar prosecution was undertaken in 1802 of the bookseller Alexander Hogg for republishing *A New and Complete Collection of the Most Remarkable Trials for Adultery*. Hogg had abbreviated the seven volumes originally published in 1779–80 to two volumes, added two new volumes to cover the years 1795–1801, and then recycled the original illustrative plates and sold the whole set (to well-heeled customers) for £1.17.0. It was the plates that caused the trouble. As the indictment weightily put it, the edition contained:

> Diverse wicked lewd impious impure bawdy and obscene prints representing and exhibiting men and women in the act of carnal copulation and in various other most indecent lewd and obscene attitudes and postures to the great displeasure of Almighty God to the scandal and reproach of the Christian religion in contempt of our said lord the king to the great offence of all civil government to the evil example of all others in the like case offending and against the peace of the said king his crown and dignity.

Hogg could hardly suggest in his own defence that if you believed that you would believe anything (the prints were pretty mild). But he did imply that this sledgehammer had descended upon a nut that earlier generations had swallowed easily enough. He claimed to be an honest hard-working man who for twenty-four years had supported wife and family as a bookseller in Paternoster Row. There he had specialized in religious, historical and scientific works, never in 'works of a political or sceptical nature'. He had bought the *Trials'* copyright in all innocence from Samuel Bladen, and Bladen had sold them openly in Paternoster Row for twenty years past, as other booksellers had as well. He knew that the plates were improper, but he had had their worst indecencies engraved out of them. Once charged, he had destroyed the plates and stopped the book's sales, at a loss of £400. In the event, the law had no mercy; what it did have were effects. By one contemporary account of 1800, the *Trials* had been among the most borrowed of all items held in lending libraries. But after this prosecution they disappeared from view. Francis Place noted in the 1820s that adultery and divorce cases were now, thankfully, always 'decently' reported: in other words, their unseemly details were censored.[37]

Historians often argue that moral policing is easily evaded. This was true in many contexts. Yet when efforts to control coincide with new social interests, and when they persist, their messages may be internalized over the years or decades. Many evangelical interventions were trivial as well as deranged, and not all succeeded immediately. Discredited and unpopular, the anti-vice society's membership shrank to 236 by 1825. Nonetheless, its impact was cumulative, certain and disproportionate to its size. The fact that no previous reformative campaign had been as hated as this one was speaks for that effect.

## Resistances

None of the booze-, women-, and laughter-fond men who have so far populated this book, nor the more sexually compliant of their women, were of the kind (initially) to care a fig for William Wilberforce and his purposes. Many were staunchly freethinking, and none would have touched anti-vice campaigns with barge-poles. As the Proclamation Society's historian demurely puts it, 'the notoriously lax morals of Fox's circle lessened the number of possible Whig recruits' to them. She forgets that this went for many Tories also.[38] Although Wilberforce attached Pitt and a small phalanx of MPs and peers to his cause, most deplored the anti-sensualism of the coming times regardless of the party they supported. When they had a religion, which was far from invariably, it was the urbane Christian utilitarianism of William Paley's *Natural Theology,* which Wilberforce damned for moral laxity.[39] Their church was worldly and relaxed, its sermons containing no more Christianity than did the writings of Cicero, as the lawyer Blackstone reported. They might pay lip-service to monogamy and oppose luxury and effeminacy axiomatically. But reason and science continued to instruct them in the 'natural' sensuality of both sexes and also in the goodness of pleasure. Many remained as ironic, satirical and ribald as their forefathers had been over the century past – and just as freethinking. Fox's dying words on life's meaning were 'It don't signify, my dearest, dearest Liz'. 'I will have nothing to do with your immortality,' Byron announced as boldly; 'we are miserable enough in this life, without the absurdity of speculating upon another.' 'I am no Platonist,' he added, 'I am nothing at all; but I would sooner be a Paulician, Manichean, Spinozist, Gentile, Pyrrhonian, Zoroastrian, than one of the seventy-two villainous sects who are tearing each other to pieces for the love of the Lord and hatred of each other.'[40] Even those who loathed Byron would have agreed with him on what was 'pure and good' about their own values: their *manly* English candour, rationality and satirical energy, for a start.

In contrast to the volumes of laudatory words that have been penned about the evangelicals, few words have been written about the thousands who deplored those virtuous people. In the long term, the evangelicals were in some sense the winning voices, and since posterity tends to celebrate winning voices, they are usually taken at their own self-valuation, as being on the angels' side. Add to that a modern sense that libertine cultures could do with taming (and that slavery, when all is said and done, was thankfully abolished), and it is not surprising that those who poured scorn on evangelicals are now virtually forgotten while their targets are put on pedestals. Yet, well into the 1820s, those who hated evangelical sanctimony harnessed the languages of satire to mock it, with little or no sense of their coming obsolescence.

Visual satire, we'll see, supports this observation, but textual satire does also. From the Tory Canningites' attacks on the new pieties, on to those of literary liberals like Lamb, Leigh Hunt, Hazlitt, Hood, Moore, Shelley and Byron, then on again to radical journalists like Cobbett, Wooler and Hone, the lampooning of the fashionably virtuous, respectable and prudish extended into the 1820s – and 'cant' was its named enemy and emblem. Literary scholars have not commonly associated satirical irony with this era. Impressed by the deepening earnestness of Romanticism, they usually think of satire as an earlier, Augustan and chiefly literary form. The sentimental novel's amazing growth, however, doesn't preclude the fact that the thirty years or so after 1790 were satire's golden age. Byron and Shelley were major satirists, and the output of both textual and graphic satire expanded hugely. Between 1789 and 1832, over 700 poetic satires were published, and over sixty of the 201 volumes of poetry published in 1820 alone can be classified as satirical.[41] That satire flourished in these years is, once stated, unsurprising. In the culture wars now unfolding, satire and sensibility reacted against and lived off each other.

Tories led the way in this reaction. This was because they thought of sensibility as a Jacobin muse, contaminated with Rousseauan associations. Even anti-slavery was 'jacobin' in their eyes, thanks to the threat it offered to interest and property. Beyond that, emoting sermonizers, sentimental philanthropists and gushing women were no more to their tastes than they were to those of enlightened liberals. The leading practitioners of conservative satire were the urbane politicians and poets behind the weekly *Anti-Jacobin: or Weekly Examiner*, published in 1797–8 as a loyalist journal under George Canning's aegis. A renegade from youthful liberal principles, Canning was now one of Pitt's under secretaries of state, and the journal drew on secret Treasury funding. Canning, John Hookham Frere and other Etonian friends, and occasionally Pitt, were its main though anonymous contributors. Sales were thought to be 'enormous' when they rose to 2,000 weekly copies, netting the publisher Wright some £500 profit by the time the journal closed in July, when Canning retired, thinking journalism too low a calling to combine with office. The journal then reinvented itself as the monthly *Anti-Jacobin Review and Magazine*, and continued until 1821.[42] In both incarnations, it castigated the Whig opposition's errors in columns headed 'lies', 'misrepresentations' and 'mistakes'. It interpreted the news in the loyalists' favour, and leaked ministerial information when convenient. Most notably, it published a series of verse satires by Canning and Frere that parodied English-Jacobin 'effusions'. These taunted the Foxites, Southey, Coleridge, Godwin, Erasmus Darwin and others then on the liberal flank (and were thought to have nudged the Lake poets towards their public recantations of French principles shortly after).[43] Though now forgotten by non-specialists, some critics regard these verses as among the most pungent satires since Dryden.

Canning paid Gillray to illustrate some of these verses in plates for separate sale (later bound in with the journal's successor). For the first time the satirical writer and engraver joined in purposeful collaboration, an example widely followed over the next twenty years.[44] The relationship was uncomfortable, and there was often a tonal disjunction between text and image. The best matches for the ludic hyperboles of graphic satire were light-hearted parodies or the comic triple meters and iambic tetrameter couplets of the colloquial Horatian mode. But Canning and Frere also aimed at the sublimity of neo-Juvenalian satire, and Gillray had to illustrate this as well. Another problem was that Gillray would insist on personalizing his protagonists, ignoring Canning's insistence that satire should avoid 'personal particulars'. A good example of this was his response to Canning's and Frere's parody of Southey's early radical sentimentalism in their verses on *The Needy Knife-grinder*. The halting rhythms of their verses were inspirationally comic:

FRIEND OF HUMANITY:

'Needy knife-grinder! Whither are you going?
Rough is the road, your wheel is out of order –
Bleak blows the blast; – your hat has got a hole in't,
        So have your breeches!' . . .
Did some rich man tyrannically use you?
Was it the squire? or parson of the parish?
        Or the attorney? . . .
(Have you not read the Rights of Man, by Tom Paine?)
        Drops of compassion tremble on my eyelids
        Ready to fall, as soon as you have told your pitiful story.'

But the knife-grinder disappoints his interrogator by replying that he tore his breeches in a drunken tavern scuffle, that he'd be glad of a sixpence to drink the gentleman's health, and that he never meddled in politics. At which betrayals, the philanthropist explodes: '*I* give thee sixpence! I will see thee damn'd first.' He then 'kicks the knife-grinder, overturns his wheel, and exit[s] in a transport of republican enthusiasm and universal philanthropy'. As they planned Gillray's illustration of the verses, Frere wrote to Gillray's friend, the amateur caricaturist Revd John Sneyd, that 'Gillray is to be here tomorrow, and Canning is to have his way with him'. 'We very much wish (as the pen and pencil must assist each other) that you would send us a sketch on the following subject': Gillray was required to follow Sneyd's design. They were overoptimistic, however. In the authors' view, Gillray's ensuing print spoilt the effect by depicting the philanthropist as the Whig Tierney. This literalized the attack as the poem refused to [fig. 221]. 'Gillray

**Fig. 221** Gillray, *The Friend of Humanity and the Knife-Grinder, – Scene, The Borough, in Imitation of Mr Southey's Sapphics* (H. Humphrey, 1797)

**Fig. 222** Gillray, *New Morality; – or – the Promis'd Installment of the High-Priest of the Theophilanthropes, with the Homage of Leviathan and his Suite* (*Anti Jacobin Review & Magazine*, 1798)

has bedevilled it and destroyed all the simplicity of the idea,' Frere complained.[45]

The mismatch between verse and image is even better exemplified in Gillray's fold-out plate for Canning and Frere's celebrated heroic couplets on 'The New Morality' (1798) [fig. 222]. The poem opens with a savage indictment of 'the *New Philosophy* of modern times [the canting sentimentality of philanthropy, that is] whose boundless mind / Glows with the general love of all mankind', and of the philanthropist who is 'A steady patriot of the world alone, / The friend of every country – but his own'. It indicts sensibility's 'shrinking softness' as it weeps 'For the crushed beetle

*fhd. August 1st 1798. by J.Wright Nº113 Piccadilly. for the Anti Jacobin Magazine & Review*  ——  *J. Gillray invt & fet*

*—ANTHROPES, with the Homage of Leviathan and his Suite.* ——

" PR_TL_Y and W_F_LD, humble, holy men,
" Give praises to his name with tongue and pen ! __
_TH_LW_L. and ye that Lecture as ye go,
" And for your pains get Pelted, praise LE PAUX ! __
_Praise him each Jacobin, or Fool, or Knave,
And your cropp'd heads in sign of worship wave ! __
_All creeping creatures, venomous and low,
PAINE, W_LL_MS, G_DW_N, H_LC_FT, praise LEPAUX ! __

"And thou LEVIATHAN ! on Ocean's brim
"Hugest of living things that sleep & swim ;
"Thou in whose nose by BURKE'S gigantic hand
"The hook was fix'd to drag thee to the land
"With ___ , ___ , and ___ in thy train,
"And W___ wallowing in the Yeasty main.
"Still as ye snort, and puff, and spout, and blow,
"In puffing, and in spouting, praise LEPAUX !__ _Vide Anti Jacobin_

first, – the widowed dove, / And all the warbled sorrows of the grove; – / Next for poor suff'ring guilt; – and last of all, / For parents, friends, a king and country's fall'. It inveighs against 'liberal justice' 'whose blood-stained book one sole decree, / One statute fills – "the people shall be free." / Free by what means? – by folly, madness, guilt, / By boundless rapines, blood in oceans spilt'. And it castigates the French Director Lépaux ('at whose nod / Bow their meek heads *the men without a God!*') and English radicals' deference to his atheist doctrines.

Gillray's illustration of these verses was too elaborate to do justice to their elevated and caustic tone, memorably influential though his print was. Grotesque statues of Justice, Philanthropy and Sensibility adorn the altar to the right, Sensibility holding a book by Rousseau and weeping over a dying bird; all three wear Jacobin *bonnets rouges*. In front of them, the hunch-backed Lépaux preaches from a book labelled *Religion de la n[ature]*, surrounded by small simian figures representing the opposition newspapers (labelled, 'Lies, blasphemy, sedition'). From the left, Lépaux is approached by a procession of all the Foxite and literary figures who populate loyalist demonology. The Duke of Bedford dominates them, because he is portrayed as a giant whale-like 'leviathan' (alluding to a reference by Burke).[46] The Bedford monster is ridden by Nicholls, Tierney, Fox and Thelwall, all with *bonnets rouges*, and followed by the swimming figures of Erskine, Norfolk, Burdett and Derby, surrounded by small grotesques representing Tom Paine and Thomas Holcroft, and by William Godwin in the form of a donkey. To the right Southey and Coleridge are given donkey's heads, Charles Lamb is a toad, and Erasmus Darwin, Joseph Priestley and Gilbert Wakefield follow, each identified by the texts he holds. Papers spilling from a 'cornucopia of ignorance' include Wollstonecraft's *Wrongs of Women*, works by Holcroft and by the sentimental poetess Perdita Robinson, and an array of the Whiggish pamphlets and speeches recently reviewed in the *Anti-Jacobin*. The print was as closely perused and as long remembered as the poem was, Southey admiring Holcroft's likeness and Godwin asking Lamb on their first meeting whether he was a toad or a frog. It inspired Cruikshank's devastating image of the *Prince of Whales* a dozen years later [fig. 251].

In revolution-haunted times, both Canning's *Anti-Jacobin* and its successor had to have it both ways. On the one hand, they could hardly fail to endorse critiques of the 'growing profligacy of manners', of 'luxury and dissipation', and of the 'most frequent, flagrant and aggravated violations of the nuptial tie' – or now and then to condemn dancing, gambling, sabbath-violation, prostitution, bull-baiting, the costs of poor relief, and illicit sex among the poor. On the other hand, they retained belief in a rational and benign human nature, a tolerance of legitimate sensual pleasures, and a mistrust of sensibility and enthusiasm. In the tradition already noted, they both insisted that their morality was 'commonsensical', 'English', and '*manly*'[47] and their characteristic weapon was ridicule, leavened by the old clubbish vulgarity: 'Peter [Pindar], thou art a puff . . . And like that other puff, a f—[ar]t'. Above all, their attacks on evangelicals' 'spiritual conceit' and 'puritan fanaticism' were incessant. Barely an issue of the journal in its later form failed to assail 'ignorant fanatics, speaking the true cant of the tabernacle'. It attacked evangelical Sunday schools for spreading uppity ideas among the poor. It charged Hannah More with hypocrisy when she fed the poor with cakes and lectured them on how much better off they were than the poor in France, while giving the rich who attended her lecture a full and lavish tea. It accused evangelicals of making money from their virtue, and attacked their indifference to elite vices and their focus on those of the poor. It questioned the hypocrisy of efforts to abolish the slave trade that ignored domestic misery, and it opposed evangelical efforts to enforce the abolition of slavery after 1807. In 1816 it denounced 'the fanatical exertions of those spurious philanthropists, who are labouring to puritanize ... the public mind, and, consequently, to destroy the best energies, and the best feelings, of *Englishmen*' [my italics]. And it declared that 'it is the dread of the predominance of this faction, who are making rapid strides towards ascendancy in the state, that renders it an imperious duty to open the eyes of the public to their real motives and views'.[48] In short, the *Anti-Jacobin* saw no irony in the fact that among its many enemies it included the one rising force that was to carry conservative reaction and remoralization across the land.

---

This hostility shaped liberal as well as Tory critiques of the coming moral order. Despite their vast disagreements on political reform and on France, both camps had been nurtured in shared Enlightened cultures, even the same schools. But the protracted exclusion from power of men of liberal or Whiggish disposition gave them added reasons for disaffection. In the early decades of the new century, it was they, chiefly, who generalized and democratized the resistance to the new virtue.

The most eloquent exponent of gentlemanly-anglican liberalism after William Paley's death in 1805 was the Revd Sydney Smith, whig, wit and scholar. In 1808–9, he wrote four damaging articles on evangelical humbuggery for the *Edinburgh Review*, assailing the anti-vice society's humbuggery in particular. Renaming it the Society for Suppressing the Vices of Persons whose Income does not exceed £500 a Year, he saw in it 'a voluntary magistracy, which creates so much disgust, that it almost renders vice popular'. Indifferent to the vices of the rich, the society reeked of 'cant and hypocrisy'. He understood why it should be so: 'To suppose that any society will ever attack the vices of people of fashion is wholly out of the question ... What gentleman so fond of suppressing, as to interfere with the vices of good company, and inform against persons who were really genteel? He knows very well that the consequence of such interference would be a complete exclusion from elegant society.' So double standards permitted the wealthy to ride a horse until it dropped 'in order to see an innocent animal torn to pieces by dogs'; but while 'any cruelty may be practised to gorge the stomachs of the rich', none was permitted 'to enliven the holidays of the poor'. Should 'the common people' be seen to enjoy themselves, 'away rush secretary, president, and committee, to . . . bring back the life of the poor to its regular standard of decorous gloom', while 'the gambling houses of St James's remain untouched'. 'Can there be anything more despicable than such distinctions as these? Those who make them seem to have for other persons' vices all the rigour of the ancient puritans – without a particle of their honesty or their courage.' Efforts to prosecute obscenity, sedition and sabbath-breaking were counter-productive, since 'indicting men into piety' produced only outward compliance, not 'inward feeling'.[49]

Smith here laid down the terms of an attack that were replayed many times subsequently. William Cobbett in 1809 declared that every one of the puritans 'is not only a staunch anti-Jacobin, but belongs also, I am told, to the *Society for the Suppression of Vice*; anti-Jacobins, anti-bull-baiters, anti-boxers, anti-revellers, and anti-dancers, anti-every thing that is calculated to draw the people together, and to afford them a chance of communicating their ideas; anti-every thing which does not tend to abject subjection'.[50] Byron weighed in, in 'English Bards, and Scotch Reviewers' (1809):

Raise not your scythe, suppressors of our vice!
Reforming saints! too delicately nice!
By whose decrees, our sinful souls to save,
No Sunday tankards foam, no barbers shave;
And beer undrawn, and beards unmown, display
Your holy rev'rence for the sabbath-day.

*The Scourge: or Monthly Expositor of Imposture and Folly*, liberal in politics and one of the magazines that followed the *Anti-Jacobin* in linking textual to visual satire, lamented with heavy irony that 'the poor have no business to laugh', making its point about the new prudery in sledgehammer irony and ribaldry: 'every unmarried female, above the age of fourteen, detected in assisting a male child, to perform the urinary office, should be committed to the county gaol . . . Of the equine race, mares and geldings alone should be permitted to approach within three miles of any populous town; and every object that bears a *phallic* outline, should be banished from our dwellings, and razed from our streets . . . rolling pins should be burnt without mercy, and pokers be driven from the parlour stove.'[51]

Leigh Hunt in the *Examiner* swelled the critical chorus. The evangelicals, he wrote, were prostituting religion 'into a servile piece of political convenience for one rank, and a mental ligature of a most debasing description for another'. 'Societies are formed to prosecute the humble exclusively,' he continued, their tracts pursuing 'the servile principle of producing the utmost possible submission from the inferior to the superior'. Ever submissive to their social betters, 'the modern school of predestination' committed itself narrowly to the 'servile creed of modern puritans'. The poor, he continued, not only had 'to be humble and thankful for everything', but also had:

> To be sober and industrious, for otherwise they cannot pay twopence or threepence a-week to half a dozen subscriptions, including one for the translation of the Bible into the Telinga! Never to meddle with politics, which lead them to alehouses and from chapel. Moreover, can they be governed better than they are governed? Never to enter a playhouse, which is the direct road to hell for them, however it may prove to their betters; nor to attend dances, nor to go to fairs, nor to cricket or nine-pins. The oftener they go to chapel the better. They are also allowed to sing psalms, as Milton says, everlastingly. Never to be merry, as all mirth leads to perdition. Never to take a boat on a Sunday, it being a part of the scheme of providence to drown all people below a certain rank who venture on the water on the sabbath-day. Never to break the sabbath by festivity of any kind, the most serious judgements attending all who do so out of the west of London.[52]

Or, again, as Hazlitt asked in his *Spirit of the Age* (1825), 'What have the SAINTS to do with freedom or reform of any kind?': 'We can readily believe that Mr Wilberforce's first object is to do what he thinks right; his next . . . is to do what will be thought so by other people . . . Mr Wilberforce's humanity will go all lengths that it can with safety and discretion: but it is not to be supposed that it should lose him his seat for Yorkshire, the smile of majesty, or the countenance of the loyal and pious. He is anxious to do all the good he can without hurting himself or his fair fame . . . He preaches vital Christianity to untutored savages; and tolerates its worst abuses in civilized states . . . There is in all this an appearance of a good deal of cant and tricking.'

These views spread down to popular levels. When in 1811 the utopian radical Thomas Spence dreamed of a return to the land, he envisaged a society that would provide 'feasts of hospitality and love' with access to 'cheering beverage' and 'strong drink' – an ancestral memory invoked here of a carnivalesque idyll that defied those 'always preaching up temperance, labour, patience and submission'.[53] And when in the 1820s moralizers attacked Pierce Egan's comic creations, *Tom and Jerry*, they were rebuffed thus by Egan's dramatist, Moncrieff: 'to those venerable noodles who complain that I and my prototype, Pierce, have made this the age of flesh, I answer – my age is better than the "age of cant".'[54]

# The prints

What, finally, was the role of graphic satire in this culture war? The answer may be predicted. Not one print that referred to evangelical or clerical endeavours between the late 1780s and the late 1820s did so without ridiculing them mercilessly. While the philosophical interventionist Jeremy Bentham appears only once in the entire catalogue of visual satire in these decades, Wilberforce features in fifty prints, and always as a canting prude. As ever, it is difficult to say whether it was the market's expectations or the engravers' and printshop proprietors' worldliness and political disaffection that determined this: the two were too intimately married to be easily distinguished. The regency decade was certainly to see a marked radicalization of print output. The rise of new City printshops less in thrall to West End custom combined with deepening hatred of the regent and his repressive governments to sharpen commentary in ways that the shops of the 1780s and 1790s would never have attempted.[55] But even in those earlier years, everything we've noted about the engravers' manners points to their own irreligiousness, and the number and vehemence of anticlerical prints proves how many people in the market shared it. Although jokes about idle, pluralist, tithe-battening, drunken and overfed parsons drew on centuries-old prototypes, they multiplied, diversified and sharpened in this period, suggesting a wide if usually covert aversion to godliness which textual evidence rarely exposes so well.

To be sure, some anticlerical prints were simply humorous. *The Vicar and Moses* (1782), for example, illustrated G. A. Stevens's comic doggerel about a drunken vicar and his clerk weaving their way from the tavern to perform

**Fig. 223** Colley(?), *The Vicar and Moses* (H. Humphrey, 1782)

a risibly intoxicated and disastrous burial: 'The body we'll bury, but pray where's the hurry / Why lord sir, the corpse it does stay / You fool hold your peace, since miracles cease, / A corpse, Moses, can't run away' [fig. 223]. The print's popularity 'among the vulgar' and its being 'often hung up on the walls of farmhouses' explains why two further versions of it were published between 1782 and 1784 (one by Rowlandson). It also explains why Vicesimus Knox deplored it for encouraging those 'who from their infancy are accustomed to behold the parson an object of derision, a glutton, and a drunkard'.[56] Jokes as mild as this were lost on some.

*WOLVES IN SHEEPS CLOATHING*

**Fig. 224** Anon., *Wolves in Sheeps' Cloathing* (W. Humphrey, 1777)

Most prints were more vicious, however. One of the printseller William Humphrey's earliest – *Wolves in Sheeps' Cloathing* [sic] (1777) [fig. 224] – had three clergymen at a wine- and meat-laden table with courtesans perched on their laps, nipples exposed as usual. Satires on tithe-fattened or debauched parsons multiplied thereafter: Dighton, Carington Bowles, Colley, Newton, Isaac Cruikshank and Rowlandson all produced them.[57] None referred to evangelical initiatives specifically until a cluster in 1793–6 mocked the king's decree that the nation support the war effort by fasting. 'A fast!' Coleridge snorted in 1795: 'A word that implies prayers of hate to the God of love – and after these a turbot feast for the rich, and their usual scanty morsel to the poor, if indeed debarred from their usual labour they can procure even this.'[58] This cue the engravers readily followed. 'Fasting and prayer, attending the church bell, / That, that's the way, good Christians, to live well!', proclaimed Newton's *Fast Day!* as it illustrated fat clerics tucking heftily into a roast joint and claret [fig. 225]. Isaac Cruikshank's *A General Fast in Consequence of the War!!* (1794) has the archbishop and lady friends at Lambeth stuff themselves on the left, while a Spitalfields family starves on the right [fig. 226]. In one of his rare flashes of social awareness, Gillray, in *Substitutes for Bread; – or – Right Honorables,*

**Fig. 225** Newton, *Fast Day!* (Holland, 1793)

**Fig. 226** Isaac Cruikshank, *A General Fast in Consequence of the War!!* (Fores, 1794)

*Saving the Loaves, and Dividing the Fishes*, shows ministers gorging themselves on the golden fishes of office while starving people protest outside.[59]

It says much about the confident milieux in which the satires were conceived and marketed that it took some years before they registered the scale of what was really afoot. Anticlericalism was one thing; a full sense of what Wilberforce and his friends were up to was another, and it dawned only slowly. Initially, only a couple of prints of note thought Wilberforce's campaigns worth commenting on at all, and they targeted the royal family chiefly. Rowlandson's *Reformation – or, the Wonderful Effects of a Proclamation!!!* (1787) – the proclamation against vice, that is, which Wilberforce got the king to issue – has the king and queen in chapel, with princely, Whig and aristocratic rakes in attendance, listening to a preacher in the implausible guise of the libertine John Wilkes [fig. 227]. While the Prince of Wales flirts with Mrs Fitzherbert and Lord North and others sleep, Fox sits draped in a penitent's sheet and wearing a placard, 'For playing cards on the Lord's day'. Behind the congregation, a wall plaque is dedicated to the memory of 'the renowned Plenipotentiary'

**Fig. 227** Rowlandson, *Reformation – or, the Wonderful Effects of a Proclamation!!!* (1787)

**Fig. 228** Gillray, *Vices Overlook'd in the New Proclamation* (H. Humphrey, 1792)

(he of the enormous phallus celebrated in Captain Morris's song) by 'two maiden ladies of this parish who tasted exquisite felicity from his prowess'.[60] A few years later, Gillray's *Vices Overlook'd in the New Proclamation* (1792) [fig. 228] has the king and queen hugging money-bags under the heading 'avarice'; the drunken Prince of Wales being taken home by watchmen under 'drunkenness'; the Duke of York sitting at a gaming-table under 'gambling', and the Duke of Clarence embracing his mistress, Mrs Jordan, under 'debauchery'. Gillray subtitled the print in ironic dedication: 'To the Commons of Great Britain, this representation of vices, which remain unforbidden by proclamation, is dedicated, as proper for imitation, and in place of the more dangerous ones of thinking, speaking, & writing, now forbidden by authority'. Because *Vices Overlook'd* appears to castigate high-born vices, Diana Donald sees it as articulating 'the sensibilities of those outside the pale of fashionable elite society', and of the 'middle class' particularly.[61] This misses the point. Humphrey's elite customers knew that the print's primary target was the proclamation's absurdity and hypocrisy rather than the vices proclaimed against. Given

**Fig. 229** Isaac Cruikshank, *The Enraget Politician or the Sunday Reformer or a Noble Bellman Crying Stinking Fish* (Fores, 1799)

a West End deeply antipathetic to puritans and meddlers, the engravers peddled a distaste for Wilberforce and his works that reflected the views of the market they aimed at. Gillray shared those views. One of his manuscript lists in 1805 shows that he planned a print on 'The society for the suppression of vice – a debate on using deception for pious end – debate on pious fraud'.[62]

As evangelical campaigning became more intrusive, mocking prints expanded their range. They ridiculed evangelical distress at the revealing dresses of French ballet dancers [figs. 167 and 168]. They exposed Lord Belgrave's double standards when with Wilberforce's support he moved for a bill to suppress the Sunday sale of newspapers and of everything except milk and mackerel: thus Isaac Cruikshank's *The Enraget* [sic] *Politician* (1799) [fig. 229] shows Belgrave getting furious at the bawling news-sellers outside his window while he ignores the din made by a fashionable rout in the grand house opposite. (A news-seller holds up a newspaper that reminds

**Fig. 230** Williams, *City Scavengers Cleansing the London Streets of Impurities!!* (Sidebotham, 1816).

purchasers that Belgrave's mother, Lady Grosvenor, had been famously tried for adultery in 1770.) Later prints mocked Lord Mayor Wood's campaign to clear the City streets of prostitutes. For example, Williams's *City Scavengers Cleansing the London Streets of Impurities!!* (1816), drawn for one of the new City printshops, Sidebotham's made its comic point about the authorities' hypocritical prurience (looking up skirts, etc.) in a composition littered with *doubles entendres*, tumbling legs and exposed thighs, with the Lord Mayor, Woods, presiding over the forcible removal of prostitutes from the city's streets while on the steps of the Mansion House the Recorder of london reads the Riot Act [fig. 230]. George Cruikshank mocked the same campaign in his Fuselian parody, *The Night Mayor* ('painted by Fuzely'), which perched Mayor Wood on a sleeping prostitute's breast, with the City Recorder, Silvester, grinning through a doorway, the subtext carrying the satirical comment on Wood's real motives: 'The Night Mayor flitting thro' the evening fogs / Traverses alleys, streets courts lane

**Fig. 231** George Cruikshank, *Making Decent – !!* (H. Humphrey, 1822)

& bogs / Seeking some love bewilder'd maid by gin oppres'd / Alights –
& ogling sits upon her downy breast.' Cruikshank's *Making Decent – !!* (1822)
lampooned Wilberforce's prudishness about Achilles's giant nude statue in
Hyde Park [fig. 231]: Wilberforce's tiny figure reaches to cover its vast fig-
leafed genitals with a top hat; 'A hint to the Society for the Suppression of
Vice,' the subtitle reads: 'This print commemorative of Anglo French brass
& true British <u>chastity</u>, is inscribed with veneration to that worthy man Mr
Willbyforce who with saintlike regard for the morals of his country has
undertaken to make the above fig[ure] decent from 10 in the mg. till dusk.'
And so on – via Hood's *The Progress of Cant* in 1825 – to 1829, when Heath's
*The March of Morality* has the overdressed ladies of the Religious Tract
Society, preceded by a beadle, hunting down indecent prints in printshop
windows, and having nude statues decently covered. The word 'cant' is
written on the society's fascia-board in the background, while placards
advertise Stockdale's pornography [fig. 232].

Even Wilberforce's anti-slavery campaign was attacked, on the grounds
that it cared more about the plight of distant slaves than it cared about the
plight of English workers. Both Gillray and Isaac Cruikshank produced
powerful plates to depict and protest at slave atrocities, but it was

**Fig. 232** Heath, *The March of Morality* (McLean, 1829)

**Fig. 233** Gillray, *Philanthropic Consolations, after the Loss of the Slave-Bill* (H. Humphrey, 1796)

Wilberforce's indifference to domestic distress that really vexed them.[63] When Parliament in 1792 agreed to the slave trade's gradual abolition, Holland issued four anti-Wilberforce plates by Newton to this effect. One, *Justice and Humanity at Home*, shows a flogged English soldier crying that he would rather be a slave than be treated thus, while a blind old man begs pitifully and a debtor looks out from a prison: Wilberforce, watching, says, 'I and my tribe must look abroad for acts of cruelty and oppression – This is so near home it is beneath our notice. My duty to my Maker teaches me thus to act.'[64] Gillray's *Philanthropic Consolations, after the Loss of the Slave Bill* (1796) has Wilberforce and Bishop Horsley consoling themselves for that year's defeat of the Anti-slavery Bill by cavorting lasciviously with two black women, one of them bare-breasted.

The most developed attack on the anti-slave men was delivered over twenty years later in George Cruikshank's *New Union Club* (1819) [fig. 234]. This compositional and comic tour de force, sized 12 by 18½ inches, would today be better known were it not for its racist postures. The idea for it came from Cruikshank's partisan friend, Frederick Marryat, the son of a plantation-owner who led the West India interest in Parliament and whose pamphlets had charged Wilberforce's African Institution with hypocrisy for ignoring the exploitation of English workers. This was the point of Cruikshank's print also. In its exuberant invective, it claimed Gillray's mantle, as its debt to Gillray's 1801 *Union Club* in composition, detailing and title show. It depicts a drunken debauch around a long table dominated by Wilberforce's chair of honour (a commode). As Wilberforces proposes a toast in the form of the 'Black Joke' (the lewd song), black people and white philanthropists consort promiscuously. Abolitionists, including Zachary Macaulay and James Stephen, canoodle with fat black women on their laps; and other figures show the outcome of miscegenation. A black man and a white woman hold a naked piebald baby between them, one side of it black, the other white. Another black woman suckles a baby whose white body is dappled in black spots. The one-legged black beggar, Billy Waters, fiddles and dances on the table (we shall meet Waters on several occasions later). The lower end of the table dissolves into a reprise of Gillray's *Union Club* punch-up. A teapot, a broken bottle and a bottle of

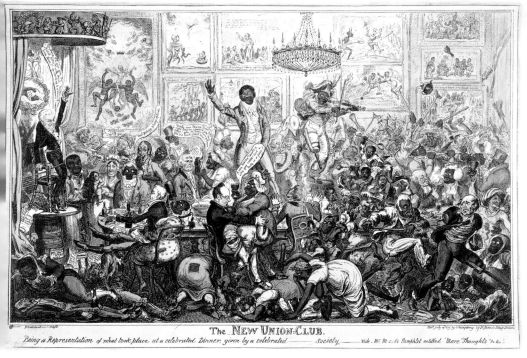

**Fig. 234** George Cruikshank, *The New Union Club* (G. Humphrey, 1819)

'Day & Martin Blacking' fly through the air. The background is crowded with waving beggars' crutches, and the floor is littered with drunken figures. All representations of black people are derogatory, and a dozen pictures on the rear wall allegorize abolitionist hypocrisies. The print is so saturated that the British Museum catalogue needs 1,700 words to describe it.

The role that mockery played in the culture war need not be laboured further. But could the ribaldry of such ripostes be sustained? 'No God and no religion can survive ridicule,' Mark Twain wrote optimistically, many decades later: 'No political church, no nobility, no royalty or other fraud, can face ridicule in a fair field, and live.' Byron had similarly hoped that ridicule was the only weapon that the English climate couldn't rust. But in this event such hopes were bound to be disappointed. The satirizing of cant endured, of course. Satire might retreat as a discrete literary and visual form, but Dickens could not invent Mrs Jellyby, Mrs Pardiggle and the Revd Mr Chadband without a vibrant tradition of anti-canting ridicule to draw on. Yet Dickens's ridicule shunned the antique bawdry, and this loss of an older, crueller, carnivalesque aggression was to mark a fundamental change – a taming.

In 1803, the evangelical *Christian Observer* published a letter which advised that ridicule was 'neither sprung from Christian love nor compatible with it'. Lacking 'the divine affection of love', satire sought only 'opportunities of private recrimination and revenge'. Then it added:

> To excite mirth without much consideration of the end in view, or of the manner of doing it, or of the feelings of others . . . to make others feel their inferiority, and to give them pain; these . . . are, I fear, almost always apparent among the motives of the humourist and the satirist. Though his professed object may be to exhibit vice to view, in its native deformity, and stripped of its disguises, and to reform the vicious; yet if he choose ridicule or satire as his instrument, let him pause before he ventures to pronounce his motives to be hallowed.[65]

It could hardly be foreseen that that cramping weasel-word, 'hallowed' and, more largely the recycling and Christianization of this formula from the Augustan theoreticians of politeness, would ring the old laughter's death-knell. Within a quarter-century or so, its validity would be seldom contested, and such bawdy aggression as survived in public print would be outlawed.

# CHAPTER SIXTEEN

# RADICAL SATIRE
# AND THE CENSORS

## 'Treason!!!': the 1790s

In March 1798, the young Richard Newton etched and published one of the most daring of the prints produced in that tense and sedition-conscious decade. His *Treason!!!* depicts a robustly plebeian John Bull, hands cheekily on hips, cocking up his buttocks to fart defiance at a poster-portrait of George III, as Prime Minister Pitt warns him 'That is treason, Johnny' [fig. 235]. The year before this, Newton had also engraved his *General Sentiment*,

and its implications were just as startling. It has Pitt being hanged by the neck, watched by his Whig opponents, Fox and Sheridan. They wear revolutionary *bonnets rouges* and gleefully utter the mock-pious wish: 'May our heaven born minister be *supported* from *above*' [fig. 236].

How did Newton get away with such risky images? Private tavern conversations were being spied upon, reported and prosecuted for statements no stronger than Newton's. Indeed, within weeks of the publication of *Treason!!!*, Pitt suspended *habeas corpus*. The Treasury

**Fig. 235** Newton, *Treason!!!* (Newton, 1798)

**Fig. 236** Newton, *The General Sentiment* (Fores, 1797)

Solicitor's papers are full of preparations for the prosecution of this or that individual for cursing the war, toasting the French, or damning Pitt, even in private tavern conversations. Spies were everywhere. And it was no defence in such cases to say that you were only joking. 'Is a laugh treason?', the bookseller William Hone was to ask incredulously when prosecuted for publishing his satirical parodies in 1817. The law replied then, as it did throughout this period, that ridicule could carry a seditious intention, and that sedition stood next to treason. Patricians could laugh at themselves within limits, but they wouldn't put up with being laughed at by common people or being threatened by radicalized rabbles. To laugh at king, church and constitution was beyond bearing. The last thirty years of George III's reign were years of tightening control, and how the satirists dealt with those controls is one of the nicest questions we must now deal with.

We'll never know whether the Crown's law officers would have called Newton to account for these prints. He fell ill shortly after *Treason!!!* appeared, and by December 1798 he was dead, in his twenty-first year. They would probably have let them pass. Visual satirists were protected by the ambivalence inherent in all graphic irony. *The General Sentiment* could be represented as an attack on Fox and Sheridan as much as a wish for Pitt's strangulation. (Gillray's *The Dog Tax* the year before had depicted Sheridan and Fox as hanged dogs gloated over by a dogs-bodied Pitt and George III, though that print was on the loyalist side, of course, and only about a dog tax.) Had *Treason!!!* been prosecuted, the court would have been obliged to debate whether Newton himself had the seditiously 'wicked purpose of ridiculing the king and royal family', or whether he was merely warning against that wickedness, as his defence would have claimed. He would also have been protected by the need to read out in court an indictment in pompous legalese that would have to describe a farting figure. This would have so punctured the law's solemnity that prosecution would have been counterproductive.

The laws limiting free expression were deeply intimidating in the short term, but had little bearing on satire's long-term taming. It wasn't legal repression that terminally silenced disaffected satirists: it was the king's bribery in 1820–1 that finally clinched it. Beyond that, the political reforms of the 1820s and the social and cultural shifts that multiplied the old laughter's enemies were more lastingly influential. London was filling with revivalists, people of sensibility, and respectable people who couldn't stand bawdry. Beyond that again, censorship usually *favours* satire by compelling artists and writers to deploy all the forms of misdirection – parody, allegories, overstatements, dream visions – that camouflage their true intentions and sow doubts about their meanings. As Lord Shaftesbury had written long before, it was 'the persecuting spirit' that gave rise to 'the bantering spirit': the greater the constraint upon the satirist, the stronger his satire.[1] Indeed, satire's purposes and audiences were radicalized in the 1810s, when the law's attack on dissidents was at its fiercest. Journalists, publishers and new 'low' printshops were then to attack corruptions and oppressions with a vehemence unprecedented in the 1790s.

That said, there's no denying the legal force that confronted critical printsellers, and booksellers and writers. The censorship of printed works *before* publication had been discarded in 1695, but that didn't stop many common-law prosecutions for seditious, blasphemous or obscene libel *after* publication in the century following. Rulings on public libel were restrictive. Blackstone's *Commentaries on the Laws of England* (1765–8) stated that the common law's sole interest was in 'the tendency which all libels have to create animosities, and to disturb the public peace'. It was no defence to claim that what the libel asserted was true (or simply funny), because 'the provocation, and not the falsity, is the thing to be punished criminally'. Holt's *Law of Libel* added in 1812 that libel 'is proportionately more criminal as it presumes to reach persons to whom special veneration is due', i.e. royalty and statesmen. It was particularly noxious when it appealed to 'passion' rather than to reason, implicitly, that is, to plebeian or vulgar readers.[2]

In and after the 1790s, statutes multiplied to cover the common law's omissions. To start with, the king issued a proclamation against tumultuous meetings and seditious writings in 1792. A year later, *habeas corpus* was suspended after Louis XVI's guillotining, notwithstanding the fact that this prerogative writ is 'unquestionably the first security of civil liberty', as the Victorian legal historian Erskine May put it. (It requires a detained person to be brought before a court for the detention's legality to be examined.) In 1795, a stone thrown at George III's coach provoked the Seditious Meetings and Treasonable Practices Acts, commonly called the Convention Bills because they aimed to stop the calling of a reformers' convention. They prohibited meetings of fifty or more people and criminalized 'constructive treason' in publications. This was followed by multiplying curbs on press freedom. Stamp duties inhibited newspaper circulation; circulating libraries and reading rooms had to be licensed; presses and typefaces had to be registered, and printers had to declare their names and addresses on all publications. By 1808 the Attorney-General was being authorized to arrest and hold for bail any publisher against whom he chose to file an '*ex officio* information': this meant that the reasons behind an indictment could be withheld.

*Habeas corpus*, again suspended in 1798, was suspended once more in 1817. At least the earlier suspensions had been during a period of revolution and war, but by 1817 France was settled under the Bourbons, and the state was threatened with no danger but domestic discontent and turbulence.[3] That didn't end it, however. In 1819, the Blasphemous and Seditious Libels Act allowed twice-convicted offenders in seditious libel cases to be transported, while another Act imposed duties on radical publications which had so far dodged them by pretending to peddle opinion rather than news. These were among Home Secretary Sidmouth's notorious Six Acts, passed to contain the public outrage at the Manchester yeomanry's 'massacre' of people attending a peaceful reform meeting at St Peter's Fields in 1819 – the infamous 'Peterloo'.

Prosecutions under these powers were too few to constitute a reign of 'terror'. Jury independence was increased by Fox's Libel Act of 1792; there were many acquittals, and *ex officio* information had to be used more warily after Hone's acquittals in 1817. All the same, the political trials that scarred these decades were no trivial matters. Although in the 1790s the best remembered of the law's targets were the artisan radicals of the London Corresponding Society, the most frequent and vulnerable targets were modest booksellers and publishers, some of them printsellers as well. The stress, costs and loss of custom that ensued from the mere threat of prosecution could lay them low. 'I am wretched; ruin and destruction await my wife and family, unless withheld by your clemency': thus Henry Delahaye Symonds plausibly pleaded when faced by prosecution for selling Tom Paine's *Rights of Man* in 1793.[4] Just as the papers of the court of the King's Bench in these years swell with prosecutions for obscene libel, so the Treasury Solicitor's papers brim with dossiers on booksellers charged for publishing Paine's and similarly subversive texts. One of those imprisoned in 1793–4 for selling Paine was the printseller William Holland. Richard Newton depicted Holland and fellow prisoners in Newgate in a watercolour entitled *Soulagement en Prison* (or 'comfort in prison') that Holland later had him engrave as a half-guinea subscription print. In a room decorated by Newton's caricatures, it showed Lord George Gordon standing extreme left (imprisoned for five years for libelling Marie Antoinette), and Holland at a table (front left) with other convicted printmen and their visitors – disaffected Paineites or London Corresponding Society members all of them, their radical sympathies proclaimed in their cropped hair and refusal to wear wigs [fig. 237].[5]

**Fig. 237** Newton, *Soulagement en Prison* (watercolour, 1793)

Another wave of prosecutions for seditious libel opened in 1809. Radicals and liberal editors caught it for seditiously libelling the Duke of York, and the radical journalist William Cobbett went inside for two years in 1810–12 for criticizing the flogging of militiamen at Ely. In 1812, the brothers Leigh and John Hunt of the liberal newspaper *The Examiner* were imprisoned for two years for libelling the regent, and Daniel Isaac Eaton was pilloried at Charing Cross for publishing Paine. Five years later, T. J. Wooler was prosecuted for seditious libel in his radical *Black Dwarf*, as, most famously, was William Hone for blasphemous libel. For republishing Paine and other pamphleteers, the freethinking Richard Carlile got six years in 1819 and was kept in near-total isolation in Dorchester jail until 1825; he got another two years for seditious libel in 1831–3. The radical Henry Hunt was sentenced to two-and-a-half years in 1820 for chairing the Peterloo meeting and for seeking justice after the militia fatally attacked it. Several writers for Carlile's *Republican* were charged, and John Hunt was fined £200 for publishing Byron's 'Vision of Judgment' in 1824. In seventy such prosecutions between 1808 and 1821, thirty-four resulted in convictions. The thirty-six prosecutions for 1821–34 resulted in twenty-seven convictions, the proportion higher than hitherto only because the government was more selective in its attack.

———•———

In these conditions, what political criticisms could printshops possibly venture in the 1790s? The answer is many more than they did. A couple did stick their necks out modestly. Before Newgate brought him to heel, Holland issued the teenage Newton's *A Bugaboo!!!* (1792) ('scare-baby'), a sour comment on the way Pitt exploited anxieties about French anarchy the better to contain sedition at home. Pitt rides on the king's back as the latter, in his royal proclamation, spouts warnings of French tortures, spies and bastilles [fig. 238]. Three years later, Holland issued Newton's *A Sociable Meeting, or Old Friends with New Faces!!!* (1795): Fox's and Sheridan's lips are padlocked by the 1795 Acts. S. W. Fores in Piccadilly was the boldest printshop proprietor. He was the first to resuscitate the padlocked-jaw motif (from a print of 1742). In *A Lock'd Jaw for John Bull*, issued in November 1795, Pitt padlocks John Bull's lips and tells him that he would

**Fig. 238** Newton, *A Bugaboo!!!* (Holland, 1792)

**Fig. 239** West(?), *A Lock'd Jaw for John Bull* (Fores, 1795)

hardly notice the lock once he'd got used to it [fig. 239]. In *A Concise Explanation of the Convention Bills!!* (in December), a Frenchman asks an Englishman, 'Pray Monsieur what be the meaning of these Convention Bills?', to which the Englishman retorts briskly and meaningfully, 'Hold your jaw!' [fig. 240]. And in *A Thinking Club!!* (probably G. M. Woodward's in January 1796), six gagged gentlemen sit around a club table in order to think about (as distinct from discuss) the question on the wall: 'How long may we be permitted to think?' 'Constitutional muzzles are sold at the

**Fig. 240** West(?), *A Concise Explanation of the Convention Bills!!* (Fores, 1795)

door,' the club rules read [fig. 241]. When George Cruikshank revived the locked-jaw motif in 1819 in his famous *A Free Born Englishman! The Admiration of the World!!! and the Envy of Surrounding Nations!!!!!*, that print, too, was issued by Fores [fig. 242]. The proprietor's initiative was always as important as the engraver's in these cases. Fores issued many loyalist and anti-Jacobin prints in the 1790s, but all the way through to 1820 his track-record as a critic of high-handed government was unmatched by any other printshop's, including Holland's.[6]

**Fig. 241** Woodward(?), *A Thinking Club!!* (Fores, 1796)

These prints, however, pretty well measure the sum total of graphic protest in the 1790s. They made their point sharply, but ventured nothing that government could really baulk at. Even Pitt affected to be amused by *A Thinking Club!!*.[7] Certainly they took very few risks in the 1790s compared with those they took two decades later. The vast majority of prints abstained from reformist or libertarian critiques, and continued to be about social and humorous subjects, Foxite disloyalties or parliamentary and international manoeuvres. The prince's errancies and Pitt's supremacy were always fair game; but the cruellest satire on the prince could be tolerated provided it was for elite consumption. Otherwise, no engraver was ever kind to plebeian radicals, Paine or sans-culottes; and they all at some point equated the Foxites with Jacobins. It was the written text that took the biggest chances, from Paine's *Rights of Man* down to Charles Piggot's exposures of high corruptions in his book, *The Jockey Club, or a Sketch of the Manners of the Age* (1792). These works aimed at popular audiences as the West End prints didn't – and that's what was dangerous. Piggot dropped heavy hints that 'all reform of government in England, as we have beheld it elsewhere, must begin and end with the people', that

**Fig. 242** George Cruikshank, *A Free Born Englishman! The Admiration of the World!!! and the Envy of Surrounding Nations!!!!!* (Fores, 1819)

A FREE BORN ENGLISHMAN !
THE ADMIRATION of the WORLD!!!
AND THE ENVY OF SURROUNDING NATIONS!!!!!

'when the shoe pinches, it is thrown aside', and that 'where the h[ei]r to the c[row]n . . . affords such testimony to his taste and attachments, the people cannot expect any benefit or relief from that quarter; and it becomes them to think seriously for themselves'. For these reflections, Pigott's publisher was fined £100 and sent to Newgate for a year (though this didn't stop the book from going through thirteen editions). The visual satirists said nothing as explicit as this. The best explanations for the printshops' caution lie in their dependence on West End custom and in the fact that most of them, in that revolution-beset decade, were real or prudential loyalists anyway. All the same, the fact that Fores and Newton got away with their prints indicates what *might* have been attempted had there been a greater will to take risks. The printshops' silence is all the stranger in view of their relative immunity from prosecution.

Two cases from 1793 illustrate this immunity. In each, the law officers rightly calculated that the best way to silence the publishers of risky images was to prosecute them for selling texts rather than prints. Thus when Holland was prosecuted at the Middlesex sessions in February 1793, the prosecution brief argued that Holland 'carried on a business full[y] as pernicious as that of disseminating seditious publications – namely the publishing and exposing to sale prints of the most indecent kind'. It explained that the (Wilberforcian) Proclamation Society had long wished to prosecute Holland for his prints (Newton's presumably), but had found it impossible to persuade customers to give evidence against him. The best way to get him (the brief made clear) was through the fact that 'a person . . . who has been long employed by us' discovered that Holland was selling one of Tom Paine's pamphlet protests at the king's proclamation against seditious publications. The agent bought a copy, and, to Holland's astonishment, had him arrested. Holland 'complained heavily of his being singled out as the only person to be prosecuted, insisted that he had only sold a very few of them [the pamphlets], and that . . . they were publickly exposed to sale by all the booksellers in London'. Unimpressed, the prosecution found it 'extraordinary that the defendant whose profession is selling of prints should chuse to begin the trade of a bookseller by selling one of the most dangerous libels that ever appeared in this country. It is for him to account for this.' Still, the prosecution had been initially provoked by Holland's prints, not the text. Holland was convicted, fined £100, charged sureties of £200 from himself and £200 from others for good behaviour on release, and put inside Newgate for a year.[8]

In the second example, the law officers charged a Birmingham bookseller, James (or William) Belcher, with selling the same Paine pamphlet. Belcher's chief offence, however, was that his shop-window displayed 'a variety of caricature prints', including Gillray's devastating image of the Prince of Wales, *A Voluptuary under the Horrors of Indigestion*, and his *The Sun in his Glory*. This last the prosecution brief described as 'representing the side features of his majesty on the top of a candlestick with rays darting therefrom for the wicked purpose of ridiculing the king and royal family' – which spoke for a complete misinterpretation of the print's loyalist intention. This display suggested that Belcher was 'a man much disaffected to government and industrious to circulate everything inimical to it and likely to stir up discontent among his majesty's subjects'. In the event, Belcher's sentence at the Warwick summer assizes was for selling Paine's pamphlet, not the prints.[9] Gillray himself was arrested in 1796 for his *The Presentation, or, the Wise Mens Offering*, the offence delivered by the 'blasphemous' title. The case, however, collapsed.

## Mary Anne Clarke: 1809

It is easy to think of the 1790s as the most heroic moment in London's populist radical history in this era. French regicide and Jacobin principles provided inflammatory models for the radical artisanate, and members of the London Corresponding Society were sensationally prosecuted then. Yet it was the 1810s that saw the most turbulent years in London's radical history. Popular passions were inflamed by the betrayals, repressions and taxes of the distressed regency years, and they exploded at last in the pro-Caroline and anti-George factionalism of 1820–1, not to mention in the Cato Street conspiracy to assassinate half the Cabinet at dinner. Throughout these years, graphic satire measured radical passions quite accurately, much more so than their 1790s predecessors had done. This was thanks to an extraordinary act of cultural appropriation that for a time seemed set to transform the very nature of the satirist's identity and calling. Dissident and humbler commentators, along with new, 'low' printshops, hijacked what had hitherto largely been an elite genre and turned it against their rulers. This briefly gave metropolitan satire a radical and popular identity that flourished until George IV's accession in 1820.

This appropriation was unprecedented. Eighteenth-century satire had in principle provided the vocabulary with which the privileged and the comfortable had commented upon, assailed and corrected each other. It hadn't referred to poor people except incidentally as servants or as anonymous plebeians. It had never addressed them, and outside carnival enactments hadn't been deployed by plebians either. Least of all had it borne a critical attack from low people upon high, for all its habitually cynical subtexts. At base, eighteenth-century satire is better thought of as a substitute for revolution rather than as a summons to it.[10] This changed in 1809. For a decade thereafter, satire was turned against the powerful by humbler people who were supposed neither to understand nor to use it. The prints disseminated by new City shops cared nothing about the enclosed parliamentary manoeuvres that had dominated print commentaries hitherto. Instead, they set about exposing the usages, corruptions and inequalities of power itself, and this to a middling market that in the 1810s went 'politics mad'. Even London's ultra-radical taverns rang with satirical songs in these years.[11] In voicing humbler people's sardonic mistrust of the powerful and by making new thoughts possible, this shifted the political world a little, and made it more like our own.

The upper classes were as disoriented by the fact of this appropriation as they were by its uses. In 1786, Charles Abbott (later the judge who sat on Hone's case in 1817) had opined that, as society became more refined, 'the variety and caprice of artificial manners' would 'multiply the objects of ridicule, and thus by perpetual exercise, improve and perfect the satiric muse'. He added that satire should name and shame scoundrels, so that 'just ideas' might spread.[12] Neither Abbott nor his contemporaries could have anticipated how the improved and perfected satiric muse would present itself to them thirty years later – let alone that it would name them as the scoundrels. Once that happened, the right order of things was overturned, and the shock was profound. During William Hone's trials in 1817, the Attorney General fumed that the lower classes shouldn't be exposed to Hone's parodies because they were 'not fit to cope with the sorts of topics which are artfully raised for them'. Lord Chief Justice Ellenborough agreed that 'the social bonds of society [would] be burst asunder' if the humble were allowed to laugh at churchmen and ministers. The Tory *Quarterly Review* felt obliged to dismiss Hone as 'a poor illiterate creature' and as 'a wretch as contemptible as he is wicked', and this verdict echoed down the century among the pious and respectable.[13]

What did most to revitalize London's radicals and satirists in 1809 were the corruption charges ensuing from the Duke of York's infatuation with the courtesan Mary Anne Clarke. For five months the scandal so dominated the printshops that they ignored Wellesley's military expedition to Portugal and Austria's declaration of war. 'The sensation in London about this nonsensical business is marvellous,' Charles Lamb wrote: 'I remember nothing in my life like it. Thousands of ballads, caricatures, lives, of Mrs. Clarke, in every blind alley.'[14] The duke was a dim-witted buffoon who is now best remembered as the grand old Duke of York who marched his men to the top of the hill and then marched them down again. Mary Anne, conversely, was an adventuress of striking beauty, and smart with it. Born of humble parents *c.*1776, she had children by a builder's son before climbing into high men's beds and favours. Soon she was entertaining so extravagantly at the duke's expense in her Gloucester Place house that when the affair ended in 1806 she was left deeply in debt. Two years later she threatened to publish the duke's gushing love letters unless he paid her the annuity she said he had promised her. In January 1809, moreover, the MP Colonel Wardle told Parliament how Mary Anne had extracted military promotions from the besotted duke (as commander-in-chief of the army) on a scale of charges payable to herself by those who applied to her. She had to defend herself for two hours before a parliamentary committee of inquiry into the corruption charges, and she did so so effectively that Wilberforce found her 'elegantly dressed, consummately impudent, and very clever: clearly got the better in the tussle'. It was 'curious,' he noted, 'to see how strongly she has won upon people', though he didn't add that, after appearing before the Commons, she earned the punning toast to 'the lady that can raise five hundred members'. The duke was acquitted of wrongdoing but had to resign his command. The story ticked on throughout the summer as recriminations and libel cases multiplied, losing its bite only as Wardle's personal interest in attacking the duke was exposed. He had been refused an army commission, had himself been one of Clarke's many lovers, and had bought her testimony by promising to furnish her house. The story ended when the duke bought Mary Anne's silence for £7,000 and a life annuity and her memoirs were suppressed. She spent the remaining forty years of her life receiving fashionable visitors in Paris.[15]

The scandal was a gift for anti-corruption radicals and printshops alike. It particularly profited the new City printshops that were rising at this time

**Fig. 243** Rowlandson, *The Bishop and his Clarke, or a Peep into Paradise* (Tegg, 1809)

because the story was serious, sexy and funny. The British Museum catalogues 121 satires on the affair, 56 of them by Rowlandson for Thomas Tegg's printshop in Cheapside. In February and March, Rowlandson produced them at a rate sometimes of one a day. Each one of them was cheerfully bawdy.[16] 'My dearest dear I hope to be in your arms,' the duke swoons in *The Bishop and his Clarke, or a Peep into Paradise,* as he lies cosily in bed with Mary Anne and gazes at her adoringly: 'ask any thing in reason and you shall have it my dearest dearest dearest love' (the title because he was the titular bishop of Osnabrück). Above the bed is pinned her list of names for promotion [fig. 243]. In *Chelsea Parade . . . the Inside, Outside, and Backside of Mrs Clarke's Premises* [fig. 244], Mary Anne, all but bare-breasted, leans from her window as the duke leaves by the front door. Wardle arrives and she encourages him up: 'Tho last not in love enter quick my guardian Angle [angel] my Sweet Widdle Waddle.' The bawd guarding the door says that Mary Anne is 'engaged five deep at present but [she] dispatch[es] quick so pray enter and your business shall be done in a crack.'

The scandal reinvigorated the radicals because it enabled Cobbett and others to establish 'no corruption' as the popular oppositional cry. Their exploitation of the story was so effective that for the first time loyalists

**Fig. 244** Rowlandson, *Chelsea Parade, or a Croaking Member Surveying the Inside, Outside, and Backside of Mrs Clarke's Premises* (Tegg, 1809)

**Fig. 245** Gillray, *The Life of William-Cobbett, – Written by Himself*: 7th plate
(H. Humphrey, 1809)

had to take the popular radicals seriously. In the 1790s, the radical enemy
at home had been located among the Foxite Whigs or otherwise left
beneath the dignity of naming. Tom Paine would be shown as a down-at-
heel tailor or as a blood-soaked sans-culotte, but for the most part radicals
were portrayed and doubtless imagined as blubber-mouthed plebeians
huddled in bedizened cellars in anonymous conspiracy (as Gillray saw
them in his *London Corresponding Society Alarm'd* (1798)). Now, however,
loyalists began to name radical foes individually. Thus Gillray's eight
scathing plates on *The Life of William-Cobbett, – Written by Himself* (1809)

cited and parodied Cobbett's own published accounts of his career to expose him as a political turncoat and braggart. In plate 7 of the sequence [fig. 245], Gillray has Cobbett announce himself 'the greatest man in the world' (excepting only Napoleon); and he is made boozily to celebrate the Clarke exposures with Horne Tooke, Burdett, Cochrane and others (each recognizable), while Wardle lies drunk on the floor, in a composition that was a reprise of Gillray's own earlier *Union Club*. In January 1809, similarly, the Tory magazine *The Satirist, or Monthly Meteor* published fifteen pages on the radicals' duplicities accompanied by a print by Samuel de Wilde, *The ROBBING Hood Debating Society*, in which radicals like Gale Jones, Hague, Captain Hogan and Finnerty (whose pamphlets had opened the attack on the Duke of York) sit at a table with ruffians, thieves and pickpockets.[17] *The Satirist* followed this in June with yet another reprise of *The Union Club*, de Wilde's *The Reformers' Dinner* [fig. 246], which lampooned a grand radical dinner held at the Crown and Anchor in Fleet Street for some 2000 people. London's radical leaders cavort at table amid overturned chairs, scattered bottles, sprawled figures on the floor and hat-waving plebeians. Lord Cochrane (naval hero, critic of naval abuses and Burdett's fellow radical Westminster MP) brandishes his sword at the crown painted on the inn sign; Burdett waves a wine-glass and a Jacobin *bonnet rouge*; Wardle holds out 'a plan for a new government'; and Major Cartwright

The Reformers' Dinner
Published for the Satirist June 1st 1809 by S. Tipper 37 Leadenhall Street

**Fig. 246** De Wilde, *The Reformers' Dinner* (for *The Satirist*, 1809)

listens to a butcher reading from a paper headed 'The Wae Ow too Rifform the Parl[iament]'.[18]

# The rise of the 'low' printshops

The grief that the printshops delivered upon the Duke of York in 1809 was as nothing compared with the onslaught on the Prince of Wales and his ministers after he became regent in 1811. It is now, not in the 1790s, that we meet satirical disaffection at its most insolent and virulent. The social thrust and content of visual satire was importantly transformed.

The press and the printshops had been fairly kind to the prince over the preceding decade, as if their comments on his affairs and extravagances had grown stale with repetition. As sexually incontinent as ever, his comic potential stayed high. It helped that his current mistress, Lady Hertford, was a woman 'of ample though well-corseted proportions', shaped rather as he was. But when George III went conclusively mad in 1811, the fact that, as regent, the profligate had real power at last imbued the attacks upon him with new venom. When he kept on his father's Tory ministers instead of putting the Whigs into office, the old Foxite friends who had supported and caroused with him for decades were outraged. 'Nought's permanent among the human race,' the quip went, 'except the Whigs not getting into place': they stayed out of place until 1830. The regent had several good political reasons for dropping the Whigs, not least the fact that the 'Delicate Investigation' of 1806–7 into his wife's infidelities had put Caroline at the Tories' mercy. The Whigs themselves, meanwhile, thought that only Lady Hertford's malign influence could explain George's ingratitude to them.[19] So radicals and Whigs alike turned to champion the rejected Caroline as she went into continental exile in 1812. In an era of mounting popular distress and unrest, the ensuing vendetta polarized political life until George IV was crowned and Caroline died in 1821.

In these conditions, textual and graphic satire often delivered their attacks in purposeful collaboration. Texts more often influenced images than vice versa.[20] Writers had long known the advantage of resorting to mock nursery rhymes and parody to camouflage their true intentions. Textual parody was difficult to prosecute, and jury verdicts against it were few. Parody was 'as old at least as the invention of printing', Hone told his prosecutors in 1817, adding that 'he had never heard of a prosecution for a parody, either religious or any other' – until his own.[21] On this principle, major parodic satires were written by Moore and Leigh Hunt, while Lamb's doggerel verses, Hone's nursery rhymes, or Byron's sardonic meters and bathetic rhymes made their points with a light-hearted jauntiness that hid their purposes even as they undercut their targets' pretensions. But cross-fertilizations could also move from image into text. When liberal writers resorted to parody or deployed puns, exaggerated analogies and calculated flippancy, they were in effect exploiting the traditional devices of graphic satire. Hone's nursery-rhyme rhythms in his scathing *Political House that Jack Built* (1819), for example, was prefigured in Rowlandson's use of 'The House that Jack Built' in a print about the riots over new prices charged at the Theatre Royal in 1809.[22] Shelley's satirical drama on the regent, *Oedipus Tyrannus, or Swellfoot the Tyrant* (published in 1820 by John Johnston), was full of the enemas, 'green bags' (which held lawyers' papers), and nicknamings of pro-Caroline caricature. The name 'Swellfoot' invoked the regent's gouty leg that Cruikshank publicized; and the play's character of 'Banknotina' referred to Cruikshank's *Bank Restriction Note* published the year before. Shelley wrote *Swellfoot* in Italy, where it is probable that he studied caricatures in the houses of the English residents in Leghorn.[23]

Regardless of the question of which came first, there are several reasons for suggesting that prints, not texts, were the strongest propagandist weapons in the war of nerves that now unfolded. Graphic attacks on the regent achieved a much greater circulation than textual satires did (only Moore's poems and Byron's 'Vision of Judgement' circulated widely at the time); nor should we forget Hogarth's wise axiom that 'ocular demonstration' carries 'more conviction' than a thousand volumes. Moreover, although graphic satires were to promote quite as much 'hatred and contempt' for regent, government and laws as any text did, the law still felt it riskier to prosecute them than the written word. It was writers who directly attacked the regent usually suffered for it. When in 1812 the Tory *Morning Post* sycophantically praised the regent as a 'conqueror of hearts' and an 'Adonis in loveliness', Leigh Hunt was provoked into a defiant riposte in his and his brother's liberal *Examiner*: 'This "exciter of desire",' he snorted, '– this "Adonis in loveliness", is a corpulent man of fifty! – in short, this *delightful, blissful, wise, pleasurable, honourable, virtuous, true,* and *immortal* prince, is a violator of his word, a libertine over head and ears in disgrace, a despiser of domestic ties, the companion of gamblers and demireps [courtesans], a man who has just closed half a century without one single claim on the gratitude of his country, or the respect of posterity!' Hunt's great diatribe earned him and his brother two years' imprisonment for seditious libel. His vehemence was later matched in Shelley's *Masque of Anarchy*, written after Peterloo in 1819: 'Last came Anarchy; he rode / On a white horse, splashed with blood; / He was pale even to the lips, / Like Death in the Apocalypse. / And he wore a kingly crown; / And in his grasp a sceptre shone; / And on his brow this mark I saw – / I am God, and King, and Law!' For fear of prosecution, that poem had to stay unpublished for another dozen years; other verse satires by Shelley had to await their publication for even longer.[24]

By contrast, the immunity of the image that had been tacitly allowed in the 1790s was explicitly though not publicly conceded in April 1812. In that month the Secretary of State sent to the Solicitor General the issue of the liberal satirical magazine, *The Scourge*, that contained *Princely Predilections*, one of George Cruikshank's earliest and most vicious full-blown caricatures on the regent [fig. 250]. Asked if the print might be prosecuted as a seditious libel, the Solicitor General's reply was emphatic: 'This is a most indecent and imprudent print *but it would require so much of difficult explanation in stating it as a libel* that it does not appear to us advisable to make it the subject of a criminal prosecution' – thus acknowledging that to describe so comic a scene in an indictment would only compound the joke.[25] Henceforth it was thought wiser (as Queen Caroline's counsel, Denman, recalled) to leave visual satires 'however offensive, to perish in their obscurity': to have prosecuted them 'would have been to play the game of the libellers'.[26]

Altogether, then, bookshops had to tread much more cautiously than printshops. Here is one measure of this from a few years later. In 1822, a Bow Street officer reported that Richard Carlile (or his wife: he was in prison) had invented a system in his little bookshop off Fleet Street that would thwart *agents provocateurs* by ensuring that the book-salesman's identity was concealed and that sales were wordless. The device consisted of 'two apertures in the back partition [of the shop] one for the receipt of money the other for the transmission of the publication from behind, over which is a round dial with numbers on it and a moveable hand which may be turned so as to point to any number. These numbers correspond with others affixed to a list of books stuck up in one side of the shop, so that any person by perusing this list may learn to what number to affix the hand of the dial.'[27] The Carliles might have been lampooning the law in this subterfuge. The fact remains that no printshop needed to resort to anything like it. It was becoming dangerous to sell obscene prints, but the most scurrilous satires on the regent were still sold as openly as ever.

In brash celebration of this licence, a revitalized and radicalized City print trade now led the visual attack on the regent. The impact of this small galaxy of new, less reputable firms has hardly been noticed by historians, but if we look for a leading agency in the public vendetta, it's here that we'll find it. Aiming at lower middle-class as well as a broader range of disaffected opinion, these shops lowered the tone as the older West End printshops no longer cared to. Thomas Tegg had already tapped the cheaper City market for prints from the Cheapside bookshop he had opened in 1804.[28] Significant others now followed his example, the regency of a highly lampoonable and despised prince their undoubted provocation.

---

First came the cheap publisher and bookseller John Fairburn, with shops in Blackfriars and Ludgate Hill. He saw the point of issuing prints from 1811 onwards. He became (after Tegg) the most prolific of the new print publishers (and later went on to match Humphrey's output with some 275 titles across 1820–27, long after Tegg had given up satire). Also in 1811, John Johnston opened his 'cheap caricature warehouse' at 101 Cheapside: his imprint appeared on some 130 sheets by the late 1820s. In 1811 again, M. Jones of Newgate Street began publishing the satirical journal *The Scourge; or, Monthly Expositor of Imposture and Folly* as a liberal riposte to the conservative *Satirist*, with many prints in it. (Johnston of Cheapside was one of the shops that sold it; it ran to nine volumes until 1815.) In January 1812, it was taken over by its printer, William Naunton Jones, of the same address: he, significantly, was a friend of Hone and George Cruikshank and was to employ the latter. Hone himself issued some ninety single-sheet titles between 1815 and 1822, from his succession of tiny Fleet Street, Old Bailey and Ludgate Hill bookshops. They included major Cruikshank sheets as well as Cruikshank's woodcuts for Hone's pamphlet parodies. Thomas Dolby awoke to the profitability of bookselling and printselling in 1817, when 'we all went politically mad', as he put it: 'finding a hubbub gathering about me concerning parliamentary reform, and a great call for all manner of books in that subject, I was obliged to throw down my apron and sleeves [as a vellum-binder] and fetch [and sell] Cobbett's *Register*. The more I fetched the more people wanted.' He was to publish twenty-eight catalogued satires against the king from 1820 to 1822.[29] J. Sidebotham, once of Dublin, worked from Newgate Street, the Strand and Bond Street, and produced some seventy-five titles between 1815 and 1820, employing Robert and George Cruikshank mostly. In 1820, John Marshall produced half-a-dozen devastating sheets against the king from Little St Martins Lane, while William Benbow, from the Strand, High Holborn and Castle Street, issued twenty-three listed titles in 1820–25, thus initiating a radical career that extended into the Chartist 1840s. From 1817, J. L. Marks published his own work from Artillery Row off Bishopsgate, though also from addresses in Soho, Covent Garden and Piccadilly. (As in all such cases, this mobility suggests financial difficulties, a febrile lifestyle, or short partnerships with others: a few of Mark's more inflammatory later prints were published by Benbow, for example).

Marks provides the best examples of these printshops' bawdy irreverence. An engraver in his own right, he had begun his career in 1814 by working for Tegg, imitating George Cruikshank's bulb-breasted female courtiers and mistresses and the regent's pineapple-shaped head; then in 1818, he pioneered the use of lithography: 'drawn and printed from stone!' many of his satires trumpeted. Littered with sexual puns and symbols, his prints achieved a uniquely inventive vulgarity. The speech bubble he gave to a female radical in a print of 1819 gives their flavour. Holding a phallic scroll and gesturing towards a phallic stick indelicately topped by a *bonnet rouge*, she declaims: 'Dear sisters, I feel great pleasure, in holding this thing-um-bob in my hand, as we see our sweethearts, and husbands, are such fumblers at the main thing, we must of course take the thing, in our own hands . . . we must pursue the point as far as it will go . . . Though we should be stark naked, we could make the whole army stand! – It is our duty as wives to assist our husbands in every push and turn.'[30] It was in this raunchy spirit that he issued prints to commemorate the London visit of the Persian ambassador's beautiful wife in 1819, for example, showing her in a blizzard of visual and verbal puns about vaginas, penises and 'stones' (testicles) and accompanied by eunuchs [fig. 247]. More importantly, the royal family was included in such attacks. The first of two lithographs on Princess Elizabeth's marriage to the corpulent Prince

**Fig. 247** Marks, *Persian Customs! Or Eunuchs Performing the Office of Lady's Maids – Dedicated to the Circassian Beauty* (Marks, 1819)

**Fig. 248** Marks, *John Bull Supporting, the Nuptial Bed!!!* (Marks, 1818)

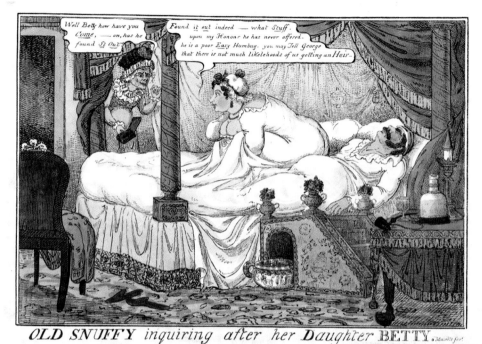

**Fig. 249** Marks, *Old Snuffy Inquiring after her Daughter Betty* (Marks, 1818)

of Hesse-Homburg in 1818, *John Bull Supporting, the Nuptial Bed!!!*, has the couple on their wedding night in a vast bed that a stooping and overtaxed John Bull has to carry on his back; the queen's and the prince's conversation around the bed is full of *doubles entendres* about penetrating the princess's 'hair' in pursuit of an 'heir', etc. [fig. 248]. The second print, *Old Snuffy* [the queen] *Inquiring after her Daughter Betty* [fig. 249], has the princess in bed next morning, bare-breasted of course, telling the queen that the prince snoring next to her hadn't 'offered' so that getting an heir would be impossible. (The print reminds one of a Richard Newton satire on Princess Charlotte's wedding night with the corpulent Prince of Württemburg in 1797: 'how he will reach her, God only knows. I suppose he has some German method.') Images like these hardly speak for the reflexive popular deference to royalty that is often assumed to characterize this era, and certainly show that there was more to Marks than cheerful vulgarity. He bludgeoned the powerful with a creative virulence – even attacking hanging law, which was an extremely rare thing to do even in the law-debating post-war years.[31]

Such were the firms that orchestrated graphic attacks on the regent for near on a decade. Their insolence far exceeded that of newspapers, or of their West End forerunners. They delivered the opening salvos against Lady Hertford's influence in 1812 and led in championing Caroline as oppositional emblem, achieving an unprecedented radicalization of graphic language, and speaking to a much wider market than their predecessors. Between 1812 and late 1820 barely a single pro-George print was published. They even hinted at the prince's taste for being fellated by Lady Hertford or at his fantasy of living in 'paradise' under his ensuing mistress, Lady Conyngham's, petticoats.[32] No court, no prince, had previously been lampooned so viciously: nor has any been so lampooned since. Despite his analogous musings about taking refuge in Mrs Parker-Bowles's private parts, the present-day Prince of Wales has had an easy time of it by comparison.

## Cruikshank and the regent

If the rise of the new printshops was bad news for the regent's equanimity, the rise of a great satirical artist was worse. With Isaac Cruikshank dead of drink in April 1811, George Cruikshank came out from his father's shadow. He had been a rather marginal figure hitherto. Hannah Humphrey had employed him to finish some of Gillray's plates, but Holland and Fores preferred to use Rowlandson, Williams and Elmes. Most of Cruikshank's early work had been for Laurie and Whittle. In his nineteenth year, however, John Johnston took him up, and it might have been Johnston who introduced him to William Jones, the *Scourge*'s printer and publisher. This was a fateful meeting. Within months, Jones commissioned Cruikshank to produce the exuberant *Dinner of the Four in Hand Club at Salthill* [fig. 42], the first of the forty-one Cruikshanks that were eventually bound into the journal. In the third of these, *Interior View of the House of God* [fig. 30], Cruikshank depicted a marginal group of observers: himself, holding a sketchbook and looking debonair, his brother Robert, William Jones and William Hone – this the earliest indication of the Hone–Cruikshank friendship. His association with these printmen turned Cruikshank into the greatest caricaturist since Gillray. In comic exuberance and inventiveness, he touched heights greater than Gillray's.[33]

It was Jones who first tested what the law would bear and thus opened the way for what followed. In the third volume of *The Scourge*, in April 1812,

**Fig. 250** George Cruikshank, *Princely Predilections or Ancient Music and Modern Discord* (Jones, *The Scourge*, April 1812)

he allowed Cruikshank to cut to the political bone with the 'indecent and imprudent' *Princely Predilections* [fig. 250] about which the Secretary of State consulted the Solicitor General, only to decide against prosecution. It was an inelegant composition, but no previous print had attempted anything like it. While earlier attacks on the prince and his court had been single-focused, this one, packed with meaningful incident, attempted a synopsis of all current court gossip. It was also accompanied by the *Scourge*'s textual commentaries on 'The Prince Regent and the Opposition' and on 'The Noble Adulterer'. It has the regent standing tipsily among his old Whig friends and new Tory ministers, his clothing disordered and garter hanging loose, as he tells a lady that he doesn't like his new Tory friends at all. Lady Hertford, to his right, holds a child's leading strings around his waist and tells him he 'will always meet with a warm friend in *Hertford*'. (Her speech bubble to this effect was scratched out in later printings (as in this illustration): Jones or Cruikshank must have taken fright at the law's interest.) A scowling Lord Hertford, behind her, wears cuckold's horns, and the Duke of York enters (right) with his latest paramour, Mrs Carey. Antlers sprout from the regent's secretary's head. On the left, a chaplain holds a paper 'Sermon on drunkenness Sunday next', while Death marches off with Lord Liverpool (because he had lately been the war minister; a month later he became prime minister). Princess Charlotte stands on the right, weeping, as she was famously inclined to do. Wellesley ('the noble adulterer') holds up a forefinger to her, his arm around his mistress Moll Raffles, while Sheridan in harlequin's dress picks John Bull's pocket. A wall-picture shows the regent, Bacchus-like, astride a cask of curaçao. He is offered a goblet by a bare-breasted woman and is surrounded by horned and other figures in suitably improper poses.

Jones and Cruikshank got away with this (Johnston, too, since his shop was one of the *Scourge*'s two main outlets), so between March and November 1812, Jones commissioned another six elaborate Cruikshank prints on the regent, all, like this one, indecent in detailing and allusion, and all saturated with venomous reference to the evolving political vendetta as they hammered home the royal brothers' depravities and infidelities, Lady Hertford's influence and the new ministers' hypocrisies.[34] The most unforgettable, because simplest in design, was *The Prince of Whales or the Fisherman at Anchor*, published in *The Scourge* on 1 May [fig. 251]. Drawing on the image of the leviathan Duke of Bedford in Gillray's *New Morality* [fig. 222], its direct inspiration was Charles Lamb's contemptuous doggerel, 'The Triumph of the Whale', published in the *Examiner* six weeks earlier:

Not a mightier whale than this
In the vast Atlantic is;
Not a fatter fish than he
Flounders round the polar sea.
See his blubber – at his gills
What a world of drink he swills,
From his trunk as from a spout
Which next moment he pours out.
. . . But about his presence keep
All the monsters of the deep;
Mermaids with their tails and singing
His delighted fancy stinging;
Crooked dolphins they surround him;
Dog-like seals they fawn around him
. . . By his bulk and by his size,
By his oily qualities,
This (or else my eyesight fails),
This should be the Prince of Whales.

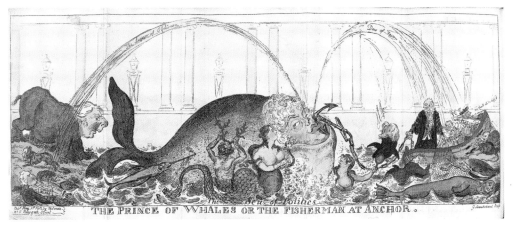

**Fig. 251** George Cruikshank, *The Prince of Whales or the Fisherman at Anchor* (Jones, *The Scourge*, April 1812)

Cruikshank duly shows a monstrous whale with the regent's fat tousled head swimming in 'the sea of politics' while it spouts 'the liquor of oblivion' over his old Whig friends Sheridan, Grenville and Grey, and 'the dew of favour' over the Tory ministers (led by the prime minister, Perceval, the 'fisherman' who has hooked him). Lady Hertford is the mermaid ogling the prince in the foreground, her husband behorned behind her. In front of the whale a smaller mermaid emerges reproachfully: Mrs Fitzherbert, long ago discarded.

In these terms *The Scourge* opened the season for harassing the regent. For twenty years between 1778 and 1797, 294 prints on the prince are catalogued (putting him fifth in the frequency of references then). In the eight years from January 1812 to December 1819, by contrast, he was targeted in 230 prints. This equalled one-seventh of all catalogued prints in those years, and ensured that the prince topped the list of satirical targets, ahead even of Napoleon. Furthermore, of these 230 prints, 94 were Cruikshank's. And such was Cruikshank's profit from the subject that his attacks on the regent made up some sixth of his total output – this in years when he was producing twice as many prints as Rowlandson and three times as many as Williams, his nearest rivals.

Cruikshank's daring increased as he got the measure of his subject and began production for other printshops. Here are a few examples. In August 1812, Johnston published his *Merry Making on the Regents* [sic] *Birth Day, 1812* [fig. 252]. At a lavish party, the regent dances with the ever-bulbous Lady

**Fig. 252** George Cruikshank, *Merry Making on the Regents Birth Day, 1812* (Johnston, 1812)

**Fig. 253** George Cruikshank, *Gent, No Gent, and Re gent!!* (Tegg 1816)

Hertford. Two demons play French horns over Lord Hertford's head; and his feet rest on a sheet headed 'The Black Joke', one of the many obscene songs that Cruikshank expected his purchasers to know.[35] Outside the palace, two figures hang from a scaffold as a poor man, burdened with emaciated children, comments that 'if rich rogues like poor ones were for to hang it would thin the land such numbers would swing upon Tyburn tree'. The regent's fondness for that same pubic 'black joke, and belly so white' was underscored in *Gent, No Gent, and Re Gent!!*, for Tegg in 1816 [fig. 253]. Its central panel, set pointedly in the past, when George still hobnobbed with the Whigs, has the 'no-gent' sitting on Lady Hertford's knee as he carouses with Fox, Sheridan, Norfolk and Colonel Hanger, his sidekick; Norfolk is beneath the table, vomiting in *Union Club* fashion. 'The Black Joke' is pinned to the wall, alongside a list of rules of the 'Cock and hen club St Gilse's [*sic*]' to which, it's implied, the five belonged. The left-hand panel parodies Sir Thomas Lawrence's idealized portrait of the 'gent' painted two years before, while the right-hand panel shows him as 're-gent', fat, with gouty legs and crutches and crowned by a Chinese headdress surmounted by a cone with bells; a Chinese dragon above his head is inscribed 'Taste' in reference to the Brighton Pavilion in which the scene is set. One of the more enduring Cruikshank jokes equated the regent's bloated physique with that of the enormous French mortar (or 'bomb', as it was called) which the Spanish had given the regent in 1816 to commemorate Wellington's Peninsular victory four years before. Cruikshank punned happily on the fact that 'bomb' was then prounounced 'bum': whence, for Hone, his *View of the R–g–t's Bomb* [fig. 254] and *Saluting the R—ts* [sic] *Bomb Uncovered on his Birth Day August 12th 1816*, in which the regent crouches in the bomb's posture backside-up, his bum kissed by one minister and ramrodded by another, watched by mistresses past and present [fig. 255]. Other engravers laboured

A VIEW of the R d Tˢ BOMB.

**Fig. 254** George Cruikshank, *A View of the R–g–t's Bomb* (Hone, 1816)

**Fig. 255** George Cruikshank, *Saluting the R—ts Bomb Uncovered on his Birth Day, August 12th 1816* (Hone, 1816)

**Fig. 256** George Cruikshank, *Royal Hobby's, or the Hertfordshire Cock-Horse!* (Tegg's *Caricature Magazine*, 1819)

**Fig. 257** George Cruikshank, *Royal Embarkation; or – Bearing Brittannia's Hope from a Bathing Machine to the Royal Barge* (Tegg, 1819)

the joke for three years to come.[36] Cruikshank also produced important single sheets for Tegg and others, some touching the comic sublime. Thus Lady Hertford rides the prince as if he were one of the newly fashionable 'hobby-horses' in *Royal Hobby's, or the Hertfordshire Cock-Horse!* ('If the rascals caricature me, I'll buy 'em all up d— me,' says the Duke of York in the background) [fig. 256]. In *Royal Embarkation; or – Bearing Brittannia's* [sic] *Hope from a Bathing Machine to the Royal Barge*, two buxom women carry the even fatter regent to a skiff from Brighton beach, his hand at one of their breasts, unerringly. 'Do my dear girls put me on board safe,' he instructs them: '. . . I have been almost suffocated in that infernal bathing machine'; from the machine peer two naked women [fig. 257].

The full range of ensuing print comment on George as regent and king can't be covered here: luckily other works have illustrated it.[37] Enough to say that the continuing virulence of the graphic attack was guaranteed by economic distress after the end of the Napoleonic wars in 1815 and then by recurrent political crises, to all of which the City shops responded unflaggingly. For Tegg, for example, the young William Heath in 1815 produced *Answer to John Bull's Complaint*, in which the regent thus dismisses the pleas of a ragged and impoverished John Bull:

> Why you unatural [*sic*] grumbler after I have done all I could to get rid of your money you still grumble. Did I not give you a fete, did I not build you a bridge [the new Blackfriars Bridge], did I not treat you with a smell of all the nice things at my feast, did I not sign the Corn Bill, did I not refuse your Address, have I not drank whole pipes of wine for fear it should be waste'd, have I not spent all your money because you should not spend it your self, have you not got the income tax to keep you sober, & as for your dress the thinner the better for the sumer [*sic*] season, so Johnny go home to work, its all for the good of your country.

A flood of prints similarly addressed radical plots, clampdowns on free expression, and the Peterloo outrage, all delivering a punch that would have been unthinkable under the market and the political conditions of the 1790s. Hone's pamphlets and sardonic doggerel were soon giving Cruikshank room to depict the peacock prince in woodcut [figs. 91, 92]; these had huge circulation. In 1817, most notably, Sidebotham issued Cruikshank's fine *Liberty Suspended! with the Bulwark of the Constitution!* in protest at the Seditious Meetings Act and the suspension of *habeas corpus*. It mocked Home Secretary Sidmouth's scaremongering about the Spencean radicals' allegedly revolutionary plotting, refusing to share his alarm [fig. 258]. In it, Lord Chancellor Eldon's green bag contains, as 'evidence against liberty', 'an old stocking full of gunpowder 3 or 4 rusty fire arms and a few bullets too large to fit the barrels!!!' From a platform formed by the base of a free printing press (a Cruikshankian icon of increasing importance), Castlereagh, Eldon and Lord Chief Justice Ellenborough display the bound and gagged body of Liberty hanged from a gibbet. On the left, the Archbishop of Canterbury intones thanksgivings for the regent's escape 'from the madness of the People', while, on the right, John Bull and the radicals (Cochrane, Cobbett, Henry Hunt and Burdett) look on, weeping. Nor did Cruikshank's *Loyal Address's & Radical Petitions, or the R—ts Most Gracious Answer to Both Sides of the Question at Once* (for Tegg in 1819) pull its political punches: the regent farts on the radical

**Fig. 258** George Cruikshank, *Liberty Suspended! with the Bulwark of the Constitution!* (Sidebotham, 1817)

leaders, Hunt, Watson and Burdett as they petition for a Peterloo enquiry, while graciously accepting loyal petitions from his toadies [fig. 76].

With George III's death in January 1820, the regent's accession as George IV, and his efforts then to divorce Caroline, the vituperation in the output of Dolby, Sidebotham, Benbow and Fairburn reached a crescendo. When Caroline landed at Dover to claim her crown in June and the king rejected her, each endorsed Caroline as an icon of wronged womanhood. When the Lords 'tried' her for immorality in August, mass demonstrations supported her; in November the Bill against her was defeated, to the printshops' as well as to popular jubilation. Altogether, some 440 catalogued prints featured Caroline and George in 1820: nearly all supported the queen. George Humphrey's St James's Street shop initially supported her, but he turned his coat in early 1821, to issue a brilliant series of loyalist prints by Theodore Lane. These rubbed home the evidence of Caroline's adulteries, thus doing much to demolish her

**Fig. 259** Marks, *Quite Well Again* (Marks, 1820)

martyr image and swing support towards the king.[38] Otherwise, the vast majority of prints 'tainted, disgraced, and vilified' the king (as the law would put it), the best of them following Cruikshank's prototype caricature. Marks's inspired *Quite Well Again* (March 1820), for example, shows the bubble-headed king sprawl drunkenly between the portly Duchess of Richmond and the equally round Lady Hertford [fig. 259], while in Marshall's *Our Fat Friend Going to Roost* (December 1820), he is carried drunkenly to bed by two tipsy and bulbous peeresses, one of them his

**Fig. 260** John Marshall, *Our Fat Friend going to Roost* (Marshall, 1820)

latest favourite, Lady Conyngham – the title appropriating the unfortunate question, 'Alvaney, who's your fat friend?' which had famously cost Beau Brummel the regent's favour [fig. 260]. Through their lethal inversions, prints like these proclaimed the common man's contempt for the great – and their sense of their own impunity too.

What effects did prints like these deliver? In an image-starved era, they helped determine how people saw their world. Cruikshank's prints, for instance, stereotyped the regent's comically oversized head, curly hair, fluffy side-whiskers, fat chops, gouty legs and corpulent, decorated body. As other engravers adopted this icon, it became impossible for the national mind to forget it. Because the production of engraved official portraits of George fell off dramatically between 1811 and 1820 (the National Portrait Gallery catalogues only three from these years, and one of those recycled a portrait of 1809), Cruikshank's caricature became the instantly recognized oppositional emblem that determined George's image for decades thereafter – just as Philipon's caricature of Louis-Philippe's pear-shaped head influenced French views of that ruler in the 1830s, when dissident Paris was fast covered in pear-shaped graffiti. As late as 1854, Thackeray's memoir of George IV was influenced by the Cruikshankian image.[39] That the Whig elites appreciated the prints is shown in two surviving collections of ephemera on the 1820 divorce drama. Each is contained in a pair of finely leather-bound volumes, the first collected by one Minto Wilson, the other by Lord Holland, Fox's nephew. Both are full of printed reports, speeches and press cuttings, but both are dominated by graphic satires: as many as 228 single-sheet prints are pasted into Holland's two volumes. Here and there Holland added wry manuscript comments on the queen's reported misadventures which reveal his own capacity for satiric visualization: 'We have on oath that beds can see, / 'Tis well they cannot speak, say we.'[40] The real impact of the prints, however, we'll register in the next chapter, in the king's desperate efforts to silence them.

## Laughter and William Hone: 1817

In view of the difficulties of prosecuting satirical *images*, it comes as no surprise that the most concerted legal attack of the 1810s, as in the 1790s, was directed against subversive *texts*. Of all the radical printmen, William Hone was this policy's most famous victim. Tried in 1817 for the blasphemous libel of publishing three pamphlet parodies of the liturgy, he owed his fame to his heroic defiance of his persecutors and his final victory. His fame should also rest on the way he trumpeted the satirist's credo, since nobody has ever trumpeted it better. 'It was not proper that the press should be shackled,' he told the court: 'The press was common property; it was a great security which every man in England felt he had against injustice.' Nor had he mocked religion, he insisted: what he had mocked was only 'a certain set of men, whose only religion was blind servility'. He had done so because they were 'little men of little minds; their measures were the objects of his contempt, and the men themselves, as ministers, were the object of his pity . . . If there was ridicule [in his parody], those who rendered themselves ridiculous, however high their station, had no right to cry out because they were ridiculed.' The aim of his parodies, he said, was to 'laugh His Majesty's ministers to scorn; he had laughed at them, and, *ha! ha! ha!* he laughed at them now, and he would laugh at them, as long as they were laughing stocks!' 'They were his vindictive persecutors, and his hypocritical persecutors; and laugh at them he would, till they ceased to be the objects of his laughter by ceasing to be ministers . . . Was a laugh treason? Surely not.'[41] That '*ha! ha! ha!*' is our satirists' response exactly.

The story began in early 1817, when the magistrates of Chelmsford in Essex reported to the law officers that a local agricultural machine-maker was circulating pamphlets that 'tended to promote hatred and contempt of His Majesty's government and laws'. Questioned, the man admitted to buying them while he was on business in London. After eating in a tavern in the Old Bailey, he had been 'attracted to a bookseller's shop by the appearance of a great number of persons' outside it: it was 'like a fair from the number of persons resorting there'. He found that they were buying up pamphlets at the cut-price rate of eight for a shilling. He bought some 'merely from curiosity' (he said), and took them home to show his family and friends. It must have seemed a piece of luck to the law officers that the shop turned out to be Hone's.

Born in 1780, Hone had early rebelled against his father's piety and his own boyhood loyalism when he read Godwin and similar radical texts. Aged sixteen, he turned atheistical or Unitarian and joined the London Corresponding Society. Struggling upwards in the book trade, he joined the Burdettite reformers, and befriended that lynchpin of Westminster politics, Francis Place. By 1812 he was hobnobbing with radically inclined pressmen like William Jones of *The Scourge*. Through Jones he seems to have been propelled towards radical publication (and also towards George Cruikshank). His output became frankly political in pamphlets against the Bourbon restoration in 1815 and against the property tax in 1816, for example, each embellished by Cruikshank woodcuts. By 1816, he was also publishing engraved single-sheet Cruikshank satires. In accounts of Hone's career, the importance of these prints has been neglected; but some of them touched brilliance. One of them, Cruikshank's *The Royal Shambles or the Progress of Legitimacy & Reestablishment of Religion & Social Order – !!! – !!!* (1816), was as inventively detailed and ambitious as any of Gillray's largest set-pieces [fig. 261]. Lampooning the celebrations of the anniversary of Louis XVIII's return to Paris, and summarizing the international concerns of metropolitan radicalism after the war, its meticulous composition made it a striven-for masterpiece that anticipated Cruikshank's *Liberty Suspended!* a year later and his *New Union Club* of 1819.[42]

Although none of this would have endeared Hone to ministers, Hone wasn't as yet uniquely conspicuous. But a brief spell of editing the *Critical Review* had loosely connected him with the advanced liberals around Leigh

**Fig. 261** George Cruikshank, *The Royal Shambles or the Progress of Legitimacy &*
*Reestablishment of Religion & Social Order – !!! – !!!* (Hone, 1816)

Hunt's *Examiner*. He drew close to Hazlitt thereafter, and would meet with
Hazlitt and Cruikshank in a Chancery Lane tavern to plot the uses of
satire.[43] By 1817 his *Reformists' Register* stood next to Cobbett's *Political Register*
and Wooler's *Black Dwarf* as an offensively critical newspaper. In it he
lampooned the government for suspending *habeas corpus*, and issued a
pamphlet parody of the litany (*The Bullet Te Deum*) on the same subject. As
he played to a popular market in his pamphlets, Hone must have known that
he was playing with fire also. The law officers already had their eyes on
Cobbett and Wooler. Cobbett left for America to avoid their attentions, but
Wooler was tried before Mr Justice Abbott for sedition in May 1817. Wooler
defended himself by arguing that his articles were written in a spirit of
ridicule; and he made the court laugh, just as Hone did seven months later.
Wooler's first trial misfired and had to be dropped, and on the second trial
he was acquitted. These failures strengthened the law officers' determination
to get Hone if they could. The trouble was that they also gave Hone a model
of how best to conduct his own defence – through mockery.

The three pamphlets that had brought Hone to the law officers' attention must have made him seem an easy as well as necessary target. From their first publication on 10 January until they were withdrawn from sale on 22 February, they sold 3,000 copies. They mocked regent, ministers and sinecurists by parodying the Church of England creed, catechism and litany respectively, and this for pennies which poor people could afford:

Q. What is your name? [the *Catechism* began].

A. Lick Spittle.

Q. Who gave you this name?

A. My sureties to the ministry . . . wherein I was made a member of the majority, the child of corruption, and a locust to devour the good things of this kingdom . . .

Q. Rehearse the articles of thy belief.

A. I believe in George, the Regent Almighty, maker of new streets and knights of the Bath, and in the present ministry, his only choice, who were conceived of Toryism, brought forth of William Pitt, suffered loss of place under Charles James Fox, were execrated, dead, and buried. In a few months they rose again from their minority; they re-ascended to the Treasury benches, and sit at the right hand of a little man in a large wig; from whence they laugh at the petitions of the people, who pray for reform, and that the sweat of their brow may procure them bread.

Or, as his *Political Litany* put it:

From a Parliament chosen only by one tenth of the tax-payers; from taxes raised to pay wholesale human butchers their subsidies; from the false doctrines, heresy, and schism, which have obscured our once glorious constitution; from conspiracies against the liberty of the people; and from obstacles thrown in the way of the exertion of our natural and constitutional rights, – *Good prince, deliver us!*

. . . That it may please ye to keep yourselves in all sobriety, temperance, and honesty of life – that ye spend not extravagantly the money raised from the production of our labours, nor take for yourselves that which ye need not, – *We beseech ye to hear us, O rulers!*

. . . That it may please ye to lead and strengthen GEORGE Prince of Wales, our present REGENT, in the true fear and knowledge of the principles whereon the people of this commonwealth placed their crown on the head of his ancestors, and continue it towards him; and that it may please ye as much as in ye lie, to keep and to defend him from battle and murder, and sudden death, and from fornication, and all other deadly sin, – *We beseech ye to hear us, O rulers!*

With the Wooler fiasco in mind, the law officers thought it would be easier to get Hone for blasphemy than for sedition. That, they wrongly thought, would stop him from making political speeches and go down better with the juries. So Hone was arrested on an *ex officio* information in May 1817 and imprisoned without being told the terms of his indictment. He was released on his own recognizances in July only because he could prove that his wife and children were starving in his absence, but he spent the rest of the year in mounting distress awaiting his fate. At last his three trials in the City's Guildhall, one for each pamphlet, were held on three successive days in December. The government tried to pack his juries with loyalists, but the rigging was exposed and in the event Hone's juries were randomly selected.

Too poor to employ counsel, Hone conducted his own defence. He did so with such audacity that each trial resulted in triumphant acquittal. The Attorney General, prosecuting, was repeatedly outmanoeuvred by Hone's insistence that his parodies ridiculed politicians rather than religion and that countless past parodies of holy texts had been published with impunity. To prove this, he lengthily cited Luther and Milton, among many others, as well as the Tory minister George Canning for his *Anti-Jacobin* parodies in 1797: 'If I am convicted he ought to follow me to my cell.' He pointed out that Gillray had used scriptural imagery parodically, not least in the caricatures commissioned by Canning. All that distinguished these predecessors from himself was that they had been 'on the right side'.[44]

Hone's presentation of himself as the common man's David confronting the ministerial Goliath played theatrically to the court's sympathy. He apologized for the poverty of his clothes, and he looked (and was) worn and ill. 'I have the pride of being independent,' he declared, but 'I have never had any property' and was 'as destitute as any man in London'. His Fleet Street bookshop was a paltry three feet wide in front, he said; he could afford to furnish only one room above his Old Bailey shop; for the past year his children had had no beds to lie in; and for two and a half years his family had been next to starving. When, therefore, he inveighed against the use of *ex officio* informations, the packing of juries, or the government's shackling of the press, or when he rebuked Mr Justice Abbott during the first trial and Lord Chief Justice Ellenborough, who took over the case during the second and third trials, for their many prejudicial interjections and inappropriate directions to the juries, the court erupted in cheers. 'Gentlemen, it is you who are trying me today,' he reminded one jury: 'His lordship is no judge of me. You are my judges – you are my only judges. His lordship sits there [only] to receive your verdict.' And when Ellenborough objected that Hone was wasting time by citing so many historical examples of parody, Hone exploded in reply, 'Wasting time, my Lord! I am to be tried, not you! When I shall have been consigned to a dungeon, your lordship will sit as coolly upon that seat as ever; you will not feel the punishment . . . I am the injured man. I am upon my trial by those gentlemen, my jury.' Sallies like these produced laughter and 'loud acclamations'. Ellenborough or Abbott would threaten furiously to clear the court or bring charges of contempt (Ellenborough: 'The first man I see laugh shall be brought up'); but within minutes laughter would erupt again.

The acquittals were predictable. At each day's not guilty verdict, people in court cried 'Long live the honest jury!' and 'An honest jury for ever!', and 'the waving of hats, handkerchiefs and applause continued for several minutes.' In the streets, *The Times* reported that 20,000 cheering people assembled: all that could be heard was 'the language of joy'. After the third and last acquittal, the lord chief justice, disgusted, rode into the jeering and spitting crowd and himself 'laughed at the hooting and tumultuous mob who surrounded his carriage, remarking that their saliva was more dangerous than their bite'; then he stopped his coach so that his coachman could buy kippers. A lot of laughter flowed around this story, but Ellenborough never sat in court again. 'The popular opinion was that Lord Ellenborough was killed by Hone's trial, and he certainly never held up his head in public after.' Ellenborough was the most vicious and execrated of judges in that harshest of systems. His humiliation by laughter was not the least element in Hone's triumph.[45]

Hone became liberal-radical London's hero. He was feted at banquets and helped by subscriptions. Luminaries like Jeremy Bentham and the Whig Dr Parr congratulated him. And the printshops celebrated. 'Sir, I heartily rejoice in your defeat of the oppressors and sincerely congratulate you on your triumph and present prospects as a result of that wicked attempt,' S. W. Fores wrote to Hone, and Fores then employed Cruikshank to squeeze the judges' humiliation for every laugh he could get.[46] *Out Witted at Last – or Big Wig in the wrong Box* showed Hone and the jury triumphing over a donkey-headed Ellenborough while a bulldog labelled 'John Bull' cocked up its leg to urinate on the prime minister's trousers [fig. 262]. In *William the Conqueror, or the Game Cock of Guildhall*, Hone is a gamecock resting a claw on a block labelled 'Trial by jury'; he cries 'cock a doodle doo!!!' over the prostrate blackbird figures representing Ellenborough and the Attorney General. A third print illustrated a songsheet entitled *Great Gobble, and Twit Twittle Twit, or Law versus Common Sense: Being a Twitting Report of Successive Attacks on a Tom Tit, his Stout Defences and Final Victory; a New Song* [fig. 263]. In it, a turkeycock with Ellenborough's head confronts a tiny tom-tit with Hone's head. The attorney general, Shepherd (shepherd's crook), is the largest among the geese that stand for the prosecuting counsel; the jury are twelve cockerels. 'Let me remind you gentlemen! of your own vile nonsense,' the tom-tit Hone says: 'Twit, twittle twit: twit, twittle twit.' Ellenborough replies: 'This is not to be borne – what! are we to be twitted to our faces; & must I stay here for ever the object of profane diversion . . .

**Fig. 262** George Cruikshank, *Out Witted at Last – or Big Wig in the wrong Box* (Hone(?), 1817)

**Fig. 263** George Cruikshank, *Great Gobble, and Twit Twittle Twit, or Law versus Common Sense* (Hone, 1817)

gobble, gobble, gobble.' The twitting of the law pleased the plebeian market, too. A twopenny verse broadsheet issued by John Fairburn celebrated *The Three Honest Juries*: 'How majestic is law! How it swells and looks big; / How tremendous its brow! And how awful its wig! / But the frown of a judge was not valued a fig – / By the verdicts of three honest juries, / Oh, the three honest juries, huzza!' The sheet was surmounted by a medallion depicting a laughing face labelled: '*Laugh like me!!!*' and '*Oh! The big wigs of old England! Laugh at the English big wigs!!*' [fig. 264].

Hone's satire had drawn on traditions of elite ridicule that stretched back through the eighteenth century. His liturgical parodies had been inspired by *John Wilkes's Catechism*, a mock-catechism of 1769, for example,

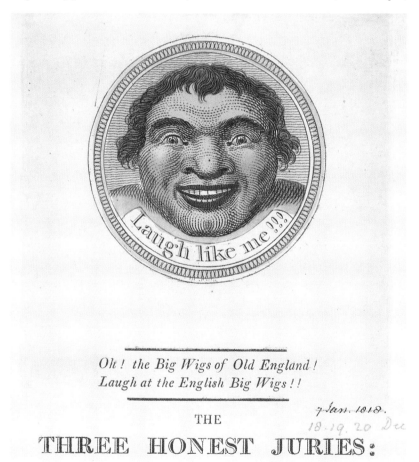

Oh! the Big Wigs of Old England!
Laugh at the English Big Wigs!!

THE

THREE HONEST JURIES:

**Fig. 264** Fairburn(?), *The Three Honest Juries: a Parody on 'The Roast Beef of Old England'* (broadsheet detail, Fairburn, 1817)

while Cruikshank's woodcuts of the regent for Hone's *Political House that Jack Built* [fig. 91] and *Queen's Matrimonial Ladder* [fig. 92] were modelled on Gillray's *Voluptuary* of 1792 [fig. 90]. Despite these continuities, Hone's attacks worked to new effect. His trials and the laughter they elicited made repressive law and its minions look asinine. His acquittals led to the curtailment if not end of *ex officio* informations and of jury-packing, and they transformed Hone himself into one of the great heroes of press freedom. No parodic satire would be plausibly prosecutable after this, and the way lay open for Hone's and Cruikshank's wickedly offensive pamphlet collaborations in the three years that followed.

Nor was it just Hone, or the jury, or press freedom that triumphed in this story. Hone's latest biographer observes how odd it seems that laughter should in this sense have been one of liberty's springs. Laughter, he notes, seems too 'trivial' to be a motor of change or the stuff of heroic resistance to repression. Readers of this book will be less surprised than he is. From the trials' outset, when the attorney general had to intone Hone's texts verbatim as he read out the indictment, it was Hone's every intention that the lawmen should be shafted on their own absurdity. This story represents the triumph of laughter. How long that triumph could last, however, was a different matter.

# CHAPTER SEVENTEEN

# THE SILENCING

The vast promise held out by the radical satires of the 1810s didn't long survive the regent's accession as George IV in 1820: the new reign marked a watershed. Politicians and adulterers continued to be ridiculed in the old ways. Single-sheet satires continued, and during the reform agitations of 1830–32 some of them recaptured the old vigour. But radical commentary henceforth turned solemn and earnest on the whole, as a new optimism about the prospects for social- and self-improvement developed. The virulent clarity of regency mockery was really quite suddenly lost, along with the open contempt that had fuelled it. The prospect of serious political reform, improving conditions and cultural shifts determined this process most deeply. But there was also a narrower cause, and this was the new king's extraordinary success in silencing the satirists.

George had endured mockery for over forty years, but both the insolence of Cruikshank's prints during the regency and the vituperation unleashed by the queen's affair exceeded anything he had suffered in his younger days. The most remarkable aspect of the king's feud with Caroline, the American minister wrote, 'was the boundless rage of the press and liberty of speech. Every day produced its thousand fiery libels against the king and his adherents, and as many caricatures, that were hawked in all the streets.' In the past, Sir M. Cholmeley, MP, complained, one had actually to enter a shop to see 'bad' caricatures; but now these things were 'thrust upon the notice of passengers; and no man could go through the streets without having his eyes insulted by the most offensive placards and comparisons of an odious kind between the highest personage and the greatest of tyrants'. 'The press now is completely open to treason, sedition, blasphemy and falsehood with impunity,' someone else objected.[1] This sustained mockery forced George as regent to become a virtual recluse at Windsor or on the royal yacht – his 'one fear' being of ridicule, as the Duke of Wellington said. It didn't get better. By October 1820, Anne Cobbett was telling her brother that 'the gentleman does not dare to show himself in London, or indeed, anywhere else; he kept himself cooped up in Windsor forest for nearly two months, and then, all of a sudden we heard of his going on board of ship at Brighton (at which place he was terribly hissed) and out to sea . . . It is a rather melancholy thing to see a king playing at hide and seek in this way.' It helped that he was still so easy a target: 'from corpulence and disease, what had once been prepossessing, and attractive, was altogether obliterated. His liaisons, which even in his youth were without sentiment, were, when he grew old, ridiculous and vulgar.'[2]

Writing years after the event, Lord Brougham recalled of the battle between George and Caroline that 'the most unmeasured attacks on the royal family from the king downwards were become as familiar as the court circular . . . They had become about as harmless, and prosecution was never thought of for a moment.'[3] This gloss was disingenous. The king never once thought the satirists were harmless, and there is no question but that he wanted them permanently silenced. His confidence increasing as Caroline's support waned with the accumulating evidence of her own adulteries, his first instinct was to reach for prosecution. He wrote to the Lord Chancellor, Eldon, in January 1821: 'My dear Lord, As the courts of law will now open within a few days, I am desirous to know the decision that has been taken by the Attorney-General upon the mode in which all the vendors of treason, and libellers, such as Benbow &c &c are to be prosecuted.' This, he added elsewhere, was:

A measure so vitally indispensable to my feelings, as well as to the country, that I must insist that no *further* loss of time should be suffered to elapse before proceedings be instituted. It is clear beyond dispute from the improvement of the public mind and the loyalty which the country is now displaying, *if properly cultivated and turned to the best advantage by ministers*, that the government [should] thereby be enabled to repair to the country and to me, those evils of the magnitude of which there can be but one opinion.[4]

The king referred to William Benbow not because Benbow's prints were more vicious than those of other printshops. Two prints that George

**Fig. 265** George Cruikshank, A *Scene in the New Farce of a Lady and the Devil* (Benbow, 1820)

Cruikshank engraved for Benbow in June 1820, for example, were by current standards rather run-of-the-mill, though that didn't stop the king from hating them. The first, *A Scene in the New Farce of a Lady and the Devil* [fig. 265], has the king and ministers comically startled by the news of the queen's landing at Dover; the second, *A Leap Year Drawing Room, or the Pleasures of Petticoat Government* [fig. 266], depicts the king ludicrously in a woman's dress and coiffeur surrounded by fawning (and bulbous) female admirers, Lady Conyngham included. Nor was Benbow even a prolific printmaker (only twenty-three of his prints are catalogued for 1820–25). All the same, this Manchester shoemaker-turned-printman was radical to the core, and his Strand bookshop was a fount of radical publication, so he was an obvious target. Newly arrived in London in 1816, Benbow had associated not only with the Westminster Burdettites and Cobbett but also with the Spencean revolutionaries, and this had cost him a year's imprisonment during the suspension of *habeas corpus* in 1817. What particularly provoked the king, however, was that between June and December 1820 Benbow published a series of scathing print and verse attacks on his deepening dependence on his new *maîtresse en titre*, Lady Conyngham. If *Leap Year Drawing Room* hinted

**Fig. 266** George Cruikshank, *A Leap Year Drawing Room, or the Pleasures of petticoat Government* (Benbow, 1820)

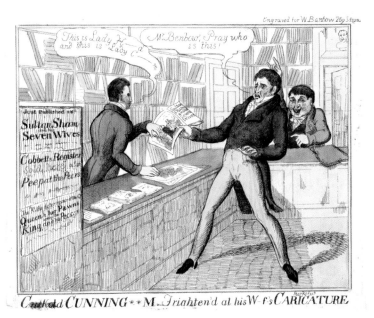

**Fig. 267** J. L. Marks, *Cuckold Cunning..m Frightend at his W–f–'s Caricature* (Benbow, 1820)

at this, one print that Benbow got J. L. Marks to engrave for him, *Cuckold Cunning..m Frightend at his W–f–'s Caricature*, publicized the Conyngham affair irrevocably [fig. 267]. This is set inside Benbow's implausibly well-appointed shop, which is plastered with advertisements for Cobbett's *Register* (which he published), 'Sultan Sham and his Seven Wives', and similarly unpleasant pamphlets. The Marquess Conyngham steps back in horror from the print of his wife and Lady Hertford that Benbow shows him: the print's subtext verses make jokes about the cuckoldry. Cut off the British Museum copy, they now survive only on the king's own copy in the Library of Congress, where they are marked 'suppressed'.

Suppression there certainly was, though it was futile. In June 1820, the Crown had already paid Benbow a hefty £100 (a lower shopkeeping family would have thought that an adequate annual income) to suppress the Cruikshank prints just mentioned, and to publish no more on the subject. In November, the Crown paid Benbow and Marks another £45 to suppress *Cuckold Cunning..m* and a further £50 to suppress the scurrilous verses beneath it. Benbow took the bribes and then ignored them. In December, his own engraving of *The R—l Cock and Chickens – or the Father of his People!!!*

**Fig. 268** Benbow(?), *The R—l Cock and Chickens – or the Father of his People!!!* (Benbow, 1820)

has George IV, gouty of foot, horned like the devil, and with devil's wings spread over his minions, holding a bottle labelled 'peoples tears' as he sits with an arm around the shoulders of 'Care-away Cunningham' (caressing her 'lasciviously', the ensuing indictment thought), while her arm dangles between his legs a little too friendlily. Britannia covers her face in shame as she sits in the background between a line of cavalry that faces 'the people', who huddle beneath a cloud labelled 'a storm gathering' [fig. 268]. It was this defiance, doubtless, that made the king insist on prosecution. The law officers duly prepared two indictments against Benbow for 'grotesque and ludicrous' seditious libels. But prosecutions for caricature still failed to impress juries. Both indictments against Benbow were thrown out by the Westminster grand jury, though not before he had sat in prison for eight months without trial, his business collapsing in consequence.[5]

It might have been to prepare for Benbow's prosecutions that at an unspecified date the Treasury Solicitor bought ninety-one of the most offensive prints published between June and December 1820.[6] Seventeen were Benbow's, but in addition there were as many as twenty issued by Fores, seventeen by Fairburn, five each by Marks and Dolby, four by Marshall, three by Johnston, and three or fewer from a half-dozen other shops. Again, however, this flexing of legal muscles came to nothing. Indeed, one of the prints tauntingly demonstrated the printshops' sense of their own immunity. *His Most Gracious Majesty Hum IVth & his Ministers Going to Play the Devil with the Satirists* bears Thomas Dolby's imprint; unsigned and undated, it looks like Cruikshank's [fig. 269]. In it, the king (or 'Hum', the poet Tom Moore's nickname for him), Wellington and other ministers drag the regent's commemorative 'bomb' (or mortar) to shoot down the satirists that plague them. Like gnats, the satirists circle in the air above them, wave 'free' printing presses on poles, or dance around the great men in mockery. 'Zounds & fury down with them!' cries the king: 'Here! Sid[mouth] you old tottering h—mb—g. Desire the bishops to come along with the tinder-box and matches! . . . dont you see! They are rediculing [*sic*] my very bomb [bum]! I tell you again, I am K—g, and be d—d to you all, and will do just as I please!!!' In one corner, George III's ghost, shrouded in black, cries: 'O my dear son! My dear son! If you prosecute them you will make their fortunes – but if you will only conduct yourself like a man and a gentleman you will destroy their profession.'

Dolby had to be allowed to get away with this print. Instead, the law resorted to the old policy of prosecuting him for selling seditious *texts*. To

**Fig. 269** George Cruikshank(?), *His Most Gracious Majesty Hum IVth & his Ministers Going to Play the Devil with the Satirists* (Dolby, 1820)

hide their involvement, the law officers passed the case to the so-called Constitutional Association. This was a loyalist subscription society formed in December 1820 (perhaps with government money), of which the Duke of Wellington was a prominent member. In May 1821, it prosecuted Dolby for describing the king's recent speech to parliament as 'a few insipid ungrammatical sentences recited by Hum and for which Hum receives a million a year'. The constitution, Dolby had added, was marked by 'religion without piety, law without reason, representatives without constituents, aristocracy without talents, a king without authority, and people without subsistence'. The case looked secure, but nobody counted on Dolby's petitioning the Commons against the 'self-denominated' Constitutional Association's assumption of the law officers' duties. In the event, he got away with having to pay £100 security against reoffending.[7]

With prosecutions failing, the king's second option was to buy up as many hostile plates, prints and copyrights as he could. According to the courtier Mrs Arbuthnot, this 'dirty work' was done for him by the head of the royal household, Bloomfield, in order 'to keep his own and Ly. Conynham's name out of them, as he has not courage to treat that sort of thing with the contempt it deserves'.[8] But this policy merely encouraged printshops to produce more scurrilous images in order to get the pay-off. So it had to be outright bribery, finally, that would do the trick; and do the trick it did.

The royal archives at Windsor reveal that between 1819 and 1822 George spent some £2,600 to achieve these silencings. The scale of this pay-off was substantial. That sum total equals some £100,000 in modern values.[9] First, in April 1819, John Johnston of Cheapside got £75 to suppress two plates and to promise 'not to publish . . . or cause to be published or printed separately or in any work, any plate or matter respecting his Royal Highness the Prince Regent'; this was followed in May 1820 by £100 to suppress a caricature and an article for the *New Bon Ton Magazine*, and by a further £35 in August to suppress a further article and plate in the same journal. Sidebotham's and Clinch's shops were also paid unspecified sums in 1819. In 1820, there were further payments as follows: £35 to J. L. Marks to suppress the satirical verses that Benbow had published anyway; £80 to Brookes to suppress two caricatures; £80 to William Clarke to suppress a poem and a plate, followed by £50 for four caricatures and a pledge 'not to publish any caricature respecting his present majesty'; and £30 to King of Chancery Lane to suppress a caricature. The king's paranoia and humiliation couldn't be measured better than by this sad list.

The most interesting payments went to the Fores family. In view of the fact that the biggest number of prints bought up by the law officers were published by S. W. Fores of Piccadilly, one might expect him to have featured prominently in the ensuing payments. In the event he got only £30 in December 1820 to suppress a print and a song on a subject already illustrated by Benbow. It may be that S. W. had hived off the riskiest works to family scions; for murkier payments were also made to H. Fores and Richard Fores, and these were substantial. Working from Panton Street, H. Fores received £70 in July 1820 to suppress a caricature. That payment was repeated in September; a further £50 was paid in October; and another £30 was paid in January to suppress a poem which was apparently a variant of Benbow's. Richard Fores, dealing from Aldgate, received £40 in May 1820 to suppress a caricature, and another £100 in June 'for the absolute purchase and total suppression of two sketches or drawings for caricatures, worked with my initials'. He also had to 'promise and undertake that I will not directly or indirectly print, engrave, or expose to sale . . .

either of the said drawings or any other caricature in any manner alluding or referring to the king and the marchioness of Hertford or Lady Conyngham or either of them'. He netted a further £50 in January 1821 for suppressing two plates, perhaps the same ones. He would have done well out of these deals were it not that the Society for the Suppression of Vice prosecuted him at Guildhall Sessions a few months later for publishing an image of 'a man and woman partly naked in the act of carnal copulation'; this put him in prison for nine months. H. Fores's Panton Street imprint was still current in 1832, but in 1821 Richard Fores disappeared from history, doubtless ruined just as his woeful petitions for mercy predicted.[10]

George IV's greatest success lay in the silencing of George Cruikshank. Cruikshank delivered his last attacks on the king in June 1820, in *A Scene in the New Farce* and *A Leap Year Drawing Room* as well as in his *'Ah! Sure such a pair was never seen so justly form'd to meet by nature'*, a representation of the king and queen as equal grotesques, which he engraved for George Humphrey's shop in St James's Street. A Windsor receipt records that the king paid Cruikshank £100 on 19 June 1820, 'in consideration of a pledge not to caricature his majesty in any immoral situation'; his brother Robert got £70 as well. A month later, both George and Robert were summoned to the Brighton Pavilion to negotiate 'with the king' further limits on their satires.[11]

When we recall that George Cruikshank had produced some ninety-four of the 230 catalogued satires on the regent between 1812 and the accession, and the best of them too, it becomes clear that this marked a moment of closure from which the satire of royalty would not easily recover. It's true that in 1823 the king was still complaining to Home Secretary Peel that 'obscene prints in the form of caricatures' were everywhere: 'there is scarcely a shop in London that deals in such trash in which the king is not exposed in some indecent or ridiculous manner. This is now become a constant practice, and it is high time that it should be put a stop to.' A print that lampooned his angling in 1826 was said to have stopped his pleasure in fishing altogether, and comic images continued to plague him until his death in 1830.[12] Still, these later mockeries not only diminished in frequency; they were also gentler, and suggested more sorrow than anger. After 1830 the graphic representation of royalty was to be unfailingly deferential, respectful or affectionate until recent times.

The bawdy, boozy George Cruikshank, 'cradled in caricature' (as he said of himself), had been Gillray's more than worthy successor. Although he lacked Gillray's versatility and imaginative range, he had been the sharpest thorn in the regent's side and the staunchest defender of free expression: he was certainly the greatest graphic satirist of the regency years. Nevertheless, this was the man who now signed up for the profits of decorum. For a few years he continued to illustrate Hone's pamphlets, until their friendship ended in 1821 when Hone found himself unable to bear Cruikshank's manic drinking. He continued to be fascinated by low life, still preferring 'the company of pugilists, journalists, jolly tars, gamblers, Grub Street hacks, Bacchanalians, and actors; often he would come home with the milk in the morning reeking of tobacco and beer and laugh while his sister-in-law scrubbed his face and his mother belaboured him with her fists'. But in 1823 he abjured satire altogether and reinvented himself as a comic magazine and book illustrator, quite without the old venom. As the years passed, his past virulence forgotten, he was to be celebrated even across the Channel (by Charles Baudelaire) for his 'inexhaustible abundance of grotesque invention' and, interestingly, for his 'delicacy of expression'.[13] By the 1840s he was a moralizing teetotaller, weakly emulating Hogarth by producing didactic teetotal 'progresses'. Twenty years on again, and he had become the grand old man of English image-making, the next best thing to an eminent Victorian, worth burying in St Paul's on his demise, which is more than Gillray could have hoped for. There was plenty of cant in him. He secretly ran two families until his death in 1878, the illicit one disclosed over a century later. But in this, among the Victorian great and good, he wasn't alone.

So how important was the bribe in achieving Cruikshank's trans-formation? It certainly tipped a balance. One hundred pounds wasn't a sum to be sniffed at in 1820, and Cruikshank, always a spendthrift, was easily bought. J. G. Lockhart described him in 1823 as a 'free-handed comical young fellow who will do anything he is paid for'. Cruikshank was also beginning to be flattered into notions of himself that were above his past and present station. Lockhart thought that he might play at being a Gillray if he liked, but that he was 'fitted for a higher walk', and could get himself a reputation 'such as Gilray [*sic*] was too sensible a fellow to dream of aspiring after'. Cruikshank was 'a thorough-bred *artist*', Lockhart insisted: 'he draws with the ease, and freedom, and fearlessness of a master. Let him do himself justice . . . let him think of Hogarth.'[14] Such blandishments were not easily resisted in an age when caricature was thought of as a mean artisan calling; and Cruikshank's vanity is well attested.

But there's more to add. Cruikshank's radical credentials had always been shaky: he could be contingently or opportunistically radical, but he wasn't radical *au fond*, any more than the rest of his family. Although he staunchly opposed curtailments of free expression, no printmaker could fail to do so, if only out of self-interest. But radicalism was another matter. Not for nothing had the Cruikshank males been infected by the 'scarlet fever' when father Isaac joined the volunteer militia in 1803: George's later patriotic satires against Napoleon were fully felt. Years later, Dickens aptly thought it 'too "radical" for good old George' to acknowledge in his teetotal prints that alcoholism was hatched as much from deprivation as from personal weakness.[15] And what we may now receive as his 'radical' output in the regency years was invariably prompted by printshop proprietors. Jones of *The Scourge*, Sidebotham, Johnson, Hone and Tegg (in his anti-regent mode) each mattered to Cruikshank's sociable soul, so that when he worked with or for them he easily took on their political colouring.

**Fig. 270** George Cruikshank, *The Age of Reason or the World Turned Topsyturvy Exemplefied in Tom Paines Works!!* (Tegg, 1819)

This, though, didn't stop him working for the conservative George Humphrey in St James's, or for *The Satirist* magazine, which was *The Scourge's* Tory rival. The only political prints he admitted to inventing independently ('*inv.*' on the plates) were paranoid about radical principles. The most vehement of these, astonishingly, were published in the last three months of 1819, just after Peterloo. Thus *The Age of Reason or the World Turned Topsyturvy Exemplefied in Tom Paines* [sic] *Works!!* crowed at the freethinking Richard Carlile's imprisonment for publishing Paine. It shows Carlile and other radicals, watched by the devil, burning the Bill of Rights, Magna Carta and emblems of church and state, while bishops and statesmen dangle from a gibbet supported by guillotines. '*No Christianity!!! – No religion!!! – No king!!! – No Lords! No Commons! No laws!!!*', a placard screams: '*Nothing but Tom Paine & universal suffrage!*' [fig. 270]. In *The Radical's Arms*, which he engraved for Humphrey in late 1819, he offered as extreme a calumny on the radicals as was ever produced in this era [fig. 271]. It beat any of Gillray's.[16]

These may be reasons enough for Cruikshank's easy abdication in 1820 from attacking the king and for his ensuing self-reinvention. None the less, for a tavern and wenching young man who had lived in and off the great tradition for thirteen years and whose father had lived off it before him, the bribe hardly sufficed alone to change his life's whole tenor. The larger truths are that a deep tide was turning in the 1820s, and that Cruikshank simply went with it. The key measure of this lies in the fact that so many of his old associates went with him.

The few printmen who stayed true to the radical or freethinking beliefs of the 1820s were stifled as their market collapsed or as the law threatened them. Some, like the much prosecuted Benbow, sustained their radical thrust by publishing erotica (though Benbow resumed his radical career later): the anti-vice society brought him to trial for obscene publication in June 1822 and again in February 1823.[17] Richard Carlile's bookshop, similarly, run by his wife while he was in prison, continued to pump out freethinking tracts with resounding titles like *An Address to Men of Science; Calling upon them to . . . Vindicate the Truth from the Foul Grasp and Persecution of Religion* (1821), as well as important tracts advocating birth control later. Unrepentant, Carlile even tried to sell an engraving of the Deity that was so imaginatively blasphemous that it apparently survives only in the Treasury Solicitor's papers, confiscated as evidence against him. Signed and addressed by Carlile (and dated 1825, according to the law officer's

**Fig. 271** George Cruikshank, *The Radical's Arms* (G. Humphrey, 1819)

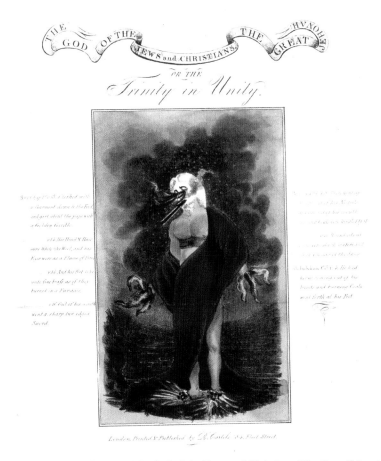

**Fig. 272** Richard Carlile, *The God of the Jews and Christians. The Great Jehovah* (1825)

inscription on the back), *God of the Jews and Christians. The Great Jehovah* ridiculed the Old Testament fantasy of the deity by taking its descriptions of him in Revelations and the psalms literally [fig. 272]. God is shown 'clothed with a garment down to the feet and girt about the paps with a golden girdle', with hair 'white like wool', with eyes 'as a flame of fire', and with 'feet like unto fine brass, as if they burned in a furnace'. Smoke comes from his nostrils and from his mouth fire so hot that 'devoured coals were kindled by it'. His mouth projects 'a sharp two-edged sword', while horns emerge from his hands and burning coals from his feet. This was an extraordinary invention for its own or any time, expressing an outrageously parodic disbelief that could be more easily depicted than spoken.[18]

Otherwise the shutters came down on commentary as risky as this. Most print and booksellers, however daring under the regency, followed Cruikshank into silence. The brave William Hone was among the first to discard the confrontational postures of 1817–21. Exhausted by his trials, he turned to the publishing of uncontroversial and successful yearbooks and antiquarian miscellanies (only to have the rights to his books bought up by Tegg after one of his many bankruptcies). By 1834, he had even seen the redeemer's light, and wrote an autobiography to explain how he'd managed to do it. His politics changed too. He was to argue that the 1832 Reform Act went too far in reforming the political system, and that the radical political unions should have been suppressed. He laboured at a self-justificatory history of parody, but never published it, and he died in 1842, the very model of the respectable publisher of items inoffensive and engaging.[19]

Robert Cruikshank also reneged. He had been as ambivalent as his brother about radical extremists.[20] By May 1821, he was rubbishing even George's libertarian moment in a brilliantly simple design entitled *All My Eye*: its title and content lampooned Hone's and his brother's eulogies on the free printing press and on Caroline as the wronged woman [fig. 273].

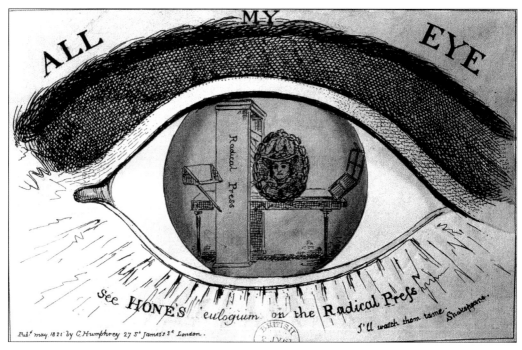

**Fig. 273** Robert Cruikshank, *All My Eye* (G. Humphrey, 1821)

John Johnston went the same way, though perhaps for different reasons. He might have become a government informer. He had been among the very first to be paid off by Carlton House in 1819. After that, the Windsor archives contain receipts for £10 paid to him in June 1820 for 'information conveyed' (about prints to be published by 'Williams of Kennington'), and for another £10 in August for 'the sketch of a caricature' and for 'information'. Shelley chose Johnston to publish his *Swellfoot the Tyrant* in 1820, but Dorothy George noted that, after only seven copies had been sold, Johnston rather too quickly surrendered all copies of it to the Society for the Suppression of Vice when the society threatened prosecution; she suspected that Johnston's relations with Carlton House explain why. Suspicion is deepened by an allusion to 'the notorious Johnson' as a vice society informer in Hood's synoptic print, *The Progress of Cant*, in 1825 [fig. 218].[21]

Thomas Tegg was probably the most predictable of the turncoats. With his sharp eye for the market, he was as natural a chameleon as Cruikshank. His instincts had also always been conservative. This was the man who on meeting Tom Paine in his youth had been struck by the great radical's 'fiend-like countenance' and who had found Paine's blasphemies intolerable. He had published Rowlandson's near-daily comments on the Mary Anne Clarke scandal in 1809 and many Cruikshank attacks on the regent thereafter, but these had been relatively safe targets: so far as the regent was concerned, Jones of *The Scourge* had already tested the risk of prosecution. Most of Tegg's other political satires were comfortably patriotic attacks on Napoleon. Like Cruikshank, he had it both ways when it paid. Both men protested at Peterloo when that disaster surprised them, but it was Tegg who issued Cruikshank's *Radical Reformer* and *Age of Reason* shortly after. By late 1820 Tegg was seeking office as a common councilman for Cheapside, and found it expedient to sign a loyal address to support the king against Caroline. Then, abruptly, he gave up publishing caricature altogether.

John Fairburn (admittedly a trade rival) was contemptuous of this volte face. His *A Snug Meeting to Get up an Ultra-Loyal Address; or a Peep at Te-a-g, Rag and Bobtail* (1821) shows Tegg in his auctioneer's box, corralling City toadies to sign the loyal address, while advertising a raffle of his past caricatures and jokes against the regent. 'I expect to be made a common council man,' he declares: '. . . And as you all know I am a loyal subject. I have sold all my old copper plates and disposed of the remaining charicatures!!!' [fig. 274]. A dog pisses on the loyal address on the floor; a portrait of the

**Fig. 274** Anon., *A Snug Meeting to Get up an Ultra-Loyal Address; or a Peep at Te-a-g, Rag and Bobtail* (Fairburn, 1821)

king surrounded by hens hangs over the fireplace; and near Tegg's rostrum lies a wry reminder of Tegg's and Cruikshank's past glories: a copy of *Royal Hobby's*, Cruikshank's unseemly satire on the regent and his brother of York which Tegg had published two years earlier.[22]

Tegg's repudiation of satire was final, however. Just as Cruikshank later suppressed all reference to the radical bawdry of his regency years (and as a result is now seldom remembered for it), so Tegg said nothing in his autobiography about his own huge contribution to caricature's popularization, and later chroniclers of his career have forgotten it also.[23] Tegg's and Cruikshank's opportunism provides one measure of the sea-change in print in these years. But deeper currents flowed as well, and it was these currents, we'll see, that they were following.

## CHAPTER EIGHTEEN

# HAPPINESS, CANT AND THE BEGGARS

## Lowest life in London

If the 'taming' of the graphic satirists owed much to the royal bribes of 1820–21, it owed most to the increasingly decorous and order-fixated expectations of their customers and the shifts in political culture that underpinned them. The new reign marked a point of renewal; but it mattered more that the quest for urban and personal disciplines intensified in the 1820s, and that at middling social levels the boundaries between high and low manners were strengthened. Humour itself was beginning to be taught good manners, to use Thackeray's phrase: the wild, coarse, reckless, ribald and '*generous*' laughter of Thackeray's boyhood was fading. There are many ways of illuminating this vast process, including those offered by political history. But the best way for the visual historian to engage with it may be by registering the fact that in and after the 1820s low life was increasingly represented as a terrain of anxiety and didactic moralization: in short, it became less and less funny. By following this line we may achieve a fair summation of profound attitudinal change. Viewed thus, some key low-life prints produced by the Cruikshank brothers present themselves as the last unapologetic flings in our great, louche, comic tradition.

It was an early portent of the brothers' movement from the virulent single-sheet satire towards comic book illustration that in 1820–21 they collaborated on thirty-six aquatints for Pierce Egan's picaresque quasi-novel, *Life in London*. Robert Cruikshank produced some similar prints for Charles Westmacott's *The English Spy* four years later. Among the best of these prints are several that illustrate London life at its very lowest and merriest – the world of the lumpen and the beggar. These images confront us with the representation of a *truly* low life, and stand on the cusp of deep change in the history of representation and mentality.

*Life in London* was first issued in a dozen monthly parts. It wasn't for plebeian readers. Each part cost 2s 6d to 3 shillings, and the book cost several guineas when bound. Its subtitle explains what it was about: *The Day and Night Scenes of Jerry Hawthorn, Esq. and his Elegant Friend Corinthian Tom, Accompanied by Bob Logic, the Oxonian, in their Rambles and Sprees through the Metropolis.* Organized around the Cruikshank plates and cheerfully littered with slang terms and Egan's characteristically random italics and capitalizations, it follows the adventures of those three gentlemanly young swells as they cross social boundaries in search of what Egan called 'real life'. The book contrasts the follies of the upper classes with the happiness of the lower and it aimed at a raffish readership long practised in crossing social boundaries also. Despite its implicit critique of upper-class hypocrisies, its political posture was acquiescent. Dedicated to George IV, its frontispiece [fig. 275] portrays the social hierarchy as a stable Corinthian column. The king and the court are at the top, supported by the nobles and the 'respectable' people. In the centre, Jerry, Tom and Logic carouse at table in the old manly manner, and the subtext cites Robert Burns: 'Here are we met three merry boys, / Three merry boys I trew are we, / And many a night we've merry been, / And many more we hope to be.' Flanking them or below them are artisans and 'tag rag and bobtails': these are either 'in' prison or 'out' of it or falling 'down'. At the base are the cellar people who have fallen, huddled in squalor. For the most part, the book accepted this order as a given.

*Life in London* became the decade's bestseller and was much plagiarized. 'We have been pirated, COPIED, traduced; but unfortunately, not ENRICHED', as Egan later complained, listing sixty-five piracies to prove it. Twopenny sheets of woodcuts and flash songs summarized the plot, while at least ten London theatres presented stage versions of the book within a year of its publication; Egan had to write a dramatization of his own to net some of the profits. Tea-trays, snuff-boxes, handkerchiefs, fans and screens were embellished with reproductions of Tom and Jerry at their pranks. The book, it was declared, achieved 'a revolution in our

**Fig. 275** George and Robert Cruikshank, *Frontispiece* to Pierce Egan, *Life in London* (1820–21)

literature, in our drama, and even in our nomenclature ... All the announcements from Paternoster Row were of books, great and small, depicting Life in London; dramatists at once turned their attention to the same subject, and tailors, bootmakers, and hatters, recommended nothing but Corinthian shapes, and Tom and Jerry patterns.'[1]

Success of this order may be built on a book's originality. Indeed, one commentator sees *Life in London*'s ways of observing the diversities of London living as so innovative that he regards it as the source of a 'popular literary modernism'.[2] This claim, however, would have been news to the Victorians. When later literary men referred to the book, it was to measure themselves against and not with it. Dickens certainly had a copy in his library, and his first novel, *The Pickwick Papers* (1836–7), begins in Egan's manner. But Dickens's own vast vision soon got the better of him, and by the end of *Pickwick* Egan's influence is exiguous. Except as a curiosity, *Life in London* didn't much recommend itself thereafter. Bulwer-Lytton's and Ainsworth's novels engaged with Egan's underworld city, but a review of Ainsworth's *Jack Sheppard* announced that no other books had so threatened public decency since 'the time of Tom and Jerry'. Although Thackeray had loved *Life in London* as a boy, and forty years later still relished the 'enjoyment of life in these young bucks of 1823 [*sic*], which contrasts strangely with our feelings of 1860', he remembered the text as 'a little vulgar'. A later memoirist dismissed *Life in London* as 'sad rubbish'. Moncrieff, the best of its many dramatizers, claimed to have 'pitched the letterpress into the fire, and [written] the play from the etchings alone'.[3]

The book's success is better explained, therefore, by what it recycled from the cultures that had hatched it. With these it shared that pleasure in metropolitan variety and low conviviality that we've met repeatedly in the foregoing chapters. It was averse to cant, and refused to judge, categorize and order. It celebrated its protagonists' innumerable forays across social boundaries precisely in the spirit of the affluent young swells who bought satirical prints. And its ironic or facetious humour was exactly that of many of the prints and illustrated books of the 1810s. *Life in London* looked backwards rather than forwards.

It would be strange were it otherwise. Egan grew up in the jobbing print world and artisan town that nurtured the satirical engravers. Apprenticed to a printer at the age of twelve in 1784, he worked as a compositor in St Martin's Lane, and then became one of the pugilistic 'Fancy', making his name with *Boxiana*, his great survey of the boxing world, in 1812. He followed this by churning out a great range of opportunistic publications, from a satire on the regent's affair with Mary 'Perdita' Robinson in 1814 to a reissue of Francis Grose's *Classical Dictionary of the Vulgar Tongue* in 1823 – this last 'revised and corrected with the addition of numerous slang phrases collected from tried authorities'. He dismissed what he called closet learning, and knew as well as any engraver that London was best understood 'by means of a free and unrestrained intercourse with society'. This knowledge wasn't 'modernist'. Rather, it echoed George Cruikshank's youthful delight in taverns full of fiddling and dancing coal-heavers in which, as he recalled (Egan-like), 'the highest and the lowest had united in harmonious fellowship . . . What a picture of life was there! It was *all life*!' It also echoed Grose's and George Parker's delight in the St Giles's boozing 'kens' (i.e. dens) to which they had resorted to gather the latest canting slang in the 1790s. It shared Parker's pride in his 'talent of easily and naturally accommodating myself to the manners of every rank in life', and chimed with Charles Lamb's pleasure in that 'London-with-the-many-sins' that delighted him more than 'all the flocks of silly sheep' appreciated by the Lake poets. Like countless such people, Egan celebrated nothing less than those boundary-denying and carnivalesque fluidities about which Victorians were to become so anxious.

The Cruikshank brothers had already illustrated *Boxiana's* early issues; their *Life in London* pictures drew on the same familiarity with rakish venues. Some of their illustrations show fashionable people at theatres, masquerades, Carlton House, Almack's assembly rooms, or in gentlemanly fencing-rooms. But their best pictures follow Egan's three young swells as they venture downwards into sleazier places: to dog- or cock-fights, the Newgate prison press-yard, the Fleet debtors' prison, low dives and coffee-shops in which the women were reliably jolly, encounters with pugilists and gamblers, punch-ups with 'peep o' day boys', or into magistrates' courts after gentlemanly 'sprees'. It was later disputed whether the pictures or Egan's text came first. The pictures seem to win. Robert Cruikshank's son Percy claimed that the book's subject-matter was first proposed by Robert after Robert had taken his brother-in-law on a tour of low-life London. Most of the prints were Robert's, and Robert enlisted Egan to provide the commentary. In later life, George characteristically announced that he had had such doubts about the book's morality that he had left two-thirds of the illustrations to Robert. According to Moncrieff, Jerry was Robert, Tom was George, and Logic was Egan, and their portraits confirm this (though others reversed the first two attributions).[4] Be all this as it may, *Life in London* was in these senses a summation of the passing culture and of its comic tradition, not a foretaste of the new. So firmly did it stand for the old culture's threatened values that Moncrieff dismissed his own and Egan's moral critics as 'venerable noodles' and insisted that he preferred the 'age of flesh' to the 'age of cant'. This so obviously paraphrased Byron's lament that 'the *cant* is so much stronger than *cunt* now a days' that one wonders whether Byron's was a widely known manly joke in these years.

At two stages in the book, Egan's young swells make excursions into the 'lowest life in London'. This becomes the title of the most engaging of the Cruikshank illustrations. Further subtitled *Tom, Jerry and Logic among the Unsophisticated Sons and Daughters of Nature at 'All Max' in the East* [fig. 276], it takes us into a grimy gaslit gin-cellar where 'the sons and daughters of nature' make merry. Five of them are black. Flashy Nance and Black Sall perch on Logic's knees and surround him with 'fields of temptation' (he is shortly to take them upstairs, the texts tells us, for mutual pleasure); Jerry plies a one-legged fiddler with gin; Tom charms Mrs Mace, the landlady; and the coal-whipper jigs to the fiddle with African Sall as her neglected

**Fig. 276** George and Robert Cruikshank, *Lowest Life in London: Tom, Jerry and Logic among the Unsophisticated Sons and Daughters of Nature at 'All Max' in the East* (in Pierce Egan, *Life in London*, 1820–21)

baby yells for attention. 'All licker to bee paed for on delivery,' a notice insists over the fireplace. Egan's text follows the picture's cues to present this low dive as an alternative arcadia that is cheerfully democratic and free of cant. It tells us that it is patronized by 'lascars, blacks, jack tars, coal-heavers, dustmen, women of colour, old and young, and a sprinkling of the remnants of once fine girls'. It was a place that permitted no distinction between its patrons: 'A card of admission was not necessary; – no inquiries were made; and every *cove* that put in his appearance was quite welcome: colour or country considered no obstacle; and *dress* and ADDRESS completely out of the question. *Ceremonies* were not in use, and, therefore, no struggle took place at ALL MAX for the master of them.' The sex on offer was democratic as well: 'The parties paired off according to fancy . . . and nothing thought of about birth and distinction. All was *happiness*, – every body free and easy, and freedom of expression allowed to the very echo.' To rub the point home, one of the swells contrasts the dive's candid generosities with the genteel hypocrisies at fashionable Almack's in the *West* End ('All Max' a pun on that upmarket venue, and 'max' slang for gin). It is 'the LOWER ORDERS of society who really ENJOY themselves', he declares:

> They eat with a good appetite, *hunger* being the sauce; they *drink* with a zest, in being *thirsty* from their exertions, and not nice in their beverage; and as to *dress*, it is not an object of serious consideration with them. Their minds are daily occupied with work, which they quit with the intention of *enjoying* themselves, and ENJOYMENT is the result; not like the rich, who are out night after night to *kill* TIME, and, what is worse, dissatisfied with almost every thing that crosses their path from the dulness of *repetition*.

Another of the friends agrees: 'among all the scenes that we have witnessed together, where the LOWER ORDERS have been taking their pleasure, I confess they have appeared ALL HAPPINESS. I am sorry I cannot say as much for the higher ranks of society.' This liberating fantasy duly licenses robustly comic Cockney dialogues which feed straight into Dickens:

> '*Vy*, Sir,' replied Mrs. *Mace*, 'that *are* black *voman*, who you *sees* dancing with *nasty Bob*, the coal-*vhipper*, is called *African Sall*, because she comes from foreign parts; and the little *mungo* in the corner, holding his arms out, is her child; yet I *doesn't* think *as how*, for all that, SALL has got any husband: but, *la!* sir, it's a poor heart that never rejoices, *an't* it, sir?'

Tom and Jerry "Masquerading it" among the Cadgers in the "Back Slums"
in the "Holy Land"

**Fig. 277** George and Robert Cruikshank, *Tom and Jerry 'Masquerading it'
among the Cadgers in the 'Back Slums' in the Holy Land* (in Pierce Egan, *Life in
London*, 1820–21)

The second *Life in London* picture that engages with London's lowest life
is darker, but something of the same joviality shines through it. It illustrates
*Tom and Jerry 'Masquerading it' among the Cadgers in the 'Back Slums' in the Holy
Land* [fig. 277].[5] (This was one of the earliest uses of the word 'slum' in its
modern meaning. 'Cadger' (still current) was canting slang for a beggar or
thief, and 'Holy Land' was a common pun on the 'St' in 'St Giles's': current
*c*.1785, it referred to the rookeries there.) In a bedizened cellar, the friends
join a carousal of merry beggars. This time Egan's text does hint at a moral
line; for, while All Max in the East was at least patronized by workers,
workers the cadgers are not. So Egan explains the mendicant scams
exposed here: 'The wretch who has also pretended to be *blind* . . . can here
*see* and enjoy all the good things of this life . . . The *chap* who has been
begging upon *crutches* through the streets, [is] the first to propose a dance . . .
The *pregnant* female . . . [removes] the *pillow* from under her stays, drinking
success to begging, and singing, ". . . A queen cannot swagger, nor get
drunk like a beggar, / Nor be half so happy as I, as I."' Nonetheless, the illustration undercuts easy disapproval. The beggars are ragged, the furniture
battered, the atmosphere raucous, and a fight breaks out in the backbround.
Yet once again happiness rules. Beggars dance merrily to the fiddling of the

one-legged and hat-befeathered black beggar, Billy Waters. The diminutive crippled figure of 'Little Jemmy' in his top hat presides at the table on the right. An old crone descends the entrance ladder without difficulty, carrying her unneeded crutches. Jerry and Logic sit amiably at table, and Tom flirts with a breast-exposing woman. The foreground business is busily communal. The only child present is a boy urinating into a beer-mug behind Piebald, the black beggar on the right; but the child expresses the cheerful anarchy of the place rather than a criticism of it. Even down to the background fight, the composition parodies the merry elite debaucheries so familiar from past satires, Gillray's *Union Club* particularly [fig. 131].

—◆—

We should be in no doubt that these low-life fantasies stood at the end of a long and generous representational tradition. A world in which couples paired off according to fancy without thought of birth and distinction, in which all was happiness and everybody was free and easy, and in which a queen couldn't be half so happy as a beggar, invoked a centuries-old idyll that had long borne its own critique of conventional life: and the merry beggar was central to it. In 1632, for example, Burton's *Anatomy of Melancholy* had related this wonderful citation from St Augustine:

> Passing by a village in the territory of Milan, I saw a poor beggar that had got belike his belly full of meat, jesting and merry; I sighed and said to some of my friends that were then with me, what a deal of trouble, madness, pain, and grief do we sustain and exaggerate unto our selves, to get that secure happiness, which this poor beggar hath prevented us of, and which we peradventure shall never have. For that which he hath now attained with the begging of some small pieces of silver, a temporal happiness, and present heart's ease, I cannot compass with all my careful windings and running in and out. And surely the beggar was very merry, but I was heavy: he was secure, but I timorous. And if any man should ask me now, whether I had rather be merry, or still so solicitous and sad, I should say, merry. If he should ask me again, whether I had rather be as I am, or as this beggar was, I should sure choose to be as I am, tortured still with cares and fears; but out of peevishness and not out of truth.

Burton then addressed the reader: 'That which S. Au[gu]stin[e] said of himself here in this place, I may truly say to thee, thou discontented wretch, thou covetous niggard, thou churl, thou ambitious and swelling toad, 'tis not want but peevishness which is the cause of thy woes, settle thine affection, thou hast enough.'[6] This beautiful fantasy had its counterpart in a genre of European beggar portraits which stretched back at least to Callot's and Rembrandt's engravings of the 1620s and 1630s. These had registered the beggar's oddity, pathos and poverty, but had neither problematized him nor caricatured him as a grotesque. Allowing him his own autonomy, they, too, used him to comment on conventional life. Rembrandt even depicted himself as a beggar – both to explore his own identity and to revel defiantly in the low-life that moralists abhorred. Finding something 'authentically heroic' in the beggar, Simon Schama has noted, his engraving 'comes eccentrically close to celebration'.[7] In London this form of sympathetic projection into the beggar's identity reached full graphic flowering within this book's timespan. This happened even as – or because – improvers were mounting ever more concerted attacks on begging.

It is true that satirical printshops had hitherto eschewed beggar commentaries as inappropriate for polite consumption. Great men might be lampooned as beggars in satirical inversion, and the satires of the 1780s and 1790s did represent St Giles's as a cant-free moral universe whose depravities chiefly pointed up the equal depravities of the rich [fig. 68]. Otherwise sympathetic beggar satires had been few. The case was different in the non-satirical depiction of beggars and street-people, however. Artists who depicted the rural poor capitulated to the deepening problematization of poverty during the 1780s; but this didn't check representations of street-people that fed an ethnographic rather than judgemental curiosity about the low other. These flowed from Pierce Tempest's reissue of Marcellus Laroon's *Cryes of the City of London* (1711), through Paul Sandby's *Twelve London Cries Done from the Life* (1765) and Rowlandson's *Cries of London* (1799), to J. T. Smith's *Vagabondiana, or Anecdotes of Mendicant Wanderers through the Streets of London, with Portraits of the Most Remarkable Drawn from Life* (1817), and even into T. L. Busby's *Costumes of the Lower Orders of London, Designed and Engraved from Nature* (1820). The genre closed with Géricault's *Pity the Sorrows of a Poor Old Man*, one of twelve lithographs of street life that he produced during his London visit in 1821: no adverse judgement here, either, for this beggar was simply wretched. Smith's thirty-one beggar engravings in *Vagabondiana* were admittedly accompanied by a text that deplored the 'disgusting

**Fig. 278** Smith, *Beggar* from *Vagabondiana, or Anecdotes of Mendicant Wanderers through the Streets of London, with Portraits of the Most Remarkable Drawn from Life* (1817)

nuisances' they caused, but his sympathetic account of mendicant history through the ages undercut this formal judgement, as did the several mendicant life stories he provided to establish beggars' valour. His engravings relished the beggars' sometimes carnivalesque garb, but none ventured into caricature and at least one of his beggars was jolly [fig. 278]. Busby's *Costumes of the Lower Orders* similarly included among its twenty-four coloured plates

BILLY WATERS.

**Fig. 279** Busby, *Billy Waters*, from his *Costumes of the Lower Orders of London* (1820)

a finely realized portrait of the carnivalesque figure of the one-legged black fiddler, Billy Waters [fig. 279]. Waters, the accompanying text reports, was 'remarkable for good humour and industry, for the feathers in his hat, the grin of his countenance, and the sudden turn and kick out of his wooden limb'. Born in America, he had lost his leg after falling from the yard-arm of the British warship *Ganymede* on which he was serving, and had had to beg to keep his wife and beloved little daughter alive ever since. Waters was familiar enough on the streets to be modelled and sold as a china pot for mantelpieces and to feature in earlier prints, Cruikshank's *New Union Club* included.[8] Then he found lasting fame with *Life in London*, though not to his advantage, as we'll see.

The two *Life in London* illustrations discussed above owe much to this tradition. That, though, isn't their only significance. They also so totally ignore the mounting textual and verbal noise about low-life morals that it is difficult not to see them as tacitly 'resistant' images in the culture war that chapter 15 has charted. The Cruikshanks might well be turning away from the old satire, but no other depictions in our long print repertoire so vigorously celebrated low-life vitality as these did. Prints of this ambition might normally be expected to lead printmakers in new directions. It is striking, however, that, outside a few immediately contemporary plagiarisms, they left no legacy whatsoever. They are the very last prints I know of in which low-life conviviality was presented as something guiltlessly to relish and be amused by. So what happened?

## Generosity and the beggars

Beggars and vagrants had always been harassed. Beggar books and cony-catching pamphlets had exposed beggar scams in the seventeenth century, and the Society for the Reformation of Manners had hounded them in the early eighteenth century. Magistrates spent a good part of their time sending beggars to houses of correction or forcibly returning them to their parishes. But in and after the 1790s anxieties about them escalated. In a period of wartime recession there simply seemed to be increasing numbers of beggars to deal with: 'every street, every alley, presents some miserable object, covered with loathesome sores, blind, mutilated, or exposed almost naked to the keen wintry blast,' Francis Grose lamented.[9] For the first time, moreover, observers tried to count them. In 1803, the merchant philanthropist Matthew Martin calculated that adults begged on average sixpence a day and children threepence, altogether extracting some £97,000 a year from London pockets. The Westminster magistrate Patrick Colquhoun put it higher, claiming in 1799 that charity cost Londoners £850,000 annually. By the winter of 1802–3, Martin further estimated that there were some 15,288 London beggars, 6,000 of them Irish.

Inevitably, reactions got harsher. A healthy reservoir of poverty might be necessary for the nation's economic well-being, Colquhoun argued, but a reservoir of the able-bodied and indigent work-shy was another matter. He wanted 'a correct system of police' to deal with it through the coordination of charitable giving and the erection of houses of industry in which 'the modest and deserving poor' would be relieved while idle and profligate beggars 'would be compelled to apply to honest labour for their subsistence'.[10] The 1815 peace added to the problem by putting discharged, crippled and pensionless servicemen on to the streets in swelling numbers. To them were added the seasonal influxes of country people desperate to earn pence from hay-harvesting around the capital. In 1815, a parliamentary committee on mendicity heard that some were actually starving. As national poor relief rose from £2 million in 1792 to £6.5 million in 1812 and £8 million in 1818, increasing numbers of improving people distanced themselves from their forebears' easy tolerances. Nearly every witness before the 1815 select committee agreed that mendicity had 'a tendency to degrade the mind' because 'when poor people once find they can easily get money by begging, they very seldom afterwards have recourse to habits of industry'. Beggars cared nothing about hard labour in Bridewell, they insisted; on discharge, they simply returned to begging. Prisons merely swelled their ranks when they 'vomited out' 5,000 prisoners annually. Those sent to their parishes returned to town, while parish relief in London was inefficiently administered, and professional beggars scorned it.

The most effective short-term solution was offered by the London Society for the Suppression of Mendicity. This was established in 1818 by the kinds of progressive professional men who were to be leading protagonists in the 'age of reform' – busy, intervening people who subscribed to the precepts of political economy and who sought to advance social discipline and efficiency on principle.[11] They did worry about suffering, but their finer natures were also disgusted by its uglier manifestations. As the Society's first report declared, 'groups of miserable objects, many in the garb of seamen, others in a state nearly approaching nudity, thronged our principal streets, or were found, night and day, upon the bridges and in the most frequented parts of town, presenting an aggregate of human suffering which it was evident no ordinary distribution of alms could hope to mitigate'. The 'revolting features of that frightful scene of human calamity' must be erased by instructing the public that 'indiscriminate almsgiving is not charity', and that assistance should be offered only to the 'industrious and deserving' and withheld from the 'idle and the vicious'. So printed tickets were supplied free to the Society's subscribers and in packets of five for a shilling to others for distribution to beggars in lieu of money. Beggars who presented their tickets at the Society's office would be fed if their accounts were plausible, but arrested and prosecuted if they looked 'professional'.[12] Alas, the Society was facing a problem that was to be endlessly refuelled as well as reinvented. Another select committee calculated in 1820 that there were still 15,000 beggars on London's streets; and while once Martin had thought that they each begged threepence to sixpence a day, and while the 1815 committee bumped this up to three to five shillings, this later committee heard that each beggar daily netted five to eight shillings. While Martin had estimated an annual cost in alms of £97,000, and Colquhoun £850,000, it was now thought to amount to £1,368,700 – 'or nearly double the present half-pay of the navy'. By 1830 the alms that beggars levied were said to amount to 'something incredibly enormous': 'they are consuming the substance of the country, without adding to its store, and rapidly increasing the amount of its poor's rates, to the lasting injury of the honest and industrious classes.'[13]

In the long term, it is well known that these discussions fed into the debate about the poor laws, eventually 'amended' in favour of more systematized harshness in 1834. The main point here, of course, is that they eroded the old sympathy for beggars. Antique stories began to multiply about their manipulativeness, immorality and organization. Francis Grose had already claimed that most beggars practised 'voluntary austerities on themselves, in order to excite compassion'. They were regulated by 'a king or superior, who appoints to every one a particular district or walk, which walks are farmed out to inferior brethren at certain daily sums . . . Natural defects or bodily misfortunes are reckoned advantages . . . He, who has neither legs nor arms, is nearly at the head of his profession.'[14] Accounts like these were amplified in the evidence heard by the 1815 Committee, most of them fantasy-laden or based on hearsay. Thus witnesses worried about the unmentionable depravities that flourished in the beggars' tenements. In Whitechapel 'they lie in a great round bed all round the room, to the tune of thirty or forty . . . very merry in the evening, and in the morning they sally forth with all sorts of deceptions'. 'Eight out of ten' were impostors. They scarified their feet to make them bleed, or bandaged themselves to pretend that they had been wounded in military or naval service. Women hired small children for the day, or feigned pregnancy to elicit pity. They divided themselves into 'companies' that were in turn subdivided into 'walks'. Each walk was considered 'a sort of property', and senior beggars got the best of them. Every morning twenty or thirty beggars erupted from Dyot Street in Seven Dials to 'branch off, five or six together, one way, another another', visiting gin shops first. Gin was the main cause of mendicity, the chaplain of Bridewell maintained. There were 'five large gin-shops, or wine-vaults as they are called, close to Seven Dials, which are constantly frequented. There is one where they go in at one door and out at another, to prevent the inconvenience of their returning the same way, where there are so many.' Beggars also had 'their rules' – and above all their carousings: 'I have seen tables set; one a very long table covered with a coarse cloth, but a clean one; and there was something roasting . . . they were going to have their dinner at the fashionable hour of seven.' 'They spend their evenings in a very riotous manner; the food that is given to them by benevolent persons they do not eat, but either throw it away or give it to the dogs.' 'These people send one of their crew to one of the eating-houses . . . and have ham, beef, and so on, brought, with knives and forks, and eat very heartily, with the property they have procured.' 'They live very well, especially if they are pretty well maimed, or if they are blind, or if they have children,' said the rector of St Clement Danes. They boasted that they made three to five shillings a day, more than an honest labourer's wage. Some were rich, from hoarding.

<hr />

Although Egan's and the Cruikshanks' low-life representations drew on the information marshalled by this mounting chorus, there is no question about their resistance to its disciplinary subtexts. The brothers were still moving only tentatively towards respectability, and discourses on poor laws, police and social discipline as yet troubled them little more than it did the raffish market they aimed at. In this sense, the uncritical jollity of *Tom and Jerry 'Masquerading it' among the Cadgers* and *Unsophisticated Sons and Daughters* was an affirmation of the old culture's resilience.[15]

Their resistance was endorsed by powerful voices. Historians in their forward-looking way tend to privilege the coming, the disciplinary voices: but here as elsewhere we shouldn't forget the eloquence of contrary critics. Plenty of people knew that wartime and post-war dislocations, though grave, were not unprecedented. Some understood that, like increases in 'crime', increases in beggary were as much functions of perception as of reality. Sir Nathaniel Conant, for example, drew on thirty-three years' experience as a Bow Street magistrate to tell the 1815 committee that beggars were no more numerous than they had been thirty years earlier: all that was afoot now was better counting. Conant was convinced that beggar impostures were uncommon, and fantasies about their wealth were ludicrous. Few arrested beggars had 'more than a shilling or two' on their persons; in his whole career he had known of only one woman 'who had a caddy in which there were nine or ten guineas hoarded'. Present laws against beggars were already excessive. If fully enforced they would cause a greater 'laceration of the mind' than the evil they aimed to cure.[16]

Moreover, until the mid-1820s, the disciplinary urge was opposed by that constellation of liberal literary figures we've met in other contexts. For the likes of William Godwin, William Hazlitt, Leigh Hunt, Charles Lamb and Thomas Hood, the beggar retained his older iconic standing. Indeed, some chose to fight the culture war around him. In 1797, Godwin admitted that professional beggars were 'the opprobrium of human nature, and that the earth would feel itself lightened by their removal'. But then, in one of the bold shifts typical of his style, he pointed out that a policy enacted mechanically out of principle would be more vicious than the corruptions it attacked: 'The case of the man who demands my charity in the streets, is often of the most pressing nature, and is therefore no proper field for experiments . . . I cannot consent to lending even my passive assistance, to the starving [of] men to death, that the laws may be reformed . . . There are some sufferings, so great and urgent, that a found morality will teach us to dispense with our general maxims, and, for no possible calculation of distant evils, to turn a deaf ear to the cries of humanity.'[17]

Charles Lamb saw it this way as well. In his 'Complaint of the Decay of Beggars in the Metropolis' (1822), he lamented the passing of what he read as the old mendicant lifestyles, and castigated the Mendicity Society as a vehicle of the new cant. Why hound beggars into workhouses, he asked, or begrudge them their small profits and nocturnal pleasures in drink? 'Reader, do not be frightened at the hard words, imposition, imposture – *give, and ask no questions* . . . Rake not in the bowels of unwelcome truth, to save a halfpenny.' Then he wheeled out the Burtonian fantasy that beggars had a dignity which sprung 'from the very depth of their desolation'. It made the beggar 'the only free man in the universe', his nakedness 'so much nearer to the being a man, than to go in livery'.[18] This notion of the beggar as the liberated obverse of the shackled bourgeois self drew on the mythic arcadia embedded in the long tradition we have noticed, as well as in goliardic texts that stretched back to the Middle Ages. 'Liberty' was its watchword. 'A fig for those by law protected! / Liberty's a glorious feast!', went the chorus of Robert Burns's 'Jolly Beggars' of 1799 – and in this spirit, in 1823, George Cruikshank illustrated the poem in ebulliently comic woodcuts [fig. 280].

Resistance also had its more intuitive expressions for it could draw on Londoners' deep familiarity with and backhanded affection for the beggars they passed every day on the streets. Street-knowledge of this kind determined people's sense of urban variety and their relation to it, and in this case it could induce a sympathetic curiosity about the beggar's character and oddity, if he was picturesque and harmless. This intuitive knowledge was capable of much greater generosity than any mendicity entrepreneur could muster. The 1815 Mendicity Committee kept hearing how pedestrians insisted on giving alms to beggars, despite advice not to. A constable who tried to arrest a beggar was sure to be surrounded and abused by a crowd: whereupon 'these beggars immediately make a resistance, by falling down and screaming; and then good-natured people interest themselves, and desire they [the constables] will not pull the poor creature about'. One constable who tried to arrest a blind beggar with his dog in St Paul's Churchyard 'had two teeth knocked out of his mouth and was very nearly killed'. The beggar 'had the impudence to say, it was his dog that begged, and not he; and if an officer interferes, the people say, "What, ill-treat a blind man!" He says he lost his eyes in the East Indies, and I believe he is blind; but he is perfectly capable of turning a wheel, or anything of that kind.' Pedestrians thought otherwise. They thought that the blind and the lame 'have a privilege', the City marshal glumly noted.[19] J. T. Smith thought otherwise also. He engraved just such a blind beggar and his dog for his *Vagabondiana*.

Beggars were regarded as the sprites or spirits of their particular patches, as Peter Ackroyd puts it; and their life-stories were relished. In 1826, for example, *The Times* was still able to devote twenty column-inches to the sad

THE BALLADMONGER

**Fig. 280** George Cruikshank, *The Balladmonger* and *The Soldier and his Doxy*: woodcuts illustrating Robert Burns, 'The Jolly Beggars' (in W. Clarke, *Points of Humour*, 1823)

life and death of the crippled beggar, Andrew Whiston. (He was the diminutive figure of 'Little Jemmy' who presides in the Cruikshanks' *Tom and Jerry among the Cadgers*.) The article called him the King of the Beggars, but he made the least plausible of kings.[20] He was only twenty-eight inches high, with a head of the same circumference. With his begging patch in the poor streets south of Blackfriars bridge, we learn that he lived in a bleak tenement room in Williams Court a couple of blocks to the east of it. He pursued his trade from a wooden truck on wooden wheels which he propelled with tiny crutches. He had once loved 'the attractive form of Miss Jane Cotters, of Shoe-lane', and was inconsolable when she died. He next wooed one Sarah Marshall, but 'she proved false, and he undone'. Everyone laughed when he was cited in a paternity case and protested the innocence that none doubted. At the end of each day, he would propel himself across the bridge in order to get drunk in Surr's wine vaults in Shoemaker Row. It was this habit that finally undid him. One night, he paid two coal-heavers in beer to hoist him home. As a joke, they carried him head-down. Whiston was later found suffocated on his vomit and slumped over the miniature table in his room.

The surgeons offered £100 for the right to dissect his corpse, but the tenants refused to surrender it until constables forced them to do so. The body was buried in a parish grave fourteen feet deep with three other coffins on top of it to deter the resurrection men.

For all its facetious touches, *The Times* article passed no judgement on Whiston's parasitic ways. Rather, it was moved by a simple curiosity about the urban grotesque. In this respect, Whiston shared the fate of many other unfortunates of the time: the twenty-inch-high 'Sicilian fairy', Caroline Crachami, for instance, who was exhibited in Bond Street for a shilling, another shilling for touching. A surgeon sold her body to the Royal College for dissection when she died in 1824; her skeleton is still there.[21]

How long, in this sobering culture, could these sympathetic expressions endure? The answer wasn't long in coming. It was foreshadowed in *Life in London*'s reception. Egan's representation of beggars living the merry and profitable lives of Old Riley amused many readers, but it stuck in the gullets of others. Beggars' duplicities and unearned pleasures obsessed them. In one dramatization of Egan's book, Billy Waters is made to complain wonderfully about the lamentable quality of his dinner: 'No capers cut for de leg ob mutton, *Bah!* No real turtle, but de mock turtle! No lem'un to him weal, no hoysters to him rup'-steak. Vat! Vat's dat I hears! No sassingers [sausages] to de turkey? – [is like] de alderman vidout him chain. Damme, landlord, me change my hotel to-morrow.' Even a penny street-broadside inspired by *Life in London* has Billy Waters singing: 'Frisk away, let's be gay, / This is cadger's holiday; / While knaves are thinking, we are drinking, / Bring in more gin and beer' – the chorus following: '. . . Now merry, merry, let us be, / There's none more happier sure than we, / For what we get we spend it free, / As all must understand!' With revelations like these on everyone's lips, Billy's street-patrons began to desert him. He had to pawn his fiddle, and would have pawned his wooden leg too, had it not guaranteed that he could never be put to the treadwheel. He died in St Giles's workhouse in 1823, allegedly cursing 'Tom Jerry' for destroying his livelihood.[22]

A significant shift in the graphic representation of beggars soon followed. The reference here is to a third Cruikshank illustration of low life, this one by Robert alone. It was one of seventy-one aquatints that he produced in 1825–6 for Charles Westmacott's *English Spy*, the best, though

*Courtiers Carousing in a Cadgers' Ken*

**Fig. 281** Robert Cruikshank, *Courtiers Carousing in a Cadgers' Ken* (from C. Westmacott, *The London Spy*, 1825–6)

more decorous, spin-off from the *Life in London* model. The print is entitled *Courtiers Carousing in a Cadgers' Ken* [fig. 281], and it draws shamelessly on the brothers' *Tom and Jerry 'Masquerading it' among the Cadgers* of four years before. But this is the better print. More ambitious in composition and working to stronger effect, it is the darkest of all exercises in the comic grotesque achieved in these years. Here at last there is a *dissociation* from rather than a celebration of the rumbustious low-life scurrility of past decades. Darkness descends; and the comic muse yields to judgement.[23]

At first we may not see this. The beggars' den is crowded and the picture energetic, and all is murky warmth, movement and deep rich colour. The laughter, the shouting and the drunken toasts are all but audible; and the sweat and the smoke are stifling. Crippled, black and Jewish beggars, aged crones, and children mingle promiscuously. The arms raised in toasts energize the scene, and nearly everyone smiles, laughs or shouts. It is only when one looks more closely that emblems of death and corruption intrude. Gallows graffiti are scratched on the back wall, while a mother and baby occupy the foreground, and they are starving. The pumpkin faces in the

567

background are leering and ghastly. Children in the foreground learn vicious ways from the pipe-smoking mother who plays cards with a man whose jaw is bound like a corpse's. A drinker vomits at the table while another is supine beneath it. At the table a tousled little girl watches the celebrations in mixed puzzlement and delight as she awaits her own certain corruption. Although the tropes of high-life debauchery are as determinedly projected on to low life as they had been in the *Life in London* plate (this is yet another print that remembers Gillray's 1801 *Union Club*), here, for the first time, the old graphic language is harnessed to the message that this isn't a world to be approved of or enjoyed, or one that could last.

For the print has some surprises. Our alienation from the scene is completed when Westmacott's text reassures us that this beggars' club is now long past. Some time ago, he tells us, we might have found in a cellar of this kind 'a scene worthy of the pencil of a Hogarth or a Cruikshank'. In past times, 'notorious impostors, professional paupers, ballad-singers, and blind fiddlers might . . . be witnessed carousing on the profits of mistaken charity and laughing in their cups at the credulity of mankind'. In past times, too, stout-hearted rakes had visited dives like this in pursuit of low nocturnal sensation. Westmacott reminds us that George Parker and Francis Grose had collected material for their canting dictionaries in such places; and (most important) that in the beggars' club 'the dissolute Lord Barrymore and Colonel George Hanger . . . are said to have officiated as president and vice-president, attended by their profligate companions'.[24] It is this last cue that Robert Cruikshank illustrates with bravado. His composition is based on a dynamic communication between beggars on the left and, on the right, four gentlemanly figures from that now distant and unlamented age. One, resting his arm on the back of the chair, is none other than the chubby-faced Prince of Wales himself (though the text dare not name him). Another, seated and raising his glass, is Charles James Fox: dead in 1806, he's not named either. Barrymore smokes his pipe on the right, while, recognizable from his hooked nose and cudgel, Colonel George Hanger (for years the prince's sidekick) raises his arms celebratorily to match the beggar's toast on the left.[25] In the prince's youth these four really had been infamous fellows in debauchery, and, although there is no evidence that together they sought titillation in venues as low as this, Barrymore might well have done so.[26] *Courtiers Carousing in a Cadgers' Ken* implies that great men behaved like this no longer. In this, a moment of closure is marked, and the text underscores the sense in which this had to be so. 'The police have now disturbed [the beggars'] nightly orgies,' it tells us, 'and the Mendicant Society [have] ruined their *lucrative* calling.' The cellar has become a twopenny lodging-house, and 'scarce a vestige remains of the disgusting depravity of former times'. Even 'the long table, where the trenchers [plates] consisted of so many round holes turned out in the plank, and the knives, forks, spoons, candle-sticks, and fire-irons *all chained* to their separate places, is no longer to be seen'.

The shifting postures in Cruikshank's low-life images, four or five years apart, illuminate a broad movement in the culture at large towards a more discipline-minded moralism. The boundary between respectable and low lifestyles was being staunchly reinforced and, like everyone else, the graphic artist soon found it nigh impossible again to cross it.

—•—

'From the lame, the halt, and the blind, have started up a race of people, whose habits, manners, and customs are peculiar to themselves,' the Mendicity Society declared in 1830; and they flourished only because people were too generous: 'the public is subjected to robbery, plunder, and murder, only because they *will* give alms to any wandering vagrant who applies to them, and this premium on idleness and vice fills the metropolis with thieves.' Luckily, however, 'the darkness' was 'dispersing': 'the middling and industrious lower classes, on whom these impostors have pressed so heavily, are beginning to understand their own interests.'[27] A quarter-century later, few disagreed that the beggar problem was receding. By 1852, Dickens could wheel out stories of beggars' jolly lives in the past, and then announce that (thanks to policemen) all that was 'gone, all gone; as defunct as the box-seat of the York mail': 'the spirit of street mendicity and mendacity is broken'.[28] Ten years later, Henry Mayhew's *London Labour and the London Poor* admitted that economic disasters and privations drove poor people to beg, and he rejected the myth of the rich beggar outright. But then he too recycled tales of beggars' carousings, organizations, kings and tricks, to conclude chillingly that there was 'a duty of the head as well as of the heart', and that our duty was 'not to waste our own interest and our resources on beings that will be content to live on our bounty, and will never return a moral profit to our charitable industry . . . [Wealth is] never meant to be lavished on mere human animals who eat, drink and sleep, and whose only instinct is to find out a

**Fig. 282** Seymour, *Beggars Beginning the Day* (McLean, 1832)

new caterer when the old one is exhausted.'[29] Indictments of the sturdy beggar were age-old; even so, a vast distance had been travelled between Georgian perceptions and this harsher Victorian one. The sense that beggars had a rightful place in the great chain of being or that they possessed their own dignity was dispensed with.

The Cruikshanks' prints of low life in 1821 had not been unaware of underworld tricks: they had celebrated the underworld's joyous conviviality despite them. Graphic culture thereafter was capable of no such acknowledgement. In 1832, R. S. Seymour's lithograph for McLean's printshop, *Beggars Beginning the Day*, could still pose as comic (the mother dropping her baby from the attic for another woman to use it for begging; one beggar preparing to strap up a perfectly good leg to make himself 'one-legged', another making himself up in the mirror to look ghastly); but the old ambivalences and energy were lost in Seymour's literalism [fig. 282]. Thereafter a few merry beggars survived in *Punch*'s jokes, but to be laughed at, not with. Otherwise, the Victorian representation of street-destitution (when not sentimental) became irrevocably squeamish and disapproving, and wit and humour were totally expelled from it. Thus a conscience-stirring depiction of *A Lodging House in Field Lane* [fig. 283] in 1848 can show exactly the kind of slum lodging-house in which the Cruikshank beggars had revelled a quarter-century earlier. The picture anticipates a new social realism, but there is no hidden play or complexity in it. The irony of the older tradition is lost, and the propagandist message dominates. So, while the beds upstairs are arranged in meaningfully promiscuous intimacy, the kitchen beneath is occupied by a dark huddle of defeated people, and under the floor a scavenger wades through a midden on mysterious business. The picture purports to be 'humanitarian', and one admits its good intentions. All the same, it keeps its distance from those people as the earlier pictures never did. Their eyes don't meet ours, nor do we enter their space. Instead, we peer into it from the safety outside, the wall removed for that purpose. Humanity is the last thing it grants them.[30]

**Fig. 283** Mason, *A Lodging House in Field Lane* (from H. Gavin, *Sanitary Ramblings: Being Sketches and Illustrations of Bethnal Green*, 1847)

The drear subtexts of this motif were to be recycled in the steel engravings that illustrated Mayhew's *London Labour*, as well as in the iconic artistic statements of Victorian philanthropy. George Cruikshank's *Taken by the Police at a Three-Penny Lodging House*, for example, in his didactic series, *The Drunkard's Daughter* (1848) [fig. 284], or Gustave Doré's *The Bull's Eye*, published a quarter-century later, both ostensibly engage with London's lowest life; but their main purpose is to show how the bull's-eye beam of the law probes the darkness to oblige the benighted figures it exposes to yield to light, law and civility. Just as fallen women in Victorian art must literally fall, so, in image after image, the underclasses must be shown defeated and suffering. To hint that their lives might be merry would be to admit that the disciplines of poor law and scientific philanthropy were failing. Indeed, not the least business of Victorian low-life representation was to reflect back to viewers their own benevolence. In Luke Fildes's

THE DRUNKARD'S CHILDREN.

Plate IV.—— URGED ON BY HIS RUFFIAN COMPANIONS, AND EXCITED BY DRINK, HE COMMITS A DESPERATE ROBBERY.—— HE IS TAKEN BY THE POLICE AT A THREE-PENNY LODGING HOUSE.

**Fig. 284** George Cruikshank, *Taken by the Police at a Three-Penny Lodging House* (from *The Drunkard's Daughter*, 1848)

*Applications for Admission to a Casual Ward* (1874), the most iconic declaration of Victorian compassion, the applicants for poor relief are required to pose as anonymous and defeated subjects (again submissive to the kindly policeman who presides over them). Fildes's engraving to the same effect for *The Graphic* was accompanied by an article rubbing home poor people's habitual drunkenness, fecklessness and indifference. His work made serious moral points about urban degradation, and some contemporaries thought of him as a latter-day Hogarth. But, as one historian puts it, 'it was as if scenes of social distress could not be tackled without allowing the audience to feel a glow of reassuring emotions: of pathos, sympathy or charity, which left them feeling munificent rather than guilty'.[31] In this spirit, William Macduff's *Shaftesbury, or Lost and Found* (1862) has two urchin shoe-blacks gaze in submissive gratitude into a printshop window at a print portraying Lord Shaftesbury, founder of the philanthropic 'shoe-black brigade'. It doesn't occur to the artist that the costly and pious prints in the window underscore the gap between their purchasers' wealth and the boys' degradation, least of all that his painting's self-regard aligns it with what Thomas Carlyle called the 'universal syllabub of philanthropic twaddle'. Again, even as the flower-girl who in her deathly pallor is obliged bleakly to pose for an engraving in Mayhew is transmogrified into Augustus Mulready's crassly sentimentalized *London Crossing Sweeper and Flower Girl* (1884), the dissociation of respectable observer from plausibly lived reality is sustained. Compare Mulready's flower-girl with Hogarth's cheery *Shrimp Girl* of the 1740s, and it is clear how in the later case inventiveness of composition is negated in its message's shallow predictability.[32]

Pictures like these, of course, sought to inform or to inspire in ways to which our earlier engravers were indifferent. They also advocated sorely needed improvements. Our criticism is compromised by the fact that we moderns now depend on policemen, order and sewers; and, by whatever devices public energy was mobilized, it was better to mobilize it thus than not at all. All the same, while they purported to depict 'reality', these images in fact made ideologically filtered statements *about* reality, and the 'reform' they advocated was advanced in the name of order and control. By earlier standards, the vision that informed them was damaged. They testified to respectable Victorians' loss of a peaceful ease with their society, and their distaste for and withdrawal from its demotic vitality. The last thing they could sustain was irony.

# FRANCIS PLACE
# AND 'IMPROVEMENT'

## Respectability

One day in the later 1820s, Francis Place – that archetype of the upwardly mobile tradesman and the closest of all observers of London's humbler lives in our era – recalled how thirty years earlier he had entered a poor street in Lambeth, south of the Thames. It was inhabited by river-fishermen and other poor people, he remembered. He had found that its ancient houses were 'perfectly black with soot and dirt, the rooms were neither painted nor whitewashed for many years together, [and] patches of paper or a rag stuck through the casement kept the cold where the glass was broken from entering. No such thing as a curtain unless it were a piece of old garment was to be seen at any window.' The womenfolk emptied their slops at their doorways, and in summer they sat on stools in the street 'without gowns on their back or handkerchiefs on their necks, their leather stays half laced and as black as the door parts, their black coarse worsted stockings and striped lindsey petticoats "standing alone with the dirt".' Lately, however, he had revisited the street to find that much had improved. Although river-fishing was declining, the people now spent their money more carefully. Nearly all the houses had white-painted sash windows and curtains; and the women wore washable clothes. Mortality rates were lower:

the 'wretched half-starved, miserable scald headed children, with ricketty limbs and bandy legs' who had once blighted streets like this were no longer to be seen. Place thought that these improvements were 'universal', and that they ensued from better education and from the modestly higher wages that encouraged people's 'desire to accumulate'. Future prospects were hopeful. 'People thus improved,' he thought, 'will struggle still further to improve their condition, and harder still to prevent degradation.' This in turn would erode their 'absurd reverence for their betters as they used to be called'. Above all, it would encourage 'a greater love of distinction'.[1]

Since this book opened with London, so it should end – with Place's view of the changes that marked the great city and of his own and others' 'improvement' within it. It also opened by discussing 'polite' and 'impolite' manners; and so it should similarly end, by addressing the transformative force in the middle ranks of life that was called 'repectability'. Both themes illuminate the erosion of the old satire in the 1820s and the coming of a more improving, decorous and ordered world.

There were many reasons why satire got tamer in the 1820s. Its cultural purchase was already being challenged by the rise of new sensibilities and of a new pietism, and by the increasing cultural presence and idealization of women. For a while, these forces had been staunchly resisted, and were in any case offset at lower social levels by the rise of disaffected regency satire. The satirists were soon silenced, however, for the king's coronation in 1821 marked a moment of renewal after his father's sixty-year reign, while the revelation of his wife's infidelities followed by her death from 'constriction of the bowel' (she was as fond of calories as her husband) marked just as firm a moment of closure.[2] Over these events loomed the final comeuppance of London's extremist radicalism. In May 1820, watched by 100,000 people outside Newgate prison, the five Cato Street conspirators who had planned to assassinate half the Cabinet at dinner were hanged for treason and ritually decapitated, their blood-dripping heads then held up to the crowd in the old-fashioned way. The political climate changed also. Most shopkeepers, craftsmen and lower professional and commercial people remained as socially and politically marginalized as ever; but more liberal Tory governments increased hopes of reform as well as some reality of it, so that for five or so years after 1822 the satirical prints' commentaries on 'Old Corruption' were all but obliterated. When at last the Whigs replaced the Tories in office, their enfranchisement of middle-class males in 1832 won hearty approval among the middling sorts of people.

But even these forces can't fully account for the transition. In these conditions a refashioned 'correctness' also took hold and, as ever, the prints show its deepening purchase. Satirical vocabularies so softened that one doubts whether a single print of the 1820s featured a buttock or a fart, let alone royal ones. Some despairing radical publishers turned to clandestine erotica to sustain their fading market, but the leading firms left that alone. Thomas Tegg abjured caricature altogether, while Humphrey's and Fores's shops virtually stopped publishing political satires and turned to comedies of domestic and middle-class manners instead. By the late 1820s, Thomas McLean was leading the print trade, and his comic scrapbooks and vignettes by Cruikshank and others spoke for a shrewd sense of what the bulk of the market now wanted.

When in 1820–21 a leading satire publisher like Tegg could turn loyalist overnight, when Cruikshank, harshest of the regent's scourges, could be so easily bribed into silence, and when even the once-defiant William Hone so swiftly discovered the profits of decorum, we're faced with such abrupt capitulations to the new order that some scepticism about the depth of such people's earlier disaffection may be called for. Moderate radicals had never been innocent of impulses that cut against their political frustrations. When Caroline landed to claim her crown in 1820, for example, William Hazlitt took the sourest view of the ensuing public fervour. 'Here,' he wrote, 'were all the patriots and jacobins of London and Westminster who scorned and hated the king, going to pay their homage to the queen and ready to worship the very rags of royalty . . . No matter what else she was (whether her case were right or wrong) – it was the mock equality with sovereign rank, the acting in a farce of state, that was the secret charm. That was what drove them mad.' Respectable people and radicals alike, he added, were only too ready to bow to 'hereditary imbecility'; for the most obsequious radical queenites had included 'the wives and daughters of popular caricaturists and of forgotten demagogues'.[3]

The truth was that many competing forms of communal and personal identification gave meaning to the lives of middling-class people: shared craft or patriotic or religious interests, for instance, and most particularly a self-differentiating view of *manners* – a more energetic insistence, that is, on the behavioural differences that should exist between a rising people and the roughs beneath and the elites above them. This explains why so many who sustained the radical anger of the regency years could, in modestly improving conditions, renege on it a mere year or two later. The postures conveyed in the words 'respectability' and 'respectable' were by no means peculiar to our era. Respectable tradesmen had kept their distance from the lowest classes and had led lives that were proper and prudent in the seventeenth century. Yet it suggests the rapid diffusion and social location of those qualities that the words that described them were unknown to Dr Johnson's *Dictionary*, even in its later eighteenth-century editions. The modern *Oxford English Dictionary* dates the first uses of 'respectability' and 'respectable' to 1785. Their currency accelerated spectacularly thereafter.

Francis Place was right to argue that the main engine behind this diffusion was a modest rise in the better shopkeepers' and craftsmen's economic expectations. Indeed, it was to cater to this rising market that the City printshops had multiplied in the 1810s, to mirror back to it its comic but also increasingly prosperous foibles. Not for nothing did Rowlandson lampoon tradesmen's aspirations and rising pretensions in prints like *The Hopes of the Fammily* [sic], *or Miss Marrowfat Home for the Holidays*

**Fig. 285** Rowlandson, *The Hopes of the Fammily, or Miss Marrowfat Home for the Holidays* (Tegg, 1809)

(1809), in which the daughter returns from the boarding-school that her alderman-butcher father can now afford, to gratify her mother by singing to the lute at the back of the shop, while her father serves the meat at the front [fig. 285]. Not for nothing, in his *Taylor Turn'd Lord* (1812), did Rowlandson mock the fancy airs even of tailors [fig. 286]. To be sure, these people's affluence shouldn't be overstated: it's minorities among them that matter here, not all of them. Most of the 30,000 or so families of London's middle sorts still had political and social exclusion to put up with, as well

**Fig. 286** Rowlandson, *Taylor Turn'd Lord* (Rowlandson, 1812)

as heavy post-war taxation. Most were chronically anxious about the impact of illness, trade depression or bankruptcy, and hopes of serious upward mobility were beyond them. As the radical journalist T. J. Wooler pointed out in 1817, many were 'now in no better a situation, and [had] worse prospects before them, than when they began life . . . Many have lived single, in hopes of one day supporting a wife, and maintaining a family in comfort; but the phantom of ease has always fled before them, at the approach of the tax-gatherer.'[4] So 'comfortable' is too strong a word to describe most of these people. Still, to this condition there were countless exceptions. Those who could snare fashionable custom or capitalize on skill were beginning to run profitable businesses. By 1822, Place noted how his former London Corresponding Society associates of the 1790s, once journeymen or shopmen and radical to a man, were 'now all in business all flourishing men'. Some (like himself) were 'rich', he wrote, and could give their children 'good educations'.[5]

When not pious, these people's tastes were still low, their humour rough, and their manners as unpolished as those of Rowlandson's butcher and tailor. But, along with the nouveaux riches 'cits', they had every interest in distancing themselves from the low people from whom they had risen. This they achieved, as Roy Porter put it, by consciously pursuing virtue. Steering between the self-indulgent depravities of the swells and the animality of the mob, they insisted that their economic rise spoke for their moral and cultural distinction. How better to establish their status than by repudiating rough habits on the one hand while cocking a snook on the other hand at the aristocratic cultures that excluded them – by insisting that their culture was more moral?[6] So people of this kind must repudiate hedonism, defend monogamy, attack obscenity and lewdness and, as evangelicals or dissenters, insist that religion embodied a crusade and not mere outward worship. In these senses, respectability may be regarded as a way of coping with inequality. Although often snobbish, it could sustain radical attitudes also, since those who had made the best of their lives could believe that others should have chances to do so equally.

Shopkeepers' and craftsmen's 'respectability' differed from what cultivated eighteenth-century people had thought of as 'politeness'. Politeness had been an elite, oppositional and socializing creed, harnessed to the pursuit of civic virtue, even if by the end of the century its Shaftesburian bases were diluted as it came to entail an outward display of the genteel graces – Shaftesbury's mere 'embroidery, guilding, colouring, daubing'. Respectable people similarly affirmed status through symbolic consumption, attitude and behaviour, but what characterized it more was that sense of personal worth that is common to upwardly mobile if still marginalized people. The key point now is that, whatever the form it took, respectability went ill with unseemly, mocking or bawdy humour. In the long term, a popular and confrontational satire, hatched from below and directed at the powerful, shared the fate of all satire in cultures that were discovering the rewards of good manners and the purchasing power to express them. In and after the 1820s, the vast promise of a radical satire that was held out during the regency years was quenched in the autodidact's po-faced aspiration.

## Francis Place's 'watershed'

Francis Place had never personally known the destitution he encountered during that early Lambeth visit of his; but he still came from humble origins. He was born in 1771 into penny-pinching poverty in a Drury Lane tenement, the illegitimate son of a sponging-house (i.e. debtors' prison) keeper who later ran a tavern. His father, he recalled, had the coarseness of the old manners. 'A resolute, daring, straightforward sort of a man, governed almost wholly by his passions and animal sensations', he was proud of his own 'sturdiness and dissoluteness', and spent his time 'drinking, whoring, gaming, fishing and fighting'. Young Place rejected this model and set about his own and others' improvement. After serving his apprenticeship in 1785–9 to a breeches-maker, he helped organize a trade strike in 1793, and suffered great hardship when the masters closed their shops against him. Between 1794 and 1797 he was active in the artisan-radical London Corresponding Society. Then, after nightmarish setbacks, he opened his own tailor's shop in Charing Cross in 1799, and within a few years turned himself into a fashionable tradesman. He stayed true to his radical principles, although his deepening utilitarian and Malthusian beliefs were to cost him the approval of radicals like Cobbett. He became a key wheeler-dealer in Westminster's radical politics, and helped Sir Francis Burdett's electoral campaigns in and after 1807. By the 1820s and 1830s, he was campaigning for popular education, free trade unions, and (with Richard Carlile) the spread of birth-control knowledge. The philosophers James Mill and Jeremy Bentham patronized him, and parliamentary committees asked his advice on questions like education and the drunkenness of the people. His was a remarkable story of upward mobility.

In middle age, Place also became the most compulsive of all chroniclers of London's humbler life, his close annotations moved by deepening optimism about his own and his class's ongoing 'improvement'. Having begun his note-taking in 1819, he was encouraged by Bentham in 1823 to record his world more systematically by producing a 'correctly detailed domestic history' and an autobiography that would show how manners had improved across his lifetime. In the event, the larger history remained unwritten, while the autobiography was so rough-hewn that it was left unpublished for 150 years. But the evidence Place assembled is now preserved in the forty-one hefty volumes of autobiographical drafts and of notes and cuttings on London politics and manners that he left at his death. Most have been well combed by historians of political radicalism, but the six volumes which he entitled 'Relating to manners and morals, 18th and 19th centuries' have been analysed less fully. They include notes on the 'grossness' of eighteenth-century books and street-songs, on the past prevalence and present diminution (he believed) of drunkenness, begging and crime, and on improvements in everything from education and travel to London's club-life.[7]

The power of observation revealed in these volumes is exceptional, for Place had the power of total recall that often characterizes lively minds bounded within small territories. Until his later years, he never lived more than a mile from the Drury Lane tenement of his birth; he lived south of the river only once, and then briefly; and only once before his late thirties did he venture more than thirty miles from London. Most of the sixteen lodgings he and his family occupied before 1799 were cramped single rooms in dank courtyards off the Strand or Holborn. His move to Charing Cross in that year took him only half a mile from his birthplace. The result of this close focus is that his voluminous notes and autobiographical musings offer as closely observed a record of workaday London as Boswell's diaries do of literary London a half-century earlier. Place had none of Boswell's introspection or subtlety. He was a clumsy, self-taught and not fully literate writer, and he lacked a sense of both irony and humour. But he monitored humble and middling-class London with an intensity that Boswell could never have attempted. He recorded the traffic outside his window, the number of horses and carts in the street, the furnishings and humble rooms of his youth, the dirtiness of casement windows in those days, the stenches of workshops, courtyards and back-alleys, the filthiness of clothes, the casual violence and ill-treatment of Jews, the prostitutes, ballad-singers and obscene picture-vendors of the Strand and Whitehall, and the bawdy cock-and-hen conviviality of apprentices, girls and publicans in the unimproved 1780s.

Place's aim in all this was single-minded. It was to reveal the truth that 'instead of mankind growing worse and worse they grow better and better and that the wisdom of our ancestors may be too highly prized'. He had no doubt that 'the progress made in [the] refinement of manners and morals' had ensued not only from 'the improvements in arts manufactures and commerce' initiated some sixty years before, but also from humble people's own efforts and from their deepening 'love of distinction'. It was the people themselves that achieved their own progress: anti-vice evangelicals and meddlers had nothing to do with it. (A freethinker, he subscribed to no religious or morally reformist societies other than the British and Foreign School Society.) The difference between 'then' and 'now' recurs throughout his papers, and never once does that difference fail to underscore 'progress'. In his youth, for example, London workmen had been 'ignorant and dissolute': now, 'the difference between skilled workmen and common labourers is as strongly marked as was the difference [then] between the workman and his employer'. 'The reformation of manners are [*sic*] almost wholly attributable to [skilled men's?] exertions.' Thanks to the rise of political societies and reading clubs, Sunday schools and new teaching methods, though helped by policing also, the outcome was certain: 'Some say we have refined away all our simplicity and have become artificial, hypocritical and upon the whole worse than we were half a century ago. This is a common belief, but it is a false one, we are a much better people now than we were then, better instructed, more sincere and kind hearted, less gross and brutal, and have fewer of the concomitant vices of a less civilized state.' In short, Place's was the most confident of all contemporary claims that English culture had reached a 'watershed' by the 1820s. It was unique in asserting that people like him were the key agents in that process.[8]

Place's vision was selective and flawed. He took the experience of his own trades circle for the whole. He had no developed sense of plebeians, and only thinly registered their miseries except when he insisted that they were diminishing. He wrote little about aristocratic, libertine London, or about high-life and low-life interpenetrations. About both the West and the East End of London he was relatively silent. And he occasionally described the sink of filth and iniquity that was his apprentice-day London so salivatingly that one discerns a suppressed relish for them. Nonetheless, his vision has authority because it was researched. It was not a mere wishful thinker, for example, who compiled his 'specimens of songs and parts of songs (from memory) sung about the streets within my recollection and without molestation'. Rather, he conscientiously called on his middle-aged cronies (Mr Tijou, 'a carver and gilder in a large way of business in Greek Street, Soho', and Richard Hayward, a struggling attorney who had been one of Place's colleagues in the London Corresponding Society) to help him remember the songs, however lewd.[9] Nor did he opine loosely about the 'grossness' of the past century's literature. Instead, he bought, read and cited closely from it. And he got many things right. Rejecting the notion that crime was increasing, for example, he knew that it was merely better recorded.

Underneath it all, however, Place's history of his times entailed a projection of his own experience of improvement on to the experiences of workaday London. In repudiating past vulgarities, in distancing himself from the low world that he and his kind had outgrown, in his priggish humourlessness, earnestness and vanity about his own distinction, he turned himself into another of the old laughter's enemies, speaking in this for many at aspirant middling levels, and announcing the coming of more sober times.

———•—•———

Place's six volumes on eighteenth-century 'manners and morals' include a great wodge of 'extracts from publications mostly sold at respectable booksellers without disguise'. The extracts are headed 'Grossness. Books etc. 1705–1795', and in them a now 'inconceivable' grossness is all he sees.[10] Blind to art, Place unfortunately wrote nothing about prints, but his comments on these extracts make it clear that he would have deplored most of them. It is easy now to sniff at his priggish responses, but he was a man of his times. His literary views were anticipated in Chalmers' survey of the *English Poets* (1810), for example (he quoted from it), and Thomas Bowdler had already sanitized Shakespeare. If a repressed voyeurism induced him to cite the worst of his texts at length or to transcribe verbatim the mind-boggling obscenities of the old street-songs, his opinions were at least conscientiously evidenced, and served to shock him into a sense of change. What results in his notes is an immodest anthology of uncensored citation that endorses his conviction that his was indeed a watershed era.

By 'grossness' Place meant sexual or scatological explicitness, and some of his citations were gross by any standard. Others, however, came from what is now thought of as the literary canon, their complex ironies quite lost on him. Thus around Defoe, Fielding and Smollett, around the earlier poets Charles Cotton and Matthew Prior, then around Rolleston's *Philosophical Dialogue Concerning Decency: To which is Added a Critical and Historical Dissertation on Places of Retirement for Necessary Occasions* (1751) (a book, he thought, that measured 'the grossness of taste of the better sort of people')[11] – and then again around more frankly scurrilous works like *On the Benefits of Farting*, Ned Ward's *London Spy*, Harris's *List of Covent Garden Ladies*, and *The Life and Adventures of William B[rad]s[ha]w Commonly Called Devil Dick* (possibly Defoe's)[12] – around each of these and more, Place's narrow judgements flow in what fast becomes a dreary predictability. 'Disgusting', 'filthy', 'vulgar', 'licentious', 'nasty', 'obscene', 'loose', 'downright bawdy', 'silly', 'bad', 'infamous', 'obnoxious', 'disgraceful': these are the words that constitute his critical vocabulary, and in each instance he registers incredulity that such things had been so widely read, not so long ago.

'It would be difficult in the present day,' Place writes of Cotton's burlesques on Virgil, for example, 'to find a man who was not perfectly low lived who would be able to find anything like wit in the whole poem. It is bad in every sense and would [now] be a disgrace to a respectable bookseller who should publish it, and no such bookseller were he to print it would find a sale for it, sufficient to cover his expenses.' To prove the point he cites Cotton's account of Venus's error when she disguises herself as a country maid: 'A great mistake in her whose bum / So oft had been god Mars his drum / When oft, full oft the lusty drum-stick, / Breaking quite through would in her bum stick.'[13] He notes, further, that the half-crown charged for Ned Ward's *Complete and Humorous Account of all the Remarkable Clubs and Societies* meant that it had been bought by master tradesmen and 'the lesser gentry', 'few of whom could now look into the book without disgust'. He notes that *Devil Dick* was published by booksellers 'nearly at the top of their trade', despite its 'filthy story' of prostitutes and its 'low-lived' adventures in crime, cross-dressing and nudity: 'these and such like adventures were common half or three quarters of a century ago, while now they are rare, many persons at those times went through a series of low, vulgar, infamous adventures, which no one goes through now.' Bad books were still being published, Place admitted, but only 'by low obscure people of bad character', and none would 'use the gross vulgar language which this book contains'. The courtesan Harriette Wilson's recent *Memoirs* of 1825 might suggest otherwise, but Place stresses that they were published by J. J. Stockdale, an 'infamous scoundrel', 'common cheat' and bankrupt, who had been 'expelled from society for several years past'. But at least Harriette's book had 'nothing in it which is grossly expressed[;] its meaning in all places is clear enough, but the words in which the meaning is conveyed are not gross and low, like those in *Devil Dick*'.

Place is surprised by the things that women had once tolerated. He scours the 1749 volume of the *Lady's Magazine or Universal Entertainer*, and clucks in disbelief at an advertisement for a soap 'which leaves behind it a most delicious agreeable and fragrant smell, when all other soaps leave a *nauseous stench*' ('soaping' or 'lathering' a metaphor for sex). He disapproves of the magazine's bawdy stories – about a girl, for example, who impregnated herself with wind-borne 'animalcules' by admitting 'this tickling agent [the wind] up her petticoats': 'very profitable for young masters and mistresses, in the *Lady's Magazine*,' he sighs. What ladies, he further asks, would now tolerate verses in their own magazine about a lady sitting cross-legged to play a gentleman at cards? 'What various charms can Celia boast, / By nature how befriended, / Whose legs are both a charm when cross'd / And charming when extended.' He is shocked when Lady Mary Wortley Montagu extolled 'the animal spirits' that sanctioned a man enjoying 'rapture with his cook maid'. And he is stunned by Matthew Prior's *Curious Maid*, who gazes at her private parts by straddling a mirror on the floor: 'And is this all, is this, she cry'd, / Man's great desire and woman's pride?' Then he relates anecdotes about Prior's sexual and alcoholic life, and shocks himself by noting Dr Johnson's approval of Prior's 'gross' poetry.

Finally, he has a field-day with *Harris's List of Covent Garden Ladies*. This, he explains, was once an annual publication 'sold openly in booksellers shop[s]'. The 1786 edition he owned contained the names of 105 women who (he quotes in disbelief) 'seem the most pleased with that refined sensation, [who] wantonly and mutually enjoy the extatic bliss, [and who] return with equal vigor . . . the meeting shower, and sigh for sigh, the gasping torrent pour'. Disgusted he might be, but Place doesn't fail then to transcribe the pinings, say, of Miss M–ll–r of New Compton Street (her price one guinea): 'Lovely man, assuage my anguish, / See supine a tender maid / Begs you will not let her languish / One good — will ease the jade.

/ Did you know how brisk her motion / You need not long f— alone; / Prince of nature's balmy lotion, / Nine inches long without the bone.' Nor does he censor the charms of Miss L—e of 30 Newman Street, whose 'seat of love' is 'supported on two marble pillows framed by the just hand of symmetry', and whose 'raven coloured harbour of bliss' is guarded by her 'blushing clytoris, now swelling with delight, now reddening with desire': 'Apply then, ye sons of pleasure, the full swell'd engine and stem the rapid torrent. Three guineas is the price.' Place did, however, think it another sign of improvement that he had had to scour a hundred bookshops before he could find a copy of *Harris's List* to quote from.

## Charing Cross and London's refashioning

The London explored in Part I of this book was a very hierarchized society but also a fluid one. The chasms between rich and poor weren't easily bridged; yet, in the metropolis, low-born and high-born men of louche disposition knew more of each other than their differing manners and ambiences might have suggested. In the convivial and sporting enthusiasms of great men on the razzle, in their controlled interminglings with Covent Garden tarts, actors, artists, publicans, pugilists or beggars, shared understandings were generated that in those conditions could make class boundaries hazy. The bawdy, sardonic and satirical casts of humour that were common to all these people were determined by the frames and opportunities of low London living. But what London once gave, it began increasingly to withhold. When – with its prize-fights, cock-fights, bull-baitings, public hangings and turbulent electoral hustings – the 'naughty old England' began to be 'improved out of existence', its 'broad-blown comic sense' was set to disappear with it.[14] By the 1820s, London was itself beginning to be washed, combed, clothed and taught good manners. This induced a new sense of separation among its people, even as it endorsed an optimism about their improvement that matched the improvement of the city itself.

By the time Place began to record it, London was a city of constant renewal. Streets were being widened, bridges built and old houses demolished; while the new Regent's Street carved out a symbolic as well as actual boundary between the West End and the old town. Place was unique in the attention he gave to these changes, for he knew that urban improvement was the material correlative of the watershed in manners that he and others were reaching. He testified to this in the close attention he gave to changes in his own narrow patch of Charing Cross, where he lived from 1799 onwards. Over several decades he noted nearly everything that moved in that territory. As he did so, he exposed those contiguities of squalor and dilapidation, of past and present grandeur, of high and low living that had informed the comic vision of his younger days, but which were being obliterated as he lived there. His papers propel us towards a microscopic view of that central territory, and their promptings we now follow.

In those of us today who have to cope with megapolitan London, an older sense of the town has become much attenuated. Victorian demolitions, modern office blocks, countless road-widenings, and the present swamp of traffic make it difficult to visualize the past realities of this once human-scaled city. In the traffic-murdered space that is now Charing Cross, therefore, it is almost impossible to imagine the conscious directional adjustments that shaped millions of past journeyings there. There, for two millennia, the east–west 'Strand' or riverside route from the City has turned sharply south to Westminster, and just as there Dr Johnson's 'full tide of human existence' simply had to flow, so it must still. But the Charing Cross houses and shops that Place knew are gone. Their friendly human disorder rematerializes in one of the precise pencil drawings of the Bavarian immigrant lithographer, George Scharf. His drawing of northern Charing Cross and St Martin's Lane on the eve of their demolition shows the

**Fig. 287** George Scharf, *Charing Cross in 1830. Looking Northward* [detail] (pencil sketch, 1830)

variformed roof patterns, shopfronts and antique taverns, the shouting notices and fascia-boards, the steps, bollards, street lights, railings, 'areas', small-paned windows and shop-window displays, which everyone took for granted before improvement had its way [fig. 287].[15]

In the seventeenth century, the vistas around Charing Cross had been only thinly developed. While St James's Park had led to open pastures to the west, you would have looked across the Thames from the coal wharfs of Scotland Yard to fields where the South Bank is now. Down Whitehall, your view would have been blocked by the Holbein Gate that opened on to the huge sprawl of Whitehall Palace. This royal domain stretched up from Westminster through the Privy Gardens (opposite the present Horse

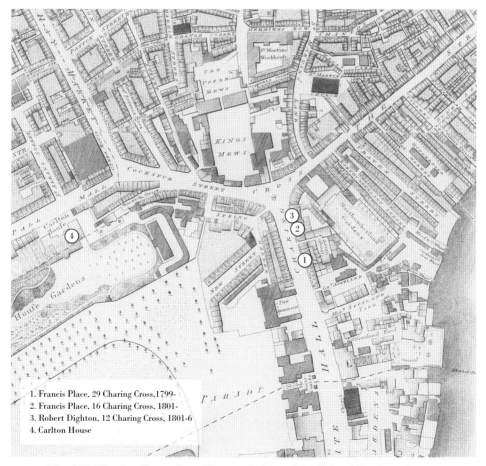

1. Francis Place, 29 Charing Cross, 1799-
2. Francis Place, 16 Charing Cross, 1801-
3. Robert Dighton, 12 Charing Cross, 1801-6
4. Carlton House

**Fig. 288** Charing Cross, from Horwood, *Plan of the Cities of London and Westminster*, 1799

Guards) to the old Scotland Yards (where the Scottish kings had lodged when paying homage to the English Crown), and right up to the tenement houses Place was to live in. In 1698 a laundrywoman accidentally burned down most of the palace, or at least, she got the blame. The court then moved to St James's Palace, and still lived there under George III. Holbein Gate was removed in 1759, so that when Place arrived all that was left of past splendour was Inigo Jones's Banqueting House in Whitehall, along with the decaying dwellings, stables and kitchens of the Scotland Yards, the Privy Gardens, and the jumble of Tudor houses and yards of which his tenements formed the northernmost part [fig. 288]. Most of this didn't last much longer. Middle and Little Scotland Yards were being demolished within Place's earshot while he lived doors away. Planted with new houses in 1820, Great Scotland Yard nine years later was to accommodate in no. 4 the headquarters of the metropolitan police, its associations thus transformed utterly. Craig's Court, rebuilt in 1702, survived from the antique jumble, while the imposing Tudor façade of Northumberland House also still loomed over Charing Cross until it was demolished for Northumberland Avenue to be driven through the site in 1874. Place's tenements were duly replaced by Victorian office buildings. Nos. 9 to 28 Charing Cross are now renamed as 1 to 39 of modern Whitehall.

In the façades of the Horse Guards and the Admiralty, the west side of the street still bears some of its old dignity. Great people lived there. Even as Place redecorated his house across the road, the Melbournes danced out their giddy sexual gavottes in Melbourne House, now the Scottish Office. Had Place looked out of his window on 12 August 1812, he would have witnessed the collapse of Byron's affair with Lady Caroline Lamb: she frantically running past into Pall Mall, pursued by servants, after Lord Melbourne had rebuked her for her sexual excesses.[16] Now gone, however, are the fine houses along the upper-western front of Charing Cross. These had once projected back into Spring Garden, a pleasure-ground built over after the Restoration, its public entertainments sent westwards to the gardens at Vauxhall. Here, in the former Huguenot chapel, J. C. Bach had directed concerts and Mozart had made his London debut. James Cox adapted the chapel for his museum of mechanical curiosities in 1772 (charging a half-guinea entry fee to keep out the rough elements), and for the next half-century the chapel remained one of London's busiest exhibition halls.[17] The learned pig that Rowlandson commemorated [fig. 8] was exhibited at no. 55. George Canning lived on the corner of Cockspur Street in 1799, and

Carlton House was a few minutes away along Pall Mall. In short, this westerly side of Charing Cross was still predominantly elegant, and it led on westwards to St James's. All the same, you had only to cross to Place's side of the street to meet otherworldly squalor.

Place's first shop and house, no. 29, was one of a line of capacious, old and disreputable tenements that had once belonged to courtiers. A lease for no. 29 survives from 1547, granted by the king. A drawing dated 1610 shows what nos. 9 to 28 had then looked like. They were three- or four-storeys high, narrow, timber-framed, gabled and lattice-windowed, and they stretched back several rooms on each floor. No. 16, to which Place moved in 1801, was 140 feet deep and contained thirty rooms. Squared-off facades were added in the eighteenth century, but other improvements were superficial.[18] The backs of the houses, Place noted, were built in an 'old fashioned style' but 'in a very expensive manner'. They had red-brick pilasters and capitals to make them look smart when viewed from the Privy Gardens. No. 16 he found 'old fashioned and very old'. Its cellar was vaulted and groined, and its front door was four feet wide and four inches thick; with barred gratings at the top and at eye-level, it was 'as strong as a gaol door'. It led on to a 'very old fashioned staircase' lit by 'a large old fashioned lamp' which burned all night.

While the western side of Charing Cross boasted fashionable concert and exhibition rooms, Place's eastern side he regarded as 'infamous'. This infamy he certainly exaggerated. In fact, craftsmen, artists and artisans still lived there, cheek by jowl with whores and rougher people in those easy proximities that characterized most of workaday London. The caricaturist Robert Dighton, for example, sold his prints at no. 12, four doors away from Place's second house. On the other hand, some of his neighbouring houses, with ground floors 'about 6 steps below the foot pavement', were indeed 'inhabited by very low dirty people'. His own no. 16 was surrounded by four public houses, three gin shops, and five houses of what he called ill fame – all frequented by 'common soldiers and common women of the lowest description'. The fourteen ancient houses in Trinity Place behind his own were dens 'of the lowest and worst description' in which nearly every room was rented by prostitutes. 'The place could not be outdone in infamy and indecency by any place in London. The manner in which many of the drunken filthy young prostitutes behaved is not describable nor would it [now] be beleived [*sic*] were it described.' The whole territory was one of saturated sensation. In 1795 in a crimping house 'of the very worst sort' (press-ganged army recruits were confined there), a man delirious from smallpox escaped on to the roof, from which 'he fell naked into the street. A mob collected and destroyed every thing the house contained'; one of the rioters was later hanged outside no. 28.[19] Bawdy song-sellers had their pitches along the Privy Garden walls, while the pillory was located in the centre of Charing Cross, under Charles I's statue and a stone's throw from Place's windows. Miscreants were exposed there at the dinner hour when streets were most crowded. Except when they cheered popular heroes like Daniel Isaac Eaton, the pillory crowd was considerably less jolly than the crowd Rowlandson depicted in one of Ackermann's *Microcosms of London* (1808–10) [fig. 289]. People were expected to pelt the victim with dead cats, eggs, cabbages and dung, women being allowed to throw from the front if they tipped the constables first. Eyes were lost and blood flowed in the mud on these occasions, and those pilloried for 'unnatural' crimes could die.[20]

**Fig. 289** Rowlandson and A. C. Pugin, *Charing Cross Pillory* (from W. H. Pyne and W. Combe, *The Microcosm of London*, Ackermann, 1808–10)

When Place moved into no. 16, its front room was occupied by a barber and then a printseller, the basement by a grocer, and the upstairs rooms by whores. The rear of the house contained the so-called Royal Bagnio. This seems to have been a part of the old Turk's Head tavern, renamed the Rummer after the original Rummer was destroyed by fire in 1750. Timber-built, it was 'very old, and the floors . . . much out of the level' when surveyed in 1811.[21] Hogarth's *Night* (1738) depicts the alley that ran down the side of no. 16 to the old Rummer's main entrance [fig. 6]. The print takes great liberties with the topography, but it does indicate the tavern and the barber's pole; and two signboards advertise bagnios, though neither is 'Royal'. The bagnio had a communicating door straight into Place's no. 16, which didn't please him at all. The baths were long associated with aristocratic orgies and purchased sex; James Boswell and William Hickey were among many rakes who had taken girls there. Place was gratified that the baths were losing money by the time he moved in. To preserve them from ruin their owner, a Strand hotel-keeper, had to let to one of his waiters 'the large and noble cold bath, the hot baths sweating room and other conveniences'. If living next to the bagnio was bad, living next to the Rummer was worse. A 'long celebrated brothel', Place called it. Samuel Pepys in 1693 had arranged to meet a highwayman in the original tavern, hoping to retrieve goods stolen from him. In 1722, the criminal hero Jack Sheppard stole two silver spoons from the tavern, his first known theft. An Old Bailey trial in 1754 of Mary Lewis for picking pockets confirms Place's view of the place:

I was coming along the Strand in company with Robert Mitchel Edwards, on the 5th of July about 10 o'clock at night, we overtook the prisoner [Mary Lewis] and another woman together, they tossed up their hoops to let us pass, and the prisoner said, Lord! every body is admiring my breast as they go along. Lord, said I, perhaps they are worth admiring, she turned round and said how do you do, my dear, will you give me a glass of wine, and took hold of my hand; with all my heart, said I, then they brought us down to the Rummer by Charing-Cross; when we came in we called for a bottle of port, we were in a room below stairs . . . Then she came to me and turned up all her clothes to her navel, and sat down on my knee, and said my dear; I said, my dear, I'll have nothing to say to you, she unbuttoned my breeches before, and pulled all out shirt and all. Then I turned round and buttoned them up again; by G—d, said she, I will be st—d [stuffed?] by you, and came and unbuttoned them again.[22]

This environment couldn't have been much worse than the Drury Lane that Place was born in. But, as he prospered, he set out to improve it. When he had first moved into no. 29 with his family and his business partner, they had done so by night to conceal the poverty of their furniture, opened their tailor-shop with a mere 1s 10d left between them. Then they hit on the idea of displaying men's fancy waistcoats in the window, the first shop in the West End (he says) to do so. Soon profits began to show, and Place began 'dancing attendance on silly people, to make myself acceptable to coxcombs'.[23] By Christmas 1800, thirty-two tailors were working for them. When his partner deserted him, Place moved to no. 16, borrowing £60 to rent the front shop, parlour and first-floor bedroom, along with a workshop backing on to Trinity Place. This outlay again impoverished him: he had 'scarcely any furniture and hardly a change of cloathes'. But business recovered and his ambitions with it, and he began to expand his domain over the whole house.

His account of what ensued nicely indicates why Tudor interiors are so rare today. First, he put in a new shopfront, 'as elegant as the place would permit'. It had 'the largest plate glass windows in London', each pane costing him £2; two further panes in the door cost £4 apiece. Then, lighting the shop brightly, he employed his men in the shop to give an impression of busyness. In 1805, having displaced the billiard-room owner from the first floor upstairs, he pulled down the house's 'enormous' chimney stack, cleared the first floor of its 'very old, small panelled wainscoating', plundered some of the bagnio's marble to make a living-room fireplace, and put in a new floor and ceiling. He 'made a capital water closet on the first floor', changed the first-floor bedroom to a kitchen, and made five other rooms 'all modern all neat and good in a very plain stile' – thus achieving 'as handsome a suite of apartments as a man with moderate views could well desire to have'. In 1812 he bought out the billiard-room owner from the second floor, and turned out 'the vagabonds who resorted to it, and made it respectable'. It helped that the deplored Rummer was taken over by Clowes the printer. By 1816 Place was able to pull down the whole back of the house, the bagnio included. At last the whole house was his, and he could claim, a little implausibly, that his business was making £2,500 a year.[24]

From his now spacious quarters, Place returned to radical politics. No. 16 became famous as a reformers' library and a headquarters of the Burdettite cause.[25] By then, the whole neighbourhood was improving. Whores still did business at Charing Cross (well beyond the mid-nineteenth century), but the Rummer and the bagnios were gone, and the houses got smarter. Fifty or so Charing Cross shopkeepers climbed up the social ladder alongside Place. The Westminster poll-book for 1818 shows that there were three Burdett-voting bootmakers, along with a Burdettite tailor, watchmaker, clothier, mapseller, eating-house keeper and victualler. These radicals were surrounded, however, by ministry-voting drapers, hatters, poulterers, grocers, fishmongers, opticians, musical instrument makers, teadealers and lottery officials. They outnumbered radical voters by three to one. This was despite Place's neighbourhood leadership of the Burdettite cause – or perhaps because of it, since his vanity was famously offensive. Doubtless what swung most of these non-radical voters was the hard-won respectability that increasing numbers of them shared.

———•———

And so this story ends in the age of improvement, as well as in the age of the cant that should be associated with it. Satire's deepening obsolescence is framed by a better-washed, better-combed and better-mannered cityscape and by mounting shopkeeper prosperity. 'Everybody complains,' William Blake had written in 1803, 'yet all go on cheerfully and with spirit. The shops in London improve; everything is elegant, clean and neat; the streets are widened where they were narrow; even Snow Hill is become almost level and is a very handsome street, and the narrow part of the Strand near St Clements is widened and becomes very elegant.'[26] Waterloo Bridge was opened in 1817, and the approaches to the new London Bridge were cleared and the first piles driven in 1824. Nash's new Regent Street was in use by now, deliberately segregating the polite west London of fine squares and terraces from the turbulent artisan London of Covent Garden and Soho, thus inserting a more than merely symbolic chasm between them. In 1821, the Theatre Royal was erected in the Haymarket to Nash's design, so that, just as St James's Street offered a vista on to the palace, St James's Square offered one on to the theatre's pedimented façade – and still does. The most resonant element in this refashioning was the king's demolition of Carlton House in 1826, scene of so much past extravagance and dissipation. Deciding that his mansion was too modest for a great monarch, George IV replaced it with the fine stuccoed houses which are now Carlton Terrace and began to reconstruct Buckingham House at the end of the Mall. A few years later, Nash's Charing Cross improvement scheme brought down the vast courtyard and stables of the King's Mews, along with the shops, taverns and courtyards on the northern sides of Charing Cross and the Strand. In lower St Martin's Lane, 515 houses went as well, many brothels and gambling dens going with them. By 1830, Trafalgar Square replaced them, the National Gallery was built, and the church of St Martin's-in-the-Fields acquired its open ambience. Carlton House's Corinthian columns were re-erected on the Gallery's façade, where they still are. Nash had intended to drive an avenue from Trafalgar Square north-east to the British Museum and Bloomsbury. This would have demolished large sections of the Seven Dials and St Giles's rookeries, but that plan was abandoned.

Even after the Great Fire, Londoners had seen nothing like town planning on this scale, and west London and the western edges of the Covent Garden parishes were transformed by it. With its new vistas, London began to offer a sense of 'circulation'. Visitors returning to it in the late 1820s would have encountered a city that looked more ordered, planned and controlled than it had been. These changes paralleled campaigns for moral and political reform, the trading classes' improvement, and 'intellect's' onward march. The demolition of an old palace and the rise of a new one, the digging of real boundaries between elite west and artisan east, the construction of new streets and bridges from north to south, the rise of shopkeeper gentility (and of the policemen that shopkeepers paid for) – doubtless it was the middle sorts of people that celebrated these most, for London's new orderliness matched their own. There was to be much optimism among the upwardly aspirant in the coming decades, both about progress and their own part in advancing it. Materially, topographically, as well as culturally, we witness the coming of a more socially differentiated, ordered and decorous world. The old laughter found it more difficult to establish a rightful place in it.

# Brief Lives

**Ackermann, Rudolph** (1764–1834): German-born printseller, publisher and art patron; settled in London in 1787 as coach-designer; opened printshop at 101 Strand in 1797 ('The Repository of Arts' from 1798); sold decorative and art prints and over 100 Rowlandson caricatures, mainly non-political; published art books and works illustrated by Rowlandson, including *Microcosm of London* (1808–9), *Tours of Dr Syntax* (1812, 1820, 1821) and *Dance of Death* (1815–16).

**Benbow, William** (1784–*c*.1852): shoemaker and dissenting preacher turned radical publisher; associate after 1816 of *William Cobbett* and *Sir Francis Burdett*; imprisoned 1817; opened printshop and bookshop in the Strand in 1820 (later in High Holborn and Castle Street); supported *Queen Caroline* and published bawdy prints and literature, issuing twenty-three catalogued titles 1820–25; detained without trial for eight months in 1821 for caricaturing *George IV*; prosecuted for pirating Byron and for obscene publication in 1822; published erotica until 1827; influential in popular radicalism and Chartism thereafter.

**Bowles, Carington** (1724–93): inherited family's print firm established in the 1690s; specialized in mezzotints and comic 'drolls', avoiding political satire; his sons Henry Carington and Henry continued the business, the latter trading as Bowles and Carver.

**Boydell, John** (1719–1804): leading City art-print dealer; pioneered commercial art market by opening Shakespeare Gallery in Pall Mall in 1789 to exhibit paintings on Shakespearian and similarly elevated subjects; the Gallery failed when the French wars closed the print export trade.

**Burdett, Sir Francis** fifth baronet (1770–1844): aristocratic radical reformer; married into Coutts's banking fortune in 1793; attacked conditions in Cold Bath Fields prison in 1798; MP for Middlesex in 1805–6 and Westminster in 1807, helped by Francis Place and radical Westminster Committee; 1810 riots in Piccadilly supported him when House of Commons found him guilty of breach of privilege and had him arrested; proposed new Reform Bill in 1818; fined and imprisoned for three months for seditious libel in 1820 when he compared the king to Nero.

**Canning, George** (1770–1827): junior minister under Pitt; paid pension to Gillray in 1797 to produce loyalist and anti-Foxite propaganda and to work for his *Anti-Jacobin Review*; prime minister in 1827.

**Carlile, Richard** (1790–1843): radical publisher and writer; a Spencean and Paineite radical, imprisoned for reprinting William Hone's parodies in 1817; in 1819 opened bookshop at 55 Fleet Street; sentenced to six years' imprisonment for seditious libel; opened Fleet Street shop in 1826; campaigned with Francis Place for birth control; two years' imprisonment in 1831 for seditious libel; became a 'Christian atheist' and lecturer.

**Caroline of Brunswick, Princess of Wales** (1768–1821): married Prince of Wales in 1795, but separated after conceiving their only child, Princess Charlotte; excluded from court; left England for Mediterranean travels in 1813, spies thereafter reporting on her lurid liaisons; returned to popular acclamation to claim her crown when George became king in 1820; faced proceedings in the Lords as the king set about divorcing her in August; excluded from the coronation in July 1821 and died three weeks later of 'constriction of the bowel'.

**Clarke, Mary Anne** (1776?–1852): courtesan taken up in 1803 by Frederick, Duke of York, commander-in-chief of the army; in return for payment, added the names of officers seeking promotion to the duke's lists of commissions; scandal erupted 1809; the duke cleared of corruption but resigned his command (resuming it in 1811); William Cobbett exploited the scandal to make 'Old Corruption' the target of metropolitan radicalism; Rowlandson produced fifty-six caricatures on the scandal for Tegg.

**Cobbett, William** (1763–1835): political journalist; son of farm labourer, self-educated; loyalist bookseller and publisher by 1796; prosecuted for libel in 1797, but an active Tory journalist until 1804; from 1802 produced *Cobbett's Weekly Political Register* until his death; wrote in the radical interest from 1804; reactivated London radicals over the Mary Anne Clarke scandal, 1809; withdrew to America in 1817–19 to avoid prosecution; pro-Caroline 1820; sought to enter Parliament in 1821.

**Conyngham, Marchioness** (1769–1861): from 1820 the last of the Prince of Wales's mistresses, much mocked because her portliness matched his.

**Cruikshank, George** (1792–1878): caricaturist and comic illustrator; son of Isaac Cruikshank and brother of Robert; learned his art in his father's studio, finishing Isaac's prints and producing drolls for Laurie and Whittle; in 1808–11 produced a great range of prints for John Johnston and other City printshops; employed by Hannah Humphrey to finish Gillray's last prints; befriended by William Hone and William Jones in 1811; engraved forty-one satires for Jones's *The Scourge* magazine, some attacking the regent, his mistresses and ministers; in work for Tegg, Hone, Fores, Fairburn, the regent and Napoleon were his chief political targets until 1820; paid £100 by George IV in June 1820 to stop satirizing him; in 1823 abjured satire and turned to comic book illustration; across a long career the most versatile and prolific of comic artists.

**Cruikshank, Isaac** (1764–1811): caricaturist, father of George and Robert; born in Edinburgh, son of a customs inspector; trained in drawing and etching before moving to London in 1783; exhibited genre subjects at Royal Academy; produced drolls for Robert Sayer's and Laurie and Whittle's printshops and political satires for Fores and Fairburn; his favoured targets were the Prince of Wales, Fox and Napoleon; engraved 345 catalogued prints from 1793–1800, but 1,350 are attributed to him across his lifetime; died of alcoholic poisoning.

**Cruikshank, (Isaac) Robert** (1789–1856): caricaturist, eldest son of Isaac Cruikshank and brother of George; midshipman on East India Company ship; first visible as satirical engraver in a satire on Mary Anne Clarke scandal 1809; prolific in caricaturing dandies 1818–19 and the royal divorce scandal 1820; his and George's silence bought by George IV in 1820; allegedly originated Pierce Egan's *Life in London* (1820–21) for which he and George produced the prints; illustrated Westmacott's *English Spy* in 1825.

**Darly, Matthew** (*c*.1720–78?) and **Mary Darly** (*fl.* 1760–81): printsellers, Matthew the leading London print publisher from the 1750s, working from the Strand until *c*.1779; 313 catalogued titles in the 1780s, ahead of Carington Bowles (111), Sayer and Bennet (70), and William Humphrey (66); specialized in humorous 'drolls'; his wife Mary sold prints from Leicester Fields, moving to 159 Fleet Street in 1780; the last prints dated 1781.

**Dent, William** (*fl.* 1783–93): specialized in coarse caricature; allegedly received 'secret service' payment to lampoon Fox and Duchess of Devonshire during 1784 Westminster election.

**Dighton, Robert** (1751–1814): engraver and printseller, son of printseller; attended Royal Academy schools 1772; worked as portrait miniaturist and watercolourist and designer of Carington Bowles's mezzotints; occasionally exhibited at Academy; famous as a concert singer; sold his own caricatures from 12 Charing Cross in 1790s; supplemented income by stealing prints from British Museum 1798–1806; not to be confused with his son Robert Dighton (*c*.1786–1865), producer of caricature portraits between 1800 and 1809.

**Dolby, Thomas** (dates unknown): book and printseller from 1817; published twenty-eight catalogued satires against the king in 1820–22; prosecuted for seditious libel.

**Fairburn, John** (dates unknown): publisher and bookseller (shops in Blackfriars and Ludgate Hill); issued prints from 1811 onwards; after Tegg, the most prolific of the new print publishers; matched George Humphrey's output with some 275 titles across 1820–27.

**Fores, Samuel William** (1761–1838): printseller and art supplier, son of a bookseller; opened business at 3 Piccadilly 1783; dominated the satirical print trade ahead of Hannah Humphrey and William Holland, with 214 known titles in the 1780s; 1789–*c*.1792 exhibited caricatures and drawings for a shilling admission; moved to 50 Piccadilly in 1795; produced loyalist prints in 1790s, otherwise consistently liberal until 1820, opposed to constraints on free expression, and pro-queen in 1820; his dominance displaced by Thomas McLean in the later 1820s.

**Fox, Charles James** (1749–1806): Whig opposition leader and Prince of Wales's closest ally; sympathies for French Revolution kept him out of office until his short spell as Foreign Secretary in 1806.

**Frederick, Duke of York** (1763–1827): George III's second son; commander-in-chief from 1798 until the Mary Anne Clarke scandal forced him to resign in 1809 (but reinstated 1811); gambler and libertine.

**George Augustus Frederick, Prince of Wales, regent and King George IV** (1762–1830): first son of George III; well educated in youth but 'too fond of wine and women' and in constant debt; consorted with the Foxite Whigs and a succession of mistresses, including Mary (Perdita) Robinson and Charles James Fox's future mistress and wife, Mrs Armitstead; secretly and illicitly 'married' the Catholic Mrs Maria Fitzherbert in 1785; discarded her in favour of Lady Jersey; agreed to marry Caroline of Brunswick in 1795 in exchange for the settlement of his debts, the marriage failing almost immediately; in 1811 assumed the regency on his father's descent into madness and 'dropped' the Whigs, ensuring their enmity and pro-Caroline stance until 1821; held responsible for government repressions that culminated in the 'Peterloo massacre' of 1819; king in 1820; vainly sought a Bill of Pains and Penalties to punish Caroline for her adulteries; regained some popularity by the time of his coronation in July 1821 (Caroline dying three weeks later); found comfort during his reign on the Marchioness Conyngham's ample bosom.

**Gillray, James** (1756–1815): caricaturist, son of strict Calvinist; educated at Moravian school until 1764; apprenticed to lettering engraver; first known satire for William Humphrey in 1775; admitted to Royal Academy schools 1778 to study stipple engraving under Bartolozzi; in 1786 returned to satire after failing as art engraver; worked for Holland and Fores, then (from 1791) exclusively for Hannah Humphrey, with whom he lodged chastely for the rest of his life; loathed 'French principles' but avoided party allegiance until George Canning in 1797 gave him a £200 annual 'pension' to produce propaganda for *The Anti-Jacobin Magazine* and its successors; led attacks on the Foxites, the Prince of Wales, and Napoleon; produced some 1,000 prints in his lifetime (one third of them 'social and personal' satires) until eyesight and mind gave way in 1809.

**Heath, William** [*pseud.* Paul Pry] (1795–1840): prolific caricaturist of the 1820s, working for Thomas McLean chiefly.

**Hertford, Marchioness** (1760–1834): Prince of Wales's intimate friend *c.*1807–20, though not apparently his mistress (despite the satirists' belief otherwise); displaced by Lady Conyngham.

**Holland, William** (1757–1815): printseller and bookseller; opened first shop in Drury Lane in 1782, alongside a publisher of flagellation literature, George Peacock; moved to 50 Oxford Street in 1786, exhibiting his prints for one shilling admission in his 'Museum of Genius' 1788–*c.*1794; in the 1780s produced ninety-five catalogued titles, behind William Humphrey (100), Hannah Humphrey (109), and S. W. Fores (214); employed Gillray in 1786 and Richard Newton from 1791; imprisoned in 1793 for selling *Paine*'s pamphlets; output fell off thereafter.

**Hone, William** (1780–1842): radical bookseller and print publisher; joined the London Corresponding Society and set up as bookseller; in 1809 entered Westminster radical circles and edited liberal *Critical Review* 1814–15; opened Old Bailey bookshop and campaigned for reform; employed George Cruikshank to produce important satires; issued around ninety satirical titles 1815–22; campaigned against restrictions on free expression in his *Reformers' Register* (1817); tried in December 1817 for publishing 'blasphemous' parodies, his defence and acquittals making him the hero of radical and liberal London; published pamphlet satires against the ministry, illustrated by Cruikshank's woodcuts (notably *The Political House that Jack Built*, which sold over 100,000 copies in fifty-four editions); collaborated with Cruikshank until 1821, whereafter Hone repudiated satire; published his *Everyday Book* (1825), *Table Book* (1827) and *Year Book* (1832), and reconverted to Christianity in 1832.

**Humphrey, George** (dates unknown): printseller; succeeded to his aunt Hannah Humphrey's St James's Street shop on her death 1818; published George Cruikshank's anti-radical plates in 1819 and loyalist prints during the Queen's affair 1820–21; turned to humorous prints thereafter, leading the trade until Thomas McLean displaced him.

**Humphrey, Hannah** (*c.*1745–1818): printseller, sister of William Humphrey; shop in Old Bond Street *c.*1779; monopolized Gillray's prints from 1791; moved to 27 St James's Street in 1797; alongside S. W. Fores headed the satirical print trade until 1810, when Gillray's output collapsed due to insanity; died 1818, leaving business to George Humphrey, her nephew; output loyalist.

**Humphrey, William** (1742?–1814?): engraver and printseller, working 1772–4 from St Martin's Lane, 1775–7 from Gerrard Street, 1777–80 from 227 Strand; published 100 catalogued titles during the 1780s (third in output after Fores and

Hannah Humphrey but ahead of Carington Bowles); published Gillray's earliest satires; turned to portrait prints thereafter.

**Jersey, Lady** (1753–1821): Prince of Wales's mistress 1793–99; inaccurately caricatured as an old hag because already a grandmother.

**Johnston, John** (dates unknown): followed Tegg by opening 'cheap caricature warehouse' at 101 Cheapside; early employer of George Cruikshank; probably introduced Cruikshank to Jones and Hone 1811; imprint on some 130 catalogued prints by the late 1820s.

**Jones, William Naunton** (dates unknown): printer and publisher of the satirical *The Scourge; or, Monthly Expositor of Imposture and Folly* (nine volumes from 1811 until closure in 1815); launched the satirists' attack on the regent by employing George Cruikshank in 1811.

**Laurie, Robert** (1755?–1836): mezzotint engraver and printseller; worked for the print publisher Robert Sayer (1724–94) of Fleet Street, whose business he took over in 1794 with James Whittle as partner; retired in 1812 (Whittle died 1818); the firm continued under Laurie's son; specialized in maps and charts, and employed Isaac and George Cruikshank to produce popular drolls.

**Liverpool, Lord** (1770–1828): Pittite minister, Foreign Secretary and prime minister 1812–27.

**McLean, Thomas** (dates unknown): printshop proprietor and publisher whose Haymarket imprint first appeared in 1821; by 1827 the leading humorous print publisher, relying on the work of William Heath ('Paul Pry'), Egerton, Alken, etc.; from 1830 sold sheets of vignettes by Heath, Seymour, etc. in *McLean's Looking Glass*.

**Marks, J. Lewis** (dates unknown): engraver and printseller: began career 1814 by working for Tegg, imitating George Cruikshank; from 1817 published his own work from Artillery Row off Bishopsgate and from Soho, Covent Garden, and Piccadilly; in 1818 pioneered the use of lithography in satires; specialized in sexualized jokes against the regent and ministers until the king bribed him into silence in 1820–21.

**Marshall, John** (dates unknown): print publisher, Little St Martin's Lane; his pro-Caroline prints forced the king to buy his silence, 1820.

**Newton, Richard** (1777–90): caricaturist and miniature painter, son of Drury Lane haberdasher; produced his own prints from 1791 while working also for

William Holland (1757–1815), his output radical and bawdy; opened his 'Original Print Warehouse' in Brydges Street, Covent Garden, 1797, but died aged twenty-one of unknown illness.

**Paine, Thomas** (1737–1809): author of *The Rights of Man*; son of Norfolk staymaker and farmer; went to America in 1774; achieved fame in 1776 with *Common Sense*, his pamphlet on the American war; having returned to England, replied to Edmund Burke's *Reflections on the Revolution in France* in Part I of his *Rights of Man* (1790); on publication of Part II (1792) fled to France to avoid prosecution; became a French citizen and member of the Convention; published *The Age of Reason*, 1793; arrested in Paris, his life saved by Robespierre's fall; returned to America in 1802, where he died; the only English writer who clearly expressed the principles of the French Revolution, his works became the textbooks for the English radical cause.

**Pitt, William (the younger)** (1759–1806): prime minister 1784–1801 and 1804–6; presided over French wars and repressions of free expression; 'stiff to everybody but a lady', he died of drink – 'old aged at forty-six, as much as if he had been ninety'.

**Place, Francis** (1771–1854): illegitimate son of debtors' prison-keeper and tavern-keeper born off Drury Lane; basic education before apprenticeship to breeches-maker in 1785; married 1791 (fifteen children eventually, seven of whom died in childhood); in 1791 led strike of breeches-makers and suffered near starvation; read Paine's *Age of Reason* in 1794 and joined the artisan-radical London Corresponding Society; opened tailor's shop at 29 Charing Cross 1799, moving to no. 16 in 1800; helped organize radical Westminster politics, working for Burdett 1807–20; in the 1820s advocated popular education and birth control and franchise extension; accepted Jeremy Bentham's principles, and compiled voluminous 'Papers' towards a history of his times; widely consulted by parliamentary committees on the morals of the poor.

**Ramberg, Johann Heinrich** (1763–1840): German-born painter and engraver; entered Royal Academy Schools to study under Benjamin West 1781; patronized by George III, for whom he produced caricatures; returned to Hanover as court painter 1792.

**Rowlandson, Thomas** (1757–1827), artist and caricaturist; son of failed City silk merchant; brought up in comfort by aunt who sent him to the Royal Academy schools 1772–8; succeeded as RA exhibitor and picturesque watercolourist; travelled widely; published occasional caricatures 1780 onwards (particularly on the 1784 Westminster election); inherited aunt's fortune 1789 but gambled most of it away; resorted increasingly to satirical engraving to supplement income; many prints published on his own account; patronized by Rudolph Ackermann who first published his work in 1797; produced fifty-six satires on Mary Anne Clarke affair for Tegg 1809, and regularly worked for Tegg thereafter.

**Sayers, James** (1748–1823): caricaturist and political propagandist, Gillray's earliest rival; most of his attacks delivered on the Foxite opposition.

**Sidebotham, J**. (dates unknown): printshop publisher from Dublin; opened shops in Newgate Street, the Strand and Bond Street; produced around seventy-five anti-regent titles 1815 20, employing Robert and George Cruikshank mostly.

**Tegg, Thomas** (1776–1846): Wimbledon grocer's son who became one of the nation's most prolific publishers; after earlier partnerships, he opened his bookshop at 111 Cheapside in 1804, moving to the Old Mansion House in 1824; prospered by the cheap republication of remaindered or out-of-copyright books; began publishing satirical prints in 1805, holding down prices by recycling old plates and aiming at middling-class purchasers; employed *Rowlandson* to attack the Duke of York in 1809 and *George Cruikshank* to lampoon Napoleon and the regent; conservative at heart, he abjured satire and declared his loyalism on George IV's accession in 1820, going on then to make his publishing fortune.

**Williams, Charles** (dates unknown): accomplished and prolific satirical engraver working between 1797 and the 1820s; early prints under the name 'Ansell'; later an imitator of Gillray; employed by Fores until George Cruikshank became Fores's chief artist *c*.1815.

**Woodward, George Murgatroyd** (1760?–1809), caricaturist, son of estate steward; first caricatures published 1790; total output of 525 catalogued titles for Holland, Fores, Ackermann and Tegg; most of his prints commented on middle-class foibles, etched by his friends Rowlandson and Isaac Cruikshank; surpassed Rowlandson in popularity in Tegg's *Caricature Magazine* (1807–9); pioneer of 'strip' caricatures; led a dissolute life.

# Abbreviations in Notes

| | |
|---|---|
| Add MSS | Additional Manuscripts, British Library |
| BL | British Library |
| BM | British Museum |
| BMCSat. | Mary Dorothy George, *Catalogue of Political and Personal Satires Preserved in the Department of Prints and Drawings in the British Museum* (1935–54) |
| BMCSat. + 5 to 11 | M. D. George's vols. 5 to 11 of BMCSat. for 1771–1832 |
| BMSat. | catalogue number of individual print(s) in BMCSat. |
| HO | Home Office papers, National Archives, Kew |
| KB | King's Bench papers, National Archives, Kew |
| *ODNB* | *Oxford Dictionary of National Biography* |
| TS | Treasury Solicitor's papers, National Archives, Kew |

# Notes

## Introduction:
## Lady Worsley's Bottom

1  The Worsley prints are described in the British Museum's *Catalogue of Political and Personal Satires* at nos. 6105–12. See also W. S. Lewis (ed.), *The Yale Edition of Horace Walpole's Correspondence* (48 vols, 1937–), vol. 25, pp. 228, 245–6; M. R. Brownell, *The Prime Minister of Taste: a Portrait of Horace Walpole* (2001), pp. 211–14. The story was long remembered. Gillray's bathhouse print hangs in the background in Isaac Cruikshank's *Sketches from Nature.!!!* (1796), on the Prince of Wales's affair with Lady Jersey (underscoring Lord Jersey's own connivance in his wife's adultery).

2  Boyd Tomkin in the *Independent*, 13 December 1996, cited by K. Harvey, 'The century of sex? Gender, bodies, and sexuality in the long eighteenth century', *Historical Journal*, 45 (4) (2002), p. 899.

3  My claim to originality may seem self-serving in view of, for example, J. Verberckmoes's ten-page research bibliography, 'Humour and history', in J. Bremmer and H. Roodenburg (eds), *A Cultural History of Humour: From Antiquity to the Present Day* (1997). But Verberckmoes's booklist covers the whole of Europe over 2,000 years, and many of the publications it lists over the past century or more are of low quality and ambition. Thanks to M. Bakhtin's seminal *Rabelais and his World*, trans. H. Iswolsky (Cambridge, 1968), there have been many more studies on humour *before* 1700 than after it, and in Germany and France than in Britain. For post-1700 Britain, the historiography of humour hardly exists. *Literary* satire has been closely studied, but through canonical texts rather than the history of manners.

4  B. Montagu, *Thoughts on Laughter* (1830), p. 44. Montagu lifted this story unacknowledged from Hazlitt, *Lectures on the English Comic Writers* (1819).

5  L. D. Schwarz, *London in the Age of Industrialisation: Entrepreneurs, Labour Force and Living Conditions, 1700–1850* (Cambridge, 1992), p. 51; G. Rudé, *Hanoverian London 1714–1808* (1971), pp. 57–8.

6  See V. A. C. Gatrell, *The Hanging Tree: Execution and the English People 1770–1868* (Oxford, 1994), Part II, 'The plebeian texts'.

7  H. Fielding, *Enquiry into the Causes of the Late Increase of Robbers* (1751), pp. 9–10; *Humphrey Clinker*, Everyman edn, p. 84; G. F. A. Wendeborn, *A View of England towards the Close of the Eighteenth Century* (trans. from German edn. of 1785–88, 2 vols, 1791), vol. I, pp. 184, 189, 287–90; C. A. G. Goede, *A Foreigner's Opinion of England* (3 vols. bound in 2, 1821, first published as *A German Visitor to England in 1802*), vol. II, pp. 52–3; Boswell, cited by J. Brewer, *The Pleasures of the Imagination: English Culture in the Eighteenth Century* (1997), p. 32.

8  Wendeborn, *A View of England*, vol. I, pp. 287–90, 184, 292.

9 E. H. Gombrich, *Meditations on a Hobby Horse and Other Essays on the Theory of Art* (3rd edn, 1978), p. 120; R. Porter, 'Seeing the past', *Past and Present* 118 (Feb 1988); introductions to P. Langford, *Walpole and the Robinocracy* (1986) and J. Brewer, *The Common People and Politics 1750–1790s* (1986).

10 Diana Donald's *The Age of Caricature: Satirical Prints in the Reign of George III* (1996) stands alone in exploring the relationship between the satires and prevailing 'mentalities', and its coverage up to 1800 or so is impressive. But it downplays the violent, bawdy and celebratory themes stressed in the present book; it is less concerned with social context, too; and it thins out after 1800. At key points I depart from her interpretations fundamentally. The doyenne of print historians was Mary Dorothy George. Everyone who studies visual satire depends on her seven-volume contribution to the *Catalogue of Political and Personal Satires Preserved in the Department of Prints and Drawings in the British Museum* (henceforth BMCSat.). Her volumes (5 to 11) cover 1771–1832 and were published 1935–54. See Sebet bibliography for further major studies.

11 W. T. J. Mitchell, *Picture Theory: Essays on Verbal and Visual Representation* (Chicago, 1994), p. 13.

12 Cf. J. de Vries, 'Introduction', in D. Freedberg and J. de Vries (eds), *Art in History, History in Art: Studies in Seventeenth-century Dutch culture* (Santa Monica, Calif., 1991); P. Burke, *Eyewitnessing: the Use of Images as Historical Evidence* (2001).

13 Walpole to Countess of Ossory, 10 Feb. 1786, and Walpole to Mann, 13 Feb. 1786 (P. Cunningham (ed.), *Letters of Horace Walpole, Earl of Oxford* (9 vols, 1891), vol. IX, pp. 39, 46); H. Angelo, *The Reminiscences of Henry Angelo* (2 vols, 1828; 1904 edn, 2 vols), vol. I, p. 330. The first print on the subject was *The Follies of a Day, or the Marriage of Figaro*, by Thomas Rowlandson's friend and travel companion, Henry Wigstead.

14 Edward Hawkins's manuscript attribution for the 'Fitz' prints was to Kingsbury (Hawkins was a major Victorian donor to the British Museum collection); for contrary attributions to Stubbs, see C. Lennox-Boyd, R. Dixon, and T. Clayton, *George Stubbs: the Complete Engraved Works* (1989), p. 374. Although the prints are in similar style, certainty about their artist is impossible. The print showing Fores's window is *The Cock of the Walk, Distributing his Favours*. Gillray also appropriated Hogarth's *After* for his fictitious depiction of the prince and Mrs Fitzherbert in the bedroom of a French inn: *The Morning after Marriage – or – a Scene on the Continent* (for Humphrey's printshop 1788), in which the prince's posture recalls the yawning wife's in Hogarth's *Marriage à la Mode*, but Gillray toned down the sexual explicitness (see fig. 142).

15 Wendeborn, *A View of England*, vol. I, p. 292; *Literary Gazette*, 3 January 1835; Hazlitt, 'Definition of wit' (1829), in T. Paulin and D. Chandler (eds), *William Hazlitt: 'The Fight' and other Writings* (2000), p. 511.

16 L. Klein, 'Liberty, manners, and politeness in early eighteenth-century England', *Historical Journal*, 32 (3), (1989), p. 588.

17 L. Klein, 'The third earl of Shaftesbury and the progress of politeness', *Eighteenth-century Studies*, 18 (2) (1984–5), p. 198.

18 The best general introduction to 'politeness' is J. Brewer, *The Pleasures of the Imagination: English Culture in the Eighteenth Century* (1997), ch. 2. The politeness paradigm owes much to Lawrence Klein's work: *Shaftesbury and the Culture of Politeness: Moral Discourse and Cultural Politics in Early Eighteenth-century England* (Cambridge, 1994); his edition of *Shaftesbury, Characteristics of Men, Manners, Opinions, Times* (Cambridge, 1999); and, among many articles, including those cited above, his 'Politeness and the interpretation of the British eighteenth century', *Historical Journal*, 45 (2002),

pp. 869–98. See also, *inter alia*, M. Cohen, *Fashioning Masculinity: National Identity and Language in the Eighteenth Century* (1996), ch. 3; P. Carter, *Men and the Emergence of Polite Society: Britain, 1660–1800* (2001). For a typical notion that a libertine woman's deviance from polite and religious values must have been 'dangerous' (was it?), see K. Wilson, 'The female rake: gender, libertinism, and Enlightenment', in P. Cryle and L. O'Connell (eds), *Libertine Enlightenment: Sex, Liberty and Licence in the Eighteenth Century* (2004), p. 102. Helen Berry purports to rethink politeness by noting elites' impolite interest in canting jargon, but sees this, disappointingly, as no more than a 'resistance' to a 'repressive civil code of outwardly conformist behaviour': 'Rethinking politeness in eighteenth-century England . . .', *Transactions of the Royal Historical Society* (sixth series), xi (2001), pp. 65–81. Paul Langford, wisely, regards the current emphasis as merely 'fashionable', and explores its limits via sceptical continental commentaries in 'British politeness and the progress of western manners: an eighteenth-century enigma', *Transactions of the Royal Historical Society* (6th series), vii (1997), pp. 53–72. How the politeness paradigm has infected the historiography on manliness and on woman is developed in chapter 4 and 12 below: except as courtesans, 'impolite' women are currently next to invisible in current historical literature.

19 These principles underpinned the argument in my book, *The Hanging Tree: Execution and the English People 1770–1868* (Oxford, 1994): pp. 238, 316. They also draw on the following: J. Le Goff, 'Mentalities: a history of ambiguities', in J. Le Goff and P. Nora (eds), *Constructing the Past: Essays in Historical Methodology* (Cambridge 1985), p. 169; R. Chartier, *Cultural History: Between Practices and Representations* (trans., 1988), p. 28; A. Burguière, 'Demography', in Le Goff and Nora (eds), *Constructing the Past*, pp. 110–11; F. Braudel, 'History and the social sciences' in his *On History* (trans., 1980), pp. 31, 35. The resistances Braudel had chiefly in mind were geographical, biological and economic; but he acknowledged that 'mental frameworks too can form prisons of the *longue durée*'. 'Ideological representations share with all systems of values a heaviness, an inertia, since their framework is made up of traditions,' G. Duby noted in his 'Ideologies in social history', in J. Le Goff and P. Nora (eds), *Constructing the Past*, p. 153.

20 B. Wilson, *The Laughter of Triumph: William Hone and the Fight for a Free Press* (2005), p. 10. The most illuminating discussion of the later eighteenth-century erosion of the public/private boundary is J. Barrell's 'Coffee-house politicians', *Journal of British Studies*, 43, no. 2 (April 2004), pp. 206–32, expanded in his *The Spirit of Despotism: Politics and Culture in the 1790s* (Oxford, 2006). For earlier, see L. E. Klein, 'Gender and the public/private distinction in the eighteenth century: some questions about evidence and analytic procedure', *Eighteenth-Century Studies*, vol. 29, no. 1 (1995), pp. 97–109; and J. Brewer, 'This, that and the other: public, social and private in the seventeenth and eighteenth centuries', in D. Castiglione and L. Sharpe (eds), *Shifting the Boundaries: Transformation of the Languages of Public and Private in the Eighteenth Century* (Exeter, 1995). On Boswell: A. Sisman, *Boswell's Presumptuous Task: Writing the Life of Dr Johnson* (2000), pp. 118, 134, 164–8.

21 Gatrell, *The Hanging Tree: Execution and the English People, 1770–1868*.

Chapter One

# London and the Pleasure Principle

1 Walpole to the Miss Berrys, 8 June 1791 in P. Cunningham (ed.), *The Letters of Horace Walpole, Earl of Orford* (9 vols, 1857–59), vol. IX, p. 324.

2 P. J. Grosley, *A Tour to London; or, New Observations on England, and its Inhabitants* (2 vols, 1772), vol. I, p. 24; Walpole to the Miss Berrys, 5 March 1791: Cunningham (ed.), *Letters of Horace Walpole*, vol. IX, p. 294.

3 Grosley, *Tour to London*, vol. I, pp. 33–7, 44–5.

4 Rev. R. J. Richardson, *Recollections, Political, Literary, Dramatic, and Miscellaneous, of the Last Half-Century* (2 vols in 1, 1856), vol. I, p. 32.

5 C. Ryskamp (ed.), *Boswell: the Ominous Years 1774–1776* (1963), p. 304.

6 Richardson, *Recollections*, vol. I, p. 14.

7 Joshua White, *Letters on England* (1810).

8 Francis Place in 1827 noted that he had seen none in St James's Street for the past six or seven years: Place Papers, vol. 4, fo. 12 (BL Add. MSS 27828).

9 G. C. Lichtenberg, *Visits to England* trans. W. H. Quarrell and M. L. Mare (1956).

10 Walpole to Miss Berry, 15 April 1791: Cunningham (ed.), *Walpole Letters*, vol. IX, p. 303.

11 See plates reproduced in M. Galinou and J. Hayes, *London in Paint: Oil Paintings in the Collection at the Museum of London* (1996), p. 159; Summerson, *Georgian London* (1988 edn), pp. 98–9; D. Cruikshank and N. Burton, *Life in the Georgian City* (1990), pp. 2, 11; C. Fox (ed.), *London World City, 1800–1840* (1992), p. 321; P. Jackson, *George Scharf's London: Sketches and Watercolours of a Changing City, 1820–1850* (1987), pp. 64–5, 120.

12 Place Papers, vol. 4, fos. 7–9 (BL Add. MSS 27828).

13 F. M. L. Thompson, 'Nineteenth-century horse sense', *Economic History Review*, 2nd ser., xxix (1), pp. 65, 77.

14 D. Masson, *Memories of London in the Forties* (1908), cited by P. Jackson, *George Scharf's London* (1987), p. 75.

15 A handful of writers had agreed that the city was indispensable to urbane sociability; a few, like Gay in *Trivia: or the Art of Walking the Streets of London* (1716), had appreciated London's pleasures without resort to moralizing. But such cases were rare. See M. Byrd, *London Transformed: Images of the City in the Eighteenth Century* (Newhaven, 1978); D. E. Nord, *Walking the Victorian Streets: Women, Representation and the City* (1995); R. Williams, *The Country and the City* (1973), pp. 154–5; J. Wolfreys, *Writing London: the Trace of the Urban Text from Blake to Dickens* (1998); J. Marriott, 'Introduction', in Marriot (ed.), *Unknown London: Early Modernist Visions of the Metropolis 1815–45* (6 vols, 2000), vol. 1.

16 Cited by F. K. Brown, *Fathers of the Victorians: The Age of Wilberforce* (Cambridge, 1961), p. 27.

17 I. Lustig (ed.), *Boswell: the English Experiment 1785–1789* (1986), p. 31.

18 F. A. Pottle (ed.), *Boswell's London Journal, 1762–1763* (New York, 1950), pp. 43–4.

19 C. Ryskamp and F. A. Pottle (eds), *Private Papers of James Boswell* (New York, 1930), vol. VII, p. 163; W. K. Wimsatt (ed.), *Boswell for the Defence, 1769–1774* (1959), p. 30.

20 Wimsatt, *Boswell for the Defence*, p. 108.

21 C. Ryskamp and F. A. Pottle (eds), *Boswell: The Ominous Years, 1774–1776* (1963), p. 111.

22 G. B. Hill (ed.), *Boswell's Life of Johnson* (6 vols, Oxford, 1934–50), vol. III, pp. 176–7; F. Brady and F. A. Pottle (eds), *Boswell in Search of a Wife, 1766–1769* (1956),

pp. 331–2; M. Byrd, *London Transformed: Images of the City in the Eighteenth Century* (Yale, 1978), p. 113.

23  *Humphrey Clinker* (1771), letter of 31 May.

24  Lamb to Wordsworth, 30 January 1801, and letter to Manning around the same date, in E. W. Marrs (ed.), *The Letters of Charles and Mary Ann Lamb* (3 vols, 1975), vol. I, pp. 248, 267.

25  'The Londoner', in P. Fitzgerald (ed.), *The Life, Letters and Writings of Charles Lamb* (6 vols, 1903), vol. IV, p. 323.

26  J. Timbs, *Anecdote Lives of William Hogarth, Sir Joshua Reynolds, Thomas Gainsborough, Henry Fuseli, Sir Thomas Lawrence, and J. W. M. Turner* (1872: republished Portsmouth, 1997), p. 209.

27  L. A. Marchand (ed.), *Byron's Letters and Journals* (13 vols, 1973–94), vol. I, p. 157.

28  Place Papers, vol. 4, folios 7–9 (BL Add. MSS).

29  Cf. also T. Malton, *Picturesque Tour through the Cities of London and Westminster . . . Illustrated . . . in Aquatint* (1792); *The London Guide, Describing Public and Private Buildings* (1782); Richard Phillips, *Modern London* (1804); D. Hughson, *Walks through London* (2 vols, 1817) and *London* (4 vols); T. Allen, *The History and Antiquities of London, Westminster, Southwark, & Parts Adjacent* (4 vols, 1827–8) and *The History and Antiquities of the Parish of Lambeth* (1826); Samuel Leigh, *Leigh's New Picture of London: . . . a Brief and Luminous Guide to the Stranger* (1819).

30  The genre extended back well beyond Ned Ward's *London Spy* of 1698. For the eighteenth century, see *Tricks of the Town Laid Open; or a Companion for a Country Gentleman* (1747); *The Countryman's Guide to London; or Villainy Detected* (1780); *The Devil upon Crutches in England; or Night Scenes in London* (1759); S. Foote, *The Devil upon Two Sticks: a Comedy* (1778); [W. Combe?], *The Devil's Wedding: a Poem . . . Exhibiting some of the most Flagitous Characters of the Present Age* (1778); [W. Combe?], *The Devil upon Two Sticks in England: being a Continuation of Le Diable Boiteux of Le Sage* (4 vols, 1790). These publications were not eclipsed in the new century: cf. G. Andrewes, *The Stranger's Guide or Frauds of London Detected* (1808). A satirical newspaper was published in 1832, entitled *Asmodeus; or, the Devil in London*, its bannerhead reading: 'In these daies, the Devil was seen publicly walking about the streets of London: Hollinshed'. For the long tradition of low-life guidebooks, see *Low Life: or, One Half of the World Knows not how the Other Half Live …*(1764); *The Midnight Spy, or, a View of the Transactions of London and Westminster, from the Hours of Ten in the Evening, till Five in the Morning; Exhibiting a Great Variety of Scenes in High and Low Life, with the Characters of Some Well Known Nocturnal Adventurers of Both Sexes* (1766); *The Complete Modern London Spy for the Present Year* (1781); *London Unmasked; or the New Town Spy* (1784); George Stevens, *The Adventures of a Speculist; or, a Journey through London* (2 vols, written 1750s?; pub. 1788); *Midnight Merriment, or, a Nocturnal Ramble through St Giles, Containing a Funny, but Faithful, Picture of that Quarter* (1805); *The Dens of London Exposed* (3rd edn, 1835); *A Peep into the Holy Land, or Sinks of London Laid Open! Forming a Pocket Companion for the Uninitiated, etc.* (1835).

31  The prototype of these later comically illustrated guides was Woodward's *Eccentric Excursions: or, Literary and Pictorial Sketches of Countenance, Character and Country … with upwards of One Hundred Prints* (1796). This was followed by Beresford's and Rowlandson's *Miseries of Human Life* (1806–7), J. A. Atkinson's derivative *Sixteen Scenes taken from the Miseries of Human Life* (1807), and Woodward's *Chesterfield Travestie, or School for Modern Manners embellished with … Caricatures* [*from*] *Rowlandson* (1808). Cruikshank's vignettes of 1818 and later inspired Dighton's, Egerton's, Alken's, and Hood's work through to the 1830s. In 1830, Southey's and Coleridge's witty satirical poem, 'The Devil's Thoughts' (1799), was republished as *The Devil's Walk*, with brilliant designs in the same spirit by Robert Cruikshank.

32 J. Marriot, 'Introduction', in vol. 1 of Marriot (ed.), *Unknown London: Early Modernist Visions of the Metropolis 1815–45* (6 vols, 2000). See fuller discussion, ch. 19 below.

33 D. E. Nord, *Walking the Victorian Streets: Women, Representation and the City* (1995), p. 48.

34 R. Paulson, *The Art of Hogarth* (1975), pp. 30 ff., 64; J. Lindsay, *Hogarth: His Art and his World* (1977), pp. 20, 157.

35 C. Baudelaire, 'Some foreign caricaturists' (1857), in P. E. Charvet (ed.), *Baudelaire: Selected Writings on Art and Literature* (1992).

36 James Boswell and William Hickey both took their women there, and Francis Place had to cope with their unseemliness when he moved in next door. See Epilogue.

37 J. Uglow, *William Hogarth: A Life and a World* (1997), pp. 299, 302–3.

38 *Diary of Capt. Edward Thompson*, 17 March 1785, in *Cornhill Magazine*, xvii (1868), p. 611, cited in Boswell's *Life of Johnson* (G. B. Hill and L. F. Powell (eds), (Oxford, 1933–50, 6 vols), vol. IV, pp. 547–8; Boswell, *Life*, vol. IV, pp. 373–4; Blake, 'On art and artists' (1800–3), in G. E. Bentley (ed.), *William Blake's Writings* (2 vols, Oxford, 1978); R. Southey, *Letters of Espriella* (1807), vol. III, p. 49.

39 The Oxford English Dictionary dates the first derogatory reference to 'a Bow-bell Cockney' at 1600, though the etymology is older than that. The word 'cit' similarly referred contemptuously to City tradesmen or shopkeepers, as in Andrew Marvell's ballad 'O ye addle-brain'd cits!' (1674), or Samuel Johnson's reference (1771) to 'the cits of London and the boors of Middlesex'.

40 See below, ch. 13. An etching like *Chaos is Come Again* (1791) (fig. 190 below) shows the very moment when, in a tumble of broken masonry and terrified people, a crowded balcony collapses in a fashionable theatre. An ink and watercolour sketch of 1805 declares *'Tis Time to Jump Out*, as two fast galloping horses tremble on the very edge of the precipice they are about to career over, the occupants of the coach they are pulling looking very alarmed. Nor, in his comic engraving of that title, are people allowed decorously to mount the Royal Academy's serpentine *Exhibition Stare Case* [staircase]: they must tumble down it head over heels, with female buttocks exposed (and stared at by the men) as dresses fly up and legs kick wildly. *'Tis Time to Jump Out* is reproduced in R. R. Wark, *Drawings by Rowlandson in the Huntington Collection* (1975), p. 139.

41 See fig. 289 for example.

42 Tegg bought the rights to Beresford's book in 1810.

43 Cf. Henry Alken, *Symptoms of Being Amused* (1822); M. Egerton, *Airy Nothings; or, Scraps and Naughts, and Oddcumshorts . . .* ( 2nd edn, 1825) (with 23 coloured plates). For the tension between 'celebratory' and critical representations of the metropolis, see D. J. Gray, 'Views and sketches of London in the nineteenth century', and W. Vaughan, 'London topographers and urban change', in I. B. Nadel and F. S. Schwarzback (eds), *Victorian Artists and the City: a Collection of Critical Essays* (New York, 1980); and C. Arscott, 'The representation of the city in the visual arts', in M. Daunton (ed.), *The Cambridge Urban History of Britain* (Cambridge, 2000), vol. III, pp. 811–832. Cf. the Cruikshank brothers' tacit indebtedness to Rowlandson's *Miseries* in George Cruikshank's *Points of Humour* and Robert Cruikshank's *Points of Misery* (1823), and their collaboration in *London Characters* (1827).

Chapter Two
## 'The West or Worst End'

1 F. Bamford and Duke of Wellington (eds), *The Journal of Mrs Arbuthnot, 1820–1832* (2 vols, 1950), July 1821.

2 Hon. Mrs Hugh Wyndham (ed.), *Correspondence of Sarah Spencer Lady Lyttelton, 1787–1870* (1912), pp. 237–8; George Keppel, Earl of Albemarle, *Fifty Years of my Life* (2 vols, 1876), vol. I, p. 327: cited in S. David, *Prince of Pleasure: the Prince of Wales and the Making of the Regency* (1999), p. 420; cf. C. Hibbert, *George IV* (1976), ch. 35.

3 R. Southey, *Letters from England* (1807; reprinted 1951, 1984, ed. J. Simmons), p. 69; R.J. Richardson, *Recollections, Political, Literary, Dramatic, and Miscellaneous, of the Last Half-Century* (2 vols, 1856), vol. I, pp. 3–5.

4 P. J. Grosley, *A Tour to London; or, New Observations on England, and its Inhabitants* (2 vols, 1772).

5 Byron, *Don Juan*, canto xi.

6 J. Barrell, in J. Chandler (ed.), *The Cambridge History of English Literature: The Romantic Period* (Cambridge, 2006).

7 Topographical details in the following from Richard Horwood's *Map of the Cities of London and Westminster*, 3rd edition by William Faden (1813); E. B. Chancellor, *Memorials of St James's Street together with the Annals of Almack's* (1922); *The Survey of London*, vol. xxix, pp. 71, 330 and *passim*; B. Weinreb and C. Hibbert, *The London Encyclopaedia* (rev. edn, 1993); J. Summerson, *Georgian London* (rev. edn, 1978); E. McKellar, *The Birth of Modern London: the Development and Design of the City 1660–1720* (Manchester, 1999).

8 A. Bourke, *The History of White's* [club] (2 vols, 1892); J. Timbs, *Clubs and Club Life in London* (1872).

9 R. Southey, *Letters from England* (1807; reprinted 1951, 1984, ed. J. Simmons), pp. 69–70.

10 *The Fruits of Experience; Or Memoir of Joseph Brasbridge, Written in his 80th and 81st Year* (2nd edn, 1824).

11 C. A. G. Goede, *A Foreigner's Opinion of England* (3 vols bound in 2, 1821, first published as *A German Visitor to England in 1802*), vol. I, pp. 127, 130. W. Carey's *The Stranger's Guide through London; Or, a View of the British Metropolis in 1808* (1808) listed four 'lounging rooms' in his discussion of the 'state of literature, &c. ', pp. 254–67.

12 J. Hemlow (ed.), *Francis Burney: Selected Letters and Journals* (Oxford, 1987), p. 270.

13 H. More, 'The *Bas Bleu* [bluestocking]: or, Conversation' (1787). When Mrs Vesey asked Benjamin Stillingfleet to attend the group, he declined since he could not afford the formal dress required for evening events. Mrs Vesey told him to come in his informal day clothes. So he did, wearing his blue worsted stockings. 'Such was the excellence of his conversation,' Boswell recorded, 'that his absence was felt as so great a loss, that it used to be said "We can do nothing without the blue stockings," and thus by degrees the title was established': Boswell, *Life of Johnson* (ed. R. W. Chapman), (Oxford, 1985), pp. 1147–8.

14 [C. Pigott], *The Female Jockey Club* (1794), p. 192; Byron, *Don Juan* (1819), Canto xi. Cf. Peter Pindar, *Nil Admirari; or a Smile at a Bishop, Occasioned by an Hyperbolical Eulogy on Miss Hannah More, by Dr Porteus . . . Moreover, an Ode to the Blue-Stocking-Club . . .* (1799); Thomas Moore, *M.P. or the Blue-Stocking. A Comic Opera* (1811).

15 *Lady's Magazine*, May 1816.

16 C. A. G. Goede, *A Foreigner's Opinion of England* (3 vols, bound in 2, 1821, first published as *A German Visitor to England in 1802*), vol. I, pp. 127, 130.

17 G. F. A. Wendeborn, *A View of England towards the Close of the Eighteenth Century* (trans. by the author from the German edition. of 1785–88, 2 vols, 1791), vol. I, pp. 311–12.

18 F. Wilson, *The Courtesan's Revenge: Harriette Wilson, the Woman who Blackmailed the King* (2003), p. 27.

19 W. S. Lewis (ed.) *The Yale Edition of Horace Walpole's Correspondence* (48 vols, 1937–), vol. 25, p. 227.

20 S. Tillyard, *Aristocrats: Caroline, Emily, Louisa and Sarah Lennox, 1740–1832* (1995), pp. 43, 67, 169.

21 Wendeborn, *A View of England*, vol. I, p. 294.

22 Hon. Mrs H. Wyndham, *Correspondence of Sarah Spencer Lady Lyttelton 1787–1870* (1912), p. 101 (dated 1810).

23 L. A. Marchand (ed.), *Byron's Letters and Journals* (13 vols, 1973–94), vol. 3 for 22 March 1814.

24 Oliver Goldsmith, 'The Present State of Polite Learning' (1754), and 'An Essay on the Theatre; or, a Comparison between Laughing and Sentimental Comedy' (1773), in A. Friedman (ed.), *The Collected Works of Oliver Goldsmith* (5 vols, Oxford, 1966), vol. I, pp. 320–2, and vol. III, pp. 209–13. Much later, both Lamb and Hazlitt were to defend Restoration comedy in similar terms against those who wished to purge it of its 'disagreeables'.

25 F. MacCarthy, *Byron: Life and Legend* (2002), pp. 256–7.

26 'The nobility and gentry are respectfully acquainted, that there will be a concert at this place on Tuesday, the 21st instant. The principal vocal parts by Mrs Barthelemon and Mr Arrowsmith. The orchestra under the direction of Mr Bathlemon [*sic*]. Admittance three shillings and sixpence each person, tea and coffee included. The doors will be opened at eight o'clock; and the concert begin at nine'. *Morning Post*, 14 November 1786.

27 *The Works of Soame Jenyns* (4 vols, 2nd edn, 1793), vol. II, p. 108; *Humphrey Clinker* (1771; Penguin, 1967), pp. 95–7; L. Stone, *Family, Sex and Marriage in England 1500–1800* (1977), pp. 485–6; L. G. Mitchell, *Charles James Fox* (Oxford, 1992). On the Duke of Norfolk, N. W. Wraxall, *The Historical and Posthumous Memoirs of Sir Nathaniel William Wraxall, 1772–1784* (2 vols, (1835), republ. 1884, 5 vols (ed. H. B. Wheatley)), vol. III, pp. 361–7; and J. Richardson, *Recollections of the Last Half Century*, vol. II, pp. 119–20.

28 B. Mitchell and H. Penrose (eds), *Letters from Bath, 1766–1767* (Gloucester, 1983), pp. 30, 75, 181, cited by M. Rosenthal, *The Art of Thomas Gainsborough* (1999), p. 25.

29 Stone, *Family, Sex and Marriage*, pp. 485–6.

30 S. David, *The Prince of Pleasure: the Prince of Wales and the Making of the Regency* (1999), p. 170.

31 'Jazey' was slang for a bob-wig; the title punned on the prince's affair with Lady Jersey.

32 I. Gilmour, *Riot, Risings, and Revolution: Governance and Violence in Eighteenth-century England* (1992), p. 349.

33 N. Tolstoy, *The Half-mad Lord: Thomas Pitt, Second Baron Camelford (1775–1804)* (1978), pp. 114–16.

34 For the following, see *Memoirs of the Life of Sir Francis Burdett . . .* (1810); *Account of the Proceedings of the Electors of Westminster, on the Commitment of their Representative Sir Francis Burdett to the Tower* (1810); Sir S. Romilly, *Memoirs of the Life of Sir Samuel Romilly, Written by Himself* (1840): 28 March–18 May 1810; TS.11.42/152; TS.11.750ff /2347; M. W. Patterson, *Sir Francis Burdett and his Times (1770–1844)* (2 vols, 1931); J. A. Hone, *For the Cause of Truth: Radicalism in London, 1796–1821* (Oxford, 1982). J. R.

Dunwiddy, 'Sir Francis Burdett and Burdettite Radicalism', *History* 65 (1980), pp. 17–31; J. Stevenson, *Popular Disturbances in England 1700–1832* (1992), pp. 226–35.

35 Patterson, *Burdett*, vol. I, p. 254.

36 Ibid., p. 259.

37 *The Times*, 9, 10, 11, 12 April 1810; Patterson, *Burdett*, vol. I, p. 278.

38 Hon. Mrs H. Wyndham, *Correspondence of Sarah Spencer Lady Lyttelton 1787–1870* (1912), pp. 97–8.

39 Patterson, *Burdett*, vol. I, p. 263.

40 C. Hibbert (ed.), *Captain Gronow: his Reminiscences of Regency and Victorian Life, 1810–1860* (1991), pp. 223–4. Of the 1815 episode, Gronow reported that in St James's Square he 'beheld, collected together, thousands of the lowest of the London rabble. These ruffians, with loud shouts, and threats of summary vengeance on the Ministers, were at the time I arrived breaking the windows of most of the houses in the square. The Life Guards were patrolling in the neighbouring streets, and, whenever they appeared, were received with volleys of stones mingled with mud, and cries of "Down with the Piccadilly butchers!"'

41 TS11/208.

42 Fores's social interest is revealed in another source as well. In 1799, his house-painter filched from his shop 'seventy-seven prints, value £17; thirty prints, value 30s.; half a quire of paper, value 3d.; five prints in gilt frames, value 2s.; [and] a glazier's diamond, value 10s.' The loss mattered enough for Fores in person to trace the painter to his lodgings in Shoreditch in order to secure his death sentence at the Old Bailey and seven years' transportation for his female accomplice. *The Proceedings of the Old Bailey*, 8 May 1799 (http://www.oldbaileyonline.org/).

43 On Fores's usual liberalism see below, chapter 16, note 6.

44 Altogether some two dozen (surviving) satires on the Burdett crisis were published between the first rioting on 6 April and Burdett's release in June. Of these, only a couple opposed him.

45 See J. Summerson, *The Life and Work of John Nash, Architect* (1980), pp. 71, 75–81 and ch. 10; H. J. Dyos, 'The objects of street improvement in Regency and early Victorian London', in D. Cannadine and D. Reeder (eds), *Exploring the Urban Past: Essays in Urban History by H. J. Dyos* (Cambridge, 1982), pp. 82–3; D. Arnold, *Re-presenting the Metropolis: Architecture, Urban Experience and Social Life in London, 1800–1840* (2000).

46 T. S. 11/42/142/Part 2/2, fos. 179ff.


## Chapter Three

# Covent Garden and the Middling Sorts

1 *The Poll Book, for Electing Two Representatives in Parliament for . . . Westminster, June 18, to July 4, 1818.*

2 G. Rudé, *Hanoverian London 1714–1808* (1971), pp. 57–8.

3 T. Smollett, *Humphrey Clinker* (1771; Everyman edn), p. 84.

4 M. Thale (ed.), *The Autobiography of Francis Place, 1771–1854* (Cambridge, 1972) p. 107; D. R. Green, *People of the Rookery: A Pauper Community in Victorian London* [St. Giles's] (1986): also in D. R. Green and A. G. Parton, 'Slums and slum life in Victorian England: London and Birmingham at mid-century', in S. M. Gaskell (ed.), *Slums* (Leicester, 1990).

5  L. D. Schwarz, *London in the Age of Industrialisation: Entrepreneurs, Labour Force and Living Conditions, 1700–1850* (Cambridge, 1992), pp. 6, 52, 59–63, 72; G. Rudé, *Hanoverian London 1714–1808* (1971), p. 56; M. Hunt, *The Middling Sort: Commerce, Gender and the Family in England, 1680–1780* (1996), p. 15.

6  G. E. Bentley (ed.), *William Blake's Writings* (2 vols, Oxford, 1978), vol. II, pp. 1535, 1582; M. Thale (ed.), *The Autobiography of Francis Place* (Cambridge, 1972), p. 199.

7  C. Ryskamp (ed.), *Boswell: The Ominous Years 1774–1776* (1963), p. 306; C. Ryskamp and F. A. Pottle (eds), *Private Papers of James Boswell* (1930), vol. VII, p. 163.

8  P. Quennell (ed.), *The Memoirs of William Hickey* (1976 edn), pp. xi, 13, 42, 48–9, 58.

9  M. Grosley, *A Tour to London; or, New Observations on England, and its Inhabitants* (2 vols, 1772), vol. I, p. 57.

10  Thale (ed.), *Autobiography of Francis Place*, p. 51n (citing Add. Ms 36625, fo. 8). On Roach's prosecution, KB28/370/5; on Holland's pornography, D. Alexander, *Richard Newton and English Caricature in the 1790s* (1998), p. 18 and n. 40.

11  For discussion of the 'debauchery prints', see chs. 4 and 9.

12  R. Cruikshank's print is in C. Westmacott, *The English Spy: An Original Work, Characteristic, Satirical, and Humorous, Comprising Scenes and Sketches in every Rank of Society* (2 vols, 1825), vol. I, p. 398. See also J. Wardroper, *The Caricatures of George Cruikshank* (1977), p. 10; R. L. Patten, *George Cruikshank's Life, Times, and Art: volume I; 1792–1835* (1992), pp. 26–8; B. Jerrold, *The Life of George Cruikshank* (1898 edn, reprint 1971), p. 106. Westmacott identifies the later club with the Brilliants, but the 'Finish' might have been a name appropriated by several dives across time: William Hickey describes a place of 'depravity and infamy' in Covent Garden which was so named and which he frequented in the 1760s (*The Memoirs of William Hickey* (ed. P. Quennell, 1976), p. 53). See further references at BMSat 9784.

13  Patten, *Cruikshank's Life, Times, and Art: Volume 1*, pp. 34–5. Bannister gave Rowlandson the idea for his Dr Syntax series, one of the great publishing successes of the 1810s: J. Adolphus, *Memoirs of John Bannister, Comedian* (2 vols, 1839), vol. I, pp. 290–1.

14  J. C. Riely, 'Horace Walpole and "the Second Hogarth"' [Bunbury], *Eighteenth-century Studies* 9 (1975–6), pp. 28–44. The Lewis Walpole Library, Yale University, contains Walpole's Bunbury collections, scatological prints included.

15  H. Angelo, *The Reminiscences of Henry Angelo* (2 vols, 1828; 1904 edn, 2 vols), vol. I, p. 335.

16  Angelo's *Reminiscences* are the chief biographical source; see also J. Hayes, 'Rowlandson', *ODNB*. At his death, however, Rowlandson left nearly £3,000 and a collection of old master and contemporary prints and paintings.

17  B. Jerrold, *The Life of George Cruikshank* (1898 edn, reprint 1971), pp. 48, 53.

18  For two years after his release from Newgate prison in 1794, Holland virtually lived off Newton, who turned out a print a week for him: Alexander, *Richard Newton*, pp. 14–15, 24, 44, 56.

19  R. L. Patten, *George Cruikshank's Life, Times, and Art: volume I, 1792–1835* (1992), p. 120; T. Clayton, 'The Bowles family' and 'Hannah Humphrey', *ODNB*. In the 1790s, Fores's wholesale price for a water-coloured print which he sold at a shilling was 7½d when sold to other shops in batches of a hundred; uncoloured prints were half that. These prices were inscribed on his prints in 1793 (e.g. on BMSat 8288): 'To those who give them away [i.e. sell] 1£ 11s 6d pr hundred plain, and 3£ 3s 0d in colours 6d Plain, s1 coloured'.

20  G. E. Bentley (ed.), *William Blake's Writings* (2 vols, Oxford, 1978), vol. II, pp. 1535, 1582; B. Jerrold, *The Life of George Cruikshank* (1882), pp. 90–4; F. W. Hackwood, *William Hone: His Life and Times* (1912), pp. 198–205; I. McCalman, *Radical*

*Underworld: Prophets, Revolutionaries and Pornographers in London, 1795–1840* (Cambridge, 1988), pp. 29–31.

21  R. L. Patten, 'Cruikshank, George', *ODNB*, citing *Spectator*, 26 Dec 1836.

22  For the words, see ch. 10.

23  Thale (ed.), *Autobiography of Francis Place*, p. 77.

24  *Lichtenberg's Visits to England*, trans. W. M. Mare and W. H. Quarrel (Oxford, 1936), p. 118.

25  Reproduced in M. D. George, *Hogarth to Cruikshank: Social Change in Graphic Satire* (1967), p. 75.

26  *The Proceedings of the Old Bailey*, 8 May 1799: (http://www.oldbaileyonline.org)

27  *The Proceedings of the Old Bailey*: (http://www.oldbaileyonline.org) *passim.*

28  J. Brasbridge, *The Fruits of Experience; Or Memoir of Joseph Brasbridge, Written in his 80th and 81st Year* (2nd edn, 1824), pp. 14, 59–60; Francis Place Papers, BL. Add. MSS. 27828, fos 30–4. For full text of 'Sandman Joe' (and similar street songs), see my *The Hanging Tree: Execution and the English People 1770–1868* (1994), ch. 4, appendix: no. 23 in Place's 'Songs within memory' (Francis Place Papers, BL Add. MSS. 27825, vol. xxxvii): this song 'was usually for a long time on Saturday nights sung in an open space at the back of St Clements in the Strand at the front of an alehouse door call'd the Crooked Billet by two women who used to sham dying away as they concluded the song – amidst roars of laughter'.

29  Thale (ed.), *Autobiography of Francis Place*, pp. 51n , 81–2, 45, 20, 57–8, 73–5, 121; B. Jerrold, *The Life of George Cruikshank* (1898 edn, reprint 1971), p. 240n.

30  G. E. Bentley (ed.), *William Blake's Writings* (2 vols, Oxford, 1978), vol. II, p. 1463.

31  The association is J. Grego's in *Rowlandson the Caricaturist* (2 vols, 1880), vol. II, pp. 229–30.

32  The sketch is reproduced in E. B. Krumbhaar, *Isaac Cruikshank : A catalogue raisonné* (Philadelphia, *c.*1966) frontispiece (cat. no. 269): Krumbhaar, who owned it, accepted its authenticity; B. Jerrold, *The Life of George Cruikshank* (1898 edn, reprint 1971) pp. 16–17, pp. 47, 240; R. L. Patten, *George Cruikshank's Life, Times, and Art: Volume I; 1792–1835* (1992), p. 91.

33  J. Grant, *Portraits of Public Characters* (2 vols, 1841), vol. II, p. 239. Cruikshank refers to Captain Morris's rude song 'The Plenipotentiary' in a detail of his *Interior View of the House of God* (1811); to 'The Black Joke' in his *Merry Making on the Regents Birth Day* (1812), his *Gent, No Gent, and Re-gent!!* (1816), and his *New Union Club* (1819); and to 'Morgan Rattler' in his *Princely Amusements* (1812).

34  Jerrold, *Life of Cruikshank*, pp. 39–40; Patten, *Cruikshank's Life, Times, and Art, Volume 1*, pp. 209–15; B. Wilson, *The Laughter of Triumph: William Hone and the Fight for a Free Press* (2005), pp. 347–8. Cruikshank later 'expiated his peccadilloes in this direction a hundredfold, and temperance never had a more enthusiastic advocate than he proved himself to be': H. Vizetelly, *Glances Back through Seventy Years* (2 vols, 1893), vol. I, pp. 107–8. For Cruikshank's quasi-bigamy, see Patten's 'George Cruikshank', *ODNB.*

35  Cf. the minatory subtext of Boitard's *The Harlots Nurse, or Modern Procuress* (*c.*1750): 'Behold the practis'd baud explore, / The nymph from head to foot all o'er, / For cupers [purchasers?] whom she's dress'd w'th care, / (A bait to catch some money'd heir) / Whose lot when she begins to fail / Is want, disease, and a tail [pudendum].'

36  S. Leech, *Thirty Years from Home; or, A Voice from the Main Deck* (1844), p. 54; and W. Robinson, *Jack Nastyface: Memoirs of an English Seaman* (1836), pp. 91–2: cited by L. Carter, 'British women during the revolutionary and Napoleonic wars, 1793–1815: responses, roles, and representations' (Cambridge University Ph. D. dissertation, 2005), pp. 165–6.

Chapter Four

# Crossing the Boundaries

1  Manliness in our period is a relatively neglected subject. For every 'gender historian' who has written about men, a hundred have written about women. Historians of the later seventeenth century have attended to manliness more extensively. They also convey a stronger sense of how its libertine expressions present 'a major obstacle to any linear theories of the civilization of manners': A. Bryson, *From Courtesy to Civility: Changing Codes of Conduct in Early Modern England* (Oxford, 1998), p. 243 and ch. 7. (See also E. Foyster, *Manhood in Early Modern England* (1999), and A. Shepard, *Meanings of Manhood in Early Modern England* (Oxford, 2003).) Historians' deference to the 'politeness' paradigm has checked a similar acknowledgement about the eighteenth century (see Introduction above). When noticed at all, 'impolite' male expressions are seen as 'rebellions' against polite or female norms. Libertinism's philosophical underpinning is only lightly noticed. Anthony Fletcher mentions a private male world of hedonism and debauchery (not measuring how public it was in fact), but he explains it in terms of the sexual double standard and men's 'anxiety' and 'reactions' against politeness and regulation (*Gender, Sex and Subordination in England, 1500–1800* (1995), ch. 16). Michelle Cohen notes a male reaction after the 1780s against politeness's Frenchified artificiality and deepening suspicion of the male fop as English sincerity became ever more valued. But whereas she and Philip Carter note the tensions between polite and manly codes, they say more about the former than the latter (M. Cohen, *Fashioning Masculinity: National Identity and Language in the Eighteenth Century* (1996), and her 'Manliness, effeminacy, and the French: gender and the construction of national character in eighteenth-century England', in T. Hitchcock and M. Cohen (eds), *English Masculinities, 1660–1800* (1999); P. Carter, *Men and the Emergence of Polite Society: Britain, 1660–1800* (2001)). Manly codes could certainly be reactive or rebellious; but they can just as well be understood as autonomous cultural expressions to which politeness itself reacted: see Introduction above, and J. Tosh, 'The old Adam and the new man: emerging themes in the history of English masculinities, 1750–1850', in Hitchcock and Cohen (eds), *English Masculinities*; P. Carter, 'Boswell's manliness' (in ibid.); and Karen Harvey, *Reading Sex in the Eighteenth Century: Bodies and Gender in English Erotic Culture* (Cambridge, 2005), ch. 4.
2  C. Lamb, 'On the artificial comedy of the last century' in E. V. Lucas (ed.), *The Works of Charles and Mary Lamb* (4 vols, 1903), vol. II, p. 142.
3  *London und Paris*, XIII, pp. 15–16; N. Tolstoy, *The Half-mad Lord: Thomas Pitt, Second Baron Camelford (1775–1804)* (1978), pp. 113, 141.
4  F. MacCarthy, *Byron: Life and Legend* (2002), p. 161; C. Hibbert, 'George IV', *ODNB*; Revd R. J. Richardson, *Recollections, Political, Literary, Dramatic, and Miscellaneous, of the Last Half-century* (2 vols in 1, 1856), pp. 267–9 (my italics).
5  Published in *The Scourge*, I, p. 431, the print is another tribute to Gillray's *Union Club*. The Four-in-Hand Club satisfied a mania among the fast set for the fast driving of four-in-hand carriages, and Barrymore was its star: R. H. Gronow, *Reminiscences and Recollections 1810–1860* (2 vols, 1985; original edn, 1892), vol. II, pp. 108–10.
6  Revd Robert Thripe, Oxford magistrate and 'man of the world', aged about sixty in 1827, to Francis Place: Place Papers, BL Add. MSS. 27827, fo. 108; MacCarthy, *Byron*, p. 64. Rowlandson's print on bucolic debauchery derives from his watercolour 'The Hunt Supper', *c.*1790: J. Hayes, *The Art of Thomas Rowlandson* (Virginia, 1990), plate 46.

7 *Boswell's London Journal, 1762–1763*, ed. F. A. Pottle (New York, 1950), pp. 43–4: see above, ch. 1.

8 G. F. A. Wendeborn, *A View of England towards the Close of the Eighteenth Century* (2 vols, 1791), vol. I, pp. 205, 207.

9 Colonel Jones to Francis Place, August 1828: Place Papers, BL Add. MSS, 27827, fo. 131.

10 L. A. Marchand (ed.), *Byron's Letters and Journals* (13 vols, 1973–94), vol. I, p. 13.

11 Boswell, *The Hypochondriack*, no. 58, July 1782.

12 P. Clark, *British Clubs and Societies 1580–1800* (Oxford, 2000), pp. 2, 10, 89; A. Sisman, *Boswell's Presumptuous Task: Writing the Life of Dr Johnson* (2000), p. 48.

13 *The Attic Miscellany* (vol. 1, 1789), pp. 8–9.

14 D. Stevenson, *The Beggar's Benison: Sex Clubs of Enlightenment Scotland and their Rituals* (2001), pp. 6–7, 33; Place Papers, BL Add. MSS. 27828, fo. 29; N. Scarfe (ed.), *A Frenchman's Year in Suffolk: French Impressions of Suffolk Life in 1784* [de la Rochefoucauld's *Mélanges sur l'Angleterre* (1784)] (Woodbridge, 1984), pp. 14–15, 188–9; G. J. Barker-Benfield, 'Sensibility', in I. McCalman, J. Mee, G. Russell, C. Tuite (eds), *The Romantic Age: British Culture 1776–1832* (Oxford, 1999), p. 103.

15 C. Hibbert (ed.), *Captain Gronow: His Reminiscences of Regency and Victorian Life, 1810–1860* (1991), pp. 226–7 (and note), 292; Wendeborn, *A View of England towards the Close of the Eighteenth Century*, vol. I, p. 197.

16 Rochefoucauld, *Mélanges sur l'Angleterre* (1784) p. 23. Rochefoucauld based his account on his experience of the Duke of Grafton's hospitality at Euston Hall, p. 21.

17 B. Faujas de Saint-Fond, *Travels in England, Scotland, and the Hebrides, etc.* (trans., 2 vols, 1799).

18 W. M. Thackeray, *The Four Georges: Sketches of Manners, Morals, Court and Town Life* (1856), pp. 355, 359; MacCarthy, *Byron*, p. 219; L. G. Mitchell, *Charles James Fox* (Oxford, 1992), p. 97.

19 W. Alexander, *The History of Women* (3rd edn, 2 vols, 1782; first edn, 1779), vol. I, pp. 475, 486, 493–4.

20 H. F. Lippincott (ed.), *'Merry Passages and Jeasts': a Manuscript Jestbook of Sir Nicholas Le Strange (1605–1655)* (Salzburg, 1974); C. Tomalin, *Samuel Pepys: The Unequalled Self* (2002), pp. 114, 153.

21 *Joseph Andrews*, Book III, ch. 3.

22 Gronow on Barrymore in Hibbert (ed.), *Gronow*, pp. 31–2.

23 W. S. Lewis (ed.), *The Yale Edition of Horace Walpole's Correspondence* (48 vols, 1937–), vol. 37, p. 166.

24 Mitchell, *Fox*, p. 14.

25 Cited by S. David, *Prince of Pleasure: the Prince of Wales and the Making of the Regency* (1999), pp. 35, 169.

26 David, *Prince of Pleasure*, p. 128, citing *Prince of W. Correspondence*, vol. II, pp. 3–4.

27 M. M. Cloake (ed.), *A Persian at the Court of King George 1809–1810: the Journal of Mirza Abul Hassan Khan* (1988), pp. 151–2; and p. 131.

28 N. W. Wraxhall, *The Historical and Posthumous Memoirs of Sir Nathaniel William Wraxall, 1772–1784* (ed. H. B. Wheatley, 1884, 5 vols) (first published in 2 vols, 1836), vol. V, p. 352ff.

29 Thackeray, *Four Georges*, p. 356.

30 Walpole, *Letters*, 21 March 1755; Mitchell, *Fox*, pp. 14, 92–3.

31 C. Pigott, *The Whig Club* (1794), cited in Mitchell, *Fox*, p. 92. Hibbert (ed.), *Gronow*, p. 77n.

32 See Mitchell, *Fox*, p. 105, and on his debts generally, pp. 100ff.

33  G. Parker, *A View of Society and Manners in High and Low Life* (2 vols, 1781), vol. I, p. ix.

34  M. Thale (ed.), *The Autobiography of Francis Place (1771–1854)* (1972), p. 85. On the Duke's social habits, see H. Angelo, *Reminiscences* (1828; 1904 edn, 2 vols), vol. I, p. 286ff. Similarly, the publican Sam House was an intimate of Fox; he appears in Rowlandson's *Samuel House* (1780) and in several satires on the 1784 Westminster election.

35  B. Reay, *Popular Cultures in England 1550–1750* (1998), pp. 217–18.

36  F. A. Pottle (ed.), *Boswell's London Journal 1762–3* (1950), pp. 272–3.

37  P. Quennell (ed.), *The Memoirs of William Hickey* (1975 edn), pp. 296–8.

38  As one print declared, *c*.1750 (*He and his Drunken Companions Raise a Riot in Covent Garden* (no imprint)), 'They sally forth and scowr the street / And play the devil with all they meet / Swagger and swear and riots make / And windows, lamps, & lanthorns break. / . . . As rudely his companions treat / All that in petticoats they meet / The women struggle, scream, and scratch / . . . In come the watch 'larm'd by the outrageous noise / And fall upon the Roaring Boys / Uplifted staves, drawn swords oppose / And stabs are well repaid with blows.' See Steele, 'The Mohock Club', *The Spectator*, 10 March 1712; John Gay, *Trivia: or, the Art of Walking the Streets of London* (1716) ('Who has not heard the *Scowrer*'s midnight fame? / Who has not trembled at the *Mohock*'s name? / Was there a watchman took his hourly rounds, / Safe from their blows, or new-invented wounds?'). See D. Statt, 'The case of the Mohocks: rake violence in Augustan London', *Social History*, 20 (2) May 1995; and N. Guthrie, '"No truth or very little in the whole story"?: a reassessment of the Mohock scare of 1712', *Eighteenth-Century Life*, 20 (2), 1996.

39  D. T. Andrew, 'The code of honour and its critics: the opposition to duelling in England, 1700–1850,' *Social History*, 5 (3), 1980; R. B. Shoemaker, 'Male honour and the decline of public violence in eighteenth-century London', *Social History* 26 (2), 2001; R. B. Shoemaker, 'The taming of the duel: masculinity, honour, and ritual violence in London, 1660–1800', *Historical Journal* 45 (3), 2002. 'Savage nobles' is J. G. Turner's neat phrase in his *Libertines and Radicals in Early Modern London: Sexuality, Politics, and Literary Culture, 1630–1685* (Cambridge, 2002), p. 166.

40  R. J. Richardson, *Recollections, Political, Literary, Dramatic, and Miscellaneous, of the Last Half-century* (2 vols, 1856), vol. II, pp. 129–30.

41  H. Angelo, *Reminiscences*, vol. I, pp. 285–8 and vol. II, p. 80.

42  N. Tolstoy, *The Half-mad Lord: Thomas Pitt, Second Baron Camelford (1775–1804)* (1978), pp. 97, 160. Gillray's *The Caneing in Conduit Street* (1796) shows Camelford attacking Lord Vancouver, who had had Camelford discharged for insolence when Camelford served under him on his naval voyage.

43  *Proceedings of the Old Bailey* (http://www.oldbaileyonline.org Ref: t17970712–55).

44  TS 11/932. The priests, however, 'went from opportunity of seeing a warm fire, and partaking the viands at the side-board with which these houses are always furnished gratis – the master of the house being in the act of turning them out, because they would not play, at the time the constables entered.'

45  Tolstoy, *The Half-mad Lord*, p. 113; Mrs H. Wyndham (ed.), *Correspondence of Sarah Spencer Lady Lyttelton 1787–1870* (1912), p. 12.

46  '. . . The sporting world in all its variety of style and costume along the road from Hyde Park Corner to Moulsay Hurst', pub. by 'Sherwood, Neely and Jones, Sept. 1st 1819'; the forty-two vignettes are numbered, implying that it was published with a commentary (Cambridge University Library).

47  G. Parker, *Life's Painter of Variegated Characters in Public and Private Life* (1789), p. 138; F. Grose, *Classical Dictionary of the Vulgar Tongue* (1785), pp. 9–10, 7–8, 385–6; Angelo, *Reminiscences*, vol. I, p. 130; *Lexicon Balatronicum: a Dictionary of Buckish Slang, University*

*Wit, and Pickpocket Eloquence . . .* (1811); [Tom Moore], *Tom Crib's Memorial to Congress . . . By one of the Fancy* (1819); on Egan's *Life in London* (1821), see ch. 18 below.

48  *Athenaeum*, October 1831.

49  M. T. W. and J. E. Payne, 'Henry Wigstead, Rowlandson's fellow-traveller', *British Art Journal*, 4 (3), (2003), pp. 27–38.

50  J. Hayes, *Rowlandson Watercolours and Drawings* (1972), plate 87, p. 181. On Angelo's friendship with Rowlandson and Rowlandson's with the Barrymores: Angelo, *Reminiscences*, vol. I, pp. 283–8 and vol. II, p. 80; and *Angelo's Pic nic; or Table Talk, Written by Himself* (1835; ed. 1905), pp. 91–2.

51  F. O'Gorman, *Voters, Patrons, and Parties: The Unreformed Electoral System of Hanoverian England 1734–1832* (1989), p. 211; Thale (ed.), *Autobiography of Francis Place*, p. 216; Rogers, *Whigs and Cities*, pp. 187, 180–4, 194; D. Miles, *Francis Place 1771–1854: The Life of a Remarkable Radical* (Brighton, 1988), p. 250.

52  Anonymous letter reproduced by Stockdale in his *Poll Book, for Electing Two Representatives in Parliament for the City and Liberty of Westminster, June 18, to July 4, 1818* (1818), p. vi. Gillray himself satirized Stockdale's social pretensions in *Effusions of the Heart; – or – Lying Jack the Blacksmith at Confession* (1798).

53  Anon., *The Patrons of Genius: a Satirical Poem with Anecdotes of their Dependants, Votaries and Toadeaters* (1798), p. 6.

54  Lewis (ed.), *Horace Walpole's Correspondence*, vol. XI, p. 220; *Athenaeum* (1 October 1831), p. 633.

55  N. Rogers, *Whigs and Cities: Popular Politics in the Age of Walpole and Pitt* (Oxford, 1989), pp. 4, 142, 146–9; O'Gorman, *Voters, Patrons, and Parties*, pp. 55, 180, 210–13, 315, 302.

56  *The Poll Book, for Electing Two Representatives in Parliament for the City and Liberty of Westminster, June 18, to July 4, 1818* (1818). By contrast, in the St James's section of Piccadilly, eighteen of the ninety tradesmen listed cast both of their votes for the ministerialist candidate Maxwell, and twenty-nine split their votes between Maxwell and the Liberal-Whig Romilly. Only seven of the ninety plumped for Burdett alone (a chemist, a bootmaker, a colourman, a carpenter, a hosier, a tailor and a saddler), and twenty-nine split their votes between Burdett and Romilly; similar patterns were apparent among the smart shopkeepers of Haymarket and the Strand.

57  By the 1820s, the middling people and their betters were being called 'middle-class' to add weight to critiques of the old order. By the middle classes, the *Examiner* declared in 1822, 'we understand all persons of moderate or very small capital; and the still greater number with no capital at all, who, by dint of a decent parentage and respectable bringing up, may hope to succeed in the world by prudence and industry' (14 April 1822). D. Wahrman, *Imagining the Middle Class: The Political Representation of Class in Britain, c. 1780–1840* (Cambridge, 1995), pp. 207, 261.

58  D. Donald, *The Age of Caricature: Satirical Prints in the Reign of George III* (1996), pp. 105–7, 99.

59  James Sayer was the only exception to this. In the 1780s and 90s (living in Norwich), his prints supported the Pittites and anti-reformers.

60  H. Fielding, *Tumble-down Dick: or, Phaeton in the Suds* (1736); G. F. A. Wendeborn, *A View of England towards the Close of the Eighteenth Century* (2 vols, 1791), vol. I, p. 292; R. Paulson, 'The joke and "Joe Miller's jests"', in his *Popular and Polite Art in the Age of Hogarth and Fielding* (1979), p. 68

61  For further discussion, see chs 16 and 17 below.

62  Angelo, *Reminiscences*, vol. I, p. 308. Not all of Bowles's output was solemn. The firm published several undidactic mezzotints about prostitution in 1772–3: *The Pantheon,*

*in Oxford Street* (above, fig. 17); *An Evenings Invitation; with a Wink from the Bagnio* (fig. 36); *Beau Mordecai Inspir'd; A Decoy for the Old as well as the Young.* And two mezzotints *à la* Carington Bowles of copulatory scenes in *Fanny Hill* are held by the BM prints and drawings dept., cat. 1954-8-18.

63 Not in the British Museum. The Lewis Walpole Library dates its copies 1800; the Huntington Library dates its 1795.

64 *The Memoirs of William Hickey* (ed. P. Quennell, 1960 edn), p. 78.

65 For example, I. Cruikshank, *The Dwarf and the Giant, or the Strong Lad of Brighton Taking off the Prince's Chum!!!* (Fores, 1795), reporting on Sir John Lade's bet with Lord Cholmondely that he could carry Cholmondely, naked, twice around the Stein at Brighton: the print imagines the spectacle, watched by the prince and bashful ladies (Cholmondely lost the bet by refusing to strip).

66 *London Literary Gazette*, no. 536 (Apr. 1827), p. 268.

67 W. M. Thackeray, *The Four Georges: Sketches of Manners, Morals, Court, and Town Life* (1855; ed. 1923), pp. 331–2.

68 D. Donald, *The Age of Caricature: Satirical Prints in the Reign of George III* (1996), pp. 99, 105–7.

## Chapter Five
# Laughing Politely

1 *The Idler*, no. 64 (1759), in W. J. Bate, J. M. Bullitt, and L. F. Powell (eds), *The Yale Edition of the Works of Samuel Johnson* (New Haven, 1963), vol. II, p. 199.

2 Boswell, *Life of Johnson*, pp. 548, 637; G. E. Bentley (ed.), *William Blake's Writings* (2 vols, Oxford, 1978), vol. II, p. 1354.

3 F. Hutcheson, *Thoughts on Laughter* (1725), pp. 19–20; *L'Encyclopédie* (1751–72), vol. XIV, p. 299; Boswell, *Life of Johnson*, p. 637.

4 For the instances cited here, see V. B. Hertzel, 'Chesterfield and the anti-laughter tradition', *Modern Philology*, 26 (1928–9), pp. 73–90.

5 G. de Rocher, *Rabelais's Laughters and Joubert's 'Traité du ris'* (Alabama, 1979), pp. 10–20, 113.

6 According to Descartes, laughter was stimulated by the tension set up when we perceive 'some small evil in a person whom we consider to deserve it: we have hatred for the evil, but joy to see it in one who deserves it'; and to this he added the impact of surprise: *The Passions of the Soul* (1649) in *The Philosophical Writings of Descartes* (Cambridge, 1985), vol. I, p. 371. He added (p. 393) that the risible stimulus must be unexpected and the evil witnessed in the person laughed at must be insignificant: 'For if it is great, we cannot believe that the one who has it deserves it [our laughter] unless we have a very bad nature or we bear much hatred towards him.'

7 Just as *L'Encyclopédie* prefaced its article 'Ris ou Rire' with a short discourse on the zigomatic muscle, so the second edition of *Encyclopaedia Britannica* (1778–83) introduced its article on laughter with this description, retained into the seventh edition of 1842: 'The eye-brows are raised about the middle, and drawn down next the nose; the eyes are almost shut; the mouth opens and shows the teeth, the corners of the mouth being drawn back and raised up; the cheeks seem puffed up, and almost hide the eyes; the face is usually red, the nostrils are open; and the eyes wet . . . Authors attribute laughter to the fifth pair of nerves, which sending branches to the eye, ear, lips, tongue, palate, and muscles of the cheek, parts of the mouth,

praecordia, &c., there hence arises a sympathy, or consent between all these parts; so that when one of them is acted upon, the others are proportionately affected.' Cf. Herbert Spencer, 'The physiology of laughter' (1860) (in *Essays: Scientific, Political, and Speculative* (3 vols, 1891), vol. II, pp. 452–66); and Charles Darwin's 'The expression of the emotions in man and animals' (1872).

8  Cureau de la Chambre, *Les characteres des passions* (Paris, 1640), pp. 225–7: English translation in *An Essay on Laughter, wherein are Displayed, its Natural and Moral Causes, with the Arts of Exciting it* (London, 1769), pp. 38–40.

9  D. Roberts (ed.), *Lord Chesterfield's Letters* (Oxford, 1992): 25 July [N.S.], 1741; 19 April [O.S.], 1749; 25 January, 19 March, 12 November [O.S.], 1750.

10  Ibid., 9 March 1748. In other letters to similar effect, Chesterfield forbade 'horse-play, romping, frequent and loud fits of laughter, jokes, waggery, and indiscriminate familiarity'. A joker 'is near akin to a buffoon; and neither of them is the least related to wit': 30 Aug. [O.S.] 1749.

11  W. S. Taylor and J. H. Pringle (eds), *Correspondence of William Pitt, Earl of Chatham* (4 vols, 1838–40), vol. I, p. 79.

12  James Beattie, *Essay on Laughter, and Ludicrous Composition* (1776).

13  A. Koestler, *The Act of Creation* (1964; 2nd edn, 1976), pp. 29–31, summarized in 'Humour and wit', *New Encyclopaedia Britannica* (15th edn), vol. XX, pp. 682–8.

14  Even in 1923 it was possible to list 363 publications on the subject, ranging from Plato and Aristotle through to Kant, Bergson and Freud: J. Y. T. Greig, *The Psychology of Laughter and Comedy* (1923). Since then, the number if not stature of laughter pundits has exploded risibly. Recent 'laughter research' tells us, for example, that a laugh 'is characterized by a series of short vowel-like notes each about 75 milliseconds long, that are repeated at regular intervals about 210 milliseconds apart'. It adds that when American women speak to men, they laugh 127 per cent more often than their male auditors do, whereas when men speak to women they laugh about 7 per cent less than the women who listen to them. Males, in short, 'are the leading humor producers and females are the leading laughers': Robert R. Provine, 'Laughter', *American Scientist* (Jan.–Feb. 1996).

15  E. Kris, *Psychoanalytic Explorations in Art* (1953), pp. 204–5.

16  Koestler, *Act of Creation*, p. 51, and in *New Encylopaedia Britannica*, vol. XX, p. 683.

17  William Hazlitt in 1819, citing Aristotle, discerned similar impulses behind both laughter and weeping: 'Tears may be considered as the natural and involuntary resource of the mind overcome by some sudden and violent emotion, before it has had time to reconcile its feelings to the change in circumstances: while laughter may be defined to be the same sort of convulsive and involuntary movement, occasioned by mere surprise or contrast (in the absence of any more serious emotion), before it has time to reconcile its belief to contradictory appearances': *Lectures on the English Comic Writers* (1819; ed. 1963), p. 5. Cf. Voltaire: 'Other animals have this muscle as well as ourselves, yet never laugh any more than they shed tears': *A Philosophical Dictionary, from the French of M. Voltaire* (orig. 1765; translated in 6 vols, London, 1824), vol. IV, pp. 299–301. (Actually, chimpanzees laugh too: see Robert R. Provine, 'Laughter', *American Scientist* (1996).)

18  Q. R. D. Skinner, *Reason and Rhetoric in the Philosophy of Hobbes* (Cambridge, 1996), pp. 198–211, 390–5, and 'Why laughing mattered in the Renaissance', *History of Political Thought*, xxii (3), Autumn 2001, pp. 418–47.

19  Hobbes, *The Elements of Law Natural and Political* (1640), ch. 9. See also his 'Human nature' (1650) (ix, 13) in F. Tonnies (ed.), *The Elements of Law, Natural and Politic* (2nd edn, 1969), pp. 41–2. For later endorsement of Hobbes's views, see Louis Poinsinet de Sivry's *Traité des causes physiques et morales du rire relativement à l'art de l'exciter* (1768)

(ed. W. Brooks, Exeter, 1986), pp. 92–6; Montesquieu's *Of the Pleasures of the Soul*, in *The Complete Works of M. de Montesquieu* (4 vols, London, 1777), p. 142 ('a certain joy in our soul' is caused by another's faults or deformity); and Basil Montagu, *Thoughts on Laughter* (1830), pp. 33–4, 40.

20  *The Spectator* (23), 27 March 1711. *The Spectator* also parodied Hobbes in no. 47: 'When we hear a man laugh excessively, instead of saying he is very merry, we ought to tell him he is very proud', *The Spectator*, ed. D. F. Bond (2 vols, Oxford, 1965), vol. I, pp. 200–4 (no.47, 24 April 1711). James Beattie, *Essay on Laughter, and Ludicrous Composition* (1776), p. 591.

21  Lord Shaftesbury, *Characteristics of Men, Manners, Opinions, Times* (1711), ed. L. Klein (Cambridge, 1999), pp. 48, 43, 31, 59.

22  F. Grose, *Rules for Drawing Caricaturas; with an Essay on Comic Painting* (1788).

23  Hutcheson, *Thoughts on Laughter*, pp. 2–4, 14, 9–10, 24–5, 29.

24  Shaftesbury, *Characteristics*, pp. 35, 50–1.

25  Beattie, *Essay on Laughter*, pp. 666–70, 683–704.

26  *The Letters of David Hume* (2 vols, Oxford, 1932), vol. II, p. 301.

27  Walter Harte, *An Essay on Satire, particularly on the Dunciad* (1730) (reprint with introduction by T. B. Gilmore, Los Angeles, 1968), p. 6; P. K. Elkin, *The Augustan Defence of Satire* (Oxford, 1973), pp. 94–5 (I am much indebted to Elkin's work in this section); Boswell, *Life of Johnson*, p. 1207. Cf. to similar effect Steele in *The Tatler* no. 61, 30 Aug 1709, and Swift in *The Examiner*, no. 38, 26 April 1711; and William Combe in 1777: cited Elkin, ibid., pp. 75–6.

28  Charles Abbott, 'On the use and abuse of satire' (1786, republished in *Oxford English Prize Essays* (Oxford 1836)), vol. I, pp. 187, 199 (cited in Elkin, *Augustan Defence of Satire*, pp. 181–3).

29  Elkin, *Augustan Defence of Satire*, pp. 70, 85.

30  V. Knox, 'On the ill effects of satire', in *Essays Moral and Literary* (3rd edn, 1782), vol. I, p. 189 and vol. II, p. 227, cited by Elkin, *Augustan Defence of Satire*, pp. 48, 52–3.

31  G. Dyer, *British Satire and the Politics of Style 1789–1832* (Cambridge, 1997), pp. 144–52.

32  *Spectator*, no. 23 (March 1711).

33  *Joseph Andrews* (1742), Book III, ch. 2.

34  Elkin, *Augustan Defence of Satire*, pp. 125–8; T. J. Mathias, *The Pursuits of Literature* (1794–7) (cited by Dyer, *British Satire and the Politics of Style*, p. 25); Abbott, 'On the use and abuse of satire', vol. I, p. 186;

35  Elkin, *Augustan Defence of Satire*, pp. 172–4, 146–60.

36  Hutcheson, *Thoughts on Laughter*, pp. 42, 27–8.

37  H. Fielding, preface to 'The history of the adventures of *Joseph Andrews*', and 'An essay on conversation', in his *Miscellanies* (1743) (ed. H. K. Miller, Oxford, 1972), pp. 123, 150–1.

38  *Essay on Laughter*, pp. 662, 602. Often, Beattie thought, this was best seen in prints: Hogarth's *The Enraged Musician* was a 'very comical mixture of incongruity and relation' (ibid., pp. 607–8).

39  Thus summarized in *Encyclopaedia Britannica* (2nd edn, 1780), p. 4031.

40  Grose, *Rules for Drawing Caricaturas* (1788), pp. 13, 15, 21.

41  *Thoughts on Laughter*, pp. 54, 39, 62–4.

42  C. A. G. Goede, *A Foreigner's Opinion of England* (3 vols, bound in 2, 1821, first published as *A German Visitor to England in 1802*), vol. II, pp. 63–4.

43  R. Porter, *Flesh in the Age of Reason* (2003), p. 296.

Chapter Six

# Bums, Farts and Other Transgressions

1  The words were Thomas Erskine's in 1793, defending the London Corresponding Society member, John Frost, against the charge of sedition: cited by J. Barrell, 'Coffee-house politicians', *Journal of British Studies*, 43, no. 2 (2004). My thanks to John Barrell for allowing me pre-publication access to this deftest of all analyses of public/private distinctions in the later eighteenth century: cf. his *The Spirit of Despotism: Politics and Culture in the 1790s* (Oxford, 2006).

2  H. F. Lippincott (ed.), *'Merry Passages and Jeasts': a Manuscript Jestbook of Sir Nicholas Le Strange (1605–1655)* (Salzburg, 1974); F. K. Brown, *Fathers of the Victorians: The Age of Wilberforce* (Cambridge, 1961), pp. 19–20; L. Picard, *Dr Johnson's London* (2000), p. 266.

3  J. Swift, *A Discourse concerning the Mechanical Operation of the Spirit, etc.*, in *Prose Works* (1941 edn), vol. XI, p. 253; G. Legman, *No Laughing Matter: Rationale of the Dirty Joke: second series* (1978), ch. 15; M. L. Apte, *Humor and Laughter: an Anthropological Approach* (New York, 1985), pp. 92–6.

4  *Merrie Conceited Jests of George Peele* (1627 and eds. 1657, 1809), p. 31; see also Hazlitt, *Shakespearian Jest Books* (2 vols, 1864), vol. II, cited in G. Legman, *No Laughing Matter*, p. 980.

5  *The Merry-thought: or, the Glass-window and Bog-house Miscellany* (1731; Augustan Reprint Society, nos 216, 221–2 (Los Angeles, 1982), part 2, p. 25; part 1, p. 20; part 2, p. 24. Cf. F. MacCarthy, *Byron: Life and Legend* (2002), p. 384.

6  R. W. Scribner, 'Demons, defecation, and monsters: popular propaganda for the German Reformation', in R. W. Scribner, *Popular Culture and Popular Movements in Reformation Germany* (1987), pp. 276–99; R. W. Scribner, *For the Sake of Simple Folk : Popular Propaganda for the German Reformation* (1981); B. Babcock, *The Reversible World: Symbolic Inversion in Art and Society* (Ithaca, NY., 1978); W. A. Coupe, *German Political Satires from the Reformation to the Second World War* (2 vols, New York, 1993); P. Burke, 'Frontiers of the comic in early modern Italy', in his *Varieties of Cultural History* (1997).

7  This motif referred back to an anti-Walpole print of 1740: the anonymous *Idol Worship, or the Way to Preferment* (1740), which had servile MPs kiss Sir Robert Walpole's colossal buttocks (reproduced in Donald, *The Age of Caricature*). Cf. also Newton's *Buonaparte Establishing French Quarters in Italy* (1797), in which the Pope submissively kisses Napoleon's buttocks.

8  Dent's *The Host of Dissenters and St Charles* (1790) shows churchmen defending themselves against dissenters by using vomit and turds as projectiles. Fox and Lord North administer a curative enema to Britannia in Gillray's *A New Administration; or – The State Quacks Administering* (1783). Isaac Cruikshank has a line of Flemishwomen pissing on invading French soldiers in *Opening the Sluices, or Holland's Last Shift* (1794); Cawse follows suit in his *Opening the Sluices or the Secret Expedition* (1799), with three Dutch fishwives urinating on retreating British soldiers in order to drown them (Britain having agreed to cease hostilities with Holland and evacuate it). In Isaac Cruikshank's *Bonne Farte Raising a Southerly Wind* (1798) Bonaparte projects from his backside a guillotine, balloons, infantry, tents, cavalry, etc., across the Channel. Elmes's *The Imperial Comet Shedding its Baneful Influence* (1811) has the infant king of Rome fart his defiance at the Pope.

9  Gillray's *Scene le Vrog House* (1782) has French admirals defecate in fear before the triumphant Admiral Rodney. See also Isaac Cruikshank's *The Renunciation of an Ex*

*Noble now Become a Republican Sans-Culotte Citizen* (1794) in fig. 210 below.

10  Gillray's *Sawney in the Bog-house* (1779) similarly recycles a long-standing lavatorial satire at the Scots' expense: reproduced in Donald, *The Age of Caricature*.

11  D. Drakard, *Printed English Pottery: History and Humour in the Reign of George III* (1992).

12  *Scene in the R—l Bedchamber; or a Slit in the Breeches!!*

13  D. Nokes, *Raillery and Rage: A Study of Eighteenth Century Satire* (Brighton, 1987), p. 80; J. N. Lee, *Swift and Scatological Satire* (Albuquerque, 1971).

14  D. Brewer, 'Prose jest-books mainly in the sixteenth to eighteenth centuries in England', in J. Bremmer and H. Roodenburg (eds), *A Cultural History of Humour from Antiquity to the Present Day* (1997), pp. 102–3. See also S. Dickie, 'Hilarity and pitilessness in the mid-eighteenth century: English jestbook humor', *Eighteenth-Century Studies*, 37 (1), 2003.

15  Ned Ward, *Remarkable Clubs and Societies* (1756: 7th edn of *The Secret History of Clubs* (1709)), p. 31. See P. Hyland introduction to *The London Spy* (East Lansing, 1993); P. Rogers, *Grub Street: Studies in a Subculture* (1972).

16  Thus *The Covent Garden Jester* tells us that 'Two were disputing, which was the noblest part of the body; one said the mouth, because it saluted first; the other said, the breech, because it sat down first: at the next meeting he that held for the mouth, saluted the other with a fart; at which he seemed angry: "Why, said he, that is the part which you held most noble, and therefore I salute you with it. "'

17  N. Elias, *The Civilising Process*, vol. I *The History of Manners* (1978); S. G. Greenblatt, 'Filthy rites', in his *Learning to Curse: Essays in Early Modern Culture* (New York, 1990), pp. 60–1. Cf. L. Roper, *Oedipus and the Devil*, p. 159; and G. K. Paster, *The Body Embarrassed: Drama and the Disciplines of Shame in Early Modern England* (Cornell, 1993).

18  Northrop Frye, 'The mythos of winter: irony and satire', in his *The Anatomy of Criticism* (New Jersey, 1957), reprinted in R. Paulson (ed.), *Satire: Modern Essays in Criticism* (1971), p. 244; Paulson, 'The central symbol of violence', ibid., pp. 344–5.

19  J. Beattie, *Essay on Laughter, and Ludicrous Composition* (1776).

20  John Brown, 'Essay on Ridicule', in *Essays on the Characteristics of the Earl of Shaftesbury* (1751), pp. 53–4.

21  P. K. Elkin, *The Augustan Defence of Satire* (Oxford, 1973), pp. 57–8, 176. Cf. J. Aden, 'Swift's "unprintables"', in L. S. Champion (ed.), *Quick Springs of Sense: Studies in the Eighteenth Century* (Athens, Georgia, 1974).

22  Laurent de Joubert, *Traité des causes du ris et tous ses accidents* (1579); G. de Rocher, *Rabelais's Laughers and Joubert's 'Traité du ris'* (Alabama, 1979), pp. 12–13, 22–6.

23  J. Nichols, *Biographical Anecdotes of William Hogarth* (1781; 1971 edn), p. 7.

24  M. Bakhtin, *Rabelais and his World* (trans. 1968), pp. 117, 120.

25  Emma Griffin, 'Popular sports and celebrations in England, 1660–1840', Ph. D. dissertation (Cambridge, 2000), pp. 1–15; B. Reay, *Popular Cultures in England 1550–1750* (1998), pp. 162–7; R. Hutton, *The Rise and Fall of Merry England* (Oxford, 1994), ch. 3. Griffin shows that most recent studies of 'popular cultures' assume that popular culture had an autonomous life that directly reflected economic and social conditions, neglecting how they were changed *politically*. Hutton notes that 'All over western and central Europe during the sixteenth and seventeenth centuries reformers attacked popular festivity and tried to enforce a stricter standard of sexual morality and of personal decorum. A sharper separation was made between the sacred and the profane and between the sophisticated and the vulgar, and an attempt was made to create a more orderly and sober, as well as a more pious society' (pp. 111–12); 'the early Tudor culture of seasonal celebration was in decline over the whole subsequent period of a century and a half' (p. 152).

26  Griffin, 'Popular sports', p. 100; R. D. Storch (ed.), *Popular Culture and Custom in*

*Nineteeth-century England* (1982), ch. 4; Sir John Fielding, *An Account of the Origins and Effects of a Police* (1758), ix–x.

27  J. Strutt, *The Sports and Pastimes of the People of England* (1801; new edn. by William Hone, 1830), pp. xl, 339, 349, 351–2; R. Southey, *Letters from England* (1807; 1984 edn), p. 362; L. Wagner, *Manners, Customs, and Observances: Their Origin and Signification* (1894), p. 426; Hutton, *Merry England*, p. 244; H. Angelo, *Reminiscences* (2 vols, 1828), vol. I, p. 408.

28  Griffin, 'Popular sports and celebrations', ch. 2 and pp. 101–2; Strutt, *Sports and Pastimes*, pp. 340, 369; Hunt in *The Examiner*, 21 December 1817, pp. 801–3; P. Burke, *Popular Culture in Early Modern Europe* (1978), ch. 9.

29  R. W. Malcolmson, *Popular Recreations in English Society, 1700–1853* (1973), p. 25; R. D. Storch, ' "Please to remember the fifth of November" : Conflict, solidarity and public order in Southern England, 1815–1900', in R. D. Storch (ed.), *Popular Culture and Custom in Nineteenth-century England* (1982).

30  Wagner, *Manners, Customs, and Observances*, p. 463.

31  T. Gretton, *Murders and Moralities: English Catchpenny Prints, 1800–1860* (1980), pp. 85, 109; *St James's Magazine*, July 1865, p. 511.

32  For these survivals, see citations in *Oxford English Dictionary*.

33  Reay, *Popular Cultures*, pp. 132–6; D. A. Reid, 'Interpreting the festival calendar: wakes and fairs as carnivals', in Storch (ed.), *Popular Culture and Custom*.

34  Malcolmson, *Popular Recreations*, p. 36; J. Brewer, 'Theatre and counter-theatre in Hanoverian politics: the mock elections at Garrett', *Radical History Review*, 22 (1979); J. Brewer, *Party Ideology and Popular Politics at the Accession of George III* (Cambridge, 1976), pp. 187–90, 310–11; F. O'Gorman, 'Campaign rituals and ceremonies: the social meaning of elections in England, 1780–1860', *Past and Present*, no. 135 (May 1992), pp. 79–115; E. P. Thompson, *Customs in Common* (1991), pp. 467–531; V. A. C. Gatrell, *The Hanging Tree: Execution and the English People 1770–1868* (Oxford, 1994), p. 93.

35  Wagner, *Manners, Customs, and Observances*, p. 439; R. Southey, *Letters from England*, pp. 78–80. Cf. C. Phythian-Adams, 'Milk and soot: the changing vocabulary of popular ritual in Stuart and Hanoverian London', in D. Fraser and A. Sutcliffe (eds), *The Pursuit of Urban History* (1983), pp. 83–104.

36  W. Hone, *The Every-day Book; or, The Guide to the Year* (2 vols, 1826), vol. II, pp. 523–7, 1195, and *The Every-day Book* (1825), vol. I, p. 630. C. Walford, *Fairs, Past and Present* (1883); S. Rosenfeld, *The Theatre of the London Fairs in the Eighteenth Century* (Cambridge, 1960); H. Cunningham, 'The metropolitan fair: a case study in the social control of leisure', in A. P. Donajgrodzki (ed.), *Social Control in Nineteenth-century Britain* (1977), pp. 163–184.

37  'Bartleme Fair', in G. A. Stevens, *Songs, Comic and Satyrical* (1782 edn), pp. 69–71. In *The Prelude*, Wordsworth described the fair as a 'parliament of monsters', filled with 'albinos, painted Indians, dwarfs . . . the horse of knowledge . . . the invisible girl . . . and puppet shows', along with musicians playing hurdy-gurdies, fiddles, kettledrums and trumpets.

38  *Gentleman's Magazine* (1817), p. 272; 'The mirror of months', 1826, in Walford, *Fairs, Past and Present*, p. 238; Hone, *The Every-day Book* (1826–7), cited in J. Mullan and C. Reid (eds), *Eighteenth-Century Popular Culture: A Selection* (2000), pp. 143–5.

39  Gatrell, *Hanging Tree*, pp. 119–23 (here re-cited), and R. Leach, *The Punch and Judy Show: History, Tradition and Meaning* (1985).

40  See Reformation examples in K. Moxey, *Peasants, Warriors, and Wives: Popular Imagery in the Reformation* (Chicago, 1989). For animal masks, Gillray's *Crumbs of Comfort or – Old Orthodox, Restoring Consolation to his Fallen Children* (1782) (among many examples).

For *memento mori*, fig. 19 above. For a world-upside-down print, see S. O'Connell, *The Popular Print in England* (1999), p. 124.

41 Angelo, *Reminiscences*, vol. I, pp. 285–8.

42 Malcolmson, *Popular Recreations*, pp. 56–8, 63, 68.

43 F. MacDonogh, *The Hermit in London* (1819–20), vol. II, pp. 118–19 (cited in P. Langford, *Englishness Identified: Manners and Character 1650–1850*, (Oxford, 2000), p. 131.

44 S. Carter, '"This female proteus": representing prostitution and masquerade in eighteenth-century English popular print culture', *Oxford Art Journal*, 22 (1), (1999), pp. 55–79.

45 T. Castle, *Masquerade and Civilization: The Carnivalesque in Eighteenth-century English Culture and Fiction* (1986), pp. 2–10, 17–19, 32–4, 51, 74–5, 90, 101–3, and passim. Castle's book is the indispensable source for all who now write on masquerade, and I draw heavily on it. Cf. C. Craft-Fairchild, *Masquerade and Gender: Disguise and Female Identity in Eighteenth-century Fictions by Women* (Pennsylvania, 1993); B. A. Babcock, '"Liberty's a whore": Inversions, marginalia, and picaresque narrative', in B. A. Babcock (ed.), *The Reversible World* (New York, 1978).

46 BMSat. 3030.

47 P. Quennell (ed.), *The Memoirs of William Hickey* (1975 edn), pp. 286, 289–90, 292; Mrs H. Wyndham (ed.), *Correspondence of Sarah Spencer Lady Lyttelton 1787–1870* (1912), p. 14.

48 *London Chronicle* (1788), p. 420.

49 David Garrick to the Countess of Burlington, 3 August 1749: 'Your Lp will se by ye enclos'd prints, that a much greater man is attack'd upon his amours, – the little Savoyard girl was certainly in the forest, and it is confidently affirm'd, that she refus'd some offers; she tells the story and grinds her musick for half a crown in the purlieus of Covt Garden – The other print, is a second and more accurate description of Miss C[hudleigh]'s dress; some say laughingly, that this is publish'd by herself, to vindicate her decency from false imputations; the gentleman talking to her in the domino [the king], may be known by his hat.' *The Letters of David Garrick* (1963), vol. I, pp. 107–8 (I am grateful to Kate Retford for this reference). Walpole reported on another masquerade held a few days later 'by the king's command for Miss Chudleigh . . . with whom our gracious monarch has a mind to believe himself in love, – so much in love, that at one of the booths he gave her a fairing for her watch, which cost him five and thirty guineas, – actually disbursed out of his privy-purse, and not charged on the civil list': BMCSat. on the Chudleigh plates, 3030–3.

## Chapter Seven

# Image Magic

1 B. Jerrold, *The Life of George Cruikshank* (1898, reprint 1971), p. 103; C. Banerji and D. Donald (eds), *Gillray Observed: The Earliest Account of his Caricatures in 'London und Paris'* (Cambridge, 1999), pp. 245–7.

2 J. Lindsay, *Hogarth: His Art and his World* (1977), pp. 138–9; Oliver Goldsmith, *The Citizen of the World* (1762 edn), p. 175; C. Williams (trans. and ed.), *Sophie in London* (1933), pp. 237, 262–3; Jerrold, *Life of George Cruikshank*, pp. 90–4; F. W. Hackwood, *William Hone: His Life and Times* (1912), pp. 198–205.

3 W. M. Thackeray, 'On the genius of George Cruikshank', *Westminster Review* (1840).

4 H. Viztelly, *Glances back Through Seventy Years: Autobiographical and other Reminiscences*

(2 vols, 1893), vol. I, p. 88; C. M. Smith, *The Little World of London* (1857), pp. 9–10. Cf. J. Brewer, *The Common People and Politics, 1750–1790s* (Cambridge, 1986), pp. 21–4, 27.

5 '*Punch* has the benevolence to announce, that in an early number of his ensuing volume he will astonish the parliamentary committee by the publication of several exquisite designs, to be called *Punch's* cartoons!' *Punch*, 24 June 1843.

6 Sir Gilbert Elliot's passing note in a letter of 1804 is the most one can expect: 'There is a new print of Gillray's, in which the state waggon is drawn by asses, and is stuck fast in a slough . . . the horses' faces are portraits of the Oppositionists': Countess of Minto (ed.), *Life and Letters of Gilbert Elliot, First Earl of Minto, from 1751 to 1806* (3 vols, 1874), vol. III, p. 319. The annual sale of newspapers in London rose from some 7 to 16 million in the second half of the century, while London dailies increased from nine to thirteen, and ten further papers appeared three times a week. M. Butler, *Romantics, Rebels and Reactionaries: English Literature and its Background 1760–1830* (1981), p. 15; Porter, *Enlightenment: Britain and the Making of the Modern World* (2000), pp. 77–8.

7 B. Stafford, *Body Criticism: Imaging the Unseen in Enlightenment Art and Medicine* (Cambridge, Mass., 1994), p. xviii. On the scant reference to caricaturists in their time, see Donald, *Age of Caricature*, pp. 22–3.

8 *Letters . . . of John Wilkes . . . to his Daughter* (4 vols, 1804), vol. III, p. 189.

9 Jerrold, *Life of George Cruikshank*, p. 103; W. S. Lewis (ed.), *The Yale Edition of Horace Walpole's Correspondence* (48 vols, 1937–), vol. 20, pp. 77–8, 90.

10 Northrop Frye, 'The mythos of winter: irony and satire', in *The Anatomy of Criticism*, (New Jersey, 1957), reprinted in R. Paulson (ed.), *Satire: Modern Essays in Criticism* (1971), p. 235; *Anecdotes of William Hogarth, Written by Himself* (1833 edn), p. 9.

11 W. M. Thackeray, 'Roundabout Papers: *de juventate*', *Cornhill Magazine*, October 1860, pp. 509–10.

12 M. Wood, *Radical Satire and Print Culture 1790–1822* (Oxford, 1994), p. 3.

13 Jerrold, *Life of George Cruikshank*, pp. 90–4; F. W. Hackwood, *William Hone: His Life and Times* (1912), pp. 198–205; Gatrell, *The Hanging Tree*, pp. 187–9.

14 W. M. Thackeray, *The Four Georges: Sketches of Manners, Morals, Court, and Town Life* (1855), ch. iv. Cf. the image invoked in the pro-Caroline pamphlet in 1820 that called the king 'a plaister of Paris figure, pretty well polished outside, quite hollow within, and covered all over with trinkets': *The King the Avowed Enemy of the Queen: a New Royal Game of Chess . . . Invented by Philoi-d'or . . .* (T. Dolby, 1820), p. 5.

15 BMSat 9, xlix.

16 *Johnsonian Miscellanies*, ii, pp. 419–20. The print was Gillray's *Apollo and the Muses, Inflicting Penance on Dr Pomposo, Round Parnassus* (Holland): BMSat 6328.

17 G. F. A. Wendeborn, *A View of England towards the Close of the Eighteenth Century* (trans. from German edn. of 1785–88: 2 vols, 1791), vol. I, p. 213.

18 L. G. Mitchell, *Charles James Fox* (Oxford, 1992), p. 14.

19 Mathias's views to this effect had high authority: his *The Pursuits of Literature* (1794–7) had achieved sixteen editions by 1812: G. Dyer, *British Satire and the Politics of Style 1789–1832* (Cambridge, 1997), pp. 25–6.

20 H. Angelo, *The Reminiscences of Henry Angelo* (1828), pp. 365–7.

21 D. Hill, *Mr Gillray the Caricaturist* (1965), p. 128; Cobbett's *Political Register*, 30 May 1818. Cobbett used the occasion to expose the bribe Gillray had received from the Tory minister George Canning: see below, ch. 9.

22 *The Times*, 8 and 15 May 1800. BMCSat. provides four further but rare examples of prosecutions for personal libel involving graphic satire. (1) In 1792, a Holborn printseller and artist, Baldrey, was fined and sentenced to three months for libelling

an Essex magistrate (BMCSat.7, xvi). (2) In a much publicized case in 1808, Sir John Carr failed in an action against the publishers of a caricature frontispiece that so attacked his abilities as a travel writer that his own publisher (Phillips) refused his latest manuscript 'for fear of ridicule' (at a loss to Carr of £700). The case was brought 'solely and exclusively on the caricatures', and not on the 'pretended criticisms'. Ellenborough summed up in favour of the rights of critics and liberty of the press, however. BMCSat.7, xvi, and BMCSat.8, xv; prints at BMSat 11081, 11084, 11089 comment on the case. (3) In 1813, caricatures were cited in a protracted legal vendetta between corrupt parish officials and their opponents: BMCSat.9, xix–xx and BMSat.11951. (4) In 1815, an action was brought at Maidstone assizes against a Miss Mary Edmunds for 'three poetical libels and two caricature drawings' accusing a local attorney, Boys, of dishonesty. Boys claimed £1000 damages and got £10: BMCSat.9, xix–xx.

23  J. T. Smith, *Nollekens and his Times* (edn. 1895), p. 87.

24  *History of the Westminster Election . . . By Lovers of Truth and Justice* (1784), p. 352 (cited BMSat6, xvii).

25  Reynolds's *Georgiana, Duchess of Devonshire, and her Daughter* (1784): M. Postle (ed.), *Joshua Reynolds: The Creation of Celebrity* (Tate Gallery, 2005).

26  On Fox and Sayers: 'James Sayers', *ODNB*, citing H. Twiss, *The Public and Private Life of Lord Chancellor Eldon* (3 vols, 1844), vol. I, p. 163, and M. D. George, *English Political Caricature: A Study of Opinion and Propaganda* (2 vols, Oxford, 1959), vol. 1, p. 169. On Fox and Norfolk, Angelo, *Reminiscences of Henry Angelo*, pp. 365–7. Fox's and Norfolk's reputations never fully recovered from this episode. Horne Tooke and the radicals attended this celebration for the first time, and 2,000 people dined in the street outside. Norfolk compared the 2,000 with those who rallied round George Washington. For this, the king also removed him from his lord lieutenancy and colonelcy of the militia. Memories of indiscretions like this helped to condemn the Foxites to virtually unbroken exclusion from government for a half-century after 1783.

27  BMSat. 9240; K. R. Johnston, 'Romantic anti-jacobins or anti-jacobin romantics?', *Romanticism on the Net*, 15 (August 1999); N. Roe, *Wordsworth and Coleridge: The Radical Years* (Oxford, 1988); W. C. Hazlitt (ed.), *Letters of Charles Lamb* (2 vols, 1886), vol. I, p. 208. See below.

28  BMSat. 8, xi.

29  Classic examples of engravers' revenge attacks are Gillray's elaborate and expensive satires on Boydell of the Shakespeare Gallery (*Shakespeare Sacrificed* (1789)), on Thicknesse (*Lieut Govern. Gall-stone, inspired by Alecto* (1790)), and on the amateur caricaturist General Davies, who was said to have slighted Gillray (*The Military Caricaturist* (1799)). The first two of these are reproduced in R. Godfrey (ed.), *James Gillray: The Art of Caricature* (2001), plates 83 and 43B. Matthew Darly in 1775 produced a vicious attack (*Ecce Homo*) on the allegedly demented artist-cum-caricaturist Henry Austin, who himself, according to the print, had been moved to 'declare & pronounce war with and against all and every printshop and printseller within and without the City of London' for their conspiring against his ambitions to open his own 'museum of drawings'.

30  Donald, *Age of Caricature*, pp. 22–24; R. P. Knight, *The Progress of Civil Society: A Didactic Poem* (1796), cited ibid., p. 23.

31  By this period even the once awesome dance-of-death motif was reduced to a joke – in Rowlandson's book series on the subject, or in Woodward's *Dance of Death Modernised* (1808). E. H. Gombrich, *Art and Illusion* (1977 edn), pp. 289–91; E. Kris, *Psychoanalytical Explorations in Art* (1952), ch. 6 and (with E. H. Gombrich) ibid., ch. 7;

R. Paulson, *Satire: Modern Essays in Criticism* (1971), pp. 340–2; R. C. Elliott, *The Power of Satire: Magic, Ritual, Art* (Princeton, N.J., 1960), pp. 87–8, 98, 261–4; F. S. Connelly, 'Profound play: the image tradition of the comic grotesque', in P. Kort (ed.), *Comic Grotesque: Wit and Mockery in German Art, 1870–1940* (New York, 2004), pp. 195–209.

32  E. J. Lovell (ed.), *Lady Blessington's Conversations of Lord Byron* (Princeton, 1969), p. 145.

33  Elliott, *The Power of Satire*, pp. 271–3.

34  Donald, *Age of Caricature*, p. 142.

35  H. J. C. Grierson (ed.), *The Letters of Sir Walter Scott* (12 vols, 1932–7), vol. IV, p. 384f. (cited BMCSat.8. xi).

36  W. S. Lewis (ed.), *The Yale Edition of Horace Walpole's Correspondence* (48 vols, 1937–), vol. 33, pp. 400–1.

37  D. Hill, *Mr. Gillray the Caricaturist* (1965), chs. 6–9 for Gillray's correspondence with *Anti-Jacobin* circle.

38  The Gillray print that ensued from the cited letter is *Billingsgate Eloquence no. 5* (dashes abbreviating the swear words); the original sketch is in BM Prints and Drawings Department: British 201. c. 06 PIV (no. 89). See also proposals for satires contained in Gillray's papers, BL Add. MSS. 27337, fos. 37–43, 110–128, 184. The BM Prints and Drawings Department database lists Gillray satires that were proposed by amateurs.

Chapter Eight

# Seeing the Jokes

1  Even in 1785, Horace Walpole was claiming that that earlier era had seen 'nothing like the present constellation' of satirists. 'Once in a year or two,' he recalled, 'Pope after many throes was delivered of an imitation of Horace, and Swift now and then sold you a bargain in short verses – [but] for the rest of the time . . . Lord Lyttelton squirted out ballads to Delia no better than what are [now] sung at Vauxhall': W. S. Lewis (ed.), *The Yale Edition of Horace Walpole's Correspondence* (48 vols, 1938–), vol. 33, p. 501.

2  James Sayers issued a print on *The Biographers [of Johnson]: Mrs Thrale, Boswell, Courtenay* (1786); Rowlandson produced twenty caricatures on Johnson's and Boswell's Highland journey: *Picturesque Beauties of Boswell* (1786), bound in two parts for 10s. 6d.

3  Of *early* eighteenth-century prints of all kinds, Sheila O'Connell bluntly reminds us that 'the vast majority do not survive': 'The print trade in Hogarth's London', in R. Myers, M. Harris and G. Mandelbrote (eds), *The London Book Trade: Topographies of Print in the Metropolis from the Sixteenth Century* (2003). Although the numbers of London printshops greatly increased in the years 1727–63 to feed a growing demand for political caricature, 'social' satires were then relatively few: H. M. Atherton, *Political Prints in the Age of Hogarth: A Study of the Ideographic Representation of Politics* (Oxford, 1974), p. 2.

4  A microfilm of the Library of Congress's prints that are unlisted in BMCSat. is available in the British Museum Prints and Drawings Department. Major US holdings are in the Lewis Walpole, Huntington, New York Public and Pierpont Morgan Libraries. While BMCSat. lists 330 satirical mezzotints for 1760–1800, a further 424 uncatalogued mezzotints have now been identified in American libraries: see John Hart's online *Catalogue of 18th-Century British Mezzotint Satires in*

*North American Collections* (http://www.lclark.edu/~jhart/home.html). Also uncatalogued are thirty-two of the 200 satires in the Baker Baker Papers, University of Durham Library (http://flambard. dur. ac. uk:6336/dynaweb/handlist/fam/baker).

5 A prospectus for the New Shakespeare Gallery in 1794 put the feasible quantity at a higher figure. It vaunted the advantage of line engraving over stipple on the grounds that 'a stroke-engraved plate . . . when well executed, is capable of producing at least two thousand good prints': D. H. Weinglass, *Prints and Engraved Illustrations by and after Henry Fuseli: A catalogue raisonné* (1994), p. xviii. H. M. Atherton (*Political Prints in the Age of Hogarth: A Study of the Ideographic Representation of Politics* (Oxford, 1974), p. 64) referred to a run of 'two or three thousand' before a print's quality was 'completely gone'. Dorothy George claimed that from the 1770s improved technology permitted good runs of between 1,000 and 1,500 (*English Political Caricature*, vol. I, p. 131).

6 *The Repeal or the Funeral of Miss Ame-Stamp*: M. D. George, *English Political Caricature* (Oxford, 1959), vol. I, p. 135.

7 *The Follies of a Day, or the Marriage of Figaro* (13 March 1786, for Fores) was by Rowlandson's friend, Henry Wigstead: H. Angelo, *The Reminiscences of Henry Angelo* (2 vols, 1828; 1904 edn, 2 vols), vol. I, p. 330.

8 Ackermann's printshop led in establishing artistic lithography in England *c*.1817. George Cruikshank used lithography for Fores in his January 1818 celebration of Hone's acquittals, *William the Conqueror, or the Game Cock of Guildhall*. At least two of Marks's bawdy satires on Princess Elizabeth's marriage (*John Bull Supporting, the Nuptial Bed!!!* and *Old Snuffy Inquiring after her Daughter Betty* (both April 1818) declared that they were 'drawn and printed from stone' (see figs. 248 and 249).

9 Fores advertised caricatures expressly for pasting on screens: see Woodward's and I. Cruikshank's six prints, *Caricature Ornaments for Screens* (Fores, 1800). B. Lynch, *The Prize Ring* (1925) illustrates Byron's screen. Pasted screens are depicted in Heath's *The Royal Milling Match* (Fores, 1811), and in a Robert Cruikshank illustration in P. Egan, *The Finish to the Adventures of Tom, Jerry, and Logic* (1830), p. 142 and facing. On print-rooms: S. Tillyard, *Aristocrats: Caroline, Emily, Louisa and Sarah Lennox 1740–1832* (1994), pp. 203–5; R. L. Patten, *George Cruikshank's Life, Times, and Art*, vol. 1: 1792–1835 (1992), p. 75; D. Donald, *The Age of Caricature: Satirical Prints in the Reign of George III* (1996), p. 21 (photograph of the Calke Abbey room; Donald provides an excellent discussion of print distribution, pp. 19ff.). For an early illustration of a room decorated with prints, see *Squire Randal's Excursion Round London* (1777), frontispiece.

10 H. Angelo, *Reminiscences of Henry Angelo* (1828), pp. 365–7. On the printshop 'lounge': C. A. G. Goede, *A Foreigner's Opinion of England* (3 vols, bound in 2, 1821, first published as *A German Visitor to England in 1802*), vol. I, pp. 130, 127.

11 N. K. Robinson, *Edmund Burke: A Life in Caricature* (1996), appx. 1, p. 194.

12 Angelo, *Reminiscences*, pp. 365–7.

13 In addition, the BM holds several volumes of 'Caricatures' that were strongly bound for 'C. B. Wilson': his name and the dates 1820–23 appear on title pages. The Reform Club in Pall Mall owns a caricature collection with 'S. W. F[ores]' stamped on the covers. A handbill in the Prints and Drawings Department of the BM headed 'Roxburgh Collection of Caricatures' advertises for sale in 1812 a collection 'bound in 24 uniform volumes' that went for 250 guineas. See S. O'Connell, 'Selling Hogarth's prints: the Hogarths, Hogarthmania, and John Boydell' (unpublished: my thanks to the author for a copy); S. O'Connell, 'The Peel collection in New York', *Print Quarterly*, March 1998, p. 66; Simon Turner, 'Fores, Samuel William', *ODNB*.

The BM prints and drawings department holds a checklist of the Rothschild collection's contents (pressmark P.6.18), along with microfilms of the Peel collection, and four microfilm spools of the prints in the Prince of Wales's collection not held in the BM (now in the Library of Congress). For the ongoing destruction of collections, cf. Sotheby's auction on 13 November 1997 of a major collection of satires and genre pieces assembled *c*.1770–1800 by a 'high titled' European.

14  Wilkes, *Letters . . . of John Wilkes . . . to his Daughter* (4 vols, 1804), vol. III, pp. 247, 315: also pp. 171, 301, 307. The unnamed prints that upset the prince might have included Gillray's *The Fall of Phaeton*, engraved for Fores in July, 1788: the prince falls from his phaeton and is about to land on Mrs Fitzherbert, whose own fall has bared her ample buttocks: a real accident, apparently, since this image was copied by several others.

15  Tillyard, *Aristocrats: Caroline, Emily, Louisa and Sarah Lennox, 1740–1832* (1995), pp. 203–5.

16  Many prints in the Baker collection are apparently lost or later removed as unseemly. The survivors are listed and their relationship to Mrs Baker's tastes are expertly discussed on the website of the Baker Baker papers, University of Durham Library. The collection contains an additional thirty or so prints dating from before her husband's death and from after her own, probably bought by her husband and son. I am grateful to Edward Higgins for advice on the collection.

17  BM Prints and Drawings Department, Inventory Reg. A. 40, and *User's Guide* (1987), p. 82. Gillray's *An Old Maid on a Journey* (1804) allegedly depicts Miss Banks as an elderly woman entering an inn carrying a print portfolio. Donald, *Age of Caricature*, pp. 17, and (for constraints on women's relationship to the satires) pp. 15–18.

18  Reproduced in M. Pointon, *Hanging the Head: Portraiture and Social Formation in Eighteenth-century England* (1993), fig. 113.

19  R. L. Patten, *George Cruikshank's Life, Times, and Art*, vol. 1: 1792–1835 (1992), p. 75 and note 18. On the destruction of the letters see J. Lees Milne, *The Enigmatic Edwardian: The Life of Reginald, Second Viscount Esher* (1986), pp. 239, 243: my thanks to Piers Brendon for this reference.

20  Cited by P. J. Corfield, *Power and the Professions in Britain, 1700–1850* (1995), p. 45.

21  Edinburgh boasted its own mild-mannered caricaturist in John Kay: see J. Kay, *Series of Original Portraits and Caricature Etchings* (2 vols, Edinburgh, 1838); H. and M. Evans, *John Kay of Edinburgh* (1973); Donald, *Age of Caricature*, pp. 19–20; S. Nenadic, 'Print collecting and popular culture in eighteenth-century Scotland', *History* (1997), pp. 221–2; L. Weatherill, *Consumer Behaviour and Material Culture in Britain, 1660–1760* (1988).

22  Le Blanc, cited in J. Lindsay, *Hogarth: His Art and his World* (1977), p. 146; Charles M. Smith, *The Little World of London* (1857), p. 242.

23  C. McCreery, 'Keeping up with the *bon ton*: the *tête-à-tête* series in the *Town and Country Magazine*', in H. Barker and E. Chalus (eds), *Gender in Eighteenth-century England: Roles, Representations, and Responsibilities* (1997).

24  BMCSat. vol. 7, xvi–xvii; Espinasse, *Reports at Nisi Prius*, iv. 97. Evidence was 'called to prove that the [Fores] collection was one of the best that could be procured of the kind, and the prices charged reasonable'. The defence's response was that it 'contained several prints of obscene and immoral subjects, exclusive of several being duplicates'. The judge referred the matter to other judges for their opinion, himself advising that 'for prints whose objects are general satire or ridicule of prevailing fashions or manners, I think the Plaintiff may recover; but I cannot permit him to do so for such whose tendency is immoral or obscene; nor for such as are libels on individuals and for which the Plaintiff might have been criminally answerable for

libel'. Fores apparently won his case. On the prints' relative immunity from prosecution, see below, chapter 16.

25  R. L. Patten, *George Cruikshank's Life, Times, and Art: volume 1: 1792–1835* (1992), pp. 172–3.

26  G. F. Berkeley, *My Life and Recollections* (4 vols, 1865), vol. IV, p. 133.

27  There had long been a semi-clandestine satirical trade in France; this escalated during the Revolution (see box of French satires 1790–1815: BM Prints and Drawings Department) but was virtually extinguished under the Bourbon restoration. On European satires see: L. Hunt, *The Family Romance of the French Revolution* (1992), p. 15; N. M. Athanassoglou-Kallmyer, *Eugene Delacroix: Prints, Politics and Satire 1814–1822* (1991); A. de Baecque, *La caricature revolutionnaire* (Paris, 1988); C. Clerc, *La caricature contre Napoléon* (1985); W. A. Coupe, *German Political Satires from the Reformation to the Second World War* (2 vols, New York, 1993); J. Cuno and C. Burlingham (eds), *French Caricature and the French Revolution, 1789–1799* (1988); P. Chu and G. P. Weisberg, *The Popularization of Images: Visual Culture under the July Monarch* (New Jersey, 1994); B. Farwell, *The Charged Image: French Lithographic Caricature 1816–48* (Santa Barbara, 1989); R. J. Goldstein, *The Censorship of Political Caricature in Nineteenth-century France* (Ohio, 1989) and *Political Censorship of the Arts in Nineteenth-century Europe* (1989); C. Langois, *La caricature contre-revolutionnaire* (Paris, 1988); J. Wechsler, *A Human Comedy: Physiognomy and Caricature in Nineteenth-century Paris* (1982).

28  G. F. A. Wendeborn, *A View of England towards the Close of the Eighteenth Century* (2 vols, 1791), vol. I, pp. 137–8; vol. II, p. 155 (I am grateful to Suzanne Mathieson for this reference); D. Alexander, *Richard Newton and English Caricature in the 1790s* (1998), p. 22. Cf. *Sayer and Bennett's enlarged catalogue of new and valuable prints, in sets, or single; also useful and correct maps and charts; likewise books of architecture, views of antiquity, drawing and copy books, &c. &c. in great variety, at No. 53, in Fleet-Street, London; where gentlemen for furniture, merchants for exportation, and shopkeepers to sell again, may be supplied with the greatest assortment, on the most reasonable terms. For 1775.* (facsimile reprint, Holland Press, 1970).

29  On the German reception of English satire, see C. Banerji and D. Donald, *Gillray Observed: the Earliest Accounts of his Caricatures in 'London und Paris'* (Cambridge, 1999), pp. 21–29.

30  R. Wolf, *Goya and the Satirical Print in England and the Continent, 1730–1850* (Boston, 1991); R. Hughes, *Goya* (2003), p. 23. Hogarth's and Gillray's influence on Goya was explored in an exhibition of *British Satirical Prints: Hogarth and his Age* at the Biblioteca Nacional, Madrid, 2001: see website.

31  N. Tolstoy, *The Half-mad Lord: Thomas Pitt, Second Baron Camelford (1775–1804)* (1978), p. 151.

32  George Cruikshank produced eight prints from Russian originals after Napoleon's retreat from Moscow: BMCSat. 9, xiv–xvi and BM 12051. After Leipzig, BMSat notes a 'wholesale international copying of political prints' to celebrate the success of international cooperation: BMCSat. 8, xiv, xl–xliii.

33  W. S. Lewis (ed.), *The Yale Edition of Horace Walpole's Correspondence* (48 vols, 1937–), vol. 21, p. 90. Cf. ibid., vol. 21, p. 487 (1761); vol. 23, pp. 5 (1768) and 496 (1784); vol. 25, p. 641 (1776); BMCSat.10, xv; M. Wood, *Radical Satire and Print Culture* (Oxford, 1994), pp. 264–71.

34  The Bowles's family firm was at 69 St Paul's Churchyard ever since its establishment *c.*1691; Carington Bowles took it over in the 1760s, and his son continued the business in partnership with Samuel Carver until the 1830s; Robert Sayer married into the Overton family's firm at 53 Fleet Street in 1748 (it was established in the 1660s); he was joined by John Bennett in the 1770s: see O'Connell, 'The print trade in Hogarth's London' and T. Clayton, *The English Print 1688–1802* (1997), p. 288.

Matthew Darly was at no. 39 in the Strand before 1780 and thereafter at 159 Fleet Street. The Strand shop is illustrated in BMSat. 4701 and 5318. Darly is portrayed in two of the 'macaroni' caricatures kept by Horace Walpole.

35 Darly's advertisement continued with a reference to female amateurs that made sense in a culture in which drawing and designing were valued female accomplishments: 'Ladies to whom the fumes of the *aqua fortis* are noxious may have their plates carefully bit and proved, and may be attended at their own houses, and have ev'ry necessary instruction in any part of engraving, etching, dry needle, metzotints [*sic*] &c. All sorts of tools for the above arts and for immediate use are neatly prepared. viz. gravers, points, oylstones, bags, grounding tools, scrapers, &c.'

36 The woman Walpole spoke to was probably the wife of T. Cornell, off Berkeley Square, where Walpole kept his town house (W. S. Lewis (ed.), *The Yale Edition of Horace Walpole's Correspondence* (48 vols, 1937–), vol. XXXIII, pp. 400–1). Cornell's was a small printshop, and its returns from print sales would have been modest. Only fifty-eight titles are attributed to it in the decade 1781–90. It is listed in Pendred's 1785 directory not as a printshop, but as a 'stationer' ('to the Prince of Wales'): G. Pollard (ed.), *The Earliest Directory of the Book Trade. By John Pendred (1785)* (1955), p. 10. The print advertising Fores's readiness to engrave amateur designs is BMSat. 6961. The Merlin database in the BM's Prints and Drawings Department details fifteen original sketches by amateurs which were engraved by Gillray and which the Museum now holds.

37 Across 1781–90 the numbers of *satirical* prints per printshop as catalogued in BMCSat. run in ascending order as follows : 25 by James Bretherton, New Bond Street; 32 by W. Dent (often via other print-shops); 41 by Mrs D'Archery, St James's Street (ceased trading in 1784); 58 by Thomas Cornell or Corneille, Bruton Street; 67 by Carington Bowles; 95 by W. Holland, Drury Lane and then Oxford Street; 100 by William Humphrey, starting in Gerrard Street, Soho, in 1777 and at 227 Strand until the mid-1780s; 109 by Hannah Humphrey, Bond Street; 214 by S. W. Fores, Piccadilly. Printshop addresses are from BMCSat. 'Introductions' and I. Maxted, *The London Book Trades 1775–1800: a Preliminary Checklist of Members* (1977) and I. Maxted, *The London Book Trades 1775–1800: a Topographical Guide* (1980). On Ackermann, BMCSat., 8 xl–xliii.

38 C. A. G. Goede, *A Foreigner's Opinion of England* (3 vols bound in 2, 1821, first published as *A German Visitor to England in 1802*), vol. III, p. 140.

39 See BMSat. 10835 for a depiction of Ackermann's Repository of Arts, and BMSat. 10118 and 11565 for Fores's shop.

40 Fores's 1794 advertisements read: 'he has fitted up his caracature [*sic*] exhibition in an entire novel stile admit 1s NB folios lent out.' 'Prints and drawings are lent out on the plan of a library,' he was announcing a few years later. In 1807, Ackermann advertised his 'circulating port-folios consisting of the choicest drawings and prints' for yearly subscription of four guineas; and he lent out caricature portfolios over weekends or overnight. BMCSat.6, xxxiii–v; 7, xlvi; 8, xl–xliii.

41 Sayer and Bennet boasted that they sold prints to 'gentlemen for furniture', while Holland in 1794 advertised his readiness to bind his caricatures into volumes, 'like those he has had the honour to make up for their Royal Highnesses the Prince of Wales and the Duke of York' (Alexander, *Newton*, pp. 21, 43).

42 BMCSat. vol. 6, p. xi note.

43 BM Prints and Drawings Department: BM receipt N.7.1.

44 Big sales could bring down the cost of fine-art prints, however. John Raphael Smith's engraving of Fuseli's *Night Mare* cost only five shillings in 1783: D. H. Weinglass, *Prints and Engraved Illustrations by and after Henry Fuseli: A catalogue raisonné* (1994), p. 55. See fig. 121.

45  D. Donald, *The Age of Caricature*, pp. 184–5, and E. E. Nicholson, 'Consumers and spectators: the public of the political print in eighteenth-century England', *History* (January 1996). Nicholson focuses narrowly on the political satires of early to mid-century, reads London's social structure simplistically ('elite' vs 'plebeian'), and has no sense of middling-class political sophistication.

46  F. W. Hackwood, *William Hone: His Life and Times* (1912), pp. 39–40.

47  Tegg's autobiography was summarized from his own MS (now lost) in the *City Press*, 6 and 13 August 1870: a copy is in the Guildhall Library. I am grateful to Tegg's descendant Mr Michael Crellin for a transcript. On Tegg, as well as on Fairburn and other publishers of the period, see also John Britton, *Specimen of the Auto-biography of John Britton* (1850); J. Grant, *Portraits of Public Characters* (2 vols, 1841), vol. II, p. 24ff.; *Real Life in London* (1821; new edn, 2 vols, 1905), vol. I, pp. 275–6; H. Viztelly, *Glances Back through Seventy Years: Autobiographical and Other Reminiscences* (2 vols, 1893), vol. I, p. 89. On the book trade generally: J. Lackington, *Memoirs of the First 45 Years in the Life of James Lackington* (1791); J. Raven, 'Selling one's life', in O. M. Brack (ed.), *Writers, Books and Trade: An Eighteenth-century Miscellany* (New York, 1994); M. Butler, *Romantics, Rebels and Reactionaries: English Literature and its Background 1760–1830* (1981), p. 15; Roy Porter, *Enlightenment: Britain and the Creation of the Modern World* (2000), pp. 77–8; J. Feather, 'The power of print: word and image in eighteenth-century London', in J. Black (ed.), *Culture and Society in Britain, 1660–1800* (Manchester, 1997), p. 59.

48  J. Raven, 'New reading histories, print culture and the identification of change: the case of eighteenth-century England', *Social History*, 23 (3) (1998), pp. 276–8; Raven, 'Books as commodities', in M. Suarez (ed.), *The Cambridge History of the Book in Britain* (Cambridge, 2004), vol. 5; Butler, *Romantics, Rebels and Reactionaries*, p. 15; Porter, *Enlightenment*, pp. 77–8; G. E. Bentley (ed.), *William Blake's Writings* (2 vols, Oxford, 1978), vol. II, pp. 1535, 1582.

49  Three volumes of *Tegg's Caricature Magazine* were issued by 1809 and another in 1821, each holding up to 500 prints, their contents depending on what prints were in stock. Advertisement at the back of Tegg's *Chesterfield Travestie: or School for Modern Manners* (1808): 'a large collection (the largest in England) of new popular humourous and political caricatures, by Woodward, Rowlandson, Cruikshanks, only 1s. each, equal to any, and superior to most, published at double the price. N. B. Please to order Tegg's new caricatures. Noblemen, gentlemen, &c., wishing to ornament their billiard or other rooms, with caricatures may be supplied 100 per cent cheaper at Tegg's caricature warehouse. Merchants and captains of ships supplied wholesale for exportation.' Earlier printshops had issued bound volumes of prints: *The Butiad, or Political Register* offered forty-three prints on political affairs in 1762–3; Matthew Darly bound prints with a title page in 1771; *Sayer and Bennett's Catalogue of Prints* for 1775 (pp. 72–4) advertised ninety-five prints 'neatly done up in half binding, price 3 guineas'.

50  Little is known about Williams, but he was an accomplished and prolific artist who worked between 1797 and the 1820s. His early work was published under the name 'Ansell'; later he became an imitator and copyist of Gillray. He was frequently employed by Fores until George Cruikshank became Fores's chief artist around 1815.

51  W. S. Lewis (ed.), *The Yale Edition of Horace Walpole's Correspondence* (48 vols, 1937– ), vol. 32, p. 304 n. and vol. 38, p. 120.

52  Walpole's 'selection' is now in the New York Public Library. Walpole had pasted another two hundred or so satires into albums in earlier years. His phrasing cited above suggests that some were thrown away. But many other Walpole-owned prints

are in the Lewis Walpole Library, Yale University; others, sold off in 1842, are now in the BM and elsewhere. Walpole had acquired every Bunbury print he could and was his chief patron, chiefly because he was a gentleman amateur knitted into Walpole's social circle: J. C. Riely, 'Horace Walpole and "the second Hogarth",' *Eighteenth-Century Studies*, 9 (1975–6), pp. 28–44.

53 Lewis (ed.), *Horace Walpole's Correspondence*, vol. 25, p. 496.

54 These included a Carington Bowles mezzotint (BMSat 4546), a Wigstead caricature of Mrs Inchbold the actress (1787, not in BM), several striking prints by James Sayers, four or five Gillrays in his maturer style of the late 1780s (BMSat. 6932, 7530, 7163, 7165, 7166), the bestselling *The Repeal, or the Funeral of Miss Ame-Stamp* of 1766; his own self-portrait, and another (BMSat. 4701); *The vis à vis* (BMSat. 5375); and *Betty the Cook's Maid's Head Drest* (BMSat. 5380).

55 BMSat 6187, 6188, 6194. Reproduced in D. Hill, *Mr Gillray the Caricaturist* (1965) and discussed p. 24.

56 For his delight in the Worsley scandal and comment on Gillray's *A Peep into Lady W!!!!!'s Seraglio*, see M. R. Brownell, *The Prime Minister of Taste: A Portrait of Horace Walpole* (2001), pp. 211–14.

57 *The Kettle Hooting the Porridge-Pot.*

58 *Gulliver Casting a Damper upon the Royal Fireworks at Lilliput*: on the Speaker's casting vote against fortifying two southern ports (BMSat. 6919).

59 Published by J. Barrow, 16 January 1783: not in BMSat., but see BMSat. 6168 for companion print.

60 BMSat. 5571.

61 Gillray, *Wouski* (after a black theatrical character) (Humphrey, 1788).

62 *Anecdotes of Painting* (1761), preface.

63 R. Paulson, *Rowlandson: A New Interpretation* (1972), p. 15; P. J. Corfield, *Power and the Professions in Britain, 1700–1850* (1995), p. 47; C. A. G. Goede, *A Foreigner's Opinion of England* (3 vols, 1821: first published as *A German Visitor to England in 1802*), vol. III, pp. 139–40.

64 Walpole to Countess of Ossory, 10 February 1786, and Walpole to Mann, 13 February 1786 (*Letters*, Cunningham ed., vol. IX, pp. 39, 46).

65 Walpole to the Miss Berrys, 27 March, 9 October 1791: Lewis (ed.), *Horace Walpole's Correspondence*, vol. XI, p. 220; Brownell, *The Prime Minister of Taste*, pp. 295–8. Gillray's *Siege of Blenheim* was long remembered. In 1824 G. Cruikshank adapted (but sanitized) this theme in a print (BMSat.14712) about a breach of promise case.

66 J. Barrell, 'The private comedy of Thomas Rowlandson', *Art History* (December 1983), pp. 426–33; C. S. Matheson, 'Viewing', in I. McCalman et al. (eds), *The Romantic Age: British Culture 1776–1832* (Oxford, 1999), p. 189; L. Klein, 'The third Earl of Shaftesbury and the progess of politeness', *Eighteenth-Century Studies* 18 (1984–5), pp. 191, 198.

## Chapter Nine

# Gillray's Dreamscapes

1 M. Grosley, *A Tour to London; Or, New Observations on England, and its Inhabitants* (2 vols, 1772), vol. I, p. 57.

2 C. Lamb, 'On the genius and character of Hogarth' (1811, revised 1818): in E. V. Lucas (ed.), *The Works of Charles and Mary Lamb* (6 vols, 1912), vol. I, p. 82.

3 R. Godfrey (ed.), *James Gillray: The Art of Caricature* (2001), p. 7; E. H. Gombrich,

*Meditations on a Hobby Horse* (1960), pp. 120–2.

4 The scene in Hogarth's *Gulliver* appears nowhere in Swift's book, but it translates the message that Swift conveys by indirection and understatement 'into an emblematic image of Gulliver's subservient "liberty"-loving folly in a country run by Hanoverian and Walpolian pygmies': R. Paulson, 'The tradition of comic illustration from Hogarth to Cruikshank', in R. L. Patten (ed.), *George Cruikshank: A Revaluation* (Princeton, 1992), p. 47.

5 W. H. Pyne [as Ephraim Hardcastle], 'Reminiscences of artists', in Pyne's *Somerset House Gazette and Literary Museum*, no. 26 (1824), pp. 409–12 (cited without acknowledgement by H. Angelo, *Reminiscences* (1828), pp. 384–9).

6 C. Banerji and D. Donald (eds), *Gillray Observed: The Earliest Account of his Caricatures in 'London und Paris'* (Cambridge, 1999), pp. 245–7. This view revised Huttner's earlier sense of Gillray as 'pleasant in company, with an effervescent wit', see pp. 55–6.

7 BM Add. MSS 27337, fos. 29, 101, 108.

8 BM Add. MSS 27337, fos 7–10; D. Hill, *Mr Gillray the Caricaturist* (1965), pp. 10–12.

9 The original amateur sketch is in the BM Prints and Drawings Department (British 201. c. 06 PIV (no. 15)). The department holds a group of drawings by amateurs supplied to Gillray at 1867–10–12–609 to 621. Some formed the basis of well-known satires like Gillray's *The King of Brobdingnag and Gulliver*. See T. Wright, *The Works of James Gillray, the Caricaturist, with the History of his Life and Times* (1873) for appendix of 'Subjects suggested to Gillray by amateurs', pp. 374–6.

10 H. Angelo, *Reminiscences*, pp. 383–4; Banerji and Donald (eds), *Gillray Observed*, pp. 55–6.

11 Reproduced in T. Hyman, 'A carnival sense of the world', in T. Hyman and R. Malbert, *Carnivalesque* (2000), p. 46. I am grateful to Timothy Hyman for a readable photocopy.

12 Add MSS. 27337, fos. 74–6.

13 Reproduced, for example, in Godfrey (ed.), *James Gillray*, plates 41A and C; for contemporary comment, see Walpole, *Letters*, 2 Sept 1790; and K. Garlick, A. Macintyre, and K. Cave (eds), *The Diary of Joseph Farington [1793–1821]* (16 vols, 1978–98), vol. I, pp. 286–7.

14 Gillray was not first engraver to break the taboo on caricaturing the king and queen: Mansell, Kingsbury and Newton had done so before him. Still, no royal caricature was as vicious as this one. Preceding satires had been limited to comments on the royal couple's parsimony: Mansell's(?), *The Constant Couple* (Fores, 1786: the king and queen sharing the same horse); Kingsbury's, *The Farm Yard* (Phillips, 1786: the couple as simple farmers); Kingsbury's, *From the Originals at Windsor* (Dowse, 1791: a travesty of Metsys's *The Misers*, showing the couple counting their money); and Newton's *A Visit to the Royal Cole Pit* (1791). How shocking the caricaturing of majesty remained is clear from the Treasury Solicitor's case against the Birmingham bookseller, Belcher, in 1793: see below, ch. 16.

15 Landseer's recollection: *Athenaeum*, no. 207 (1831), p. 667.

16 Hill, *Mr Gillray the Caricaturist*, p. 81.

17 R. W. Buss (on Cruikshank's authority), in *English Graphic Satire* (privately printed, 1874), pp. 128–9 (cited by R. L. Patten, *George Cruikshank's Life, Times, and Art*: vol. 1: *1792–1835* (1992), p. 84). In fact, most of Gillray's prints were planned before engraving, and his surviving notebooks are covered in sketched designs and notes on protagonists and postures.

18 Godfrey, *Gillray*, p. 221.

19 'Fox and Sheridan pick [John Bull's] pockets, Pitt runs him through a coffee grinder, the French enslave him, and George III madly accosts him.' Paulson notes: '. . . His

sufferings are constant and, in most cases, undeserved, and he frequently shows more common sense than his tormenters.' Bull is the only figure who is not in a state of chronic self-delusion, yet he is also, significantly, the only major protagonist in Gillray who is not a real person. In any case, 'all his sympathetic qualities are countered by his gross face, body, actions and words', for Bull has 'no brains, few words, and hardly any personal identity': R. Paulson, 'The grotesque, Gillray, and political caricature', in his *Representations of Revolution (1789–1820)* (1983), pp. 190, 195, 211.

20 M. Butler, 'Art for the people: Blake, Gillray and Wordsworth', in her *Romantics, Rebels and Reactionaries: English Literature and its Background* (1982), p. 56; Paulson, 'The grotesque, Gillray, and political caricature', pp. 189, 193–5.

21 Banerji and Donald (eds), *Gillray Observed*, pp. 55–6.

22 W. Hone, *The Three Trials of William Hone* (1817; reprinted with introduction by W. Tegg, 1876), pp. 35, 36, 40–1, 122 (for Hone and his trials see below, chapter 16). Cobbett on Gillray's bribe: *Weekly Political Register*, 33 (1818), p. 625. For correspondence between Gillray and the Canning circle, J. Bagot, *George Canning and his Friends* (2 vols, 1909); and Hill, *Mr Gillray the Caricaturist*, chs 6–10. Gillray's pension lapsed on Pitt's resignation, since no protégé of Canning's would be supported by the new prime minister, Addington. But Cobbett later thought that it must have been restored in 1807, so fierce were Gillray's attacks then on the ministry of the 'Talents' (*Political Register*, 30 May 1818). Gillray's correspondence with the Canningites continued through the medium of Sneyd, secrecy being its essence, Sneyd pressing Gillray not to name names, 'which in these times of inquiry seems to frighten all publick men'.

23 Northcote cited by D. Donald, *The Age of Caricature: Satirical Prints in the Reign of George III* (1996); W. M. Thackeray, 'On the genius of George Cruikshank', *Westminster Review* (1840).

24 Banerji and Donald (eds), *Gillray Observed*, pp. 245–7.

25 *Anecdotes of William Hogarth* (1833 edn), pp. 8–9, 17, 32–3.

26 Citations from Blake from his handwritten marginalia in his copy of Reynolds' *Works*: G. E. Bentley (ed.), *William Blake's Writings* (2 vols, Oxford, 1978), vol. II, pp. 1450, 1459–61, 1467, 1470, 1535, 1582. His strictures on Reynolds are at their fullest in his satirical rhymes 'On Art and Artists' (1800–3).

27 The term 'phantasmagoria' was coined in 1802 to advertise a commercial exhibition of light-projected optical illusions. Gillray used the word as a title for one of his prints a year later.

28 N. Powell, *Fuseli: The Nightmare* (1973), pp. 20, 27, 39ff.

29 For a complete catalogue of engraved versions of *The Nightmare*, along with derivations and parodies, see D. H. Weinglass, *Prints and Engraved Illustrations by and after Henry Fuseli: A catalogue raisonné* (1994), pp. 55–73; for the five-shilling price of the authorized 1783 engraving, p. 55. Powell, *Fuseli*, Appendix II provides an incomplete list of *Nightmare* parodies; Donald, *Age of Caricature*, pp. 69–71, adds two more.

30 *Shakespeare-Sacrificed* (1789); *A Witch, upon a Mount's Edge* (1791); *Wierd-Sisters* (1791); *An Angel, Gliding on a Sun-beam into Paradise* (1791); *Sin, Death, and the Devil* (1792); *The Nuptial-bower* (1797); and *A Peep into the Cave of Jacobinism* (1798). The first three drew on Fuseli's work for the Shakespeare Gallery, the next three on his work for the Milton Gallery. Hill, *Mr Gillray the Caricaturist*, pp. 90, 147–8.

31 Cited in Godfrey, *Gillray*, p. 11.

32 Hogarth's and Gillray's influence on Goya was explored in an exhibition of *British Satirical Prints: Hogarth and his Age* at the Biblioteca Nacional, Madrid, 2001. See also R. Wolf, *Goya and the Satirical Print in England and the Continent, 1730–1850* (Boston,

1991); R. Hughes, *Goya* (2003), p. 23. On Gillray's influence on Blake: Godfrey, *Gillray*, p. 11; D. V. Erdman, 'William Blake's debt to James Gillray', *Art Quarterly*, xii (1949), pp. 165–70; D. V. Erdman, *Blake: Prophet against Empire* (1977).

33 R. Paulson, 'The grotesque, Gillray, and political caricature', in *Representations of Revolution (1789–1820)* (1983), pp. 182–3.

34 Their prototypes are the grotesque female figures in *The Miser's Feast* and *The Injured Count..[es]s* of 1786: see figs. 146 and 147).

35 Gillray's explicit dreamscapes include two versions of *Tom Paine's Nightly Pest* (1792), in which the sleeping Paine is beset by nightmare visions of judges and gallows before he flees to France to escape prosecution for *The Rights of Man*, Part 2. But not all his dreamscapes are horrific. In *The Lover's Dream* (1795), the sleeping Prince of Wales is beset by visions of his parents, mistresses, and Princess Caroline (whom he had consented to marry if his debts were paid). Similarly in *Delicious Dreams! – Castles in the Air! – Glorious Prospects!* (1808) the Cabinet, in drunken stupor after dinner, dream of Napoleon's defeat and capture.

36 Banerji and Donald (eds), *Gillray Observed*, pp. 116, 118, 245–7.

37 One might add the incubi, demons, scaffold visions and decapitated bodies that haunt Tom Paine or Fox in several prints; or the demons that plague the imposter Thicknesse in one of Gillray's most ambitious if now obscure prints, *Lieut Goverr Gall-Stone, inspired by Alecto; – or the Birth of Minerva* (1790) – 'one of the most sustained, complex and savage visual attacks ever sustained by a single individual' (and another measure of Gillray's unforgiving nature) (Godfrey, *James Gillray*, p. 84). Nightmare visions fill Gillray's *Hopes of the Party* (1791), in which George III is decapitated by Fox and the Whigs outside the Crown and Anchor tavern, while the queen and Pitt are hanged from lamp brackets. *Promis'd Horrors of the French Invasion* sustains similar imaginings.

38 For an excellent discussion of *The Apotheosis*, see Donald, *The Age of Caricature*, pp. 69, 176–7; also Godfrey, *Gillray*, plates 56, 57. In a rare retrospect on Gillray's and others' caricatures written in 1835, this print was thought to 'border on the sublime': *Literary Gazette*, Jan., no. 937, (1835), p. 1.

39 H. Angelo, *The Reminiscences of Henry Angelo* (1828), p. 363.

40 BL Add. MSS 27337; Hill, *Mr Gillray the Caricaturist*, pp. 81–5.

41 J. Brewer, *The Pleasures of the Imagination: English Culture in the Eighteenth Century* (1997), p. 76; G. F. A. Wendeborn, *A View of England towards the Close of the Eighteenth Century* (2 vols, 1791), vol. II, p. 156; James Barry, *A Letter to the Dilettanti Society* (1798), p. 23, cited by Donald, *Age of Caricature*, p. 23; on Dick v. Dick, *The Scourge: or Monthly Expositor of Imposture and Folly* (9 vols, 1811–15), vol. III, pp. 34–5.

42 The Shakespearean scholar, George Steevens, 'is often at Mrs. Humphrys paint [*sic*] shop, and likely enough supplies the Latin motto's to Gilrays prints,' Farington noted in 1797: *The Diary of Joseph Farington* (ed. K. Garlick and A. Macintyre), vol. III, pp. 927–8.

43 J. Bagot, *George Canning and his Friends* (2 vols, 1909), vol. I, pp. 56–7.

44 Bentley (ed.), *William Blake's Writings*, vol. II, pp. 1604–5.

45 The most immediate progenitor of *The Union Club* was an anonymous and dim little magazine etching of the Union Club, from which Gillray lifted some of his own print's personnel and the caption verses: 'We'll join hand in hand, all party shall cease, / And glass after glass, shall our Union increase, / In the cause of Old England we'll drink down the sun, / Then toast Little Ireland and drink down the moon!' (BMSat. 9698).

46 H. Alken, *A Touch at the Fine Arts; Illustrated by Twelve Plates* (1824), plate 11; and an Alken plate for Surtees's *Jorrocks's Jaunts and Jollities* (184).

'Mixed feelings: the Enlightenment and sexuality', in P.-G. Bouce (ed.), *Sexuality in Eighteenth-Century Britain* (1982); R. Porter, *Enlightenment: Britain and the Creation of the Modern World* (2000), pp. 258–65; J. G. Turner, 'The properties of libertinism,' in R. P. Maccubin (ed), *'Tis Nature's Fault: Unauthorized Sexuality during the Enlightenment* (Cambridge, 1985); G. S. Rousseau and R. Porter (eds), *Sexual Underworlds of the Enlightenment* (Manchester, 1987). For Carlile's comment: TS11/43, part 2, pp. 179–80.

22  P. Cryle and L. O'Connell (eds), *Libertine Enlightenment: Sex, Liberty and Licence in the Eighteenth Century* (2004), pp. 2–4.

23  L. A. Marchand (ed.), *Byron's Letters and Journals* (13 vols, 1973–94), vol. I, p. 19.

24  Rolleston's probable authorship is noted in the Cambridge University Library copy.

25  Experiences on the Grand Tour underpinned a good deal of the anthropologizing common to this kind of text. Cf. the above with P. Beckford, *Familiar Letters from Italy, to a Friend in England* (1805), letter xlvii: 'Your ladies [in England] take even an unnecessary trouble to conceal the necessities of nature; here [in Siena] we hand our ladies to the very door of the water-closet': A. Brilli, *English and American Travellers in Siena* (Siena, 1987), p. 110.

26  Cf. M. Madan, *Thelypthora; or, a Treatise on Female Ruin* (1780–81); J. H. Lawrence, *The Empire of the Nairs* (1811) (the Nairs, or Nayars, were a military caste of Malabar who practiced polyandry).

27  Hamilton's letter and Knight's *Account* were republished by J. C. Hotten in 1865 as *Discourse on the Worship of Priapus*: this edition, pp. 13, 16–17. On the influence of the discovery of sexually explicit classical materials, see W. Kendrick, *The Secret Museum: Pornography in Modern Culture* (New York, 1987).

28  List of possible prints on the back of a pen-and-wash sketch for a satire: reproduced in T. Hyman and R. Malbert, *Carnivalesque* (2000), p. 46. I am grateful to Timothy Hyman for a photocopy of the original.

29  In his *The Progress of Civil Society, A Didactic Poem* (1796).

30  M. Clarke and N. Penny (eds), *The Arrogant Connoisseur: Richard Payne Knight 1751–1824* (Manchester, 1982), pp. 61–2; G. Carabelli, *In the Image of Priapus* (1996), pp. 84–6.

31  I. Jenkins and K. Sloan, *Vases and Volcanoes: Sir William Hamilton and his Collection* (1996), p. 101; Clarke and Penny, *Arrogant Connoisseur*, p. 63; Carabelli, *Priapus*, p. 27.

32  Carabelli, *Priapus*, pp. 19–22, 27, 29, 54; Clarke and Penny, *Arrogant Connoisseur*; R. Trumbach, 'Erotic fantasy and male libertinism in Enlightenment England', in L. Hunt (ed.), *Invention of Pornography*, p. 279.

33  G. E. Bentley, *The Stranger from Paradise: A Biography of William Blake* (2001), p. 136; P. Ackroyd, *Blake* (1995), p. 154.

34  R. Porter and L. Hall, *The Facts of Life: The Creation of Sexual Knowledge in Britain, 1650–1950* (1995), pp. 108–11; B. Brandon Schnorrenberg, 'A true relation of the life and career of James Graham, 1745–1794', *Eighteenth-century Life*, 15 (1991), pp. 58–75 (q.v. for visual satires on Graham); P. Otto, 'The regeneration of the body: sex, religion and the sublime in James Graham's "Temple of Health and Hymen"', *Romanticism on the Net*, 23 (August 2001).

35  For the earliest account of the Medmenham Abbey libertines, see C. Johnstone, *Chrysal; or, the Adventures of a Guinea* (4 vols, 1760–5; many editions thereafter). For a key to its allusions and members: W. Davis, *Olio of Bibliographical and Literary Anecdotes and Memoranda* (1814), pp. 13–21. Also L. Cust and S. Colvin (eds), *History of the Society of Dilettanti* (1898); C. Harcourt-Smith, *The Society of Dilettanti* (1932); R. Fuller, *Hell Fire Francis* (1939); D. McCormick, *The Hell-Fire Club* (1958). The most accurate (and sceptical) summary of the Medmenham Abbey circle is J. Sambrook's entry on

the 'Franciscans [monks] of Medmenham' in *ODNB*.

36  D. Stevenson, *The Beggar's Benison: Sex Clubs of Enlightenment Scotland and their Rituals* (2002).

37  Carabelli, *Priapus*, p. 2.

## Chapter Eleven

# Philosophy and Raking

1  F. A. Pottle (ed.), *James Boswell's London Journal, 1762–1763* (1950), pp. 251–6; F. A. Pottle (ed.), *Boswell on the Grand Tour: Germany and Switzerland 1764* (1953), pp. 37, 127; C. Ryskamp and F. A. Pottle (eds), *Private Papers of James Boswell* (New York, 1930), vol. VII, p. 163. L. Stone counts Boswell's conquests in *The Family, Sex and Marriage in England, 1500–1800* (1977), p. 487.

2  P. Quennell (ed.), *The Memoirs of William Hickey* (1976 edn), passim and pp. 21, 23; on Norfolk, N. W. Wraxhall, *The Historical and Posthumous Memoirs of Sir Nathaniel William Wraxall, 1772–1784* (5 vols, edited by H. B. Wheatley, 1884), vol. III, pp. 361–7.

3  P. J. Grosley, *A Tour to London; or, New Observations on England, and its Inhabitants* (2 vols, 1772), cited by L. Picard, *Dr Johnson's London* (2000), p. 198.

4  Cf. *The School of Venus: The Postures of Love Described in Two Instructive and Confidential Dialogues between a Wife and a Virgin*, published by the bookseller Lewis McDonald of St Martin's Fields, and prosecuted for obscene libel in 1788: KB28/347/5. Cf. A. D. Harvey, *Sex in Georgian England: Attitudes and Prejudices from the 1720s to the 1820s* (1994), pp. 21–29.

5  Johnson penned a heavily ironic poem of advice to the young Sir John Lade when that young man reached his majority in 1780, little anticipating how energetically Lade would follow its predictions: 'When the bonny blade carouses, / Pockets full, and spirits high, / What are acres? What are houses? / Only dirt, or wet or dry. / If the guardian or the mother / Tell the woes of wilful waste, / Scorn their counsel and their pother / You can hang or drown at last'.

6  S. Tillyard, *Aristocrats: Caroline, Emily, Louisa and Sarah Lennox, 1740–1832* (1995), pp. 72–3.

7  L. G. Mitchell, *Charles James Fox* (1992), pp. 9–13, 15, 93, 97–8.

8  R. J. Richardson, *Recollections, Political, Literary, Dramatic, and Miscellaneous, of the Last Half-century* (2 vols, 1856), vol. II, pp. 129–30.

9  F. A. Pottle, *Boswell's London Journal 1762–1763* (1950), pp. 272–3.

10  After this episode, Wordsworth was badly wounded by Hazlitt's reviews, so he might have embroidered the story for Crabbe Robinson and Benjamin Haydon. For their accounts see E. W. Marrs (ed.), *The Letters of Charles and Mary Anne Lamb* (Cornell, 3 vols, 1978), vol. III, p. 127. A. C. Grayling belittles the story: *The Quarrel of the Age: The Life and Times of William Hazlitt* (2000), pp. 89–90.

11  Hamilton's and Emma's relationship and 1791 marriage had been much publicized: *Town and Country Magazine*, XXII, (1 Dec., 1790), p. 483; and *Bon Ton Magazine*, I (1 Oct., 1791), p. 243.

12  Emma's 'attitudes' were widely publicized in Rehberg's twelve etchings, *Drawings Faithfully Copied from Nature at Naples* (1794). These were parodied in 1807 by substituting the young Emma with the mature fat Emma, in twelve bound prints published by Hannah Humphrey, entitled *A New Edition Considerably Enlarged and Humbly Dedicated to all Admirers of the Grand and Sublime* (1807). The artist was not

given, but the fat figure's resemblance to Gillray's *Dido* suggests that the artist was Gillray: I. Jenkins and K. Sloan, *Vases and Volcanoes: Sir William Hamilton and his Collection* (1996), plate 193(b).

13  They were easy targets for Gillray's mockery, for she was tall and willowy and he comically fat and short: Gillray's *A Peep at Christie's; – or – Tally-ho, & his Nimeny-pimmeny taking the Morning Lounge* (1796) (Lord Derby and Miss Farren inspect the pictures at Christie's); and *The Marriage of Cupid and Psyche* (1797), on the couple's marriage. Sayer's print is *A Peep behind the Curtain at Widow Belmour* – one of Miss Farren's Drury Lane roles, her nakedness a comment on the theatre manager Sheridan's penny-pinching management.

14  F. MacCarthy, *Byron: Life and Legend* (2002), pp. 130, 335–40; L. A. Marchand (ed.), *Byron's Letters and Journals* (13 vols, 1973–94), vol. I, p. 161.

15  C. Tomalin, *Mrs Jordan's Profession: The Story of a Great Actress and a Future King* (1994), p. 90.

16  A. Aspinall, *The Correspondence of George, Prince of Wales, 1770–1812* (8 vols, 1963–), vol. II, p. 130n.

17  Published in the *London Magazine*, August 1820: I am grateful to Dr Louise Carter for this reference.

18  *Letters . . . of John Wilkes . . . to his Daughter* (4 vols, 1804), vol. III, p. 247. Fores led the way in exposing the illicit marriage by issuing Wicksteed's *The Follies of a Day, or the Marriage of Figaro* in March 1786 and the flow of prints he published on the subject was sustained thereafter. On prosecuting *A Voluptuary* see below, ch. 16.

19  N. K. Robinson, *Edmund Burke: A Life in Caricature* (1996), appx. 1, p. 194.

20  M. T. W. and J. E. Payne, 'Henry Wigstead, Rowlandson's fellow-traveller', *British Art Journal*, 4 (3), (2003), pp. 27–38.

21  For subsequent incursions into the bedroom, see Isaac Cruikshank's *Oh! Che Boccone!* ('Oh! what a mouthful!') (Fores, 1795) (fig. 22); I. Cruikshank's *Three Weeks after Marriage* (1795, again for Fores) (the prince in bed with the bare-breasted princess who waves his helmet and feathers in triumph while Mrs Fitzherbert chastises him for his betrayal; a cat and dog fight in foreground); Gillray's *The Grand-Signior Retiring* (1796) (Lord Jersey conniving in his wife's adultery by escorting the prince to his wife's bed and tipping his nightcap deferentially); Gillray's *The Jersey Smuggler Detected; – or – Good Cause for Separation: Marriage Vows Are False as Dicers Oaths* (1796) (Caroline, her child in her cot in the next room, discovers her husband in bed with Jersey: the final separation is imminent).

22  J. Barrell, 'Coffee-house politicians', *Journal of British Studies*, 43, no. 2 (April 2004); Mitchell, *Fox*, pp. 9–13, 93, 97–8.

23  *Trials for Adultery: Or, the History of Divorces* (1780), vol. VI, pp. 88–9; the print is reproduced in L. Stone, *The Road to Divorce: England 1530–1987* (Oxford, 1990), plate 26.

24  R. Shoemaker, 'Male honour and the decline of public violence in eighteenth-century London', *Social History*, 26 (2), p. 208.

25  *Letters . . . of John Wilkes . . . to his Daughter* (4 vols, 1804), vol. III, p. 161. The print was advertised in D. Jordan and E. J. Pratt, *Jordan's Elixir of Life . . . Or, a Collection of all the Songs sung by Mrs Jordan* (1789).

26  The first title was republished by J. C. Hotten in 1872. Cf. 'Pisanus Fraxi' [C. R. Ashbee?], *Index Librorum Prohibitorium: Being Notes . . . on Curious or Uncommon Books* (1877), pp. 374–5.

27  Reproduced in R. Godfrey, *James Gillray and the Art of Caricature* (2001), p. 67.

28  The print is an adaptation of Gillray's modest satire on Lady Charlotte Campbell, noted for her figure-revealing clothing, *Modern Elegance* (Humphrey, 1795). *Tinglebum*

is the same figure, altered by erasion and watercolour additions (BMSat 8720). Gillray in 1785 put out his flagellation satire, *Westminster School* (again unsigned), in which Fox, in the guise of Dr Busby the headmaster, birches the bare-bottomed Pitt and his supporters. This was published by Ridgeway, the publisher of the flagellatory verse satire, *The Rolliad*. Gillray's *The Royal Joke; or Black Jack's Delight* (1788) has the Prince of Wales with Mrs Fitzherbert across his knees, publicly smacking her bottom. Holland's interest in flagellatory satires is further suggested by his publishing Newton's *A Forcible Appeal for the Abolition of the Slave Trade* (1792): ostensibly abolitionist, this depicted a little too lasciviously the whipping of a naked female slave.

29  Sources for the following are Jesse Foot (Bowes's surgeon from 1777), *The Lives of Andrew Robinson Bowes, Esq., and the Countess of Strathmore: Written from Thirty Three Years Professional Attendance, from Letters, and other well Authenticated Documents* (1810), and *The Confessions of the Countess of Strathmore, Written by Herself* (1793). The story is well told in R. Arnold, *The Unhappy Countess and her Grandson John Bowes* (1957). The Durham Record Office holds a full catalogue of the Strathmore divorce papers: this underpins my chronology of the countess's several proceedings against Bowes. I am indebted to Richard Higgins of Durham University Library for invaluable advice on this. Bizarrely, the present Earl of Strathmore denied me direct access to the papers, first until the queen mother was dead, and that tragic moment having passed, secondly in order to 'protect' the royal family's sensitivities: the grounds being that the Bowes are direct ancestors of the present queen. Other sources include: *The Trial of Andrew Robinson Bowes and Others for a Conspiracy against Mary Eleanor Bowes, Countess of Strathmore* (1787); *A Full, True and Particular Account of the Trial of Andrew Robinson Stoney Bowes . . . for an Assault on Lady Strathmore* (1787); J. Stephens, *A Full and Accurate Report of the Trial between – Stephens Esq., Trustee to Eleanor Bowes . . . and Andrew Robinson Stoney Bowes* (1788); *The Trial of Andrew Robinson Bowes Esq., for Adultery and Cruelty . . .* (1789). For other elements in the story, see *Gentleman's Magazine*, vol. LVI, pp. 991, 993, 1079; vol. LVII, p. 88; vol. LIX, p. 269; vol. LX, p. 665; vol. LXX, p. 488; *London Chronicle*, 7 February 1785, 29 November 1786, 30 May 1787; *Morning Post*, 3 January 1777. *The Times* index 1791ff. is rich in references to Andrew Bowes's later misdeeds and ensuing court appearances, the countess's death, funeral, etc. The Strathmore story is not included in L. Stone's *Road to Divorce* or his *Broken Lives*. The countess's dramatic poem is *The Siege of Jerusalem* (privately printed, 1774: BL).

30  *The Confessions of the Countess of Strathmore*, pp. 37–41; Foot, *Lives of . . . Bowes and the Countess of Strathmore*.

31  For the duel, see A. Spencer (ed.), *Memoirs of William Hickey* (4 vols, 1913–25), vol. I, pp. 287–93 (omitted in Quennell's edition).

32  Godfrey, *Gillray*, p. 68.

33  Hawkins was the BM's keeper of antiquities from 1826 to 1867, and his collection is now part of the BM's own. *The Miser's Feast*, *Flaybum*, and *The Injured Count* are reproduced in Godfrey, *Gillray*, plates. 19, 24, 25, but Godfrey does not explore their interrelationship. D. Hill, *Mr Gillray the Caricaturist* (1965), p. 140, mentions *Flaybum* only in passing, though he accepts that it was commissioned by Bowes (as does BMSat).

34  For the following: *Morning Post*, 14 and 24 November 1786; *Gentleman's Magazine*, vol. LVI (1786), pp. 991, 993, 1079ff.

35  Mary Farrer, *An Appeal of an Injured Wife against a Cruel Husband* (1788).

36  Walpole to Lady Ossory, 5 February 1785. Walpole also wrote to Lady Ossory about the abduction (1 December 1786): 'The town ringing about your old neighbour Countess Strathmore, and the enormous barbarities of her husband, who beat her

for six days and nights . . . for which the myrmidons of the King's Bench have knocked his brains out – almost.' W. S. Lewis (ed.), *The Yale Edition of Horace Walpole's Correspondence* (48 vols, 1937– ), vol. 33, pp. 401–2, 539–40. See also Wilkes, *Letters . . . of John Wilkes . . . to his Daughter* (4 vols, 1804), vol. III, p. 161; P. Quennell (ed.), *The Memoirs of William Hickey* (1976 edn), p. 217.

## Chapter Twelve

# What Could Women Bear?

1 W. S. Dowden (ed.), *The Journal of Thomas Moore* (1983), vol. 1, p. 155 (27 March 1819): punctuation emended.

2 A. Fletcher, *Gender, Sex, and Subordination in England, 1500–1800* (1995); J. Tosh, 'What should historians do with masculinity?', in R. Shoemaker and M. Vincent (eds), *Gender and History in Western Europe* (1998), pp. 77–8.

3 The term is Peter Gay's in *The Bourgeois Experience*: vol. I: *The Education of the Senses* (1984).

4 G. B. Hill and L. P. Powell (eds), *Boswell's Life of Johnson* (1934–50), pp. 53–4; anon., *The Female Aegis; or, the Duties of Women from Childhood to Old Age and in Most Situations of Life Exemplified* (1798), p. 135; Revd J. Bennett, *Letters to a Young Lady on a Variety of Useful and Interesting Subjects* (1789), vol. 1, pp. 6–10; John Gregory, *A Father's Legacy to his Daughters* (1774), pp. 16–17.

5 R. W. Chapman (ed.), Boswell, *Life of Johnson* (Oxford, 1985), pp. 393–4. Contrast W. Alexander, *The History of Women* (1779), vol. II, pp. 220–1: 'Almost all nations . . . have agreed in requiring the most absolute unconditional fidelity on the part of the woman; while, on that of the man, greater latitude has been given . . . A shorter way of explaining the matter would have been, to have said, that men are generally the framers and explainers of the law.'

6 H. More, *Strictures on the Modern System of Female Education* (1799), pp. 105–6.

7 S. Tillyard, *Aristocrats: Caroline, Emily, Louisa and Sarah Lennox, 1740–1832* (1995), pp. 263–81.

8 P. Sabor and L. E. Troide (eds), Frances Burney, *Journals and Letters* (2001), pp. 157–61, 349–53.

9 The classic statement that women were increasingly forced into 'separate spheres' around the turn of the century is L. Davidoff's and C. Hall's in *Family Fortunes: Men and Women of the English Middle Class, 1780–1850* (1987). Revisionist historians, however, are now attending to women's practices as distinct from discourses *about* them. See A. Vickery, *The Gentleman's Daughter: Women's Lives in Georgian England* (1998); L. Colley, *Britons: Forging the Nation, 1707–1837* (1992), ch. 6; C. Midgeley, *Women Against Slavery: The British Campaigns, 1780–1870* (1992); C. Sussman, *Consuming Anxieties: Consumer Protest, Gender, and British Slavery, 1713–1833* (Stanford, 2000); H. Guest, *Small Change: Women, Learning, and Patriotism, 1750–1810* (Chicago, 2000); Elaine Chalus, 'Elite women, social politics, and the political world of late eighteenth-century England', *Historical Journal*, 43 (2000); A. Vickery (ed.), *Women, Privilege, and Power in British Politics, 1750 to the Present* (Stanford, 2001); S. Knott and B. Taylor (eds), *Women, Gender, and Enlightenment* (2005); Louise Carter, 'British women during the revolutionary and Napoleonic wars, 1793–1815' (Cambridge Ph.D. dissertation, 2005).

10 Kathleen Wilson, for example, takes very seriously the impact of the contemporary critics who condemned the libertine Teresia Phillips. Phillips was aware of the

opprobrium her loose career invited, but whether she regarded her defiance as 'dangerous' (Wilson's word) is debatable. More striking is her indifference to her critics, and the space she claimed to express it: see K. Wilson, 'The female rake: gender, libertinism, and Enlightenment', in P. Cryle and L. O'Connell (eds), *Libertine Enlightenment: Sex, Liberty and Licence in the Eighteenth Century* (2004), p. 102.

11  C. Ryskamp (ed.), *Boswell:The Ominous Years 1774–1776* (1963), p. 320.

12  K. Wilson, '*The female rake*', p. 100. On Strathmore, see ch. 11.

13  N. Tolstoy, *The Half-mad Lord: Thomas Pitt, Second Baron Camelford (1775–1804)* (1978), p. 94.

14  B. Taylor, *Mary Wollstonecraft and the Feminist Imagination* (Cambridge, 2003).

15  British Museum Prints and Drawings Department.

16  F. MacCarthy, *Byron: Life and Legend* (2002), pp. 171–2.

17  Fordyce continued: 'By dint of assiduity and flattery, fortune and show, a female man shall sometimes succeed strangely with the women: but to the men an amazon never fails to be forbidding': *Sermons to Young Women* (1766), pp. 104–5.

18  D. Wahrman, '*Percy*'s Prologue: from gender play to gender panic in eighteenth-century England', *Past and Present*, 159 (1998), p. 117; D. Wahrman, *The Making of the Modern Self: Identity and Culture in Eighteenth-century England* (2004), pp. 21, 40–2. On the disapproval of fops and macaronis as symptoms of politeness's corruptions, see P. Carter, 'Men about town: representations of foppery and masculinity in early eighteenth-century urban society', in H. Barker and E. Chalus (eds), *Gender in Eighteenth Century England: Roles, Representations and Responsibilities* (1997), and P. Carter, *Men and the Emergence of Polite Society* (2000).

19  The military camps established at Cox's Heath in Kent and at Warley in Essex in anticipation of a French invasion became the foci of fashionable London sightseers, led by the Duchess of Devonshire. She set up a ladies' auxiliary corps, designing for it a uniform that combined elegance with masculinity, using a tailored version of a man's riding coat over a close-fitting dress, as in this print. The *Morning Post* commented on her leadership of 'the beauteous Amazons on Coxheath', charming 'every beholder with their beauty and affability': A. Foreman, *Georgiana, Duchess of Devonshire* (1999), p. 65.

20  A Foxite pamphlet, *History of the Westminster Election . . . By Lovers of Truth and Justice* (1784), p. 352, refers to a supposed 'Secret Service ledger' with the item: 'To several print shops £2,000' and 'To Mr. — [Dent] for his indecent engravings £500': BMSat VI, xvii. See, for example, Dent's *The Dutchess Canvassing for her Favourite Member* (fig. 95).

21  See S. O'Connell, *The Popular Print in England, 1550–1850* (1999), pp. 109–19; for early illustrated German examples, see K. Moxey, *Peasants, Warriors, and Wives: Popular Imagery in the Reformation* (Chicago, 1989). On 'warrior women', D. Dugaw, *Warrior Women and Popular Balladry, 1650–1850* (Chicago, 1989). Dugaw admittedly notices a decline after *c*.1800 in the numbers of women said to have gone to war for adventure rather than for love, as well as in the production of their stories (pp. 67–8).

22  L. Stone, *The Family, Sex and Marriage in England, 1500–1800* (1977), p. 533; L. G. Mitchell, *Charles James Fox* (Oxford 1992), p. 15; A. Vickery, 'Golden age to separate spheres? A review of the categories and chronology of English women's history', *Historical Journal* 36, 2 (1996), p. 399; Lord Wharncliffe (ed.), *Letters and Works of Lady Mary Wortley Montagu* (1837), vol. II, p. 160. On the Lades, see C. Pigott, *The Jockey Club* (1793), part III, pp. 43–4, and A. Aspinall, *The Correspondence of George, Prince of Wales, 1770–1812* (8 vols, 1963– ), vol. II, p. 130n.

23  Cited by F. Wilson, *The Courtesan's Revenge: Harriette Wilson, the Woman who Blackmailed the King* (2003), p. 44.

24  Countess of Minto (ed.), *Life and Letters of Gilbert Elliot, First Earl of Minto, from 1751 to 1806* (3 vols, 1874), vol. I, p. 264 (8 January 1780).

25  *Public Characters* (1799), pp. 519–20; S. Tillyard, *Aristocrats: Caroline, Emily, Louisa, and Sarah Lennox, 1740–1832* (1995), pp. 155–61.

26  The Weimar journal *London und Paris* (1800), cited in P. Wagner, *Eros Revived: Erotica of the Enlightenment in England and America* (1988), p. 128; P. Wagner, 'Trial reports as a genre of eighteenth-century erotica', *British Journal for Eighteenth-century Studies*, V, I (1982), pp. 117 23.

27  Judith Baker Baker Papers, Durham University Archives (http://flambard.dur.ac.uk:6336/dynaweb/handlist/fam/baker).

28  These were republished from the magazine in *The Covent Garden Jester* (1785), the source cited here. Replete with dismal but non-erotic engravings, and (to judge from its price of sixpence for eighty-eight pages) selling to middling- and middle-class purchasers, this offered itself as 'a curious collection of funny jokes, amorous pranks, anecdotes, merry stories, smart repartees, waggeries, droll adventures, double entendres, whims, frolicksome tales, wise sayings, humbugs, witty quibbles, witty jests, puns, bon mots, and many laughable tricks'. Most jokes were recycled from earlier jest-books, with references updated. The joke below about the young lady's watch appeared in *Joe Miller's Jests* of 1739 (many subsequent editions), and probably originated earlier than that, see R. Paulson, 'The joke and Joe Miller's jests', in his *Popular and Polite Art in the Age of Hogarth and Fielding* (1979), p. 75.

29  Ellen Weeton, *Journal of a Governess* (1936; republished as *Miss Weeton's Journal of a Governess*, introduction by J. J. Bagley, 1969), vol. 1, pp. 116, 76, 294.

30  Walpole to the Countess of Ossory, 27 January and 10 February 1786 (P. Cunningham (ed.), *The Letters of Horace Walpole, Fourth Earl of Orford*, (1906), vol. IX, pp. 37, 40. The print and the sketches are in Walpole's scrapbooks, New York Public Library, and are reproduced and discussed in Donald, *The Age of Caricature*.

31  R. Southey, *Letters from England* (1807; ed. J. Simmons, 1984), p. 291.

32  Ibid.; Donald, *Age of Caricature*, ch. 3.

33  Southey, *Letters from England*, pp. 76, 291.

34  Marilyn Yalom, *A History of the Breast* (1997), p. 120. For the parallel refashioning of male clothes, see ch. 15 below.

35  Countess of Minto (ed.), *Life and Letters of Gilbert Elliot, First Earl of Minto, from 1751 to 1806* (3 vols, 1874), vol. II, p. 133 and note.

36  D. Le Faye (ed.), *Jane Austen's Letters* (Oxford, 1995), Austen to Cassandra, 8 January 1801; J. Ashelford, *The Art of Dress: Clothes and Society 1500–1914* (1996), p. 178.

37  M. A. Clarke, *Memoirs of Mrs. Mary Anne Clarke . . . including Appropriate Remarks on her Conduct towards the Duke of York* (1809), p. 64 (confiscated edn: TS11/120); *Sporting Magazine*, IV, 228, July 1794, cited at BMSat 8571.

38  L. Pollock, *Forgotten Children: Parent–Child Relations from 1500 to 1900* (1983), p. 215; Yalom, *History of the Breast*, p. 106. For some excruciatingly over-theorized commentaries on this transition, see Mary Jacobus, 'Incorruptible milk: breast-feeding and the French revolution', in S. Melzer and L. Rabine (eds), *Rebel Daughters: Women and the French Revolution* (Oxford, 1992); R. Perry, 'Colonizing the breast: sexuality and maternity in eighteenth-century England', in J. Fout (ed.), *Forbidden History: The State, Society, & the Regulation of Sexuality in Modern Europe* (Chicago, 1992); Barbara C. Gelphi, 'Significant exposure: the turn-of-the-century breast', *Nineteenth-century contexts*, 20, (1997). On the padding of bellies to imitate pregancy, cf. 'The pad warehouse' in *Bon Ton Magazine* (III, 64 (1793), illustrating a shop selling pads. Many prints (by Gillray, I. Cruikshank, Newton, etc.) mocked the fashion.

39 *True Briton*, cited BMSat. 8905, i.e. Fores's *The Gallery of Fashion* (1796). This print shows five women in current fashions: 1) *A la Turk* – turbanned, bare-breasted; 2) *A la Grec* – high-waisted dress hanging from below the defined breasts; 3) *A la Cité* – a dress intended to be like 2, but distorted by the wearer's obesity (a conventionally adverse comment on the *nouveau riche* 'cit'); 4) *A la St James* – a back view of a woman with a long striped overdress and a grotesque turban; 5) *A la St Giles* – bare breasted, with apron, tuck-up dress and cap.

40 'Manners and character of the age', *Anti-Jacobin Review*, 34 (2 July 1798) (4th edition, vol. 2), p. 566.

41 Other versions of Rowlandson's print were published subsequently: Marks's *The Benefit of a Plaster or a Cure for a Cold* (1820), and O. Hodgson's *Cure for a Scold* (n. d., 1830s) (Bodleian Library: John Johnson Collection, box 6, Trade & Scraps).

42 Thus the cruelty of Rowlandson's plate on Lady Archer's morning cosmetic transformation, *Six Stages of Mending a Face* (1792) (fig. 21) is softened by the fact that its twin, *Six Stages of Marring a Face*, exposes the face of the pugilist ruffian, the Duke of Hamilton, increasingly battered and bloodied as he boxes.

43 For Clarke scandal see chapter 16.

44 First engraved by Newton in 1792, the motif was popular enough to be plagiarized by the low print firm Sidebotham in the version reproduced here, *c*.1810 (BMSat. 11696), and again by Marks around 1820 (BMSat. 14098).

45 Preface to *The Battle of the Books*, cited by P. K. Elkin, *The Augustan Defence of Satire* (Oxford, 1973), p. 85.

46 Caroline Lennox, Charles Fox's mother, to her sister in S. Tillyard, *Aristocrats: Caroline, Emily, Louisa and Sarah Lennox, 1740–1832* (1995), pp. 100–101.

## Chapter Thirteen
# The Libertine's Last Fling

1 Photographic copies of the alleged Cruikshanks are in the British Museum Prints and Drawings Department, cat. 1977–u-478; the Carington Bowles(?) mezzotints are at cat. 1954–8–18. For other contemporary English erotic caricatures, unattributed, see ibid. 1977-u-470-4. On Blake, see D. V. Erdman and C. T. Magno (eds), *The 'Four Zoas' by William Blake: A Photographic Facsimile of the Manuscript with Commentary on the Illuminations* (1987), p. 14; S. Curran and J. A. Wittreich, *Blake's Sublime Allegory* (1973), pp. 182–94 and plates; A. Lincoln, *Spiritual History: A Reading of William Blake's* 'Vala or The Four Zoas' (1995), pp. 58–9. Turner's erotic images have been discovered carefully concealed by Ruskin in the Turner bequest to the Tate Gallery: *Guardian* 31 December 2004. See also P. Webb, *The Erotic Arts* (1975), pp. 150–61 and plates 108–12.

2 *The Scourge: or Monthly Expositor of Imposture and Folly* (1811–15), vol. 1 (1 May 1811), pp. 378–9. For Richard Fores's prosecution in 1821 for publishing a print depicting 'a man and woman partly naked in the act of carnal copulation', KB28/479/28.

3 The fullest collection of (fifty) reproductions is in G. Schiff, *The Amorous Illustrations of Thomas Rowlandson* (1969). A selection was republished 'for the artist's friends' by J. C. Hotten, *c*.1872, as *Pretty Little Games for Young Ladies and Gentlemen. With Pictures of Good Old English Sports and Pastimes* (British Library).

4 A. P. Oppé, *Thomas Rowlandson: His Drawings and Water Colours* (edited by Geoffrey Holme, 1923). J. Hayes, 'Rowlandson, Thomas (1757–1827)', *ODNB*, makes no mention of his erotica, nor does R. Paulson, *Rowlandson: A New Interpretation* (1972),

pp. 17–18 and *passim*: Rowlandson's 'drawings are far more important than the prints, which at their best are bare indications of the richness of the drawings on which they are based'. See also J. Grego, *Thomas Rowlandson* (1880), p. 18; B. Falk, *Thomas Rowlandson: His Life and Art* (1949); R. Paulson, 'Rowlandson, Wilkes, Fox, Sheridan, & Co. : The comic/picturesque': in his *Representations of Revolution 1789–1820* (New Haven, 1983). For a catalogue of Rowlandson's erotica, Henry S. Ashbee [as Pisanus Fraxi], *Centuria librorum absconditorum* (1879), pp. 346–98.

5  Margaret Mead, 'Sex and censorship in contemporary society', *New World Writing*, III, New American Library (1953).

6  J. Cuno and C. Burlingham (eds), *French Caricature and the French Revolution, 1789–1799* (1988), and J. Cuno, 'Obscene humor in French revolutionary caricature . . . David's *The Army of Jugs* and *The English Government*', in J. A. W. Heffernan (ed.), *Representing the French Revolution* (1992).

7  Margaret Jacob, 'The materialist world of pornography', in Lynn Hunt (ed.), *The Invention of Pornography: Obscenity and the Origins of Modernity, 1500–1800* (New York, 1993), pp. 181–2. The essays in Lynn Hunt's volume have shaped most recent discussions of the subject; but see also W. Kendrick, *The Secret Museum: Pornography in Modern Culture* (1996); L. Sigel, *Governing Pleasures: Pornography and Social Change in England, 1815–1914* (2002); K. Harvey, *Reading Sex in the Eighteenth Century: Bodies and Gender in English Erotic Culture* (Cambridge, 2005).

8  'She naked stood whilst I with joy adore / the finest shape I ne'er had seen before / Her little pretty panting bubbies were as white as snow and as the chrystal clear / I something saw which was but thinly hair'd . . .', etc. : KB28/347/4 and KB28/387/2. Texts of these kinds may explain T. Hitchcock's prim generalization that the eighteenth-century erotic was 'rather sad and absurd', showing 'the prudery, sexual and emotional immaturity . . . of the participants': in T. Hitchcock and M. Cohen (eds), *English Sexualities, 1700–1800* (1998), pp. 21–2.

9  C. Blackledge, *The Story of V: Opening of Pandora's Box* (2003).

10  Never more so than in a print like *Platonic Love: None but the Bold Deserve the Fair*, an idea filched from Bunbury and engraved for Tegg in 1807, in which an elderly military officer resplendent in uniform but without arms or legs poignantly woos a young woman above a quotation from *Othello*. See also a small masterpiece among his comic ink and watercolour drawings, *A French Frigate Towing an English Man O'war into Port* (*c*.1790) (an old, portly, one-legged sea-dog is led arm in arm by a smiling and beautiful courtesan): R. R. Wark, *Drawings by Thomas Rowlandson in the Huntington Collection* (San Marino, Calif., 1975), plate facing p. 26.

11  J. Hayes, 'Rowlandson, Thomas (1757–1827)', *ODNB*.

12  His numbed responses to naval and other disasters might have been connected with his brother's unfortunate death at sea in the 1780s: M. T. W. Payne, 'The explosion of Rowlandson's brother', *Burlington Magazine*, 147 (2005), pp. 552–4.

13  H. Angelo, *Reminiscences* (2 vols, 1828), vol. II, pp. 324–6; vol. I, p. 180 and vol. II, pp. 222–4.

14  Wark, *Drawings by Thomas Rowlandson in the Huntington Collection*, p. 26; Paulson, *Rowlandson*, p. 29; Paulson, 'The grotesque, Gillray, and political caricature', p. 210.

15  M. Rosenthal, *The Art of Thomas Gainsborough* (1999), p. 273; Angelo, *Reminiscences*, vol. I, p. 262; A. Meyer, 'Parnassus from the foothills: the Royal Academy viewed by Thomas Rowlandson and John Wolcot (Peter Pindar)', *British Art Journal*, 3 (2), (2002), pp. 32–43.

16  BMSat dates this '1800?', but I. Jenkins and K. Sloan suggest *c*.1791, illustrating it in plate 192 of their *Vases and Volcanoes: Sir William Hamilton and his collection* (1996). See ch. 11 for other satires on Hamilton's and Emma's relationship.

17 'Gee ho Dobbin', in Francis Place's 'Songs within memory', no. 33 (Place Papers, BL Add. MSS. 27825, vol. xxxvii).

18 Paulson's and others' commentaries on plate 3 of *Rake's Progress* (1735) are discreetly self-censoring (e.g. in Paulson's *Hogarth's Graphic Works* (1989)). Most scholars note that the copper dish brought in by the servant entering right is to be used by the posture-girl who is undressing in the foreground, but none notes that the lit candle he carries is to be used by her vaginally. The text of *The Black Joke* which the ballad singer in the Hogarth print (r.) sings from her broadsheet is also invariably censored: for the words, see ch. 10.

19 Gronow blamed the prince for leading Barrymore astray: 'his acquaintance with the prince ruined Lord Barrymore both in mind, body, and estate': *Reminiscences and Recollections 1810–1860* (2 vols, 1985; original edn, 1892), vol. II, pp. 257–8. Cf. H. Angelo, *Reminiscences*, vol. I, pp. 283–8; vol. II, p. 80. On Angelo's friendship with Rowlandson and hence Rowlandson's with Barrymore, see Angelo, *Reminiscences*, and *Angelo's Pic nic; or Table Talk, Written by Himself* (1835; ed. 1905), pp. 91–2.

20 A. Aspinall, *The Correspondence of George, Prince of Wales, 1770–1812* (8 vols, 1963– ), 8 September 1796.

21 *Amorous, Eccentric, and Whimsical Anecdotes, of the Late Celebrated Old Q . . . and his Numerous Sultanas. Also, Memoirs of his Life, and Fashionable Intrigues; with the Follies and Frolics of Maria Brown . . . and other Ladies of his Grace's Harem* (1810?); cf. *The Piccadilly Ambulator; or Old Q. Containing Memoirs of the Private Life of that Ever-green Votary of Venus!* (2 vols, 1808); R. J. Richardson, *Recollections, Political, Literary, Dramatic, and Miscellaneous, of the Last Half-century* (2 vols, 1856), vol. II, p. 122. Memoirs by Henry Angelo, Gronow, Wraxall and others comment extensively on Queensberry and others.

22 L. A. Marchand (ed.), *Byron's Letters and Journals* (13 vols, 1973–94), vol. I, pp. 5, 157–65; F. MacCarthy, *Byron: Life and Legend* (2002), p. 73.

23 P. Quennell, *Byron: The Years of Fame* (1935), p. 372.

24 Marchand (ed.), *Byron's Letters and Journals*, vol. V, p. 542.

25 F. MacCarthy, *Byron*, pp. 365–6, 414–15.

26 E. J. Lovell (ed.), *Lady Blessington's Conversations of Lord Byron* (Princeton, 1969), p. 172.

27 Marchand (ed.), *Byron's Letters and Journals*, vol. VI, p. 232.

28 MacCarthy, *Byron*, p. 536.

## Chapter Fourteen
# Taming the Muse: The Long View

1 Review of John Leech's *Pictures of Life and Character* in *Quarterly Review*, XCVI (December 1854), pp. 79–80. Thackeray was closely associated with *Punch*, and Leech had been his schoolfellow and friend.

2 J. Hannay, *Satire and Satirists* (1853), cited in G. Dyer, *British Satire and the Politics of Style, 1789–1832* (Cambridge, 1997), p. 139; A. Lang, 'Letter to Dickens', in *Letters to Dead Authors* (1886). The Whig wit, Sidney Smith, had anticipated Lang's point in 1809. The costs of 'improvement' were such, he thought, that he would prefer the old cruelty: 'Give us back our wolves again – restore our Danish invaders – curse us with any evil, but the evil of a canting, deluded and Methodistical populace': *The Wit and Wisdom of Sydney Smith* (1860), p. 67.

3 H. Angelo, *Reminiscences* (2 vols, 1828), vol. I, pp. 283–4; Southey, *Letters from England* (1807; 1984 edn), pp. 362–3.

4 R. I. and S. Wilberforce, *The Life of William Wilberforce* (5 vols, 1838), vol. V, p. 211;

F. K. Brown, *Fathers of the Victorians: the Age of Wilberforce* (Cambridge 1961), p. 11.

5  M. Thale (ed.), *The Autobiography of Francis Place, 1771–1854* (Cambridge, 1972), pp. 91, 82 (probably written in 1824 (cf. p. xxvii)); Place Papers, BL Add. MSS 27827, fo. 45; W. M. Thackeray, *The Four Georges: Sketches of Manners, Morals, Court, and Town Life* (1855; 1923 edn), p. 361; R. J. Richardson, *Recollections, Political, Literary, Dramatic, and Miscellaneous, of the Last Half-century* (2 vols, 1856), vol. II, pp. 225–6.

6  E. Bulwer-Lytton, *England and the English* (2 vols, 1833), vol. II, pp. 106–7.

7  Place Papers, BL. Add. MSS 27825.

8  D. Wahrman, *Imagining the Middle Class: The Political Representation of Class in Britain, c. 1780–1840* (Cambridge, 1995), pp. 226–7, 381–2, 398, 408.

9  D. Donald, *The Age of Caricature: Satirical Prints in the Reign of George III* (1996), p. 184; M. D. George, *English Political Caricature: A Study of Opinion and Propaganda* (2 vols, Oxford, 1959), vol. II, p. 203.

10  J. S. Mill, 'The spirit of the age' (1831), in G. L. Williams (ed.), *Mill on Politics and Society* (1976), p. 171.

11  Cited in M. J. Quinlan, *Victorian Prelude: A History of English Manners 1700–1830* (1965), p. 255; W. Cobbett, *Advice to Young Men* (1829).

12  Thale (ed.), *Autobiography of Francis Place*, pp. 82, 91.

13  M. Mason, *The Making of Victorian Sexuality* (Oxford, 1994), pp. 114–15.

14  Richardson, *Recollections*, vol. II, pp. 225–6.

15  Mason, *Victorian Sexuality*, pp. 126, 130.

16  George, *English Political Caricature*, vol. II, p. 257.

17  *Encyclopaedia Britannica*, 9th edn (1876), vol. V, p. 105.

18  Isaac Cruikshank's composition recycled the excretory motifs of *A Petitioning, Remonstrating, Reforming, Republican*, a weaker Darly print of 1782 that mocked the reform associations.

19  Q. Bell, *Victorian Artists* (1967), p. 63; on Leech, see S. Houfe, *John Leech and the Victorian Scene* (1984).

20  J. C. Reid, *Thomas Hood* (1963), p. 103; *The Examiner*, 3 February 1839.

21  C. Baudelaire, 'Some foreign caricaturists' (1857), in P. E. Charvet (ed.), *Baudelaire: Selected Writings on Art and Literature* (1992). Dickens's review of *The Drunkard's Children* (in *The Examiner*, 8 July 1848) is republished in M. Slater (ed.), *Dickens' Journalism: The Amusements of the People and Other Papers . . . 1834–51* (1996), pp. 102–7. As Dickens wrote to Forster, the work was 'very powerful indeed', but 'the philosophy of the thing, as a great lesson' was 'all wrong', since Cruikshank failed to have the drinking begin 'in sorrow, or poverty, or ignorance' – this 'too "radical" for good old George, I suppose'. The prints nonetheless sold 'by tens of thousands', and were staged as a theatrical melodrama.

22  J. Hayes, 'Rowlandson', *ODNB*; D. Alexander, *Richard Newton and English Caricature in the 1790s* (1998), p. 55.

23  W. M. Thackeray, *The English Humourists of the Eighteenth Century* (1851; Oxford, 1913 edn), p. 31; Dyer guides much of this argument: *British Satire*, pp. 7, 13, 139–42, 158–64.

24  *The Examiner*, 30 December 1848.

25  John Ruskin, 'The art of England', lecture V: 'The fireside: John Leech and John Tenniel' (1883), in E. T. Cook and A. Wedderburn, *The Works of John Ruskin*, vol. XXXIII (1908), p. 359ff.

26  Thus M. Mason in his *The Making of Victorian Sexual Attitudes* (1994), pp. 215–16, 222–3, and his *The Making of Victorian Sexuality* (1994), p. 5.

27  P. Gay, *The Bourgeois Experience, Victoria to Freud*: vol. 1, *The Education of the Senses* (1984), pp. 280–1. For fuller elaboration, see my *The Hanging Tree: Execution and the*

*English People, 1770–1868* (Oxford, 1994), part III.

28  Thomas Carlyle, *Memoirs of the Life of Sir Walter Scott* (6 vols, Edinburgh, 1837), cited in Iris Origo, *Images and Shadows: Part of a Life* (1970), p. 178.

29  S. Freud, *Civilization and its Discontents*, translated by David McLintock (2002 edn), p. 34.

30  Veber's *L'impudique Albion* (1901), e.g., showed George V's face as Britannia's buttocks: W. Feaver, *Masters of Caricature from Hogarth and Gillray to Scarfe and Levine* (New York, 1981), p. 122. For the German comic grotesque, culminating, for example, in Grosz, see P. Kort (ed.), *Comic Grotesque: Wit and Mockery in German Art, 1870–1940* (New York, 2004).

31  B. Falk, *Thomas Rowlandson: His Life and Art* (1949); G. Schiff, *The Amorous Illustrations of Thomas Rowlandson* (New York, 1969).

## Chapter Fifteen
# The Age of Cant

1  E. J. Lovell (ed.), *Lady Blessington's Conversations of Lord Byron* (Princeton, 1969), p. 13; L. A. Marchand (ed.), *Byron's Letters and Journals* (1976), vol. VI, p. 232 and vol. V, p. 542.

2  Northrop Frye, 'Towards defining an age of sensibility', *English Literary History*, 23 (1956), pp. 145–8, 150.

3  V. A. C. Gatrell, *The Hanging Tree: Execution and the English People, 1770–1868* (Oxford, 1994), ch. 7; J. Mullan, *Sentiment and Sociability: The Language of Feeling in the Eighteenth Century* (Oxford, 1988), pp. 29–42; J. Dwyer, *Virtuous Discourse: Sensibility and Community in Late Eighteenth-century Scotland* (Edinburgh, 1987), pp. 55–7; G. J. Barker-Benfield, *The Culture of Sensibility: Sex and Society in Eighteenth-century Britain* (Chicago, 1992), ch. 1.

4  Frances Burney, *Journals and Letters* (edited by P. Sabor and L. E. Troide, 2001), p. 109. On this female renaissance, see R. Porter, *Enlightenment: Britain and the Creation of the Modern World* (2000), pp. 286, 327 and ch. 12; Barker-Benfield, *Culture of Sensibility*, ch. 1; G. Dyer, *British Satire and the Politics of Style 1789–1832* (Cambridge, 1997), pp. 140–43; J. Brewer, *The Pleasures of the Imagination: English Culture in the Eighteenth Century* (1997), p. 78.

5  R. Southey, *Letters from England* (1807; reprinted 1951, 1984, edited by J. Simmons), p. 453.

6  Barker-Benfield, *Culture of Sensibility*, p. xvii; on Fry, see Gatrell, *The Hanging Tree*, pp. 389–94.

7  Cited by M. Mason, *The Making of Victorian Sexual Attitudes* (Oxford, 1994), pp. 7, 218–19.

8  P. Langford, *Englishness Identified: Manners and Character, 1650–1850* (2001), pp. 159–73; L. Stone, *The Family, Sex and Marriage in England, 1500–1800* (1977), p. 533.

9  Louise Carter, 'British women during the revolutionary and Napoleonic wars, 1793–1815' (Cambridge Ph. D. dissertation, 2005), pp. 21–2. For earlier views to this effect, see W. Alexander, *The History of Women* (3rd edn, 2 vols, 1782; first edn, 1779), vol. I, pp. 475, 486, 493–4.

10  A. Johns-Putra, 'Satirizing the courtly woman and defending the domestic woman: mock epics and women poets in the Romantic age', *Romanticism on the Net*, article no. 15.

11 Austen to Martha Lloyd, 16 February, 1813, in D. Le Faye (ed.), *Jane Austen's Letters* (Oxford, 1995).

12 A. Vickery, *The Gentleman's Daughter: Women's Lives in Georgian England* (1998), pp. 213–23.

13 M. Cohen, 'Manliness, effeminacy, and the French: gender and the construction of national character in eighteenth-century England', in T. Hitchcock and M. Cohen (eds), *English Masculinities, 1660–1800* (1999), p. 60 (citing *inter alia* W. Alexander, *The History of Women from the Earliest Antiquity to the Present Time* (2 vols, 1779)).

14 Gillray, Rowlandson, the Cruikshanks and Williams produced classic debauchery prints well into the 1810s. They would not have so multiplied and sold had they not connected with male purchasers' 'resistant' tastes.

15 D. Kuchta, 'The making of the self-made man: class, clothing, and English masculinity, 1688–1832', in V. de Grazia (ed.), *The Sex of Things: Gender and Consumption in Historical Perspective* (1996); A. Ribeiro, *Fashion in the French Revolution* (1988), pp. 115–17, 127; J. Ashelford, *The Art of Dress: Clothes and Society 1500–1914* (1996), pp. 173–83. See also L. Davidoff and C. Hall, *Family Fortunes: Men & Women of the English Middle Class, 1780–1850* (1987), ch. 9. On women's fashion in the 1790s see above, ch. 12.

16 F. MacCarthy, *Byron: Life and Legend* (2002), pp. 365, 413; L. A. Marchand (ed.), *Byron's Letters and Journals*, vol. I, p. 18; E. J. Lovell (ed.), *Lady Blessington's Conversations of Lord Byron* (Princeton, 1969), p. 213.

17 Dyer, *British Satire*, pp. 52–4, 150–8.

18 Twenty years later the print's depiction of the Presbyterian ranter William Irving still earned Hood the Irvingites' 'abuse and anathema': *Eclectic Review*, n. s. XIX (March 1846), p. 288. For Lamb's puff: *New Monthly Magazine* 1826 (1), p. 232. J. C. Reid's *Thomas Hood* (1963) reproduces the print as a pull-out.

19 BMSat 15326. The print's subtext cites the speech reported in *The Oriental Quarterly Magazine*, as repeated in *The News of Sunday*, 24 April 1826.

20 J. Austen to Fanny Knight (in 1813), in D. Le Faye (ed.), *Jane Austen's Letters* (Oxford, 1995), p. 280; Godwin, 'Autobiographical fragment' (1800).

21 The reference is to the Constitutional Association as described by a bookseller and printseller whom it had tried to prosecute for seditious inclinations: T. Dolby, *Memoirs of Thomas Dolby . . . late Printer and Publisher, of Catherine Street, Strand . . . by Himself* (1827), cited by J. Wardroper, *Kings, Lords and Wicked Libellers: Satire and Protest 1760–1837* (1973), p. 225.

22 F. K. Brown, *Fathers of the Victorians: The Age of Wilberforce* (Cambridge, 1961), p. 332.

23 B. Hilton, *The Age of Atonement: The Influence of Evangelicalism on Social and Economic Thought 1785–1865* (1988), p. 6.

24 R. Fellowes, *Religion without Cant; or, a Preservative against Lukewarmness and Intolerance; Fanaticism, Superstition and Impiety* (1801), cited in Brown, *Fathers of the Victorians*, p. 176; *The Works of Sydney Smith* (2 vols, 1859), vol. I, pp. 131–8.

25 Viscountess Knutsford, *Life and Letters of Zachary Macaulay* (1900), pp. 268–9; Brown, *Fathers of the Victorians*, pp. 108, 379–85.

26 The Proclamation Society followed the model of the Society for the Reformation of Manners of 1691–1738. On prosecutions see D. Thomas, *A Long Time Burning: The History of Literary Censorship in England* (New York, 1969), ch. 9; J. Innes, 'Politics and morals: the reformation of manners movement in later eighteenth-century England', in E. Eckhart (ed.), *The Transformation of Political Culture: England and Germany in the Late Eighteenth Century* (Oxford 1990), p. 68; A. Hunt, *Governing Morals: A Social History of Moral Regulation* (Cambridge, 2000), ch. 3.

27 The SSV's first members included eight parish clergy, five lawyers, two surgeons, a

government clerk, a stockbroker, and two booksellers. By 1804, parish clergy comprised 15 per cent of members, and a few peers did come in; but most members were professional and commercial men and their womenfolk: *Sermon . . . before the Society for the Suppression of Vice . . . by R. Watson. To which are added the plan of the society, a summary of its proceedings, and a list of its members* (1804). See also M. J. D. Roberts, 'The Society for the Suppression of Vice and its early critics, 1802–1812', *Historical Journal* (1983); *idem,* 'Making Victorian morals? The Society for the Suppression of Vice and its critics, 1802–1886', *Historical Studies* xxi (1984); Brown, *Fathers of the Victorians,* pp. 428–44; Mason, *Victorian Sexual Attitudes,* pp. 68–73. Membership declined in the 1820s, but the society remained episodically active until the 1880s.

28  T. Clayton, 'Bowles family' and 'John Bowles', *ODNB.*

29  *Report to the Society for the Suppression of Vice* (1825), p. 47; Brown, *Fathers of the Victorians,* pp. 429–31.

30  *London Chronicle,* 23 November 1802.

31  *The Scourge: or Monthly Expositor of Imposture and Folly* (1811–15), vol. 1 (1 May 1811), pp. 378–9.

32  *Parliamentary Debates,* vol. XXXI, pp. 568–70, 614–17, 690–1.

33  HO44/1/77-9 (3 April 1820).

34  Cruikshank's print fronts an anonymous pamphlet, *Shakespeare and Honest King George versus Parson Irving and the Puritans* (1824).

35  Place Papers, BL Add. MSS. 27825, vol. XXXVII, fos. 144–5.

36  His petitions for mercy are in National Archives, HO17/92 (RL 47 and Mh 7).

37  TS11/944/3434; KB28/401/29; Francis Place papers, BL Add. MSS.

38  Innes, 'Politics and morals', pp. 80–88.

39  Brown, *Fathers of the Victorians,* pp. 34, 15, 19; Mason, *Victorian Sexual Attitudes,* pp. 49–52; Hilton, *Atonement,* p. 5.

40  F. MacCarthy, *Byron: Life and Legend* (2002), p. 143.

41  Dyer, *British Satire,* pp. 8, 11, chapter 2, and Appendix. Dyer's work corrects Elkin's statement, for example, that 'satire fell into decline in the latter part of the eighteenth century . . . because both friends and enemies no longer took for granted that there was something there that really needed or was worth defending': P. K. Elkin, *The Augustan Defence of Satire* (Oxford, 1973), p. 70.

42  K. Garlick and A. Macintyre (eds), *The Diary of Joseph Farington* (16 vols, 1978–98), vol. III, pp. 972, 993, 1046; E. L. de Montluzin, *The Anti-Jacobins, 1798–1800: The early contributors to the 'Anti-Jacobin Review'* (1988), pp. 1–53.

43  The attack on Coleridge and Southey in 'New Morality' was out of date, however. The two poets had already, as Coleridge put it, 'snapped their squeaking baby-trumpets of sedition' and no longer considered themselves radicals: E. L. Griggs (ed.), *Collected Letters of Samuel Taylor Coleridge* (6 vols, Oxford, 1956–71), vol. I, p. 397.

44  On Gillray's 'pension' from the Canningites, see ch. 9. By yoking visual to textual satire, *The Anti-Jacobin; or Weekly Examiner* set a precedent for its immediate spin-off, the monthly *Anti-Jacobin Review and Magazine* (1798–1821), for the Tory *The Satirist; or Monthly Meteor* (1808–14), and for the Whiggish *Scourge; or Monthly Expositor of Imposture and Folly* (1811–15) (see below, ch. 16). Each of the *Anti-Jacobin's* issues carried fold-out plates by Gillray, Rowlandson or the young George Cruikshank, among others. *The Anti-Jacobin; or Weekly Examiner* contained two Gillrays: *The Friend of Humanity and the Knife-Grinder,* with Canning's text, p. 15; and *New Morality* , p. 283. Its successor, *The Anti-Jacobin Review and Magazine,* contained five Gillrays in its first volume: *Peep into the Cave of Jacobinism* (no accompanying text); *New Morality* (text pp. 115–16); *Evidence to Character* (text pp. 284–92); *Doublures of Character* (no text); *Two Pair of Portraits* (text pp. 574–9). Vol. 2 contains three Rowlandsons which proved

that when needs must and payment was in prospect this least political of engravers could turn his hand to Tory satire as readily as Gillray. The three are *A Charm for Democracy* (an elaborate attack on the radical press, radical pamphleteering, and the Opposition), *An Irish Howl*, and *A Peep into the Retreat at Tinnehinch*.

45 *Anti-Jacobin Review & Magazine*, vol. I, p. 115; D. Hill, *Mr Gillray the Caricaturist* (1965), pp. 71–2; J. Bagot, *Canning and his Friends* (1909), vol. I, pp. 137–43.

46 In his *Letter to a Noble Lord* (1796) Burke referred to Bedford as 'the Leviathan among all the creatures of the Crown . . . [who] plays and frolicks on the ocean of the royal bounty'. Isaac Cruikshank had illustrated this in his *The Modern Leviathan!!* (1796, for Fores), Gillray's model.

47 Dyer, *British Satire*, pp. 52–4, 150–8.

48 Brown, *Fathers of the Victorians*, pp. 170, 168–7, 220–1, 369–70.

49 *The Works of Sydney Smith* (2 vols, 1859), vol. I, pp. 131–8.

50 *Political Register*, vol. XV (Jan–June 1809) p. 611.

51 Vol. II (1 Sept., 1811), pp. 202–8.

52 *The Examiner*, 31 August 1823.

53 I. D. McCalman, *Radical Underworld: Prophets, Revolutionaries and Pornographers in London, 1795–1840* (Cambridge, 1988), p. 47.

54 P. Egan, *Finish to the Adventures of Tom and Jerry* (1828), p. 21.

55 See ch. 16.

56 Knox cited at BMSat. 6130.

57 See Dighton's *A Master Parson Returning from Duty* (Sayer, 1782) and *A Master Parson with a Good Living* (Carington Bowles, 1782); Colley's *The Old Sow in Distress, or the Country Parson's Return from Tithing* (Humphrey, 1786); Rowlandson's *Tithe Pig* (Fores, 1790); Isaac Cruikshank's *Parsonic Piety: Good Precepts but Bad Example* (Fores, 1794) and *Pious Propensities, or Clerical Dissipations* (Fores, 1794); and a cluster of Newton prints for Holland: *Enjoying an Old Friend* (1795), *A Clerical Alphabet* (1795) and *A Priest Ridden Village* (Holland, 1796).

58 Coleridge cited BMSat 8428; 'A farce,' Charles Pigott called the fast, in a passage with modern relevance: 'The people called on to go to church and neglect their business, while ministers are celebrating their carousals, and getting drunk at each others' houses. An impious mummery, or rather blasphemy. We are told of our national sins, and, in expiation of them, are instructed to beseech the God of Peace to bless our exterminating principles of war; to set ourselves up as a people distinct, on whom, exclusively, he ought to shower his benign protection, and to crown our efforts, in destroying countless millions of his creatures': *Political Dictionary Explaining the True Meaning of Words* (1795).

59 Gillray addressed the print in his characteristically tortured but ironic subtext: 'To the Charitable Committee, for reducing the high price of corn, by providing substitutes for bread in their own families, this representation of the hard shifts made by the framers and signers of the philanthropic agreement [the ministers], is most respecfully dedicated.' In similar spirit I. Cruikshank's *General Fast* (Fores, 1796) showed a grotesque 'general' over the subtext: 'Of all the great generals Europe can boast / In her annals of war, in times present and past / None so handy each season to call to his post / As that meagre old general, General Fast.'

60 Probably published by Holland: BMSat 7182. On Captain Morris's 'The New Plenipotentiary', see ch. 10.

61 D. Donald, *The Age of Caricature: Satirical Prints in the Reign of George III* (1996), p. 99.

62 Reproduced in T. Hyman, 'A carnival sense of the world', in T. Hyman and R. Malbert, *Carnivalesque* (2000), p. 46. I am grateful to Timothy Hyman for an enlarged photocopy.

63 Gillray's *Barbarities in the West Indies* (1791) and Cruikshank's *Abolition of the Slave Trade* (Fores, 1792).

64 The other three Newton prints for Holland were: *Cruelty and Oppression Abroad* (plantation slaves dance merrily as Wilberforce declares that, although he knows this happy scene to be true, he is 'pledg'd to my brethren to smother truth' out of duty to his Maker); *The Blind Enthusiast* (Wilberforce, blindfolded and wearing cap and bells, ignoring the figure of Justice who declares the plantation owners 'not guilty'); and *A Forcible Appeal for the Abolition of the Slave Trade* (depicting a slave-flogging). This last might be construed as pro-abolitionist were not for an alternative target indicated in a later edition retitled *Practical Christianity*. Possibly Holland was aiming it at those with a taste for flagellation prints: D. Alexander, *Richard Newton and English Caricature in the 1790s* (1998), p. 116; Alexander reproduces *A Forcible Appeal*. Photographic copies of these rare prints are in the Menil Collection, 'Satires', Warburg Institute, London.

65 Cited by Dyer, *British Satire*, p. 146.

## Chapter Sixteen

# Radical Satire and the Censors

1 G. Dyer, *British Satire and the Politics of Style 1789–1832* (Cambridge, 1997), pp. 72–3; R. C. Elliott, *The Power of Satire: Magic, Ritual, Art* (New Jersey, 1966), p. 265.

2 For the following: D. Thomas, *A Long Time Burning: The History of Literary Censorship in England* (New York, 1969), ch. 8; W. Wickwar, *Struggle for the Freedom of the Press 1819–32* (1928), pp. 18–28, 118–19; Dyer, *British Satire*, pp. 71–4; C. Emsley, 'An aspect of "Pitt's Terror": prosecutions for seditious libel during the 1790s', *Social History* (1981).

3 T. Erskine May, *Constitutional History of England 1760–1860* (3rd edn, 3 vols, 1882), vol. III, ch. XI, pp. 10–24.

4 Delahaye Symonds: TS11/944/3419.

5 They included Thomas Lloyd, Delahaye Symonds, James Ridgeway, Charles Pigott, Daniel Holt, Daniel Isaac Eaton, John Frost, William Williams, Dr Watson, Joseph Gerrald: for full explication of the watercolour, see D. Alexander, *Richard Newton and English Caricature in the 1790s* (1998), pp. 36–8.

6 Dorothy George thought it 'difficult to associate Fores with political principles' since he accepted £30 in December 1820 for suppressing a song and an engraving on a subject illustrated by Benbow (BMCSat. 10, xlviii–lxix); D. Alexander similarly claims that Fores produced 'tory-inclined prints' (*Richard Newton*, p. 17). The only real grounds for these views are that Fores had led the way in mocking the Prince of Wales in the 1780s – whence John Wilkes's comment in 1788 on 'two most extraordinary prints . . . for which the prince's solicitor is prosecuting Fores' (see above, ch. 8, and *Letters . . . of John Wilkes . . . to his Daughter* (4 vols, 1804), vol. III, pp. 247, 315). But a longer view of Fores's output otherwise suggests a consistently liberal disposition. His 'protest' prints (after these of 1795–6) include: *The Sedition Hunter Disappointed* (1798: against false imprisonment of a Winchester carpenter for having 'damned Mr Pitt and the war' in a tavern); Williams's *The Balance of Justice* (1802: against the execution of naval mutineers); pro-Burdett prints in the 1810s (ch. 2 above); protests at the use of government spies in 1817, including Cruikshank's *Conspirators; or, Delegates in Council* (Sidmouth, Reynolds and Castlereagh at a table with three spies and a large bag of docketed papers, John Bull looking

through the window in horror), and the anonymous *More Plots!!! More Plots!!!*; G. Cruikshank's celebrations of Hone's acquittals in 1817 and Williams's equal celebrations, *Law versus Humanity or a Parody on British Liberty* and *William the Conqueror* (1817); and, most bravely, *A May Day Garland for 1820* (1820), the only critical response in graphic satire to the executions of the Cato Street conspirators (the ministers Sidmouth, Castlereagh, Gifford, Vansittart, Canning, Chief Justice Abbott, and others caper around the conspirators' decapitated and impaled heads, while Edwards, the execrated government spy who broke the case, plays the fiddle top right). More of Fores's prints (20) than of any other printshop's were included in the 91 anti-king prints called in by the Solicitor-General in late 1820 (TS11/115) (see next chapter). For Fores's support of William Hone in 1817, see below.

7  K. Garlick, A. Macintyre, and K. Cave (eds), *The Diary of Joseph Farington* (16 vols, 1978–84), vol. I, p. 137 (24 January 1796).

8  The prosecution brief is in TS11/175. *The Times* briefly reported Holland's arrest by warrant on an indictment from the Middlesex grand jury; the trial itself is not reported (18 December 1792). See also Alexander, *Richard Newton*, pp. 34–8.

9  Paine's *Letter Addressed to the Addressers on the Late Proclamation* denounced as a 'hackneyed nonsensical falshood' the fantasy that the British constitution was the envy of the world. A 'system of tyranny, injustice, and oppression', it was good only 'for courtiers, placemen, pensioners, boroughholders and the leaders of parties', and bad 'for at least 99 parts of the nation out of an hundred': TS11/578/189. The other Gillrays named in Belcher's prosecution were *Farmer George and Ch—l—tte Going to Market*, and *Farm House at Windsor*. Other (and earlier) caricatures on the monarch and consort, by Kingsbury, Newton etc., passed unchecked.

10  D. Nokes, *Raillery and Rage: A Study of Eighteenth Century Satire* (Brighton, 1987), pp. 17–19.

11  I. D. McCalman, *Radical Underworld: Prophets, Revolutionaries and Pornographers in London, 1795–1840* (Cambridge, 1988), pp. 118–24.

12  C. Abbott, 'On the use and abuse of satire' (1786), in *Oxford English Prize Essays* (Oxford, 1836), vol. I, p. 181.

13  As late as 1882, one editor of state trials could still dismiss Hone's satires as 'contemptible' and exclude Hone's trials from his volumes because their substance 'could not now be reproduced without offence to religious feeling': G. L. Browne, *Narratives of State Trials in the Nineteenth Century* (2 vols, 1882), vol. II, p. vi.

14  W. C. Hazlitt (ed.), *Letters of Charles Lamb* (2 vols, 1886), I, 397 (28 March 1809).

15  BMCSat. 8, xxx–xxxiii and entries on individual prints; W. Cobbett, *History of the Regency and the Reign of King George the Fourth* (1830); K. D. Reynolds, 'Clarke, Mary Anne', *ODNB*; Anna Clark, *Scandal: The sexual politics of the British Constitution* (2003), ch. 7.

16  See other examples, figs. 180, 181, 198, 212. In March, Tegg bound them as a *Complete Collection of Caricatures relative to Mrs Clarke*. Tegg capitalized further on the scandal by issuing fourteen portraits to illustrate it, along with a *Life of Mary Anne Clarke*, which he claimed sold 13,000 copies at 7s 6d each. John Johnston of 'Johnston's Cheap Caricature Warehouse No 101 Cheapside' intended to follow Tegg's example: he advertised 'a new caricature on Mrs. Clarke every day price one Shilling and two each' – an advert without fulfilment, however (BMCSat. 8, xliii).

17  *The Satirist* was one of the earliest journals to follow the *Anti-Jacobin's* example in binding in prints to illustrate its articles (its first volume having announced that it admired, loved and revered the British constitution above 'all the other political fabrics of the earth'). The title of *Robbing Hood Society* punned on the Robin Hood debating society, which Henry Fielding and others in the 1750s had ridiculed as a

forum for ignorant tradesmen; it had now re-emerged as the radicals' 'British Forum'.

18 Otherwise obscure to caricature, de Wilde's main satirical work was for this journal. On the radicals' revival generally, and the Crown and Anchor dinner particularly, see Cobbett's *Political Register*, 6 May 1809; M. Roberts, *The Whig Party: 1807–1812* (1965), p. 246; J. A. Hone, *For the Cause of Truth: Radicalism in London, 1796–1821* (Oxford, 1982), pp. 173–6; P. Spence, *The Birth of Romantic Radicalism: War, Popular Politics, and English Radical Reformism, 1800–1815* (Aldershot, 1996), pp. 125–6; F. Burdett, *Parliamentary Reform: . . . Meeting at the Crown and Anchor Tavern* (1809); Place Papers, BL Add. MSS 27850, fos 111–12; Crabb Robinson, *Reminiscences*; C. Lofft, *On the Revival of the Cause of Reform* (1809), p. 3n; Anon., *Sir Frantic the Reformer; Or, the Humours of the Crown and Anchor* (1809).

19 E. A. Smith, *George IV* (1998) gives the most favourable explanation of George's dropping of the Whigs, as he does of other royal actions.

20 Cf. Cruikshank's *Prince of Whales*, or Williams's print, *Love and Law i.e. A Venial Misfortune or Crim. Con. Modifyd* (for Tegg, 1813), in which a handsome adulterous couple are made lengthily to cite verses by Tom Moore in *The Examiner* (10 January 1813), including, from the man: 'Come fly to these arms, nor let beauties so bloomy / To one frigid owner be tied, / The prudes may revile, and the old ones look gloomy, / But dearest we've Law on our side . . .'; the woman advises caution since her lover is not the equal of a prince who 'might kick down decorum', and the regent proves the point by walking off right with Lady Hertford and Lord Ellenborough. The moral: 'Plate sin with gold, / And the strong lance of justice hurtless breaks; / Arm it in rags, a pigmy's straw doth pierce it'.

21 W. Hone, *The Three Trials of William Hone* (1817; W. Tegg's edn, 1876), p. 23. Parody's immunity had been demonstrated in 1794, when D. I. Eaton was acquitted of seditious libel for publishing his *Politics for the People; Or Hog's Wash*, in which he had disguised the king as a game-cock, 'a haughty, sanguinary tyrant, nursed in blood and slaughter from his infancy' who terrorized the other farmyard animals: *Proceedings of the Old Bailey* (http://www.oldbaileyonline.org, Ref: t17940219–71).

22 R. L. Patten, *George Cruikshank's Life, Times and Art*, vol. I 1792–1835 (1992), p. 67.

23 K. N. Cameron, *Shelley: The Golden Years* (1974), ch. 9 and notes, p. 628; BMCSat. 10, xv.

24 Shelley's other political works of 1819, including his sonnet 'England in 1819' ('An old, mad, blind, despis'd, and dying king, / Princes, the dregs of their dull race, who flow / Through public scorn – mud from a muddy spring . . .'), had to await publication by his wife in 1839. His dramatic satire at the regent's expense, *Oedipus Tyrannus, or Swellfoot the Tyrant* (1819), was bought up by the anti-vice society after only seven copies had been sold; the society also prosecuted his *Queen Mab* for infidelism.

25 TS11/580/1913 (my italics). Such was the risk that the wording of an indictment might provoke mirth that the law officers excluded the funnier bits of offending texts from indictments whenever they could. In November 1817, they advised against including matter in the indictments against Richard Carlile that might 'excite risibility': TS24/1/11.

26 Cited BMCSat. 9, xliv, note 1.

27 TS11/45/174 and (for its application in another of Carlile's shops in 1823) TS11/47/182.

28 On Tegg, see above, ch. 9.

29 T. Dolby, *Memoirs of Thomas Dolby . . . late Printer and Publisher, of Catherine Street, Strand . . . Written by Himself* (1827), p. 108.

30 *Much Wanted a Reform among Females* (1819) (reproduced in Donald, *The Age of Caricature.*)

31 Marks's *Blood Hounds Let Loose: On the Opinion of (Twelve) Good Judges!!! – !!! – !!!* (1818) attacked the judges' taste for hanging on the evidence of agents provocateurs: twelve judges unleash savage dogs (labelled with the names of well-known agents provocateurs) on to two youths who take flight beneath a notice, 'Beware of Man Traps', while four bodies hang from a gibbet in the background. In February four young men and women had been hanged for forgery, while the agents provocateurs were pardoned despite being convicted of felony. Only one other print of this time attacked hanging law so overtly: Fores's *A May Day Garland for 1820* (1820). Newton's print was *The First Interview, or an – Envoy from Yarmony to Improve the Breed* (1797).

32 Williams's *State Mysteries, a Vision of Pall Mall* (1813, in *The Scourge*), and Elmes's *King Cupid in the Corner – Playing Bo Peep* (Benbow, 1820): both reproduced in K. Baker, *George IV: A Life in Caricature* (2005), which gives an excellent sample of the satires on George.

33 On *The Scourge*, see R. L. Patten, *George Cruikshank's Life, Times, and Art*, vol. 1, pp. 99–101. R. J. H. Douglas lists Cruikshank's prints for *The Scourge* in *The Works of George Cruikshank Classified and Arranged* (1903), pp. 248ff.

34 The first of the six, *Princely Amusements, or the Humors of the Family* (1 March, 1812) was one of the earliest salvoes against the regent after his dropping of the Whigs. Attending mainly to the regent's and his brothers' sexual dalliances, it sets up Caroline as the wronged wife (she leaves the room while the regent dances comically with Mrs Fitzherbert and his daughter); Fox's portrait on the wall is upside down to make its accusatory point. References to the regent's discarded mistresses are multiple, and the bawdy implications are underscored by a music-sheet entitled 'Morgan Rattler &c'. Though this ditty's deathless lines are not transcribed, worldly perusers would have known them: 'First he niggled her then he tiggled her, / Then with his two balls he began to batter her / At every thrust, I thought she'd bust / With the terrible size of his Morgan Rattler' (Francis Place recorded the words: BL Add. MSS. 27825). The sequence includes *The Coronation of the Empress of the Nairs* (September), *An Excursion to R—[agley] Hall* (the Hertfords' seat) (October: reproduced in J. Wardroper, *The Caricatures of George Cruikshank* (1977)), and *The Court of Love, or an Election in the Island of Borneo* (November). In these, diversely, Lady Hertford, naked in a bath, proclaims 'the freedom of the sex & the supremacy of love'; the regent chooses ministers and household according to their skills in adultery; Lord Yarmouth (the Hertfords' dissolute son) announces that he is 'vice all over'; a buxom woman in spurs tells grenadiers to go and 'satisfy' Lady Buckinghamshire; Lord Melbourne cavorts with two St Giles's prostitutes; Sheridan is drunk between bailiffs, one holding a paper reading 'Poor fellow his magic wand is broken' – etc.

35 *The Black Joke* had been alluded to by Hogarth in *The Rake's Progress*, and Cruikshank often alluded to it too. For its verses, see above, chapter 11.

36 Hone's broadside accompanying the print versified as follows: 'Oh, what a bomb! Oh, heaven defend us! / The thought of bombs is quite tremendous!' Another sixpenny coloured woodcut broadside, *The Yacht for the R—t's B—m*, complained at the regent's expenditure on a £60,000 pleasure-boat at a time of national distress: 'If you knew how immense / Was the building expence – / And this when the nation was failing – / Of a place for this B—m / You would think it a hum, / That it must have a vessel to sail in.' Marks's *The Munchauseness of Herford!! Mounted on the R—t's Bomb* (1819) has Lady Hertford sit astride the regent's 'bomb' holding a match to the touch-hole, a miniature of the regent between her spherical breasts: 'I'll set

light to the Touch-ole and see if it will give the bomb ['bum'] any extra motion, and should a couple of balls give a mortal blow to R—d [Richmond, her latest rival], it will be a lucky stroke.'

37 Notably K. Baker's *George IV: A Life in Caricature* (2005).

38 Humphrey had earlier published (and Benbow, unexpectedly, printed) *Horrida Bella: Pains and Penalties versus Truth and Justice*, a bound sequence of alphabet-led parodic verses in the queen's favour, each alphabetical page illustrated by a 7 x 5 inch watercoloured print. It was offensive enough to be called in by the Treasury Solicitor (TS 11/120). The Caroline saga is much studied: see Anna Clark, 'Queen Caroline and the sexual politics of popular culture in London, 1820,' *Representations*, 31 (1990), pp. 47–68; T. Laqueur, 'The Queen Caroline affair: politics as art in the reign of George IV,' *Journal of Modern History* (1982), pp. 417–66; A. Clark, *Scandal: The Sexual Politics of the British constitution* (2003), ch. 8. For good selections of the Caroline prints see also E. A. Smith, *A Queen on Trial: The affair of Queen Caroline* (1993); M. D. George, *English Political Caricature:A Study of Opinion and Propaganda* (2 vols, 1959), vol. II, ch. x.

39 D. S. Kerr, *Caricature and French Political Culture, 1830–1848: Charles Philipon and the Illustrated Press* (Oxford, 2000). On Thackeray, see above, ch. 8.

40 The Holland volumes are entitled *The Trial of Queen Caroline*; the others, bearing Minto Wilson's bookplate, *Minutes of Evidence on the Queen's Trial*; both sets in the Cambridge University Library. BMCSat. 10, xvii, note 4, comments briefly on the Holland volumes.

41 W. Hone, *The Three Trials of William Hone* (1817; reprinted with introduction by W. Tegg, 1876), pp. 107, 125–6, 163: this verbatim record of each of Hone's three trials is the chief source for what follows. Pre-trial information is from Treasury Solicitor's papers, TS11/44/164. Key studies are F. W. Hackwood, *William Hone, His Life and Times* (1912) and B. Wilson, *The Laughter of Triumph: William Hone and the Fight for a Free Press* (2005). See also D. Thomas, *A Long Time Burning: The History of Literary Censorship in England* (1969); Olive Smith, *The politics of Language 1791–1814* (1984); M. Wood, *Radical Satire and Print Culture 1790–1822* (Oxford, 1994); J. Marsh, *Word Crimes: Blasphemy, Culture and Literature in Nineteenth-century England* (1998); D. Nash, *Blasphemy in Modern Britain: 1789 to the Present* (1999). Ten of Hone's and rival loyalist pamphlets are reproduced in facsimile and well introduced in E. Rickword (ed.), *Radical Squibs and Loyal Ripostes: Satirical Pamphlets of the Regency period 1819–1821* (1971). For Wooler's case (below): TS11/43, parts 4/1 and 2.

42 *The Royal Shambles* was advertised on another print (BMSat 12048) for an expensive four shillings, there described as 'handsomely and appropriately coloured, a new grand elaborate processional caricature on a plate 22 inches wide'.

43 Wilson, *The Laughter of Triumph*, pp. 128–31, 310.

44 The fact of Gillray's pension from Canning was disclosed though not proved by Hone in the course of his trials; when the Attorney General denied his allegation, Hone replied that he 'had it from the relations of that gentleman'. Two of Gillray's prints cited by Hone during the trials were *The Presentation – or – the Wise Mens Offering* (1796) (on the birth of Princess Charlotte, George's only known child), and *Disciples Catching the Mantle:– the Spirit of Darkness Overshadowing the Priests of Baal* (1808) (in which Pitt is borne upwards to Immortality). The first print's 'blasphemous' title was said to have led to Gillray's threatened prosecution in the ecclesiastical court, a threat that might have put Gillray at Canning's mercy, for the 'pension' of 1797 soon followed. The second print was a Canningite idea that appeared in the *Anti-Jacobin Review*, March 1807; it was based on Sayers's *Elijah's Mantle* (1807), which called on the ministry to make Pitt's mantle their own.

45  W. C. Townsend, *The Lives of Twelve Eminent Judges of the Last and of the Present Century* (2 vols, 1846), vol. I, p. 388; Campbell, *The Lives of the Chief Justices of England* (3 vols, 1849–57), vol. III, p. 225.

46  Fores added that he had heard that Lord Ellenborough had himself once written a parody of a divine service, just as Hone had (Fores to Hone, 2 January 1818: Hone's *General Correspondence*, vol. XIII (i), BL Add. MSS. 40120, fo. 91).

Chapter Seventeen

# The Silencing

1  R. Rush, *Memoranda of a Residence at the Court of London . . . from 1819 to 1825* (2 vols, 1845), vol. I, p. 311; C. Grenville, *Memoirs of the Court of George IV* (2 vols, 1859), vol. I, p. 68 (30 August 1820); Cholmeley in *Parliamentary Debates*, vol. V, p. 1118 (6 June 1821), probably referring to Heath's *Nero Fiddled when Rome was Burning* (1820, for Fores), which took its cue from Caroline's counsel, Denman's, speech comparing George IV to Nero.

2  L. Strachey and R. Fulford (eds), *Greville's Memoirs 1814–60* (8 vols, 1938), vol. I, p. 322; Anne to James Cobbett, cited E. A. Smith, *A Queen on Trial: The Affair of Queen Caroline* (1993), p. 114; Rev. R. J. Richardson, *Recollections, Political, Literary, Dramatic, and Miscellaneous, of the Last Half-century* (2 vols in 1, 1856), pp. 267–9.

3  *Edinburgh Review*, April 1838: cited BMCSat. 10, xi. Dorothy George's introduction to BMCSat. 10 is indispensable to the following discussion. She abbreviated her evidence in *English Political Caricature: A Study of Opinion and Propaganda* (2 vols, 1959), vol. II, ch. x.

4  H. Twiss, *The Public and Private Life of Lord Chancellor Eldon* (3 vols, 1844), vol. II, p. 413; Buckingham, *Memoirs of the Court of George IV* (2 vols, 1859), vol. I, p. 107.

5  KB28/477/76 and 77.

6  The ninety-one prints are preserved in TS11/115.

7  *Parliamentary Debates* (1821), vol. V, p. 1114; KB 28/477/94 and 75. A Hone–Cruikshank pamphlet, *Slap at Slop*, helped discredit the Association by parodying Stoddart's newspaper, the *New Times*, which had supported it.

8  F. Bamford and Duke of Wellington (eds), *Journal of Mrs Arbuthnot* (2 vols, 1950), vol. I, p. 147.

9  The £2,600 estimate is J. Wardroper's: *Kings, Lords and Wicked Libellers: Satire and protest 1760–1837* (1973), p. 213. Details otherwise from BMCSat. 10, xlviii–l. Further summaries are in C. Hibbert, *George IV*, vol. 2, p. 157, and R. L. Patten, *George Cruikshank's Life, Times, and Art, vol. 1 1792–1835* (1992), pp. 62–76.

10  KB28/479/28. For Richard Fores's mercy petitions, see ch. 15, note 36 above.

11  Patten, *Cruikshank's Life, Times, and Art*, p. 176; BMCSat. 10, xii, xl–xli.

12  C. S. Parker, *Sir Robert Peel . . . from his Private Correspondence* (1891), vol. I, p. 336. The fishing print was Williams's *A King-fisher* (for Fores).

13  C. Baudelaire, 'Some foreign caricaturists', in *Selected Writings on Art and Literature* (ed. and trans. P. E. Charvet, 1972, repr. 1992), pp. 23–4.

14  [J. G. Lockhart], 'On George Cruikshank', *Blackwood's Magazine*, vol. XIV (July 1823), pp. 18–26.

15  M. Slater (ed.), *Dickens's Journalism: The Amusements of the People and other Papers . . . 1834–51* (1996), pp. 102–7.

16  Other late-1819 prints in the same vein were *A Radical Reformer, – (i.e.) a Neck or Nothing Man!* (reviving the iconography of the 1790s with a guillotine-monster that

echoes Gillray's in *The Genius of France Triumphant* (1795)), and *Death or Liberty! Or Britannia & the Virtues of the Constitution in Danger or Violation from the Grt Political Libertine, Radical Reform!* (for Humphrey): this shows Death, wearing the mask of Liberty, trying to ravish Britannia as she braces herself against a rock labelled 'Religion' and defends herself with a flaming sword labelled 'The Laws'. Cruikshank's (and Tegg's) anti-radical outbursts in 1819 might be construed as typical of the moderates' response to the radicals' feuds and excesses. But extremism had most damaged the radical cause in 1816–17, when Henry Hunt and Cobbett had squabbled with the Burdettites and the Westminster committee and Hunt had flirted with Spenceans like Dr Watson. Cruikshank hadn't worried much then. His *Liberty Suspended!* (March 1817) had mocked ministerial scaremongering about the Spenseans (albeit at Sidebotham's behest) (fig. 258). He had also illustrated Hone's *Bartholomew Fair Insurrection; and the Pie-bald Pony Plot!*, a pamphlet satire mocking the Home Secretary's belief that armed rioters led by Thistlewood, Preston and others would assemble at Bartholomew Fair for a general insurrection on 6 September. As late as 1871, Cruikshank reactivated both Gillray's anti-sans-culotte motifs of the 1790s and his own guillotine-monster of 1819 in a vicious single-sheet satire on the Paris Commune: *An Awful Lesson to the World for All Time to Come. The Leader of the Parisian Blood Red Republic, or the Infernal Fiend* (John Johnson Collection, Bodleian Library, Oxford).

17  BMCSat. 10, xlix–l.

18  Carlile's *God* is in TS24/3/132.

19  J. Wardroper, *The World of William Hone* (1997), pp. 16–17; B. Wilson, *The Laughter of Triumph: William Hone and the Fight for a Free Press* (2005), ch. 13.

20  He engraved a vicious satire on them in 1818: *Modern Reformers in Council, – or – Patriots Regaling* (Humphrey 1818), which shows Henry Hunt presiding over a rabble of Spencean revolutionists.

21  BMCSat. 10, l–li.

22  Fairburn had earlier issued dozens of verse satires against the regent, along with serious radical publications like John Wade's *The Black Book; or, Corruption Unmasked! Being an Account of Places, Pensions and Sinecures*. But soon even he had to admit that there was no profit in mocking the new king.

23  J. J. and P. P. Barnes, 'Tegg, Thomas (1776–1846), *ODNB*. For Tegg's autobiography, see above, ch. 8, note 54.

## Chapter Eighteen
# Happiness, Cant and the Beggars

1  C. Hindley, *The Life and Times of James Catnach, Late of Seven Dials, Balladmonger* (1878), p. 111 (citing J. C. Hotten's introduction to a later edition of *Life in London*). Egan sourly reviewed how *Life in London* was pirated in his introduction to his later spin-off *Finish to the Adventures of Tom, Jerry, and Logic, in their Pursuits through Life in and out of London* (1828), pp. 3–44.

2  J. Marriott (ed.), *Unknown London: Early Modernist Visions of the Metropolis, 1815–45* (2 vols, 2000), pp. xxvi–xxvii.

3  P. Ackroyd, *Dickens* (1990), p. 204 (for John Foster's review of Bulwer-Lytton and Ainsworth); W. M. Thackeray, 'Roundabout Papers: *de juventate*', *Cornhill Magazine*, October 1860, pp. 509–10; H. Vizetelly, *Glances Back Through Seventy Years: Autobiographical and Other Reminiscences* (2 vols, 1893), vol. I, pp. 12–13.

4  C. Hindley, *The True History of Tom and Jerry* (1888), p. xiv. Dorothy George accepted that the pictures led the text: BMCSat. 10, 277. R. L. Patten finds the evidence too thin to adjudicate either way: *George Cruikshank's Life, Times, and Art*, vol. 1, *1792–1835* (1992), pp. 222–5. Egan's world is explored in J. C. Reid, *Bucks and Bruisers: Pierce Egan and Regency England* (1971).

5  According to E. Partridge's *Dictionary of the Underworld* (3rd edn, 1968), the verb 'to slum' was first recorded in 1718 to refer to the act of burglary. In 1812, J. H. Vaux (*Vocabulary of the Flash Language*: compiled 1812, published 1819) listed 'slum' as a noun referring variously to a 'room', to a criminal trick or plan, or to canting slang itself. In both *Boxiana* (1812) and *Life in London*, Egan used it to refer to a room inhabited by the poor: whence the word's present meaning.

6  *Anatomy of Melancholy* (Oxford, 3 vols, 1990), vol. II, p. 160.

7  S. Schama, *Rembrandt's Eyes* (1999), p. 304.

8  Waters features in Cruikshank's *Landing the Treasures* (1819: a satire on Ross's polar expedition), and later in Thomas Hood's *The Progress of Cant* (1825), clamouring for the abolition of the treadwheel (fig. 218 above). For his appearance in Cruikshank's *New Union Club*, see fig. 234. The experiences of the radical mulatto James Wedderburn were strikingly like Waters's: I. McCalman, *Radical Underworld: Prophets, Revolutionaries and Pornographers in London* (Cambridge, 1988), pp. 51–6.

9  F. Grose, *The Grumbler: Containing Sixteen Essays* (1791), pp. 34–5.

10 M. Martin, *Substance of a Letter, Dated 3d March, 1803, to the Right Honourable Lord Pelham, on the State of Mendicity in the Metropolis* (1803, reprinted 1811); Colquhoun, *The State of Indigence, and the Situation of the Casual Poor in the Metropolis, Explained* (1799).

11 Its first management committee included Martin and Colquhoun, the Quaker William Allen, active in many reform enterprises (including anti-slavery), David Ricardo, the political economist, the scientist William Frend, once Thomas Malthus's tutor at Cambridge, William Tooke, FRS, the radical MP Joseph Hume, and W. H. Bodkin, the Society's secretary, later a barrister, judge and MP.

12 Between March and December 1818, 3,284 cases were registered and 16,827 meals were supplied. Of this sorry host, the biggest groups were countrypeople (1,022) and Irish (927); 720 others had London parishes of origin, and 427 were foreign. The biggest congregation (876) lived in St Giles's; 691 had no place of residence at all; 564 applicants were found to be impostors or confirmed vagrants: they were prosecuted and 385 of them imprisoned. Another 1,222 were sent to their London parishes for relief, and 184 to their country parishes. One hundred and twenty-two were clothed, relieved and sent to sea, while 216 were given employment and partly clothed and 186 were given tools and means of support. But 92 were sent to workhouses and 69 to hospitals; and 54 'foreigners' were sent 'abroad'. While 286 were found able to support themselves, 146 were refused relief in workhouses, and 137 absconded: *First Report of the Mendicity Society* (1819). The Society remained active throughout the 1820s and 1830s; in various forms it outlasted the century: H. Mayhew, *London Life and London Labour* (4 vols, 1851–62), vol. IV, pp. 399–401, summarizes the Society's casework from 1818 to 1860.

13 E. Brenton, *A Letter to the Committee of Management of the Society for the Suppression of Mendicity* (1830), pp. 6–8.

14 Grose, *The Grumbler*, pp. 34–5, and his *Dictionary of the Vulgar Tongue*, pp. 385–6.

15 Egan and Robert Cruikshank stayed true to this position for several years yet. In 1828, Robert illustrated Egan's *Finish to the Adventures of Tom, Jerry, and Logic, in their Pursuits through Life in and out of London* with thirty-six further images of cheerful low-life debauchery (cf. the cock and hen club, fig. 32 above), while Egan's book itself was to repeat *Life in London*'s view that 'the poorer classes of society seem to enjoy

life with greater happiness than their superiors; indeed, there is an indescribable sort of *jollity* about their behaviour': see p. 276 and facing plate. Robert Cruikshank published a pamphlet of satires on the new policing in 1833, ironically entitled *[Robert] Cruikshank v. the New Police; Showing the Great Utility of that Military Body, their Employment, etc.*

16  1815 Select Committee, pp. 37–41.

17  William Godwin, *The Enquirer: Reflections on Education, Manners and Literature in a Series of Essays* (1797), Part II, ch. 3, pp. 185–200, 'Of Beggars'.

18  C. Lamb, 'A complaint of the decay of beggars in the metropolis', *The London Magazine*, V (1822), 532–6; reprinted in his *Essays of Elia* (1823). Cf. Thomas Hood's satire on H. Bodkin, secretary to the Mendicity Society, in *Odes and Addresses to Great People* (1825).

19  1815 Select Committee, pp. 16, 20; L. Rose, *'Rogues and Vagabonds': Vagrant Underworlds in Britain, 1815–1985*, p. 18.

20  *The Times*, 5 and 10 April 1826. Many had been called beggar kings in the seventeenth and eighteenth centuries – most famously, the author of the first semi-authentic beggar's autobiography, *The Life and Adventures of Bampfylde-Moore Carew* (1745; edited by C. H. Wilkinson, Oxford, 1931). In the nineteenth century, the title was commonly bestowed on those assumed to rule their fellow mendicants from lodging houses or gin-shops (by allocating begging patches, for example). The title was also appropriated by the occasional beggar-author: cf. G. A. Brine, *The King of the Beggars: The Life and Adventures of George Atkins Brine: A True Story of Vagrant Life* (1883). But titles claimed by street-beggars themselves were probably self-parodic, although fantasy ascriptions from above might be internalized and enacted.

21  G. Wood, *The Smallest of all Persons Mentioned in the Record of Littleness* (1998).

22  His funeral was commemorated in a broadside woodcut showing his coffin carried by coalheavers and followed by the diminutive Andrew Whiston on his trolley: C. Hindley, *The Life and Times of James Catnach (Late of Seven Dials), Ballad Monger* (1878), pp. 135–6.

23  [Charles Westmacott], *The English Spy: An Original Work, Characteristic, Satirical, and Humorous, Comprising Scenes and Sketches in Every Rank of Society: Being Portraits of the Illustrious, Eminent, Eccentric, and Notorious. Drawn from the Life by Bernard Blackmantle* (2 vols, 1825–6). Not every low-life print in *The English Spy* was as dark as *Couriers Carousing. The Wake, – or Last Appearance of Teddy O'Rafferty, a Scene in the Holy-Land*, depicting a St Giles's Irish wake with a background fight that again draws on Gillray's *Union Club*, was as exhilaratingly comic as any print in the old tradition.

24  Ibid., pp. 28–9.

25  Hanger had appeared in this guise in well over sixty caricatures from 1786 until 1800, thus becoming the twentieth most often caricatured person in graphic satire: BMCSat. indexes, and N. K. Robinson, *Edmund Burke: A Life in Caricature* (New Haven, 1996), p. 194.

26  On Barrymore, see chs. 4 and 11 above.

27  E. Brenton, *A Letter to the Committee of Management of the Society for the Suppression of Mendicity* (1830), pp. 6–8.

28  'The new policeman walks, with slow and measured steps, along dismantled or demolished streets, once the beggar's, the veritable beggar's hotel, his lavatory, his tiring-room, his harem. Streets, too, which once rang with mendicant melody or malediction, are now purged and live cleanly . . . The beggar has nightmares now; his blue lettered and numbered enemy haunts him in his dreams.' Charles Dickens, 'Departed beggars', *Household Words* (May 1852).

29  *London Labour and the London poor* (4 vols, 1851–62), vol. III (1851), p. 316; vol. IV

(1862), pp. 432–3, 448, 393.

30 The print appeared in H. Gavin's reform-advocating *Sanitary Ramblings: Being Sketches and Illustrations of Bethnal Green*. For discussion of images like this, see C. Fox, 'The development of social reportage in English periodical illustration during the 1840s and early 1850s', *Past & Present*, 74 (February 1977), pp. 90–111.

31 C. Fox, *Londoners* (1987), p. 199.

32 For colour reproductions, see L. Lambourne, *Victorian Painting* (1999), plate 407 (Fildes), and M. Galinou and J. Hayes, *London in Paint: Oil Paintings in the Collection of the Museum of London* (1996), plates 125 (Macduff) and 132 (Mulready).

## Epilogue
## Francis Place and 'Improvement'

1 Francis Place Papers, BL Add. MSS. 27827, fos. 49–55.

2 As the printseller Thomas Dolby recalled, when Caroline arrived in England to claim her crown the satirists were provoked 'into stinging activity', but the publicity given to her adulteries meant that 'the public madness subsided before the poor queen died; the rage was over'. *Memoirs of Thomas Dolby . . . Late Printer and Publisher, of Catherine Street, Strand . . . Written by Himself* (1827), pp. 149–50.

3 F. Swinnerton (ed.), *Conversations of James Northcote, Esq., R. A. . . . by William Hazlitt* (1949), p. 89.

4 T. J. Wooler, 'The folly of the middle classes in supporting our present system', *Black Dwarf*, 12 February 1817.

5 M. Thale (ed.), *The Autobiography of Francis Place, 1771–1854* (Cambridge, 1972), p. 199 (henceforth *Autobiography*).

6 R. Porter, 'Mixed feelings: the Enlightenment and sexuality', in P.-G. Bouce (ed.), *Sexuality in Eighteenth-century Britain* (1982), pp. 319, 325.

7 Place Papers, BL Add. MSS. 27825–30; *Autobiography*.

8 *Autobiography*, pp. 82, 91; Francis Place, *Improvement of the Working People: Drunkenness and Education* (1834), pp. 1–2 (in Add. MSS. 27825). Add. MSS. 27827 includes Place's 1836 draft commentary on J. S. Mill's *Civilization* (with whose pessimism he disagreed): he hoped, he stated there, that he would 'yet have health and leisure to adduce, arrange, and publish a satisfactory account of the real and beneficial advance of every thing whose tendency is the improvement and happiness of mankind'; he insisted that the common people's progress had been greater than that of the upper classes to whom Mill mainly attended.

9 On the songs, see V. A. C. Gatrell, *The Hanging Tree: Execution and the English People* (Oxford, 1994), ch. 4 and its appendix. *Autobiography*, pp. 51, 175, 272; BL Add. MSS. 27825 (vol. xxxvii), fos. 165–7.

10 Place's notes on this theme are variously dated 1824, 1826, 1827 and 1836: e.g. BL Add. MSS. 27825, fos. 13, 47, 96.

11 This book is discussed above, ch. 10.

12 This last title is not in the British Library catalogue, but the catalogue records the sixth edition (1772) of Defoe's *The Political History of the Devil* (1726), to which was prefixed *Anecdotes of a Scoundrel; Or, Memoirs of Devil Dick: a Well-known Character*.

13 Charles Cotton's *Scarronides or Virgil Travestie* (1664) went through some half-dozen eighteenth-century editions, ending with one in 1807. Place devoted thirty-eight double-sided folios to his discussion of this work.

14 A. Lang, 'Letter to Dickens', in *Letters to Dead Authors* (1886).

15  For Scharf, see P. Jackson, *George Scharf's London: Sketches and Watercolours of a Changing City, 1820–1850* (1987).

16  F. MacCarthy, *Byron: Life and Legend* (2002), p. 176.

17  R. D. Altick, *The Shows of London: A Panoramic History of Exhibitions, 1600–1862* (Cambridge, Mass., 1978), p. 69.

18  Topographical details *passim* are drawn from Place's *Autobiography*; Horwood's *Map of the Cities of London and Westminster* (1799; updated by W. Faden, 1813); G. H. Gater and E. P. Wheeler, *Survey of London: The Parish of St Martin-in-the-Fields* (1935), vol. XVI, Part I: 'Charing Cross'; and B. Weinreb and C. Hibbert, *The London Encyclopaedia* (1993 edn). My thanks to John Barrell for correcting some topographical details in this discussion.

19  For the 1795 crimping house (and other) riots, coincidentally rooted in much the same topographical analysis of Charing Cross as mine, see J. Barrell, *The Spirit of Despotism: Invasions of Privacy in the 1790s* (Oxford, 2006), ch. 1. He corrects M. Thale's editorial assumption that the Charing Cross hanging Place remembered was of a Gordon rioter in 1780 (*Autobiography*, pp. 228–9 and note 1).

20  Gatrell, *Hanging Tree*, pp. 69–70; cf. BL Add. MSS. 27826, fo. 172.

21  *Survey of London*, vol. XVI, plates 110, 85, 86 and pp. 252–3; *Autobiography*, p. 211. The original Rummer burned down in 1750 in a fire that had started next door in the house of John Rocque (printseller and creator of the best of eighteenth-century London's surveyed maps): *General Advertiser*, 8 November 1750. The Rummer then seems to have taken over the premises of the old Turk's Head. A lease of 1767 referred to the back of number 16 house as 'formerly . . . the Turk's Head . . . now used as a bagnio': *Survey of London*, vol. XVI, p. 248; *Autobiography*, p. 228. Correspondence with John Barrell has helped me unpick this intricacy.

22  Later, the witness found that the woman had absconded with his purse, but she was acquitted thanks to good character references and because it was his word against hers: but nobody thought the prosecutor's account otherwise implausible. See *Proceedings of the Old Bailey* at ⟨http://www.oldbaileyonline.org⟩, refs t16931 206–24 for Pepys and the highwayman and refs t17540717–24 for Mary Lewis's theft; and *Oxford Dictionary of National Biography* for Jack Sheppard.

23  *Autobiography*, p. 216.

24  *Autobiography*, *passim*, esp. pp. 191–3, 201, 211–12, 216, 224.

25  G. Wallas, *The Life of Francis Place* (1898), p. 176.

26  G. E. Bentley (ed.), *William Blake's Writings* (2 vols, Oxford, 1978), vol. II, pp. 1584–5.

# Select Bibliography

The place of publication (here and in the notes) is London except where otherwise indicated

Alexander, D., *Richard Newton and English Caricature in the 1790s* (1998)

Atherton, H. M., *Political Prints in the Age of Hogarth: A Study of the Ideographic Representation of Politics* (Oxford, 1974)

Baker, K. (with K. Fogerty), *George IV: A Life in Caricature* (2005)

Banerji, C. and Donald, D. (eds), *Gillray Observed: The Earliest Account of his Caricatures in 'London und Paris'* (1999)

Barrell, J., 'The private comedy of Thomas Rowlandson', *Art History* vol. 6 (4), (1983)

Bindman, D., *Hogarth and his Times* (1996)

Bindman, D., *The Shadow of the Guillotine: Britain and the French Revolution* (1989)

Bills, M., *The Art of Satire: London in Caricature* (2006)

Brewer, J., *The Common People and Politics 1750–1790s* (1986)

Clayton, T., *The English Print, 1688–1802* (1997)

Cohn, A. M., *George Cruikshank: A catalogue raisonné of the Work Executed during the Years 1806–1877* (1924)

Coupe, W. A., *German Political Satires from the Reformation to the Second World War* (2 vols, 1993)

Cuno, J. and Burlingham, C. (eds) *French Caricature and the French Revolution, 1789–1799* (1988)

Donald, Diana, *The Age of Caricature: Satirical Prints in the reign of George III* (1996).

Dyer, G., *British Satire and the Politics of Style, 1789–1832* (Cambridge, 1997)

Elkin, P. K., *The Augustan Defence of Satire* (Oxford, 1973)

Falk, B., *Thomas Rowlandson: His Life and Art: a Documentary Record* (1949)

George, Mary Dorothy, *English Political Caricature: A Study of Opinion and Propaganda* (2 vols, Oxford, 1959)

George, Mary Dorothy, *Hogarth to Cruickshank: Social Change in Graphic Satire* (1967).

Godfrey, R., *English Caricature, 1620 to the Present* (1984)

Godfrey, R., *James Gillray: The Art of Caricature* (2001)

Gombrich, E. H., *Art and Illusion* (1960 and later edns)

Gombrich, E. H., *Meditations on a Hobby Horse* (1963)

Grego, J., *Rowlandson the Caricaturist: A Selection from his Works, with Anecdotal Descriptions of his Famous Caricatures and a Sketch of his Life, Times, and Contemporaries* (2 vols, 1880)

Hallett, M., *The Spectacle of Difference: Graphic Satire in the Age of Hogarth* (1999)

Hayes, J. T., *Rowlandson: Watercolours and Drawings* (1972)

Hill, D., *Mr Gillray the Caricaturist: A Biography* (1965)

Hill, D., *The Satirical Etchings of James Gillray* (1976)

Hill, D. (ed.), *Fashionable Contrasts: Caricatures by James Gillray* (1966)

Hunt, T. L., *Defining John Bull: Political Caricature and National Identity in Late Georgian England* (2003)

Jerrold, W. B., *The Life of George Cruikshank* (1882)

Kris, E. and Gombrich, E.H., 'The principles of caricature', in Kris, E., *Psychoanalytic Explorations in Art* (1953)

Krumbhaar, E. B., *Isaac Cruikshank: A catalogue raisonné with a sketch of his life and work* (Philadelphia, c.1966)

O'Connell, S., *The Popular Print in England, 1550–1850* (1999)

Patten, R. L., (ed.), *George Cruikshank, a Revaluation* (1973–4)

Patten, R. L., *George Cruikshank's Life, Times, and Art: vol. I: 1792–1835* (1992)

Paulson, R., *Hogarth: His Life, Art and Times* (3 vols, 1971–96)

Paulson, R., *Representations of Revolution, 1789–1820* (New Haven, 1983)

Paulson, R., *Rowlandson: A New Interpretation* (1972)

Redgrave, S., *A Dictionary of Artists of the English School: Painters, Sculptors, Architects, Engravers and Ornamentists, with Notices of their Lives and Works* (1874)

Reid, G. W., *Descriptive Catalogue of the Works of George Cruikshank* (1871)

Rickword, E. (ed.), *Radical Squibs and Loyal Ripostes: Satirical Pamphlets of the Regency Period, 1819–1821* (1971)

Riely, J., *Rowlandson Drawings from the Paul Mellon Collection* (1978)

Smith, E. A., *A Queen on Trial: The Affair of Queen Caroline* (1993)

Uglow, J., *William Hogarth: A Life and a World* (1997)

Vogler, R. A., *The Graphic Works of George Cruikshank* (1980)

Wardroper, J., *Kings, Lords and Wicked Libellers: Satire and Protest, 1760–1837* (1973)

Wardroper, J., *The Caricatures of George Cruikshank* (1977)

Wark, R. R., *Drawings by Thomas Rowlandson in the Huntington Collection* (1975)

Wolf, R., *Goya and the Satirical Print in England and the Continent, 1730–1850* (Boston, 1991)

Wood, M., *Radical Satire and Print Culture, 1790–1822* (Oxford, 1994)

Wright, T., *A History of Caricature and Grotesque in Literature and Art* (1865)

Wright, T., *Historical and Descriptive Account of the Caricatures of James Gillray* (1851)

Wright, T., *The Works of James Gillray, the Caricaturist, with the History of his Life and Times* (1873)

# Index

*Note:*

Page numbers in **bold** indicate chapters.

An asterisk next to the an entry indicates that a brief biography of the person may be found in 'Brief Lives'

Discussions of illustrations and illustrations themselves are separately indexed in 'Index of Artists' Works'

# Index of Artists' Works

*Note:*
Prints are listed alphabetically by artist.

Page numbers in **bold** refer to illustrations, otherwise numbers refer to discussions in the text.